Customer Equity Management

Customer Equity Management

Roland T. Rust
Robert H. Smith School of Business
University of Maryland

Katherine N. Lemon
Wallace E. Carroll School of Management
Boston College

Das Narayandas
Harvard Business School

PEARSON
Prentice Hall

Upper Saddle River, New Jersey 07458

All rights reserved. No part of this book may be reproduced, stored in a retrieval system, or transmitted, in any form or by any means, electronic, mechanical, photocopying, recording, or otherwise, without the prior written permission of the copyright holder. The copyright on each case in this book unless otherwise noted is held by the President and Fellows of Harvard College and they are published herein by express permissions. Permissions requests to use individual Harvard copyrighted cases should be directed to the Permissions Department, Harvard Business School Publishing, 300 North Beacon Street, Watertown, MA 02472.

Case material of the Harvard Graduate School of Business Administration is made possible by the cooperation of business firms and other organizations which may wish to remain anonymous by having names, quantities, and other identifying details disguised while maintaining basic relationships. Cases are prepared as the basis for class discussion rather than to illustrate either effective or ineffective handling of an administrative situation.

Library of Congress Cataloging-in-Publication Data

Rust, Roland T.
    Customer equity management/Roland T. Rust, Katherine N. Lemon, Das Narayandas.
      p. cm.
    Includes bibliographical references and index.
    ISBN 0-13-141929-3
      1. Customer equity—Management. I. Lemon, Katherine N. (Katherine Newell)
        II. Narayandas, Das. III. Title.

HF5415.527.R87 2004
658.8′12—dc22
                                                                                                   2004057256

Acquisitions Editor: Katie Stevens
Editor-in-Chief: Jeff Shelstad
Editorial Assistant: Rebecca Lembo
Media Project Manager: Peter Snell
Marketing Manager: Eric Frank
Marketing Assistant: Nicole Macchiarelli
Managing Editor: John Roberts
Permissions Supervisor: Charles Morris
Production Manager: Arnold Vila
Manufacturing Buyer: Michelle Klein
Cover Design: Jayne Conte
Cover Illustration: Digital Vision/Getty Images
Composition: Integra
Full-Service Project Management: Progressive Publishing Alternatives
Printer/Binder: Phoenix Book Tech

Credits and acknowledgments borrowed from other sources and reproduced, with permission, in this textbook appear on appropriate page within text.

Copyright © 2005 by Pearson Education, Inc., Upper Saddle River, New Jersey, 07458.
Pearson Prentice Hall. All rights reserved. Printed in the United States of America. This publication is protected by Copyright and permission should be obtained from the publisher prior to any prohibited reproduction, storage in a retrieval system, or transmission in any form or by any means, electronic, mechanical, photocopying, recording, or likewise. For information regarding permission(s), write to: Rights and Permissions Department.

Pearson Prentice Hall™ is a trademark of Pearson Education, Inc.
Pearson® is a registered trademark of Pearson plc
Prentice Hall® is a registered trademark of Pearson Education, Inc.

Pearson Education LTD.
Pearson Education Singapore, Pte. Ltd
Pearson Education, Canada, Ltd
Pearson Education–Japan

Pearson Education Australia PTY, Limited
Pearson Education North Asia Ltd
Pearson Educación de Mexico, S.A. de C.V.
Pearson Education Malaysia, Pte. Ltd

10 9 8 7 6 5 4 3 2 1
ISBN 0-13-141929-3

To Chiharu (RTR)
To Loren and Thomas (KNL)
To Sunitha, Rohan, and Amit (DN)

Brief Contents

Preface   xii

PART I: TOOLS FOR UNDERSTANDING AND ANALYZING CUSTOMER EQUITY   1

Chapter 1   Introduction to Customer Equity Management Strategy   1
Chapter 2   The Customer Equity Approach and the Customer Management Plan   22
Chapter 3   Customer Equity Analysis   91
Chapter 4   Measuring Customer Equity   141

PART II: DEVELOPING STRATEGIES FOR CUSTOMER EQUITY MANAGEMENT   194

Chapter 5   Customer Selection   194
Chapter 6   Building and Managing Brand Equity   237
Chapter 7   Building and Managing Value Equity   267
Chapter 8   Managing Relationship Equity   313
Chapter 9   Managing Customer Relationships Using Multiple Touch Points in Multi-Channel Settings   363

PART III: MEASURING, MONITORING, AND EVALUATING CUSTOMER EQUITY MANAGEMENT STRATEGY   381

Chapter 10   Strategic Implementation: Investing for Maximum Impact   381
Chapter 11   Managing Customer Profitability in Industrial Markets   424
Chapter 12   The Role of CRM Technologies in Customer Management   460
Chapter 13   How Customer Management Is Changing Marketing   500
Index   541

Contents

Preface   xii
Acknowledgments   xv
About the Authors   xvii

PART I: TOOLS FOR UNDERSTANDING AND ANALYZING CUSTOMER EQUITY   1

CHAPTER 1   Introduction to Customer Equity Management Strategy   1

Brief Overview of the Strategic Customer Equity Management Approach   2
Why Strategic Customer Equity Management Is Important Now   4
What Is to Be Gained from Understanding Strategic Customer Equity Management?   4
Summary   5
Review Questions and Exercises   5
Case 1-1   Snapple   6

CHAPTER 2   The Customer Equity Approach and the Customer Management Plan   22

The Customer Equity Approach   23
  Role of Value Equity   24
  Role of Brand Equity   24
  Role of Relationship Equity   25
Introducing Customer Management Strategies   26
  Value Strategies   26
  Brand Strategies   27
  Relationship Strategies   27
  Value-Brand Strategies   28
  Value-Relationship Strategies   28
  Relationship-Brand Strategies   28
  Mixed Strategies   29
The Customer Management Plan   29
  Customer Equity Analysis—Data Collection   29
  Customer Equity Analysis—Firm and Competitor Performance   31
  Strategy Development   31
  Measuring, Monitoring, and Evaluating   31

Summary   33

Review Questions and Exercises   33

Appendix 1   Customer Equity Exercise: Interviewing a Customer   34

Appendix 2   Return on Marketing: Using Customer Equity to Focus Marketing Strategy   42

Case 2-1   Xerox: Book-In-Time   69

Case 2-2   Coca-Cola's New Vending Machine (A): Pricing to Capture Value, or Not?   83

CHAPTER 3   Customer Equity Analysis   91

Analyzing the Market   91

Analyzing the Firm's Performance   93

Comparing the Firm's Performance to That of Its Competitors'   96

Determining the Magnitude of the Opportunity   98

What Do We Learn from the Analysis? Where Should the Firm Focus?   100

Summary   101

Review Questions and Exercises   101

Case 3-1   The Brita Products Company   103

Case 3-2   Harrah's Entertainment, Inc.   117

CHAPTER 4   Measuring Customer Equity   141

Brand Switching and Customer Lifetime Value   141

Modeling the Switching Matrix   145

Return on Investment   146

Cross-Sectional versus Longitudinal Data   146

Summary   150

Review Questions and Exercises   150

Case 4-1   Aerosphere Airlines (A)   151

Case 4-2   Aqualisa Quartz: Simply a Better Shower   152

Case 4-3   Calyx & Corolla   166

PART II: DEVELOPING STRATEGIES FOR CUSTOMER EQUITY MANAGEMENT   194

CHAPTER 5   Customer Selection   194

Effective Customer Management Strategy   194

Customer Selection   195

Customer Roles and Management   198

Customer Selection Decision Accountability   199

Customer Selection Decision Evaluation Basis and Data Quality   199

Summary   201

Review Questions and Exercises   201

Case 5-1   Granny's Goodies, Inc.   202

Case 5-2   Fabtek (A)   224

Case 5-3   Fabtek (B)   235

CHAPTER 6   Building and Managing Brand Equity   237

Brand Equity: What Is It and Why Does It Matter?   237

When Brand Equity Matters Most   238

How Can a Firm Grow Brand Equity?   240

Building Brand Awareness: The Customer Communications Strategy   241

Attitude Toward the Brand: Brand Positioning Strategy   242

Corporate Citizenship and Ethics: Doing the Right Things and Doing Things Right   243

Summary   246

Review Questions and Exercises   247

Case 6-1   Eastman Kodak Company: Funtime Film   248

Case 6-2   ALLOY.com: 252

Case 6-3   Brand Report Card Exercise   262

CHAPTER 7   Building and Managing Value Equity   267

Value Equity: The Firm's Ability to Balance the Customer's Value Equation   268

When Value Equity Matters Most   270

Drivers of Value Equity   271
  Quality   271
  Price   274
  Convenience   277

Summary   279

Review Questions and Exercises   279

Case 7-1   KONE: The MonoSpace® Launch in Germany   280

Case 7-2   The Medicines Company   297

CHAPTER 8   Managing Relationship Equity   313

Different Approaches to Managing a Customer Relationship Over Time   313
  Foot-in-the-Door Approach   313
  All-at-Once Approach   316

Managing Different Customer Types Concurrently   319
  Quadrant 1: High Price—High CTS   321
  Quadrant 2: High Price—Low CTS   322

Contents

        Quadrant 3: Low Price—Low CTS   323
        Quadrant 4: Low Price—Low CTS   324

Summary   325

Review Questions and Exercises   325

Case 8-1   WESCO Distribution, Inc.   326

Case 8-2   Arrow Electronics, Inc   347

CHAPTER 9   Managing Customer Relationships Using Multiple Touch Points in Multi-Channel Settings   363

Multi-Channel Marketing: The Firm's Perspective   363
    Choosing Between the Various Options in Multi-Channels   364

The Customer's Perspective   365

Summary   366

Review Questions and Exercises   366

Case 9-1   Eddie Bauer, Inc.   367

PART III: MEASURING, MONITORING, AND EVALUATING CUSTOMER EQUITY MANAGEMENT STRATEGY   381

CHAPTER 10   Strategic Implementation: Investing for Maximum Impact   381

Quick Review: How Did We Get to This Point?   381

Evaluating Potential Marketing Actions   383

Opportunity for Hands-On Analysis   385

Tracking Results and Monitoring the Process   386
    Measure Customer Equity over Time   386
    Test Versus Control   388

Summary   389

Review Questions and Exercises   390

Case 10-1   Aerosphere Airlines (B)   391

Case 10-2   Customer Value Measurement at Nortel Networks—Optical Networks Division   392

Case10-3   Hilton H Honors Worldwide: Loyalty Wars   410

CHAPTER 11   Managing Customer Profitability in Industrial Markets   424

Managing Customers for Revenue   426
    The SCW Index   426
    Price Paid Index   427

Managing Customers for Profit   428

Summary   428

Review Questions and Exercises   429

Case 11-1   Hunter Business Group: TeamTBA   430

Case 11-2   CMR Enterprises   442

CHAPTER 12 The Role of CRM Technologies in Customer Management   460

Background   460

Fitting Strategy with Functional Design   461

Integration—Stakeholders   462

Integration—Critical Touch Points   462
Front Office and Back Office   462
Operational and Analytical   463
Internal and External   463
Multi-Channel and Cross Channel Coordination   464

Implementation Stumbling Blocks   464

How to Measure Success   465

Industry Overview   465

Industry Trends   466

Summary   467

Review Questions and Exercises   467

Case 12-1   Moore Medical Corporation   468

Case 12-2   SaleSoft, Inc.   482

CHAPTER 13 How Customer Management Is Changing Marketing   500

How Customer Equity Analysis Changes Marketing   500

Customer Management and Marketing Accountability   501

Summary   501

Review Questions and Exercises   502

Case 13-1   Customer Profitability and Customer Relationship Management at RBC Financial Group (Abridged)   503

Case 13-2   Citibank: Launching the Credit Card in Asia Pacific (A)   519

Index   541

Preface (for Instructors)

HOW THE BOOK IS STRUCTURED

In *Customer Equity Management,* we present the concepts and analytic tools necessary to understand the concept customer equity management. These concepts and tools are presented in a clear and concise format, and are interspersed with cases that allow the reader to integrate and apply the concepts in real-world settings. This combination of new tools and case applications provides instructors with flexibility in teaching the material, and provides students with the opportunity to practice and use new tools. Specifically, the book is structured as follows:

Part I (Chapters 1–4) outlines the framework for customer management used throughout the book. In particular, following the introductory Chapter 1, Chapter 2 presents the key components of customer equity: value equity, brand equity, and relationship equity. The chapter introduces distinct customer management strategies to show how the three components work, independently and together, to grow the long-term value of the firm through the ultimate source of that value—the firm's customers. Finally, this chapter outlines the customer management plan—a point-by-point plan for developing and implementing customer management strategy.

Chapter 3 describes customer equity analysis. This chapter focuses on the specific steps in the analysis that are necessary for a firm to begin to develop a strategic customer management plan: analyzing the market, analyzing the firm's performance, comparing the firm's performance to its competitors, and determining where the firm should focus its efforts.

In order for the customer equity approach to be truly effective, it is necessary to understand how to put the approach into practice. Chapter 4 provides a detailed look at the underlying mathematical models used in measuring customer equity. A case study provides opportunities to apply and practice the analysis tools at the end of Chapter 4.

Part II (Chapters 5–9) examines how to select customers and provides distinct customer management strategies. Effective customer management strategy begins with careful selection of customers or opportunities to serve. Chapter 5 focuses on the importance of customer selection decisions. Having selected the opportunities to serve, firms then need to formulate and implement strategies to satisfactorily and profitably serve customers and opportunities. Chapters 6, 7, and 8 examine brand equity, value equity, and relationship equity, respectively, in detail. Each chapter defines and explains the importance of each component of customer equity and the circumstances and contexts in which it is likely to be a key consideration in managing the customer relationship. In addition, the chapters examine the key, actionable drivers of brand, value and relationship equity, and describe the types of strategies firms can use to build customer equity through each driver.

Chapter 9 moves the discussion from customer management strategy formulation to customer interaction management. Successful customer relationship management is built on effective management of vendor-initiated and customer-initiated contacts. This chapter shows how firms can leverage interactive technologies to have two-way communications with customers using multiple channels concurrently, to learn more about their customers, and to enhance the value of their offerings.

Part III (Chapters 10–13) focuses on measuring, monitoring and evaluating results. Once the appropriate customer mix has been determined and the firm has determined key actions that will grow long-term profitability, it is important to measure and monitor the effects of marketing actions. Chapter 10 provides an introduction to the analyses necessary to evaluate potential marketing strategies and to determine which marketing actions will have the strongest effect on long term profitability through customer equity. This chapter explains how firms can evaluate distinct marketing investment opportunities to determine which marketing actions will have the strongest ROI. It also discusses the importance of considering competitive actions and how to evaluate the success (or failure) of a marketing initiative. A case study allows further investigation at the end of Chapter 10.

Chapter 11 highlights the difficulty that business marketers face as they attempt to manage profitability of individual customers. We review existing methodologies used by firms to link their customer management effort (costs) with revenues received at the level of individual customers. The chapter then details aggregate methodologies (for example, managing customer segments for profits rather than individual customers) that can be used by firms that do not have the systems in place to accurately measure costs and revenue streams at the individual customer level.

Chapter 12 discusses CRM software products and how they integrate with key customer management strategies. We also examine typical implementation issues to help ensure initial success and the eventual demonstration of ROI by measures defined in the planning process. Finally, we look at specific vendor products in the market, their application, and how current marketing trends are impacting CRM software.

The final chapter of the book provides a look to the future. Chapter 13 focuses on the ways in which customer management is changing the nature of the marketing function itself. By bringing together the new customer management tools and new customer management approach discussed throughout the book, we examine the ways in which marketing is in the process of transforming from a product and transaction focus to a customer and relationship focus, and what this will mean for firms seeking to grow profitability during this transformation.

KEY FEATURES

This book has been developed as a tool for managers, students, and professors. To facilitate learning, it is organized around the strategic customer equity management plan for developing profitable marketing strategies. The chapters are short, and focused on key topics. The book contains real tools, including two cases on the accompanying CD using proprietary analytic software tools developed by the authors. Relevant cases are included to enable students to apply their new knowledge and tools in real-world situations.

WHO SHOULD READ THIS BOOK

Anyone in marketing, management, or finance who wants to grow the long-term value of the firm will find this book valuable. In particular, students and practitioners who want to learn cutting-edge strategic tools will gain much from this book. Undergraduate or MBA students who have taken a basic marketing course and want to master advance marketing strategy will find the book useful. The book is also appropriate for executive development and corporate training. Finally, marketing professionals and consultants will also enjoy this book.

Acknowledgments

We gratefully acknowledge the contributions of our colleague, Valarie Zeithaml (University of North Carolina), co-author with Roland and Kay on many publications related to customer equity, who contributed many of the ideas in this book. Thanks also to Kevin Clancy (Copernicus Marketing Consulting) who has helped us to implement many of these ideas, and to Tony Zahorik (Burke Institute), Tim Keiningham (Ipsos Loyalty), and Ray Kordupleski (Customer Value Management, Inc.), whose work with Roland on return on quality provided the basis for many of the ideas in this book. Many thanks to Tim Donnelly, Kay's graduate research assistant, who compiled the first draft of Chapter 12: The Role of CRM Technologies in Customer Management.

Thanks to the team at Prentice-Hall; especially Wendy Craven, who had the vision to champion the book, Katie Stevens and Rebecca Lembo, and thanks to our expert copyediting team at Progressive Publishing Alternatives, especially Heather Meledin. Thanks to Roland's colleague, P. K. Kannan for test-driving the pre-production version of the book in his CRM class. Thanks also to Keith McKay and his colleagues at Village Software for helping to develop the software used in the book, and to David Fisher for preparing the software for classroom use. Thanks to Kay's research assistants at Boston College: Dwight Branch, Shirley Galarza, Lenka Hanzlik, and Mac Steenrod for researching background material for the book.

We would like to thank Dean Kim Clark, the members of the Division of Research, and Professor David Bell, as Marketing Area Unit Head at the Harvard Business School for their support of our efforts. We also want to thank Professor Ben Shapiro and Kash Rangan for their mentorship and support in shaping the customer management concepts presented in this book. We are also indebted to Barbara Trissel for all her help over the years. Thanks also to Ph.D. student Tuck Siong Chung.

We would also like to acknowledge the many colleagues who have allowed us to include their materials in the book. These include Professors David Bell, John Deighton, Robert Dolan, John Gourville, Charles "Kip" King III, Rajiv Lal, Andrew McAfee, Youngme Moon, Rowland Moriarty, V. G. Narayanan, V. Kasturi Rangan, Walter Salmon, Stowe Shoemaker, and Gordon Swartz.

We also wish to thank the professors that reviewed our manuscript and helped us to publish. These reviewers include:

Ruth Bolton, *Arizona State University*
Joe Cannon, *Colorado State University*
Paul Christ, *Westchester University*
Tom Collinger, *Northwestern University*
Uptal Dholakia, *Rice University*
Guy Gessner, *Canisius College*

Carol Gwin, *Baylor University*
Michel Kostecki, *University of Neuchatel*
Barak Libai, *Tel-Aviv University*
Debi Mishra, *Binghamton University*
Linda M. Mitchell, *Lyndon State*
Peter Verhoef, *University of Groningen*
Scarlett Wesley, *University of South Carolina at Columbia*

Finally, we would like to extend a special, heartfelt thank you to our family, colleagues, and friends for all of their continued support throughout the process of writing the textbook.

About the Authors

Roland T. Rust holds the David Bruce Smith Chair in Marketing at the Robert H. Smith School of Business at the University of Maryland, where he is Chair of the Marketing Department and directs the Center for Excellence in Service. His lifetime achievement honors include the American Marketing Association's Gilbert A. Churchill Award for Lifetime Achievement in Marketing Research, the Outstanding Contributions to Research in Advertising award from the American Academy of Advertising, the AMA's Career Contributions to the Services Discipline Award, Fellow of the American Statistical Association, and the Henry Latané Distinguished Doctoral Alumnus Award from the University of North Carolina at Chapel Hill. He has won best article awards for articles in *Marketing Science, Journal of Marketing Research, Journal of Marketing* (twice), *Journal of Advertising*, and *Journal of Retailing*, as well as MSI's Robert D. Buzzell Best Paper Award (twice). His book, *Driving Customer Equity* (written with Valarie Zeithaml and Katherine Lemon) won the 2002 Berry-AMA Book Prize for the best marketing book of the previous three years. His work has received extensive media coverage, including a *Business Week* cover story and an appearance on *ABC World News Tonight with Peter Jennings*. He is the founder and Chair of the AMA Frontiers in Services Conference, and serves as founding Editor of the *Journal of Service Research*. Professor Rust also is an Area Editor at *Marketing Science* and *Production and Operations Management*, and serves on the editorial review boards of the *Journal of Marketing Research, Journal of Marketing*, and the *Journal of Interactive Marketing*. He has consulted with many leading companies worldwide, including such companies as American Airlines, AT&T, Chase Manhattan Bank, Dow Chemical, DuPont, FedEx, IBM, Nortel, Procter & Gamble, Sears, Unilever, and USAA. E-mail: *rrust@rhsmith.umd.edu*.

Katherine N. Lemon, Ph.D., is an associate professor of marketing at the Wallace E. Carroll School of Management, Boston College. She is a recognized leader in the areas of customer equity, customer asset management and marketing strategy. Lemon serves on the editorial boards of the *Journal of Marketing, Journal of Service Research, Journal of the Academy of Marketing Science, International Journal of Electronic Commerce* and the *Journal of Interactive Marketing*, and on the Academic Council of the American Marketing Association. She has received multiple best-article awards for her research, including the *Journal of Marketing* and the *Journal of Service Research*, and is a recipient of the American Marketing Association's Berry Book Award and of the 2003 and 2004 Marketing Science Institute Robert D. Buzzell Best Paper Award. Lemon's prior books include *Driving Customer Equity: How Customer Lifetime Value is Reshaping Corporate Strategy* (2000, with Rust and Zeithaml), and *Wireless Rules* (2001, with Newell). She teaches courses focusing on customer equity, dynamic customer relationship management, marketing strategy, and marketing ROI. Lemon has consulted with and taught senior executives at leading global companies including Microsoft, Eli Lilly and Company, Timberland, IBM, Pearson Education, Siemens Corporation, Hewlett-Packard, Citigroup, Deloitte, HSBC, Ericsson, Textron, The Capital Markets Company (CAPCO), Copernicus Marketing, and the US Office of Thrift Supervision, and in executive development programs at Wharton and Duke. She has also been an invited and keynote speaker at numerous industry conferences around the world. E-mail: *katherine.lemon@bc.edu*.

Das Narayandas, Ph.D. is Professor of Business Administration at the Harvard Business School. He is currently the course head of the First-year Marketing course in the MBA program and is the Chair of the Business Marketing Strategy for senior sales and marketing executives at the Harvard Business School. He was the Class Day faculty speaker for the MBA Class of 2001 and Class of 2004. He also received the award for teaching excellence from the MBA Class of 2000 and the MBA Class of 2003. Professor Narayandas' background includes over six years of management experience in sales and marketing for various multinational firms that involved field sales and sales force management, new product development, alliance formation, and marketing communications. His articles have appeared in the *Journal of Marketing, Journal of Service Research, Journal of Marketing Research, Sloan Management Review, the Journal of the Academy of Marketing Science* and other publications. He serves on the editorial board of the Journal of the *Academy of Marketing Science* and the *Journal of Service Research*. He has been quoted in publications such as the *Economist*, and *U.S. World and News Report* amongst others. Das has developed and executed in-house training programs for such companies as Arrow Electronics, Compaq, Merrill Lynch, Oce, Tata Group, Northrop Grumman, and Liberty Mutual among others. He has also consulted for 3M, Adecco, Microsoft, Nortel, Praxair, and other companies in the areas of Customer Management, Strategic Marketing, Pricing, and Salesforce Management. His current research interests focus on business-to-business marketing and management of customer relationships. E-mail: *nnaryandas@hbs.edu*.

PART I: TOOLS FOR UNDERSTANDING AND ANALYZING CUSTOMER EQUITY

CHAPTER 1
Introduction to Customer Equity Management Strategy

Consider these Scenarios:

◆ The chief marketing officer of a telecommunications firm is faced with a dilemma: invest $2 million to develop a frequent user program to reduce customer churn, or spend $2 million to improve customer service support through the company's Web site and its toll-free number. Which investment will bring it the greater return?

◆ The product manager of a global pharmaceutical company must choose among:
- Investing $5 million in the technology to build a consumer database,
- Spending $1 million on a direct marketing campaign,
- Accepting the ad agency's recommendation of a $2 million media buy for next year.

What should the product manager do?

◆ The marketing VP of a leading retailing firm is considering reducing prices by 5 percent across the board but eliminating in-store sales and price promotions. How can this executive determine if this is the best use of the firm's marketing resources?

Which of these investments will have the greatest impact on customer relationships and long-term profitability? How should the executives decide? Firms today face key marketing challenges that cross traditional functional boundaries:

- What's the best way to attract new customers?
- How do I keep current customers happy and make sure they don't switch to competitors?
- What's most important to my customers?
- How do I know which customers are most important to my business?
- How do I build my business without resorting to endless price promotions?

The answers to these questions require a deep understanding of customer managment. Marketing strategy is, at its core, customer strategy. What's the goal of marketing strategy? Firms seek to attract and retain customers who will purchase goods and services from them at a rate that enables the firm to grow profitably over the long term. How should a firm do this? That's what this book is all about.

◆ BRIEF OVERVIEW OF THE STRATEGIC CUSTOMER EQUITY MANAGEMENT APPROACH

The strategic customer equity management framework presented in this book has four critical steps: (1) customer analysis; (2) firm and competitor analysis; (3) strategy development and design; and (4) measure, monitor, and evaluate the strategy. This framework is outlined in Figure 1-1. The task begins with an analysis of the market and what is most important to customers in the firm's market. This analysis includes a key measurement and analysis tool—customer equity.[1] *Customer equity* is defined as the total of the discounted lifetime values summed over all of the firm's current and potential customers.[2] This is followed by an in-depth understanding of how well the firm and its key competitors are doing with respect to customer equity. These two analyses then enable the firm to determine where to focus its efforts to maximize long-term profit—by growing the value of each customer and by reducing costs where appropriate.

FIGURE 1-1 Strategic Customer Equity Management Framework

Customer Analysis
↓
Firm and Competitor Analysis
↓
Strategy Development and Design
↓
Measure, Monitor, and Evaluate

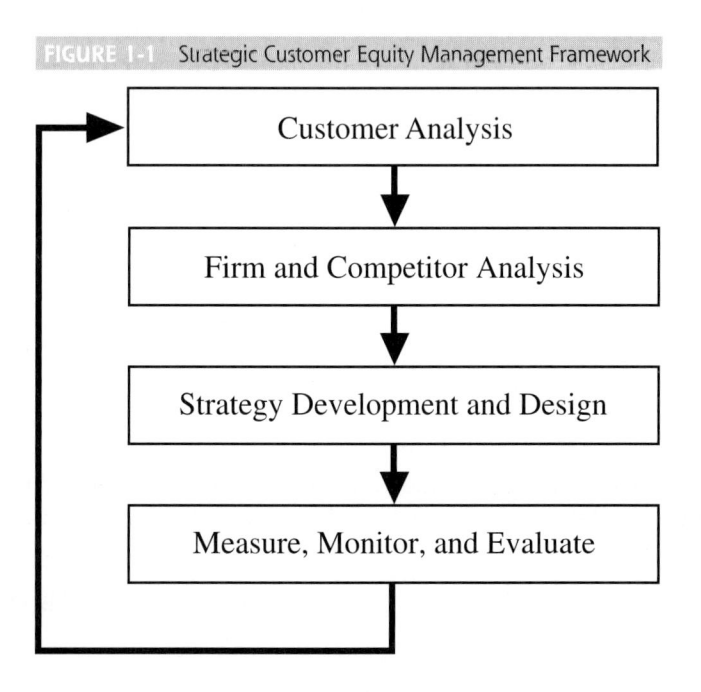

[1] Roland T. Rust, Valarie A. Zeithaml, and Katherine N. Lemon, *Driving Customer Equity: How Customer Lifetime Value Is Reshaping Corporate Strategy* (New York: The Free Press; 2000).
[2] Robert C. Blattberg, and John Deighton, "Managing Marketing by the Customer Equity Test," *Harvard Business Review* 75, no. (4) (1996): 136–44.

◆ BOX 1-1 ◆

The Volkswagen Group Cracks New Markets with the Help of CRM

The German company Volkswagen Group is an international automobile manufacturer that realizes the importance of managing customer relationships. The company is launching several international customer relationship management initiatives with the intent to expand the initiative to other markets.

The size and potential of the largely untapped Chinese market makes initiatives targeted at that country highly lucrative and a great opportunity for Volkswagen. The company created a customer relationship management (CRM) database as part of an effort to improve its ability to communicate with current and potential customers there and in other emerging markets. The CRM system will track prospective customers through the purchase process, from initial awareness to purchase intent, and will allow VW to uncover the reasons shoppers do and do not purchase. Using this information, VW is able to create a comprehensive customer profile of various market segments, enabling the company to be more cost-effective in its communications with customers. Customer relationships will be enhanced with communication through appropriate channels such as telemarketing, e-mail, Internet, and direct mail. In addition to this, VW's advertising and media plans will be tailored to the findings of the CRM database, again allowing the company to communicate most effectively with customers.

Volkswagen has also implemented CRM systems in Indonesia as part of an effort to reposition VW as a more upscale brand. The CRM system will include managing a customer database, and will affect direct and interactive marketing campaigns. The program will also highlight the most profitable segments of the Indonesian market, enabling VW to focus on these segments. Volkswagen will be able to understand what drives perceptions of its brand in Indonesia, and will be able to market its automobiles more effectively to the appropriate segments.

SOURCES: Leithen, Francis, "VW Eyeing Luxury Niche to Drive Lift on Indon Targets," *AdAgeGlobal* (September 20, 2002). Normandy, Madden, "Shanghai VW Drives Tailor-made CRM Plan," *AdAgeGlobal* (April 1, 2002).

Once its focus is determined, the firm can begin the task of developing and implementing its customer strategy. The first task is to select the appropriate mix of customers. Then, the firm must determine the strategy or strategies it will use to grow the value of those customers—to grow its customer equity. The firm can focus its efforts on brand strategies, value strategies, or relationship strategies, or a mix of these, depending on the outcome of the analysis.

Finally, it is critical to measure, monitor, and evaluate the results of the strategy. By understanding the effects of each marketing initiative on customer profitability and customer equity, the firm can reevaluate its strategic choices and implement any changes necessary to respond to changes in customer needs or market forces.

◆ WHY STRATEGIC CUSTOMER EQUITY MANAGEMENT IS IMPORTANT NOW

The economy has shifted from being goods driven to one that is service driven. Customers and firms have shifted from focusing on transactions to focusing on relationships. This has led to a fundamental shift from marketing products to managing customers.[3] It is important to develop and implement strategies that have a strong customer focus, but that do not overlook the importance of product, brand, price, channels, competition, or information technology. Finally, in a context in which firms are continually evaluated on their financial results, it is imperative to have strategic tools that enable firms to link customer management efforts to financial outcomes.[4]

In this book, you will gain the essential tools for meeting these challenges, and for developing profitable marketing strategies. In so doing, you will master new models and methods for analysis, strategy development, and evaluation. Most important, you will learn to trade off one marketing investment for another to determine the best allocation of marketing resources. Overall, you will gain significant knowledge that will enable you to move forward in your marketing or management career.

◆ WHAT IS TO BE GAINED FROM UNDERSTANDING STRATEGIC CUSTOMER EQUITY MANAGEMENT?

Returning to the examples at the beginning of this chapter, the telecom Chief Marketing Officer would be able to determine that the return on investment (ROI) of the customer support investment was significantly greater than the ROI of the loyalty program. The pharmaceutical product manager would learn that the more expensive consumer database would result in a much higher return than the less expensive, direct marketing campaign or advertising buys. Finally, the retail marketing VP would find out that the everyday low pricing strategy would have to be combined with other relationship-building strategies to be successful in the long term. In today's and tomorrow's competitive and financially accountable markets, understanding how to manage customers for long-term profit will be critical.[5]

---

[3]Paul D. Berger, Ruth N. Bolton, Douglas Bowman, Elton Briggs, V. Kumar, A. Parasuraman, and Creed Terry, "Marketing Actions and the Value of Customer Assets: A Framework for Customer Asset Management," *Journal of Service Research* 5 (August 2002); 39–54.
[4]Roland T. Rust, Katherine N. Lemon, and Valarie A. Zeithaml, "Return on Marketing: Using Customer Equity to Focus Marketing Strategy," *Journal of Marketing* 68 (January 2004); 109–127.
[5]See Ruth N. Bolton, Katherine N. Lemon, and Peter Verhoef, "The Theoretical Underpinnings of Customer Asset Management: A Framework and Propositions for Future Research," *Journal of the Academy of Marketing Science* (forthcoming); John Hogan, Katherine N. Lemon, and Roland T. Rust, "Customer Equity Management: Charting New Directions for the Future of Marketing," *Journal of Service Research* 5 (August 2002); 4–12; and Robert C. Blattberg, Gary Getz, and Jacquelyn S. Thomas, *Customer Equity: Building and Managing Relationships as Valuable Assets* (Boston: Harvard Business School Press, 2001).

Summary

A fundamental shift has occurred in marketing, from managing and marketing products to understanding and managing customers. This necessitates an understanding of the customer management process and the value of customers to the firm—the firm's customer equity. There are four steps in the customer equity management process:

1. Analyze the customers
2. Analyze the firm and its key competitors
3. Design and develop marketing strategy
4. Measure, monitor, and evaluate the strategy

Review Questions and Exercises

1. Think of a product or service that you purchase or pay for regularly (e.g., mobile phone, plan, groceries, fast food, airline tickets). Estimate how valuable you are as a customer to the firm from whom you make the purchase. Consider in your estimation how often you purchase, the monetary value of each purchase, how likely you are to continue purchasing this product or service, and the firm's approximate cost of having you as a customer.
2. Consider the Volkswagen example in this chapter. What do you think Volkswagen gains from its investment in a CRM /customer relationship–building program? How will the additional information Volkswagen gains regarding its customers enable Volkswagen to market to its customers differently?

◆◆◆ Snapple

Case 1-1

John Deighton

You remember the '80s, Philip?
– Of course.
God hated the '80s.
– He didn't like anything?
He liked Snapple.
– God liked Snapple?
Not all the flavors.

—FROM A 1998 EPISODE OF "CHICAGO HOPE,"
A NETWORK TELEVISION DRAMA

Arnie Greenberg, Leonard Marsh, and Hyman Golden had been friends since high school. In 1972, they went into business selling all-natural apple juice to health food stores in Greenwich Village under the brand name *Snapple*. By the late 1980s, their brand had achieved near-cult status on both coasts of the United States, with its iced teas particularly in demand. It had taken 15 years, they said, to become an overnight success.

In 1994 Quaker bought Snapple for $1.7 billion. The vision had been to combine Snapple with Gatorade, an earlier and very successful acquisition, to form a powerful beverage business unit. Snapple, however, did not thrive: sales fell in each of the next four years, and in 1997 Quaker despaired and sold the brand to Triarc Beverages for $300 million. In the fallout that followed, both Quaker's chairman of 16 years and its president resigned.

Mike Weinstein, CEO of Triarc Beverage Group, reflected on the acquisition. "At $300 million, Snapple is not a steal by any means. It's in decline, and when that happens to a brand it's seldom that it comes back. We're in a fashion business here, and when your imagery isn't fashionable, often that's the end. But we've talked to a lot of consumers and we did a lot of qualitative research, and we've decided that in this case the brand still has inherent strength. People feel good about it. It will respond to the right marketing stuff."

1972–1986: THE ORIGINS OF THE BRAND

Arnie Greenberg's family ran a sardine and pickle store in Ridgewood in Queens, New York. His friends Leonard Marsh and Hyman Golden helped him in the store, and in turn he helped them to manage their window-washing business. In the climate of the 1960s, Arnie encouraged the family to stock health foods. The three saw the popularity of natural no-preservative fruit juices in the store, and teamed up with a California-based juice company to manufacture and distribute a bottled apple drink. Eventually they broke away from the California partner and founded their own company—Unadulterated Food Products—and the Snapple brand.[1] "100% Natural" became Snapple's mantra.

The business grew slowly using internally generated funds. It outsourced production and product development and built a network of distributors across New York City. Where possible, it sought individual distributors working for their

---

The case was prepared by John Deighton. Copyright © 1999 by the President and Fellows of Harvard College. Harvard Business School Case 599-126.

[1] Drawn from Cynthia Riggs, "Snapple Cracks Tough Pop Market," *Crain's New York Business*, August 14, 1989 and Cara Trager, "Niche Entrepreneurs," *Beverage World*, October 1989.

own account, and found as a result that the business needed to broaden the product line to keep distributors occupied. It added carbonated drinks, fruit-flavored iced teas, diet juices, seltzers, an isotonic sports drink, and even a Vitamin Supreme. Some succeeded and many failed, but premium pricing on the successful products covered losses on the failures. Revenues and profits grew with expansion of distribution into New Jersey and Pennsylvania. In 1984 annual turnover was $4 million and it doubled by 1986 to $8 million.

In response to pleas from Snapple's distributors, the founders commissioned advertising. Jonathan Bond and Richard Kirshenbaum, who managed the Snapple account later, described this early advertising as follows:

> When tennis star Ivan Lendl was featured in several ads, the idea didn't quite come off. (He) kept mispronouncing the name as "Shnapple." Luckily the ads were so bad that they didn't do the brand any harm. Had those schlocky ads been just a little better, they actually would have been worse for Snapple. The ineptness of the ads actually came off as charming, just like the cluttered packaging.[2]

Snapple was just one of many small beverage brands aspiring to appeal to young, health-conscious urban professionals in the 1980s. Napa Naturals, Natural Quencher, SoHo, After the Fall, Ginseng Rush, Elliot's Amazing, Old Tyme Soft Drink, Manly Sodas, Syfo, and Original New York Seltzer were some of the many contenders in what eventually came to be called the New Age or Alternative beverage category.

1987–1993: THE GLORY YEARS

The vision of many entrepreneurial founders was to exit via acquisition. For example, the founders of SoHo, Connie Best and Sophia Collier, took sales to $25 million and then sold the company to liquor giant Seagram in 1989 for $15 million. They explained that they were handing off to a buyer with deeper pockets.

Seagram expanded distribution and advertising, dismantling the independent distribution network in favor of its own wine cooler distribution chain.

The Snapple founders, however, decided to cope with the next stage of growth by hiring professional management. They turned to Carl Gilman, a beverage industry veteran from Seven-Up, to run sales and marketing. Gilman used focus groups to tell him how to improve Snapple's label design. He increased the advertising budget to $1 million, and intensified the independent distributor system throughout the East Coast. He viewed expansion to the West Coast as premature and a dilution of effort. "The stronger we build the East Coast, the more the West Coast will want us."[3]

The distribution system grew until Snapple had a network of 300 small, predominantly family-owned distributors servicing convenience chains, pizza stores, food service vendors, gasoline stations, and so-called mom-and-pop stores. A press story described the work as "salesman, truck loader, driver, heavy lifter and bill collector, all in one."[4] Distribution in Boston was in the hands of Ted Landers, who had married into a Boston beer distribution company and now employed 11 people and several trucks to serve what he called the up-and-down-the-street business in soft drinks:

> In 1985 we were distributing several brands of single-serve beverage, SoHo and others. We saw lots of excitement around Snapple, and Snapple was doing its own distribution in Boston—about 250,000 cases a year—so we went to them and offered to grow their volume, which we did, up to a million cases a year. We invested in coolers and vending machines for convenience stores, and talked up the product. We visited supermarkets, but they wanted slotting allowances and service calls, which can put a strain on my pocket book, so we stayed away from

---

[2]Jonathan Bond and Richard Kirshenbaum, *Under the Radar* (New York: John Wiley and Sons, 1998).

[3]Trager, op cit.
[4]Glen Collins, "On the Front Lines of the Beverage Wars: The Life of a Snapple Distributor, Surviving Robbers, Illegal Parkers and the Usual Cutthroat Competition," *The New York Times,* December 3, 1997.

them in the main. Supermarkets were no more than 10% of my volume in 1994.

Nationally, supermarkets accounted for about 20% of Snapple's sales.

Snapple's promotion was an offbeat blend of public relations and advertising. The story of the three founders' success in an industry dominated by multinational behemoths was told many times in many media. Advertising agency Kirshenbaum, Bond & Partners created a spokesmodel for the brand in the form of Wendy Kaufman, a former truck dispatcher with a brash New York attitude. Wendy received paid exposure in the brand's advertising, but her eccentric personality also attracted unpaid media attention. She appeared on television shows such as *Oprah and David Letterman,* where she read Letterman's "Top 10 Least Favorite Snapple Drinks," and was interviewed by *USA TODAY*. At times she attracted 2,000 letters a week. She made appearances at retail stores, and accepted invitations to sleepovers, Bar Mitzvahs, and prom dates.

In a similar vein, the brand sponsored the radio programs of two very popular 1980s exponents of shock radio. Howard Stern specialized in tasteless and often outrageously sexist humor, and Rush Limbaugh built a following as an advocate of right wing political and social ideas delivered in a style that combined protracted ranting with acid sarcasm. In exchange for sponsorships on both shows, the brand received on-air endorsement and sometimes became the subject of Stern's banter and Limbaugh's rants. Stern got to know the founders of the business personally and conveyed to his listeners a genuine and infectious regard for the products and the people behind them.

Kirshenbaum, Bond adopted "100% Natural" not only as an advertising line, but as the test which all marketing actions had to pass:

Everything should and would be natural and real. We would use real people in real circumstances. Everything that happened on a Snapple shoot was real. And we would run on air only what really happened, even if it didn't turn out the way we scripted it. We got a letter from a woman who claimed that her dog Shane came running every time he heard a Snapple cap being opened. We called him "Shane, the wonder dog." But when we got there and tried it, nothing happened. The dog just sat there. So we ran the spot with the dog just lying there.[5]

On a summer day in Hempstead, Long Island, Snapple invited consumers to a Snapple Convention. Over 5,000 people sent the required $5 and 20 Snapple labels, and participated in a day of Snapple-themed fun and games. A Snapple fashion show was won by a woman in a dress made of Snapple caps.

Growth in the Alternative beverage category was explosive, with Snapple leading the way. Snapple sales grew from $80 million in 1989 to $231 million in 1992 and $516 million in 1993. Competition grew commensurately, though Snapple's share remained steady at about 30%–40% of the rather hard-to-define category. (See Exhibits 1, 2, 3, 4, and 5 for estimates of the growth and structure of the market and brand.) Brands like Clearly Canadian and Mistic appeared and Coke and Pepsi were rumored to be entering. Seagram, however, failed to benefit from the market's expansion, and sold SoHo for an estimated $1 million in 1992. Efforts to replicate its wine cooler success in the Alternative category had been unsuccessful. Industry observers attributed its difficulties to raising price, to tampering with flavors, and to dropping the patchwork of small distributors in favor of large liquor wholesalers. Seagram's president explained, "We are a large company and we should be operating large businesses."[6]

In 1992, the three Snapple founders sold control of the company to a Boston private investment bank—the Thomas H. Lee Company—in a leveraged buyout and subsequent public offering. In 1994 with sales running at $674 million, Lee sold it to Quaker Oats for $1.7 billion in cash.

---

[5]Bond and Kirshenbaum, op. cit.
[6]Eben Shapiro, "A Soda Seagram Didn't Swallow," *The New York Times,* March 21, 1992, p. 37.

Growth of Snapple

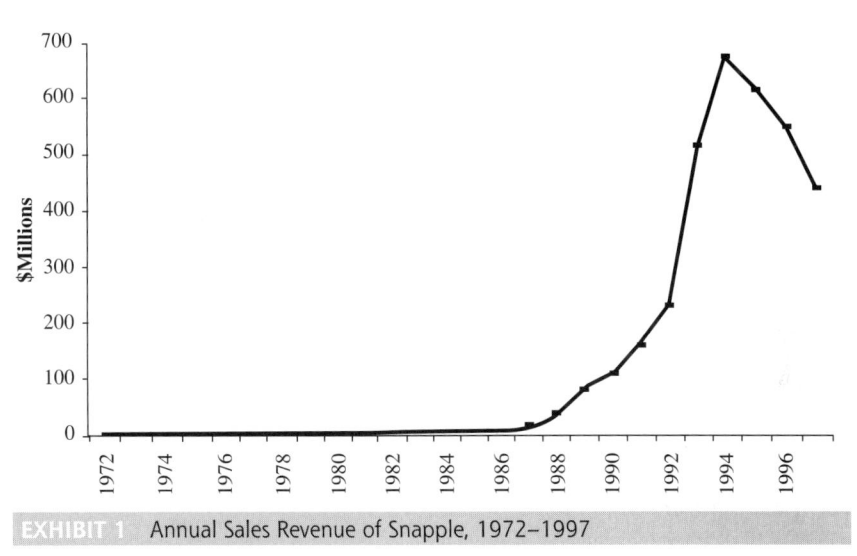

EXHIBIT 1 Annual Sales Revenue of Snapple, 1972–1997

Source: Various published sources.

1994–1997: QUAKER TAKES COMMAND

Quaker in 1994 was a food company with four main areas of business: grain-based foods, bean-based foods, pet foods, and beverages. The first three were relatively mature, while the beverage business, consisting entirely of the Gatorade brand, had been growing vigorously. Gatorade

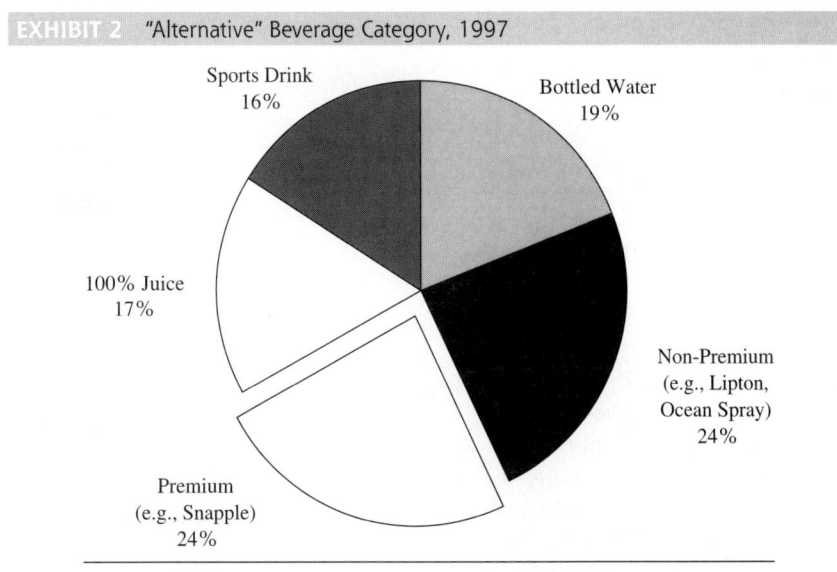

EXHIBIT 2 "Alternative" Beverage Category, 1997

- Sports Drink 16%
- Bottled Water 19%
- Non-Premium (e.g., Lipton, Ocean Spray) 24%
- Premium (e.g., Snapple) 24%
- 100% Juice 17%

Total Alternative Berverage Category: $5 Billion at Wholesale
The Alternative category represents 10% of the non-alcoholic beverage industry.

Source: Triarc Company estimates.

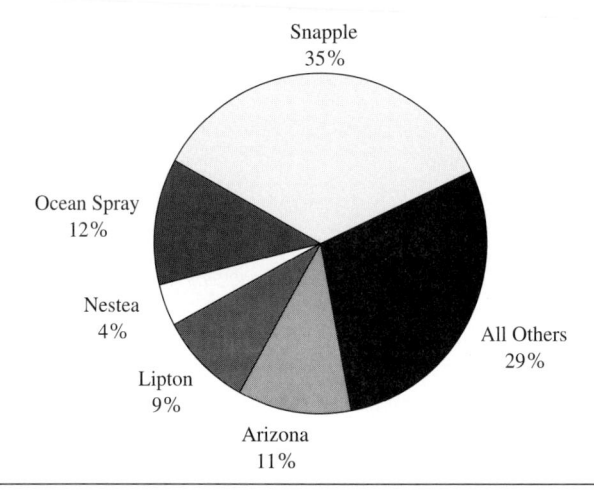

Snapple 35%
Ocean Spray 12%
Nestea 4%
Lipton 9%
Arizona 11%
All Others 29%

Total Supermarket Alternative Beverage Category:- $0.3 Billion at Wholesale

EXHIBIT 3 Supermarket Brand Shares, 1997

Source: Triarc Company estimates.

contributed $1.1 billion of the company's $5.95 billion turnover in that year.

Gatorade's origins were in a research project at the University of Florida in the early 1960s to find a way to replenish fluids lost during exercise. The product, an uncarbonated orange-flavored mix of water, salts, and sugars, was tested on the school's football team, the Gators. It came to the notice of the sports world when the Gators beat Georgia Tech in the 1969 Orange Bowl and Bobby Dodd, the losing coach, explained to *Sports Illustrated*: "We didn't have Gatorade. That

EXHIBIT 4 Snapple Flavors

		Percent of Cases in 1996
1.	Lemon Tea	15%
2.	Kiwi Strawberry	7
3.	Mango Madness	5
6.	Peach Tea	5
5.	Pink Lemonade	5
4.	Diet Peach Tea	4
7.	Fruit Punch	4
8.	Raspberry Tea	4
9.	Diet Lemon Tea	3
10.	Diet Raspberry Tea	3
Top 10 of 50 flavors		55%

Source: Triarc Company estimates.

Per 24-Bottle Case	
Retailer's price to consumer	$19 in supermarket, $24 on street
Distributor's selling price to retailer	$15 to supermarket, $19 to street
Manufacturer's selling price to distributor	$10
Cost of goods (contract manufacturing)	$ 6
Advertising and promotion	$ 2
Profit before general and administrative costs	$ 2

EXHIBIT 5 Snapple Pro Forma Income Statement

Source: Triarc Company estimates.

Note: "Street" means street vendors, delicatessens, restaurants, recreation areas, etc.

made the difference." A small packaged goods marketing firm, Stokey-Van Camp, acquired the brand, took sales to nearly $100 million, and sold it to Quaker in 1983. Quaker took its sales to $1 billion in a decade.

Within the company, management attributed this growth to three main factors.[7] First, Quaker expanded the line. When Quaker bought the business, Gatorade was sold in 32-ounce bottles. Quaker added a 16-ounce glass bottle for the convenience store trade and 64-ounce and gallon plastic bottles for sale in supermarkets, and expanded from three to eight flavors. Second, Quaker increased promotional support. The brand became more visible in the major sports leagues, with Michael Jordan of the Chicago Bulls basketball team as a spokesman, and touchline visibility in the National Football League's televised games. Third, Quaker improved Gatorade's distribution significantly. Internationally, it entered 26 foreign markets. Domestically, it improved coverage of the market and lowered its cost-to-serve by using the same logistics system that distributed Quaker's breakfast cereals and snacks. It shipped Gatorade in full truckloads from Quaker-owned manufacturing plants to the warehouses of the larger supermarket chains and the wholesalers who serviced smaller retail chains and independent supermarkets. From these warehouses Gatorade was combined with other grocery products to make up full truckload deliveries direct to retail stores.

Despite its success, some speculated that Gatorade could be an even larger brand in the hands of a company with more scale in beverages. Indeed there was speculation that Quaker, no stranger to takeover rumors, might be acquired for the Gatorade asset. In 1993 Quaker had explored a joint venture with Coca-Cola to develop overseas sales, but talks had broken down. Domestically, Quaker felt that Gatorade was weak in what it called the *cold channel,* comprising street vendors, delicatessens, restaurants, recreation areas, and so on, and distinguished from the so-called *warm channel,* comprising mainly supermarkets. About 60% of Gatorade's sales moved through the warm channel. Quaker believed that there were two million points of

---

[7]Kevin Francella, "Gatorade Takes the Heat: Interview with Quaker Oats Co. Gatorade Vice President for Sales, U.S. and Canada, David Williams," *ASAP,* January 15, 1994.

availability for soft drinks in the United States, and Gatorade was represented in 200,000.[8]

The president of Quaker's beverage division explained the decision to acquire Snapple: "Gatorade put Quaker in the beverage business; this substantially broadens our position. Quaker has the vision of becoming a very large beverage company."[9] Quaker's chairman and CEO declared, "We expect to create the most innovative distribution system in the beverage industry, one which combines the very best of the two organizations and enhances the value to our trade customers through more merchandising, more points of sale, and more in-store refrigeration equipment. The great advantage to consumers is that you will be able to buy Snapple and Gatorade in many more locations than you can today."[10] Leonard Marsh of Snapple agreed, "Quaker has the resources and management skills to take Snapple to the next level of success."[11] Snapple was expected to benefit from Quaker's packaging experience, supply chain expertise, and modern information systems capabilities. For example, Quaker sought to eliminate the substantial cost of middlemen in Snapple's warm channel by shipping direct from factory to supermarket warehouses, while at the same time using Snapple's middlemen to take Gatorade to the cold channel. Gatorade's market strengths in the U.S. South seemed to complement Snapple's strengths in the Northeast and West Coast.

It was clear to Quaker executives that Snapple's imagery was different from Gatorade's. Management talked of Gatorade as a "lifestyle" brand and Snapple as a "fashion" brand. They knew that consumers pictured Gatorade as a beverage for those who worked out or played vigorous sports, and such lifestyles were a relatively stable factor in the culture. The imagery of the Snapple brand was more fashion-sensitive, quirky and on the edge. But Snapple was now a brand with annual sales of $674 million, and the task of transitioning it from the edge to the mainstream, from fashion to lifestyle, seemed within reach.

Quaker recognized the need to integrate Snapple's entrepreneurial culture with its own. They retained Gilman and other Snapple senior management on short-term contracts. However, as a large corporation, Quaker saw risks to being associated with people who made a living cultivating controversy, as Howard Stern and Rush Limbaugh did, and terminated both relationships along with Wendy Kaufman's role. Terminating Stern was not a simple matter. For many months after he had been dropped he railed against Quaker, urging listeners to stay away from "Crapple."

Quaker charged Gilman to work with Quaker executives to rationalize distribution of Gatorade and Snapple. Teams went out to the 300 distributors to propose that they cede Snapple's supermarket accounts to Quaker in exchange for the right to distribute Gatorade to the rest of their accounts. In meeting after meeting, however, distributors resisted Quaker's proposals. They had worked for years to get into the blue-chip supermarket accounts, and were disinclined to give them up. Most distributors held contracts into perpetuity. Despite protracted negotiations with individual distributors and with distributor councils, no channel rationalization was achieved.

As Quaker introduced Snapple in larger pack sizes and in greater assortments, they met limitations on distributor trucks and retail display space in the cold channel. In addition, it appeared that Snapple played a less utilitarian role in consumers' lives than Gatorade, which lent itself to large-pack sizes because when people drank it they were thirsty and were looking to be rehydrated, often in team settings. Snapple, on the other hand, sold best in 16-ounce single-serve containers.

Snapple sales peaked in 1994 at $674 million, and declined each year until by 1997 sales were $440 million. Several changes in management did not help to reverse the trend. In the latter years Quaker hired Mike Schott, Harvard MBA of 1972 who had been the executive who had built Poland Spring bottled water to national prominence, but to no avail. Quaker was rumored to have discussed the sale of Snapple with Procter & Gamble, Pepsi, and Cadbury

---

[8]Ibid.
[9]Donald Uzzi quoted in Juline Liesse, "Quaker Ups the Ante by Buying Snapple but Food Giant Denies Move was Anti-takeover," *Advertising Age,* November 7, 1994.
[10]William D. Smithburg quoted in Andrew Kaplan, "Distribution Shifts Ahead for Gatorade/Snapple," *U.S. Distribution Journal,* December 15, 1994.
[11]Kaplan, ibid.

Schweppes, but in March 1997, Triarc came forward to buy the brand.

1997: TRIARC ACQUIRES SNAPPLE

Triarc Companies was an investment company with a long history of buying and selling troubled assets. Its controlling shareholders were Nelson Peltz, a member of Forbes list of 500 richest Americans since 1989, and Peter May, his longtime partner. Their beverage assets at the time were Mistic Brands, a fruit juice and tea business acquired in 1995 for $97 million, and Royal Crown Cola (RC). Mistic's sales at the time were $140 million.

Managing the Triarc beverage brands was Mike Weinstein, who by coincidence had been a 1972 Harvard Business School sectionmate of Mike Schott. Weinstein explained how he came to be working at Triarc and charged with trying to salvage Snapple:

> I graduated from Lafayette College in 1970 and applied to a couple of business schools including Harvard. Much to my surprise they accepted me. I went there with no particular goal other than to improve my general business skills. In my first year I was interviewing for summer jobs, not doing particularly well, and my marketing prof called me in and asked how the hunt was going. I said "not real well." He told me he had a friend at Pepsi who was looking for an intern. I interviewed and got an offer. Since that was my only job offer, I ended up in beverages.
>
> I liked the industry a lot so when I got my MBA, I joined Pepsi. I worked in their bottling operation, so while my classmates were going to work in a jacket and tie, there was I in a pair of jeans going out on a merchandising crew. But I thought it would be good to learn the business from the bottom up. After three years in bottling I spent some time in brand management. It wasn't classic P&G stuff, but more focused on distribution and promotion—key drivers in the beverage business.
>
> In 1981 an opportunity came along to join a small beverage company called A&W Root Beer, part of United Brands, as VP Marketing. I jumped at it. After a few years, A&W went through a leveraged buyout in which I was a participant. Back in those days you could do highly leveraged deals. We had a million dollars in equity and a hundred million in debt. Luckily the business was really strong, the company went public and we paid down all the debt in a few years. I eventually got promoted to president and in 1993 the company was sold to Cadbury for over $300 million, generating a really nice return for us all.
>
> When that happened I was 45 and decided to go home. I knew I'd eventually go back to work but wanted to enjoy life for a while. One morning while I was doing laps at a pool I decided to write down everything I knew about the soft drink industry. So I wrote a manual I later named "The Complete Insiders Guide to the U.S. Soft Drink Industry." It started as a small pamphlet but later turned out to be 280 pages of how the business works. That led me into beverage consulting and I started a one-person consulting business called Liquid Logic. I used the manual in seminars for people who wanted to know more about the industry—suppliers, ad agencies, promotion companies, etc.
>
> I was hired to do due diligence on a small company—Mistic Beverages—a premium beverage company that competed with Snapple. When that deal fell through, we put our own deal together. We wrote a business plan and went out to raise money. We found Triarc, who already owned RC and was interested in expanding their beverage holdings. The deal closed in August 1995 and I stayed with Triarc to get Mistic back on a growth path.
>
> I remember distinctly Peltz talking about buying Snapple during that time period. I didn't think a lot about it because I was sure Quaker wouldn't sell at a reasonable price. I always thought Snapple was a great brand because we'd met it as a competitor of Mistic. Right before Christmas in 1996 I was on a plane with Peltz and he said, "You know, we're going to get Snapple." I told him it was a great brand and he'd have to find someone to run it. He goes "What are you talking about, you're going to run it." I said "I don't do that, I'm a small-company guy." After all, Snapple was over twice the size of Mistic and RC combined, and taking on something that

big worried me a lot. Plus the brand was in a tailspin. We were just in the process of absorbing RC and here it was just a few months later and I was going to be asked to take on the beast that beat Quaker.

A Strategy for Snapple

In late 1997 Weinstein sat down with Ken Gilbert, recently recruited from a major advertising agency to the position of senior vice president of marketing at Triarc, to assess Snapple's situation and to set priorities for reversing the brand's slide.

On the table in front of Gilbert was a study written by a New Jersey group that specialized in the application of anthropological methods to marketing problems (excerpted in Exhibit 6). The study was recommended by Snapple's advertising agency, Deutsch, Inc., to help develop an overall communications strategy to revitalize the brand. Specifically, the study investigated Snapple's

---

EXHIBIT 6 Analysis of the Snapple Brand

THE CULTURAL LOGIC OF THE SNAPPLE BRAND EXTRACTS FROM A REPORT PREPARED BY THE CULTURAL ANALYSIS GROUP FOR DEUTSCH, INC., NOVEMBER 1997

OBJECTIVES

- Who are core users of Snapple, and how is the Snapple brand expressed in their lives?
- How does Snapple intersect with key trends and values in contemporary life?
- What binds consumers to the brand?
- Why do formerly heavy users step away from Snapple, and reduce their consumption?
- Ultimately, what is the meaning of Snapple in people's lives? How can we develop a positioning that transcends demography and geography?

METHOD

- 72 in-home interviews in 4 markets

2 developed markets:	2 undeveloped markets:
• New York	• Dallas
• Seattle	• St. Louis

- Divided evenly by age:
    $\frac{1}{2}$ were with ages 18–29
    $\frac{1}{2}$ were with ages 30–44
- Divided into three groups:
    1. Long-time loyalists (3+ years), heavy users (4+ times/wk.)
    2. New to franchise heavy users (where Snapple has become their favorite non-carbonated beverage in the last year)
    3. Lapsed users, former heavy users who continue to drink it (1–4 times/mo.)

THE MEANING OF SNAPPLE

- **Snapple defined by what it is not.** It is suspended between:

    depravity <----> Snapple <----> --- deprivation
    (colas)   --- (water, carrot juice, etc.)

CHAPTER 1 Introduction to Customer Equity Management Strategy   **15**

It may substitute for cola, but is by no means conceptually equivalent. Snapple use is driven, and defined in large part, by a reaction against colas:

Colas = Modernity:	*Snapple = Reaction to Modernity:*
unnatural	natural
artificial image	real
impersonal	personal
uniformity, exclusion	diversity, inclusiveness
mass production	variety, individualism
authority	anti-authority, irreverence

It is not necessarily New Age, nor a return to the past, but a bit of both. By "alternative," users do not mean drop-outs, sullen and alienated. Snapple is not like water. Snapple is a treat: Unlike water, "You can't carry it around without drinking it."

Water	*Snapple*
should drink it	want to drink it
good for you	fun
empty	full
"tasteless"/"dull"	vivid sensory experience

- ***Snapple is seen in experiential terms.*** There is something essentially sensual about Snapple: It tickles, rouses, lingers, wakes up the mouth, reminds one of the beach, or of walking barefoot in the grass. It is full of variety, full of imagination, full of flavor, more variety than any competitor, more new combinations. The packaging (complexity of the label, stippling on bottle) plays out the taste experience. Drinking a Snapple is engaging, not something you do on autopilot.
- ***Snapple has in-betweenity.*** Snapple drinkers inhabit the vast middle ground between:

Don't care what I put into my body	⟵⟶	Snapple drinkers	⟵⟶	Really serious about health

There's a Goldilocks quality: "Not too thick, not too thin, not too sweet, not too tart." Not a child's drink, but not middle-aged either. It is middle class. Colas = inner city, ghetto, and Evian, Perrier = jet set. Every Snapple drink is a blend. Snapple reaches across beverage categories. It's for when you're on the go = in-between activities. Snapple ratifies and intensified transitional periods.

PIVOTAL CHARACTERISTICS

- ***Authentic*** The brand pivots on trust. It makes implicit health claims. Its name conveys healthiness:

    snap ⟶ active, ⟶ healthy
    apple ⟶ healthy

The fruitiness claim works on the same level as the vegetable content of V8 juice. Fruit is healthy, Snapple is fruity, so Snapple is healthy. If it is seen as faux fruit juice (e.g., Sunny Delight,

(Continued)

EXHIBIT 6 (cont.)

Kool-Aid, etc.), then its claims (All natural ingredients, Made from the best stuff on earth) become just so much hype and Snapple drinkers are chumps. As a brand there is a Johnnie Walker character to Snapple. It can flicker from optimum and premium to impure and inauthentic.

- **Fun** It's irreverent. Serious and Snapple go together like oil and water. To some extent fun is a category characteristic, differentiating all such beverages from serious health drinks, but Snapple is fun in a way unduplicated by any other brand of soft drink. It is informal, natural, personal, and playful. That partly derives from full taste, and partly because it represents a break from mundane roles and responsibilities. It is not "a pure escape" but of a circumscribed and portable sort, one which is easily resealed and apportioned. The playfulness is reinforced by imaginative use of names, e.g., Melon Berry, Kiwi Strawberry, Mango Madness.

- **Personal** There's so much variety to choose from. You can find yourself within the brand. The diversity within Snapple Brand makes it a model for a multicultural society. There's a creative dimension that enhances and enlarges who you are. The logic of Snapple is very like the logic of contemporary music, a creative fusion of styles and genres. Snapple as a brand is constantly revising what it is. There is the image of a small, caring company. It is almost too individualistic. It is not a family drink. Snapple in the refrigerator increases family tension.

- **Vividly Sensual** Snapple tastes good or it is nothing. Luxury today is being redefined. It need not be a big purchase.

| Conspicuous consumption | ┄┄> | understated functional luxury "luxury that does" | ┄┄> | personally real, sensation saturated experiences |

Sensuality is based on contrast and Snapple is replete with contrast. It is smooth but complex, with a blend of different flavors and tastes both exotic and immediate, stimulating and soothing.

RUMORS

There are a disproportionate number of rumors about Snapple, initially fueled by Snapple's mysterious and unsettling florescence. They typically start with GenXs studying the label and detecting a slave ship or the letters KKK, combined with a cynical worldview where conspiracies are rampant, and a taste for celebrating the down and out.

Rumors have suggested that Snapple is anti-abortion, anti-gay, donating money to Jesse Helms, and that Rush Limbaugh has a major investment with Snapple. The rumors vary but the themes are remarkably consistent. They are not about the product, but about the company, the "owners." Snapple is in an analogous situation to the Body Shop, which is also the subject of a disproportionate number of rumors.

The issue is not the truth or falsity, or even impact on sales, but rather the underlying message, which is one of a deep sense of betrayal, perhaps over implicit health claims, or a fear that Snapple is not alternative but rather reactionary.

WHAT IS DRIVING DECREASED CONSUMPTION?

There appears to be no "Great Attractor" sucking consumers away from the brand, rather a drift away in all directions, toward water, back to sodas, to other competitors in the category, e.g., AriZona, Fruitopia. No competing brand stands out. Most competitors within the category were seen as inferior, even by lapsers, e.g., "too sweet." Some drink less Snapple juice and add ice tea.

There is also natural attrition, caused by problems of distribution: "I can't find my flavor anymore," or "My grocery store has only peach diet tea and kiwi strawberry and I'm getting tired of kiwi strawberry" or "Coke made them take the Snapple coolers out at [my] high school."

There are health issues, especially with the 30–44 age group, a wake-up call from the doctor, increasing health sophistication. Non-lapsers often were not label readers.

Authenticity was a concern, especially with the 18–29 age group, who are very sensitive to being tricked: "It even costs more than real juice," or the contrast between Snapple's small company image and the [actual] size of the company.

Fashionability and negative social pressure were sometimes explicit. A young male in St. Louis: "I used to drink a lot of Snapple, AriZona is newer," or a 40-year-old artist in New York: "It's no longer avant guarde." More often they were implicit, a feeling you get carrying or drinking Snapple in public, often expressed as a lack of presence: "You just don't see it anymore," "What happened to Wendy?" There was a feeling that Snapple has lost its focus and no longer appeals to the imagination. "I heard they fired Wendy."

FASHION

Established brands may wax and wane, but do not follow a fashion trajectory (even fashion labels — Ralph Lauren, Calvin Klein, etc.). Established brands are like animal species — each has its own niche, and as its environment changes, the brand either evolves or becomes extinct.

New Age concepts and health behaviors are often more like hula-hoops (e.g., TM, The Water Diet, Ab Roller, etc.). Desirability increases or decreases with perceived popularity. Fashion is fueled by social competition. Much of Snapple's problem is that it behaves more like a "fashion water" than an established brand. Its product differentiation is weak. It lacks a compelling reason for use. It is not embedded in daily rituals and routines.

SOCIAL REINFORCEMENT

The amount of Snapple consumed is highly correlated with intensity of Snapple use in the respondent's immediate social environment. It's not that Snapple is a social beverage — it is rarely shared, and it is not true that those who drink Snapple with others (e.g., lunch with colleagues) are more likely to be a loyalist.

Rather, Snapple use needs to be socially reinforced. It is not physiologically addictive, and it lacks the conceptual coherence that drives bottled water (good for you, purifying, intimations of working out) or Gatorade (replenishment, intensity, etc.).

ADOPTION PROCESS

Adoption, becoming a heavy user, is typically extended over several years. Most "new" drinkers had been aware of Snapple as far back in time as long-term loyalists. Many have been drinking Snapple for years. Conversion to heavy use is typically no sudden revelation, but an extended process.

(Continued)

EXHIBIT 6 (cont.)

Snapple drinking flows through friendship networks. "Significant others" stand out as a key influence. Flow tends to be from female to male. Among females, "we talk about everything." Among guys, it typically works differently. It is based on observing what friends order, how much they wanted it, etc. But generally adopters try not to imitate immediately.

If it comes from Mom, it becomes sacred.

USAGE

A high percentage of purchases are single bottles for immediate consumption: "I could save money by buying in bulk, but I don't." Snapple fits with sandwiches and delis, not fast food. Usage fluctuates seasonally, diurnally, and cyclically: "I drink Snapple when I drive on long trips." It's an individualistic, atomistic experience, normally not social or familial.

Snapple moments tend to be on the go, between here and there, yet for many loyalists it's not truly an impulse buy: "That first 15 minutes when I get home from work . . . I don't answer the phone. I sit down and have a Snapple." It is part of a salesman's routine stop for gas, part of taking baby for a morning stroll, a way to get through early morning class, "breakfast at Dunkin' Donuts, then home with a Snapple while I do the crossword in the morning newspaper."

REGIONAL DIFFERENCES

New York	Seattle	Dallas	St. Louis
The Region:			
"The Big Apple"	Apples grow here	Gatorade huge here	
Active to the point of being frenetic	High employment mobility and diversity (people exploring different career options)	Ambitious, dynamic, materialistic, engaged economically robust, open to change, gregarious, entrepreneurial	Little in-migration
New York has always been characterized by immigrant mindset, a sense of renewal and starting afresh	Like New York, Seattle has a fairly large and influential gay population	Janus faced—forward looking combined with a certain reverence for the past, a search for tradition	If Dallas is searching for tradition, St. Louis has found it—much more traditional, stable, centered
Individualism run amok	Mix and match—innovation, growth, vitality based on recombination, fusion of diverse elements	Individualistic in a characteristically Texas, "do things my way" manner, but tempered by tremendous enthusiasm for team sports	Individualism is attenuated, emphasis on what connects friends, family, community, more of adaptive, defensive stance toward life
Health conscious	Active, outdoors, health-oriented		
Strong artistic community	Strong artistic community, spiritually conscious, exploratory, embrace of the exotic		

CHAPTER 1 Introduction to Customer Equity Management Strategy

The Brand in the Region:

Snapple has gone from being fashion forward to mainstream	Most supermarkets have a juice bar, more sophisticated competition, e.g., Odwalla, Sobe	Snapple has gone from being fashion forward to being peripheral	Less health sophistication, Snapple more likely to be seen as "healthy"
The brand's presence feeds on itself		Little or no knowledge of the company, almost no rumors	

PROFILE OF SNAPPLE DRINKERS

Active approach to life, suffused with youthful attitude, outdoors. Snapple is not for the idle. But Snapple is not the drink of the really serious athlete. The Snapple drinker is open to new experiences, not particularly suspicious. Looking for things to help them step back from life. Tendency for best friends to be less stable, more "alternative," and looking for some of that in their own life. Sense of being on the way somewhere, interested in improving themselves, moving up. Snapple itself was a model of come-from-nowhere, make-it-big-time, success.

They are in control, not on a power trip, it is control of themselves. The reaction against colas is a matter of taking back control of their lives. The bottle plays directly to this sense of control: "Just fits in your hand," the screw-on lid. Snapple is a way to "seize the moment." There is an individualistic ethos and it resonates to individuals (or entities) making a comeback.

Drinkers fit a fairly narrow taste profile, like sweet things, often dislike carbonation ("Makes me burp," "It burns"). The drinker is not attracted to pure juice: "too citrusy," "too acidic," "too thick." It's not for health nuts, but for people who cleave toward fulsome and flavorful foods like Tex-Mex, lobster/shrimp, chocolate.

MEANING OF WENDY

Wendy embodies the essential Snapple qualities. A low-level employee in customer relations, a nobody, who's now a celebrity, she exemplifies the entrepreneurial story that endears many ambitious individuals to Snapple. She and the original set of commercials personify the fun, genuine, personal, whimsical, and creative dimensions of the brand, the bottom-up popularity. She's like one of their friends, a little odd but all the more endearing.

Wendy reaches all Snapple drinkers but *not* with equal efficacy. In New York and Seattle, people are more likely to read Wendy on multiple levels. In New York individuals tend to be much more familiar with the Snapple story, and Wendy Kaufman is familiar in terms of lived experience: "I know people like that." Wendy plays least well in the heartland, where she seems more "exotic" than "could be anyone." In Dallas and St. Louis respondents see Wendy as "funny," "friendly," "full of life," "energetic, not Madison Avenue slick."

CONCLUSIONS AND IMPLICATIONS

- *Regional ethos.* Areas that are most "settled," self-satisfied, are least susceptible to Snapple's "subversive" appeal. Areas with a postmodern mindset—a playful exuberance, expression of vivid sensuality (personal authenticity), and mix and match ethos—are Snapple territory.
- *Authenticity is pivotal.* Overstating or misrepresenting Snapple's health benefits does more harm than good. Snapple needs to be just healthy enough. Feeling better about yourself is an integral part of the Snapple experience, but it need not be the most important part.

(Continued)

EXHIBIT 6 (cont.)

- ***Corporate image influences brand image.*** It need not be a small company, but should be a caring company. Like social reinforcement, corporate image provides justification for use. Snapple needs to stand for something.
- ***Intermediate/interstitial character of Snapple is both strength and weakness.*** As a strength, it broadens the customer base and market niche and is a source of symbolic power. As a weakness, the brand can move quickly from hero to villain. (In mythology, interstitial figures frequently play the role of "trickster.")
- ***Social influence.*** Intensity of Snapple use is closely correlated with social presence. (Serious Snapple drinkers are far more likely to be surrounded by other Snapple drinkers.)
- ***Become more established.*** Must move Snapple from a "fashion water" to a staple brand like Pepsi, Coke, and Sprite with well-defined benefits and image.
- ***Develop sensuality of the Snapple experience.*** As with apples, there is an emphasis on mouth feel. Consumption is not a rational act, as water consumption is. Unlike sodas, Snapple is both soothing and stimulating.
- ***Snapple moments.*** Fold Snapple into personal, daily rituals—time out from the mundane, transitional moments, sense of "letting go," both restorative and sensual. Link to trend away from a mechanistic vision of health toward a more holistic, "good for you," being good to yourself, getting back in touch, de-stressing vision.
- ***Community marketing strategies.*** Build on brand's personal, local character.

---

consumers, the culture they live in, and the dynamics of the ready-to-drink beverage category.

The strategic team at Deutsch felt that the research provided Triarc with some solid direction. The study had uncovered enough evidence to show that the brand had connected strongly with consumers in its early years because it had done things differently by being real, human, and avoiding the expected marketing slickness consumers had grown suspicious of. As they saw it, the research showed that the many changes Quaker had instituted went directly against these principles. Consumers had felt betrayed, because Snapple had "sold-out."

Weinstein seemed more reserved in his attitude to the study. "Don't get me wrong, I'm not against research, but there are many things in the fashion world that you can't research. Consumers have a hard time telling you what they want, and sometimes you have to look at what's working in the category. The big thing in this industry is what's new, what's moving, what's hot. If someone comes out with an urn-shaped product, it's not that I want to copy it, but I might say what's the bigger picture here? Is it about size, or color, or just what is it? Here's something new from AriZona." He pointed to a bottle of AriZona Iced Tea whose top-to-bottom shrink-wrapped label with a willow motif gave it the appearance of a hand-painted Chinese ceramic container. "This packaging has impact. It will be noticed by anyone who looks at the beverage display."

Weinstein continued, "This category has so many segments—teas, fruit drinks, diets, water. Could we get into water, without being the cheapest water? Could we be in the sports drink business without competing head-to-head with Gatorade? I'd love to be in the chocolate beverage business.

"We know that we can sell around 200,000 cases of just about anything. We talk to key distributors and see whether they think we have a good idea. If they take it we know within the first month based on reorders whether we have a product that's selling or not. If we don't do consumer research, if we do product development in-house, if we do our own label design, we can be in the market with a new concept for $50,000 to $75,000 investment plus working capital for ingredients."

Gilbert defended the usefulness of the study. "Ask anyone what Snapple stands for and you'll hear the same words: quirky, offbeat. That's ok as far as it goes, but it's hardly satisfying as the endpoint. It's superficial. This study gives me a richer sense of what we have to work with. Granted, it does not narrow the field of play. It does not exactly make my job easy. But that's the nature of the brand. People make Snapple their own, so it ends up meaning lots of different things to lots of different people. Snapple users are really very average, normal people but the brand helps them to think of themselves as offbeat."

Weinstein smiled. "I like to think that a Snapple drinker is anyone with lips. How would it be if we developed products first and then found out which segment they appealed to? The main thing is to keep moving the ball forward. We can't get mired in the mud." ∎

CHAPTER 2
The Customer Equity Approach and the Customer Management Plan

In determining a marketing strategy, firms first need to determine their objectives—what will constitute a successful marketing strategy. In a customer-focused marketing strategy, or customer management strategy, the critical objective is to maximize customer equity, which provide the basis for the comparison of strategic marketing alternatives.[1] Customer equity is a valid measure by which to evaluate all marketing expenditures on the same basis. Customer lifetime value offers such a metric at the individual customer level. Understanding how to grow and manage customer equity is a complex endeavor. This chapter focuses on:

- Presenting the key components of customer equity: value equity, brand equity, and relationship equity.
- Introducing distinct customer management strategies to show how these components work, independently and together, to grow the long-term value of the firm through the ultimate source of that value—the firm's customers.
- Outlining the customer management plan—a point-by-point plan for developing and implementing customer management strategy.

---

[1]Customer equity was first defined in this context by Robert C. Blattberg and John Deighton, "Manage Marketing by the Customer Equity Test," Harvard Business Review 74 (July–August 1996); 136–44.

THE CUSTOMER EQUITY APPROACH[2]

Consider the issues facing a typical brand manager, product manager, or marketing-oriented CEO:

> How do I manage the brand? How will my customers react to changes in the product or service offering? Should I raise prices? What is the best way to enhance the relationships with my current customers? Where should I focus my efforts?

In a typical day, a marketing executive is barraged with all of these questions. And, not surprisingly, the executive's answers to these questions will all have an influence (positive or negative) on customer lifetime value and, therefore, on the firm's customer equity.

These questions (and the many others that face a marketing executive each day) can be broken down into three key components of customer equity. The first of these is value equity. Value equity represents the customer's objective evaluation of the firm's product and/or service offerings. The second, brand equity, represents the customer's subjective view of the firm and its offerings. Finally, relationship equity represents the customer's view of the strength of the relationship between the customer and the firm. Within each of these components are specific, incisive actions the firm can take to enhance value, brand, or relationship equity. It is the link between these actionable drivers and customer equity that provides the mechanism for firms to respond quickly to changing customer needs and a changing competitive marketplace.

◆ BOX 2-1 ◆

What is the Concept of Customer Lifetime Value?

Customer lifetime value is a measure of the future financial value of the customer's purchases with an organization. It takes into account the following aspects:

- How much the customer spends on each purchase with the firm (and how much profit is generated as a result),
- How often the customer purchases from the firm,
- How likely the customer is to remain (or become) a customer of the firm in the future,
- How much it costs to serve the customer,
- The organization's discount rate [for calculating the net present value (NPV) of the future purchases].

Customer lifetime value is a measure of the future profit flows from the customer to the firm, adjusted for the customer's future probability of purchasing from the firm, and appropriately discounted to the present.

---

[2]This framework is based on work by Roland T. Rust, Valarie A. Zeithaml, and Katherine N. Lemon, *Driving Customer Equity: How Customer Lifetime Value is Reshaping Corporate Strategy* (New York: The Free Press, 2000).

ROLE OF VALUE EQUITY

Value is the keystone of the customer's relationship with the firm. If the firm's products and services do not meet the customer's needs and expectations, the best brand strategy and the strongest retention and relationship marketing strategies will be insufficient. *Value equity* is defined as the customer's objective assessment of the utility of a brand, based on perceptions of what is given up for what is received. This definition arises out of a significant body of literature investigating customer perceptions of value.[3] This research in the areas of customer value and perceived value has defined three key drivers that influence value: quality, price, and convenience. Quality encompasses the physical and nonphysical aspects of the product and service offerings under the firm's control. The power FedEx holds in the marketplace is in no small part due to its maintenance of high-quality standards for delivery. Price represents the aspects of "what is given up by the customer" that the firm can influence. Priceline.com (www.priceline.com) has taken advantage of the power of price as a marketing tool. Convenience encompasses those actions the firm can take to reduce the customer's costs and efforts in doing business with the firm. Home delivery restaurants, such as Domino's Pizza, seek to capitalize on the importance of convenience to busy consumers. Together, quality, price, and convenience represent the three drivers available to the firm to grow value equity.

ROLE OF BRAND EQUITY

Where value equity is driven by perceptions of objective aspects such as quality, price, and convenience, brand equity is built through image and meaning. A brand serves three vital roles. First, it acts as a 'magnet' to attract new customers to the firm. Second, it can serve as a reminder to customers about the firm's products and services. Finally, a brand can become the customer's emotional tie to the firm. Brand equity has often been defined, very broadly, to include an extensive set of attributes that influence customer choice.[4] However, in our effort to separate the specific components of customer equity, *brand equity* requires a narrower focus, and is defined as the customer's subjective and intangible assessment of the brand, above and beyond its objectively perceived value.

The key drivers of brand equity are as follows: brand awareness (or familiarity), brand attitude (and associations), and corporate ethics.[5] The first driver, brand awareness, encompasses the tools under the firm's control that can influence and enhance brand awareness, particularly marketing communications. The focus on

---

[3]For more information on customer perceptions of value, see the following: Bradley T. Gale, *Managing Customer Value*, (New York: The Free Press, 1994); A. Parasuraman, "Reflections on Gaining Competitive Advantage Through Customer Value," *Journal of the Academy of Marketing Science* 25, no. 2 (1997); 154–61; Robert B. Woodruff, "Customer Value: The Next Source for Competitive Advantage," *Journal of the Academy of Marketing Science* 25, no. 2 (1997), 139–53; Valarie A. Zeithaml, "Consumer Perceptions of Price, Quality, and Value: A Means-End Model and Synthesis of Evidence," *Journal of Marketing*, 52 (July 1988); 2–22.
[4]See David A. Aaker, *Managing Brand Equity* (New York: The Free Press, 1991); David A. Aaker, *Building Strong Brands* (New York: The Free Press, 1995); Kevin L. Keller, *Strategic Brand Management: Building, Measuring, and Managing Brand Equity*, 2nd ed. (Upper Saddle River, N.J.: Prentice Hall, 2002).
[5]In addition to Aaker (1991, 1995) and Keller (2002), see Isabelle Maignan, O. C. Ferrell, and G. Thomas Hult, "Corporate Citizenship: Cultural Antecedents and Business Benefits," *Journal of the Academy of Marketing Science* 27, no. 4 (1999); 455–69; and Susan Fournier, "Consumers and Their Brands: Developing a Relationship Theory in Consumer Research," *Journal of Consumer Research* 24 (March 1998); 343–73.

media advertising by pharmaceutical companies for their prescription products (e.g., Zyban, Viagra, Claritin) is designed to build brand awareness and encourage patients to ask their doctors for these drugs by name. Second, attitude toward the brand encompasses the extent to which the firm is able to create close connections or emotional ties with the consumer. This second driver of brand equity is most often influenced through the specific nature of the media campaigns, and may be more directly influenced by direct marketing. Kraft's strength in consumer food products exemplifies the importance of brand attitude by developing strong consumer attitudes toward its key brands such as Kraft Macaroni and Cheese and Philadelphia Cream Cheese. The third driver, corporate ethics, encompasses specific actions the firm can take to influence customer perceptions of the organization, for example, community sponsorships or donations, firm privacy policy, and ethical dealings with employees. Home Depot has enhanced its brand equity by strongly supporting community events, and by encouraging its employees to do likewise. These three drivers—brand awareness, brand attitude, and corporate ethics—serve as the building blocks of brand equity.

ROLE OF RELATIONSHIP EQUITY

Consider a firm with a great brand and a great product. The company may be able to attract new customers to its product with its strong brand, and keep customers by meeting their expectations consistently. Is this enough? Given the significant shifts in the economy—from goods to services, from transactions to relationships—the answer is no. Great brand equity and value equity may not be strong enough to hold the customer. What's needed is a way to "glue" the customers to the firm, enhancing the stickiness of the relationship. Relationship equity represents the strength of the relationship between the customer and the firm. *Relationship equity* is defined as the tendency of the customer to stick with the brand, above and beyond the customer's objective and subjective assessments of the brand.

Consider the set of actions under the firm's control that may enhance relationship equity. Prior research in the area of customer relationship management reveals that the key drivers of relationship equity are loyalty programs, affinity programs, community-building programs, and knowledge-building programs.[6] Loyalty programs encompass the set of actions that firms may take to reward customers for specific behaviors with tangible and intangible benefits. From airlines to liquor stores, from Citigroup to Diet Coke, the loyalty program has become a staple of many firms' marketing strategy. Firms may also reward customers for specific behavior with intangible benefits. For

---

[6]For additional background on relationship marketing see: James C. Anderson, and James Narus, "A Model of Distributor Firm and Manufacturer Firm Working Partnerships," *Journal of Marketing* 54, no. 1 (1990); 42–58; Grahame R. Dowling and Mark Uncles, "Do Customer Loyalty Programs Really Work?" *Sloan Management Review* 38 (Summer 1997); 71–82; Evert Gummeson, *Total Relationship Marketing—Rethinking Marketing Management: From 4 P's to 30 R's* (Oxford, UK: Butterworth-Heineman, 1999); Piyush Kumar, "The Impact of Long-Term Client Relationships on the Performance of Business Service Firms," *Journal of Service Research* 2 (August 1999); 4–18; Gil Mcwilliam, "Understanding the Benefits and Costs of Web Communities," *Sloan Management Review* (forthcoming); Frederick Newell, *loyalty.com: Customer Relationship Management in the New Era of Internet Marketing* (New York: McGraw-Hill, 2000).

example, US Airways' Chairman Preferred–status customers receive complementary membership in the US Airways Club.

Affinity programs seek to create strong emotional connections with customers, linking the customer's relationship with the firm to other important aspects of the customer's life. Consider the wide array of affinity Visa and MasterCard choices offered by FirstUSA (in the thousands, at last count) that are designed to encourage increased use and higher retention levels. Community-building programs seek to increase the stickiness of the customer's relationship with the firm by linking the customer to a network of similar customers. In the United Kingdom, for example, soft drink manufacturer Tango has created a Web site (www.tango.com) that has built a virtual community with their key segment, the nation's young people.

Finally, knowledge-building programs increase relationship equity by creating structural bonds between the customer and the firm, making the customer less willing to recreate the customer–firm relationship with an alternative provider. The most oft-cited example of this is Amazon.com, but learning relationships are not limited to cyberspace. Firms such as British Airways have developed programs to track customer food and drink preferences, thereby creating bonds with the customer by anticipating their needs while simultaneously reducing costs. Taken together, these actions—loyalty programs, special benefits, affinity programs, and community building and knowledge building programs represent the drivers of retention equity. These drivers provide opportunities for the firm to maximize the likelihood of customer repurchase, maximize the value of a customer's future purchases, and minimize the likelihood of the customer switching to a competitor.

◆ INTRODUCING CUSTOMER MANAGEMENT STRATEGIES

In order to determine the appropriate customer management strategy, it is imperative to understand which of the three drivers of customer equity—value, brand, or relationship—is the most critical to the development of the firm's customer equity. This requires a customer equity analysis of the firm's customers and of the market. Once the firm has determined which component is most critical, a specific strategic approach can be developed. Most firms, having constrained resources, must trade off efforts between value equity, brand equity, and relationship equity. Depending on the importance of customer equity drivers in the industry, different strategies apply. Figure 2-1 illustrates specific strategic approaches the firm can employ.

VALUE STRATEGIES

If value equity is the most critical customer equity driver, the firm's emphasis should be on honing the actionable drivers of value. The firm should consider efforts that focus on quality, price, and convenience, with the exact allocation of effort dependent on the relative impact of each of these on value equity. Consider a division of a global high-tech manufacturer that markets stereo components to automobile manufacturers. The firm determined that value equity was the most important component of customer equity, and that it was not doing as well as its competitors on this component. Clearly, a value strategy was called for. On closer analysis, the key "value" attribute on which to

CHAPTER 2 *The Customer Equity Approach and the Customer Management Plan*   **27**

FIGURE 2-1 The Strategy Triangle

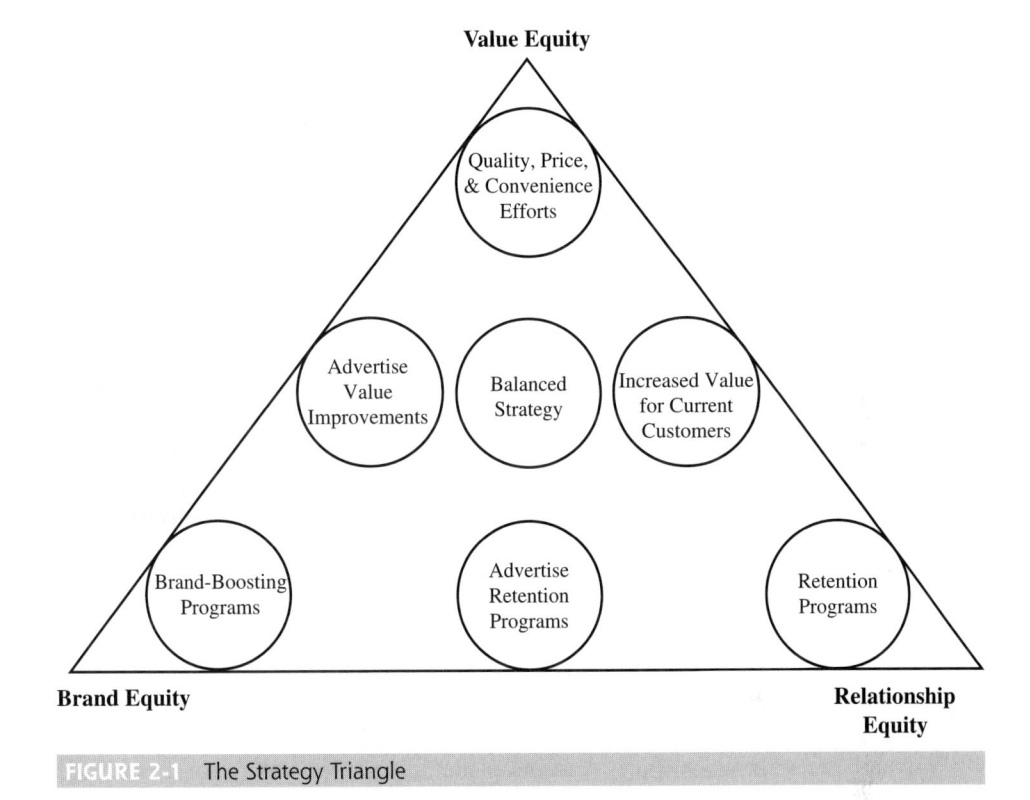

(Triangle diagram with vertices labeled Value Equity (top), Brand Equity (lower-left), and Relationship Equity (lower-right). Circles inside contain: Quality, Price, & Convenience Efforts; Advertise Value Improvements; Balanced Strategy; Increased Value for Current Customers; Brand-Boosting Programs; Advertise Retention Programs; Retention Programs.)

focus was increasing the consistency of quality of the delivered product. The firm determined that efforts focusing on improving this attribute would have the most dramatic effect on growing customer equity. Value strategies form the top of the Strategy Triangle in Figure 2-1.

BRAND STRATEGIES

When brand equity dominates, the focus of the firm should be on activities that will build the brand—for example, an integrated marketing communications approach to build brand awareness or strengthen consumer attitude toward the brand. In the facial tissues category (e.g., Kleenex, Scotties), brand equity is the most important factor. If one of the brands, say, Scotties, were weaker in brand equity, the firm would need to (1) determine which of the drivers of brand equity was most in need of improvement (brand awareness, brand attitude, or corporate ethics), and (2) take action to build brand awareness, improve attitude toward the brand, or improve company (brand) ethics. Brand strategies anchor the lower-left corner of the Strategy Triangle.

RELATIONSHIP STRATEGIES

Likewise, if relationship equity is most important, the firm should focus on loyalty programs and other relationship management actions. The consumer telecommunications industry (especially long-distance and cell-phone companies) has long struggled with reducing customer churn. Finding ways to boost relationship equity will be of utmost importance for these industries (and for the emerging competition for local-phone business as well). Relationship strategies form the lower-right corner of the Strategy Triangle.

VALUE-BRAND STRATEGIES

It is possible that two customer equity drivers will be important. For example, if both value equity and brand equity are crucial, but relationship equity is less important, the firm might focus on connecting its marketing communications (and other brand-boosting efforts) to specific aspects of value, such as quality or convenience. In other words, in such a case the firm's advertising should be focused less on creating image or developing emotional connections, and focused more on communicating objective benefits of the firm's offering. For example, United Airlines has advertised the creation of a new business class with more legroom. Similarly, Southwest Airlines' "Need to Get Away" campaign focuses on its low-price fares to vacation destinations.

VALUE-RELATIONSHIP STRATEGIES

If value equity and relationship equity are key, but brand equity is not as critical, the firms might concentrate on retaining current customers by increasing current customers' perceptions of objective value, perhaps by adding additional services, providing special convenience, or providing limited price discounts. In the high-tech computer server industry, one might expect value and relationship to be critical. A firm may need to focus on value (improving product quality) and on relationship (improving the management of the business relationship). For example, if the firm determined that those customer-facing employees directly responsible for the relationship with the customer (sales, technical support, marketing) did not understand what created value for the customer (e.g., specific elements of consistency in quality), a combination value/relationship strategy would be appropriate. In terms of relationship, the firm could listen to the customer more (to determine the dimensions of quality on which it needed to improve). In terms of value, the firm would focus on improving its follow-through on a quality improvement strategy.

RELATIONSHIP-BRAND STRATEGIES

Similarly, it is possible that relationship equity and brand equity are both important, but value equity is less essential. Here, the firm may choose to emphasize the benefits of the firm's retention programs through its marketing communications. One way of thinking about this is to view the firm's existing customers as the primary targets of the firm's communications, rather than to focus on new customers. For example, Tweeter, Etc., a large regional consumer electronics chain, sends an annual color catalog to its current customer base. Their rationale? Customers will consider adding video and stereo components while they are looking at the catalog in their living room or media room. Tweeter is already there, in a sense, to spur them into thinking about these purchases.

MIXED STRATEGIES

In rare cases, the firm may find that no customer equity driver, or pair of drivers, dominates. In such cases, the firm would be best served by embarking on a balanced strategy, with value equity, brand equity, and relationship equity receiving equal weight. Consider the strategic approach of grocery stores in today's competitive marketplace. They must focus on value (low prices, quality produce), and brand (awareness advertising, the destination store for the weekly shopping trip), yet cannot avoid relationship strategies (frequent-purchase cards and customer-specific coupons).

It is important to note that the final determination regarding strategic priorities and specific improvement efforts must include a careful financial analysis of the anticipated outcome from the investment.[7] Top priority should be given to improvement efforts that (1) are related to a customer equity driver that is important in the industry, (2) are related to a driver (and sub-driver) on which the firm's performance is sub-par, and (3) project an acceptable rate of financial return if implemented successfully.

Overall, the customer equity approach outlines three critical components of customer equity—value equity, relationship equity, brand equity. Based on analysis of the importance of each component, and the firm's performance in each area relative to competitors, the firm can determine the appropriate strategy or mix of strategies.

◆ THE CUSTOMER MANAGEMENT PLAN

The customer management plan (Table 2-1) represents a roadmap for developing customer management strategy. Using the customer equity framework described above, it outlines a step-by-step approach to analysis, strategy development, and strategic evaluation. Steps 1 through 4 focus on analysis. Steps 5 through 7 focus on strategy development. Steps 8 through 10 focus on monitoring and measuring the results.

CUSTOMER EQUITY ANALYSIS—DATA COLLECTION

In developing a customer management plan, the first step is to complete a customer equity analysis. First, the analysis of the market is completed, with a determination of the key components and drivers of customer equity for the industry. It is important to gather information directly from customers to determine customer perceptions of how

---

[7]This approach follows Roland T. Rust, Anthony J. Zahorik, and Timothy L. Keiningham, "Return on Quality (ROQ): Making Service Quality Financially Accountable," *Journal of Marketing* 59 (April 1995); 58–70; and Roland T. Rust, Valarie A. Zeithaml, and Katherine N. Lemon, *Driving Customer Equity* (New York: The Free Press, 2000).

TABLE 2-1 Customer Management Plan

1. *Analysis I.* Analyzing the Market. Determine the key drivers (and sub-drivers) of customer equity for your market.
2. *Analysis II.* Analyzing Your Firm's Performance. Determine how you are doing in terms of customer equity and in relation to your competitors:
   a. How are you doing (performance) on all drivers?
   b. How are you doing on key drivers (those most important to customers)?
      i. Where are your necessary points of parity (on what attributes do you have to be "good enough")?
      ii. Where are your opportunities for differentiation (where can your firm really shine)?
   c. What portion of the customer equity share do you hold in your market? What portion do your competitors hold?
3. *Analysis III.* Comparing Your Performance to That of Your Competitors. Analyze the past and intended future behavior of the customers in your market (yours and your competitors'). By examining the switching matrix, determine if:
   a. Customers are switching from you to your competitors (bad indicator).
   b. Customers are switching from your competitors to you (good indicator).
   c. Customers are staying with your firm and you have a high share of retained customers (good indicator).
   d. Customers are staying with your competitors and they have a high share of retained customers (bad indicator, or indicator of key opportunity).
4. *Analysis IV.* Determining Where to Focus Your Efforts.
   a. Given the examination in (a), (b), and (c) above, determine key weaknesses to overcome.
   b. Given the examination in (a), (b), and (c) above, determine key opportunities.
5. *Strategy Development and Design I.* Given the analysis above, determine key priorities and where the analysis suggests key resources should be invested.
6. *Strategy Development and Design II.* Determine the appropriate mix of customers and appropriate target customers. Particularly if you determine you need to gain additional customers from your competitors, you need to determine which customers to select.
7. *Strategy Development and Design III.* Given the appropriate set of current and target customers, if you determine that the maximum ROI would come from:
   a. Improving brand equity, then you need to focus on brand building strategies and managing brand equity.
   b. Improving value equity, then you need to focus on value building strategies and managing value equity.
   c. Improving the relationship and growing relationship equity, then you need to focus on managing relationship equity, relationship building strategies, and relationship touchpoints and personalization.
8. *Measure, Monitor, and Evaluate I.* Once you have determined the appropriate customer mix and the key actions to grow long-term profitability, you need to measure and monitor the results.
9. *Measure, Monitor, and Evaluate II.* If necessary, utilize appropriate CRM software that will enable you to collect the appropriate data to measure and monitor the success of your customer management efforts.
10. *Measure, Monitor, and Evaluate III.* On a recurring basis, analyze the key drivers and sub-drivers of customer equity and determine your performance relative to your critical (and rising) competitors. Then follow steps 1 through 9 again.

the firm and its competitors are performing, and to determine what is most important to customers.

There are multiple approaches to collecting the information necessary to conduct the analysis. The Customer Equity Exercise (See Appendix 1 at the end of this chapter) is a survey that can be used to implement a qualitative approach to data collection. The survey takes approximately 45 minutes, and is done in an in-person, one-on-one interview format. Such a qualitative approach is often useful for firms that have only a few customers, or very large enterprise customers.

Implementation of a quantitative statistical analysis is somewhat more complex. To complete a quantitative analysis of the market, firms need to field a cross-sectional survey. An example of such a survey can be found in the article, "Return on Marketing: Using Customer Equity to Focus Marketing Strategy," in Appendix 2 of this chapter. This article also describes the statistical analyses that can be utilized to determine which components are most important in building customer equity (e.g., value, brand, or relationship).

CUSTOMER EQUITY ANALYSIS—FIRM AND COMPETITOR PERFORMANCE

Once the customer information is collected, the next step is to analyze the firm's performance to determine how the firm is doing in terms of customer equity and its components. Then, the firm's performance is compared to its competitors, to determine how the firm stacks up relative to the competition, and to determine customer trends (e.g., are customers moving to the firm or switching away from the firm?). Finally, specific areas of weakness and opportunity can be determined.

STRATEGY DEVELOPMENT

Following the analysis, the next steps in the customer management plan focus on strategy development. The first task is to determine key priorities and the focus of the strategy (e.g., value, brand, relationship, or a mix of strategies). Second, the firm must determine the appropriate mix and selection of customers to serve. This step is critical, as not all customers are profitable for the firm to serve. Specific approaches for customer selection are outlined in Chapter 5. Next, specific strategies are developed, focusing on building brand, value, or relationship equity. Each strategic approach suggests specific actions the firm might take and specific types of marketing investments.

MEASURING, MONITORING, AND EVALUATING

The final steps in the customer management plan focus on measuring, monitoring, and evaluating the customer strategy. Once a strategy has been determined and implemented, it is important to examine how the firm's efforts are linked to long-term profitability. Firms may also find it helpful to utilize customer relationship management systems (e.g., CRM software, databases) to assist in the monitoring efforts. The final step in the customer management plan is to reanalyze the key components of customer equity and to determine how the firm is doing. In other words, this is a dynamic process, and needs to be done on a recurring basis, usually at least annually.

◆ BOX 2-2 ◆

Boise Renames, Rebrands, and Refocuses

Chances are that right now, not many people will have heard of Boise Cascade, the Boise, Idaho-based paper and office product manufacturer. However, with Boise Cascade's innovative marketing campaigns and recent name change, that relative obscurity is certain to change.

Boise Cascade changed its trade name to Boise, to launch a new brand identity that would more accurately reflect the full scope and focus of its business. Boise Cascade represented the traditional wood products and manufacturing focus of the business; Boise would now encompass the office supplies sector with its broadening selection of products.

"We are very pleased to introduce our new name and launch our new corporate identity" George J. Harad, chairman and chief executive announced last year. "Our new brand allows us to maintain continuity with Boise Cascade's distinguished heritage, while more clearly reflecting the business transformation we have undergone over the past several years."

The company has recently focused on designing innovative solutions for home and office, as illustrated by the change from Boise Cascade Office Products to Boise Office Solutions. The name change was only one aspect of the repositioning effort to reclaim the lead position in consolidating the office supply market.

Boise wanted a compelling sales tool that would offer a form of "infotainment" for its core customer segment of administrative assistants. The "Work Around the World" ad campaign was introduced in 2002, primarily through postcards and pocket reference guides with phone numbers for major airlines, car rental firms, and travel-related services. In addition, a 36-page flyer and direct-mail catalog was distributed, and a Web overlay with ExecutivePlanet.com offered visitors tips about working in other countries, from arranging business meetings to dining etiquette.

However, Boise's most successful campaign was the "You've Got to Have Personality" series, which both entertained and informed consumers. Boise hoped to present the brand as having superior operations and services, while promoting the company's 35 years of experience and expertise in the business world. Again, the target of the campaign was administrative assistants, a group composed primarily of women ages 18 to 54 who had at least a high school diploma, and an average salary ranging from $15,000 to $40,000.

To that end, Boise and ad agency Momentum joined with Spectrum Development, creator of an exclusive personality color-typing system, to create a test targeted at this specific audience. The test was not time consuming, but would generate enough interest so its takers would pass it on to coworkers and discuss test results it.

The marketing team hoped that their audience would take the time to learn more about themselves and, subsequently, Boise Cascade. They sent out a flyer inserted in direct-mail catalogs to 300,000 potential customers, and also included one with each order shipped out. The campaign proved to be a great success; the products promoted in the catalogs with the flyer inserts saw their sales increase by 15.8 percent, and Web traffic at the Boise site increased by 30 percent.

SOURCES: "Boise Cascade Launches New Brand Identity," *Times-News*, Twin Falls, ID. March 15, 2002. "Work Around the World," *Brandweek*, March 18, 2002.

CHAPTER 2 *The Customer Equity Approach and the Customer Management Plan* 33

Summary

When developing a customer-focused marketing strategy, the critical objective is to maximize customer equity—the total of the discounted lifetime values summed over all of the firm's current and potential customers. The three key components of customer equity are value equity, brand equity, and relationship equity. Firms must determine which of these components is the most important determinant of future customer behavior, and develop a strategy that enhances customer perceptions of value, brand, or relationship. The process by which a firm can determine the key drivers of customer equity is called the customer management plan. The four major steps in developing and executing a customer management plan are

1. Analysis of the Market:
   a. Analyze the market—your current and potential customers.
   b. What are the most important drivers and sub-drivers of customer equity?
2. Analysis of Your Firm and Key Competitors:
   a. Analyze your firm's performance.
   b. Compare your firm's performance to competitor performance.
   c. Determine where to focus your efforts.
3. Strategic Development:
   a. Determine key priorities.
   b. Select customers.
   c. Determine strategic focus. (Brand? Value? Relationship? Mix of Strategies?)
4. Measure, Monitor and Evaluate:
   a. Determine strategic trade-offs.
   b. Monitor key metrics.
   c. Reanalyze the drivers of customer equity.
   d. Reevaluate strategic priorities.

The customer management plan allows firms to develop marketing strategies that will focus resources on those efforts that will grow the value of the firm's customer base, thereby growing the value of the firm.

Review Questions and Exercises

1. Consider the soft drink industry and the strong competition among the key players (e.g., Coke and Pepsi). Given the nature of the products in this category and the competitive environment, which strategic approach would Coke or Pepsi be most likely to incorporate in an attempt to improve its customer equity—a value, brand, or relationship strategy? Why?
2. Visit the Dell Computer Web site (www.dell.com). Using the information available there, consider how Dell approaches its customers in its Consumer Business Division. How does Dell communicate information about value (quality, price, convenience)? Information about brand (brand awareness, brand attitude, corporate ethics)? Information about relationship (loyalty programs, affinity programs, community of customers, customized customer information)? What does this tell you about what Dell might think is most important to its customers?

◆ ◆ ◆ **Appendix 1**

Customer Equity Exercise: Interviewing a Customer

DIRECTIONS FOR CUSTOMER EQUITY EXERCISE INTERVIEW

1. **Goal of the Exercise.** The goal of this exercise is to begin to understand what motivates your customer to do business with you. Specifically, you will ask a customer a series of questions to learn more about what matters most when that customer considers doing business with you.

2. **Choosing a Customer.** Please choose an external customer (someone outside the company for whom you or your organization provides products and/or services), or, if you work mainly within your organization, choose an internal customer (someone inside the company for whom you provide products and/or services)
   - As you consider the customer you choose for this exercise, please consider the following:
     1. This should be a customer with whom you currently do business.
     2. Ideally, this should also be a customer who has the option of doing business with someone else (your competitors).
   - If you do not now work for a company that has a customer you may interview, please interview someone you know who is a customer for a product or service with the following characteristics:
     1. A product, type of shop, or service that offers several choices in the marketplace [e.g., overnight mail service, coffee shop, supermarket, home service (such as cleaning or gardening)], or consumer good purchased on a regular basis (such as coffee, snacks, soft drinks)
     2. A product, type of shop, or service that the customer purchases from regularly (e.g., at least once per month)

3. **Conducting the Survey.** It is very important that you conduct this survey ***in person***, if at all possible. If this is not possible, it is acceptable to conduct the survey over the telephone. Please do not mail, fax, or e-mail the survey to your customer. Part of the exercise is the experience of the *interaction between you and your customer*.

4. **Specific Directions for the Survey.**
   - There are 20 questions on the survey (attached).
   - It should take about 45 minutes to complete.
   - Please note that the comments in *italics* are notes for you, and should not be read to your customer.
   - Please get your customer's agreement to spend the 45 minutes with you before your start.
   - Also, please let the customer know that this information will be used only to better understand the customer's needs, and that you are very appreciative of the customer taking the time to talk with you about these issues.
   - Please go through the survey before you meet with your customer—taking a few notes as to how best to "customize" the questions to meet your (and the customer's) specific

CHAPTER 2 *The Customer Equity Approach and the Customer Management Plan*   35

requirements (e.g., if you provide only *services*, and no *products*, cross out the word *product* wherever it appears).
5. **Final Note.** Have fun. This is a great opportunity to gain a better understanding of your customers. You might even learn something about yourself or your organization as well!

PARTICIPANT TO COMPLETE

Before the Interview
Customer name _____.
What they purchase from you (or what product/service) _____.
Approximate volume of current business (in €, $, units, hours—per month or year) _____.
Why did you choose this customer?

After the Interview
What did you learn that surprised you?

POSSIBLE INTRODUCTION FOR CUSTOMER INTERVIEW

Thank you for agreeing to participate in this customer interview. The goal of this interview is for me to gain a greater understanding of your customer needs, so that our organization can serve you better. I will be asking you a set of questions (about 20), so that I can learn more about what matters most to you when you consider doing business with us.

The entire interview should take no more than 45 minutes. Is now a good time for us to talk, or should we schedule a specific time?

I want to assure you that this information will be used only to better understand your needs. I appreciate your willingness to take this time to talk with me about these issues.

Ready? Great, let's get started.

QUESTIONS TO ASK YOUR CUSTOMER

I'd like to start by asking you a series of questions of what is important in choosing a supplier for the types of products and/or services we provide.

For the following questions, on a scale of 1 to 5, with 1 being "would never prevent us from buying from a supplier" and 5 being "would always prevent us from buying from a supplier":

To what extent would each of the following, **if not to your standard,** prevent you from buying from a supplier?

1. Quality of Product or Service

1	2	3	4	5
would never prevent	could possibly prevent	might prevent	could definitely prevent	would always prevent

2. Price of Product or Service

1	2	3	4	5
would never prevent	could possibly prevent	might prevent	could definitely prevent	would always prevent

3. Brand Perceptions of Product or Service

1	2	3	4	5
would never prevent	could possibly prevent	might prevent	could definitely prevent	would always prevent

4. Relationship with Company

1	2	3	4	5
would never prevent	could possibly prevent	might prevent	could definitely prevent	would always prevent

5. On a scale of 1 to 5, with 1 being "poor" and 5 being "excellent," how would you rate us on each of the attributes we just talked about?

   a. Quality of Product or Service

1	2	3	4	5
poor	below average	average	above average	excellent

   b. Price of Product or Service

1	2	3	4	5
poor	below average	average	above average	excellent

   c. Brand Perception

1	2	3	4	5
poor	below average	average	above average	excellent

   d. Relationship with Company

1	2	3	4	5
poor	below average	average	above average	excellent

Now I'd like you to think about your other potential suppliers for these products or services. In addition to our organization, from which two key suppliers do you purchase? (or alternatively, ask Who do you see as our organization's key competitors?)

Supplier #1:_____

Supplier #2:_____

Note: If your customer feels uncomfortable about naming the competitors, just ask them to think of them as supplier #1 and supplier #2. Then, in the questions that follow, refer to supplier #1 and supplier #2.

6. How would you rate each of the two suppliers you listed above?

   Supplier #1:
   a. Quality of Product or Service

CHAPTER 2   *The Customer Equity Approach and the Customer Management Plan*   **37**

1	2	3	4	5
poor	below average	average	above average	excellent

b. Price of Product or Service

1	2	3	4	5
poor	below average	average	above average	excellent

c. Brand Perception

1	2	3	4	5
poor	below average	average	above average	excellent

d. Relationship with Company

1	2	3	4	5
poor	below average	average	above average	excellent

Supplier #2:
a. Quality of Product or Service

1	2	3	4	5
poor	below average	average	above average	excellent

b. Price of Product or Service

1	2	3	4	5
poor	below average	average	above average	excellent

c. Brand Perception

1	2	3	4	5
poor	below average	average	above average	excellent

d. Relationship with Company

1	2	3	4	5
poor	below average	average	above average	excellent

7. Thinking about the quality of the product (or service), what influences your perceptions of quality?

    Consider suggesting or probing for some of the following:
    - quality of the physical product or service product
    - quality of the service delivery or service environment
    - defect rate; consistency; reliability; defect-free repairs
    - convenience; ease of use; locations; availability; responsiveness
    - specific features of the product
    - special features; innovativeness; state of the art

What is most important (about quality)?

What is least important (about quality)?

8. Thinking about the price of the product, what influences your perceptions of price?
    Consider suggesting or probing for some of the following:

- regular prices
- price changes over time
- how price compares to competition
- discounts: volume-based; sale prices
- contract terms: long-term contracts, payment terms

What is most important (about price)?

What is least important (about price)?

9. Thinking about your perceptions of the brand of the product, what influences your perceptions of the brand?
    Consider suggesting or probing for some of the following:

- Customer perceived "fit" with the brand (e.g., how the supplier's brand perceptions fit with your company's brand perceptions in the marketplace)
- Information about or communication with company
- Prior experience with the brand
- Well-known brand
- Related products or services
- Word-of-mouth from other customers
- Company or brand ethics

What is most important (about the brand)?

What is least important (about the brand)?

10. Thinking about the relationship with the company, what influences your perceptions about your relationship with a company?
    Consider suggesting or probing for some of the following:

- Frequent purchase/reward programs (loyalty programs)
- Special Recognition (best customer programs)
- Relationship with individuals from company
- Responsiveness to requests; anticipation of requests
- "User groups"

CHAPTER 2   *The Customer Equity Approach and the Customer Management Plan*   **39**

- Customized products and/or services
- Company learning about our specific needs over time

What is most important (about the relationship)?

What is least important (about the relationship)?

[For the following questions (11–14), utilize the item the customer noted as most important for each attribute (from questions 7, 8, 9, 10).]

11. When we talked about quality, you said _____ was most important. Again, on a scale of 1 to 5, with 1 being "poor" and 5 being "excellent":
    How would you rate us on that aspect of quality?

1	2	3	4	5
poor	below average	average	above average	excellent

    How would you rate each of the two suppliers you listed above?

    Supplier #1:

1	2	3	4	5
poor	below average	average	above average	excellent

    Supplier #2:

1	2	3	4	5
poor	below average	average	above average	excellent

12. When we talked about price, you said _____ was most important. Again, on a scale of 1 to 5, with 1 being "poor" and 5 being "excellent":
    How would you rate us on that aspect of price?

1	2	3	4	5
poor	below average	average	above average	excellent

    How would you rate each of the two suppliers you listed above?

    Supplier #1:

1	2	3	4	5
poor	below average	average	above average	excellent

    Supplier #2:

1	2	3	4	5
poor	below average	average	above average	excellent

13. When we talked about brand perceptions, you said _____ was most important. Again, on a scale of 1 to 5, with 1 being "poor" and 5 being "excellent":
    How would you rate us on that aspect of brand perceptions?

1	2	3	4	5
poor	below average	average	above average	excellent

    How would you rate each of the two suppliers you listed above?

    Supplier #1:

1	2	3	4	5
poor	below average	average	above average	excellent

    Supplier #2:

1	2	3	4	5
poor	below average	average	above average	excellent

14. When we talked about relationship with the company, you said _____ was most important. Again, on a scale of 1 to 5, with 1 being "poor" and 5 being "excellent":
    How would you rate us on that aspect of the relationship?

1	2	3	4	5
poor	below average	average	above average	excellent

    How would you rate each of the two suppliers you listed above?

    Supplier #1:

1	2	3	4	5
poor	below average	average	above average	excellent

    Supplier #2:

1	2	3	4	5
poor	below average	average	above average	excellent

15. Overall, thinking about all the things we've talked about, when you consider purchasing our products or services, what is most important to you?

Now, just a few questions to finish up:

16. What percent of your requirements (for our particular products or services) do you currently purchase from our organization?

    _____%.

17. In addition to our organization, approximately what percent of your requirements do you purchase from the suppliers you mentioned above?

    Supplier #1: _____% of requirements _____

    Supplier #2: _____% of requirements _____

CHAPTER 2 *The Customer Equity Approach and the Customer Management Plan*   **41**

18. Thinking about next year, what percent of requirements do you anticipate purchasing from each of the three identified suppliers (our organization and two others)?

    Us: _____% of requirements

    Supplier #1: _____% of requirements

    Supplier #2: _____% of requirements

19. To what extent do you expect your requirements to be different next year? *(Read scale, have customer choose one and circle.)*

1	2	3	4	5
Substantially Reduced	Somewhat reduced	Same	Somewhat increased	Substantially increased

20. As we finish up, we've talked quite a bit about what is important to you when doing business with us. Is there anything else that comes to mind that our organization (or I) could do to serve you better?

    [Please thank your customer for his or her time:]

    Thank you for taking the time to talk with me about these issues. Understanding what is important to you will enable us to serve you better.

Copyright 2003: Katherine N. Lemon, Roland T. Rust and Valarie A. Zeithaml.

◆ ◆ ◆ Appendix 2

Roland T. Rust, Katherine N. Lemon, & Valarie A. Zeithaml

Return on Marketing: Using Customer Equity to Focus Marketing Strategy

The authors present a unified strategic framework that enables competing marketing strategy options to be traded off on the basis of projected financial return, which is operationalized as the change in a firm's customer equity relative to the incremental expenditure necessary to produce the change. The change in the firm's customer equity is the change in its current and future customers' lifetime values, summed across all customers in the industry. Each customer's lifetime value results from the frequency of category purchases, average quantity of purchase, and brand-switching patterns combined with the firm's contribution margin. The brand-switching matrix can be estimated from either longitudinal panel data or cross-sectional survey data, using a logit choice model. Firms can analyze drivers that have the greatest impact, compare the drivers' performance with that of competitors' drivers, and project return on investment from improvements in the drivers. To demonstrate how the approach can be implemented in a specific corporate setting and to show the methods used to test and validate the model, the authors illustrate a detailed application of the approach by using data from the airline industry. Their framework enables what-if evaluation of marketing return on investment, which can include such criteria as return on quality, return on advertising, return on loyalty programs, and even return on corporate citizenship, given a particular shift in customer perceptions. This enables the firm to focus marketing efforts on strategic initiatives that generate the greatest return.

The Marketing Strategy Problem

Top managers are constantly faced with the problem of how to trade off competing strategic marketing initiatives. For example, should the firm increase advertising, invest in a loyalty program, improve service quality, or none of the above? Such high-level decisions are typically left to the judgment of the chief marketing or chief executive officers, but these executives frequently have little to base their decisions on other than their own experience and intuition. A unified, data-driven basis for making broad, strategic marketing trade-offs has not been available. In this article, we propose that trade-offs be made on the basis of projected financial impact, and we provide a framework that top managers can use to do this.

Financial Accountability

Although techniques exist for evaluating the financial return from particular marketing expenditures (e.g., advertising, direct mailings, sales promotion) given a longitudinal history of expenditures (for a review, see Berger et al. 2002), the approaches have not produced a practical, high-level model that can be used to trade off marketing strategies in general. Furthermore, the requirement of a lengthy history of longitudinal data has made the application of return on investment (ROI) models fairly rare in marketing. As a result, top management has too often viewed marketing expenditures as short-term costs rather than long-term investments and as financially unaccountable (Schultz and Gronstedt 1997). Leading marketing companies consider this problem so important that the Marketing Science Institute has established its highest priority for 2002–2004 as "Assessing Marketing Productivity (Return on Marketing) and Marketing Metrics." We propose that firms achieve this financial accountability by considering the effect of strategic marketing expenditures on their customer equity and by relating the improvement in customer equity to the expenditure required to achieve it.

Customer Equity

Although the marketing concept has reflected a customer-centered viewpoint since the 1960s (e.g., Kotler 1967), marketing theory and practice have become increasingly customer-centered during the past 40 years (Vavra 1997, pp. 6–8). For example, marketing has decreased its emphasis on short-term transactions and has increased its focus on long-term customer relationships (e.g., Håkansson 1982; Storbacka 1994). The customer-centered viewpoint is reflected in the concepts and metrics that drive marketing management, including such metrics as customer satisfaction (Oliver 1980), market orientation (Narver and Slater 1990), and customer value (Bolton and Drew 1991). In recent years, customer lifetime value (CLV) and its implications have received increasing attention (Berger and Nasr 1998; Mulhern 1999; Reinartz and Kumar 2000). For example, brand equity, a fundamentally product-centered concept, has been challenged by the customer-centered concept of customer equity (Blattberg and Deighton 1996; Blattberg, Getz and Thomas 2001; Rust, Zeithaml, and Lemon 2000). For the purposes of this article, and largely consistent with Blattberg and Deighton (1996) but also given the possibility of new customers (Hogan, Lemon, and Libai 2002), we define *customer equity* as the total of the discounted lifetime values summed over all of the firm's current and potential customers.[1]

Our definition suggests that customers and customer equity are more central to many firms than brands and brand equity are, though current management practices and metrics do not yet fully reflect this shift. The shift from product-centered thinking to customer-centered thinking implies the need for an accompanying shift from product-based strategy to customer-based strategy (Gale 1994; Kordupleski, Rust, and Zahorik

1993). In other words, a firm's strategic opportunities might be best viewed in terms of the firm's opportunity to improve the drivers of its customer equity.

Contribution of the Article

Because our article incorporates elements from several literature streams within the marketing literature, it is useful to point out the relative contribution of the article. Table 1 shows the contribution of this article with respect to several streams of literature that influenced the return on marketing conceptual framework. Table 1 shows related influential literature streams and exemplars of the stream, and it highlights key features that differentiate the current effort from previous work. For example, strategic portfolio models, as Larreché and Srinivasan (1982) exemplify, consider strategic trade-offs of any potential marketing expenditures. However, the models do not project ROI from specific expenditures, do not model competition, and do not model the behavior of individual customers, their customer-level brand switching, or their lifetime value. Our model adds to the strategic portfolio literature by incorporating those elements.

Three related streams of literature involve CLV models (Berger and Nasr 1998), direct marketing–motivated models of customer equity (e.g., Blattberg and Deighton 1996; Blattberg, Getz, and Thomas 2001), and longitudinal database marketing models (e.g., Bolton, Lemon, and Verhoef 2004; Reinartz and Kumar 2000). Our CLV model builds on these approaches. However, the preceding models are restricted to companies in which a longitudinal customer database exists that contains marketing efforts that target each customer and the associated customer responses. Unless the longitudinal database involves panel data across several competitors, no competitive effects can be modeled. Our model is more general in that it does not require the existence of a longitudinal database, and it can consider any marketing expenditure, not only expenditures that are targeted one-to-one. We also model competition and incorporate purchases from competitors (or brand switching), in contrast to most existing models from the direct marketing tradition.

---

[1]For expositional simplicity, we assume throughout much of the article that the firm has one brand and one market, and therefore we use the terms "firm" and "brand" interchangeably. In many firms, the firm's customer equity may result from sales of several brands and/or several distinct goods or services.

TABLE 1 Comparing the Return on Marketing Model with Existing Marketing Models

Type of Model	Exemplars	Strategic Trade-Offs of Any Marketing Expenditures Calculated?	ROI Modeled and Calculated?	Explicitly Models Competition?	Calculation of CLV?	Can Be Applied to Most Industries?	Net Present Value of Revenues and Costs?	Brand Switching Modeled at Customer Level?	Statistical Details?
Strategic portfolio	Larreché and Srinivasan (1982)	Yes	No	No	No	Yes	Yes	No	Yes
CLV	Berger and Nasr (1998)	No	No	No	Yes	No	Yes	No	Yes
Direct marketing: customer equity	Blattberg and Deighton (1996); Blattberg, Getz, and Thomas (2001)	No	Yes	No	Yes	Yes	Yes	No	Yes
Longitudinal database marketing	Bolton, Lemon, and Verhoef (2004); Reinartz and Kumar (2000)	Yes	Yes	No, unless panel data	Yes	No	Yes	No, unless panel data	Yes
Service profit chain	Heskett et al. (1994); Kamakura et al. (2002)	No	No	No	No	No	No	No	Yes
Return on quality	Rust, Zahorik, and Keiningham (1994, 1995)	No	Yes	No	No	Yes	Yes	No	Yes
Customer equity book	Rust, Zeithaml, and Lemon (2000)	Yes	Yes	Yes	Yes	Yes	Yes	No	No
Return on marketing	Current paper	Yes	Yes	Yes	Yes	Yes	Yes	Yes	Yes

The financial-impact element of our model is foreshadowed by two related literature streams. The service profit chain (e.g., Heskett et al. 1994; Kamakura et al. 2002) and return on quality (Rust, Zahorik, and Keiningham 1994, 1995) models both involve impact chains that relate service quality to customer retention and profitability. The return on quality models go a step farther and explicitly project financial return from prospective service improvements. Following both literature streams, we also incorporate a chain of effects that leads to financial impact. As does the return on quality model, our model projects ROI. Unlike other models, our model facilitates strategic trade-offs of any prospective marketing expenditures (not only service improvements). We explicitly model the effect of competition—an element that does not appear in the service profit chain or return on quality models. Also different from prior research, our approach models customer utility, brand switching, and lifetime value.

Finally, we compare the current article with a recent book on customer equity (Rust, Zeithaml, and Lemon 2000) that focuses on broad managerial issues related to customer equity, such as building a managerial framework related to value equity, brand equity, and relationship equity. The book includes only one equation (which is inconsistent with the models in this article). Our article is a necessary complement to the book, providing the statistical and implementation details necessary to implement the book's customer equity framework in practice. The current work extends the book's CLV conceptualization in two important ways: It allows for heterogeneous interpurchase times, and it incorporates customer-specific brand-switching matrices. In summary, the current article has incorporated many influences, but it makes a unique contribution to the literature.

Overview of the Article

In the next section, on the basis of a new model of CLV, we describe how marketing actions link to customer equity and financial return. The following section describes issues in the implementation of our framework, including data options, model input, and model estimation. We then present an example application to the airline industry, showing some of the details that arise in application, in testing and validating our choice model, and in providing some substantive observations. We end with discussion and conclusions.

LINKING MARKETING ACTIONS TO FINANCIAL RETURN

Conceptual Model

Figure 1 shows a broad overview of the conceptual model that we used to evaluate return on marketing. Marketing is viewed as an investment (Srivastava, Shervani, and Fahey 1998) that produces an improvement in a driver of customer equity (for simplicity of exposition, we refer to an improvement in only one driver, but our model also accommodates simultaneous improvement in multiple drivers). This leads to improved customer perceptions (Simester et al. 2000), which result in increased customer attraction and retention (Danaher and Rust 1996). Better attraction and retention lead to increased CLV (Berger and Nasr 1998) and customer equity (Blattberg and Deighton 1996). The increase in customer equity, when considered in relation to the cost of

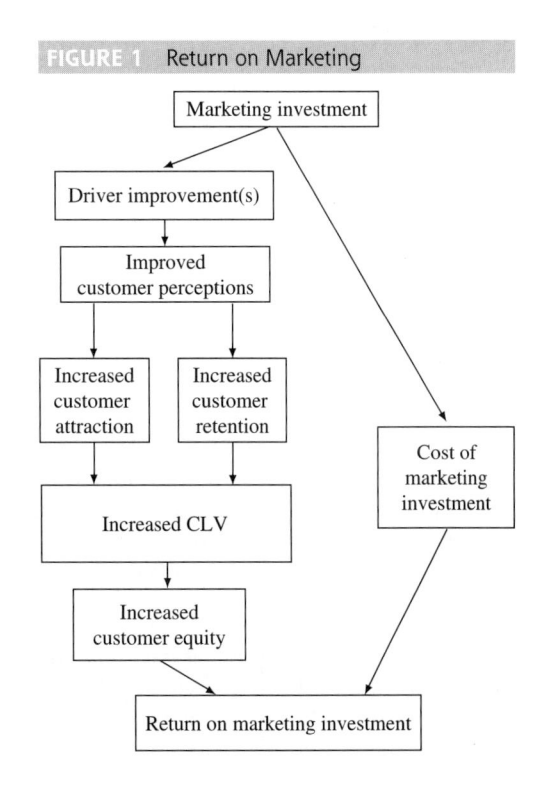

FIGURE 1 Return on Marketing

marketing investment, results in a return on marketing investment. Central to our model is a new CLV model that incorporates brand switching.

Brand Switching and CLV

It has long been known that the consideration of competing brands is a central element of brand choice (Guadagni and Little 1983). Therefore, we begin with the assumption that competition has an impact on each customer's purchase decisions, and we explicitly consider the relationship between the focal brand and competitors' brands. In contrast, most, if not all, CLV models address the effects of marketing actions without considering competing brands. This is because data that are typically available to direct marketers rarely include information about the sales or preference for competing brands. Our approach incorporates information about not only the focal brand but competing brands as well, which enables us to create a model that contains both customer attraction and retention in the context of brand switching. The approach considers customer flows from one competitor to another, which is analogous to brand-switching models in consumer packaged goods (e.g., Massy, Montgomery, and Morrison 1970) and migration models (Dwyer 1997). The advantage of the approach is that competitive effects can be modeled, thereby yielding a fuller and truer accounting of CLV and customer equity.

When are customers gone? Customer retention historically has been treated according to two assumptions (Jackson 1985). First, the "lost for good" assumption uses the customer's retention probability (often the retention rate in the customer's segment) as the probability that a firm's customer in one period is still the firm's customer in the following period. Because the retention probability is typically less than one, the probability that the customer is retained declines over time. The implicit assumption is that customers are "alive" until they "die," after which they are lost for good. Models for estimating the number of active customers have been proposed for relationship marketing (Schmittlein, Morrison, and Columbo 1987), customer retention (Bolton 1998), and CLV (Reinartz 1999).

The second assumption is the "always a share" assumption, in which customers may not give any firm all of their business. Attempts have been made to model this by a "migration model" (Berger and Nasr 1998; Dwyer 1997). The migration model assigns a retention probability as previously, but if the customer has missed a period, a lower probability is assigned to indicate the possibility that the customer may return. Likewise, if the customer has been gone for two periods, an even lower probability is assigned. This is an incomplete model of switching because it includes purchases from only one firm.

In one scenario (consistent with the lost-for-good assumption) when the customer is gone, he or she is gone. This approach systematically understates CLV to the extent that it is possible for customers to return. In another scenario (consistent with the migration model), the customer may leave and return. In this scenario, customers may be either serially monogamous or polygamous (Dowling and Uncles 1997), and their degrees of loyalty may vary or even change. We can model the second (more realistic) scenario using a Markov switching-matrix approach.[2]

Acquisition and retention. Note that the brand-switching matrix models both the acquisition and the retention of customers. Acquisition is modeled by the flows from other firms to the focal firm, and retention is modeled by the diagonal element associated with the focal firm. The retention probability for a particular customer is the focal firm's diagonal element, as a proportion of the sum of the probabilities in the focal firm's row of the switching matrix. Note that this implies a different retention rate for each customer × firm combination (we show the details of this in a subsequent section). This describes the acquisition of customers who are already in the market. In growing markets, it is also important to model the acquisition of customers who are new to the market.

The switching matrix and lifetime value. We propose a general approach that uses a Markov switching matrix to model customer retention, defection, and possible return. Markov matrices have been widely used for many years to model brand-switching behavior (e.g., Kalwani

---

[2]It is also possible to model the share-of-wallet scenario that is common to business-to-business applications by using the concept of fuzzy logic (e.g., Varki, Cooil, and Rust 2000; Wedel and Steenkamp 1989, 1991).

and Morrison 1977) and have recently been proposed for modeling customer relationships (Pfeifer and Carraway 2000; Rust, Zeithaml, and Lemon 2000). In such a model, the customer has a probability of being retained by the brand in the subsequent period or purchase occasion. This probability is the retention probability, as is already widely used in CLV models. The Markov matrix includes retention probabilities for all brands and models the customer's probability of switching from any brand to any other brand.[3] This is the feature that permits customers to leave and then return, perhaps repeatedly. In general, this "returning" is confused with initial "acquisition" in other customer equity and CLV approaches. The Markov matrix is a generalization of the migration model and is expanded to include the perspective of multiple brands.

To understand how the switching matrix relates to CLV, consider a simplified example. Suppose that a particular customer (whom we call "George") buys once per month, on average, and purchases an average of $20 per purchase in the product category (with a contribution of $10). Suppose that George most recently bought from Brand A. Suppose that George's switching matrix is such that 70% of the time he will rebuy Brand A, given that he bought Brand A last time, and 30% of the time he will buy Brand B. Suppose that whenever George last bought Brand B he has a 50% chance of buying Brand A the next time and a 50% chance of buying Brand B. This is enough information for us to calculate George's lifetime value to both Brand A and Brand B.[4]

Consider George's next purchase. We know that he most recently bought Brand A; thus, the probability of him purchasing Brand A in the next purchase is .7 and the probability of him purchasing Brand B is .3. To obtain the probabilities for George's next purchase, we simply multiply the vector that comprises the probabilities by the switching matrix. The probability of purchasing Brand A becomes $(.7 \times .7) + (.3 \times .5) = .64$, and the probability of purchasing Brand B becomes $(.7 \times .3) + (.3 \times .5) = .36$. We can calculate the probabilities of purchase for Brand A and Brand B as many purchases out as we choose by successive multiplication by the switching matrix. Multiplying this by the contribution per purchase yields George's expected contribution to each brand for each future purchase. Because future purchases are worth less than current ones, we apply a discount factor to the expected contributions. The summation of these across all purchase occasions (to infinity or, more likely, to a finite time horizon) yields George's CLV for each firm. Note that if there are regular relationship maintenance expenditures, they need to be discounted separately and subtracted from the CLV.

The bridge of actionability. We assume that the firm can identify expenditure categories, or drivers (e.g., advertising awareness, service quality, price, loyalty program) that influence consumer decision making and that compete for marketing resources in the firm. We also assume that management wants to trade off the drivers to make decisions about which strategic investments yield the greatest return (Johnson and Gustafsson 2000). The drivers that are projected to yield the highest return receive higher levels of investment. Connecting the drivers to customer perceptions is essential to quantify the effects of marketing actions at the individual customer level. Therefore, it is necessary to have customer ratings (analogous to customer satisfaction ratings) on the brand's perceived performance on each driver. For example, Likert-scale items can be used to measure each competing brand's perceived performance on each driver, perceptions may vary across customers.

The firm may also want to assemble its drivers into broader expenditure categories that reflect higher-level resource allocation. We refer to these as "strategic investment categories." For

---

[3] The Pfeifer and Carraway (2000) Markov model considers only one brand and does not capture brand switching. Its states pertain to recency rather than brand.

[4] Actually, George's CLV also depends on word-of-mouth effects (Anderson 1998; Hogan, Lemon, and Libai 2000), because George may make recommendations to others that increase George's value to the firm. To the extent that positive word of mouth occurs, our CLV estimates will be too low. Similarly, negative word of mouth will make our estimates too high. Although these two effects, being of the opposite sign, tend to cancel out to some extent, there will be some unknown degree of bias due to word of mouth. However, word-of-mouth effects are notoriously difficult to measure on a practical basis.

example, a firm may combine all its brand-equity expenditures into a brand-equity strategic investment category, with the idea that the brand manager is responsible for drivers such as brand image and brand awareness.

Modeling the Switching Matrix

Thus, the modeling of CLV requires modeling of the switching matrix for each individual customer. using individual-level data from a cross-sectional sample of customers, combined with purchase (or purchase intention) data, we model each customer's switching matrix and estimate model parameters that enable the modeling of CLV at the individual customer level.

The utility model. In addition to the individual-specific customer-equity driver ratings, we also include the effect of brand inertia, which has been shown to be a useful predictive factor in multinomial logit choice models (Guadagni and Little 1983). The utility formulation can be conceptualized as

$$\text{Utility} = \text{inertia} + \text{impact of drivers.} \quad (2.1)$$

To make this more explicit, U_{ijk} is the utility of brand k to individual i, who most recently purchased brand j. The dummy variable LAST_{ijk} is equal to one if j = k and is equal to zero otherwise; X is a row vector of drivers. We then model

$$U_{ijk} = \beta_{0k}\text{LAST}_{ijk} + \mathbf{X}_{ik}\boldsymbol{\beta}_{1k} + \varepsilon_{ijk} \quad (2.2)$$

where β_{0k} is a logit regression coefficient corresponding to inertia, $\boldsymbol{\beta}_{1k}$ is a column vector of logit regression coefficients corresponding to the drivers, and ε_{ijk} is a random error term that is assumed to have an extreme value (double exponential) distribution, as is standard in logit models. The β coefficients can be modeled as either homogeneous or heterogeneous.[5] For the current exposition, we present the homogeneous coefficient version of the model. In a subsequent section, we build and test alternative versions of the model that allow for heterogeneous coefficients. The model can also be estimated separately for different market segments.

The individual-level utilities result in individual-level switching matrices. Essentially, each row of the switching matrix makes a different assumption about the most recent brand purchased, which results in different utilities for each row. That is, the first row assumes that the first brand was bought most recently, the second row assumes that the second brand was bought most recently, and so on. The utilities in the different rows are different because the effect of inertia (and the effect of any variable that only manifests with repeat purchase) is present only in repeat purchases.

Consistent with the multinomial logit model, the probability of choice for individual i is modeled as

$$\begin{aligned} P_{ijk*} &= \Pr[\text{individual i chooses brand K*,} \\ &\quad \text{given that brand j was most} \\ &\quad \text{recently chosen}] \\ &= \exp(V_{ijk*}) \sum_k \exp(V_{ijk}) \end{aligned} \quad (2.3)$$

where V represents the deterministic component of utility. Thus, the individual-level utilities result in individual-level switching matrices, which result in an individual-level CLV.

Brand switching and customer equity. To make the CLV calculation more specific, each customer i has an associated J × J switching matrix, where J is the number of brands, with switching probabilities P_{ijk}, indicating the probability that customer i will choose brand k in the next purchase, conditional on having purchased brand j in the most recent purchase. The Markov switching matrix is denoted as $\mathbf{M_i}$, and the 1 × J row vector $\mathbf{A_i}$ has as its elements the probabilities of purchase for customer i's current transaction. (If longitudinal data are used, the $\mathbf{A_i}$ vector will include a one for the brand next purchased and a zero for the other brands.)

For brand j, d_j represents firm j's discount rate, f_j is customer i's average purchase rate per unit time (e.g., three purchases per year), v_{ijt} is customer i's expected purchase volume in

---

[5]To the extent that heterogeneity in the regression coefficients exists, the state dependence effect will likely be overestimated (Degeratu 1999; Frank 1962). This would result in underestimation of the effects of the customer equity drivers, which means that the effect of violation of this assumption would be to make the projections of the model more conservative. However, it has been shown that our approach to estimating the inertia effect performs better than other methods that have been proposed (Degeratu 2001).

a purchase of brand j in purchase t,[6] π_{ijk} is the expected contribution margin per unit of firm j from customer i in purchase t, and $\mathbf{B_{it}}$ is a 1 × J row vector with elements B_{ijt} as the probability that customer i buys brand j in purchase t. The probability that customer i buys brand j in purchase t is calculated by multiplying by the Markov matrix t times:

$$\mathbf{B_{it}} = \mathbf{A_i M_i^t}. \quad (2.4)$$

The lifetime value, CLV_{ij}, of customer i to brand j is

$$CLV_{ij} = \sum_{t=0}^{T_{ij}} (1+d_j)^{-t/f_i} v_{ijt} \pi_{ijt} B_{ijt}, \quad (2.5)$$

where T_{ij} is the number of purchases customer i is expected to make before firm j's time horizon, H_j (e.g., a typical time horizon ranges from three to five years), and B_{ijt} is a firm-specific element of $\mathbf{B_{it}}$. Therefore, $T_i = \text{int}[H_j f_i]$, where int[.] refers to the integer part, and firm j's customer equity, CE_j, can be estimated as

$$CE_j = \text{mean}_i(CLV_{ij}) \times POP, \quad (2.6)$$

where $\text{mean}_i(CLV_{ij})$ is the average lifetime value for firm j's customers i across the sample, and POP is the total number of customers in the market across all brands. Note that the CLV of each individual customer in the sample is calculated separately, before the average is taken.

It is worth pointing out the subtle difference between Equation 5 and most lifetime value expressions, as in direct marketing. Previous lifetime value equations have summed over time period, and the exponent on the discounting factor becomes −t. However, in our case, we are dealing with distinct individuals with distinct interpurchase times (or equivalently, purchase frequencies f_i). For this reason, we sum over purchase instead of time period.[7] The exponent $-t/f_i$ reflects that more discounting is appropriate for purchase t if purchasing is infrequent, because purchase t will occur further into the future. If $f_i = 1$ (one purchase per period), it is clear that Equation 5 is equivalent to the standard CLV expression. If $f_i > 1$, the discounting per purchase becomes less than the discounting per period, to an extent that exactly equals the correct discounting per period. For example, for $f_i = 2$, the square root of the period's discounting occurs at each purchase.[8]

We can also use the customer equity framework to derive an overall measure of the company's competitive standing. Market share, historically used as a measure of a company's overall competitive standing, can be misleading because it considers only current sales. A company that has built the foundation for strong future profits is in better competitive position than a company that is sacrificing future profits for current sales, even if the two companies' current market shares are identical. With this in mind, we define *customer equity share* (CES, in Equation 7) as an alternative to market share that takes CLV into account. We calculate customer equity share for each brand j as

$$CES_j = CE_j / \sum_k CE_k. \quad (2.7)$$

ROI

Effect of changes. Ultimately, a firm wants to know the financial impact that will result from various marketing actions. This knowledge is essential if competing marketing initiatives are to be evaluated on an even footing. A firm may attempt to improve its customer equity by making improvements in the drivers, or it may drill down

---

[6]To simplify the mathematics, we adopt the assumption that a customer's volume per purchase is exogenous. We leave the modeling of volume per purchase as a function of marketing effort as a topic for further research.

[7]If standard marketing costs (e.g., retention promotional costs) are spent on a time basis (e.g., every three months), they may either be discounted separately and subtracted from the net present value or be assigned to particular purchases (e.g., if interpurchase time is three months, and a standard mailing goes out every six months, the mailing cost could be subtracted on every other purchase).
[8]We should also note that the expression implies that the first purchase occurs immediately. Other assumptions are also possible.

further to improve subdrivers that influence the drivers (e.g., improving dimensions of ad awareness). This requires the measurement of customer perceptions of the subdrivers about which the firm wanted to know more.

A shift in a driver (e.g., increased ad awareness) produces an estimated shift in utility, which in turn produces an estimated shift in the conditional probabilities of choice (conditional on last brand purchased) and results in a revised Markov switching matrix. In turn, this results in an improved CLV (Equations 4 and 5). Summed across all customers, this results in improved customer equity (Equation 6). We assume an equal shift (e.g., .1 rating points) for all customers, but this assumption can be relaxed if appropriate, because our underlying modeling framework does not require a constant shift across customers.

Projecting financial impact. It is often possible to devote a strategic expenditure to improve a driver, but is that investment likely to be profitable? Modern thinking in finance suggests that improved expenditures should be treated as capital investments and viewed as profitable only if the ROI exceeds the cost of capital. Financial approaches based on this idea are known by such names as "economic value-added" (Ehrbar 1998) or "value-based management" (Copeland, Koller, and Murrin 1996). The increased interest in economic value-added approaches has attracted more attention to ROI approaches in marketing (Fellman 1999).

The discounted expenditure stream is denoted as E, discounted by the cost of capital, and ΔCE is the improvement in customer equity that the expenditures produce. Then, ROI is calculated as

$$\text{ROI} = (\Delta CE - E)/E. \qquad (2.8)$$

Operationally, the calculation can be accomplished by using a spreadsheet program or a dedicated software package. Note, though, that even if ΔCE is negative, the ROI expression still holds.

IMPLEMENTATION ISSUES

Cross-Sectional Versus Longitudinal Data

Our approach requires the collection of cross-sectional survey data; the approach is similar in style and length to that of a customer satisfaction survey. The survey collects customer ratings of each competing brand on each driver. Other necessary customer information can be obtained either from the same survey or from longitudinal panel data, if it is available. The additional information collected about each customer includes the brand purchased most recently, average purchase frequency, and average volume per purchase. The logit model can be calibrated in two ways: (1) by observing the next purchase (from either the panel data or a follow-up survey) or (2) by using purchase intent as a proxy for the probability of each brand being chosen in the next purchase.

Obtaining the Model Input

The implementation of our approach begins with manager interviews and exploratory research to obtain information about the market in which the firm competes and information about the corporate environment in which strategic decisions are made. From interviews with managers, we identified competing firms and customer segments; chose drivers that correspond to current or potential management initiatives; and obtained the size of the market (total number of customers across all brands) and internal financial information, such as the discount rate and relevant time horizon. In addition, we estimated contribution margins for all competitors. If there was a predictable trend in gross margins for any firm in the industry, we also elicited that trend. From exploratory research, using both secondary sources and focus group interviews, we identified additional drivers, which we reviewed with management to ensure that they were managerially actionable items. On the basis of the combined judgment of management and the researchers, we reduced the set of drivers to a number that allows for a survey of reasonable length. The drivers employed typically vary by industry.

Estimating Shifts in Customer Ratings

The calculation of ROI requires an estimate of the rating shift that will be produced by a particular marketing expenditure. For example, a firm may estimate that an advertising campaign will increase the ad awareness rating by .3 on a five-point scale. These estimates can be obtained in several ways. If historical experience with similar expenditures is available, that experience can be used to approximate the ratings shift. For example, many marketing consulting firms have developed a knowledge base of the effects of marketing programs on measurable indexes. Another way, analogous to the decision calculus approach (Blattberg and Deighton 1996; Little 1970), is to have the manager supply a judgment-based estimate. The manager may reflect uncertainty by supplying an optimistic and a pessimistic estimate, the outcome would be considered sensitive to the rating shift estimate, indicating the need for more information gathering. Another limited cost approach is to use simulated test markets (Clancy, Shulman, and Wolf 1994; Urban et al. 1997) to obtain a preliminary idea of market response. Finally, the marketing expenditure can be implemented on a limited basis, using actual test markets, and the observed rating shift can be monitored (e.g., Rust et al. 1999; Simester et al. 2000).

Calibrating the Data

It is typical in many sampling plans to have respondents with different sampling weights, w_i, correcting for variations in the probability of selection. We can use the sampling weights directly, in the usual way, to generate a sample-based estimate of market share, which we denote as MS_{sample}. If the sample is truly representative, MS_{sample} should be equal to the actual market share, MS_{true}. To make the sample more representative of actual purchase patterns, we can assign a new weight, $w_{i,new} = (MS_{true}/MS_{sample}) \times w_i$ to each respondent, with market shares corresponding to that respondent's most recently chosen brand, which will correct for any sampling bias with respect to any brand. The implied market share from the sample will then equal the actual market share.

If purchase intent rather than actual purchase data is used, the application must be done with some care. Previous researchers have long noted that purchase-intention subjective probabilities occasionally may be systematically biased (Lee, Hu, and Toh 2000; Pessemier et al. 1971; Silk and Urban 1978). We assume that the elicited purchase intentions, p_{ij}, of respondent i purchasing brand j in the next purchase need to be calibrated. In general, we assume that there is a calibrated probability, p^*_{ij}, that captures the true probability of the next purchase. These probabilities can be calibrated in two possible ways. First, if it is possible to follow up with each respondent to check on the next purchase, we can find a multiplier K_j for each brand that best predicts choice. (We set K_j for the first brand arbitrarily to one, without loss of generality, to allow for uniqueness.) The K's can be quickly found using a numerical search. If p^*_{ij} is the stated probability of respondent i choosing brand j in the next purchase, the calibrated choice probability is $p^*_{ij} = K_j p_{ij}/\Sigma_k K_k p_{ik}$. Second, if checking the next purchase is not possible, it is still possible to calibrate the purchase intentions by making an approximating assumption. Assuming that the market share (as the percentage of customers who prefer a brand) for each brand in the near future (including each respondent's next purchase) is roughly constant, we employ a numerical search to find the K_j's (again setting $K_1 = 1$) for which $MS_{true} = mean_i(p^*_{ij})$.

Model Estimation

Principal components regression. In this application, as in customer satisfaction measurement, multicollinearity is an issue that needs to be addressed (Peterson and Wilson 1992). For this reason, we adopt an estimation approach that addresses the multicollinearity issue. Principal components regression (Massy 1965) is an approach that combats multicollinearity reasonably well (Frank and Friedman 1993), yet it can be implemented with standard statistical software. Principal components regression is a two-stage procedure that is widely known and applied in statistics, econometrics, and marketing (e.g., Freund and Wilson 1998; Hocking 1996; Naik, Hagerty, and Tsai 2000; Press 1982). Principal components multinomial logit regression has been used successfully in the marketing literature, leading to greater analysis interpretability and coefficient stability (e.g., Gessner et al. 1988).

The idea is to reduce the dimensionality of the independent variables by extracting fewer principal components that explain a large percentage of the variation in the predictors. The principal components are then used as independent variables in the regression analysis. Because the principal components are orthogonal, there is no multicollinearity issue with respect to their effects. In addition, eliminating the smallest principal components, which may be essentially random, may reduce the noise in the estimation. Because the principal components can be expressed as a linear combination of the independent variables (and vice versa), the coefficients of the independent variables can be estimated as a function of the coefficients of the principal components, and the coefficients (after the least important principal components are discarded) may result in better estimates of the driver's effects. Estimation details are provided in Appendix A.

Importance of customer equity drivers. The results from the model estimation in Equation 2 provide insight into which customer equity drivers are most critical in the industry in which the firm competes. When examining a specific industry, it is useful to know what the key success factors are in that industry. Ordinarily, this might be explored by calculating market share elasticities for each driver. However, that approach is not correct here, because the drivers are intervally scaled rather than ratio scaled. This means that it is incorrect to calculate percentages of the drivers, as is necessary in the calculation of elasticities. Moreover, our focus is customer equity rather than market share. To arrive at the impact of a driver on customer equity, we need to determine the partial derivative of choice probability, with respect to the driver, for each customer in the sample. That is, if a driver were improved by a particular amount, what would be the impact on customer choice and, ultimately, on CLV and customer equity? Appendix A provides details of these computations and significance tests for the drivers.

AN EXAMPLE APPLICATION

Data and Sampling

Survey items. We illustrate our approach with data collected from customers of five industries. We assume three strategic investment categories: (1) perceived value (Parasuraman 1997; Zeithaml 1988), (2) brand equity (Aaker and Keller 1990), and (3) relationship management (Anderson and Narus 1990; Gummeson 1999). The three categories span all major marketing expenditures (Rust, Zeithaml, and Lemon 2000). We drew heavily on the relevant academic and managerial literature in these areas to build our list of drivers and ensured that the drivers could be translated into actionable expenditures. The resulting survey contained questions pertaining to shopping behavior and customer ratings of each driver for the four or five leading brands in the markets we studied. In addition, several demographics questions were asked at the end of the survey. We selected industries (airlines, electronics stores, facial tissues, grocery, and rental cars) that represented a broad set of consumer goods and services. To save space, we present the details for the airline industry analysis only; however, our approach was similar across the other four industries. The complete list of the survey items used in our analysis of the airline industry appears in Appendix B.

Population. We obtained illustrative data from two communities in the northeastern United States: an affluent small town/suburb and a medium-sized city that adjoins a larger city. Respondents were real consumers who had purchased the product or service in the industry in question during the previous year. Demographic statistics suggest that the sample is representative of similar standard metropolitan statistical areas in the United States, with the exception of generally high levels of education and income. For example, in the small town (with a population of approximately 20,000), the average age of the respondent was 47, the average household had two adults and one child, the average household income was $91,000, and the average years of education was 17. In the larger city, the average age was somewhat lower (39 years), the average household had two adults and one child, the average household income was $70,000, and the average years of education was similar to that of the small town.

Sampling. We obtained respondents from three random samples. The first sample, drawn from the city population, answered questions about electronics stores and rental car companies. The second sample, also drawn from the city population, addressed groceries and facial tissues. The third sample, drawn from the small town, focused on airlines. Potential respondents were contacted at random by recruiters from a professional market research organization (by telephone solicitation or building intercept). The screening process consisted of two criteria: (1) the respondent had purchased from the industry in the past 12 months, and (2) the respondent had a household income of at least $20,000 per year. Respondents agreed to participate and received $20 compensation for completing the questionnaire. In the electronics stores and rental cars survey, 246 consumers were approached: 153 were eligible, 144 cooperated, and 7 were disqualified, resulting in a total of 137 total surveys completed. In the groceries and facial tissues survey, 177 consumers were approached: 124 were eligible, 122 cooperated, and 4 were disqualified, resulting in a total of 118 surveys completed. In the airline survey, 229 consumers were approached: 119 were eligible, 105 cooperated, and 5 were disqualified, resulting in a total of 100 surveys completed.

Data collection and preliminary analysis. Data were collected in December 1998 and January 1999 at the firm's offices in each location. The respondents came to the facility to complete the pencil-and-paper questionnaire, which took about 30 minutes. They were then thanked for their participation and compensated. In addition, we obtained aggregate statistics on the small town and city (e.g., percentage of population that uses rental cars, average spent at grocery store) from secondary sources and used them in subsequent analysis. For purposes of financial analysis, we used local population and aggregate usage statistics for predominantly local industries (electronics stores and groceries) and national statistics for predominantly national industries (airlines, facial tissues, and rental cars). Although our random samples may not be fully representative of U.S. users, we extrapolated to the national market for national industries to show the type of dollar magnitudes that can arise given a large population. Because our examples are illustrative, truly precise dollar estimates are unnecessary.

Data were cleaned to eliminate obvious bad cases and extreme outliers. Because listwise deletion of cases would have resulted in too many cases being removed (even though only a relatively small percentage of responses were missing for particular items), we employed mean substitution as our missing data option for all subsequent analyses.[9] Because we suspected that the relationship drivers would affect primarily repeat purchasers, we collected relationship items only for the brand most recently purchased.[10] We mean centered the relationship-related drivers for the cases in which the brand considered was the previously purchased brand, and we set them equal to zero for the cases in which the brand considered was different from the previously purchased brand. This enabled the "pure" inertia effect to be separated from the relationship effect of the drivers.

Choice Model Results

Principal components analysis results. We reduced the dimensionality of the predictor variables in each industry by conducting a principal components analysis. We used an eigenvalue cutoff of .5, which we judged to provide the best trade-off between parsimony and managerial usefulness.[11] The airline analysis began with 17 independent variables, and we retained 11 orthogonal factors. Table 2 shows the loadings on the rotated factors. The resulting factor structure is rich. All the factors are easily interpretable. The few negative loadings are small and insignificant; they are zero for all practical purposes. All drivers load on only one factor, and many (e.g., inertia, quality, price, convenience, trust, corporate citizenship) load on their own unique factor.

There is some degree of discrimination among the value, brand, and relationship strategic investment categories in that drivers in the three

---

[9]Mean substitution can result in biased estimates, but in our judgment, the additional effort of employing a more sophisticated missing values procedure (e.g., data imputation) was not justified in this case, given the relatively low percentage of missing values.
[10]This decision was based solely on the researchers' best judgment. Our model does not require this.
[11]The 1.0 eigenvalue cutoff (Kaiser 1960) is typically employed in marketing, but it is just one of many possible cutoff criteria (for two alternatives, see Cattell 1966; Jolliffe 1972). As Kaiser (1960, p. 143), who proposed the 1.0 cutoff, points out, "by far [the] most important viewpoint for choosing the number of factors [is] . . . psychological meaningfulness." In other words, the cutoff should be chosen such that the results are substantively meaningful, which is our justification for using the particular cutoff level that we chose.

TABLE 2 Factor Loadings: Airline Industry

Driver	F1	F2	F3	F4	F5	F6	F7	F8	F9	F10	F11
Inertia	−.013	−.004	.033	.038	.015	.116	−.024	**.984**	.029	.043	.002
Quality	.097	.058	.174	.076	.147	.212	.014	.049	.068	**.904**	.083
Price	.044	−.007	.128	.054	.078	.023	.039	.030	**.975**	.059	.034
Convenience	.078	.068	.219	.161	.043	**.830**	.066	.163	.018	.260	−.015
Ad awareness	−.031	.130	.038	**.938**	−.010	.022	.048	−.011	.074	.101	.058
Information	.216	−.077	.248	**.656**	.322	.299	−.207	.125	−.038	−.058	.016
Corporate citizenship	.011	.122	.150	.093	**.880**	.001	.256	.021	.077	.137	.006
Community events	.021	.100	.188	−.042	.226	.051	**.921**	−.026	.041	.011	.029
Ethical standards	−.016	.044	**.605**	.105	.458	.266	.028	−.034	.104	.109	.218
Image fits my personality	.098	.112	**.878**	.107	.069	.092	.203	.058	.110	.142	.081
Investment in loyalty program	**.921**	.044	.090	.032	−.007	−.060	.018	.014	−.003	.137	−.103
Preferential treatment	**.898**	.087	.082	−.002	.022	−.071	−.029	.032	−.007	.077	.104
Know airline's procedures	**.708**	.232	−.022	.116	.029	.166	.058	−.033	.010	−.069	.240
Airline knows me	**.681**	.309	−.073	−.059	−.001	.356	−.012	−.061	.136	−.075	.219
Recognizes me as special	.214	**.851**	.069	.077	−.036	.042	.138	−.004	−.044	.118	.092
Community	.175	**.876**	.065	.031	.166	.035	−.015	.001	.036	−.042	.129
Trust	.246	.227	.179	.069	.041	−.003	.031	.006	.038	.091	**.889**

Notes: Loadings greater than .5 are shown in bold.

strategic action categories of different drivers do not correlate highly on the same factors. As we expected, the strategic investment categories, value, brand, and relationship are not unidimensional. The drivers that constitute the categories can be grouped for managerial purposes as managers consider them, but drivers in a particular strategic investment category may be quite distinct in the customer's mind.

Logit regression results. Using the resulting factors as independent variables, we conducted multinomial logit analyses, using the analysis we described previously. Table 3 shows the coefficients that arise from the multinomial logit regression analysis, highlighting the significant factors. Using Equations A1–A9, we converted the factor-level results to the individual drivers. The resulting coefficients, standard errors, and test statistics are shown in Table 4. All the drivers are significant and have the correct sign, but some drivers have a larger effect than others. The most important drivers span all three strategic investment categories. In addition to the drivers, inertia has a large, significant impact (.849, $p < .01$). Among the value-related drivers, convenience has the largest coefficient (.609), followed by quality (.441); for brand-related drivers, direct mail information has the largest impact (.638), followed by ad awareness (.421) and ethical standards (.421). The loyalty program (.295) and preferential treatment (.280) are the most important relationship-related drivers.

Model Testing and Validation

We tested and validated the core choice model in several different ways. We tested for brand-specific effects, heterogeneity of response, a more general covariance matrix, and the reliability of the coefficient estimates.

Brand-specific effects. The model in Equation 2 assumes that there are no brand-specific effects. We tested the validity of this assumption by including brand-specific constants in the model of Equation 2. Testing the

CHAPTER 2 The Customer Equity Approach and the Customer Management Plan

TABLE 3 Logit Regression Results: Airline Industry

Independent Variable	Coefficient	Standard Error	b/s.e.	p
F1	.325**	.122	2.65	.008
F2	−.031	.118	−.26	.795
F3	.421*	.210	2.00	.045
F4	.459	.285	1.61	.107
F5	.212	.228	.93	.352
F6	.331*	.159	2.08	.037
F7	−.081	.279	−.29	.771
F8	.633**	.100	6.36	.000
F9	.034	.164	.21	.835
F10	.184	.147	1.26	.209
F11	−.033	.115	−.29	.772
Log-likelihood	= −98.46			
Chi-square (11 degrees of freedom) = 69.246**				

*$p < .05$.
**$p < .01$.

significance of the more complicated model can be accomplished through the use of a nested-likelihood-ratio chi-square test (in the airline application, this involves three degrees of freedom, reflecting a number of brand-specific constants that is equal to the number of brands minus one). The resulting nested model comparison was not significant ($\chi^2_3 = .977$), from

TABLE 4 Driver Coefficients: Airline Industry

Driver	Coefficient	Standard Error	b/s.e.
Inertia	.849	.075	11.341*
Quality	.441	.041	10.871*
Price	.199	.020	9.858*
Convenience	.609	.093	6.553*
Ad awareness	.421	.099	4.242*
Information	.638	.082	7.819*
Corporate citizenship	.340	.045	7.617*
Community events	.170	.024	6.974*
Ethical standards	.421	.053	7.901*
Image fits my personality	.390	.050	7.874*
Investment in loyalty program	.295	.027	10.956*
Preferential treatment	.280	.026	10.857*
Know airline's procedures	.238	.027	8.779*
Airline knows me	.249	.041	6.108*
Recognizes me as special	.167	.017	9.771*
Community	.151	.016	9.412*
Trust	.203	.023	8.725*

*$p < .01$.

which we conclude that brand-specific constants are not required.[12]

Heterogeneity of response. It is reasonable to suspect that there may be unobserved heterogeneity of response across the respondents. That is, expressed in terms of Equation 2, the βs may be different across respondents. To test this, we employed a random coefficients logit model (Chintagunta, Jain, and Vilcassim 1991) in which we permitted the driver coefficients to be distributed as an independent multivariate normal distribution. The log-likelihood improved from −97.58 to −93.24, which is an insignificant improvement (χ^2_{11} = .8.68). Therefore, we conclude that the random coefficients logit formulation does not produce a better model and that it is not worthwhile in this case to model unobserved heterogeneity in the parameters.

Correlated errors. Another way the independence from irrelevant alternatives property can be violated is if the error terms in Equation 2 are correlated. For example, it is possible that people who prefer American Airlines more than the model predicted will systematically dislike Southwest Airlines more than the model predicted. To address this issue, we turned to a multinomial probit model (Chintagunta 1992). In this model, the error terms in Equation 2 are assumed to be normally distributed rather than extreme value, and they are permitted to have a general covariance matrix.

Our original logit model is no longer a constrained version of the more complicated model, so we cannot do the nested likelihood-ratio chi-square test. However, by comparing the general multinomial probit model with a multinomial probit model in which the error terms are assumed to be independent, we can address the issue of whether modeling the more general covariance matrix is useful. This results in a nested test. We found that the uncorrelated errors version of the model resulted in a log-likelihood of −98.46 (slightly worse than the multinomial logit log-likelihood) and that the more general model produced a log-likelihood of −97.57. The improvement is insignificant (χ^2_3 = .82). We also can compare the general multinomial probit model with the original multinomial logit model by using the Akaike information criterion. The improvement from −97.58 to −97.57 does not compensate for the additional three estimated parameters (we would need a log-likelihood improvement of at least 3.0), suggesting that the general multinomial probit model is not better than our multinomial logit model. Thus, we conclude that the more general covariance matrix is not warranted.

Coefficient reliability. Given our relatively small sample size (96 usable data points after the data are cleaned), we were unable to pursue split-half tests or complete holdout samples. However, to further understand the reliability of our model estimates, we randomly split our sample into three parts (A, B, and C) and estimated our model on AB, AC, and BC. The mean range (and median range) of the coefficient estimates across the 11 factors was .14; that is, on average, the swing between the largest and smallest coefficient estimate across the three samples was .14, which comes out to about .6 standard errors, on average. Thus, the model appears to produce reasonably stable coefficient estimates.

CLV

Using Equation 5, we calculated CLV for American Airlines for each respondent in our airline sample. To operationalize the equation, we assumed a time horizon of three years, a discount rate of 10%, and a contribution margin of 15%. The 15% figure was approximately equal to the average operating margin for the industry for the five years preceding the survey, according to annual reports of the four firms we studied (since our study, airline industry operating margins have declined). We also based our contribution margin figures in the other four industries on financial data from annual reports. To extend the CLV figures to the firm's U.S. customer equity, we used U.S. Census data to determine the number of adults in the United States (187,747,000), and we then combined this with the percentage of U.S. adults who were active users of airline travel (23.3%), yielding a total number of U.S. adult airline customers of 43,745,051. To approximate the total customer

---

[12]This nested chi-square was also insignificant in the other four industries that we studied (electronics = 6.79, facial tissues = 1.00, grocery = 5.82, and rental cars = .28).

FIGURE 2 Distribution of CLV: American Airlines

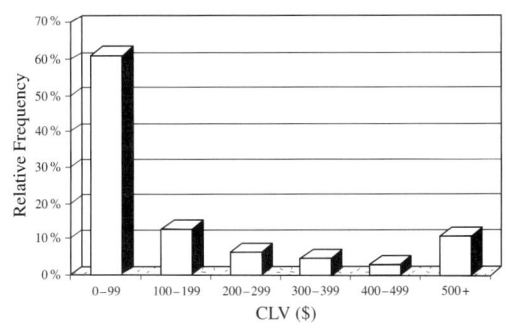

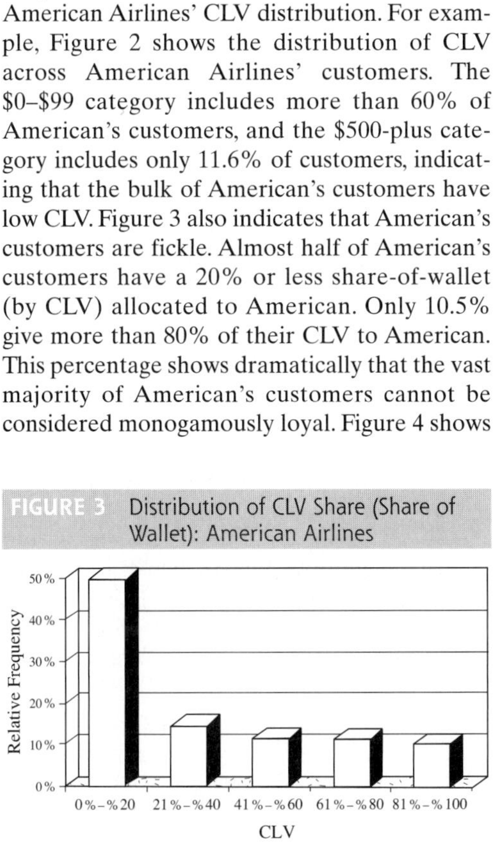

FIGURE 4 Percentage Customer Equity by CLV Category: American Airlines

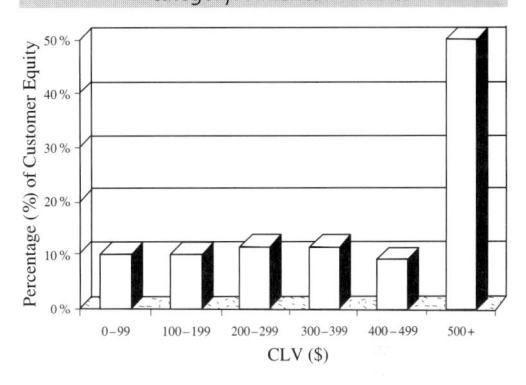

equity, we multiplied this number by the average CLV across our respondents. Note that though we used average CLV to project customer equity, we calculated CLV at the individual customer level for each customer in the sample.

Customer loyalty and CLV. Some insights can be obtained from examining American Airlines' CLV distribution. For example, Figure 2 shows the distribution of CLV across American Airlines' customers. The $0–$99 category includes more than 60% of American's customers, and the $500-plus category includes only 11.6% of customers, indicating that the bulk of American's customers have low CLV. Figure 3 also indicates that American's customers are fickle. Almost half of American's customers have a 20% or less share-of-wallet (by CLV) allocated to American. Only 10.5% give more than 80% of their CLV to American. This percentage shows dramatically that the vast majority of American's customers cannot be considered monogamously loyal. Figure 4 shows

FIGURE 3 Distribution of CLV Share (Share of Wallet): American Airlines

a startling picture of the percentage of American's customer equity that is contributed by each CLV category. The $0–$99 category, though by far the largest (more than 60% of American's customers), produces less than 10% of American's customer equity. In contrast, the $500-plus CLV category, though only 11.6% of American's customers, produces approximately 50% of American's customer equity.

Comparison with the lost-for-good CLV model. Previously, we proposed that some models of CLV that do not account for customers' returning systematically underestimate CLV and customer equity (for an exception, see Dwyer 1997). Using the airline sample, we explored the degree to which this was true. The lost-for-good model is simply a constrained version of our switching model, such that all probabilities of switching from another brand to the focal brand are zero. In other words, to calculate the results, we considered only the customers who were retained from the first purchase. When the customer chose another brand, we gave a probability of zero to any further purchase from the focal brand. For American Airlines, our brand-switching model gives a customer equity of $7.303 billion. Without accounting for switching back, the estimated customer equity declines to $3.849 billion. Thus, the lost-for-good model provides a systematic underestimation of customer equity that, in this case, is an understimation of 47.3%.

Customer equity and the value of the firm. It has been suggested (Gupta, Lehmann, and Stuart 2001) that customer equity is a

TABLE 5 Projected ROI from Marketing Expenditures

Company (Industry)	Area of Expenditure	Geographic Region	Investment	Amount Improved	Percentage Improvement in Customer Equity	Dollar Improvement in Customer Equity	Projected ROI
American (airlines)	Passenger compartment	United States	$70 million	.2 rating point	1.39%	$101.3 million	44.7%
Puffs (facial tissues)	Advertising	United States	$45 million	.3 rating point	7.04%	$58.1 million	29.1%
Delta (airlines)	Corporate ethics	United States	$50 million	.1 rating point	1.68%	$85.5 million	71.0%
Bread & Circus (groceries)	Loyalty programs	Local market	$100,000	.5 rating point in two measures	7.04%	$87,540	−12.5%

reasonable proxy for the value of the firm. Our analysis of American Airlines provides some support for this idea. Multiplication of American's average CLV ($166.94) by the number of U.S. airline passengers (43,745,051) yields a total customer equity for American of $7.3 billion. Given American's opening share price for 1999 ($60) and its number of shares outstanding at that time (161,300,000) (AMR Corporation 1999), we calculate a market capitalization of $9.7 billion. Because our projection ignores profits from international customers and nonflight sources of income, our customer equity calculation is largely compatible with American's market capitalization at the time of the survey.

Projected Financial Return

Our framework enables the financial impact of improvement efforts to be analyzed for any of the usual marketing expenditures. For example, American Airlines recently spent a reported $70 million to upgrade the quality of its passenger compartments in coach class by adding more leg room. Is such an investment justified? To perform an analysis such as this, we estimated the amount of ratings shift and the costs incurred in effecting the ratings shift. We then used the ratings shift to alter (for each respondent) the focal brand's utility, switching matrix, and CLV (see Equations 2–5), which, when averaged across respondents and projected to the size of the population (see Equation 6), resulted in a revised estimate for the firm's customer equity. In this way, and using the discount rate and contribution margin we discussed previously, we analyzed the recent American Airlines seating improvement. We used the $70 million cost figure reported by the company.

If we assume that the average for the item that measures quality of the passenger compartment (a subdriver of quality) increases by .2 rating points on the five-point scale, our analysis (see Table 5) indicates that customer equity will improve by 1.39%, resulting in an improvement in customer equity of $101.3 million nationally, or an ROI of 44.7%, which indicates that the program has the potential to be a large success. Table 5 shows the results of similar analyses from the other four industries. For example, a $45 million expenditure by Puffs facial tissues to improve ad awareness by .3 rating points would result in a $58.1 million improvement in customer equity and an ROI of 29.1%.[13]

It is even possible to measure the financial impact of corporate ethical standards or corporate citizenship. For example, if Delta spent $50 million to improve customers' perceptions of Delta's ethical standards by .1 rating points, this would project to a customer equity improvement

---

[13]To conserve space, we show the details only for the airline example, but the details of the other industry examples are similar.

of $85.5 million (a 1.68% increase). Such findings may cause some airlines to reconsider practices such as canceling flights that are not full in order to be profitable.

Not all investments will project to be profitable. For example, suppose that the grocery store Bread & Circus decides to spend $100,000 in the local retail area to improve its loyalty program ratings across two measures by .5 points. The projected benefit is not enough to justify the expenditure, and the ROI is −12.5%.

The preceding examples illustrate only some of the marketing expenditures that can be evaluated by means of the customer equity framework. Any marketing expenditure can be related to the drivers of customer equity, measured, and evaluated financially. This capability enables a firm to screen improvement ideas either before application or after a test market has nailed down the expected degree of improvement.

Model Sensitivity

The preceding analyses are based on point estimates, but how sensitive is the ROI model to errors of estimation or measurement? Sensitivity to errors of estimation can be analyzed by considering the sampling distribution of β_x. Appendix A shows how to construct confidence intervals for β_x. Then, by applying the end points of the confidence interval to the ROI model, it is possible to analyze the sensitivity of ROI to estimation error. In general, this error is of more concern on the low side, because overoptimism may result in inappropriate expenditures. With this in mind, we suggest calculation of a coefficient, $\beta_{\bar{x}}$, which will be greater than the true value only 5% of the time. Assuming that there is a large n, this is calculated as

$$\beta_{\bar{x}} = \beta_x - 1.645(\text{standard error of } \beta_x). \quad (2.9)$$

Then, $\beta_{\bar{x}}$ can be used to produce "conservative" projections of the customer equity change and the ROI. This can be done by inserting $\beta_{\bar{x}}$ directly into the customer equity calculations. For example, if we calculate a conservative estimate of customer equity impact for the American Airlines example in Table 5, we obtain a $93.9 million increase in customer equity, or a 1.29% increase. This would result in a 34.2% ROI, indicating that even a conservative estimate shows a quite favorable return.

Sensitivity to errors of measurement can be addressed by considering the sampling distribution of the sample mean. In Equation A5 in Appendix A, unlike the case in regression analysis, the level of a variable affects the extent to which a change in the variable affects choice and thus utility, CLV, and customer equity. By evaluating the end points of the confidence interval for the sample mean of a variable to be improved, we can thus obtain a confidence interval for the ROI that will result from a shift in that variable. We performed this analysis for the Delta Airlines corporate ethics example in Table 5. A 95% confidence interval for the mean on the corporate ethics variable was 3.346 ± .188, which results in a 95% confidence interval for corporate ethics improvement of $83.1 million/$87.8 million and a 95% confidence interval for ROI of 66%/76%.

If the projected rating shift results from a test market, the sampling distribution of the rating shift can also be employed to generate a confidence interval. Under the assumption that the sources of error are independent, which is not unreasonable, it would then be straightforward to simulate an all-inclusive confidence interval for ROI, incorporating errors in the model coefficient estimate, estimated sample mean, and estimated shift that are based on an assumption of a multivariate normal distribution with orthogonal components.

DISCUSSION AND CONCLUSIONS

Contributions to Theory and Practice

We make several contributions to marketing theory and practice. First, we identify the important problem of making all of marketing financially accountable, and we build the first broad framework that attempts to address the problem. We provide a unified framework for analyzing the impact of competing marketing expenditures and for projecting the ROI that will result from the expenditures. This big-picture contribution extends the scope of ROI models in marketing, which to date have focused on the financial impact of particular classes of expenditure and have not addressed the general problem of comparing the impact of any set of competing marketing expenditures. Our work is the first serious attempt to address this issue in its broadest form: the trading off of any strategic marketing alternatives on the basis of customer equity. Marketing Science Institute member companies have identified this research area as the most important problem they face today.

Second, we provide a new model of CLV, incorporating the impact of competitors' offerings and brand switching; previous CLV models have ignored competition. We also discount according to purchase rather than time period. Previous CLV models have been limited to the consideration of purchases made in prespecified time units, which is realistic for some businesses (e.g., subscription services, sports season tickets) but not for others (e.g., consumer packaged goods). By discounting according to purchase, at the individual level, our model is more widely applicable. The approach set out previously considers customer equity for the entire relevant competitive set, which has two advantages over existing approaches. First, this approach considers the expected lifetime value of both existing customers and prospective customers, thereby incorporating acquisition and retention (for the focal firm and competitors) in the same model. Second, by explicitly considering competitive effects in the choice decision, it is possible to use the model to consider the impact of competitive responses on the firm's customer equity.

Third, we provide a method for estimating the effects of individual customer equity drivers, testing their statistical significance, and projecting the ROI that will occur from expenditures on those drivers. We present a principal components multinomial logit regression model for estimating the Markov brand-switching matrix, and we separate the driver effects from the inertia effect. The identification and measurement of key drivers has been a process widely and successfully employed in the fields of customer satisfaction measurement and customer value management (e.g., Gale 1994; Kordupleski, Rust, and Zahorik 1993). We extend this idea to customer equity. By doing so, companies can answer questions such as, "Should we spend more on advertising, or should we improve service quality?" and "Which will have a bigger effect?"

Fourth, customer equity provides a theoretical framework for making the firm truly customer centered, and it is applicable to a wide variety of market contexts and industries. Basing strategic investment on the drivers of customer equity is an outside-in approach that directly operationalizes these fundamental marketing concepts. In other words, the customer equity approach provides a means of making strategic marketing decisions inherently information driven, which is consistent with the long-term trends of decreasing costs for information gathering and information processing.

Fifth, application of the customer equity framework is consistent with practical management needs. The results provide insight into competitive strengths and weaknesses and an understanding of what is important to the customer. By contrasting the firm's customer equity, customer equity share, and driver performance with those of its competitors, the firm can quickly determine where it is gaining or losing competitive ground with respect to the value of its customer base. In addition, the model results include the distribution of CLV across the firm's customer, the distribution of CLV share (discounted share-of-wallet) across the firm's customers, and the percentage of the firm's customer equity provided by the firm's top X% of customers. Collectively, the information gives useful information about how to segment the firm's customers on the basis of importance. Finally, the mathematical infrastructure of our framework can be implemented by means of widely available statistical packages and spreadsheet programs, and we have conducted all the analyses by using only standard, commercially available software packages.

Limitations and Directions for Further Research

In this article, we have developed and illustrated a practical framework for basing marketing strategy on CLV and customer equity. As with any new endeavor, there is much work yet to be done. Specifically, we have determined seven key areas for further research. First, the effects of market dynamics on customer equity should be examined. For example, if the market is rapidly expanding or rapidly shrinking, an assumption of stable market size is inappropriate. In such markets, it would be necessary to model the changing size of the market and relate that to customer equity. This also implies the explicit modeling of a birth and death process for customers in the market. New-to-the-world products and services and markets in which firms are expanding globally are examples of contexts in which we believe this will be particularly important.

Second, our model assumes that there is one brand or product in the firm and does not consider cross-selling between a firm's brands or products. We believe that the model we have described provides a solid foundation for firms to understand what drivers customer equity in a given brand or product category. However, because many firms have multiple offerings and hope to encourage customer cross-buying of these products, it will be important to understand the influence of the drivers of customer equity on customer cross-buying behavior and to incorporate the impact of cross-selling on customer equity. This is particularly important for firms that rely on customer cross-buying behavior for long-term customer profitability (e.g., financial service firms).

Third, we adopt the assumption that a customer's volume per purchase is exogenous. An extension of this research would permit volume per purchase to vary as a function of marketing effort. For example, it will be important to understand whether marketing effort that may result in forward buying (e.g., short-term price discounts) have a long-term effect on customer equity.

Fourth, there is a need to develop dynamic models of CLV and customer equity. Traditional models of CLV have been adopted from the net-present-value approach in the finance literature. Understanding how the value of the firm's customers (and overall customer equity) changes over time will enable managers to make even better marketing investments. There is also an opportunity to develop richer models of CLV that incorporate a deeper understanding of consumer behavior.

Fifth, there is an opportunity to relate customer equity to corporate valuation (Gupta, Lehmann, and Stuart 2001). This should involve the evaluation of corporate assets, liabilities, and risk, as well as the estimated customer equity. Sixth, applications of this framework and further empirical validation of its elements would be useful, especially across different cultures. For example, in what kinds of cultures are various drivers more important or less important, and why? Seventh, although our model incorporates competition, it makes no provision for competitive reactions. An extension of this work might involve a game theoretic competitive structure in order to understand the effects of potential competitive reactions to the firm's intended improvements in key drivers of customer equity.

Summary

We have provided the first broad framework for evaluating return on marketing. This enables us to make marketing financially accountable and to trade off competing strategic marketing investments on the basis of financial return. We build our customer equity projections from a new model of CLV, one that permits the modeling of competitive effects and brand-switching patterns. Customer equity provides an information-based, customer-driven, competitor-cognizant, and financially accountable strategic approach to maximizing the firm's long-term profitability.

APPENDIX A
ESTIMATION DETAILS

Principal Components Regression

The independent variables for the principal components analysis are all the drivers and the LAST variable. The vector $\mathbf{X}_{ijk}$ denotes the original independent variables for each customer i by previously purchased firm j by next-purchase firm k combination. Treating the customer by firm combinations as replications, we extract the largest principal components of $\mathbf{X}_{ijk}$ and rotate them using varimax rotation to maximize the extent to which the factors load uniquely on the original independent variables, thereby aiding managerial interpretability. The vector $\mathbf{F}_{ijk}$ denotes the rotated factor. These form the independent variables for our logit regression, which we describe subsequently.

Expressing Equation 2 in terms of the underlying factors leads to the following:

$$U_{ijk} = \mathbf{F}_{ijk}\gamma + \varepsilon_i, \quad (A.1)$$

where γ is a vector of coefficients.

From factor analysis theory, it is known that the factors are linear combinations of the underlying variables $\mathbf{X}_{ijk}$. In other words, there exists a matrix $\mathbf{A}$ for which $\mathbf{F}_{ijk} = \mathbf{X}_{ijk}\mathbf{A}$. However, the idea of the principal components analysis was to discard the potentially muddling effects of the least important components. Denoting **A*** as the subvector of **A** that corresponds to the reduced factor space (discarding the principal components that do not meet the eigenvalue cutoff) and **γ*** as the estimated **γ** that corresponds to the reduced space, Equation A1 can be expressed as

$$\hat{U}_{ijk} = (\mathbf{X}_{ijk}\mathbf{A}^*)\boldsymbol{\gamma}^* = \mathbf{X}_{ijk}(\mathbf{A}^*\boldsymbol{\gamma}^*), \quad (A.2)$$

where $\hat{U}_{ijk}$ is the estimated utility, which means that $\boldsymbol{\beta}^* = \mathbf{A}^*\boldsymbol{\gamma}^*$ can be the estimated coefficient vector. In other words, the coefficients of $\mathbf{X}_{ijk}$ are obtained by multiplying the regression coefficients obtained from the logit regression on the factors by the factor coefficients that relate the drivers to the factors.

Logit Estimation

Usually in multinomial logit regression, the observed dependent variable values are ones and zeroes, corresponding to the purchased brand (1 = "brand was purchased," 0 = "brand was not purchased"). This will be the case if the next purchase is observed from a longitudinal panel or follow-up survey. However, if purchase intent is used as a proxy for next purchase, the dependent variable values will be proportions that correspond to the stated (or calibrated) purchase intention probabilities. This does not create any difficulties. From Equation 9, we have $U_{ijk} = \mathbf{F}_{ijk}\boldsymbol{\gamma}^* + \varepsilon_i$, after discarding the principal components that did not meet the cutoff. Using the laws of conditional probability, we can express the likelihood of a particular parameter vector **γ*** given respondent i's observed next purchase (or purchase intention) vector $\mathbf{p}^*_i$ as

$$L(\boldsymbol{\gamma}^*|\mathbf{p}^*_i) = \sum_{j=1}^{J} L(\boldsymbol{\gamma}^*|Y_{ij}=1)P(Y_{ij}=1)$$
$$= \sum_{j=1}^{J} L(\boldsymbol{\gamma}^*|Y_{ij}=1)p^*_{ij}, \quad (A.3)$$

where Y_{ij} equals one if customer i chooses brand j and equals zero otherwise, the likelihoods on the right side are the usual 0–1 logit likelihood expressions obtained as in Equation 3, and p^*_{ij} is the element of $\mathbf{p}^*_i$ that corresponds to firm j. The resulting likelihood for the sample is then the product of the individual likelihoods across the respondents. It is easily shown that with this adjustment in the likelihood, the standard logit regression maximum likelihood algorithms can be employed (Greene 1997, p. 916, 1998, pp. 520, 524). The same adjustment of the likelihood does not affect the derivation of the asymptotic distribution of the regression coefficients[14] (as is evident in McFadden's [1974, pp. 135–38] work), which means that the usual chi-square statistics, as given in standard logit software such as LIMDEP, can still be employed, even if the $\mathbf{p}^*_{ij}$ vector is not all zeroes and ones.

From Equation 3, it is easily shown that the partial derivative of probability of choice with respect to utility, for respondent i and firm k, is[15]

$$D_{ik} = \partial P_{ik}/\partial U_{ik}$$
$$= \left\{\left[\sum_{k^*}\exp(U_{ik^*})\right][\exp(U_{ik})]\right.$$
$$\left.-[\exp(U_{ik})]^2\right\}\bigg/\left[\sum_{k^*}\exp(U_{ik^*})\right]^2$$
$$= [\exp(U_{ik})]\bigg/\left[\sum_{k^*}\exp(U_{ik^*})\right]$$
$$\times \left[\sum_{j\neq k}\exp(U_{ik})\bigg/\sum_{k^*}\exp(U_{ik^*})\right]$$
$$= p^*_{ik}\left\{\left[\sum_j \exp(U_{ij}) - \exp(U_{ik})\right]\bigg/\left[\sum_{k^*}\exp(U_{ik^*})\right]\right\}$$
$$= p^*_{ik}(1 - p^*_{ik}). \quad (A.4)$$

Then, from Equation A2 we have

$$\partial P_{ik}/\partial \mathbf{X}_{ijk} = \partial P_{ik}/\partial U_{ik} \times \partial U_{ik}/\partial \mathbf{X}_{ijk} = (\mathbf{A}^*\boldsymbol{\gamma}^*)D_{ik}$$
$$= (\mathbf{A}^*\boldsymbol{\gamma}^*)p^*_{ik}(1 - p^*_{ik}). \quad (A.5)$$

---

[14]Actually, convergence is faster, because the probabilities of next purchase are given directly, so the law of large numbers does not need to be evoked with respect to the dependent variable.

[15]For convenience, we suppress the j subscript for D, P, and U, because for any customer i in the sample, j is fixed.

This equation shows how each customer's brand-switching matrix will change given a change in any driver (or changes in more than one driver). This result is nonlinear and implies diminishing returns for any driver improvement. By applying the altered switching matrix in Equation 4, reestimating CLV by using Equation 5, and aggregating across customers by using Equation 6, we find the impact on customer equity.

The relative importance of each driver, measured as the impact of a marginal improvement in the driver on utility, can also be addressed as a proportion of the total marginal impact summed across all drivers. In other words, the importance of driver X is the per-unit amount that it contributes to utility, and the relative importance is that amount expressed as a percentage.

$$\text{Importance} = \sum_{c=1}^{C} (A_{cx}\gamma_c), \text{ and} \quad (A.6)$$

Relative importance

$$= \left[\sum_{c=1}^{C} (A_{cx}\gamma_c) \Big/ \sum_{x^* \in S_d} \sum_{c=1}^{C} (A_{cx^*}\gamma_c)\right] \times 100, \quad (A.7)$$

where C is the set of retained principal components, A_{cx} is the factor coefficient relating driver x to factor c, and γ_c is the logit coefficient corresponding to factor c.

In addition, we address the statistical significance of the drivers. The coefficients, γ_c, as estimated by the logit model, are distributed asymptotically normally, and mean and variance are estimated and reported by standard logit regression software. If the estimated logit coefficient and variance of the estimate for factor c are $\hat{\gamma}_c$ and σ_c^2, respectively, and $\beta_x = \Sigma_c A_{cx}\gamma_c$ is the coefficient estimator for driver x, then, if we assume that the $\hat{\gamma}_c$'s are distributed independently, β_x is a linear combination of independent normal distributions and thus is also normally distributed. Specifically:

$$\text{Standard error of } \beta_x = \left(\sum_c A_{cx}^2 \sigma_c^2\right)^{\frac{1}{2}}, \quad (A.8)$$

which results asymptotically in the following z-test for β_x:

$$z = \beta_x \Big/ \left(\sum_c A_{cx}^2 \sigma_c^2\right)^{\frac{1}{2}}, \quad (A.9)$$

which is easily calculated from the results of the principal components analysis (for A_{cx}^2) and logit analysis (for β_x and σ_c^2).

Computational Issues in Estimating CLV

If the time horizon, is long or the customer's frequency of purchase is high, there may be many purchases expected before the time horizon, which increases computation considerably. Therefore, it is useful to make a simplifying approximation that can speed up the computation. In practice, the expected purchase probabilities, B_{ijt}, approach equilibrium and change little after about 15 purchases. This enables us to employ the approximation that the purchase probabilities do not change after 15 purchases. If $T_i \leq 15$, we can estimate CLV_{ij} as in Equation 5. However, if $T_i > 15$, we can simplify the calculations. Let $CLV_{ij}(15)$ denote the lifetime value of customer i to firm j in 15 purchases, as calculated by Equation 5, and let $CLV_{ij}^*(T_i)$ and $CLV_{ij}^*(15)$ denote the lifetime values that would occur (through T_i purchases and 15 purchases, respectively) if the purchase probabilities were constant and equal to $B_{ij,15}$.[16] The expected lifetime value of the purchases beyond purchase 15 can be approximated as $CLV_{ij}^*(T_i) - CLV_{ij}^*(15)$. This is helpful because CLV^* can be viewed as a net present value of an annuity, and it can be calculated in closed form because the probabilities $B_{ij,15}$ are constant. Expressing the individual-specific discount rate per purchase as $d_i^* = d_i^{-1/f_i}$, we have the standard expression for the net present value of an annuity:

$$CLV_{ij}^*(t) = v_{ijt}\pi_{ijt}B_{ij,15}(1/d_i^*)[1 - (1 + d_i^*)^{-t}], \quad (A.10)$$

---

[16]We could also use the equilibrium probabilities. In practice, there is little difference between the two.

from which we obtain the estimated lifetime value of

$$\text{Estimated CLV}_{ij} = \text{CLV}_{ij}(15) + \text{CLV}_{ij}*(T_i) - \text{CLV}_{ij}*(15). \quad \textbf{(A.11)}$$

APPENDIX B
EXAMPLE SURVEY ITEMS (AIRLINE SURVEY)

Here are some examples of survey items that might be used to measure customer equity and its drivers. These items are from the survey that we used to analyze the airline market. (The headings in this Appendix are for explanatory purposes and would not be read to the respondent.)

Market Share and Transition Probabilities

1. Which of the following airlines did you most recently fly? (please check one)
2. The next time you fly a commercial airline, what is the probability that you will fly each of these airlines? *Probability (please provide a percentage for each airline, and have the percentages add up to 100%)*

Size and Frequency of Purchase

3. When you fly, how much on average does the airline ticket cost?
   _____ less than $300
   _____ between $300 and $599
   _____ between $600 and $899
   _____ between $900 and $1199
   _____ between $1200 and $1499
   _____ between $1500 and $1799
   _____ between $1800 and $2099
   _____ $2100 or more
4. On average, how often do you fly on a commercial airline?
   _____ once a week or more
   _____ once every two weeks
   _____ once a month
   _____ 3–4 times per year
   _____ once a year
   _____ once every two years, or less

Value-Related Drivers

5. How would you rate the overall quality of the following airlines? (5 = "very high quality," 1 = "very low quality")
6. How would you rate the competitiveness of the prices of each of these airlines? (5 = "very competitive," 1 = "not at all competitive")
7. The airline flies when and where I need to go. (5 = "strongly agree," 1 = "strongly disagree")

Brand-Related Drivers (5 = "Strongly Agree," 1 = "Strongly Disagree")

8. I often notice and pay attention to the airline's media advertising.
9. I often notice and pay attention to information the airline sends to me.
10. The airline is well known as a good corporate citizen.
11. The airline is an active sponsor of community events.
12. The airline has high ethical standards with respect to its customers and employees.
13. The image of this airline fits my personality well.

Relationship-Related Drivers (5 = "Strongly Agree," 1 = "Strongly Disagree")

14. I have a big investment in the airline's loyalty (frequent flyer) program.
15. The preferential treatment I get from this airline's loyalty program is important to me.
16. I know this airline's procedures well.
17. The airline knows a lot of information about me.
18. This airline recognizes me as being special.
19. I feel a sense of community with other passengers of this airline.
20. I have a high level of trust in this airline.

Roland T. Rust is David Bruce Smith Chair in Marketing, Director of the Center for e-Service, and Chair of the Department of Marketing, Robert H. Smith School of Business, University of Maryland (rrust @ rhsmith.umd.edu). Katherine N. Lemon is Associate Professor, Wallace E. Carroll School of

Management, Boston College (e-mail: lemonka @ bc.edu). Valarie A. Zeithaml is Roy and Alice H. Richards Bicentennial Professor and Senior Associate Dean, Kenan-Flagler School of Business, University of North Carolina, Chapel Hill (e-mail: zeithamv @ bschool.unc.edu). This research was supported by the Marketing Science Institute, University of Maryland's Center for e-Service, and the Center for Service Marketing at Vanderbilt University. The authors thank Northscott Grounsell, Ricardo Erasso, and Harini Gokul for their help with data analysis, and they thank Nevena Koukova, Samir Pathak, and Srikrishnan Venkatachari for their help with background research. The authors are grateful for comments and suggestions provided by executives from IBM, Sears, DuPont, General Motors, Unilever, Siemens, Eli Lilly, R-Cubed, and Copernicus. They also thank Kevin Clancy, Don Lehmann, Sajeev Varki, Jonathan Lee, Dennis Gensch, Wagner Kamakura, Eric Paquette, Annie Takeuchi, and seminar participants at Harvard Business School, INSEAD, London Business School, University of Maryland, Cornell University, Tulane University, University of Pittsburgh, Emory University, University of Stockholm, Norwegian School of Management, University of California at Davis, and Monterrey Tech; and they thank participants in the following: American Marketing Association (AMA) Frontiers in Services Conference, MSI Customer Relationship Management Workshop, MSI Marketing Metrics Workshop, INFORMS Marketing Science Conference, AMA A/R/T Forum, AMA Advanced School of Marketing Research, AMA Customer Relationship Management Leadership Program, CATSCE, and QUIS 7.

References

Aaker, David A. and Kevin Lane Keller (1990), "Consumer Evaluations of Brand Extensions," *Journal of Marketing*, 54 (January), 27–41.

AMR Corporation (1999), Annual Report, [available at http://www.amrcorp.com/ar1999/shareholders.html].

Anderson, Eugene (1998), "Customer Satisfaction and Word-of-Mouth," *Journal of Service Research*, 1 (1), 5–17.

Anderson, James C. and James Narus (1990), "A Model of Distributor Firm and Manufacturer Firm Working Partnerships," *Journal of Marketing*, 54 (January), 42–58.

Berger, Paul D., Ruth N. Bolton, Douglas Bowman, Elten Briggs, V. Kumar, A. Parasuraman, and Creed Terry (2002), "Marketing Actions and the Value of Customer Assets: A Framework for Customer Asset Management," *Journal of Service Research*, 5 (1), 39–54.

—— and Nada I. Nasr (1998), "Customer Lifetime Value: Marketing Models and Applications," *Journal of Interactive Marketing*, 12 (Winter), 17–30.

Blattberg, Robert C. and John Deighton (1996), "Manage Marketing by the Customer Equity Test," *Harvard Business Review*, 74 (July–August), 136–44.

——, Gary Getz, and Jacquelyn S. Thomas (2001), *Customer Equity: Building and Managing Relationships as Valuable Assets*. Boston: Harvard Business School Press.

Bolton, Ruth (1998), "A Dynamic Model of the Duration of the Customer's Relationship with a Continuous Service Provider: The Role of Satisfaction," *Marketing Science*, 17 (1), 45–65.

—— and James Drew (1991), "A Longitudinal Analysis of the Impact of Service Changes on Customer Attitudes," *Journal of Marketing*, 55 (January), 1–9.

——, Katherine N. Lemon, and Peter C. Verhoef (2004), "The Theoretical Underpinnings of Customer Asset Management: A Framework and Propositions for Future Research," *Journal of the Academy of Marketing Science*, 32, forthcoming.

Cattell, Raymond B. (1966), "The Scree Test for the Number of Factors," *Multivariate Behavioral Research*, 1 (2), 245–76.

Chintagunta, Pradeep (1992), "Estimating a Multinomial Probit Model Using the Method of Simulated Moments," *Marketing Science*, 11 (4), 386–407.

——, Dipak Jain, and Naufel Vilcassim (1991), "Investigating Heterogeneity in Brand Preferences in Logit Models for Panel Data," *Journal of Marketing Research*, 28 (November), 417–28.

Clancy, Kevin J., Robert S. Shulman, and Marianne Wolf (1994), *Simulated Test Marketing*. New York: Lexington Books.

Copeland, Tom, Tim Koller, and Jack Murrin (1996), *Valuation: Measuring and Managing the Value of Companies*. New York: John Wiley & Sons.

Danaher, Peter J. and Roland T. Rust (1996), "Indirect Financial Benefits from Service Quality," *Quality Management Journal*, 3 (2), 63–75.

Degeratu, Alexandru M. (1999), "Estimation Bias in Choice Models with Last Choice Feedback," *International Journal of Research in Marketing*, 16 (4), 285–306.

—— (2001), "A simple Way to Reduce Estimation Bias in Some Dynamic Choice Models," *Marketing Letters*, 12 (3), 271–78.

Dowling, Grahame R. and Mark Uncles (1997), "Do Customer Loyalty Programs Really Work?" *Sloan Management Review*, 38 (Summer), 71–82.

Dwyer, F. Robert (1997), "Customer Lifetime Valuation to Support Marketing Decision Making," *Journal of Direct Marketing*, 11 (4), 6–13.

Ehrbar, Al (1998), *EVA: The Real Key to Creating Wealth*. New York: John Wiley & Sons.

Fellman, Michelle Wirth (1999), "Report on ROI," *Marketing News*, (April 12), 1, 13.

Frank, Ildiko E. and Jerome H. Friedman (1993), "A Statistical View of Some Chemometrics Regression Tools," *Technometrics*, 35 (May), 109–135.

Frank, Ronald E. (1962), "Brand Choice as a Probability Process," *Journal of Business*, 35, 43–56.

Freund, Rudolf J. and William J. Wilson (1998), *Regression Analysis: Statistical Modeling of a Response Variable*. San Diego: Academic Press.

Gale, Bradley T. (1994), *Managing Customer Value*. New York: The Free Press.

Gessner, Guy, Wagner A. Kamakura, Naresh K. Malhotra, and Mark E. Zmijewski (1988), "Estimating Models with Binary Dependent Variables: Some Theoretical and Empirical Observations," *Journal of Business Research*, 16 (1), 49–65.

Greene, William H. (1997), *Econometric Analysis*. Upper Saddle River, NJ: Prentice Hall.

—— (1998), Plainview, NY: Econometric Software, Inc.

Guadagni, Peter M. and John D. C. Little (1983), "A Logit Model of Brand Choice Calibrated on Scanner Data," *Marketing Science*, 2 (Summer), 203–238.

Gummeson, Evert (1999), *Total Relationship Marketing-Rethinking Marketing Management: From 4 P's to 30 R's*. Oxford, UK: Butterworth-Heineman.

Gupta, Sunil, Donald R. Lehmann, and Jennifer A. Stuart (2001), "Valuing Customers," Marketing Science Institute Report No. 10–119.

Håkansson, H., ed. (1982), *International Marketing and Purchasing of Industrial Goods: An Interaction Approach*. Chichester, UK: John Wiley & Sons.

Heskett, James L., Thomas O. Jones, Gary W. Loveman, W. Earl Sasser Jr., and Leonard Schlesinger (1994), "Putting the Service-Profit Chain to Work," *Harvard Business Review*, 72 (2), 164–74.

Hocking, Ronald R. (1996), *Methods and Applications of Linear Models*, Wiley Series in Probability and Statistics. New York: John Wiley & Sons.

Hogan, John E., Katherine N. Lemon, and Barak Libai (2000), "Incorporating Positive Word of Mouth Into Customer Profitability Models," working paper, Carroll School of Management, Boston College.

Jackson, Barbara B. (1985), *Winning and Keeping Industrial Customers*. Lexington, MA: D. C. Health and Company.

Johnson, Michael D. and Anders Gustafsson (2000), *Improving Customer Satisfaction, Loyalty, and Profit*. San Francisco: Jossey-Bass.

Jolliffe, I. T. (1972), "Discarding Variables in a Principal Components Analysis. I. Artificial Data," *Applied Statistics*, 21, 160–73.

Kaiser, Henry F. (1960), "The Application of Electronic Computers to Factor Analysis," *Educational and Psychological Measurement*, 20 (1), 141–51.

Kalwani, Manohar U. and Donald Morrison (1977), "A Parsimonious Description of the

Hendry System," *Management Science*, 23 (January), 467–77.

Kamakura, Wagner A., Vikas Mittal, Femando de Rosa, and José Afonso Mazzon (2002), "Assessing the Service Profit Chain," *Marketing Science*, 21 (3), 294–317.

Kordupleski, Raymond, Roland T. Rust, and Anthony J. Zahorik (1993), "Why Imporving Quality Doesn't Improve Quality," *California Management Review*, 35 (Spring), 82–95.

Kotler, Philip (1967), *Managerial Marketing, Planning, Analysis, and Control*. Englewood Cliffs, NJ: Prentice Hall.

Larreché, Jean-Claude and V. Srinivasan (1982), "STRATPORT: A Model for the Evaluation and Formulation of Business Portfolio Strategies," *Management Science*, 28 (9), 979–1001.

Lee, Eunkyu, Michael Y. Hu, and Rex S. Toh (2000), "Are Consumer Survey Results Distorted? Systematic Impact of Behavioral Frequency and Duration on Survey Response Errors," *Journal of Marketing Research*, 37 (February), 125–33.

Little, John D. C. (1970), "Models and Managers: The Concept of a Decision Calculus," *Management Science*, 16 (8), 466–85.

Massy, William F. (1965), "Principal Components Regression in Exploratory Statistical Research," *Journal of the American Statistical Association*, 60 (March), 234–56.

———, David B. Montgomery, and Donald G. Morrison (1970), *Stochastic Models of Buying Behavior*. Cambridge: Massachusetts Institute of Technology Press.

McFadden, Daniel S. (1974), "Conditional Logit Analysis of Qualitative Choice Behavior," in *Frontiers in Econometrics*, Paul Zarembka, ed. New York: Academic Press.

Mulhern, Francis J. (1999), "Customer Profitability Analysis: Measurement, Concentration, and Research Directions," *Journal of Interactive Marketing*, 13 (Winter), 25–40.

Naik, Prasad, Michael R. Hagerty, and Chih-Ling Tsai (2000), "A New Dimension Reduction Approach for Data-Rich Marketing Environments: Sliced Inverse Regression," *Journal of Marketing Research*, 37 (February), 88–101.

Narver, John C. and Stanley F. Slater (1990), "The Effect of a Market Orientation on Business Profitability," *Journal of Marketing*, 20 (October), 20–35.

Oliver, Richard L. (1980), "A Cognitive Model of the Antecedents and Consequences of Satisfaction Decisions," *Journal of Marketing Research*, 17 (November), 460–69.

Parasuraman, A. (1997), "Reflections on Gaining Competitive Advantage Through Customer Value," *Journal of the Academy of Marketing Science*, 25 (2), 154–61.

Pessemier, Edgar A., Philip Burger, Richard Teach, and Douglas Tigert (1971), "Using Laboratory Brand Preference Scales to Predict Consumer Brand Purchases," *Management Science*, 17 (February), B371–B375.

Peterson, Robert A. and William R. Wilson (1992), "Measuring Customer Satisfaction: Fact and Artifact," *Journal of the Academy of Marketing Science*, 20 (1), 61–71.

Pfeifer, Phillip E. and Robert L. Carraway (2000), "Modeling Customer Relationships as Markov Chains," *Journal of Interactive Marketing*, 14 (2), 43–55.

Press, S. James (1982) *Applied Multivariate Analysis*. Malabar, FL: Robert E. Krieger Publishing.

Reinartz, Werner (1999), "Customer Lifetime Value: An Integrated Empirical Framework for Measurement, Antecedents, and Consequences," doctoral dissertation, Department of Marketing, University of Houston.

——— and V. Kumar (2000), "On the Profitability of Long Lifetime Customers: An Empirical Investigation and Implications for Marketing," *Journal of Marketing*, 64 (October), 17–35.

Rust, Roland T., Timothy L. Keiningham, Stephen Clemens, and Anthony Zahorik (1999), "Return on Quality at Chase Manhattan Bank," *Interfaces*, 29 (March–April), 62–72.

———, Anthony J. Zahorik, and Timothy L. Keiningham (1994), *Return on Quality:*

Measuring the Financial Impact of Your Company's Quest for Quality. Chicago: Probus Publishing.

———, ———, and ——— (1995), "Return on Quality (ROQ): Making Service Quality Financially Accountable," *Journal of Marketing*, 59 (April), 58–70.

———, Valarie A. Zeithaml, and Katherine N. Lemon (2000), *Driving Customer Equity: How Customer Lifetime Value Is Reshaping Corporate Strategy*. New York: The Free Press.

Schmittlein, David C., Donald G. Morrison, and Richard Columbo (1987), "Counting Your Customers: Who Are They and What Will They Do Next?" *Management Science*, 33 (January), 1–24.

Schultz, Don E. and Anders Gronstedt (1997), "Making Marcom an Investment," *Marketing Management*, 6 (3), 40–49.

Silk, Alvin J. and Glen L. Urban (1978), "Pre-Test-Market Evaluation of New Packaged Goods: A Model and Measurement Methodology," *Journal of Marketing Research*, 15 (May), 171–91.

Simester, Duncan I., John R. Hauser, Birger Wernerfelt, and Roland T. Rust (2000), "Implementing Quality Improvement Programs Designed to Enhance Customer Satisfaction: Quasi-Experiments in the United States and Spain," *Journal of Marketing Research*, 37 (February), 102–112.

Srivastava, Rajendra K., Tasadduq A. Shervani, and Liam Fahey (1998), "Market-Based Assets and Shareholder Value: A Framework for Analysis," *Journal of Marketing*, 62 (January), 2–18.

Storbacka, Kaj (1994), *The Nature of Customer Relationship Profitability*. Helsinki: Swedish School of Economics and Business Administration.

Urban, Glen L., John R. Hauser, William J. Qualls, Bruce D. Weinberg, Jonathan D. Bohlmann, and Roberta A. Chicos (1997), "Information Acceleration: Validation and Lessons from the Field," *Journal of Marketing Research*, 34 (February), 143–53.

Varki, Sajeev, Bruce Cooil, and Roland T. Rust (2000), "Modeling Fuzzy Data in Qualitative Marketing Research," *Journal of Marketing Research*, 37 (November), 480–99.

Vavra, Terry G. (1997), *Improving Your Measurement of Customer Satisfaction*. Milwaukee: ASQ Quality Press.

Wedel, Michel and Jan-Benedict Steenkamp (1989), "A Fuzzy Clusterwise Regression Approach to Benefit Segmentation," *International Journal of Research in Marketing*, 6 (4), 241–58.

——— and ——— (1991), "A Clusterwise Regression Method for Simultaneous Fuzzy Market Structuring and Benefit Segmentation," *Journal of Marketing Research*, 28 (November), 385–96.

Zeithaml, Valarie A. (1988), "Consumer Perceptions of Price, Quality, and Value: A Means-End Model and Synthesis of Evidence," *Journal of Marketing*, 52 (July), 2–22.

Copyright of Journal of Marketing is the property of American Marketing Association and its content may not be copied or e-mailed to multiple sites or posted to a listserv without the copyright holder's express written permission. However, users may print, download, or e-mail articles for individual use.

Case 2-1 Xerox: Book-In-Time

V. Kasturi Rangan

The New Way to Market, Order, Print, and Fulfill Books One at a Time, Just in Time, Worldwide

Ranjit Singh, senior V.P., Internet and Software Solutions, and Frank Steenburgh, senior V.P. and General Manager, Graphic Arts, pondered the possibilities for commercializing what some considered a breakthrough printing process. Xerox's Book-In-Time (BIT) system could produce one 300-page book for $7, which was an enormous business advantage in a market where such economies were available to printers only when lot sizes exceeded 1,000 copies. A printing system, consisting of a document printer, color cover printer, and a binder, could add up to as much as a $1.5 million sale for Xerox, and open new business segments at printers who already owned Xerox equipment. Naturally, some senior executives viewed BIT as a terrific opportunity to expand the company's copying and printing equipment portfolio. Michael Ruffolo, President, Document Solutions Group, had instructed Singh and Steenburgh to craft a commercialization plan in three months, in time for a divisional review by June 1, 1999. According to Ruffolo:

> We would like to approach it with an open mind and consider the full gamut of opportunities. We could offer a service to authors, publishers, wholesalers/retailers, and book printers, or we could also be selling selected components and modules to different players in the book value chain. Successful commercialization is the challenge. We know that the technology works

and will only get better as we shape our marketing plan in the next year.

Singh had spent 10 years turning around software/solutions-related initiatives for businesses big and small, and Ruffolo 10 years with computing and telecommunications giants NCR and AT&T, before they had converged at Xerox in the past 18 months. Among his responsibilities, Michael Ruffolo had worldwide profit responsibility for developing, marketing, and delivering document products, services, and solutions through global industry businesses dedicated to Manufacturing, Financial Services, Graphic Arts, and the Public Sector. Xerox recorded over $7.0 billion in annual sales to these four industries in 1998. Stated Ruffolo, "The sales resources to successfully commercialize Book-In-Time lies in our Graphics Arts Business, which calls on the publishing and printing market. What we need is a successful start-up plan and a way to transition it to scale." Frank Steenburgh, head of Graphic Arts, was a Xerox veteran with over 25 years of sales, marketing, and product development experience in the printing and publishing marketplace.

XEROX CORPORATION

Xerox, with 1998 revenues of $19.4 billion, a net income of $1.69 billion before a restructuring charge, and an operating profit margin of 13.6%, was one of the great comeback stories of the decade. Whereas in the 1980s it was a stand-alone, black-and-white, analog copier company, by 1999 it had transformed itself into a networked, color, digital company that sold document solutions to its customers worldwide.

In 1998, the company's operations were organized by four business groups:

The case was prepared by Professor V. Kasturi Rangan with research assistance from Jay Sinha. Copyright © 1999 by the President and Fellows of Harvard College. Harvard Business School Case 599-119.

Office documents   The largest of Xerox's four business units, with worldwide sales of $10 billion in 1998, this group sold black and white digital and light lens copiers and color copiers/printers to offices.

Production systems   With worldwide revenues of $5 billion in 1998, this group manufactured and sold large production publishing and printing systems. The company had made a decisive move in the nineties to embrace the digital world. Indeed, its future thrust was on document technology enabled by computers and digital printers in a networked environment. The company had launched the highly successful DocuTech Production Publisher in 1990, which accounted for over $2 billion of its 1998 revenues.

Channels group   Given the rapid explosion of the SOHO (Small Office Home Office) market segment in the eighties, Xerox chose to approach this fragmented market through conventional retail channels (office supply stores like Staples, Office Max, and Office Depot, mass merchandisers like Sears, and superstores like Wal-Mart) and value added resellers (e.g., Pinacor, Tech Data). This unit, with 1998 sales of $1.4 billion, was one of the fast-growing businesses within Xerox. It essentially sold the lower end of the Office Document product line through retail and reseller outlets.

Document services group   This $3 billion group provided industry consulting, systems integration, network services and outsourcing to major accounts. This fast-growing Xerox business (approximately 40% growth rate in 1998) served over 6,000 client companies in 40 countries.

Until 1998, Xerox's Customer Operations, with approximately 15,000 sales reps and 20,000 service technicians, sold the products and services of the four business groups. But in January 1999, Xerox announced a series of initiatives designed to allow the company to better capitalize on growing digital market opportunities and create greater value for customers and shareholders by aligning by industry rather than geography.

"We believe these changes will better align Xerox to serve its diverse customers, increase the effectiveness, efficiency, and breadth of our distribution channels, and provide an industry-oriented focus for global document services and solutions," stated Xerox President and Chief Operating Officer G. Richard Thoman. "This migration to an industry global account and solutions focus will evolve over the next couple of years. Our goal is to have our large customers view us as 'strategically relevant' to their businesses," he added.

As a result of the 1999 changes, the Document Solutions Group, headed by Ruffolo (see Figure A), was not only responsible for the sales of all products, services, and solutions to the Graphic Arts, Manufacturing, Financial Services, and Public Sector businesses, but also had accountability for the three business units that comprised the former Document Services Group.

The Book-In-Time project reported to the Internet and Software Solutions unit headed up by Ranjit Singh. This group was charged with commercializing PARC-developed (Palo Alto Research Center, Xerox's in-house research lab) technology and building software platforms across various industry segments. Book-In-Time was one among a handful of promising new projects such as Docushare and Print Xchange. John Stempeck had headed up the Book-In-Time project from 1996–1998, before moving on to a different job. He was instrumental in moving the project through its incubation to its current commercialization phase. Ranjit Singh was brought in from a different business unit of Xerox to guide the commercialization of the various new project ideas.

Xerox's group of research laboratories, especially PARC, was highly reputed for its breakthrough inventions. According to an authoritative book:

> Highly visible contributions in information technology from PARC gave rise to a new computing paradigm that became populated by an amazing array of techniques and technologies, including personal computing, client-server architecture, graphical user interfaces, local area networks, laser printing, bit maps, page description languages, and object-oriented programming. It was also true, however, that some of these technologies were better exploited commercially by other entrepreneurs. The most famous example is the Graphical User Interface (GUI) system that launched

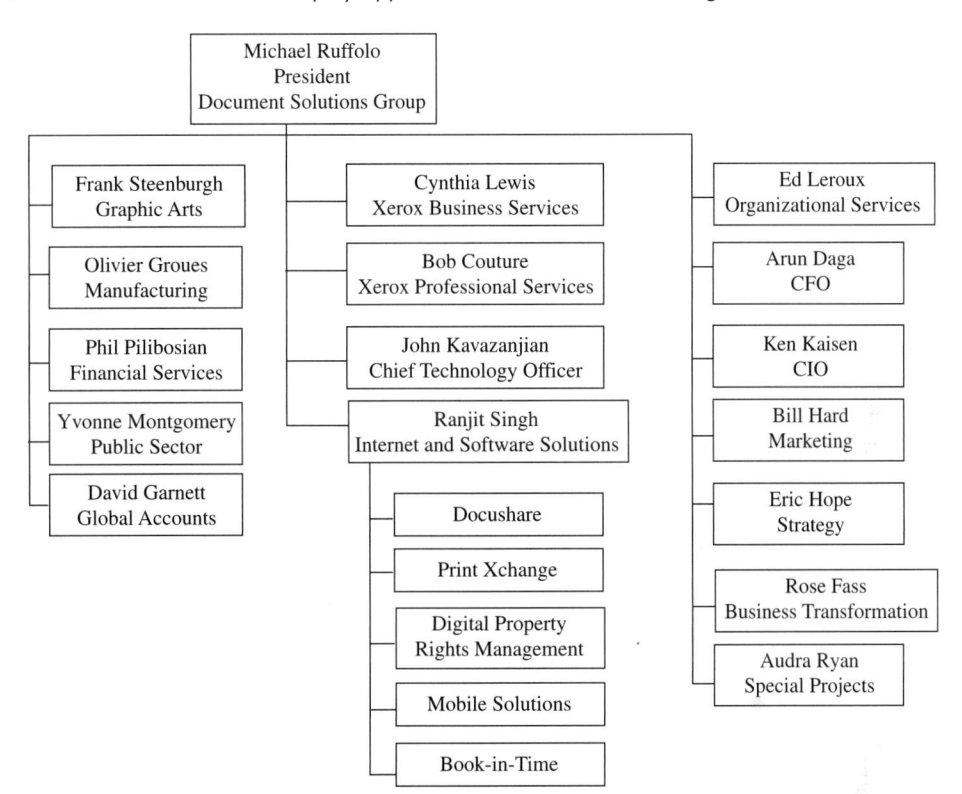

CHAPTER 2 The Customer Equity Approach and the Customer Management Plan

FIGURE A Document Solutions Group

```
                        Michael Ruffolo
                        President
                        Document Solutions Group
```

Reporting to Michael Ruffolo:

- Frank Steenburgh — Graphic Arts
- Olivier Groues — Manufacturing
- Phil Pilibosian — Financial Services
- Yvonne Montgomery — Public Sector
- David Garnett — Global Accounts
- Cynthia Lewis — Xerox Business Services
- Bob Couture — Xerox Professional Services
- John Kavazanjian — Chief Technology Officer
- Ranjit Singh — Internet and Software Solutions
  - Docushare
  - Print Xchange
  - Digital Property Rights Management
  - Mobile Solutions
  - Book-in-Time
- Ed Leroux — Organizational Services
- Arun Daga — CFO
- Ken Kaisen — CIO
- Bill Hard — Marketing
- Eric Hope — Strategy
- Rose Fass — Business Transformation
- Audra Ryan — Special Projects

Apple Computer as a serious personal computer player.[1]

Xerox had sold GUI to Apple for what many managers at Xerox and Apple now consider "a song." GUI was only one among several inventions that Xerox licensed out in the 1970s and 1980s for little return. Its inability to seize on certain commercial opportunities during this period was explained by its managers:[2]

- Investment was technology focused but failed to consider how the customer would evolve into the technology's use.

- Insulated [ourselves] from rapidly emerging markets because of commitments to existing markets.

At that time, many within Xerox considered its strength to be in Sales and R&D, with its workforce of 15,000 sales reps and 20,000 service technicians respected as one of the best in the business; its weakness, as a lack of ability to envision changing market needs and influence its evolution. Xerox had considerably altered its new product commercialization process to address a number of these problems.

Xerox followed a rigorous phase-gate process in evaluating new projects and bringing them to market. Called TTM (time to market), the process broadly had five phases, starting with the idea-generation stage where usually a white paper was prepared regarding the technology/business opportunity, followed by prototyping and initial announcement. Depending on the success of the

---

[1] "Research and Change Management in Xerox," by Mark B. Myers, Chapter 4, *Engines of Innovation*, edited by Richard S. Rosenbloom and William J. Spencer.
[2] Ibid.

project through the first three stages, the fourth step was broad commercialization. The final phase involved the implementation of an after-sales service and customer satisfaction plan. From phase to phase, a senior management team thoroughly evaluated the technology and business parameters for ultimate success. The Book-In-Time project was one of a dozen in Michael Ruffolo's portfolio, having consumed about $5 million of R&D and an operating budget of $1 million/year during the last two years in phases 2 and 3. The project had reached the initial announcement stage and would soon need a firm business plan before broad commercialization.

Ranjit Singh interpreted the phase-gate review process as follows:

> The structured process was designed for big pieces of equipment involving considerable engineering and tooling up. In reality, for Internet- and software-type products, we whip the project through only three steps. Prototyping and commercialization go hand-in-hand. We need to think big, start small, and scale up fast.

According to Singh, scale-up was crucially dependent on the robustness of the technology. "It is a constant juggling game," added Singh. "Say I have $50 million for seven projects. This year I know we will kill two or three and replace them with new projects with better business potential. The trick is to make those decisions fast and decisively and move to commercialize hot prospects."

BOOK INDUSTRY OVERVIEW

In 1997 the book market was valued at $92 billion in worldwide sales (at the end user/consumer level); printing expenditures amounted to about $20 billion. A total of 8.5 billion books were printed worldwide.[3] The United States accounted for 2.4 billion books valued at $21 billion in retail sales. The book market was growing at approximately 5% per year, of which 68% of titles were in paperback format and 32% in hard cover; 69% of titles were non-fiction and 31% were fictional.

Products within the U.S. book publishing industry could be divided into the following six major categories: adult trade, juvenile trade, mass market, professional, college, and ELHI (elementary and high school). Trade books, representing the largest share of the book market, encompassed all general interest publications, such as adult and juvenile fiction, nonfiction, advice, and how-to books. See Table A for book sales by market segment.

As the U.S. economy began to recover in the mid-1990s, the outlook for the book publishing industry also began to improve. Shifting demographics pointed toward higher enrollment levels in schools and colleges, while the federal government appeared likely to increase funding for libraries and the arts. Many publishers expected growth among medical and healthcare-related titles to correspond with the concerns of the aging U.S. population, as well as growth in professional and technical titles to support rapid changes in office technology. In general, industry analysts expected the U.S. book market to grow at 6% to 8%.[4]

Market research by Xerox revealed that:

- 53% of books were selected by subject, only 22% due to author's reputation.
- Publisher name/imprint was simply not a factor in the consumer's reason for purchase of a particular book.
- 55% of books were planned purchases and 45% were bought on impulse.
- 81% of books were bought for oneself, whereas 19% were purchased as a gift.

While Xerox did not break up its research by professional and scientific versus popular books, a wide dispersion was believed to exist on the above numbers between the two groups.

THE DISTRIBUTION VALUE CHAIN

Nearly 77% of all book sales in the United States were made to customers, institutions, or retail chains, and 23% were routed through wholesalers. Figure B sketches the flow of products from publishers to channels to markets. Exhibit 1 provides further detail on units sold and average price points by channel category.

Publishers The book publishing industry faced many changes entering the mid-1990s. Observers noted that the industry, once characterized as

---

[3]Source: Xerox.

[4]U.S. Industry Profiles, Printing and Publishing.

TABLE A U.S. Book Sales by Segment ($millions)

	1992	1995	1996	1997
Adult trade, Total	3,484.2	4,234.1	4,195.4	4,095.2
Hardbound	2,222.5	2,646.9	2,586.0	2,410.2
Paperbound	1,261.7	1,587.2	1,609.4	1,685.0
Juvenile, Total	1,177.4	1,326.7	1,447.6	1,358.0
Hardbound	850.8	836.6	867.7	887.7
Paperbound	326.6	490.1	579.9	470.3
University press	280.1	339.7	349.3	367.8
Religious, Total	907.1	1,036.9	1,093.4	1,132.7
Bibles, hymnals, & prayer books	260.1	293.0	294.8	285.4
Other religious	647.0	743.9	798.6	847.3
Mass-market paperbacks	1,263.8	1,499.6	1,555.1	1,433.8
Book clubs	742.3	976.1	1,091.8	1,145.3
Mail order	630.2	559.5	579.5	521.0
Professional, Total	3,106.7	3,869.3	3,985.0	4,156.4
Business	490.3	617.6	721.4	NA
Law	1,128.1	1,400.4	1,429.8	NA
Medical	622.7	809.3	815.8	NA
Technical & scientific	865.6	1,042.0	1,018.0	NA
College texts & materials	2,084.1	2,324.8	2,485.8	2,669.7
El-Hi texts & materials	2,080.9	2,466.2	2,619.1	2,959.6
Standardized tests	140.4	167.3	178.7	191.4
Subscription reference	572.3	670.8	706.1	736.5
Other	449.0	476.0	493.2	510.0
Total net sales	16,918.5	19,947.0	20,780.0	21,277.4

Source: Association of American Publishers. NA-Not Available

gentlemanly and literary, had quickly become more cutthroat and businesslike. *National Review* cited as evidence the trend for large publishing houses to replace long-time chief executives, best known for their "literary sensibilities," with industry outsiders steeped in "modern management techniques." As a result, many employees within the publishing industry shifted focus from building relationships with authors and carefully tailoring manuscripts to cutting costs and analyzing profit and loss statements.[5] An industry insider noted that an increasing trend among modern-day publishing houses was to move the profit targets higher and higher, from the historical 8% to 10% to 12% to 15%.[6]

Over 40,000 companies participated in the book publishing industry in the mid-1990s. However, the industry was dominated by several giant publishing houses. According to *Trade Book Publishers, 1996: Analysis by Category*, the top 12 trade book publishers accounted for nearly 85% of the overall U.S. book publishing market. These large publishers consolidated many of the smaller imprints in the early 1990s in order to cut costs and reposition themselves for the onset of electronic publishing. However, this concentration of power among relatively few publishers led to criticism from some quarters regarding the quality and diversity of materials published. Industry observers saw an increasing role for smaller presses to publish works of literary quality that did not necessarily have enormous sales

---
[5]Ibid.
[6]Ibid.

U.S. Publishers
2.36 Billion Books

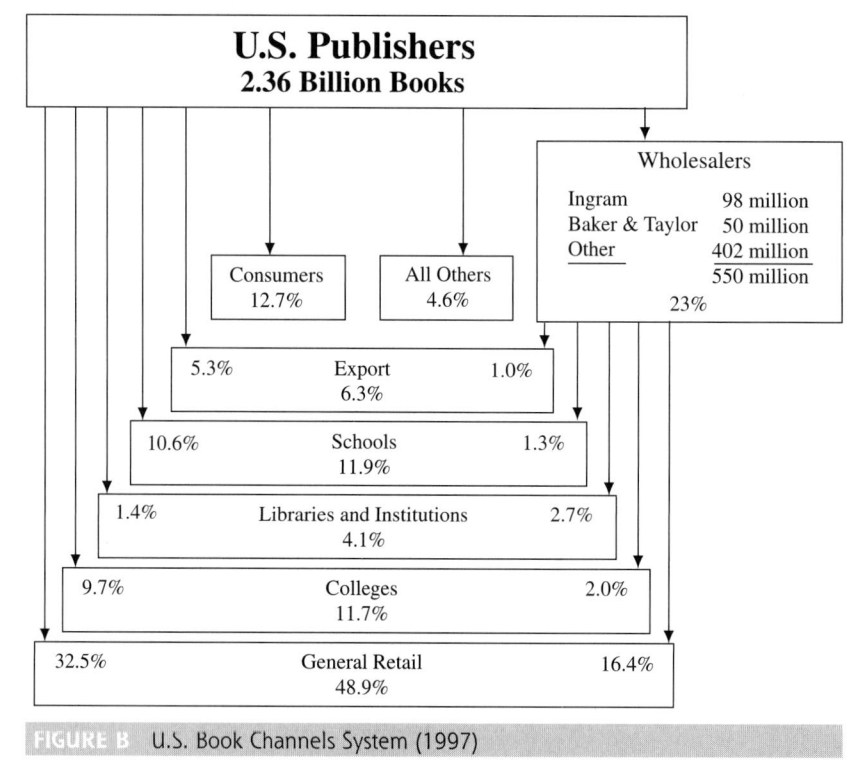

Wholesalers	
Ingram	98 million
Baker & Taylor	50 million
Other	402 million
	550 million
	23%

Consumers 12.7%	All Others 4.6%	
5.3%	Export 6.3%	1.0%
10.6%	Schools 11.9%	1.3%
1.4%	Libraries and Institutions 4.1%	2.7%
9.7%	Colleges 11.7%	2.0%
32.5%	General Retail 48.9%	16.4%

FIGURE B U.S. Book Channels System (1997)

Source: Xerox.

potential. (See Table B for the world's leading book publishers.)[7]

Printers According to industry sources, the worldwide printing market was worth about $20 billion. The industry had been relatively stable through the 1990s, with modest increases in revenue. Employment in the industry had been decreasing slowly as more and more aspects of the printing process were being automated and computer controlled. See Table C for the leaders in this market.

R. R. Donnelley, Quebecor, and Banta were the leaders in book printing. The industry was fragmented, with as many as 40,000 printing presses in the United States alone. According to Jack Klasnic, an industry consultant, the top 25 accounted for about 25% of industry volume. Of the remaining, 500 printers accounted for another 25% of industry volume and the rest for the remaining 50%. Small presses (less than 20 employees) usually focused on brochures, pamphlets, and the like because they did not have the appropriate offset printing machinery (35" × 23" press) to gain production economies for book printing. A large percentage, 95% or more, of all print jobs were accomplished by the offset printing process, machinery for which was supplied by industry giants like Heidelberg from Germany. The printing machinery industry was consolidated with Heidelberg, accounting for nearly 50% of worldwide market share, followed by Mitsubishi (from Japan) and MAN-Roland (also from Germany). The market size for printing machines was estimated to be about $10 billion worldwide in 1997. The cost of a 35" × 23", 4-color web press (i.e., paper fed in rolls) was between $1 million and $2 million, but when one added the cost of all the ancillary equipment on the printing line, costs could run upwards of $5 million.

Among the other printers shown in Table C, some such as Hallmark and American Greetings

[7]Ibid.

CHAPTER 2   *The Customer Equity Approach and the Customer Management Plan*   **75**

	Dollars	*Units*	*$/Unit*	*Dollar Share*	*Unit Share*
Sales to retail/consumer:					
Publisher sales to general retailers	$5,379,200,000	766,400,000	$7.02	27%	32%
Publisher sales to consumers	2,855,900,000	298,700,000	9.56	14	13
Wholesaler sales to general retailers	1,754,300,000	386,200,000	4.54	9	16
Total	$9,989,400,000	1,451,300,000	$6.88	50%	61%
Sales to other channels:					
Publisher sales to colleges	$2,855,900,000	228,000,000	$12.53	14%	10%
Publisher sales to libraries & institutions	780,700,000	33,600,000	23.24	4	1
Publisher sales to schools	2,714,500,000	251,000,000	10.81	13	11
Publisher sales for export	1,291,100,000	125,100,000	10.32	6	5
Publisher sales to all other	217,400,000	107,600,000	2.02	1	5
Wholesaler sales to colleges	348,000,000	47,100,000	7.39	2	2
Wholesaler sales to libraries & institutions	1,379,300,000	62,800,000	21.96	7	3
Wholesaler sales to schools	341,100,000	30,400,000	11.22	2	1
Wholesaler sales for export	201,300,000	23,200,000	8.86	1	1
Total	$10,129,300,000	908,800,000	$11.15	50%	39%
Total sales by channel (from either publisher or wholesaler)					
General retail	$7,133,500,000	1,152,600,000	$6.19	35%	49%
Consumers	2,855,900,000	298,700,000	9.56	14	13
Colleges	3,203,900,000	275,100,000	11.65	16	12
Libraries & institutions	2,160,000,000	96,400,000	22.41	11	4
Schools	3,055,600,000	281,400,000	10.86	15	12
Export	1,492,400,000	148,300,000	10.06	7	6
All other	217,400,000	107,600,000	2.01	1	5
Total	$20,118,700,000	2,360,100,000	$8.52	100%	100%

EXHIBIT 1   1996 Distribution Channel Analysis

Source: Company documents.

were specialized in-house support for the company's greeting card operations. World Color Press was heavily into magazine covers. Others like Deluxe Corporation specialized in printing checks, and Moore Corporation in business forms. But with the advent of electronic cash and advanced word processing software, the check printers like Deluxe and form printers like Moore were considering alternate markets. A large percentage (95% and more) of all print jobs were accomplished by the offset printing process, which involved developing the text on a metal plate for imprinting on paper. This required printers to buy printing presses from suppliers like Heidelberg. Xerox's digital printers like DocuTech served a complementary market, mainly office printing of documents. Xerox, IBM, and OCE (a Dutch-based operation partly owned by Siemens) were the three main providers of equipment to this nearly $5 billion worldwide market. Xerox was the clear leader, with a 50% share.

Wholesalers

Ingram, the largest wholesaler, traded close to 100 million books in 1997. Its nearly half a million titles in stock was the most extensive of any book wholesaler in the world. Ingram was renowned for its superb 24-hour to 48-hour shipping service to its retailers. It received most of its

TABLE B World's Leading Book Publishers (1997)

Company	Sales $ (B)	World Share (%)	Brief Description
1. Bertelsmann	$5.0	5.4	Bertelsmann publishing was part of Bertelsmann AG of Germany, the 3rd largest media company in the world, with interests in publishing, music, television, online, film, and radio. In March 1997, it had finalized a $1.5 billion deal to acquire Random House (#6).
2. Warner Books	$4.0	4.3	Warner Books, the publishing arm of the media giant Time Warner, Inc., also had interests in film, television, and publishing.
3. Simon & Schuster	$2.4	2.6	Simon & Schuster, one of the world's largest educational book publishers and publishing arm of media blockbuster Viacom, was heavily involved in the Internet, published books under imprints such as Macmillan, Prentice Hall, and Scribner.
4. Pearson	$2.0	2.2	Pearson Books, a publishing unit of Pearson, the United Kingdom media group, published books under the imprint of Penguin and Ladybird.[8]
5. Readers Digest	$1.7	1.8	Readers Digest Assn. engaged in publishing and direct marketing, creating and delivering products, including magazines, books, recorded music collections, home videos, and other products.
6. Random House	$1.6	1.7	Random House Inc. was the world's largest English-language general trade book publisher.
7. Groupe de la Cite	$1.5	1.6	Groupe de la Cite was France's #1 book publishing house and one of France's leading CD-ROM publishers.
8. Grupo Planeta	$1.4	1.5	Grupo Planeta was a Spanish company involved in publishing and sales of reference books and important works.
9. Hachette Liure	$1.4	1.5	Hachette Liure was a French book publisher and distributor.
10. Reed Books	$1.3	1.4	Reed Books, the publisher of Reed Illustrated Books, which produced *The Joy of Sex*, Marks & Spencer cookery books, and Sir Terrance Conran's The *Essential Garden Book*, had been sold in a £33mill. management buyout. The creation of the new company Octopus Publishing Group ended Reed Elsevier's foray into consumer publishing.
11. Harcourt Brace	$1.2	1.3	Harcourt Brace was the publishing and educational services subsidiary of Harcourt General, Inc., a premier global provider of educational products and services.
12. HarperCollins	$1.0	1.1	HarperCollins was owned by News Corp. Ltd., a giant media company based out of Australia.
Total	$23.1	25.0	

Source: Compiled from public sources by casewriter.

---

[8] Pearson Books also owned Simon & Schuster. It bought the company from Viacom for $4.6 billion in 1998.

TABLE C	Printing Companies with the Highest Sales, Ranked by Sales in 1996 ($millions)

1. R. R. Donnelley & Sons (Chicago, IL), $6,599.0 million
2. Hallmark (Kansas City, MO), $3,600.0
3. Quebecor Printing Inc. (Quebec, Canada), $3,110.3
4. Moore Corp. Ltd. (Ontario, Canada), $2,517.7
5. American Greetings Corp. (Cleveland, OH), $2,172.3
6. Deluxe Corp. (St. Paul, MN), $1,895.7
7. World Color Press Inc. (New York, NY), $1,641.4
8. Banta Corp. (Menasha, WI), $1,083.8
9. Quad/Graphics (Pewaukee, WI), $1,002.1
10. Treasure Chest Advertising Co., Inc. (Glendora, CA), $900.0

Source: American Printer, American Printer's 100 + (annual), July 1995, p. 28 +.

orders electronically and operated warehouses in seven locations. Ingram was the logistics backbone behind Internet retailer Amazon.com's rise to fame. In November 1998, however, it was announced that the $600 million (in sales) wholesaler was acquired by the retail chain of Barnes & Noble for $600 million in cash and stock. Industry commentators speculated that this must have been a welcome deal for both. Net margins at the wholesale level were rumored to be at 1% to 2%, and that combined with inventory turns of only 4 to 5, made it a very difficult business in which to make money.

The #2 wholesaler, Baker & Taylor, operated two business units. The first was Baker & Taylor Books, which supplied books, books on tape, calendars, and other information services to more than 100,000 libraries, schools, and bookstores in the United States and abroad. It sold some 50 million books a year from about 25,000 publishers. The second unit, Baker & Taylor Entertainment, supplied videos, CDs, cassette tapes, interactive games, CD-ROMs, and software to some 25,000 libraries and retailers in the United States. It offered more than 50,000 video titles and 70,000 audio titles. The company had recently launched Replica Books, a unit that published and sold licensed out-of-print titles—to both the parent company and other wholesalers—at a premium of about $5 over the original price.[9] All Replica Books were produced on Xerox DocuTech production systems.

Retailers

Even though the U.S. market was served by nearly 12,000 independent retailers, the top four retail chains—Barnes & Noble, Borders, Crown, and Books-A-Million—accounted for over 75% of market share. The top two, Barnes & Noble (sales $2.5 billion, 700 stores) and Borders (sales $1.8 billion, 300 stores), dominated the market. A unique aspect of the Barnes & Noble and Borders strategy was their extensive network of 25,000- to 30,000-square-foot superstores. Unlike mall-based bookstores, many of these superstores were stand-alone, aimed at the destination shopper. Superstores offered comfortable browsing areas, coffee bars, and special events such as book signings, author readings, and children's story hours. They were usually open longer hours (9 a.m. to 11 p.m.), and generally provided for a variety of customer conveniences.

Barnes & Noble and Borders reported pretax net margins of 3% to 5% and inventory turns of about 2%. The independent bookstores fared worse, and many were barely profitable. Many independents believed that the big superstores were able to eke out a 3% to 5% additional rebate from publishers for a variety of promotional and merchandising activities that the smaller stores could not match.

Apart from retail consolidation and the growth of superstores, the other major buzz in the industry was online retailing. Amazon.com, with 1998 sales of about $540 million (and net losses of

---

[9]"Leadership Online: Barnes & Noble vs. Amazon.com," by Pankaj Ghemawat, HBS case No. 798-063, May 26, 1998.

about $50 million), had created a distribution model whereby it offered readers nearly two million titles from its wholesalers' and publishers' stock, even though it carried only about 2,000 of the fastest-moving titles in its own inventory. By eliminating retail margins, Amazon was able to offer deep discounts of 20% to 30% on many titles. Shipping was effected from its distribution facilities and was usually fulfilled within two to five days of receiving the order, depending upon which books it had in stock and which it had to order from wholesalers. Customers paid shipping charges. Amazon was renowned, not only for its excellent customer service, but also for its unique ability to assemble a database of a community of customers with similar reading tastes. Thus, as part of selecting a book, a customer would be able to access peer comments on a book and also Amazon's recommendation for similar books. Both Barnes & Noble and Borders copied Amazon's popular model. Bertelsmann had paid $200 million for a 50% equity stake in Barnes & Noble's online spin-off.

ECONOMICS OF THE VALUE CHAIN

On a typical 300-page paperback book, retail-priced at $25, a 48% margin would be paid to the trade. Of the publisher's selling price, nearly 20% covered manufacturing costs (paper, printing, and binding), 20% covered author royalties, rights, and permissions, overhead was about 30% including sales and marketing costs, and when the 25% costs of book returns were factored in, publishers could earn about a 5% margin at best. The practice of accepting unsold books in the pipeline had long been an industry tradition, and while the return percentage varied over book categories (nearly 40% for mass-market paperbacks to 15% for professional texts), the cost of accepting the returned books and disposing of them at discount prices added a huge cost burden to the publishing industry. By comparison, Internet retailers like Amazon.com returned less than 2% of their wide selection, giving publishers a reason to consider alternative models of production and distribution.

Cost per book was a function of print run size. For example, per-unit fixed costs for mass-market paperback publishers was low because the number of copies printed was large—often more than 500,000 in the first run. By contrast, a specialized professional book printed in a small quantity incurred the same composition and plant costs that would be required to print a general interest title expected to sell many copies. For a book with a short run, these fixed costs were spread over a smaller number of books, raising the per-unit cost.

The following example for a typical 300-page book from an offset printing process details the up-front cost elements. After the text was composed on a word processor, a film was made as an intermediate process, usually 16 pages to a sheet. At a cost of $50 to $75 a sheet, that meant a $1,000 cost. The films were then converted to plates for mounting on the printing rollers, which added an additional $1,500 cost. On top of it, if one included $1,000 for the labor involved in mounting the plates on the print roll and the depreciation cost of the machinery to make the film and the plates (about $500,000 to $750,000 capital cost), the first book carried with it an overhead of $3,500 to $5,000.

The cost of acquiring the paperback rights to a successful hardcover title or buying the rights to an unreleased book by a popular author could run into the millions of dollars. When these costs were spread over a high-volume output, the author's fee was within a range that enabled publishers to eke out a profit. But when books flopped, the publishers took a beating. By comparison, authors of professional books were usually paid a flat royalty rate (10% to 15% of retail selling prices) only after the books were sold.

Trade and paperback publishers generally printed far more copies than they expected to sell to the book-buying public. They permitted retailers to return all unsold books for a full refund. This was costly to the publishers because returns entailed handling, freight, processing, and disposal at a lower price through alternative channels. On average, roughly 25% of all publishers' book shipments were returned by retailers in any given year, although the actual percentage varied widely by category. Millions of dollars were spent by both publishers and retailers to ship unsold books back and forth. Other variables affecting the return rate were the relative sizes of a publisher's backlist and frontlist. A publisher with many backlist nonfiction titles usually had much lower returns than a publisher that emphasized new fiction, because a frontlist title by definition was new to the market, while a backlist title such as *Tom Sawyer* was tried

TABLE D Unit Cost Versus Run Lengths (300-page softcover book)

Book Run Lengths	38" Web Press	40" Sheet-fed Press (or roll fed)	28" Sheet-fed Press	Short-Run Digital Printer	Book-In-Time
Less than 25					$6.90
25	$179.42	$169.64	$228.29		$6.90
50	90.07	85.29	114.70		$6.90
100	45.39	43.12	57.89	$11.47	$6.90
250	18.59	17.82	23.82		$6.90
500	9.66	9.38	12.46	$3.85	$6.90
1000	5.19	5.16	6.78		$6.90
2000	2.95	3.06	3.94		$6.90
3000	2.21	2.35	2.99		$6.90
4000	1.84	2.01	2.51		$6.90
5000	1.62	1.80	2.23		$6.90

and true. On average, about 25% to 30% of a publisher's sales came from titles on its backlist.[10]

BOOK ACQUISITION

The books that made up a publisher's list arrived in a variety of ways: some as completed manuscripts, either by an author or through a literary agent; others were "commissioned," whereby a contract was signed before the author started writing the work.[11]

When a finished manuscript arrived, its initial destination was the editorial department. Here it was usually allocated to an editor who was responsible for judging its merits for publication. In some cases, the editor did not independently evaluate the manuscript but sent it to outside experts.[12] This was usual for highly specialized or technical works. After the manuscript had been read and evaluated, a decision was made on its acceptance, rejection, or revision. If accepted, it took between nine months to a year for the book to appear in print.

Commissioned works followed a somewhat different course. A contract for them was usually signed on the basis of a proposal agreed to between the publishing house and the writer. It was rare for a house to decline to publish a commissioned book, unless the completed manuscript did not meet the terms of the proposal.

BOOK-IN-TIME PROJECT AT XEROX

Book-In-Time was a digital, low-cost, order-to-fulfillment system for the on-demand printing of books. Xerox's unique technology had been optimized for custom lengths of as low as one but could economically handle up to 1,200 or more as Table D shows.

The biggest advantage of the Book-In-Time system was the cost for run lengths of 1,000 and below. Table D presents the approximate costs of four types of offset printing and a comparison of Xerox's Book-In-Time system. At run lengths of less than 25 books, other printing methods would have to incur a minimum cost of $5,000 or so, whereas Book-In-Time could conceivably deliver at a cost of $6.90 per book.

Beyond a run length of about 1,200 copies, the traditional printing method was extremely efficient because of the tremendous speeds at which the printing presses were able to print the multiple copies. Moreover, Xerox's Book-In-Time was a sheet-fed rather than a web- (or roll-) fed operation, thus limiting the possibilities for binding and finishing. But sheet-fed presses were more flexible, especially with respect to changeover and set-up time between operations.

Over the years, Xerox engineers had perfected a system whereby any book transcript that

---

[10]*Standard & Poor's, Industry Surveys-Publishing*, April 23, 1998.
[11]I. See R. Escarpit, *The Book Revolution* (London: Harrap, UNESCO).
[12]M. Lane, *Books and Publishers* (Lexington Books, 1970).

was digitally stored in a central server could be downloaded to a DocuTech production printer, resulting in a high-quality printed book block. The multicolored (laminated) cover would be simultaneously printed on a DocuColor machine and would come together with the book-block at the binding machine. The system was capable of printing a 300-page book at the rate of one book per minute. In order to facilitate the printing of books that were out of print or which did not have a digital input file, Xerox engineers had designed a system where the material could be accurately scanned to yield a digital starting point. This usually cost about $150 for a 300-page book, and an additional $100 for the cover. This step was followed by a "mastering" phase that enabled an optimal set-up for the printing process to follow. Currently it took Xerox technicians close to a full 8-hour shift to master one book, but process development was under way to cut it down by at least half or more. Even though the system was not currently configured to provide hardbound books, developers at Xerox thought it was only a matter of time before the feature would be built in. The production process is shown in Exhibit 2.

The typical list price of the main components of the production process were:

1. Xerox DocuColor 40 (with front end) — $195,000
2. DocuTech 6180 Production Printer — $330,000
3. Horizon Binder — $80,000
4. Scanner and related software/hardware — $150,000
5. Server/glue software — $140,000

John Stempeck and his team of about 15 engineers operating out of Xerox facilities in Burlington, Massachusetts, attempted to estimate the size of the market for Book-In-Time. "The market is enormous," offered Stempeck:

> In the United States alone, about 50,000 new titles and about 1.5 million repeat titles

EXHIBIT 2

Sample Implementation Scenario

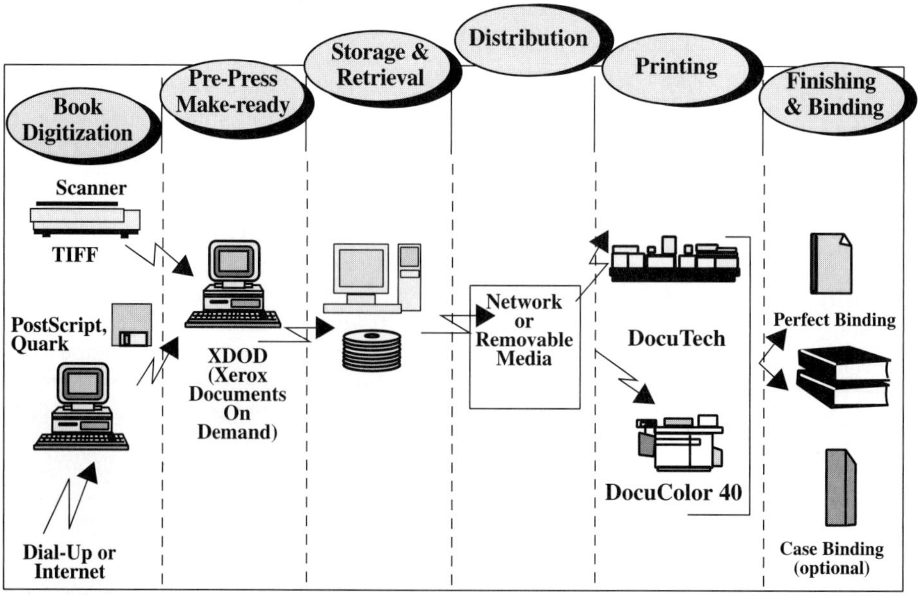

Source: Company documents

were printed last year. But the real interesting statistic for us is the 1 million titles that were out of print. Of course, worldwide (including the United States) that number turns out to be 1 million new titles and 25 million repeat titles printed last year and a whopping 20 million titles out of print. One has to only ask the question—Why were these titles out of print? Obviously because the demand was too low. Here is where our low volume technology can be a big boon for the industry.

Added Ranjit Singh: "In the digital world, the market becomes instantaneously global, so the potential market is about twice as big. Currently, small runs are usually sent out to the Far East because of the lower costs, but that means an 8 to 12 week lag time. We are talking about 24-hour shipment."

The market for on-demand, short-run books was not confined to the tail end of a typical book lifecycle alone. Even at the front end, review copies, complimentary copies, and galley proofs were usually printed in lots of less than one thousand. Even before the books went out of print, each subsequent edition was for small lots as well.

An internal Xerox study had projected the following estimates of U.S. volume that could be converted to "on demand" (see Table E).

John Kavazanjian, Chief Technology Officer, offered this perspective:

We are up against entrenched ways of doing business, all the way from production to distribution, sales, and marketing. Breaking this traditional mindset requires a paradigm shift in the way in which we approach the market, and that is not easy. It is not whether the digital revolution will occur; it will and, indeed, ten years from now, the world will be a very different place. Our dilemma is to spot that window in the next three to seven years when the real change will take place. We have to be ready to move when the window opens.

Xerox's two big challengers in the digital printing industry were IBM and OCE. IBM's equivalent digital printing equipment would cost the user about $3 million (compared to $1.5 million for Xerox). IBM's equipment was roll fed and according to Stempeck "occupied much more space." In terms of print quality, there was no apparent difference between IBM and Xerox. In terms of costs, experts thought Xerox had an advantage in small runs (less than 1,000) and IBM in long runs. Ingram, the largest book wholesaler in the United States, had leased IBM equipment and had entered into an exclusive agreement with IBM to operate a press by the name of Lightning Print. The main function of Lightning Print was to provide support for Ingram's wholesaling operation by reducing its inventory of infrequently ordered books. Lightning Print, however, sold its

TABLE E On Demand Conversion Potential

Category	Market Share %	Number of Books (millions)	On Demand Conversion Potential (%)
Trade	36	864	2
Textbooks			
Subscription reference	1	24	100
College	7	168	50
Elementary—high school	10	240	4
University press	1	24	50
Professional	7	168	50
Subtotal:	26	624	37
Mass-market paperbacks	23	552	n/a
Religion	7	168	n/a
Book club	5	120	n/a
Mail order	4	96	n/a
TOTAL	100	2,400	—

excess capacity in the open market. OCE, on the other hand, was not as active in the United States as it was in Europe. But IBM's printing division was rumored to be up for sale. The printing division, with $2 billion in 1997 sales, was up for sale at about $2.5 billion.[13]

A Lightning Print publicity release claimed that 140 publishers had used its services to print and distribute books. Ingram had placed Lightning Print's On Demand titles in its Advance Plus systems, which provided information of availability of its books to 13,000 bookstores and 9,300 libraries.

Meanwhile, Xerox in Germany had struck an arrangement with Georg Lingenbrink GMBH, the leading German book wholesaler, which marketed under the name Libri. System infrastructure and system operations were based on newly developed software by Xerox and Deutsche Telekom. This was to ensure customer-oriented data administration and the protection of electronic files against charges and access of third parties. Customer-related print releases and invoicing based on orders entered were guaranteed. Monthly statistics about the electronic title stock as well as the number of books ordered gave the publisher and Libri important economical control data. Libri obtained the simple reproduction rights for the Book on Demand titles from the publisher. The calculation and fixing of the retail price were carried out by the publisher on the basis of the usual trade margins and the production costs offered by Libri. After the editing of the print master, Libri produced two samples for acceptance by the publisher. After that the publisher generally had very little to do. At the end of the month, Libri credited the publisher's account with the margin based on actual customer offtake. Exhibit 3 provides a line drawing of the Book-In-Time concept.

Xerox also ran a document technology center (DTC) in Waltham, Massachusetts. Modeled after the German operation, the Waltham facility was completely equipped with the full array of digital scanning, printing and building equipment. The National Academy Press had entered into an arrangement with

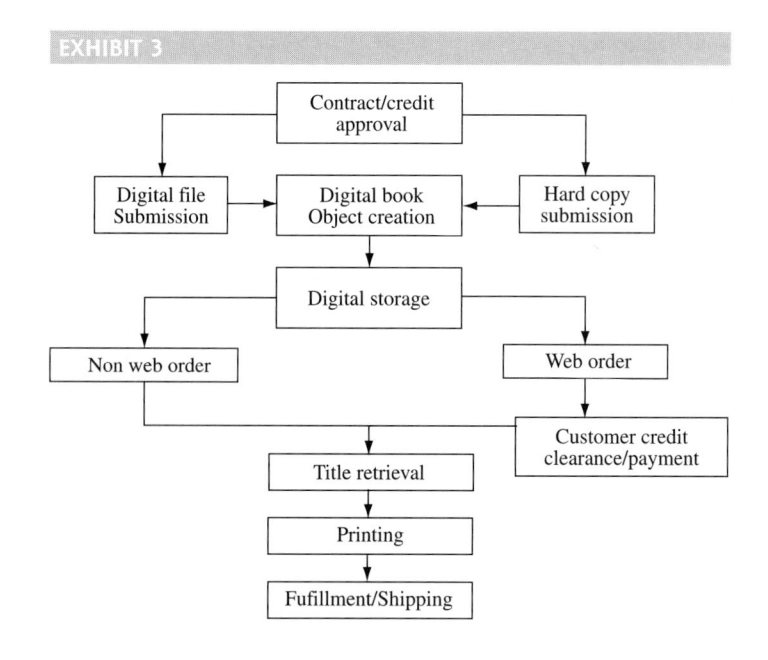

---

[13]"IBM Seeks Buyer for Global Network," *Wall Street Journal*, September 1, 1998, p. A3.

EXHIBIT 3

DTC to transfer 500 titles to its operations. The Libri and DTC facilities served as prototyping centers for the Book-In-Time team. The pure operating costs (omitting R&D) at each center could be covered at a production volume of 250,000 books at 25% margin. While the Libri facility was managed as an "outsourcing" operation, the Waltham DTC was owned and operated by Xerox.

OPTIONS

Michael Ruffolo did not wish to leave any opportunities unexplored, including the option of setting up a chain of technology centers to get into the actual book production business. This could involve work on behalf of publishers, printers, wholesalers, retailers, or even direct customers and consumers. Stempeck envisioned the upside potential of the Book-In-Time brand value, "Imagine, we will be able to deliver a book that will look the same as the original, be delivered in the same timeframe, and be reasonably priced to any market around the world. In other words, we are striving to create a can of Coca Cola!" Stempeck had even toyed with the idea of service franchising, as well. But for the time being, senior managers at Xerox were actively evaluating two options:

1. The Graphic Arts sales force had already expressed an interest in undertaking the task of selling the Book-In-Time system of equipment to all potential buyers in the value chain, from publishers and book printers to retailers. Of course, there always was the possibility that customers would ease into the production operations by buying system components first. Indeed, many commercial printers already owned many of the parts of the BIT system. It appeared to be a matter of integrating many of those pieces into a system, combined with software and services that leveraged Xerox's present organization. Frank Steenburgh had expressed, "If this is the way we want to do it, I believe we have real synergy."

2. The other option under active consideration was best articulated by Ranjit Singh: "We could expand our chain of document technology centers to get into the book production business. In essence, we would provide this as an 'on-demand' service. Naturally, we would have to consider the channel implications for our Graphic Arts customers." ■

◆◆◆ Coca-Cola's New Vending Machine (A): Pricing To Capture Value, or Not?

Case 2-2 Coca-Cola's New Vending Machine (A): Pricing To Capture Value, or Not?

Charles King III and Das Narayandas

On December 17, 1999, the Wall Street Journal ran a front-page story headlined "Tone Deaf: Ivester Has All Skills of a CEO but One: Ear for Political Nuance." The article detailed how Coca-Cola Chairman and Chief Executive Officer M. Douglas Ivester's handling of one flap after another cost him the Coke Board's confidence, eventually leading him to abruptly announce that he would step down from his position in April 2000.

One of the many events highlighted concerned Ivester's comments about Coke's new

---

The case was prepared by Professors Charles King III and Das Narayandas. Copyright © 2000 by the President and Fellows of Harvard College. Harvard Business School Case 500-068.

vending machine technology. The article reported:

> A few months later came another public relations gaffe. Asked by a Brazilian newsmagazine about Coke's testing of vending machines that could change prices according to the weather, Mr. Ivester gave a theoretical response that came across as both a defense of the technology and a confirmation that it would hit the streets. "Coca-Cola is a product whose utility varies from moment to moment," he said. "In a final summer championship, when people meet in a stadium to have fun, the utility of a cold Coca-Cola is very high. So it is fair that it should be more expensive. The machine will simply make this process automatic."
>
> A Coke spokesman says the remarks were taken out of context. Though the company had tested the technology in a lab, it never had an intention of introducing it, the spokesman says, and [Coke] bottlers confirm this. Nevertheless, the CEO's answer created a flap, seeming to cast the company as one that wasn't customer-friendly.

The article also pointed out that:

> To Mr. Ivester, the accountant, the concept [of changing prices based on the ambient temperature] was just the law of supply and demand in action. To the board, the ensuing flap was Murphy's Law at work.

Note: For a consumer-product company that, in the words of a person close to the board, "is a giant image machine," the pummeling of Coke's image was increasingly intolerable.

Earlier, on October 28, 1999, the *New York Times (NYT)* had reported that Coke was testing vending machines that could raise prices in hot weather (see Exhibit 1). The *NYT* story precipitated an immediate response from the Coca-Cola Company (see Exhibit 2 for the company press release posted on the firm's Web site on the same day), triggered a lampoon in the *Philadelphia Inquirer* on October 31, 1999 (see Exhibit 3), and generated national and international controversy (see Exhibit 4). ■

EXHIBIT 1 Text of the Article that Appeared in the *New York Times* on October 28, 1999.

Coke Tests Vending Unit That Can Hike Prices in Hot Weather

by Constance L. Hays

[T]aking full advantage of the law of supply and demand, Coca-Cola Co. has quietly begun testing a vending machine that can automatically raise prices for its drinks in hot weather.

"This technology is something the Coca-Cola Co. has been looking at for more than a year," said Rob Baskin, a company spokesman, adding that it had not yet been placed in any consumer market.

The potential was heralded, though, by the company's chairman and chief executive in an interview earlier this month with a Brazilian newsmagazine. Chairman M. Douglas Ivester described how desire for a cold drink can increase during a sports championship final held in the summer heat. "So, it is fair that it should be more expensive," Ivester was quoted as saying in the magazine, *Veja*. "The machine will simply make this process automatic." The process appears to be done simply through a temperature sensor and a computer chip, not any breakthrough technology, though Coca-Cola refused to provide any details Wednesday.

While the concept might seem unfair to a thirsty person, it essentially extends to another industry what has become the practice for airlines and other companies that sell products and services to consumers. The falling price of computer chips and the increasing ease of connecting to the Internet has made it practical for companies to pair daily and hourly fluctuations in demand with fluctuations in price even if the product is a can of soda that sells for just 75 cents.

The potential for other types of innovations is great. Other modifications under discussion at Coca-Cola, Baskin said, include adjusting prices based on demand at a specific machine. "What could you do to boost sales at off-hours?" he asked. "You might be able to lower the price. It might be discounted at a vending machine in a building during the evening or when there's less traffic."

Vending machines have become an increasingly important source of profits for Coca-Cola and its archrival, Pepsico. Over the last three years, the soft-drink giants have watched their earnings erode as they waged a price war in supermarkets. Vending machines have remained largely untouched by the discounting. Now, Coca-Cola aims to tweak what has been a golden goose to extract even more profits.

"There are a number of initiatives under way in Japan, the United States, and in other parts of the world where the technology in vending is rapidly improving, not only from a temperature-scanning capability but also to understand when a machine is out of stock," said Andrew Conway, a beverage analyst for Morgan Stanley. "The increase in the rate of technology breakthrough in vending is pretty dramatic."

Bill Hurley, a spokesman for the National Automatic Merchandising Association in Washington, added: "You are only limited by your creativity, since electronic components are becoming more and more versatile."

Machines are already in place that can accept credit cards and debit cards for payment. In Australia and in North Carolina, Coke bottlers use machines to relay, via wireless signal or telephone, information about which drinks are selling and at what rates in a particular location. The technology is known as intelligent vending, Baskin said, and the information gathered and relayed by Internet helps salespeople to figure out which drinks will sell best in which locations.

"It all feeds into their strategy of micro-marketing and understanding the local consumer," Conway said. "If you can understand brand preferences by geography, that has implications for other places with similar geography."

Coca-Cola and its bottlers have invested heavily in vending machines, refrigerated display cases, coolers, and other equipment to sell their drinks cold. Over the last five years, Coca-Cola Enterprises, Coke's biggest bottler, has spent more than $1.8 billion on such equipment. In support, Coca-Cola has spent millions more on employees who monitor and service the equipment. In 1998 alone, it spent $324 million on such support to its biggest bottler.

And last week, Coke's chief marketing officer unveiled the company's plan to pump more sales of its flagship soft drink, Coca-Cola Classic. The program includes a pronounced emphasis on Coke served cold.

Sales of soft drinks from vending machines have risen steadily over the last few years, though most sales still take place in supermarkets. Last year, about 11.9 percent of soft-drink sales worldwide came from vending machines, said John Sicher, the editor of Beverage Digest,

(Continued)

EXHIBIT 1 (cont.)

an industry newsletter. In the United States, about 1.2 billion cases of soft drinks were sold through vending machines.

In Japan, some vending machines already adjust their prices based on the temperature outside, using wireless modems, said Gad Elmoznino, director of the Trisignal division of Eicon Technology, a Montreal-based modem maker. "They are going to be using more and more communications in these machines to do interactive price setting," he said.

Industry reactions to the heat-sensitive Coke machine ranged from enthusiastic to sanctimonious. "It's another reason to move to Sweden," one beverage industry executive sniffed. "What's next? A machine that X-rays people's pockets to find out how much change they have and raises the price accordingly?"

Bill Pecoriello, a stock analyst with Sanford C. Bernstein, applauded the move to increase profits in the vending-machine business. "This is already the most profitable channel for the beverage companies, so any effort to get higher profits when demand is higher obviously can enhance the profitability of the system further," he said.

He pointed to a possible downside as well. "You don't want to have a price war in this channel, where you have discounting over a holiday weekend, for example," he said. "Once the capability is out there to vary the pricing, you can take the price down." A Pepsi spokesman said no similar innovation was being tested at the No. 2 soft-drink company. "We believe that machines that raise prices in hot weather exploit consumers who live in warm climates," declared the spokesman, Jeff Brown. "At Pepsi, we are focused on innovations that make it easier for consumers to buy a soft drink, not harder."

Source: Copyright (c) 1999 by the New York Times Co. Reprinted by permission.

EXHIBIT 2 On October 28, 1999, the Coca-Cola Company Posted the Following Press Release on its Corporate Web site.

Statement on Vending Machine Technology

ATLANTA, October 28, 1999 - Contrary to some erroneous press reports, The Coca-Cola Company is not introducing vending machines that raise the price of soft drinks in hot weather.

We are exploring innovative technology and communication systems that can actually improve product availability, promotional activity, and even offer consumers an interactive experience when they purchase a soft drink from a vending machine.

Our commitment for 113 years has been to putting our products within an arm's reach of desire. Offering the products that people want at affordable prices is precisely why Coca-Cola is the favorite soft drink of people in nearly 200 countries around the world.

The new technologies we're exploring will only enhance our ability to deliver on that promise.

Source: Coca-Cola Company Web site: *http://www.coke.com*.

EXHIBIT 3 Text of the Article that Appeared in the *Philadelphia Inquirer* on October 31, 1999.

Have a Coke, and Big Brother is Sure to Smile

by Jeff Brown

Now for the latest evidence that the world is going to hell in a handbasket: The Coca Cola Co., seeking new ways to make thirst pay, is working on a weather-sensing vending machine that will raise prices when it's hot. Isn't that immoral? I mean, if a man crawls in from the desert dying of thirst, would you demand a C-note for a glass of water?

No, but a Coke . . . that's different. It's just an indulgence. So what's wrong with charging what the market will bear more when it's hot, less when it's cold?

In fact, computer chips may soon enable vending machines to constantly adjust prices according to any number of factors that cause momentary fluctuations in supply and demand, not just weather.

So, some busy fall evening in the not-too-distant future, you sidle up to a well-lit Coke machine in South Philly. The box has no buttons, does not display any prices. A spotlight shines on your face as sensors zoom in on your vital signs. A head-high video screen flickers on.

The machine sees you're in jeans, not a suit, so it scans its library of personalities, skipping the erudite Englishman and the slinky French model. It displays the good-natured face of Sylvester Stallone.

"Yo!" the Coke machine calls. "What can I do ya for?" Sly smiles, thinking of his royalty, perhaps.

"A Coke Classic, please."

"No problem. Four bucks."

"Whoa! They're 50 cents at the supermarket."

The machine pauses while its accent analyzer determines you aren't from the neighborhood.

"You see a supermarket around here?" it says. "Four dollars."

You decide to bluff. "Look, the machine around the corner gave me a Pepsi for half that."

"When?"

"A couple of hours ago."

"Yeah, it's rush hour now. You won't get a two-dollar soda anywhere." The head on the screen shakes from side to side sympathetically. Then the red and white machine goes silent, letting you sweat. This is going to be tougher than you'd thought. You pull out your Palm Pilot X, link to the Internet, and go to sodamachines.com.

"There are 14 soda machines within four blocks," you report, holding up the Palm Pilot for the machine to see. "You're telling me I can't beat four dollars?"

The Coke machine tallies the 90 seconds it has expended on this negotiation. Its motion sensor detects two customers moving around impatiently behind you. Its atomic clock reports that rush hour is winding down.

"Okay, three dollars," it offers, peeved.

"No way." You stuff your wallet into your pants and step back.

The Coke machine focuses an infrared scanner on your lips, calibrating your thirst. It counts its inventory and finds a surplus of Diet Coke. Its hard drive whirs for a second.

"I'll give you a Coke Lite for $2.50," it offers resentfully.

"Terrible aftertaste," you say.

"With a bag of nuts."

"Nah."

"Look, pal, if you're not buyin' move along."

(Continued)

EXHIBIT 3 (cont.)

> Traffic is getting lighter. The two people behind you give up and leave.
> "All right," the box grumbles.
> You deposit two dollars, get your can, and turn to go.
> "How about those peanuts?" the machine asks hopefully. "Fifty cents."
> "I'm allergic," you answer.
> The machine pauses a nanosecond while electrons zip around its circuits. It's a week day. Rush hour. Statistics suggest you work nearby. You'll be back. The machine activates its customer relations software.
> "Have a nice evening, bud," it calls as you turn away, the face smiling widely.
> "Hey!" it calls. "I'm a soft touch today. Just got my circuits cleaned. Don't expect a deal like this next time!"
> As you disappear around the corner, the machine counts its remaining cans, assesses the odds of making a sale this late in the day, and looks at how it's doing on its sales goal-a little behind. It cranks up the volume on its Rocky voice and calls out to the nearly empty street.
> "Coke Classic! Get your Coke Classic here!"
> "Only a dollar!"

Source: Reprinted with permission of the *Philadelphia Inquirer*.

EXHIBIT 4 Excerpts from an Article that Appeared on the About.com Web site on November 3, 1999.

Mean Vending Machines

by John S. Irons

This past weekend the news wires were all buzzing about the latest idea to come from the world of soft drinks. Coca-Cola is apparently considering creating a new kind of vending machine that would test the outside temperature and adjust the price of a can of soda upwards when it is warmer outside. Here's some of the typical reactions to the idea:

- "a cynical ploy to exploit the thirst of faithful customers" (San Francisco Chronicle)
- "lunk-headed idea" (Honolulu Star-Bulletin)
- "Soda jerks" (Miami Herald)
- "latest evidence that the world is going to hell in a handbasket" (Philadelphia Inquirer)
- "ticks me off" (Edmonton Sun)

What did they think the Coca-Cola company was doing anyway? Selflessly providing the world with a glorious beverage to further the goals of all mankind? Why should all these people be suddenly offended by a company trying to maximize profits?

"Price discrimination" is the term economists use to describe the practice of selling the same good to different groups of buyers at different prices. In the Coke case, the groups of buyers are segmented by the outside temperature (i.e., Jill when it is hot outside vs. Jill when it is cold). If possible, a company would like to charge a high price to those who place a high value on the good, while charging less to those that do not.

So, are you personally offended by Coke's plan to charge more for soda's when it is warm outside? Well, you had better get over it pretty quickly; there is already plenty of price discrimination out there, and there is MUCH more to come.

CHAPTER 2 *The Customer Equity Approach and the Customer Management Plan* **89**

RAMPANT PRICE DISCRIMINATION

Price discrimination is quite common. Ever wonder why hardcover books are produced first and are so much more expensive than paperback books? Or, why it is so much cheaper to buy airline tickets far in advance? Or, why there are student discounts? Or, why matinee prices are cheaper for movies? Ever tried to buy a soda from a vending machine at a hotel or at a movie theater?

All these examples are attempts by sellers to charge different people different prices for the same good.

Much of the price discrimination in the economy may in fact be quite hidden. How do you know that the Crate and Barrel catalogue you just received has the same price for you as for someone living in another zip code? Those with a 90210 zip code see higher prices on their catalogues.

WHY IS THE VENDING MACHINE DIFFERENT?

In principle, the temperature sensitive vending machine is no different from any other form of price discrimination.

Although, I do think the idea that the process is automatic generates some additional discomfort it is the idea that technology can effectively gauge our buying interests. The heat sensitive machine is a small step toward applying machine "intelligence" to profit maximization.

If you think that the vending machine idea is worrisome, just wait the Internet will be the most sophisticated price discriminator the world has ever seen. Smart vending machines will be the least of your worries. Online vendors such as Amazon.com may know quite a lot about you your past purchasing habits, your Internet preferences, your zip code, etc, and they may want to use this information to adjust prices. Did you buy a Stephen King book last month? Maybe you'd like to buy another, more expensive, Grisham novel this month with a smaller "discount" chosen just for you.

The Internet is much better than the "real world" at price discrimination, because it is so much easier to change prices. In fact they can set a price just for you. It's hard to imagine a traditional store doing this ("Hey, here comes John. Quick, raise the price of the new Krugman Book."). But for an on-line e-commerce store, this is feasible and, with a clever programmer on the payroll, quite easy.

Not all bad: Discrimination means increased efficiency. Actually, price discrimination can actually increase the overall efficiency of a market.

A loss of economic efficiency may occur when a company has some ability to set prices and there is no discrimination. The seller must pick a price that balances their desire to charge a high price to those that really want a product, with their desire to sell a higher overall quantity to those that are not willing to pay very much for it. Because of this, there are trades which would benefit both buyer and seller that do not happen the resulting price is "too high" and the total quantity traded is "too low."

By identifying individual groups of consumers, a seller can provide an additional unit at a lower price to someone who before would have been priced out of the market. The company would now be willing to do this since they would not have to sacrifice profits by lowering prices for the high-demand group.

In the Coke case, some consumers—those who drink Cokes on hot days—will be worse off since they must pay a higher price, while some consumers those who drink Coke on cold days

(*Continued*)

EXHIBIT 4 *(cont.)*

will be better off since they will receive a lower price. The Coca-Cola Company, of course, will be better off. The sum total will be positive (pick your favorite Introduction to Economics textbook to see why).

Would you really be as offended if it was described as a discount on cold days?

So, if you are still stewing about the potential of higher Coke prices, I suggest you stock up the refrigerator and put some of that retirement money into Coca-Cola stock.

Source: © 1999 by John S. Irons (economics.about.com), licensed to About.com. Used by permission of About.com Inc., which can be found on the Web at *www.about.com*. All rights reserved.

CHAPTER 3

Customer Equity Analysis

Before a firm can develop customer management strategies, it must first understand the market in which it operates and the customers in that market. This chapter describes customer equity analysis. In this chapter, we will focus on the specific steps in the analysis that are necessary before a firm can begin to develop a strategic customer management plan. There are four critical steps in the analysis process:

- Analyzing the market
- Analyzing the firm's performance
- Comparing the firm's performance to its competitors'
- Determining the magnitude of the opportunity.

◆ ANALYZING THE MARKET

The first step is an analysis conducted at the market or industry level. It is important to understand what influences customers to purchase and repurchase in a specific market before examining an individual firm's performance in the market. Consider the following example.

The results from an initial customer equity analysis for a large global electronics firm are presented in Figure 3-1. The results presented throughout this chapter were developed from data gathered using the Customer Equity Exercise in Appendix 1 at the end of Chapter 2.

This firm's customers are large automobile manufacturers located worldwide, and the firm competes with two other global electronics firms in this market.[1]

Clearly, customers in this firm's market of automobile manufacturers place the most importance on value equity: the drivers of quality, price, and convenience are most important to this market. Figure 3-2 provides a more in-depth look at the analysis for the global electronics market, examining the importance of the key drivers of each component of customer equity. For this market, quality and convenience are the key drivers of value equity. Overall, brand equity is not very important, but within brand equity, corporate ethics is somewhat important. Finally, in relationship equity, loyalty

---

[1] The results presented throughout the chapter are based on real data collected from customers of large global manufacturers and service firms. However, the names of the firms, the industries, and the data have been disguised for confidentiality reasons.

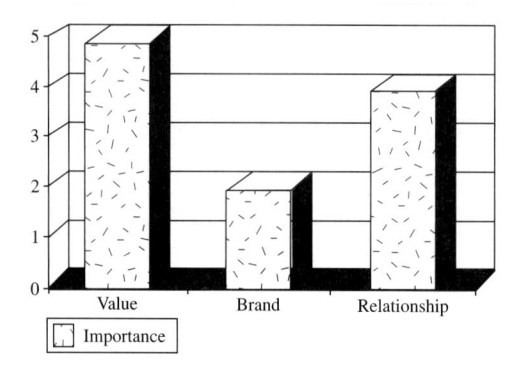

FIGURE 3-1 Importance of Customer Equity Components

or affinity programs are not important, but getting to know the customer and developing programs based on knowledge of the customer appears to be important.[2]

We can drill down even further under each of the drivers to examine which sub-drivers are most important to customers in this market. Let's take a magnified look at the sub-drivers of quality, as shown in Figure 3-3.

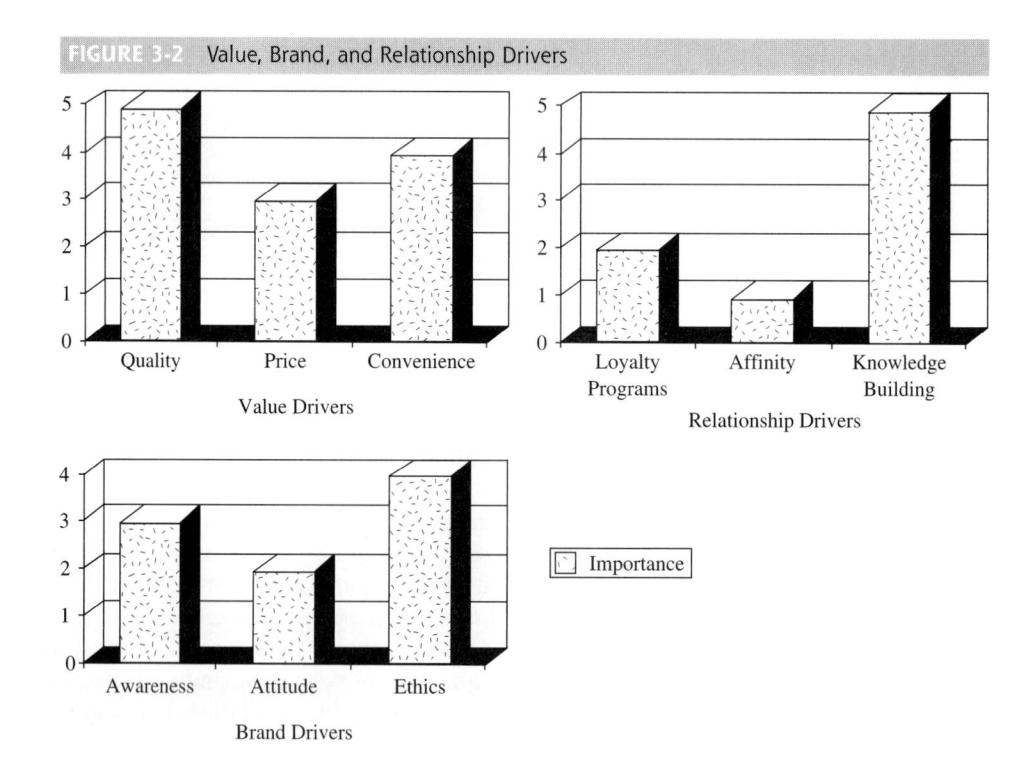

FIGURE 3-2 Value, Brand, and Relationship Drivers

---

[2]See Evert Gummeson, *Total Relationship Marketing—Rethinking Marketing Management: From 4 P's to 30 R's* (Oxford, UK: Butterworth-Heineman, 1999); Piyush Kumar, "The Impact of Long-Term Client Relationships on the Performance of Business Service Firms," *Journal of Service Research* 2 (August 1999): 4–18.

FIGURE 3-3 Sub-Drivers of Quality

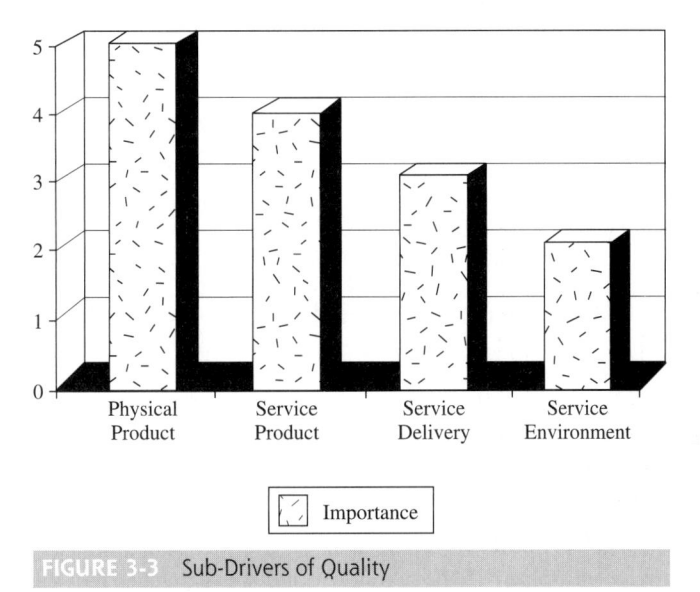

Here, we can see that, for this market, getting the physical product and service product right is most important. Specifically, for this market, consistent product quality is most important. The actual environment in which the product or service is delivered is not very important.

Overall, in examining this global electronics market, we can see that value is the most important component of customer equity. Within value, quality is the most important driver. The most important sub-driver of quality appears to be consistency of the physical product.

◆ ANALYZING THE FIRM'S PERFORMANCE

Once the firm has determined the key components and drivers of customer equity in the market, the next step is to analyze the firm's performance in each of these areas. Continuing with the global electronics firm example, let's take a look at this firm's performance in Figure 3-4.

From the graph, we can see that the firm is doing better on brand equity than it is on either value or relationship equity. This result should concern the firm, as we determined that value and relationship equity are more important to customers in this market than is brand equity. Therefore, it is useful to examine the firm's performance on the drivers in more detail, to gain a more complete picture of how the firm is doing relative to customer expectations.[3] The analysis in Figure 3-5 shows that the firm is very strong in terms

---

[3]For more information on the role of customer expectations, see Richard L. Oliver, *Satisfaction: A Behavioral Perspective on the Consumer* (Boston: Irwin/McGraw-Hill, 1997); and Rashi Glazer, Joel H. Steckel, and Russell S. Winer, "The Formation of Key Marketing Variable Expectations and Their Impact on Firm Performance: Some Experimental Evidence," *Marketing Science* 8, no. 1 (1989): 18–34.

◆ BOX 3-1 ◆

Starbucks Uses CRM to Increase Brand Equity

Starbucks is a brand that millions of people around the world automatically associate with coffee drinks they stop in for each day. Building such a strong brand equity has required the creation and maintenance of a positive in-store customer experience, along with the continuing development and innovation of Starbucks products. Joe Turner, manager of data analysis and strategy at Starbucks, notes that the company was hesitant to climb on to the customer relationship management (CRM) bandwagon in the late 1990s. Starbucks realized that its CRM initiative needed a strategic fit in order for the initiative to be successful. However, successful implementation of CRM technology has enabled Starbucks to shift its business focus from products and channels to the customer. The company did this in 2002 by introducing the Starbucks Card, a declining-balance store card.

Starbucks uses the card as a platform for product development and customer retention strategies and in 2002 alone sold over 5 million cards, amounting to $70 million in sales. Store cards may be purchased at a Starbucks or on the company's Web site, and accounts can be reloaded in stores, online, or by phone. The Starbucks Card encourages repeat visits and is convenient for customers, eliminating the need for cash and decreasing transaction time at the point of sale.

The card also allows Starbucks to monitor customer buying behavior, and to identify changes in purchase patterns when new products are introduced. The Starbucks Card also serves as a platform for customer appreciation and loyalty programs, and will pave the way for more direct communications with customers and to enhance the customer experience through further product development.

Starbucks continues to build its brand through the development of products and services by staying abreast of customer needs and tastes. A steady stream of new beverage offerings attracts new customers and helps retain current customers. Starbucks' ability to provide a first-rate experience for customers is enhanced with CRM technology.

SOURCES: Interview by Lenka Hanzlik, Boston College Research Assistant to Professor K. Lemon, with Joe Turner, manager of data analysis and strategy, Starbucks Corporation, March 2003. Drake Bennett, Kate Carlisle, Chester Dawson, and Stanley Holmes, "Planet Starbucks," *BusinessWeek,* September 9, 2002. W. A. Lee, "Starbucks Brews a Model for Prepaid Cards," *Bank Technology News,* June 2002. James Peters, "Starbucks' Growth Still Hot; Gift Card Jolts Chain's Sales," *Nation's Restaurant News,* February 11, 2002. "Carding Customers," *Specialty Coffee Retailer,* March 2002. Sarah Theodore, "Expanding the Coffee Experience: Starbucks Keeps Sales Brewing with New Products, Innovation, and Global Expansion," *Beverage Industry,* October 2002.

---

of the drivers of brand equity, and the results are somewhat mixed for relationship equity. Of most concern is the firm's weak performance on the quality driver of value equity. This should not be surprising, given the high level of importance customers place on quality in this market.

To gain additional insight into where the firm is failing in terms of quality, we drill down further, as before. The analysis in Figure 3-6 shows that the firm is performing well on service delivery and service environment—two sub-drivers that, unfortunately, are not very important to the customers. However, on the physical product and service product sub-drivers, the firm does not appear to be performing well at all. This analysis

CHAPTER 3 *Customer Equity Analysis* **95**

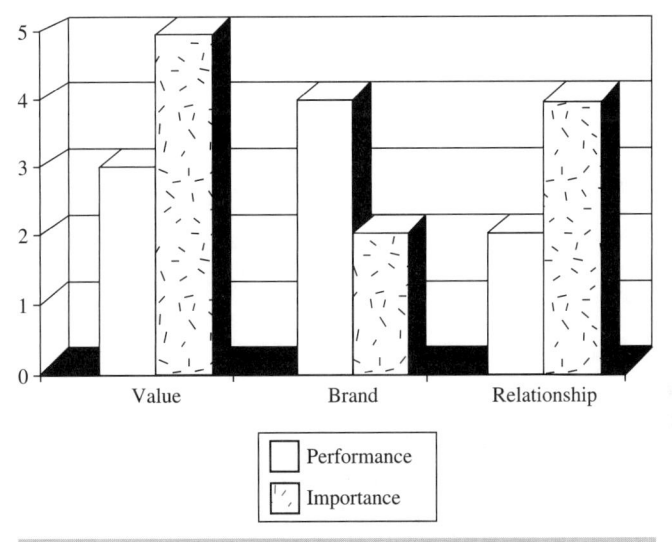

FIGURE 3-4 The Firm's Performance Versus Importance

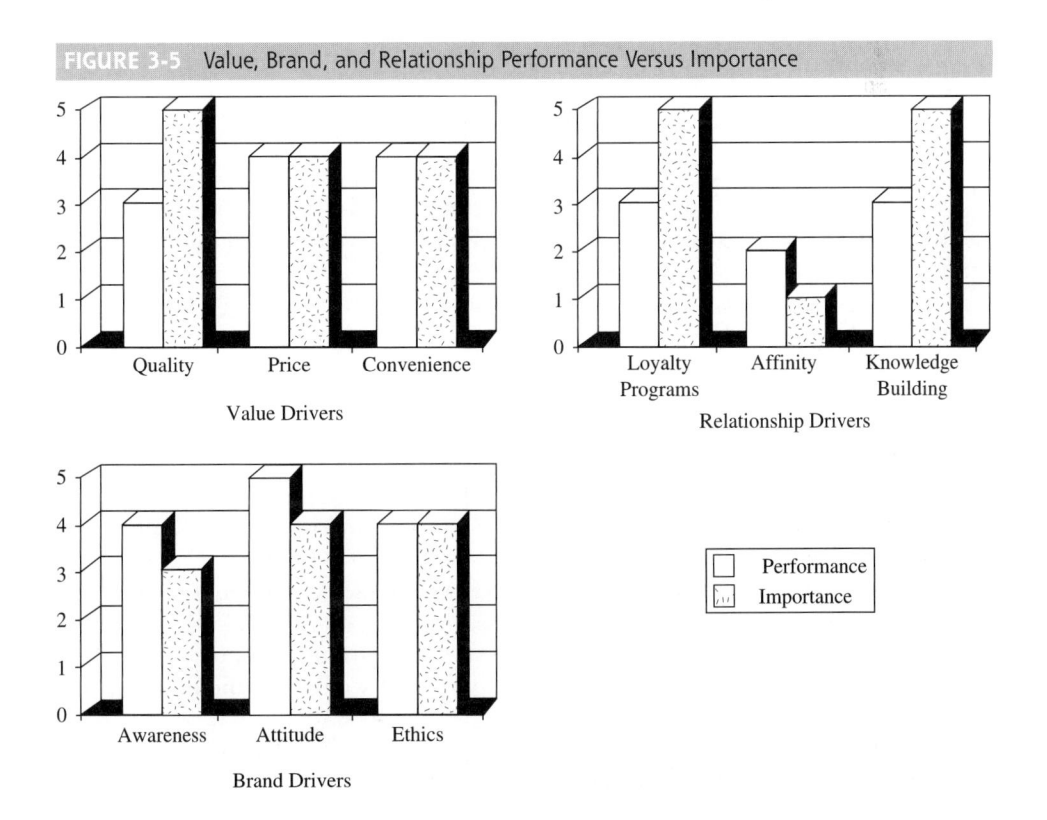

FIGURE 3-5 Value, Brand, and Relationship Performance Versus Importance

Value Drivers

Relationship Drivers

Brand Drivers

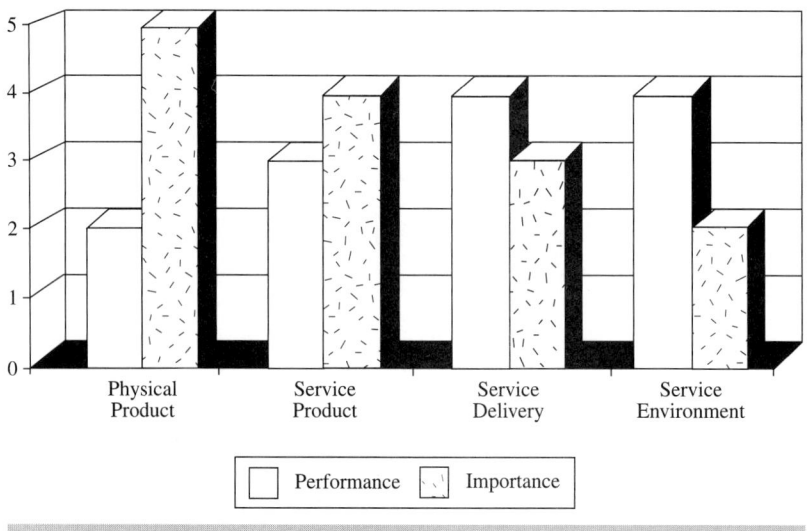

FIGURE 3-6 Sub-Drivers of Quality: Performance Versus Importance

suggests two specific areas in which the firm can improve that will have a significant impact on its customer equity.

◆ COMPARING THE FIRM'S PERFORMANCE TO THAT OF ITS COMPETITORS'

Before making strategy decisions based on this analysis, however, it is necessary to add competitors to the analysis.[4] In Figures 3-7 and 3-8, we can see how the firm's two key competitors are performing on value, brand, and relationship equity, and the drivers of each.

From Figure 3-7, we can see that Supplier 2 is currently a bigger threat to the firm in this market than is Supplier 1. Supplier 2 is performing well on the component that customers care most about—value equity, although Supplier 2 is not doing as well on the relationship component.

In considering each firm's performance on brand, value, and relationship, we can begin to see where each firm's current strengths and weaknesses may be. Supplier 1 appears to be strongest in brand equity and weakest in value equity. Supplier 2 appears to be strongest in value equity and weaker in brand and relationship equity, but shows no major weak components.

In digging deeper by examining the drivers of each component, we see (in Figure 3-8) that, in terms of value, Supplier 1 is deficient in quality and price, two areas that are important to the customers. Supplier 2's strength appears to be in its ability to deliver on quality, although it appears somewhat weaker in the areas of price and

---

[4]Shelby D. Hunt and Robert M. Morgan, "The Comparative Advantage Theory of Competition," *Journal of Marketing* 59 (April 1995): 1–15.

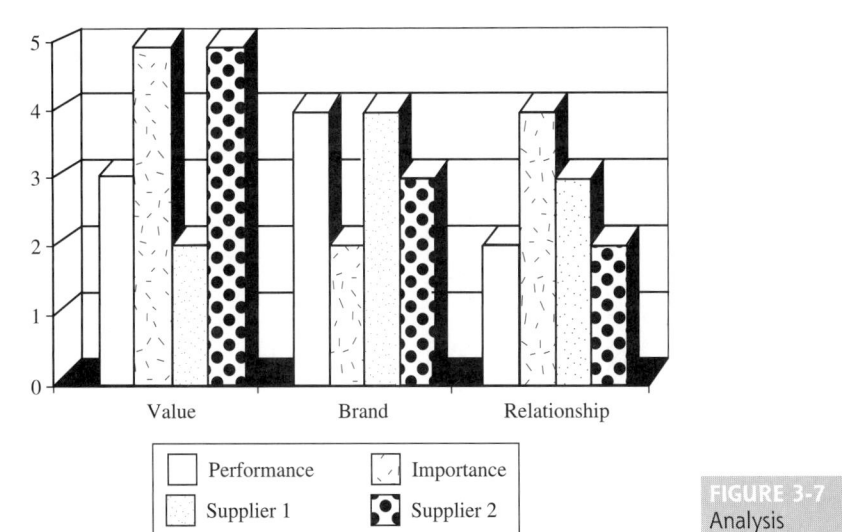

FIGURE 3-7 Competitive Analysis

convenience. For the drivers of brand equity, Supplier 1 is strong on all three drivers, while Supplier 2 is weak, especially in the area of brand awareness. This may suggest that Supplier 2 is new to this market. Supplier 1 is stronger on drivers of relationship equity, while Supplier 2 is not.

FIGURE 3-8 Competitive Analysis: Value, Brand, and Relationship Drivers

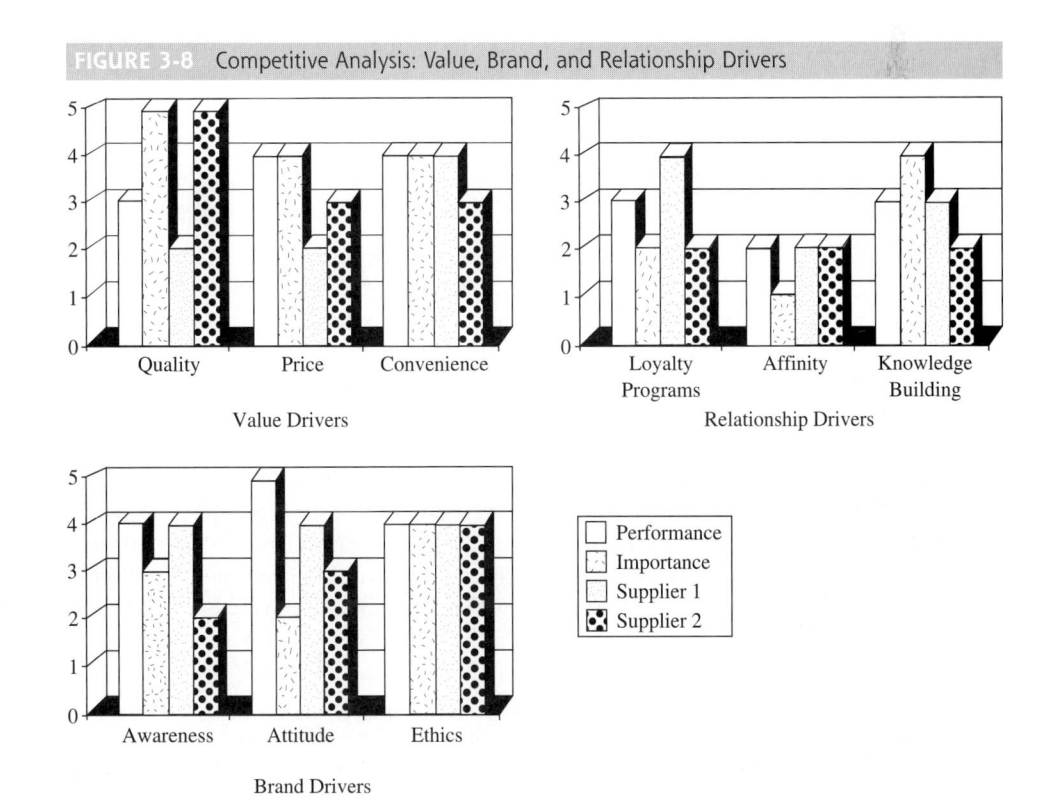

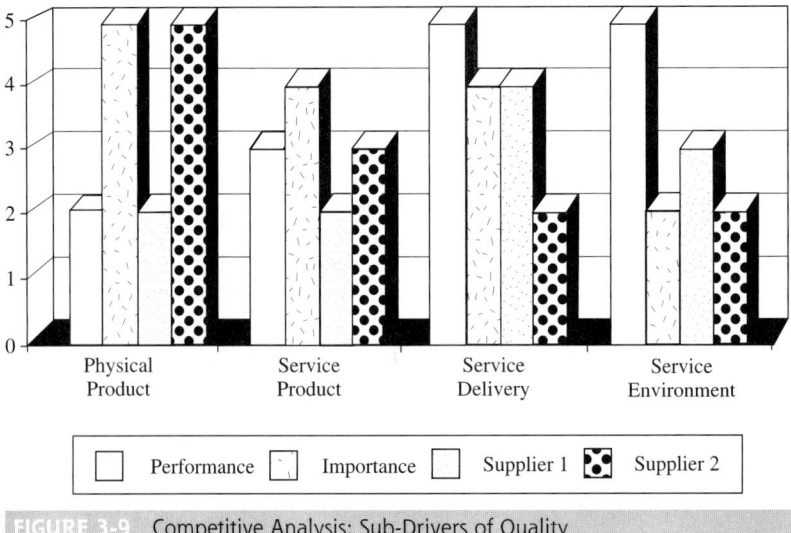

FIGURE 3-9 Competitive Analysis: Sub-Drivers of Quality

Finally, we examine the sub-drivers of quality for each of the competitors in Figure 3-9. In this chart, we can see that Supplier 2's performance on the physical product sub-driver of quality is significantly higher than the performance of the firm or Supplier 1. Supplier 2 is also performing adequately on the intangible aspects of the product—the service product. However, Supplier 1 appears to be stronger on service delivery and service environment.

DETERMINING THE MAGNITUDE OF THE OPPORTUNITY

To complete the analysis and to begin to determine where to focus the firm's efforts, it is important to understand the magnitude of the potential opportunities. How large is the market in terms of customer equity—that is, what are the future profit opportunities this market represents?[5] What portion of the overall market's customer equity is currently held by the firm? What portion is currently held by competitors? One can think of this analysis as analogous to a market share analysis. However, market share is a measurement tool that allows the firm to see how things are only in the present. Customer equity share provides a tool for the firm to understand where it stands relative to its competitors in the future. Customer equity share for the firm and its two competitors can be seen in Figure 3-10. For this market, the total customer equity (in US$) is approximately $30 million. Therefore, the firm holds 20 percent, or $6 million, Supplier 1 holds 35 percent or $10.5 million, and Supplier 2 holds the largest customer equity share of $13.5 million.[6]

---

[5]See Rajendra K. Srivastava, Tasadduq A. Shervani, and Liam Fahey, "Market-Based Assets and Shareholder Value: A Framework for Analysis," *Journal of Marketing* 62, no.1 (1998): 2–18.
[6]See also Sunil Gupta, and Donald R. Lehmann, "Customers as Assets," *Journal of Interactive Marketing* 17, no.1 (2003): 9–24.

FIGURE 3-10 Customer Equity Share

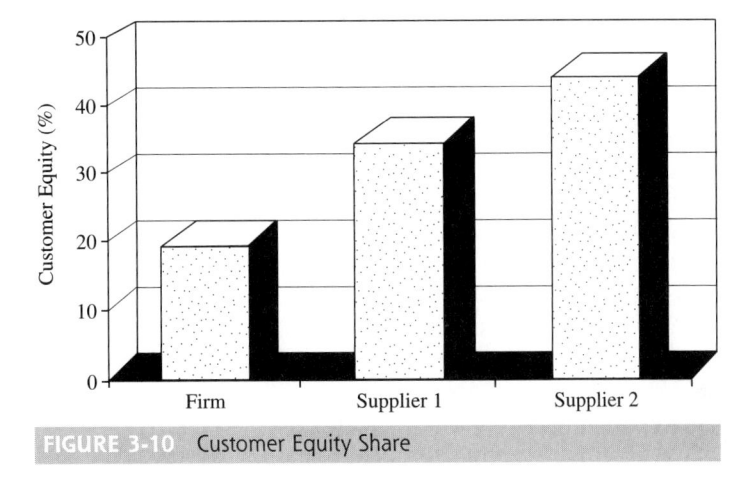

Analysis of customer switching trends in the market also tells an interesting story. The highlighted portion of the switching matrix in Figure 3-11 provides additional intuition for Supplier 2's strong customer equity.

We can see that, based on customers' last purchases, the firm held a market share of 35 percent (see right column of Figure 3-11). However, based on customers' next purchases, the firm would garner only about 20 percent of customers' business. Alternatively, consider Supplier 2. In terms of last purchase, Supplier 2 held a share of only 25 percent; but in terms of next purchase, Supplier 2's share jumps to 55 percent. Customers are clearly *switching away from* the firm and Supplier 1, and *switching to* Supplier 2. Therefore, when considering the value of the customer in terms of *future* purchases, Supplier 2 is clearly in the best position.

FIGURE 3-11 Brand Switching Matrix

		Firm (%)	Supplier 1 (%)	Supplier 2 (%)	Totals for last purchase (%)
	Next Purchase				
Last Purchase	Firm	15	5	15	35
	Supplier 1	5	20	15	40
	Supplier 2	0	0	25	25
	Totals for next purchase	20	25	55	100

WHAT DO WE LEARN FROM THE ANALYSIS? WHERE SHOULD THE FIRM FOCUS?

At this point in the analysis, we can now begin to determine how the firm is actually doing and where key opportunities may lie. We need to answer a series of seven questions:

1. What is most important to the customers in this market?
2. How is the firm doing on those aspects that are most important?
3. How are competitors doing on those important aspects?
4. What must we do at least as well as our competitors (points of parity)?
5. On what aspects do we need to do better than our competitors?
6. What key weaknesses must we overcome?
7. What, if any, opportunities for differentiation do we see?

Let's answer each question.

1. What is most important to the customers in this market?
   - Component: value equity
   - Driver: quality
   - Sub-driver: physical product

2. How is the firm doing on those aspects that are most important?
   - Value equity: not very well
   - Quality: not very well
   - Physical product: not very well

3. How are competitors doing on those important aspects?
   - Supplier 1: not very well
   - Supplier 2: very well—we should worry

4. What must we do at least as well as our competitors (points of parity)?
   - We must perform as well as (or better than) our competitors on those aspects that are most important to the customers in the market (e.g., physical product quality).

5. On what aspects do we need to do better than our competitors?
   - We may want to perform better than our competitors on those aspects that are important to customers, but not the most critical element (e.g., service product, corporate ethics, knowledge building).

6. What key weaknesses must we overcome?
   - Improve on value: We must improve on the driver of quality and, in particular, the sub-driver of physical product.
   - Improve on relationship: We should improve on the knowledge-building driver and appropriate sub-drivers that are important to the customer in this area.

7. What, if any, opportunities for differentiation do we see?
   - Possibilities: service product, price, convenience, or knowledge-building programs.

Summary

This concludes the customer equity analysis. A complete analysis of the importance of each component, driver, and sub-driver is useful to determine key areas of weakness or specific areas of opportunity. In particular, firms should:

- Determine which components, drivers, and sub-drivers of customer equity are most important for customers in its market.
- Analyze the firm's performance and performance of competitors on each component, driver and sub-driver.
- Analyze how each firm in the market is doing in terms of customer equity, customer equity share, and the customer switching matrix.
- Determine where the firm should focus its efforts, in terms of areas of weakness to overcome, areas in which it needs to achieve parity with competitors, and opportunities for differentiation.

Review Questions and Exercises

1. What could a frequently purchased consumer goods [FPCG] manufacturer such as Gillette, Procter and Gamble, or Unilever expect to be the key driver of customer equity: value, brand, or relationship? Why?
2. Assume that you are the marketing manager for a large discount retailer such as Wal-Mart or Carre Fours. How would you find the information to answer the following questions from the Customer Equity Analysis framework:
   a. What is most important to the customers in this market?
   b. How is the firm doing on those aspects that are most important?
   c. How are competitors doing on those important aspects?
   d. What must we do at least as well as our competitors (points of parity)?
   e. On what aspects do we need to do better than our competitors?
   f. What key weaknesses must we overcome?
   g. What, if any, opportunities for differentiation do we see?
3. Consider the importance and/perfomance charts in Figures 3-12 and 3-13 for a logistics and parcel delivery company we'll call WorldPak. A WorldPak executive recently interviewed a key customer. Information gained during the interview follows:
   - This customer is evaluated to be worth $4.2 million in terms of customer lifetime value to WorldPak. However, the executive also learned that the customer is seriously considering giving about 50 percent of its business to a competitor (one of the competitors listed on Figures 3-12 and 3-13).
   - In terms of value drivers, the customer believes that *on-time delivery* is the most important aspect of quality; *price consistency/fairness* is the most important aspect of price; and *around the clock availability* (with quick response) is the most important aspect of convenience.
   - In terms of brand drivers, the customer believes that *consistent sales representative contact* is the most important aspect of brand awareness; *sincerity and professionalism* are most important in terms of brand perceptions; and *hiring practices* is the most important aspect of brand ethics.
   - In terms of relationship drivers, the customer believes that *fair treatment of good customers* is the most important aspect of loyalty programs; *connecting with other customers* to learn new ideas about logistics and shipping is the most important aspect

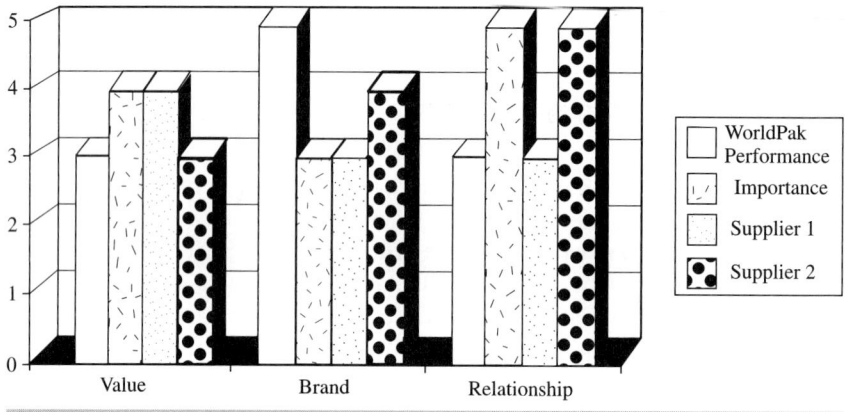

FIGURE 3-12 Customer Equity Analysis: WorldPak

of affinity; and *a sales representative who knows the customer's business* is the most important aspect of knowledge building.

Given this information, please answer the following questions:
- What is most important to the customer?
- Where is WorldPak performing well? Poorly?
- Where is WorldPak most vulnerable to competition?
- What additional questions would you like to ask this customer?
- In which area or areas (value, brand, or relationship) do you think WorldPak should invest to improve its relationship with this customer?

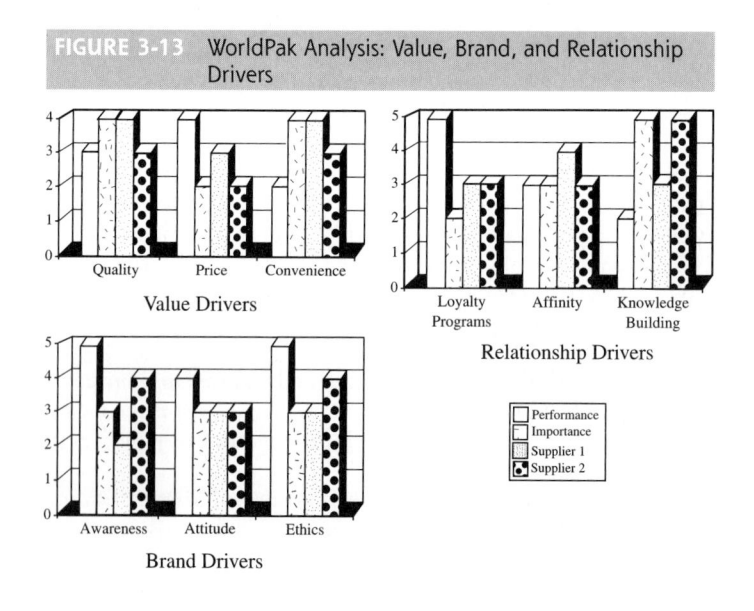

FIGURE 3-13 WorldPak Analysis: Value, Brand, and Relationship Drivers

Case 3-1   The Brita Products Company

John Deighton

In 1987 when Charlie Couric saw his first Brita pitcher he thought, "A homemade alternative to bottled water!" Here was a product that, with the right marketing support, could be very successful. Couric, a marketing executive with the Clorox Company charged with finding new business ideas, had been browsing health food stores in California when he came across the quirky home water pitcher-and-filter system made by a small German company, Brita GmbH. He proposed that Clorox acquire the right to market Brita in the United States, and in 1988 they did so. Couric reflected:

> In the early years we had to beg the corporation to invest. Some of my colleagues viewed the pitcher as another waffle iron—used once and then tossed into the basement. We saw it differently. We looked at the repeat purchasing of filters, and to us the strategy was obvious. This was a race to put a pitcher on every kitchen countertop, at a loss if necessary.

Clorox supported Couric's deficit-spending proposal, and a decade later Brita had grown to become one of Clorox's biggest brands. It had rewarded Couric's faith, spearheading the growth of a home water filtration industry in the United States. More than 17 million Brita pitchers had been sold, and each pitcher sale started a stream of filter sales. The Brita brand was generating close to $200 million revenues a year.

Now, in 1999, Couric was keeping an eye on a different water purification product launched by a small competitor, PUR. It was a filter that screwed onto kitchen faucets.[1] Clorox had its own version of the faucet-mounted filter ready for launch, and again a debate had developed over whether to deficit-spend. Some counseled that the faucet-mount had the power to disrupt the pitcher product, and Brita had no choice but to pour money into another race to build another installed base, this time in faucet-mounted products. Others argued that faucet-mounts served a different niche of the water purification market from pitchers, and the two could live side by side. A third group argued that Brita should do nothing to foster faucet-mounts. Its priority, they argued, was to invest to defend its installed base of pitchers and the associated filter revenue stream. Money spent on promoting a faucet-mount would only erode the pitcher base and interrupt its stream of filter revenues. They pointed out that PUR was a small, loss-making firm, too weak to succeed at creating a new category, particularly when the early adopters of home water filtration all had pitchers in their homes.

THE CLOROX COMPANY

The Clorox Company was a major manufacturer and marketer of laundry additives, household cleaners, charcoal, auto care products, cat litter, and home water purifiers. In January 1999, Clorox bought First Brands, a $1.2 billion manufacturer of plastic wraps and bags, auto care products, cat litter, and home fireplace products. Revenues of the two companies combined would have been $3.9 billion in 1998. Some of the well-known U.S. consumer brands that would come under common ownership following the merger were:

Clorox	First Brands
Armor All car care products	STP automotive products
Fresh Step cat litter	Scoop Away cat litter
S.O.S. steel wool pads	Ever Clean cat litter
Hidden Valley salad dressing	Johnny Cat cat litter

The case was prepared by Professor John Deighton. Copyright © 1999 by the President and Fellows of Harvard College. Harvard Business School Case 500-024.

[1] Faucet-mounted filters were not themselves a new product—Teledyne had sold one since the 1960s without much success. However, the introduction of solid carbon block technology in 1995 improved performance and increased consumer interest.

Kingsford charcoal
Clorox laundry bleach
Soft Scrub cleaners
Brita water filtration systems
Formula 409 spray cleaner
Tilex cleaners
Pine-Sol cleaner
Liquid Plumr
StarterLogg fire starters
HearthLogg fire logs
Glad plastic wraps and bags

Under Chairman and CEO G. Craig Sullivan, Clorox followed a strategy of building dominant brands, pursuing international expansion and acquiring promising businesses. Some 85% of Clorox brands were first or second in their categories. Sales beyond the United States would reach 20% of revenues after the First Brands merger, up from 18% for Clorox alone.

THE BRITA PRODUCTS COMPANY

Brita GmbH, a family-owned corporation headquartered in Tanusstein, Germany, made a variety of industrial and consumer water filtration products. Before Couric called, it had struggled without much success to sell its home water filtration system in the United States, most recently through a Canadian agent. After vigorous negotiation, in September 1988 it agreed to let Clorox form a subsidiary, Brita USA, to be the sole U.S. distributor of Brita products. Clorox would buy filters from Brita GmbH and design and make its own pitchers. Couric became President and General Manager of Brita USA.

For four years, Brita USA struggled. The costs of building distribution, designing products, and promoting the concept dwarfed the small base of sales. Couric persevered, however, because early surveys of users suggested to him that a Brita customer would have a remarkable lifetime value. Each pitcher sale would start a flow of filter sales. Over 80% of pitcher buyers were still using the product a year later and many were telling friends to try it and were giving it as gifts. In the 1990s, the product took hold like crabgrass. By 1999, an estimated 13% to 15% of the 103 million households in the United States were using a Brita pitcher. Brita had created a home water purification industry worth $350 million at retail, and held a 70% revenue share.

The Product

The Brita pour-through filtration system comprised a two-compartment pitcher and a replaceable filter (Exhibit 1). Tap water, poured into the upper compartment, flowed under gravity through the filter into the lower compartment, filling it in about five minutes.

The filter had two elements. Activated carbon reduced chlorine, sediment, and odors, and an ion-exchange resin removed any heavy metals such as lead, copper, mercury, and cadmium, as well as temporary water hardness (calcium and magnesium). The benefits were threefold. Filtered water tasted better, it did not deposit scale when boiled, and, to the extent that it might have contained harmful heavy metals, [heavy-metals] were extracted. The filter did not screen out microorganisms such as cryptosporidium and giardia, two sources of gastrointestinal illness that were potentially fatal to people with compromised immune systems.

The pitcher system was sold with a single filter in place. Filters required replacement every two months or after filtering 40 gallons of water. Brita supplied calendar stickers to help users track when a filter needed replacement. Filters were sold in packs of one, three, and five.

Consumer Attitudes and Behavior

Over the decade of the 1990s, the safety of tap water became a topic of growing concern to U.S. households. In one well-publicized case, two wells supplying the drinking water for the Boston suburb of East Woburn, Massachusetts, were found to be contaminated with industrial solvents, coincident with a number of cases of leukemia. The incident was the subject of a book and a 1998 motion picture, *A Civil Action*. In that year the U.S. Environmental Protection Agency declared that about 10% of the sediment under U.S. surface waters is "sufficiently contaminated" with toxic pollutants to pose a health threat to humans and wildlife. Later that year, Congress began requiring municipal water authorities to say when contaminant levels

CHAPTER 3 *Customer Equity Analysis* **105**

EXHIBIT 1   1993 Advertising

HOW IT WORKS.

Just fill with tap water. The Brita Water Filtering Pitcher does the rest.

The tap water enters Brita's patented, replaceable filter. It's both registered by the EPA and certified by NSF's laboratory.

Here's where the magic happens. 93% of the lead and copper is removed. Sediment, water hardness, chlorine taste and odor are all dramatically reduced.

Brita works so well, it's the nation's best-selling portable water filter system.

In just minutes, you get a half gallon of great tasting water at a fraction of the cost of bottled water. Cheers.

BRITA® Water Filtering Pitcher

Available in Standard and Ultra models.
For more information or the store nearest you, call 1-800-44-BRITA.

© 1993 BRITA (USA) INC.

(*Continued*)

106 PART I *Tools for Understanding and Analyzing Customer Equity*

EXHIBIT 1 (cont.)

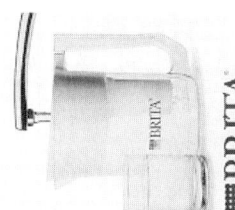

exceeded federal regulations. In Milwaukee in 1993, 403,000 people were made sick and 111 died when the parasite cryptosporidium entered the municipal water supply. By the end of the decade, a poll by *USA TODAY*, CNN, and Gallup found that 47% of respondents preferred not to drink water straight from the tap.[2]

---

[2]Eisler, Peter, Barbara Hansen, and Aaron Davis. "Lax oversight raises tap water risks." *USA TODAY*, October 21, 1998, p. 15A.

Sales of bottled water from U.S. supermarkets and home delivery services grew rapidly during the decade. By 1997, bottled water made up 8% of all the liquids that people paid to drink and was the industry's fastest-growing category (Exhibit 2). In that year, 45% of households bought still (noncarbonated) water in supermarkets and 27% bought carbonated water. The average price paid for still water was about a dollar per 128-ounce container, and carbonated brands averaged about three dollars (Exhibit 3).

EXHIBIT 2 Growth of Segments of the U.S. Beverage Market

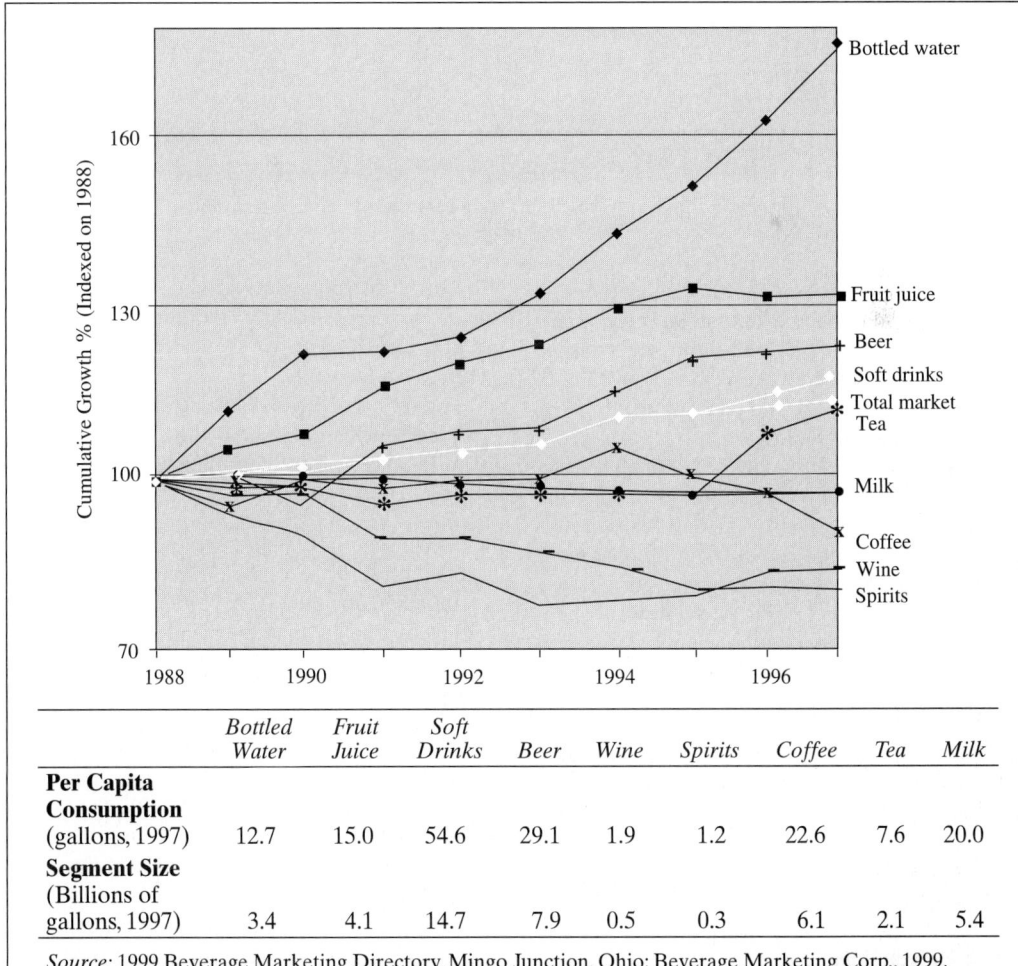

	Bottled Water	Fruit Juice	Soft Drinks	Beer	Wine	Spirits	Coffee	Tea	Milk
Per Capita Consumption (gallons, 1997)	12.7	15.0	54.6	29.1	1.9	1.2	22.6	7.6	20.0
Segment Size (Billions of gallons, 1997)	3.4	4.1	14.7	7.9	0.5	0.3	6.1	2.1	5.4

Source: 1999 Beverage Marketing Directory, Mingo Junction, Ohio: Beverage Marketing Corp., 1999.
Total Per Capita Consumption = 144.7 gallons in 1997.
Total Beverage Consumption = 44,500,000,000 gallons in 1997.

	Percent of Households Buying	Price per 128-oz. Unit
Still Water Brands	44.77%	$1.03
Dannon	6.27%	$2.09
Arrowhead	4.57%	$0.95
Poland Spring	4.47%	$1.39
Sparkletts	4.05%	$0.86
Chrystal Geyser	3.85%	$2.13
Evian	2.61%	$5.49
Hinckley & Schmitt	2.38%	$1.36
Private label	17.73%	$0.68
Carbonated Water Brands	26.83%	$3.70
Canada Dry	5.69%	$4.97
Schweppes	4.66%	$5.85
Vintage	2.65%	$2.44
Clearly Canadian	1.75%	$11.66
Perrier	1.31%	$9.47
Private Label	12.52%	$2.78

EXHIBIT 3 Major Brands in the Bottled Water Category (supermarkets only)

Source: Information Resources Inc., "Marketing Fact Book," January–December 1997, http://fic.wharton.upenn.edu/iri/factbook.

A 1998 survey[3] found that two-thirds of Americans claimed to be familiar with the expert recommendation to drink eight, eight-ounce servings of water a day, yet only one in five drank that quantity of water and 44% drank three or fewer water servings daily.

A 1999 survey[4] found that 72% of all respondents, and 89% of young adults, voiced some concern about the quality of their household's water supply. A majority of households used either bottled water or some water purification system to limit their exposure to public water supplies. The number taking no precautions declined from 47% in 1995 to 35% in 1999 (Exhibit 4).

Market Performance

Brita used the term "systems" to refer to pitchers and faucet-mounted units, and "filters" for the replacement filters. System sales were sluggish for the first four years after launch, but filter sales grew more rapidly (Exhibit 5). In the early years Couric compared performance in the United States to the first years of the product's life under other Brita distributors in Canada and the United Kingdom, and the similarity of the profiles gave him, as early as 1991, the confidence to persevere:

> We saw that trial in the United States in the early 1990s was running between the Canadian and the U.K. levels. Close to 25% of buyers told us that they had given a Brita pitcher as a gift. Another reassuring sign was that surveys were finding that more than 80% of those who had tried the pitcher were still using it a year later. The same surveys reported that they were buying 2 or 3 filters a year. Each year we tried to relate filter sales to past pitcher sales. We found that when we estimated our installed base at 80% of those who had bought a system in the previous five years, and assumed that the installed base bought 2.5 filters a year, the resulting forecasts of filter sales each year were close to reality.

Management tracked system market share in units and filter share in dollars (Exhibit 6). Brita's

---

[3]Yankelovich Partners conducted a survey of 3,003 Americans for the Nutrition Information Center at The New York Hospital—Cornell Medical Center and the International Bottled Water Association. The study is described at http://www.bottledwater-web.com/news/news3.html.

[4]"1999 National Consumer Water Quality Report," Lisle, IL: Water Quality Association, 1999.

From a survey of 1,007 adults conducted between January 14 and 17, 1999. Sample is projectable to all U.S. adults over age 18.

Expressed concerns about household water quality (% of respondents):

	1995	1997	1999
Expressed any concern	75	75	72
Health contaminants (net)	54	50	48
Bacteria			9
Aesthetics (net)	61	60	56
Smell and/or taste	45	42	40
Appearance	33	26	26
Hardness	38	39	36
Sediments	43	40	38

Expressed concerns about household water quality by age in 1999 (% of respondents):

	18–24	25–34	35–44	45–54	55–64	65+
Expressed any concerns	89	79	79	70	59	56
Health contaminants	67	56	58	45	36	25

Use of water treatment device (% of respondents):

	1995	1997	1999
No device used	47	41	35
Bottled water	36	37	38
System	27	32	38
Table-top pitcher	5	12	16
System on faucet	9	11	11
Whole house system	10	7	8
Softener	10	9	9

Use of water treatment device by region of country in 1999 (% of respondents):

	North East	North Central	South	West
Bottled water	33	32	42	43
Table-top pitcher	24	12	17	12
System on faucet	9	10	10	14
Whole house system	10	8	7	10
Softener	5	21	4	6

EXHIBIT 4 Water Quality: Consumer Attitudes and Behavior

Source: Water Quality Association: 1999 National Consumer Water Quality Report.

share of combined system and filter market revenues had been steady, in the range of 65% to 75% from 1995 to 1999. System unit shares were far more volatile. In July 1998, for example, system sales doubled over the previous year and Brita's share increased ten points in response to a so-called "bogo" (buy one, get one free) promotion on pitchers, intended to preempt a PUR competitive launch. Filter sales had been less responsive to sales promotion activity by manufacturers.

BRITA UNIT SALES ('00)

	1989	1990	1991	1992	1993	1994	1995	1996	1997	1998
Systems	171	194	202	302	546	1,056	2,030	3,363	4,565	5,266
Filters	402	581	876	1292	2,205	4,458	8,164	15,246	23,293	27,413

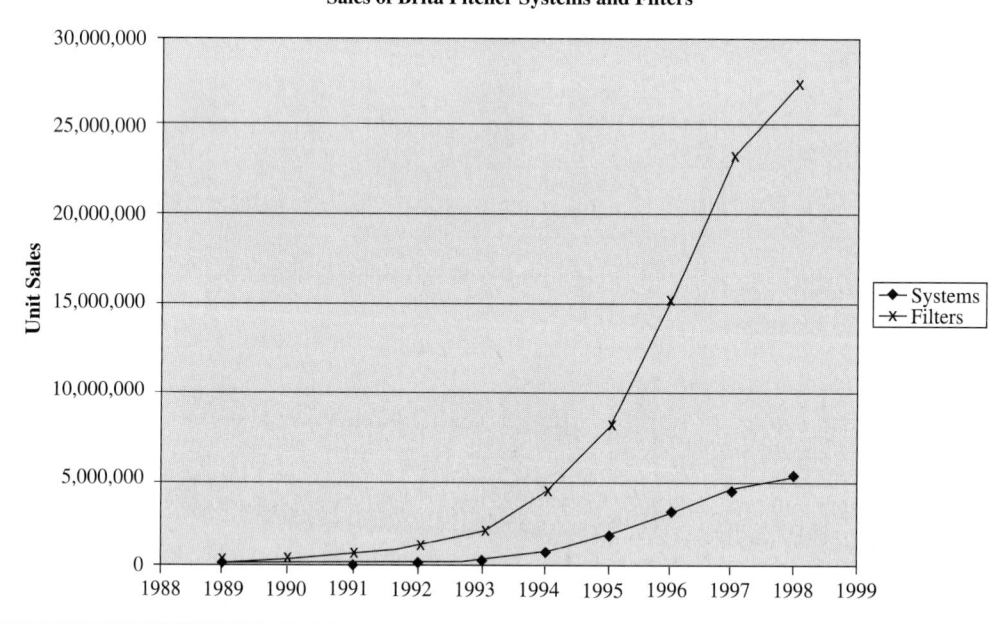

EXHIBIT 5 Brita Unit Sales, 1989 to 1998

Source: Company records (approximate and unaudited).

Brita bought pitchers from contract manufacturers at a cost per unit of $7.80. Filters were purchased from a manufacturing plant owned jointly by Clorox and Brita GmbH for $2.05 per unit, inclusive of a 3% royalty to Brita GmbH. (Profits from this plant were not material.) At the prices Brita charged retailers in 1999, pitchers earned a contribution to fixed costs of 48.6% of Brita's net revenue, and filters earned 50.0%. After advertising and trade promotions, Brita USA earned a net return on sales of 24%, the highest of all Clorox business units. Although advertising spending worked to the benefit of both pitchers and filters, trade promotions were used mainly to secure trade support for pitchers. Exhibit 7 summarizes the income statement of the brand in 1998.

Distribution

At inception, Brita's main retail outlet had been a health foods chain. Its competitors were in stores that stocked housewares, like Sears and Wal-Mart. Couric believed, however, that the product would flourish in Clorox's traditional base, grocery and drug outlets, and drove distribution in that direction.

	Brita Distribution	
	1992	*1998*
Department stores	27%	13%
Mass merchandisers	31%	34%
Grocery stores	11%	14%
Club stores	31%	21%
Drug stores	–	12%

SYSTEMS

	1992	1993	1994	1995	1996	1997	1998
Pitchers (thousands of units)	375	640	1,405	2,636	4,381	5,689	6,307
Brita	82%	82%	75%	77%	77%	80%	83%
PUR	–	–	–	–	–	4%	8%
Rubbermaid	–	–	–	–	–	7%	4%
All others	18%	18%	25%	23%	23%	11%	5%
Faucet Mounts (thousands of units)	1,186	782	602	659	898	1,249	1,291
PUR	–	–	–	9%	30%	67%	74%
Teledyne	23%	23%	30%	43%	43%	27%	23%

FILTERS

	1992	1993	1994	1995	1996	1997	1998
Filter sales ($millions, retail)	$20.5	$26.5	$38.7	$63.3	$82.3	$116.3	$154.7
Brita	32%	43%	59%	65%	75%	75%	75%
Teledyne	25%	20%	15%	10%	9%	7%	4%
PUR	0%	0%	0%	1%	2%	8%	17%
Omni	12%	13%	8%	8%	5%	3%	2%
Sears	7%	6%	3%	2%	2%	1%	1%
Pollonex	7%	4%	2%	1%	1%	0%	1%

EXHIBIT 6 Retail Market Shares (United States, all retail outlets)

Source: Company records, assembled from data from Industrial Market Research Inc. and Information Resources, Inc.

Note: Retail audit estimates may not agree precisely with Brita's sales records because they are extrapolated from a sampling of retail stores.

This pattern of channel evolution, in which high margin retailers like department stores pioneered a new category, only to lose share to lower margin retailers, was known among marketers generally as a "class to mass" strategy. Couric explained his strategy:

> Our version of "class to mass" had three elements. We wanted to be established in class, first in mass, and alone in grocery. So we created a line of upscale pitchers called Ultra for department stores, appropriate for their 35% mark-up structure. We sold the standard pitcher, inherited from Germany but manufactured locally, in mass merchants like Target and Wal-Mart and in drug and grocery stores. They marked it up 25%. We designed a bonus pack system and a 5-pack of filters to appeal to club retailers when they became important in the early 1990s.

> Keeping these various classes of trade happy is an enormous challenge. We are continuously building the system and seeing cracks appear. Eventually perhaps we'll be driven out of "class," but we aim to make it last as long as possible. We need the breadth of distribution and variety of products to support our $30 million advertising budget, and to provide a channel for introducing and establishing future new products.

> One way we attempt to keep the peace among our classes of trade is by insisting that no retailer advertise a Brita line at below the price that we set. We call it a MAP (minimum advertised price) policy. We reimburse retailers for featuring our products in their display advertising, but if they feature us at below the MAP, then we won't pay. The only exception we make is on the standard pitcher. We let them deal as much as they like on that item.

	Total ('000)	Per Unit
Brita Pitcher Systems		
Unit sales	5,266	
Revenues	$79,800	$15.16
Cost of goods sold	41,100	7.80
Gross margin	38,700	7.36
Consumer promotion	4,000	
Feature price reductions	5,000	
Other trade spending	7,000	
Brita Filters		
Unit sales	27,413	
Revenues	$112,400	$4.10
Cost of goods sold	56,200	2.05
Gross margin	56,200	2.05
Consumer promotion	1,000	
Feature price reductions	1,000	
Other trade spending	1,000	
Combined Brita Systems and Filters		
Combined revenues	$192,000	
Combined gross margins	94,900	
Advertising	30,000	
Combined consumer and trade promotions	19,000	
Net income before G & A	45,900	

EXHIBIT 7 Revenue and Net Income of Brita Systems and Filters, 1998

Source: From company records, modified to preserve confidentiality of margin information but without altering the relative magnitudes of margins.

Positioning and Advertising

Brita's advertising in the United States emphasized a taste benefit. Couric explained:

> Initially people had no clue about the concept of a pitcher product. I remember on the cab ride back to the airport after our first trade show in Chicago I explained the concept in lengthy detail to the cab driver and when I was finished he said, "You screw it onto the faucet, right?" I realized then that we had to tell people how the product worked, so we split the advertising message 50/50 between how it works and how it tastes. Today, now that our product is more well known, we are able to be more focused about the taste benefit.
>
> We decided on taste for three reasons. First, research showed that when we talk taste, we get a health benefits halo. When we talk health, we don't communicate the idea of taste. Second, we noted that the whole bottled water industry had been built without reference to health. Third, I wanted to be at the top of the mountain. I didn't want competitors overtaking us. If we focused on lead removal, say at 93%, someone else could claim to take out 95%. With taste, we could say it first, say it loudest, and we could own the benefit. By now, with $100 million of cumulative advertising on the taste claim behind us, we are impossible to dislodge.
>
> When we started eleven years ago, the water filtration category had low credibility. It was being investigated all the time for improper or false claims. We didn't want to get into a claims war. Our advertising needed

to be pure and simple. We showed mountain streams, waterfalls, and the outdoors. We promised clear, crisp, refreshing water, which is what we delivered. Today we own the waterfall imagery.

Competition

Brita's success attracted competitors in droves. Among the brand names that entered the market were Culligan, Electrolux, Sunbeam, Kenwood, Corning, Melitta, PUR, Rubbermaid, Teledyne, Omni, and Mr. Coffee. None had succeeded in challenging Brita's leadership, which remained in the range of 65% to 75% across the decade. In 1999, the only competitor with double-digit market share was PUR, the brand of a small, publicly held U.S. corporation, Recovery Engineering. This company made, in addition to water filters, a line of portable drinking water systems for outdoor enthusiasts and desalinators for marine and military use.

At the January 1998 International Housewares Show in Chicago, a dozen manufacturers unveiled new water filtration products or extensions to existing lines. The products appeared to be designed to attack niches not currently served by Brita. "Number 1 is always going to be under attack," Brian Barton, brand manager at Rubbermaid, told the press covering the trade show. "When you have 80% of the market share there's only one way to go and that's south."[5]

Several products took health and safety positions in reaction to Brita's taste appeal. Number 2 brand, PUR, announced that it would spend $40 million in advertising and promotion to support its line of faucet-mount and pitcher filters. The spend included a $15 million outlay for PUR Plus, a new pitcher system touted as the most technologically advanced to date. The PUR filter would remove contaminants such as cryptosporidium and giardia. PUR representatives described a promotional program that would begin with a six-month infomercial running on national cable television, to be followed by a schedule of 30-second spots on cable and spot network TV that would point out the differences between PUR and current pitchers. Sunbeam, known for blenders and toasters, announced the launch of Fresh Source, a product that removed microbiological cysts as well as chlorine and lead. Sunbeam would back the product with an estimated $10 million of advertising. Number 3 manufacturer Teledyne unveiled a faucet-mount product at the show.

At the trade show, Brian Sullivan, President and CEO of Recovery Engineering, Minneapolis, was quoted as saying, "If you ask consumers if they want more contaminants taken out or less, they'll say more. People will pay more for a higher-performing product." PUR's pitcher was considerably more expensive than Brita's standard product. A Brita representative responded, "The way we see the market, this business is geared more towards taste. Consumers are interested in taste. Bacteria is way down the list."[6]

In a $30 million ad campaign unveiled in the month of the Chicago show, Brita did not mention harmful impurities. A TV spot dubbed "There Was a Time" features shots of rushing streams set against a backdrop of mountains and a dark, brooding sky. "There was a time when it was perfect," the voice-over says. "You can have this taste . . . again."

Rubbermaid had launched a low-priced product in 1997, which used a technology similar to Brita's while attacking it on price/performance. Rubbermaid claimed that its filter could cleanse 800, 8-oz. glasses of water versus 560 for Brita at the same price. In 1998 the company repackaged its pitcher product and announced a portable 16-oz. bottle with a carbon filter built into the cap. Rubbermaid had not advertised its pitcher in 1997, and sales had been disappointing. At the trade show they pledged to step up promotion under a new team led by Cathryn Rings, the former head of Procter & Gamble's Max Factor cosmetics business. Rings announced at the trade show, "We're going to try some classic P&G marketing."

THE FAUCET-MOUNTED FILTER ENTRY

Prior to 1995, Brita executives expressed little interest in faucet-mounted water filtration systems. Of the 50 countries in which Brita GmbH did business, only Japan had a significant faucet business, and that was attributed to space

---

[5]Mehegan, Sean. "Sunbeam, recovery loading up $$ to take on Brita in water filtration." *Brandweek*, Vol. 39, Iss. 3, January 19, 1998, p. 12.

[6]Op cit., p. 12.

constraints in Japanese kitchens. In 1994 and 1995, however, they saw a faucet segment forming. Recovery Engineering Inc. launched a faucet-mounted product under the PUR brand name with some success. In 1995, Brita hired an outside design company to design a faucet-mount.

Functionally, water from a pitcher was different from water filtered through a faucet-mounted filter. In favor of pitchers, they were usually stored in refrigerators, so pitcher water was cold while faucet water was not. In those parts of the country where tap water was "hard" and left scale deposits and scum when boiled, only pitcher filters but not faucet filters would eliminate hardness. In favor of faucet-mounts, the water passed through at higher pressure than through pitcher filters, so finer filters could be used that could screen for microorganisms and offer protection against cryptosporidium and giardia. Also, pitcher-filtered water tasted crisper, with lower pH. Finally, faucet-filtered water cost significantly less per glass because the filter lasted longer. Where pitcher water cost 15 to 20 cents per gallon, faucet-filtered water cost perhaps half.

Were these differences significant to consumers? Did Brita stand for good tasting water, or how you get it? The Brita team debated whether the faucet-mount would be perceived as another way to deliver Brita water. Or would the consumer decide that they were buying something quite different, perhaps even so different that some might consider it a good idea to own both a pitcher and a faucet-mount?

As Brita's filtration technology played no part in the faucet-mount design, Clorox was not obliged to use the Brita name on this product. If it did so, however, it was required to pay Brita GmbH a royalty that, under the 1988 agreement, would be between 3% and 4% of sales depending on the magnitude of sales. It would also be bound by the non-compete clause of the comprehensive agreement that limited sales of products with the Brita name to North America. Conversations with the retail trade, however, revealed a distinct preference for carrying the faucet-mount under a well-known name like Brita.

The direct cost of the faucet-mount system was estimated to be $15.00 and the direct cost of a replacement faucet filter would be $3.00. Pitcher filters could not be used in faucet-mounts.

Would a faucet-mount cannibalize pitcher and pitcher filter sales? Perhaps, some speculated, the pitcher was a starter product, and customers who had learned to go back to drinking tap water would graduate up to the more convenient and sophisticated faucet unit. To explore these and other questions, Clorox commissioned a simulated test market[7] from ACNielsen Vantis, a division of the ACNielsen BASES group.

Market Simulation Study for the Faucet Filter

In the ACNielsen Vantis study, 567 respondents, characterized as water-involved[8] and drawn from eight markets across the United States, were intercepted in shopping malls, brought to rooms containing simulated retail store shelves, and asked to choose from a display of water filtration systems.

Respondents were assigned to one of three rooms. Each room displayed ten products currently available in the market. In addition, two displayed a prototype of the Brita Faucet Filter

---

[7]Simulated test market studies have a long history, dating back to the 1970s when Alvin J. Silk and Glen Urban began research at MIT's Sloan School to seek ways to forecast demand for new products without incurring the costs and public exposure of full-scale test markets. Today simulated test markets are regularly relied on to forecast in-market performance without the need to build production capacity, expose marketing plans to competitive scrutiny, and wait six or twelve months to read results. Their evolution is described in Kevin J. Clancy, Robert S. Shulman, and Marianne Wolf, *Simulated Test Marketing: Technology for Launching Successful New Products*, New York, NY: Lexington Books, 1994. ACNielsen Vantis serves services and durable goods industries with a brand of simulated test market methodology, BASES, that derives from work that began in the Pillsbury Company in the 1960s, found a temporary home in Booz-Allen & Hamilton (the name is an acronym for Booz-Allen Sales Estimation System), was spun off in a leveraged buyout in 1977, and is now a division of the A. C. Nielsen Company.
[8]A water-involved respondent was one who either owned a filtration device or bought bottled water, and described him or herself as not satisfied with the quality of their water.

System, one priced at $34.99 and the other at $39.99. The third had no Brita Faucet Filter System on display, to serve as the control cell of the experiment. In the first two rooms, subjects saw print advertising for Brita and PUR faucet-mounted filters.

Consumers were first asked to rate how likely it was that they would buy any of the displayed items in the next two months. They were then asked to identify their first, second, and third choice of item. Finally, they were asked a series of questions about the test product, the Brita Faucet Filter System. Vantis offered the Brita team the following conclusions from the study:

- The Faucet Filter increased the likelihood of buying a product from the Brita line.
- However, it did not increase interest in the filtration category as a whole, so that the combined pitcher and faucet-mounted market was not expected to expand.
- Though higher priced, the Brita Faucet Filter generated similar levels of purchase intention to the Brita Spacesaver Pitcher.

- About half the Brita pitcher owners who bought the Faucet Filter system would continue to use the pitcher in conjunction with the faucet product.
- Both Brita and PUR's faucet filters were perceived to be superior to the Brita pitcher in removing contaminants, and in convenience. However, only Brita's faucet filter was perceived to improve the water's taste.
- Unit sales and perceptions of value for the faucet mount were strong at both the $39.99 and $34.99 prices, and sales would not be significantly impacted if the PUR price was dropped by $5.00.

The study projected that unit sales of the faucet-mount in its first year would lie between 350,000 and 1,395,000 units. Half of this volume would come from consumers who would otherwise have bought a Brita pitcher. Whether sales would be at the high or low end of the range depended on how aggressive was Brita's marketing investment, and how competitors responded. Ten scenarios were generated by combining the following factors and levels:

	Low	High	Very High
Consumer advertising	$5.4 million	$11.1 million	$15 million
Consumer promotion	$2.0 million	$ 3.0 million	$ 4 million
Feature price reductions	$1.8 million	$ 2.3 million	$ 2.8 million
Other trade spending (displays, racks, etc.)	$3.2 million	$ 6.1 million	$ 9 million

The ten scenarios gave rise to the following ten sales forecasts:

Scenario	Minimum Advertised Price ($5.00 off List)	Consumer Promotion and Trade Spending	Consumer Advertising	Competitive Pricing	First Year Unit Sales Forecast
1	$34.99	Low	Low	Low	340,000
2	$34.99	Low	Low	Current	350,000
3	$29.99	Low	Low	Low	395,000
4	$34.99	High	High	Low	970,000
5	$29.99	High	High	Low	1,125,000
6	$29.99	High	High	Current	1,160,000
7	$34.99	High	Very High	Current	1,205,000
8	$34.99	Very High	Very High	Current	1,245,000
9	$29.99	Very High	High	Current	1,350,000
10	$29.99	Very High	Very High	Low	1,395,000

Each scenario resulted in a sales and income forecast. For example, scenario 2 led to the following forecast:

Total households	75.86 million
Product awareness resulting from $5.4 million advertising	13%
Distribution (% of market reached)	72%
List price (30% of sales assumed to occur at list)	$39.99
Feature price (70% of sales assumed to occur at the feature price)	$34.99
Trade promotion	$3.2 million (low)
Consumer promotion	$2.0 million (low)
Competitive pricing	current levels
Total sales (units)	350,000

Brita USA had not asked Vantis for a forecast of sales of replacement filters. The proposed product had an LED filter replacement indicator, which would likely increase compliance with filter replacement recommendations. Each filter would treat 100 gallons of water, about four months' output from a typical kitchen faucet, before the indicator would signal that it was due for replacement.

COURIC'S DECISION

Couric prepared to call his marketing team together to hear their views on how to take the Brita brand forward. He anticipated that he would hear three points of view: keep the focus on building the installed base of pitchers, shift the budget to encourage the installed base to buy more filters, or put the weight of resources behind building a whole new installed base in faucet-mounts.

He saw many demands on the Brita marketing budget besides the faucet-mount product launch. Household pitcher penetration was slowing, and yet six out of seven households did not have one. Could there be segments who had not responded to the broad appeals of the first decade, but who might well respond to more targeted communication efforts—specific appeals to singles and to parents of young children, for example? Perhaps investing in direct mail or other highly targeted marketing tools could cultivate demand in these niches. Then there was the filter opportunity. Brita had never invested in the direct cultivation of filter demand, beyond in-store promotion.

On his desk in the corner office were Recovery Engineering's published financial results for the quarter ending January 3, 1999. Its quarterly sales were up $1 million on the previous quarter to $19.5 million, but its net loss had more than doubled to $7.2 million. Its stock was trading at $10, down from $35 in mid-1998. Recovery Engineering had raised capital in an Initial Public Offering in 1997 on the claim that it had a technological edge over Brita. To be sure, PUR had been first to market with a number of new features: the first cryptosporum filter for pitchers, the first mechanical device to indicate when to replace a filter, and the first widely distributed faucet filter. But as Couric weighed how much urgency to put behind the faucet-mount launch, he found comfort in PUR's flow of red ink.

A Fax and a Phone Call

Couric's fax began transmitting. Over the line came a report from the Clorox field sales director, with a sketch of a display that had been seen that morning in the Schaumburg, Illinois, branch of Target Stores, in the store's large water filtration section. A sign over the display had read:

Which water filtration product is right for me?

How do different water filters give me great-tasting water and protect my family?

Choose your level of protection:

- •   Lead, chlorine.
- •• Lead, chlorine, cryptosporidium, giardia.

- • • Lead, chlorine, cryptosporidium, giardia, Lindane (a pesticide), Atrazine (a herbicide), asbestos.
- • • • Lead, chlorine, cryptosporidium, giardia, Lindane (a pesticide), Atrazine (a herbicide), asbestos, benzene, TTHMC.

All product claims are NSF® certified to national public health standards.

Beneath the sign he had seen five PUR systems and four Brita systems mounted on identical backing cards labeled with one, two, three, or four bullets. No PUR system had fewer than two bullets and the PUR Ultimate Faucet Mount had the maximum, four. Not a single Brita system had more than one bullet.

Simultaneously, Couric's phone rang. His investment bankers were advising that Procter & Gamble, the world's largest consumer products company and Clorox's most respected competitor, was about to close a deal at $35 per share for control of PUR. ∎

◆◆◆ Harrah's Entertainment Inc.

Case 3-2 Harrah's Entertainment Inc.

Rajiv Lal

The results are impressive enough that other casino companies are copying some of Harrah's more discernible methods. Wall Street analysts are also beginning to see Harrah's—long a dowdy also-ran in the flashy casino business—as gaining an edge on its rivals. Harrah's stock price has risen quickly in recent weeks as investors have received news of the marketing results. And the company's earnings have more than doubled in the past year.

—WALL STREET JOURNAL, MAY 4, 2000[1]

Philip G. Satre, Chairman and Chief Executive Officer of Harrah's Entertainment Inc., read with satisfaction the *Wall Street Journal* article about Harrah's. The story discussed the company's marketing success in targeting low rollers, the 100% growth in stock price and profits in the year to December 1999, and the revenue growth of 50% which significantly outpaced the industry (see Exhibit 1).

The case was prepared by Dean's Research Fellow Patricia Martone Carrolo and Professor Rajiv Lal. Copyright © 2001 by the President and Fellows of Harvard College. Harvard Business School Case 502-011.
[1]Christina Binkley, "Lucky Numbers: Casino Chain Mines Data on Its Gamblers, and Strikes Pay Dirt—'Secret Recipe' Lets Harrah's Target Its Low-Rollers at the Individual Level— A Free-Meal 'Intervention'," *Wall Street Journal*, May 4, 2000.

The $100 million investment in information technology seemed to be paying off.

But that day Satre was more interested in the marketing activities that had contributed to these results (see Exhibits 2a–2f). He asked Gary Loveman, then Chief Operating Officer, and his team of "propeller heads" two questions. He wanted to know "how much" these marketing efforts had contributed to Harrah's overall performance, and if these marketing results were a one-shot event or could be achieved year after year, especially as the competition introduced similar programs.

GAMBLING IN THE UNITED STATES

The United States had a long and complicated relationship with gambling. Early religious settlers felt that it was immoral. Yet the limited entertainment options of the frontier meant that gaming parlors coexisted, often uneasily, with churches.

	Year Ended December 31		
	1999	1998	1997
Revenues			
Casino*	$2,424,237	$1,660,313	$1,338,003
Food and beverage	425,808	231,568	196,765
Rooms	253,629	153,538	128,354
Management fees	75,890	64,753	24,566
Other	131,403	78,320	78,954
Less: Casino promotional allowances	(286,539)	(184,477)	(147,432)
Total revenues	$3,024,428	$2,004,015	$1,619,210
Operating expenses			
Direct			
Casino	$1,254,557	$ 868,622	$ 685,942
Food and beverage	218,580	116,641	103,604
Rooms	66,818	41,871	39,719
Depreciation of buildings, riverboats, and equipment	188,199	130,128	103,670
Development costs	6,538	8,989	10,524
Write-downs, reserves and recoveries	2,235	7,474	13,806
Project opening costs	2,276	8,103	17,631
Other	690,404	467,999	383,791
Total operating expenses	$2,429,607	$1,649,827	$1,358,687
Operating profit	594,821	354,188	260,523
Net income	$ 208,470	$ 102,024	$ 99,388

EXHIBIT 1 Consolidated Statements of Income (thousands, except per-share amounts)

Source: Harrah's Entertainment Inc.

*A breakdown of Casino revenues by regions is as follows:
Western region—$730.1 million, Central region—$970.9 million and Eastern region—$723.3 million.

During the 1950s, Benjamin "Bugsy" Siegel, a known gangster, saw an opportunity to elude California's strict ban on gambling and also quench its citizens' thirst for gaming. Siegel traveled to Nevada, since the state had tolerated gambling in the 1930s during the construction of the Hoover Dam, and built a luxury Caribbean-style hotel and casino called the Flamingo in Las Vegas. To attract gamblers, Las Vegas began offering inexpensive hotel rooms, food, free drinks, and well-known entertainers. Performers such as Frank Sinatra and Elvis Presley played to full houses there.

In 1978 casinos spread to Atlantic City and then to states like Colorado, Louisiana, and South Dakota. The early 1980s saw casino resorts become more popular for guests and businesses alike, and casino growth was poised to increase dramatically by decade's end. Casino gambling was approved in Iowa, Illinois, Mississippi, Missouri, and on many Native American reservations. In 1989 Iowa became the first state to allow gambling on riverboat casinos.

Also in the late 1980s, Stephen Wynn almost single-handedly changed Las Vegas by taking gambling to the next level when he built the Mirage resort. The casino resort had a shark tank, a wild animal haven, and an artificial erupting volcano. Others soon followed suit. Old casinos such as the Sands, the Hacienda, and the New Frontier were demolished. New casinos like the Luxor—a glass version of the Great Pyramid with copies of Egyptian monuments and statues of the pharaohs—were built to attract tourists looking for entertainment.

> **# of Guests**—The number of guests in a particular month. The largest quantity typically indicates selection month.
> **Hotel %**—percent of guests who stayed in the hotel.
> **Red %**—percent of guests redeeming *any* offer in a month.
> **# of Trips**—Trips (can be multiple consecutive days) captured on the Casino Management System. The Harrah's loyalty card had to be used to capture this information.
> **# of Days**—The number of individual days a customer visited Harrah's during a month.
> **Theo(theoretical) Win**—On average, what we would expect the profitability of the customers to be based on their play in the **month**.
> **Observed Win**—Actual profitability for the casino for the ***month***.
> **Complimentary (Comp) Amount**—Comp dollars provided to customers in the month (and does not include cost of the offer redeemed).
> **Complimentary (Comp) %**—Comp dollar amount as a percentage of theoretical win.

EXHIBIT 2A Glossary of Terms in Exhibits 2b–2f

Source: Harrah's Entertainment Inc.

Although many new casinos were introduced in various cities in the early to late 1990s, by 1999, Nevada and Atlantic City still claimed over 40% of the $31 billion in total gambling revenue in the United States (see Exhibit 3).

Las Vegas, the largest U.S. gaming market, was a unique destination city and, during the late 1990s, became a mecca for national conventions and "must-see" mega resorts. Vacationers could easily spend a week visiting all of the major casinos and other attractions in Las Vegas, or simply sit poolside, go to a show or shop, and enjoy fine dining. Wynn's $1.6 billion Bellagio Hotel, inspired by Italy's Lake Como region, opened in October 1998 with an 8.5-acre lake and 1,400 fountains.[2] According to data compiled by the Las Vegas Convention and Visitors Authority (LVCVA), the average Las Vegas visitor in 2000 was expected to spend $1,329 during a 3.7 day stay—50% on gambling, 20.6% on lodging, and the remainder on meals, shopping, transportation, shows, and sightseeing.

Unlike Las Vegas, Atlantic City was more of a "day tripper's" destination. Approximately 30% of its visitors arrived by charter bus and generally stayed for less than a day. The winter cold made the Boardwalk less appealing to tour group business.[3] In 1999, there were 12 hotel/casinos, of which 10 were located on or near the famous Atlantic City Boardwalk. Only one new casino had been built in Atlantic City since 1987: the Taj Mahal, opened in 1990.[4]

The geographic expansion of legalized and state-supervised gambling broadened the industry's customer base. People who had never seen the bright lights of Las Vegas nor strolled the Boardwalk in Atlantic City were being lured to riverboats in states like Iowa and Louisiana, land-based casinos in Detroit and New Orleans, and casinos on Native American land in various states. By 1999, riverboat-type casinos were operating in six states, and Native American-owned facilities were in business in over 12 states.[5]

COMPANY BACKGROUND

The man who industrialized gambling, William Fisk Harrah—26-year-old charmer, pathological car lover, and bingo entrepreneur—arrived in Reno, Nevada, in May 1937 and commenced

---
[2]Tom Graves, "Standard & Poor's Industry Surveys—Lodging and Gaming," August 17, 2000.

[3]Brian Maher and Jennifer Smith, "Credit Lyonnais Securities (USA) Inc.—Gaming Industry Highlights," March 6, 2001.
[4]Tom Graves, "Standard & Poor's Industry Surveys—Lodging and Gaming," August 17, 2000.
[5]Ibid.

EXHIBIT 2B New Business Program Analysis

Sign-Up Month	New Customers		1 Month After Signup		2 Months After Signup		3 Months After Signup	
	Customers	Theoretical	Customers	Theoretical	Customers	Theoretical	Customers	Theoretical
1-Apr-99	1022	$31,992	125	$10,857	103	$10,478	85	$10,093
1-May-99	837	44,673	133	10,772	134	15,799	102	10,950
1-Jun-99	825	46,291	135	13,231	128	10,941	91	12,823
1-Jul-99	808	45,725	162	24,712	137	23,229	109	26,629
1-Aug-99	742	43,423	164	17,494	103	11,122	97	11,817
1-Sep-99	760	42,257	141	20,102	118	15,744	104	18,995
1-Oct-99	990	54,935	178	26,086	151	24,168	148	16,080
1-Nov-99	1064	63,687	225	28,657	182	23,824	142	21,988
1-Dec-99	772	41,494	143	15,906	149	16,517	94	13,229
1-Jan-00	986	$46,502	206	$20,041	193	$22,123	92	$12,476

	Customers					Revenues			
	1st Month	2nd Month	3rd Month	1st–3rd		1st Month	2nd Month	3rd Month	1st–3rd
1-Apr-99	12%	10%	8%	31%	1-Apr-99	34%	33%	32%	98%
1-May-99	16	16	12	44	1-May-99	24	35	25	84
1-Jun-99	16	16	11	43	1-Jun-99	29	24	28	80
1-Jul-99	20	17	13	50	1-Jul-99	54	51	58	163
1-Aug-99	22	14	13	49	1-Aug-99	40	26	27	93
1-Sep-99	19	16	14	48	1-Sep-99	48	37	45	130
1-Oct-99	18	15	15	48	1-Oct-99	47	44	29	121
1-Nov-99	21	17	13	52	1-Nov-99	45	37	35	117
1-Dec-99	19	19	12	50	1-Dec-99	38	40	32	110
1-Jan-00	21%	20%	9%	50%	1-Dec-99	43%	48%	27%	118%

Source: Harrah's Entertainment Inc.

Note: The first two columns report the number of new customers signed up in a particular month and the predicted worth of these customers. Offers, of varying type and value, were sent to each new customer that played at Harrah's, and were redeemable one month, two months, and three months after their first visit. The following columns report the number of customers who came back to Harrah's in the subsequent months and predicted worth of these customers. For example, in April 1999, 1,022 new customers came to Harrah's and their predicted worth was $10,857 compared to $31,992, the predicted worth of the 1022 customers who signed up in April. Similarly, 103 of the customers who signed up in April returned in June, and 85 returned in July, with no demonstrable change in predicted worth for the pool. Each month brought a new vintage of customers signing up.

EXHIBIT 2C Loyalty Program (frequency upside)—Offer Behavior Change by Offer and Month

Offer	Report Period	# of Guests	Hotel %	Red %	# of Trips	Trips per Guest	# of Days	Days per Trip	Hours	Hours per Day	Theo Win	Observed Win	Comp Amt.	Comp %	Avg. Theo Win per Trip	Avg. Theo Win per Day	Avg. Theo Win per Hour
PRE	Jan-99	21*	24%	5%	20	1.0	34	1.7	109	3.2	$7,770	$12,745	$1,361	18%	$389	$229	$71
	Feb-99	28	18	11	28	1.0	50	1.8	166	3.3	11,957	15,436	2,434	20	427	239	72
	Mar-99	30	17	10	28	0.9	41	1.5	148	3.6	6,596	(1,432)	799	12	236	161	45
	Apr-99	40	23	18	40	1.0	61	1.5	173	2.8	5,051	6,100	845	17	126	83	29
	May-99	36	14	8	36	1.0	64	1.8	218	3.4	9,000	5,838	1,585	18	250	141	41
	Jun-99	**953**	**29**	**22**	**978**	**1.0**	**1,709**	**1.7**	**6,496**	**3.8**	**267,907**	**270,836**	**42,514**	**16**	**274**	**157**	**41**
POST	Jul-99	133*	25	31	153	1.2	252	1.6	987	3.9	74,275	95,263	12,558	17	485	295	75
	Aug-99	146	26	44	172	1.2	286	1.7	870	3.0	43,240	51,900	8,987	21	251	151	50
	Sep-99	166	40	58	188	1.1	362	1.9	1,270	3.5	70,824	94,739	16,110	23	377	196	56
	Oct-99	152	42	53	178	1.2	319	1.8	1,286	4.0	58,354	87,082	12,300	21	328	183	45
	Nov-99	102	52	55	111	1.1	198	1.8	761	3.8	29,095	50,920	7,151	25	262	147	38
	Dec-99	83	42	41	98	1.2	167	1.7	554	3.3	23,187	38,983	4,304	19	237	139	42
Total		1,890	31%	32%	2,030	1.1	3,543	1.7	13,037	3.7	$607,256	$728,410	$110,948	18%	$299	$171	$47

*To be read as, of the 953 customers who received an offer in June, 21 customers had patronized the casino in January and 133 customers patronized the casino in July.

Note: Harrah's identified a list of potentially loyal customers who could increase the number of trips that they made to Harrah's. An offer was sent to a total of 953 customers in June, redeemable in July, August, and September. Each offer consisted of three individual offers—one for each month, at an average incremental cost to Harrah's of $40 per each redeemed offer. The type and level of offer was similar in value and type to what the customer had historically received. The offer was different for customers of different perceived worth to Harrah's but was predominately cash and food based. Exhibit 2c tracks the behavior of this pool of 953 customers before and after the offer was sent in June. While, on average, only 30 of these 953 customers were visiting Harrah's between January and May, the number jumped to an average of 150 per month during the subsequent months. The theoretical win from these customers also increased accompanied with the increase in offer redemptions. Harrah's calculated the profitability of these programs by comparing the incremental theoretical wins to the incremental cost of the program.

Source: Harrah's Entertainment Inc.

EXHIBIT 2D Loyalty Program (budget upside)—Offer Behavior Change by Offer and Month

Report Period	# of Guests	Hotel %	Red %	# of Trips	Trips per Guest	Days	Days per Trip	Hours	Hours per Day	Theo Win	Observed W(L)	Comp. Amt.	Comp %	Avg. Trip	Avg. Day	Avg. Hour
Jun-99	235	0%	37%	368	1.6	401	1.1	767	1.9	$13,544	$18,011	$88	1%	$37	$34	$18
Jul-99	241	0	33	374	1.6	405	1.1	878	2.2	16,931	15,699	182	1	45	42	19
Aug-99	284	0	26	427	1.5	474	1.1	1,015	2.1	18,710	22,042	233	1	44	39	18
Sep-99	302	0	26	528	1.7	611	1.2	1,247	2.0	23,520	20,004	603	3	45	38	19
Oct-99	578	0	40	1,028	1.8	1,135	1.1	2,109	1.9	28,905	31,918	534	2	28	25	14
Nov-99	267	0	50	577	2.2	649	1.1	1,193	1.8	23,646	39,205	318	1	41	36	20
Dec-99	291	0	75	721	2.5	830	1.2	1,528	1.8	32,105	63,248	668	2	45	39	21
Jan-00	250	0	62	583	2.3	686	1.2	1,228	1.8	27,370	30,952	617	2	60	40	22
Feb-00	247	0	63	581	2.4	679	1.2	1,237	1.8	36,885	39,060	1,550	4	63	54	30
Mar-00	288	0	67	717	2.5	852	1.2	1,529	1.8	43,318	59,028	1,927	4	60	51	28
	3,802	0%	44%	7,025	1.8	7,897	1.1	15,443	2.0	$327,763	$447,149	$8,214	3%	$47	$42	$21

Note: Exhibit 2d tracks a group of customers with an upside budget potential. In October, 578 customers were selected and mailed offers that were redeemable in November, December, and January. In January, these customers were evaluated again as high budget upside and sent additional offers intended to capture a larger share of budget in February, March, and April. Each offer consisted of one coupon per month.

The offers provided an unconditional cash incentive for visiting and a larger play-based incentive to increase play. For example, a customer would receive $5 for visiting and $20 for playing to a $200 level of theoretical wins, $30 for playing to a $300 level, and so forth. The value of the unconditional offer was typically less than they had previously received via direct mail; however, the conditional part was significantly greater—resulting in a direct mail piece that was only slightly more costly to Harrah's, about $15 compared to $10 in the past.

Source: Harrah's Entertainment Inc.

EXHIBIT 2E Retention Program—Offer Behavior Change by Offer and Month

Offer	Report Period	# of Guests	Hotel %	Red %	# of Trips	Trips per Guest	# of Days	Days per Trip	Hours	Hours per Day	Theo Win	Observed W/(L)	Comp Amt.	Comp %	Avg. Theo win per Trip	Avg. win per Day	Avg. win per Hour
	Jul-98	5,980	0%	14%	8,695	1.5	11,079	1.3	27,882	2.5	$1,603,196	$1,691,024	$312,370	19%	$184	$145	$57
	Aug-98	5,041	0	13	7,284	1.4	9,330	1.3	22,962	2.5	1,325,049	1,366,126	209,748	16	182	142	58
	Sept-98	3,098	0	17	4,369	1.4	5,416	1.2	12,791	2.4	705,836	1,008,256	106,832	15	162	130	55
	Oct-98	1,444	1	21	2,272	1.6	2,661	1.2	6,303	2.4	354,198	483,471	55,006	16	156	133	56
	Nov-98	326	2	16	478	1.5	553	1.2	1,213	2.2	63,140	94,869	9,242	15	132	114	52
	Dec-98	10	10	0	14	1.4	16	1.1	25	1.6	1,293	1,729	54	4	92	81	51
	Jan-99	362	4	14	366	1.0	441	1.2	1,086	2.5	60,999	68,786	9,089	15	167	138	58
	Feb-99	3,578	0	22	4,140	1.2	5,325	1.3	12,676	2.4	661,868	803,336	105,703	16	160	124	53
	Mar-99	4,592	0	24	5,659	1.2	7,114	1.3	16,967	2.4	900,992	1,048,778	130,620	14	159	127	53
	Apr-99	4,052	0	22	5,166	1.3	6,597	1.3	16,488	2.5	911,712	1,040,968	123,737	14	176	138	55
	May-99	3,576	0	22	4,637	1.3	5,850	1.3	15,134	2.6	810,873	967,491	114,451	14	175	139	54
	Jun-99	3,325	0	23	4,492	1.4	5,710	1.3	14,113	2.5	806,390	863,057	108,807	13	180	141	57
	Jul-99	3,934	0	21	5,606	1.4	7,074	1.3	18,357	2.6	1,160,901	1,099,528	179,247	15	207	164	63
	Aug-99	3,769	0	20	5,277	1.4	6,827	1.3	17,713	2.6	1,047,831	1,293,718	169,202	16	199	153	59
	Sep-99	3,197	1	20	4,476	1.4	5,737	1.3	15,139	2.6	922,912	1,031,069	124,268	13	206	161	61
	Oct-99	2,882	1	22	3,982	1.4	5,057	1.3	13,743	2.7	760,428	918,241	105,493	14	191	150	65
	Nov-99	2,589	1	21	3,455	1.3	4,397	1.3	11,750	2.7	635,578	815,021	91,749	14	184	145	54
	Dec-99	2,151	1	21	2,834	1.3	3,597	1.3	10,144	2.8	595,359	562,899	71,643	12	210	168	59
Total		53,906	0%	20%	73,202	1.4	92,781	1.3	234,484	2.5	$13,328,555	$15,163,367	$2,027,261	15%	$182	$144	$57

Source: Harrah's Entertainment Inc.

Note: The report shown in Exhibit 2e summarizes the visitation patterns for a group of customers whose patronage was declining in the second half of 1998. These customers had significantly reduced their aggregate frequency to Harrah's casinos. Based on their historical pattern of behavior, Harrah's had expected to see them in December but hadn't.

In order to reinvigorate relationships with these customers, Harrah's sent a direct mail offer to approximately 8,000 customers in January of 1999 that was redeemable in February, March, and April. One cash coupon was sent per month, with the amount varying by customer worth. If these customers returned to Harrah's, they were put into the loyalty-marketing program and managed according to their upside potential. The program seemed to be working even though the cost of the offer had gone up from $30 to $40.

EXHIBIT 2F Consolidation of Play (theoretical win) by Customer

Customer IDs	Q1	Q2	Q3	Q4	1998	Q1	Q2	Q3	Q4	1999	Attrition	New	Change
1	$ 800	$ 700	$ 300	$ —	$1,800	$ 800	$ 900	$ 900	$ 200	$ 2,800	0	0	$1,000
2	—	—	—	—	—	120	—	80	—	200	0	1	—
3	—	60	—	60	120	80	60	—	50	190	0	0	70
4	—	—	—	—	—	—	—	80	—	80	0	1	—
5	—	60	40	60	160	—	—	—	—	—	1	0	—
6	—	60	120	220	400	150	70	80	70	300	0	0	(100)
7	—	40	—	—	40	40	—	50	70	160	0	0	120
8	80	80	—	—	160	60	60	80	80	280	0	0	120
9	—	1,200	2,000	500	3,700	—	2,500	1,500	4,000	8,000	0	0	4,300
10	—	60	—	—	60	20	50	20	50	140	0	0	80
11	80	—	40	80	200	120	80	220	—	420	0	0	220
12	—	40	40	40	120	50	50	50	50	200	0	0	80
13	—	—	—	—	—	—	—	—	150	150	0	1	—
14	800	1,500	1,200	800	4,300	1,100	1,500	1,200	1,400	5,200	0	0	900
15	7,000	2,500	—	—	9,500	5,000	6,000	—	480	11,480	0	0	1,980
16	—	—	—	—	—	—	60	70	70	200	0	1	—
17	—	—	—	—	—	—	40	40	—	80	0	1	—
18	300	400	500	500	1,700	900	900	700	400	2,900	0	0	1,200
19	40	40	—	—	80	50	50	—	—	100	0	0	20
20	50	—	—	50	100	40	40	40	—	120	0	0	20
21	—	30	30	—	60	40	30	30	—	100	0	0	40
22	400	600	—	—	1,000	—	—	280	—	280	0	0	(720)
23	—	1,000	—	—	1,000	—	600	280	—	880	0	0	(120)
24	50	—	—	—	50	100	—	—	150	250	0	0	200
25	2,000	2,000	2,200	1,500	7,700	2,100	2,200	3,000	1,500	8,800	0	0	1,100
26	—	—	—	—	—	60	—	—	—	60	0	1	—
27	30	—	30	50	110	—	—	—	—	—	1	0	—
28	40	40	50	—	130	—	—	—	—	—	1	0	—

29	40	40	–	–	80	20	40	–	40	100	0	0	20
30	–	–	60	60	120	–	–	–	–	–	1	0	–
31	100	–	80	–	180	–	–	80	90	210	0	0	30
32	–	60	30	–	90	40	40	50	40	130	0	0	40
33	30	–	–	100	130	60	–	50	–	160	0	0	30
34	–	–	4,000	2,000	6,000	3,500	50	1,000	–	4,500	0	0	(1,500)
35	50	70	–	–	320	–	–	–	–	–	1	0	–
36	–	–	200	200	200	–	–	600	–	600	0	0	400
37	60	–	40	–	100	40	40	60	80	220	0	0	120
38	–	–	200	–	200	–	240	100	90	430	0	0	230
39	50	–	60	–	110	–	260	–	–	260	0	0	150
40	–	–	–	40	40	60	60	40	–	160	0	0	120
41	120	–	–	–	120	–	–	–	–	–	1	0	–
42	–	–	200	–	200	150	100	80	60	330	0	0	130
43	40	40	60	–	140	–	–	70	60	130	0	0	(10)
44	–	–	–	–	–	70	60	80	–	270	0	1	–
45	400	400	400	500	1,700	800	800	700	500	2,800	0	0	1,100
46	–	40	–	40	80	–	60	70	–	130	0	0	50
47	–	50	–	–	50	40	–	40	260	340	0	0	290
48	–	–	–	–	–	–	–	–	120	120	0	1	–
49	–	–	70	–	70	–	140	70	60	270	1	0	200
50	–	–	–	–	–	–	3,000	1,500	70	4,570	0	1	–
51	40	40	–	–	80	70	70	50	–	190	0	0	110
52	60	120	–	–	180	–	150	–	80	230	0	0	50
53	120	60	60	60	240	–	–	–	–	–	1	0	–
54	40	–	30	–	70	40	50	50	40	180	0	0	110
55	40	60	–	–	100	50	60	90	50	250	0	0	150

(Continued)

EXHIBIT 2F (cont.)

Customer IDs	Q1	Q2	Q3	Q4	1998	Q1	Q2	Q3	Q4	1999	Attrition	New	Change
56	–	–	60	–	60	–	50	–	70	120	0	0	60
57	50	–	–	100	150	40	60	70	70	240	0	0	90
58	60	40	–	–	100	80	–	–	50	130	0	0	30
59	–	–	–	70	70	60	–	–	–	60	0	0	(10)
60	70	–	–	–	70	60	50	–	70	180	0	0	110
61	40	40	–	30	110	50	30	50	50	180	0	0	70
62	50	50	–	–	100	880	500	400	600	2,380	0	0	2,280
63	20	–	–	60	80	40	50	50	70	210	0	0	130
64	30	–	40	–	70	–	–	–	–	–	1	0	–
65	–	–	–	–	–	–	200	200	200	600	0	1	–
66	60	120	200	–	380	70	80	50	100	300	0	0	(80)
67	60	–	120	–	180	220	60	–	220	500	0	0	320
68	150	–	–	80	230	100	140	200	80	520	0	0	290
69	20	–	60	–	80	50	–	80	–	130	0	0	50
70	–	120	–	80	200	200	–	220	–	420	0	0	220
71	40	–	40	40	120	80	50	–	150	280	0	0	160
72	–	40	60	–	100	30	40	50	50	170	0	0	70
73	–	70	–	30	100	–	80	–	–	80	0	0	(20)
74	–	–	–	–	–	150	–	150	–	300	0	1	–
75	60	40	–	50	150	60	100	60	80	300	0	0	150
76	800	400	700	800	2,700	700	800	300	–	1,800	0	0	(900)
77	40	50	100	–	190	–	–	–	–	–	1	0	–
78	–	–	–	–	–	80	–	70	–	150	0	1	–
79	400	–	–	–	400	–	480	–	180	660	0	0	260
80	400	400	–	600	1,400	220	1,500	1,400	–	3,120	0	0	1,720
81	400	–	–	–	400	–	–	–	300	300	0	0	(100)
82	–	–	–	–	–	80	80	80	70	310	0	1	–
83	–	–	–	–	–	80	–	50	–	130	0	1	–

84	—	—	600	—	600	—	—	520	—	—	0	0	(80)
85	—	40	—	40	80	—	—	—	320	—	0	0	240
86	—	—	200	—	200	—	—	—	—	—	1	0	—
87	400	500	—	600	1,500	500	700	600	—	2,400	0	0	900
88	70	200	400	—	670	—	—	500	—	500	0	0	(170)
89	—	3,300	2,200	—	5,500	1,500	1,400	1,500	2,000	6,400	0	0	900
90	400	—	400	—	800	—	—	—	780	780	0	0	(20)
91	60	—	—	30	90	50	50	—	—	100	0	0	10
92	—	—	—	1,000	1,000	320	260	—	—	580	0	0	(420)
93	1,000	—	400	—	1,400	—	—	1,100	—	1,100	0	0	(300)
94	—	600	400	—	1,000	—	—	—	—	—	1	0	—
95	—	—	200	—	200	100	260	—	80	440	0	0	240
96	—	—	50	—	50	40	50	—	60	150	0	0	100
97	—	—	—	1,000	1,000	—	—	—	—	—	1	0	—
98	40	20	30	—	90	40	—	—	120	160	0	0	70
99	—	200	600	—	800	200	—	1,100	—	1,300	0	0	500
100	50	—	—	60	110	—	200	—	—	200	0	0	90
Average	176	176	190	115	656	219	282	221	165	885			
Actives	52	47	45	36	86	60	61	61	52	88			
Max	7,000	3,300	4,000	2,000	9,500	5,000	6,000	3,000	4,000	11,480			
Min	—	—	—	—	—	—	—	—	—	—			
Total	17,630	17,620	18,840	11,530	65,620	21,850	28,200	22,080	16,340	88,470			

Source: Harrah's Entertainment Inc.

	1995	1996	1997	1998	1999
Traditional					
Total Nevada	$ 7,366.4	$ 7,420.2	$ 7,802.7	$ 8,064.1	$ 9,020.5
Las Vegas Strip	3,607.4	3,579.6	3,809.4	3,812.4	4,488.5
Atlantic City	3,747.6	3,814.6	3,905.8	4,032.2	4,164.2
Total	$11,113.9	$11,234.8	$11,708.5	$12,096.3	$13,184.7
Riverboats	$ 4,732.0	$ 5,549.2	$ 6,437.9	$ 7,299.6	$ 8,332.2
Native American	$ 4,175.9	$ 4,731.3	$ 5,779.3	$ 7,890.9	$ 8,426.3
Other	$ 430.3	$ 639.0	$ 772.9	$ 873.9	$ 1,199.8
Total United States	$20,452.1	$22,154.4	$24,698.6	$28,160.7	$31,143.0

EXHIBIT 3 Total Gaming Revenue in the United States, 1995–1999 ($millions)

Source: Gaming Commissions and Merrill Lynch estimates.
Note: Other includes Colorado, Delaware, Detroit, and South Dakota.

his casino operations.[6] In 1939, Harrah opened a bingo parlor in the two-block gambling heart of Reno, Nevada, which had legalized gambling eight years earlier. In 1942, Harrah opened a casino, equipping it with blackjack, a dice table, and 20 slot machines.[7] In 1946, the company, by now called Harrah's, expanded and added roulette to the card and dice tables and began serving liquor. The spotless, glass-fronted, plush-carpeted casino was a sharp contrast to the rough frontier-type betting parlors of the time.

In 1955, Harrah bought a dingy casino on the southern shore of Lake Tahoe, and four years later, he relocated the casino across the highway to create the world's largest single structure devoted to gambling. The new casino had a 10-acre parking lot and an 850-seat theater-restaurant that drew star entertainers. Next, Harrah constructed the highest building in Reno—a 24-story hotel across the street from his casino—and then, in 1973, he opened an 18-story hotel in Lake Tahoe. Every room came with a view of the lake and a marble-finished bathroom.

By 2000, Harrah's Entertainment, Inc., was well-known in the gaming industry and operated casinos in more markets than any other casino company. Harrah's had 21 casinos in 17 different cities, including operations in all five major traditional casino markets (Las Vegas, Lake Tahoe, Laughlin, Reno, and Atlantic City). The company also owned or operated casinos in Joliet and Metropolis, Illinois; East Chicago, Indiana; Vicksburg and Tunica, Mississippi; Shreveport, Lake Charles, and New Orleans, Louisiana; and Kansas City and St. Louis, Missouri. In addition, Harrah's managed a number of Native American casinos located in Arizona, North Carolina, and Kansas.[8] In summary, Harrah's operated land-based, dockside, riverboat, and Indian casino facilities in all of the traditional and most of the new U.S. casino entertainment jurisdictions (see Graphic A).

EARLY STRATEGY

Satre, who joined Harrah's in 1980 as Vice President, General Counsel, and Secretary before becoming CEO in 1984, reflected on his first moves:

> Initially I focused on people more than anything else and I thought that was a sustainable competitive position at that time.

---

[6] Leon Mandel, *William Fisk Harrah, The Life and Times of a Gambling Magnate*, Garden City, NY: Doubleday & Co., 1982, p. 1.
[7] Harrah's Entertainment Inc.
[8] Jason Ader, Mark Falcone, and Eric Hausler, "Outside the Box: Exploring Important Investor Issues—Harrah's Entertainment, Inc.—Reaping the Benefits of Total Rewards," Bear Stearns Equity Research, November 10, 2000.

CHAPTER 3 *Customer Equity Analysis* **129**

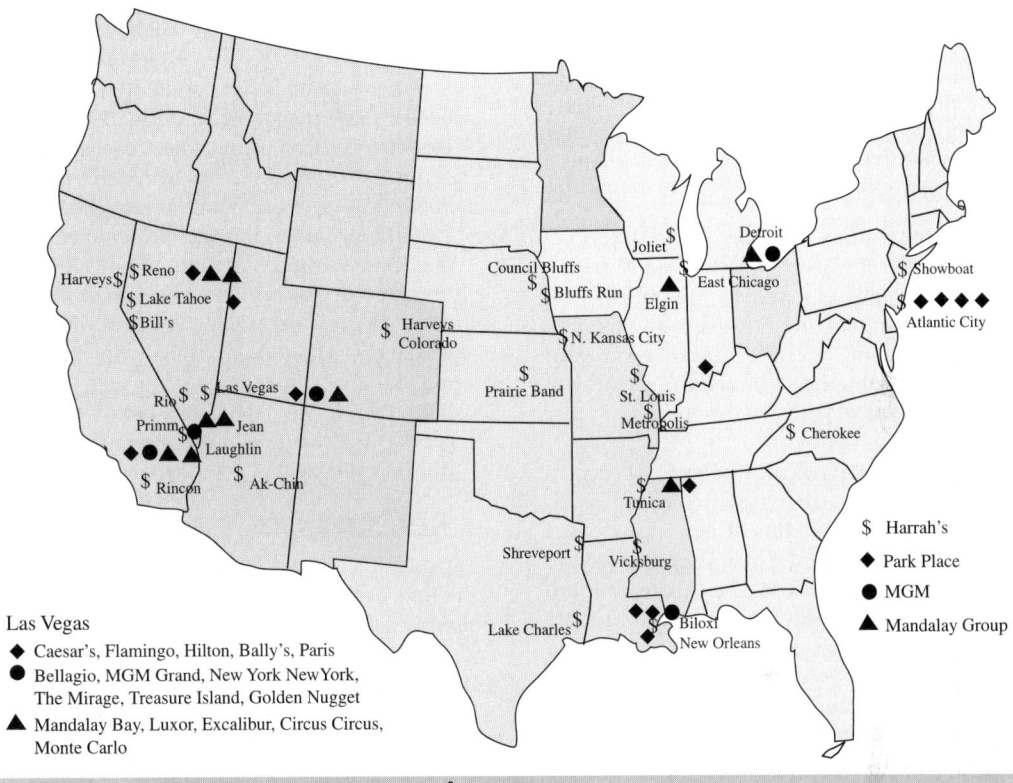

GRAPHIC A Harrah's Operations, early 2000[9]

Las Vegas
- ◆ Caesar's, Flamingo, Hilton, Bally's, Paris
- ● Bellagio, MGM Grand, New York New York, The Mirage, Treasure Island, Golden Nugget
- ▲ Mandalay Bay, Luxor, Excalibur, Circus Circus, Monte Carlo

Legend:
- $ Harrah's
- ◆ Park Place
- ● MGM
- ▲ Mandalay Group

Source: Harrah's.

The strategy seemed to be working in the early 1990s as Harrah's led the way to take advantage of legalized gambling in many states beyond Nevada and New Jersey. These new markets provided Harrah's with explosive growth and a highly profitable business.

I also started a program to communicate with customers who won over a certain amount in our jackpots. I asked them which other casinos they had visited and planned to visit. I was amazed at the amount of cross-market visitation from these customers and yet we received only a small fraction of their gaming dollars when they visited Las Vegas and Atlantic City. At the same time, we were developing rewards programs based on tracking cards (akin to frequent shopper cards) at each of our different properties. The rewards took totally different forms at each property because each property was pretty autonomous.

Satre frequently talked with John Boushy, then the head of marketing/IT, about how much better it would be if customers could use the same loyalty card at every Harrah's location. That way Harrah's would know more about customer play at each property. Harrah's first investment toward this goal was the Winner's Information Network, a national database. The plan was to follow up with both a common card and common analytical tools for making decisions that were based on the data from tracking customers' play.

Customer Loyalty as a Core Competency

By the mid-1990s, competitors had entered the new markets with better and flashier properties. The Mirage in Las Vegas had set

---
[9]Rio and Showboat were Harrah's properties.

a new standard and began to spawn imitators. With no new jurisdictions planning to legalize gambling, Harrah's was facing the formidable task of growing the business in a limited market. Satre realized that the people strategy was not sufficient to grow patronage and play at existing casinos:

> I remember reading *The Discipline of Market Leaders*, which I shared with the management of the company. The book's fundamental thrust was that you could become a leader based on one of three competencies: innovations of product, cost structure, or relationships/customer intimacy.
> We saw MGM and Mirage trying to innovate—creating highly themed environments that had lots of new experiences for their customers. Whether it was the theme park at the MGM or the dolphin tank and the tigers at Mirage.... In the early '90s, these companies were put up on a mantel as the companies to show where the industry was headed. Anyone who came to Las Vegas would say, "you guys [Harrah's] are living in the past." I told them that this would be great if you were starting from scratch, but if you were a 50-year-old company, the capital costs of making "must-see" properties would be enormous.
> While there was great temptation to go down that path because it was exciting to try to design and build, we ultimately decided against it: customer loyalty was really our competency and we decided that we could become an industry leader based on that skill.

But by early 1998, the company's performance was not meeting Satre's expectations. He realized that Harrah's did not have the marketing horsepower to implement the strategy across all properties in a consistent manner. The company had excellent technology and great operations but not effective marketing. He expressed his concerns to Sergio Zyman, then Chief Marketing Officer at the Coca-Cola Company and a noted authority on consumer marketing whom he knew through the Coca-Cola/Harrah's strategic alliance. Satre recalled:

> I went to see Sergio to get references for people that I might hire into a marketing job. He was a quick study, and said, "You are heading in the wrong direction. You don't need a marketing executive. How is your marketing executive going to implement in a company that has a history of autonomous operations and marketing is so tied to your operations strategy? You need a COO who is a marketer—who can implement your marketing, but make sure it goes through all the properties, and that there is no hiccup or interruption between the corporate strategy and what is implemented at the property level.

A NEW APPROACH

Satre turned to Gary Loveman to fill this void. At the time Loveman was on the HBS faculty in the service management area and had worked with Harrah's as a consultant for five years. Satre felt that Loveman would help the company move "from an operations-driven company that viewed each property as a 'standalone business,' to a marketing-driven company with a focus on our target customers and what it took to build their loyalty to the Harrah's brand." The board supported Satre's recommendation to hire Loveman as Harrah's COO. He joined Harrah's in 1998 bringing his atypical range of experience. Loveman described his challenge at Harrah's in the following way:

> In 1998, we were sitting on all this transactional data but not using it effectively. The statistic that jumped out and bit me was that for customers who visited Harrah's once a year or more, we got 36 cents out of their gaming dollar. Hence, they were visiting our competitors and showing remarkably little loyalty to Harrah's. That was the principal anomaly around which we organized everything else, and since then it has been an all-inclusive effort to envelop customers with reasons to be loyal.
> The Total Gold program, launched in Fall 1997, was intended to increase customer loyalty in a variety of ways, and it was supported by a lot of other marketing interventions that all had the same mission. They all

intended, for example, to attract a 60-year-old lady from Memphis, Tennessee, on a Friday night, as she and her husband were thinking about where to go in Tunica, Mississippi, where Harrah's is one of 11 casino alternatives. We wanted people to think "Harrah's, Harrah's, Harrah's" in the same way that they went to the same hairdresser, cobbler, and auto mechanic. All of our tools were a means to that end.

To achieve this goal, Loveman launched four major initiatives: changing the organization structure, building the Harrah's brand, delivering extraordinary service, and exploiting relationship marketing opportunities.

A New Organization Structure

His first priority was to build a new organizational structure. Harrah's division presidents and their subordinates in brand operations, information technology, and marketing services, started reporting to Loveman instead of to the CEO (see Exhibit 4). This emphasized that customers belonged to Harrah's and not simply to one of its casinos. Loveman explained:

Changing the organizational structure was a major accomplishment in light of the fact that historically, as with all our competitors today, each property was like a fiefdom, managed by feudal lords with occasional interruptions from the king or the queen

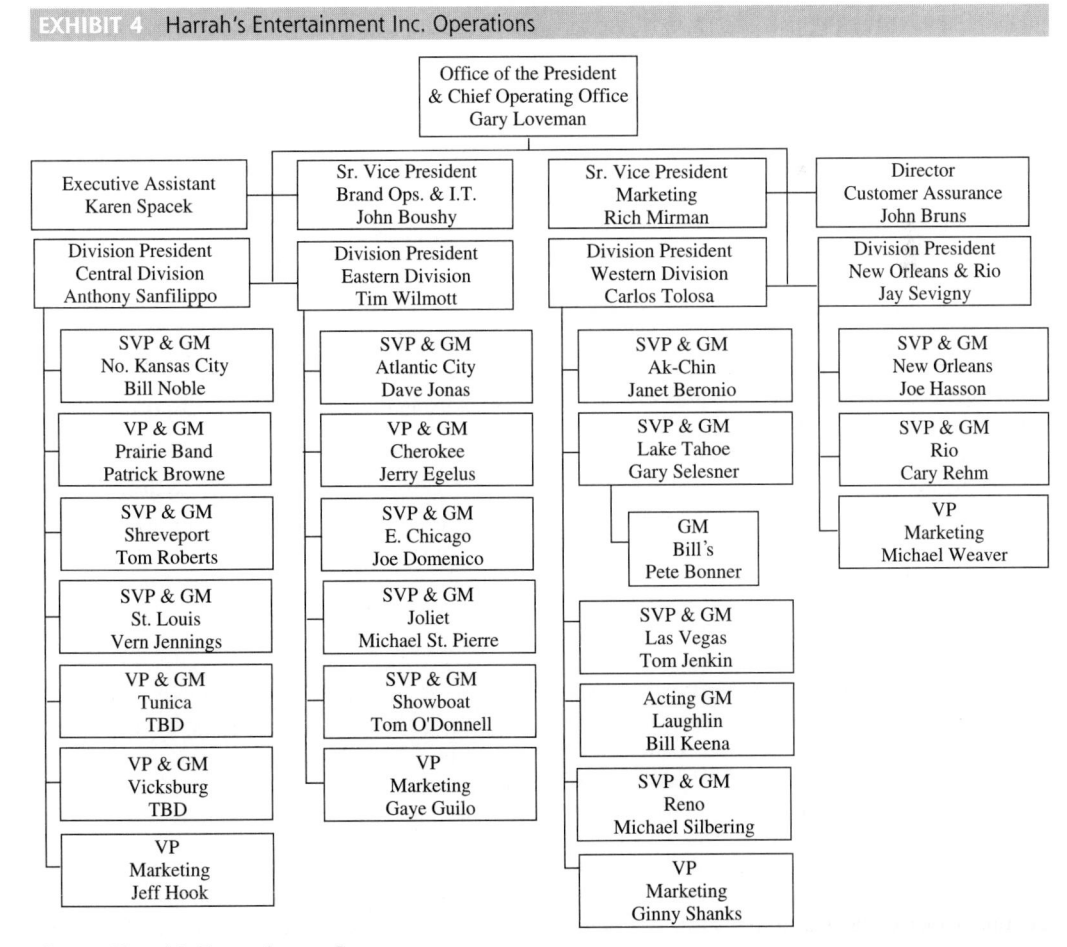

EXHIBIT 4 Harrah's Entertainment Inc. Operations

```
                    Office of the President
                   & Chief Operating Office
                        Gary Loveman

Executive Assistant   Sr. Vice President      Sr. Vice President       Director
   Karen Spacek       Brand Ops. & I.T.          Marketing         Customer Assurance
                        John Boushy             Rich Mirman            John Bruns

Division President    Division President     Division President     Division President
  Central Division     Eastern Division       Western Division      New Orleans & Rio
 Anthony Sanfilippo      Tim Wilmott           Carlos Tolosa            Jay Sevigny

    SVP & GM              SVP & GM               SVP & GM              SVP & GM
  No. Kansas City        Atlantic City            Ak-Chin              New Orleans
    Bill Noble           Dave Jonas           Janet Beronio            Joe Hasson

    VP & GM               VP & GM               SVP & GM               SVP & GM
   Prairie Band           Cherokee              Lake Tahoe                Rio
  Patrick Browne         Jerry Egelus         Gary Selesner            Cary Rehm

    SVP & GM              SVP & GM                                        VP
    Shreveport            E. Chicago               GM                  Marketing
   Tom Roberts          Joe Domenico             Bill's            Michael Weaver
                                               Pete Bonner
    SVP & GM              SVP & GM
     St. Louis              Joliet               SVP & GM
  Vern Jennings       Michael St. Pierre         Las Vegas
                                                Tom Jenkin
    VP & GM               SVP & GM
     Tunica               Showboat              Acting GM
      TBD              Tom O'Donnell             Laughlin
                                                Bill Keena
    VP & GM                 VP
    Vicksburg             Marketing              SVP & GM
      TBD                Gaye Guilo               Reno
                                             Michael Silbering
      VP
    Marketing                                      VP
    Jeff Hook                                   Marketing
                                               Ginny Shanks
```

Source: Harrah's Entertainment Inc.

who passed through town. Each property had its own P&L and its own resource stream, and the notion that you would take a customer and encourage them to do their gaming at other properties was not common practice. It required a lot of leadership from my boss and the people who ran these businesses to adopt this strategy and encourage customers to spend their money at Harrah's locations broadly rather than simply at their property.

Brand and Service

Next, because Harrah's had little meaningful brand differentiation in the casino industry, Loveman set out to develop a brand that had a gaming orientation and was centered on what the research told them was the most profound emotion of gaming—the feelings of anticipation and exuberance. He explained:

> People go to a casino because it makes them feel "exuberantly alive." That is what they are buying. They don't believe that they are going to win on average, but when they win, they have a ball. With every bet, gamblers anticipate the possibility of winning. Many described the adrenaline rush, the high, the pounding of their hearts and the tingling in their bodies that they feel when they were gambling. With every bet, they hoped to be able to sustain the level of fantasy that gambling provided. One gambler stated: "When you look up and you see that it's a hit and that you're going to get paid off, it's a tingling from my toes on up to the top of my head that comes into my body. That's what makes me want to put more money into the machines."

Harrah's research showed casino entertainment provides consumers a momentary escape from the problems and pressures of their daily lives. Gaming customers share the "exuberantly alive" feeling that risk-taking affords the likes of mountain climbers and skydivers, though casinos provide a far safer playing field. "So we focused all of our advertising around the feeling of exuberance," explained a Harrah's manager. Since Loveman's arrival, Harrah's spent $15–20 million per year in advertising to communicate the feeling of anticipation to the general audience.

Improving service was also important to the brand image. Harrah's was known for having the "friendliest employees." However, Loveman believed that the service was good but not distinguished. He recognized the need for better service on his very first night on the casino floor:

> I stopped and asked a gentleman who was playing a slot machine, "How are you doing tonight, sir?" and he said, "Shitty." It dawned on me that my parents had not taken me through the "How are you—shitty" dialogue. I did not know what to say. The same experience was repeated more than once that night and I found myself not wanting to ask that question any more. But that is the world my employees live in every day. Providing service in this environment is tricky because most guests end up losing while playing in a casino. We had not trained our people to deal with these kinds of situations. We wanted to deliver a world-class service experience that would transcend this issue.

Finally, Harrah's put in place a variety of interventions at the employee level—service process design, reward and recognition, measurement of executives—in as pervasive a fashion as possible to make service demonstrably better. Harrah's thereafter won the award for "best service" from *Casino Player*, the magazine of choice in the casino industry, for three years in a row.

Customer Relationship Management

The third and the most important initiative was to implement marketing tools and programs across all Harrah's properties. Loveman disbanded the existing marketing function and rebuilt it with people who preferred slide rules to mock-ups. Richard Mirman, a former University of Chicago math whiz, left Booz Allen & Hamilton to join the new team as Senior Vice President of Relationship Marketing. Under Mirman marketing became a very quantitative undertaking. Loveman explained:

> Customer Relationship Management (CRM) at Harrah's consists of two elements: Database Marketing (DBM) and the Total Gold program. The Total Gold program motivates customers to consolidate their

TABLE A Theoretical Win

Theoretical Win from a Customer per day = A × B × N × H

A = the house advantage on a game (e.g., 6% hold on slot machines)[10]
B = the average bet (e.g., $ 1)
N = the number of bets per hour (a good slot machine player can pull the lever almost 15 times per minute)
H = the number of hours played per day.

Source: Harrah's.

play, and the data collected through the program allows us to execute direct marketing strategies that increase the efficiency and effectiveness of our marketing dollars.

The big innovation by Mirman and his group of "propeller heads" (David Norton, Vice President of Loyalty Marketing and Dave Kowal, Vice President of Loyalty Capabilities and Revenue Management) was development of quantitative models to accurately *predict* "customer worth"—the theoretical amount the house expects to win, over the long term, from a customer based on his level of play (see Table A). Historically, the casino industry had determined customers worth based only on observed play. Our ability to accurately predict play enabled us to begin building relationships with customers based on their future worth, rather than on their past behavior.

While it was simpler to make this prediction for a slot machine player, it was significantly more complicated for table game play. The transactional data collected ever since the launch of the Total Gold card in 1997 was used to build these models and forecast customer worth. Mirman called it Harrah's secret recipe.

Database Marketing (DBM) DBM changed the way Harrah's invested in its customers. Consider the case of Ms. Maranees, reported in the *Wall Street Journal* article, who received invitations to two tournaments, along with vouchers for $200, all courtesy of Harrah's Entertainment Inc. According to Loveman:

These decisions were made using the decision science tools to predict customer worth rather than relying on observed worth from her first visit to the casino. While she would be considered a lousy customer based on her short visit to Harrah's, with the help of the information generated from one visit and one visit alone, Harrah's concluded otherwise by submitting her profile to the database. She was probably a great customer, but a great customer of Harrah's competitors. It makes sense to invest in converting her to a Harrah's customer. In the past, she would not have shown up on the radar screen.

Proactive Marketing: Opportunity-Based Customer Segmentation—As soon as players used their Total Gold cards, Harrah's began to track their play preferences, betting patterns, where they liked to eat in the casino and whether they stayed the night, how often they visited, how much and how long they played. Combined with the basic information contained on the application card, which included birth date and home address, Harrah's could begin to develop a sophisticated customer profile. Harrah's estimated that 26% of players provided 82% of revenues, with avid players spending approximately $2,000 annually.[11]

---

[10] The hold referred to the theoretical amounts a particular machine retains for the house over an extended period. In this case, the machine would theoretically return to the player $94 for every $100 played. Persistent players would eventually lose all their money.

[11] Jason Ader, Mark Falcone, and Eric Hausler, "Outside the Box: Exploring Important Investor Issues—Harrah's Entertainment, Inc.—Reaping the Benefits of Total Rewards," Bear Stearns Equity Research, November 10, 2000, p. 5.

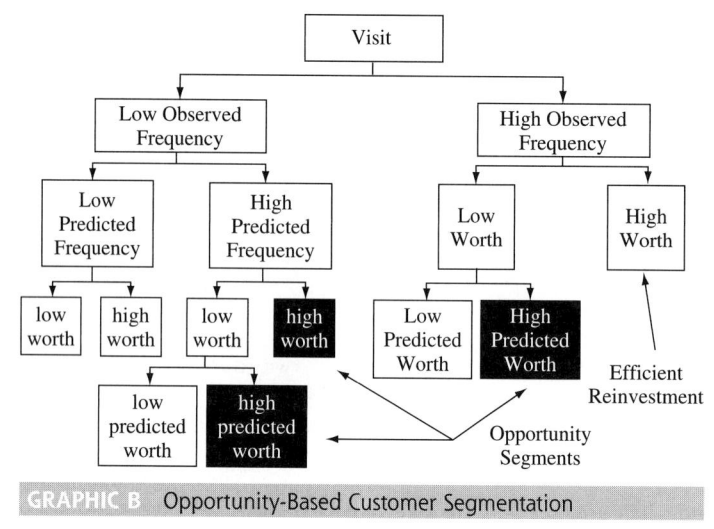

GRAPHIC B: Opportunity-Based Customer Segmentation

Source: Harrah's.

These "avid experienced players" that tended to play in multiple markets became Harrah's target customers.

Using this detailed information for every customer, Harrah's predicted potential customer playing behavior at Harrah's properties. Harrah's compared observed to predicted behavior and identified opportunity segments based on a disparity between predicted and observed values. As shown in Graphic B, there were three key opportunity segments for Harrah's as well as a segment where reinvestment could be rationalized. Harrah's used customized marketing to achieve specific objectives such as driving incremental frequency, budget, or both. (See Exhibit 5 for an overview of the potential messages and types of offers that Harrah's sent to customers. Exhibit 6 provides a typical letter to a customer.)

Marketing Experiments—Harrah's quantitative approach also made it possible to conduct "marketing experiments" and track customers over time. This helped Harrah's discover the right marketing instrument, for the right behavior modification, for the right customer. As an example, Harrah's chose two similar groups of frequent slot players from Jackson, Mississippi. Members of the control group were offered a typical casino-marketing package worth $125—a free room, two steak meals, and $30 of free chips at the casino. Members of the test group were offered $60 in chips. The more modest offer generated far more gambling, suggesting that Harrah's had been wasting money giving customers free rooms.[12] Harrah's tracked the gambling behavior of the customers in the test and control group over the next several months to conclude that the "less attractive" promotion was indeed more profitable. Using such techniques, Harrah's eradicated the practice of "same day cash" at most of its properties—the process by which casinos returned a portion of a customer's bet each day with the hope that the customer would play it. Loveman explained:

As we were looking for incremental business, we thought that giving people things today had no effect on their decisions when they were ready to go gambling again. We used the test and control methodology to gradually ramp back "same day cash" from 5% to zero. We saved half of it and gave back the rest to customers as incentives for the next visit. My operators were convinced that they would have screaming customers. By tracking customers over time, we could show the operators

---

[12]Binkley, op cit.

EXHIBIT 5 Segment Communication Program

Segment Number	Segment Description	Reinvestment	Hotel Coupon	Goal of Contract	Redemption Window	Letter Tone	Letter Messages
1	Local, lodger		no, maybe too high worth only	probably don't mail			note: do not want locals in hotel as there is no incremental value generated
2	Local, nonlodger		no	probably don't mail			note: do not want locals in hotel as there is no incremental value generated
3	New, lodger	normal to high	yes	get back for second trip	longer	introductory	welcome, explain Total Rewards
4	New, nonlodger	highest	yes	get back for a second trip as a lodger	longer	introductory	welcome, explain Total Rewards, want in the hotel, explain why our hotel is the best
5	Existing, 1 trip in last 12 months, lodger	normal	yes	thanks	longer	friendly	thanks, make sure you stay with us on your next trip
6	Existing, 1 trip in last 12 months, nonlodger	higher	yes	thanks	longer	friendly	thanks, want in the hotel, reinforce the hotel as the place to stay
7	Existing, 2+ trips in last 12 months, lodger	normal	yes	thanks	longer	appreciative	thank our best guests
8	Existing, 2+ trips in last 12 months, nonlodger	higher	yes	thanks	longer	appreciative	Thank our best guests, want in the hotel (these guests likely to stay with competitors or be day trip guests)

Source: Harrah's Entertainment Inc.

> Dear Steve,
>
> All of us want you to know how much we appreciate your recent Harrah's visit. It's always gratifying when good, loyal customers like you keep coming back. But the bottom line is, WE WANT YOU TO BRING ALL YOUR PLAY TO HARRAH'S. That way, you'll earn even bigger rewards, more often . . . just by playing at Harrah's. To thank you again for your recent play we've enclosed these valuable rewards. Why settle for less anywhere else?
>
> It may be cold outside, but the action and winning are hotter than ever inside. But don't take our word for it. [Ask Veronica Hale of Goldsby, Oklahoma. She just won $42,468 playing Harrah's one dollar Red, White and Blue slot machine.] At Harrah's you're always a winner when you use your Total [Gold] card. The more you use it, the more you can count on receiving exclusive discounts, comps for meals and hotel stays, even CASH REWARDS near the middle of each month. Right now, you can count on enjoying special happenings like these:
>
> Offer:
>
> Offer:
>
> Remember, nobody rewards loyal players better or bigger than Harrah's. So doesn't it just make good sense to bring even more of your play to Harrah's? After all, the more you play using your Harrah's card, the more it pays. And the sooner you can move up to Harrah's next level of exclusive rewards and recognition. Make the most of your play. Come back to Harrah's now!
>
> Best of Luck Always,
>
> Name
> Vice President and General Manager
>
> P.S.: With all that Harrah's has to offer, just imagine how much greater your rewards could be if you only play Harrah's.

EXHIBIT 6 Sample Letter to Loyal Customers (low actual and high predicted frequency)

Source: Harrah's Entertainment Inc.

that they could eliminate "same day cash" without adversely affecting their business. Today, "same day cash" does not exist anywhere except to a very modest degree at Harrah's Nevada destination properties. Our industry has it everywhere and they advertise against us. The piece that is critical for us is to get our internal folks to recognize that we need to do things that drive incremental revenues.

Harrah's believed it had developed a customer-centric approach to direct marketing. There were three key phases to a customer relationship. The first phase, "new business," was focused exclusively on customers new to the brand or to the property. Harrah's goal with its new business program was to encourage customers to take a second and third trip. The second phase, "loyalty," was focused on customers known for at least six months or three trips. Harrah's goal with its loyalty program was to extend continuously the relationship. The final phase, "retention," was focused on customers who had broken their historical visitation pattern. Harrah's goal with its retention program was to reinvigorate customers who had demonstrated signs of attrition. By using IT and decision science tools, Harrah's developed a variety of direct marketing programs to establish relationships with new customers, strengthen relationships with loyal customers, and reinvigorate relationships with customers who had shown signs of attrition.

Results from Data Base Marketing—Loveman and his team focused on results from the following programs:

- New Business Program

The New Business Program was designed to improve the effectiveness at converting new Total Gold members into loyal customers. The program used predicted customer worth (theoretical wins) to make more effective investment decisions at the customer level—thus allowing the particular offer to be more competitive with what the customer was currently receiving from their existing scenario of choice. This resulted in a more effective and more profitable new business program. Exhibit 2b illustrates the impact of such a program at a property.

- Loyalty Program—Frequency Upside

This program was designed to identify customers that, Harrah's predicted, were only giving Harrah's a small share of their total spending in a particular market. Harrah's capabilities enabled property marketers to develop programs that offered incentives for these customers to visit Harrah's properties more frequently—i.e., switch a trip from a competitor to Harrah's. Exhibit 2c tracks the behavior of a pool of 953 customers before and after the offer was sent in June. Harrah's calculated the profitability of these programs by comparing the incremental theoretical wins to the incremental cost of the program.

- Loyalty Program—Budget Upside

Harrah's also identified customers with budget upside—customers who were only giving a small share of their gaming budget to Harrah's on each trip. In most cases, a customer's allocation of budget was directly related to the order in which they visited casinos on a particular trip—the first stop received the largest share, the second received the second largest, and so on. Therefore, the objective of this program was to encourage the customer to visit Harrah's first and thereby capture the majority of the single casino trips. Exhibit 2d tracks a group of customers with an upside budget potential. Harrah's was less sure if this program was working.

- Retention Program

The objective of Harrah's Retention Program was to reinvigorate customers who had broken their historical visitation pattern or had demonstrated other signs of attrition. Harrah's tested a variety of offers with customer segments to determine how much to reinvest in retaining loyal guests. The report shown in Exhibit 2e summarizes the visitation patterns for a group of customers whose patronage was declining in the second half of 1998. These customers had significantly reduced their aggregate frequency to Harrah's casinos. Based on their historical pattern of behavior, Harrah's had expected to see them in December but hadn't. The effects of the program are evident from tracking the behavior of 8,000 customers who received a direct mail offer in January 1999.

Having worked on the system for more than two years, Mirman and his team recognized that the full potential of these ideas would be realized only if these capabilities could be used at the local property level. Therefore, they made significant efforts in educating the local property managers and their marketing teams about the potential and effective use of these Data Base Marketing capabilities. Mirman and his group had to contend with the fact that marketing efforts at a property were ultimately the responsibility of the property manager and decided on how the Data Base Marketing efforts were integrated with their knowledge of the local market.

Mirman and his team accomplished these goals using a technology platform that was designed to track and manage transactions in casinos. However, it was generally acknowledged that execution of marketing programs based on the most current customer information was possible but required further investments.

The Total Rewards Program The Total Gold program was designed to facilitate and encourage the cross-market visitation patterns of Harrah's customers. Through market research, Harrah's realized that a significant share of business was lost when Harrah's loyal customers visited destination markets like Las Vegas, but did not stay or play at a Harrah's during their visit. Harrah's estimated that more than a $100 million of lost revenue was generated by Harrah's customers in Las Vegas alone. The Total Program was intended to capture this lost business by making it easier for customers to earn and redeem rewards seamlessly at any of Harrah's properties across the country.

To execute Total Gold, Harrah's designed a completely integrated information technology network that linked all their properties together. The network enabled customer level information, like customer gaming theoretical value, to be shared in real time across the various casinos. This technology was then patented so as to bar Harrah's competitors from replicating what Phil Satre believed to be the company's future.

As a result of Total Gold, cross-market revenues (i.e., revenue generated from a customer in a market other than the one they signed up for) have grown significantly—from 13% in 1997 to 23% in 2000. At the Harrah's Las Vegas property alone, cross-market revenue now generates nearly 50% of the property's total revenue. Mirman says, "our cross-marketing effort is what enables our Las Vegas property to compete against properties like the Belaggio and the Venetian (multibillion dollar properties that are right next door to Harrah's Las Vegas). Mirage Resorts spent $1.8 billion to develop Bellagio to attract customers, we developed a distribution strategy that invites customers to our properties. A subtle but powerful difference."

In July 1999, Mirman and his team revamped the program and called it Total Rewards. The motivation behind the change was the realization that even in local markets, Harrah's was only capturing a small share of the customer's gaming budget. The intention was to develop Total Gold into more of a loyalty program that would complement the direct mail strategy described earlier. Mirman added,

> Total Gold was a revolutionary technological innovation, but it lacked a number of the marketing fundamentals necessary to make it a true loyalty program. A loyalty program gives customers the incentive to establish a set of goals and then provides them with a very clear criteria for how to achieve them. Airlines have done a very good job at giving customers the incentive to aspire to earn free travel. Frequent flyer members have been trained to consolidate their travel on a particular airline until they have flown 25,000 miles and earn a free ticket. We wanted our customers to think about earning a complimentary steak dinner or a membership to our tiered card program.

The program is designed to encourage customer loyalty or consolidation of play both within a particular trip and across multiple trips or over the course of a calendar year. To promote the consolidation of play over the course of a trip, The Total Reward program provides a Reward Menu that translates reward credits to the various complimentary offerings. This menu enables customers to understand exactly what compliments are available and exactly what level of play is necessary to earn them. For the annual incentives to drive more frequency, Harrah's added two additional tier levels to the program. Total Rewards became a tiered customer loyalty program, consisting of Total Gold (no minimum customer worth), Total Platinum (theoretical customer worth $1,500 annually), and Total Diamond (theoretical customer worth $5,000 annually). The two programs, represented by different colored plastic cards, have accumulating benefits that are highly valued by the customers. The criteria to earn a membership into the program is based on a customer's annual accumulation of reward credits.

According to Mirman, there was also an emotional component to the Total Rewards program. "We want customers to think . . . I want to go to Harrah's because they know me and they reward me like they know me, and if I went somewhere else they would not."[13] Even though Harrah's knew everything about the customers' gaming behavior, customers were not concerned about privacy issues because they perceived the rewards and mail offers to be valuable to their specific needs. The company awarded 3 billion points during its first year of Total Rewards and had 16 million members in late 1999. Total Rewards seemed to be having an impact on play consolidation based on the theoretical worths described in Exhibit 2f, for a sample of 100 customers.

---

[13]Richard H. Levey, "Destination anywhere. Harrah's Entertainment Inc.'s Marketing Strategy," *Direct*, 1999.

Signing up Customers To encourage sign-ups and play, Harrah's held give-away events for all cardholders at each property. Harrah's gave away houses, cars, million dollar prizes, trips (to great vacation destinations), jewelry, and the like. All one had to do to participate was to enroll in the Total Reward program and play. Customers knew that all these goodies came from the play being recorded.

COMPETITION

Harrah's competed with numerous casinos and casino hotels of varying quality and size. Park Place Entertainment Corporation, with revenues of $2.5 billion, was the industry leader in 1998. A spin-off of Hilton Hotels, it owned 18 casinos and 23,000 hotel rooms, including Paris Las Vegas, Caesars, the Flamingo, Bally Entertainment Casinos, and Hilton Casinos. Park Place's gambling operations included resorts in Las Vegas, Atlantic City, New Orleans, and Biloxi, Mississippi, as well as Australia and Canada. The company seeks to maintain geographic diversity to reduce regional risk and provide more stable income streams. It strives to cluster properties in key locations to control operating expenses, reduce overhead and enhance revenue through cross-marketing. Acquisitions are an integral part of the company's overall strategy and a diverse customer base is served through a variety of properties such as Caesars for the high-end market to the Flamingo for the value segment.

With $1.52 billion in revenues, Mirage Resorts mainly operated casinos in Las Vegas, but the company also had operations and tropical theme parks in Mississippi, New Jersey, and Argentina. Some of its better-known properties were the Mirage, Treasure Island, the Golden Nugget, and the Bellagio. Mirage is the leader in the Las Vegas strip gaming market targeting the upper-middle and premium segments of the market. It controlled approximately 60% of the high-roller market. Its strategy has been to develop high profile "must see" attractions. "We don't think of Mirage Resorts in terms of concrete and marble, games and shows, payrolls and budgets. We strive to create great resorts, each accommodating guests with a distinctive signature of charisma and style."[14] Mirage invests handsomely in its properties because "the presentation assumes that our guests appreciate and warrant fine quality, authenticity, and moments of unexpected, yet delightful grandeur."[15]

In 1998, Circus Enterprises, Inc., had revenues of $1.47 billion and owned about 10 casino resorts, including Circus Circus, the Edgewater, Excalibur, and Luxor. The company had casinos in Nevada, Mississippi, and Illinois. The strategy of the company is well stated in its 1999 annual report. "In Las Vegas, we are designing, piece by piece, spectacle by spectacle, the most ambitious, fully integrated gaming resort complex in the world—a fantasy of castles, glass pyramids, golden skyscrapers and more. One day we will own or control close to 20,000 hotel rooms along a single, continuous mile in the world's leading entertainment destination."[16] The most recent project, Mandalay Bay, was inaugurated on March 2, 1999. The property's attractions include, an 11-acre tropical lagoon featuring a sand-and-surf beach, a three-quarter-mile lazy river ride, a 30,000-square-foot spa and other entertainment attractions.

Trump Hotels & Casino Resorts, Inc., was also among the leaders in the gambling industry with several casinos such as Trump Plaza, Taj Mahal, and Trump Marina, all in Atlantic City, and a riverboat casino on Lake Michigan. Owned by Donald Trump, the casinos had revenues of about $1.4 billion. With no growth in revenues, and $133 million loss on top of the losses in the previous two years, 1999 was not a good year for the company. Donald Trump, chairman, took on the additional responsibility of Acting President and CEO. His stated goal for the company was "to increase profitability by targeting better margin business coupled with a relentless pursuit of cost controls and efficient operations without diminishing the Trump experience our valued customers expect when they visit our properties."[17] The company had a major presence in Atlantic City. With the largest poker room in Atlantic City, the Taj Mahal is

---

[14]Mirage Resorts annual report, 1998.
[15]Mirage Resorts annual report, 1999.
[16]Circus Circus annual report, 1999.
[17]Trump Hotel and Casino annual report, 1999.

a "must-see" property in the Trump portfolio. The Trump Plaza targets the lucrative high-end drive-in slot customer and The Trump Marina is geared toward younger affluent customers but does not exclude its traditional base, middle and upper-middle market segments.

As part of its integrated marketing strategy, the Trump card was an important tool in its portfolio. Gamers were encouraged to register and use their cards at slot machines and table games to earn rewards based on their level of play. The computer systems kept records of cardholders playing preferences, frequency and denomination of play and the amount of gaming revenues produced. The management at the casino provided complimentary benefits to patrons with a demonstrated propensity to wager. A gamer's propensity to wager was determined by their gaming behavior at casinos in Atlantic City. It was important that a patron's gaming activity, net of rewards, was profitable to the casinos. The information collected though the Trump card was also used in sending direct mail offers to customers expected to provide revenues based on their past behavior and were offered more attentive service on the casino floor.[18]

Finally, on the East Coast, Harrah's competed with the largest Native American casino. The Foxwoods Resort and Casino, run by the Mashantucket Pequot tribe in Connecticut, grossed about $1 billion a year. Harrah's faced only local competition in many of the remaining markets.

THE GAMBLE

As Satre stared out the window at the new construction that was taking place at the hotel next door, he tapped his fingers on the dense exhibits and thought about the term "Pavlovian marketing," once used by Mirman to describe these efforts. He hoped the reinvigoration campaign begun with Loveman's hiring would work, because Harrah's needed customer loyalty to stave off the onslaught of entertainment options from the competition. "The farther we get ahead and the more tests we run," Loveman had argued, "the more we learn. The more we understand our customers, the more substantial are the switching costs that we put into place, and the farther ahead we are of our competitors' efforts. That is why we are running as fast as we can." ■

---

[18]Paragraph excerpted from Trump Hotel and Casino's annual report, 1999.

CHAPTER 4

Measuring Customer Equity

We have thus far described how to use customer equity as a strategic tool, but for this approach to be truly effective, it is necessary to know how to put the approach into practice by measuring customer equity. In this chapter, we explore the customer equity model in more detail, and show how to implement it in practice.

◆ BRAND SWITCHING AND CUSTOMER LIFETIME VALUE

Marketing activities are designed to influence customer perceptions and actions. In terms of the customer equity approach, a marketing activity should produce an improvement in at least one of the drivers of customer equity. This will lead to improvements in customer perceptions, which will lead to an improvement in customer attraction and retention. If customers are more likely to be acquired and retained, this will lead to an increase in customer equity and customer lifetime value.[1] To incorporate both customer acquisition and retention into the same model, we must consider the idea of *brand switching*.

Brand marketers have long known that an important factor in brand profitability was the extent to which their customers repurchased, and the extent to which they could lure customers away from market competitors. We begin, then, with the idea that competition can have an influence on a customer's purchase decision. Therefore, it is

---

[1]For more information on the link between marketing actions and customer perceptions, see Duncan I. Simester, John R. Hauser, Birger Wernerfelt, and Roland T. Rust, "Implementing Quality Improvement Programs Designed to Enhance Customer Satisfaction: Quasi-experiments in the U.S. and Spain," *Journal of Marketing Research* 37 (February 2000): 102–112. For research investigating the link between improving customer acquisition and retention and improving customer lifetime value, see the following: Jacquelyn S. Thomas, "A Methodology For Linking Customer Acquisition to Customer Retention," *Journal of Marketing Research* 38; no. 2 (2001): 262–68; Peter Danaher, and Roland T. Rust, "Indirect Financial Benefits from Service Quality," *Quality Management Journal*, 3, no. 2 (1996): 63–75; Fredrick Reichheld, *The Loyalty Effect: The Hidden Force Behind Growth, Profits, and Lasting Value* (Boston: Harvard Business School Press, 1996); and Paul D. Berger and Nada I. Nasr, "Customer Lifetime Value: Marketing Models and Applications," *Journal of Interactive Marketing* 12 (Winter, 1998): 17–30. For additional insight into the relationship between customer attraction, customer retention, and customer equity, see Robert C. Blattberg and John Deighton, "Manage Marketing by the Customer Equity Test," *Harvard Business Review*, 74 (July–August 1996): 136–44; and Robert C. Blattberg, Gary Getz, and Jacquelyn S. Thomas, *Customer equity: Building and Managing Relationships as Valuable Assets* (Boston: Harvard Business School Press, 2001).

important to consider the customer's likelihood of purchasing the focal brand and competitive brands when thinking about customer lifetime value. However, many early models of customer lifetime value examined customer potential future purchase behavior without considering competing brands. By including information about the focal brand *and* competing brands, the resulting model can include both customer acquisition (attraction) and retention in the context of brand switching.[2] This enables firms to model customer flows from one competitor to another, analogous to brand switching models in consumer packaged goods.[3] Therefore, competitive effects can be modeled, yielding a fuller, more accurate accounting of customer lifetime value and customer equity. This approach also allows for two typical customer behaviors that traditional models cannot incorporate: (1) customers who leave a firm and then return—a migration model,[4] and (2) customers who typically purchase consistently from multiple firms—a share-of-wallet approach.

With this in mind, consider a specific example. Suppose Alpha Corporation has a customer, Anna. If Anna bought from Alpha last time, there is a probability (say, 0.8) that she will come back to purchase from Alpha the next time. If she bought from Beta Corporation last time, then there is some probability (say, 0.3) that she would buy from Alpha the next time, and some probability (say, 0.6) that she would again buy from Beta. If there are three firms in the market—Alpha, Beta, and Gamma—then the switching matrix might look like Figure 4-1. The switching matrix gives the probability that Anna will purchase a particular brand, given a particular purchase the previous time.

If we know which brand Anna purchased last (say, Alpha), and what her switching matrix is, then it is possible to project the probability of Anna's purchasing a particular brand for any of her future purchases. For example, if Anna bought from Alpha last time, then the switching matrix says that the probabilities of her next purchase are 0.8 for Alpha, .1 for Beta, and .1 for Gamma. For the following purchase, her probability of choosing Alpha is $[(0.8 \times .8) + (.1 \times .3) + (.1 \times .1)] = .68$. The first term says that she bought from Alpha and then Alpha again. The second term is a purchase from Beta, followed by a purchase from Alpha, and the third term is a purchase from Gamma followed by a purchase from Alpha. We can do a similar calculation for the probabilities of Beta and Gamma on the second purchase. Furthermore, we can also do a similar computation for the third purchase, fourth purchase, and so on. Notice that although Anna's brand switching matrix stays the same, her probabilities of purchase change. This happens because purchase is "sticky," in that purchasing a brand one time typically increases the probability of purchasing that brand next time.

---

[2]Alternative approaches [e.g., Robert C. Blattberg and John Deighton, "Manage Marketing by the Customer Equity Test," *Harvard Business Review* 74 (July-August 1996): 136–44; and Robert C. Blattberg, Gary Getz, and Jacquelyn S. Thomas, *Customer Equity: Building and Managing Relationships as Valuable Assets* (Boston: Harvard Business School Press, 2001)] examine the trade-offs of allocating resources either to attraction or retention. However, as many expenditures affect both attraction and retention, the brand switching approach can provide a view that is both more comprehensive (as it includes competition) and more granular, as it enables the firm to examine the effects of specific marketing actions on customer lifetime value.

[3]See, for example, William F. Massy, David B. Montgomery, and Donald G. Morrison, *Stochastic Models of Buying Behavior* (Cambridge, MA: MIT Press, 1970).

[4]See Dwyer F. Robert, "Customer Lifetime Valuation to Support Marketing Decision Making," *Journal of Direct Marketing*, 3 no. 4 (1989): 8–15; and Paul D. Berger and Nada I. Nasr, "Customer Lifetime Value: Marketing Models and Applications," *Journal of Interactive Marketing* 12 (Winter 1998); 17–30.

	To			
From		Alpha	Beta	Gamma
	Alpha	.8	.1	.1
	Beta	.3	.6	.1
	Gamma	.1	.2	.7

FIGURE 4-1 The Brand Switching Matrix

Knowing the probabilities of purchase is not enough to figure out customer lifetime value. One must also factor in the average purchase rate per unit time, the average purchase volume per purchase, and the expected contribution margin per purchase. We also need to know the company's investment horizon and its discount rate.

◆ BOX 4-1 ◆

Avis U.K.'s Customer Equity Efforts

Automobile rental agency Avis is launching customer management initiatives to help improve customer satisfaction and the effectiveness of its direct marketing efforts. Avis U.K. is planning to integrate information gathered in the customer complaint process with basic customer information. Information regarding customer complaints will be gathered from five channels: e-mail, fax, letter, telephone, and the Internet, and will provide a deeper understanding of customer needs. More detailed customer information will enable Avis to segment its customers and create customer profiles, which will improve the effectiveness of future direct marketing efforts in the United Kingdom.

Avis measures customer loyalty each year by having its customers rate those factors they feel are important, such as service quality, price, safety of its fleet, and convenience. This knowledge allows Avis to track those improvements that will be most effective in increasing customer satisfaction. For example, the Avis Preferred program was created to cater to those customers who rent frequently and value speed of exchange over the other factors. This program, which has over a million members, also enables Avis to look at the buying behavior of its customers. Avis carefully manages the customer experience to deliver excellent service, which drives customer satisfaction and loyalty, and has helped Avis improve market share in its airport segment.

Sources: Thomas Mucha, "The Payoff for Trying Harder," *Business 2.0,* July 2002. Michael Rosser, "Avis to Field All Contact Through e-CRM System," *Precision Marketing*, July 27, 2001.

To give a simple example of how customer lifetime calculations work, let's assume that the firm's investment horizon is two years, and Anna purchases every other year. From Figure 4-1 we know that the probabilities of purchase for Anna this year (given that she purchased Alpha last time) are 0.8 for Alpha, 0.1 for Beta, and 0.1 for Gamma. If she purchases Alpha this year, then in two years the probabilities of purchase would again be 0.8 for Alpha, 0.1 for Beta, and 0.1 for Gamma. If she instead purchases Beta this year, then the probabilities in two years would be (the second row of Figure 4-1) 0.3 for Alpha, 0.6 for Beta, and 0.1 for Gamma. If she instead purchases Gamma this year, then the probabilities in two years would be (row three of Figure 4-1) 0.1 for Alpha, 0.2 for Beta, and 0.7 for Gamma. By multiplying the probabilities, we can then ascertain that Anna's probabilities of purchase in two years are $(.8 \times .8) + (.1 \times .3) + (.1 \times .1) = .68$ for Alpha, $(.8 \times .1) + (.1 \times .6) + (.1 \times .2) = .16$ for Beta, and $(.8 \times .1) + (.1 \times .1) + (.1 \times .7) = .16$ for Gamma.

That tells us Anna's brand choice probabilities, but how much are those potential purchases worth? Let us suppose that the firm uses a discount rate of 10 percent per year, that Anna purchases one unit each time, and that the contribution to profit from a unit is $50. Let us consider Anna's customer lifetime value to brand Alpha. They have an 80 percent chance of getting her first purchase, which means an expected contribution of $50 × .80 = $40. Anna's second purchase will be in two years, again with $50 contribution, but this time there is only a 68 percent chance that Anna will purchase from Alpha, leading to an expected contribution of $50 × .68 = $34. But remember that that purchase is in two years, meaning that the amount needs to be discounted by a factor equal to $(1 + \text{discount rate})^{-2} = (1.10)^{-2} = .826$. This means that Alpha's expected contribution in two years is worth $34 × .826 = $23.21. Adding up the contributions from Anna's purchases, Anna's customer lifetime value to Alpha is $40 + $23.21 = $63.21.

We can use these ideas to obtain a general formula for the customer lifetime value of any customer. To show how this formula works, let's relate it to Anna's example. Let B_{jt} be the probability that Anna buys brand j in purchase t (for brand Alpha, the B_{jt}'s are .8 for $t = 0$ and .68 for $t = 1$, where t indexes the purchase. Let v_j be her average purchase volume when buying brand j (= 1 for Anna), f is her frequency of purchase (= .5 for Anna), π_j is the average contribution per unit when Anna purchases brand j ($50 in this case), T_j is the expected number of purchases that Anna will make before firm j's time horizon (= 2 in this case), and d_j is firm j's discount rate (.10), then Anna's customer lifetime value to firm j can be estimated to be:

$$CLV_j = \sum_{t=0}^{T_j}(1 + d_j)^{-t/f} v_j p_j B_{jt}$$

This formula results in exactly the same calculation that we did for Anna, but it is written in a very general way, so that any customer's lifetime value can be calculated.[5]

Firm j's customer equity is defined as the sum of the customer lifetime values across all of the market's customers (if we want to get fancy, we can consider both current and future customers). This can be estimated from a representative sample of the customers

---

[5]Note that this approach to incorporating frequency of purchase into customer lifetime value is also utilized in Rajkumar Venkatesan and V. Kumar, "A Customer Lifetime Value Framework for Customer Selection and Resource Allocation Strategy," *Journal of Marketing* (forthcoming).

in the market. To simplify, suppose there are two customers in the sample—Anna ($63.21 lifetime value) and Bill ($48.97 lifetime value). Our estimate of the average lifetime value of Alpha's customers is then ($63.21 + $48.97)/2 = $56.09. Suppose that Alpha's market has 20,000 customers. That being the case, Alpha's estimated customer equity is the average customer lifetime value multiplied by the number of customers ($56.09 × 20,000) = $1,121,800. Expressing this as a general formula, if we have customers i from the sample, firm j's customer equity, CE_j, is estimated as

$$CE_j = \text{mean}_i(CLV_{ij}) \times POP$$

where $\text{mean}_i(CLV_{ij})$ is firm j's average lifetime value for customers i across the sample ($56.09 in this case), and POP is the total number of customers in the market, across all brands (20,000 in this case).[6]

MODELING THE SWITCHING MATRIX

From the previous section we see that modeling the switching matrix goes a long way toward figuring out customer lifetime value and customer equity. From a managerial standpoint, it is now important to realize that the switching matrix is partially under the firm's control. For example, if the firm improves its service, that will likely result in a higher customer retention rate. In other words, Alpha Corporation might increase Anna's probability of repurchasing Alpha from 0.8 to perhaps .85 or .90. In the case of many customers, this would mean a lot of money to Alpha. But how much would the switching probabilities change?

Again, we look for ideas from the traditional marketing literature. Marketing has long modeled choice in terms of the utility of the competing options, consistent with economic theory. A popular way of doing this is known as logit regression.[7] In words, we assume:

Pr (brand j) = [exp(utility of brand j] / [sum {exp(utility)} across all brands]

Let us consider i. Let U_{ijk} be the utility of brand k to customer i, given that he or she most recently purchased brand j. Let $LAST_{ijk}$ be a variable that is equal to 1 if $j = k$, and otherwise is equal to zero. Let X_{ikl} be drivers of firm k's utility to customer i, and let β_0 and β_{ikl} be logit regression coefficients. Then our expression for utility is

$$U_{ijk} = \beta_{0k} LAST_{ijk} + \sum_l b_{ikl} X_{ikl} + \varepsilon_{ijk}$$

where ε_{ijk} is an error term assumed to have a special distribution, known as "extreme value." Expressing this in words, we have

Utility = Inertia effect + Effect of drivers + Random error

---

[6]Recent research suggests that there is a strong link between customer equity and overall firm value; see Sunil Gupta, Donald R. Lehmann, and Jennifer A. Stuart, "Valuing Customers," *Journal of Marketing Research* 41 (February 2004): 7–18.

[7]Logit models were first made popular in marketing modeling the effects of marketing mix variables on brand choice [see, for example, Peter M. Guadagni and John D. C. Little, "A Logit Model of Brand Choice Calibrated on Scanner Data," *Marketing Science* 2 (Summer 1983): 203–238)].

with the drivers being drivers of value equity, brand equity, and relationship equity. Because utility is something that occurs differently for each individual customer, each customer will also have his or her own separate switching matrix and customer lifetime value.

RETURN ON INVESTMENT

We have seen that customer equity is summed up over the customer lifetime values of individual customers, customer lifetime value is driven in large part by the brand switching matrix, the brand switching matrix is driven by brand utility, and brand utility is driven by drivers of value equity, brand equity, and relationship equity. As marketing managers, we would like to make marketing investment decisions that pay off. Suppose, for example, that we are considering increasing service quality, a driver of value equity. There will be a cost of making the improvement, perhaps made up of an up-front expenditure, plus ongoing expenditures. Using standard calculations from finance, we can fairly easily figure out the net present value of our expenditures. But how do we figure out whether the expenditure will pay off?

The key is to project how much a particular driver (e.g., customer ratings of service quality) will increase if we make the expenditure. This can be done either by managerial judgment (guesswork guided by experience), by comparison with similar historical changes, or by using a test market or partial roll-out to get a more precise estimate. Once we know how much the driver will improve, we can then track the effect through the chain of effects shown in Figure 4-2. The mathematics of doing this is not difficult, but it is very involved and tedious. For this reason, researchers have developed computer software that can make many of the calculations automatically. Case 4-1 at the end of the chapter gives you the opportunity to try out such software to analyze customer equity in the airlines industry.

CROSS-SECTIONAL VERSUS LONGITUDINAL DATA

To get the customers' appraisals of the drivers, we need to collect survey data similar to those collected for customer satisfaction surveys. In the survey, we need to collect all of the information (e.g., purchase volume, purchase frequency, most recent brand purchased, purchase intentions, etc.) required to estimate customer lifetime value.

Even better than getting past purchase and purchase intention data, though, would be to observe customers' behavior over time. If the purchase history could be connected with the customers' appraisal of the drivers, then we would eliminate any potential bias with respect to intentions being different from behavior. Such longitudinal panel data are occasionally available (keep in mind that we need data from the customers of all firms in the market), but that is rare. If we do not have such data, then it may be advisable to seek to calibrate the intentions data by comparing their predictions to actual sales data, either for a sample of customers, or in the aggregate.

Suppose a major restaurant chain wants to analyze its customer equity and project the return on investment that might result from particular marketing initiatives. The first thing that the organization must do is to conduct exploratory research that will permit the chain to identify the drivers of value equity, brand equity, and relationship equity.

FIGURE 4-2 Return on Marketing

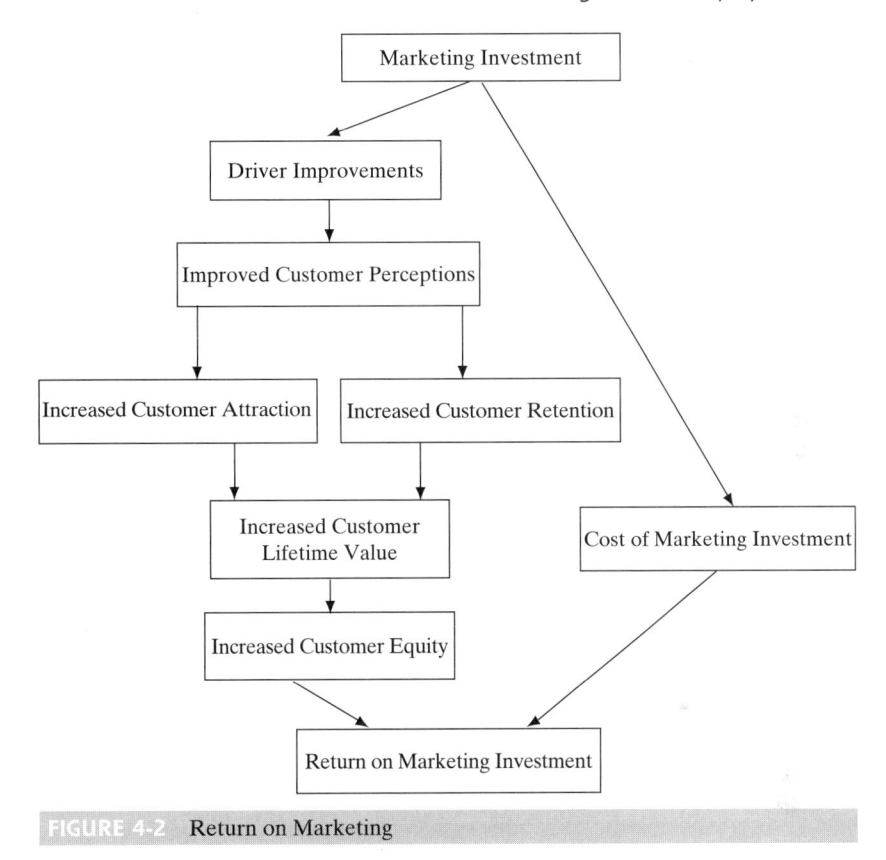

```
Marketing Investment
    │
    ├──────────────┐
    ▼              │
Driver Improvements│
    │              │
    ▼              │
Improved Customer Perceptions
    │       │      │
    ▼       ▼      │
Increased   Increased
Customer    Customer
Attraction  Retention
    │       │      │
    └───┬───┘      ▼
        ▼      Cost of Marketing Investment
    Increased Customer
    Lifetime Value
        │          │
        ▼          │
    Increased Customer Equity
        │          │
        ▼          ▼
    Return on Marketing Investment
```

The chain conducts a series of focus group interviews to find out what is important to customers within each of the three drivers of customer equity. Figure 4-3 shows an illustrative set of drivers for the restaurant chain. Note that all of the drivers are actionable. For example, the chain might improve its offerings by buying better quality ingredients. Restaurant visibility might be improved by running more ads. Frequent buyer cards might be touted by signage or by having the waitstaff solicit such business at checkout. Individual survey items would be based on each of the drivers. For example, food quality might be measured by asking customers to rate the following statement on a scale of 1 to 5 (5 = strongly agree to 1 = strongly disagree); The quality of food at this restaurant is excellent.

Next, decisions regarding data sampling need to be made. If secondary data are to be used, then the firm needs a list, at least in principle, of customers within the industry (or just a list of the population, if the product is used by a high proportion of the population). Good statistical practice requires that a "probability sample" be employed—that is, there should, at least in principle, be a known probability of selection for everybody in the population.[8] Random sampling of one form or another is then used to draw the sample.

---

[8] For detailed descriptions of appropriate sampling procedures, see David A. Aaker, V. Kumar, and George S. Day, *Marketing Research,* 8th ed., (New York: Wiley Text Books, 2003).

> ### ◆ BOX 4-2 ◆
>
> ## Vail Resorts Uses Research to Capture Customers
>
> Vail Resorts, Inc., is one of the premier resort operators in North America, with reparate business units focusing on mountain operations, lodging, and real estate. Serving over 1.6 million guests annually in Vail, Colorado, alone, the company seeks to optimize and customize guest experiences by compiling customer data and using them to improve service. With a significant portion of its revenues generated by repeat customers, it has become a company priority to build stronger and more profitable relationships with these customers. A focus on customer management has enabled Vail Resorts to evolve and change according to customer preferences and to market to a targeted audience with customized service offerings and promotions.
>
> Information technology systems are in place across the company's properties that compile data such as ticket sales, lodging reservations, restaurant visits, conference events, retail sales, ski school bookings, and rental equipment transactions. DataStage, a leading data integration solution software package that is also Vail Resort's CRM software, aggregates this information and sends it to the customer data warehouse. Marketing managers then use these data to profile groups of guests and identify preferences and trends, allowing Vail Resorts to reach new and existing guests with additional service offerings.
>
> Vail Resorts also utilizes customer management technology to optimize the online visitor experience. Online behavior, such as which Web pages are viewed, is closely monitored by NetGenesis software. This information has allowed the company to change the way the Web site is designed, and has enabled Vail Resorts to refine its marketing campaigns. In better understanding online visitors, the company can also better communicate with customers off-line.
>
> Through the implementation and utilization of customer management strategies, Vail Resorts has been able to compile quality customer information that will allow the company to better serve and market to its more than 4 million annual visitors.
>
> ---
>
> *Sources:* "Vail Resorts Fuels Continued Market Expansion with Ascential's Enterprise Data Integration Platform," *PR Newswire,* May 20, 2002. "CustomerCentric Solutions Enables Vail Resorts to Measure Online Customer Behaviors and Trends," *PR Newswire,* June 17, 2002. "New Technology at Vail Resorts Takes Online Booking to New Heights," *Business Wire,* October 7, 2002. Vail Resorts, Inc., *2001 Annual Report.*

Given the results of the survey, we estimate the choice model. Table 4-1 shows the logit regression coefficients for the drivers. The coefficients and their significance yield a lot of useful information. We see, for example, that inertia plays a large role in restaurant choice. Service quality, food quality, and dining room atmosphere are important drivers of value equity at this restaurant chain, whereas price and speed are not. All of the brand equity drivers are important, including sensitivity to minority groups. Among the relationship equity drivers, that waitstaff know the customers' names appears especially important.

Suppose that management now wishes to investigate the likely return on investment from improving service quality, the driver with the largest Z-score. If a service training program costs $4.5 million, discounted, and will produce an estimated average improvement of 0.5 in the service quality rating, does this pay off or not? Suppose the customer equity calculations say that customer equity will increase by $5.0 million if

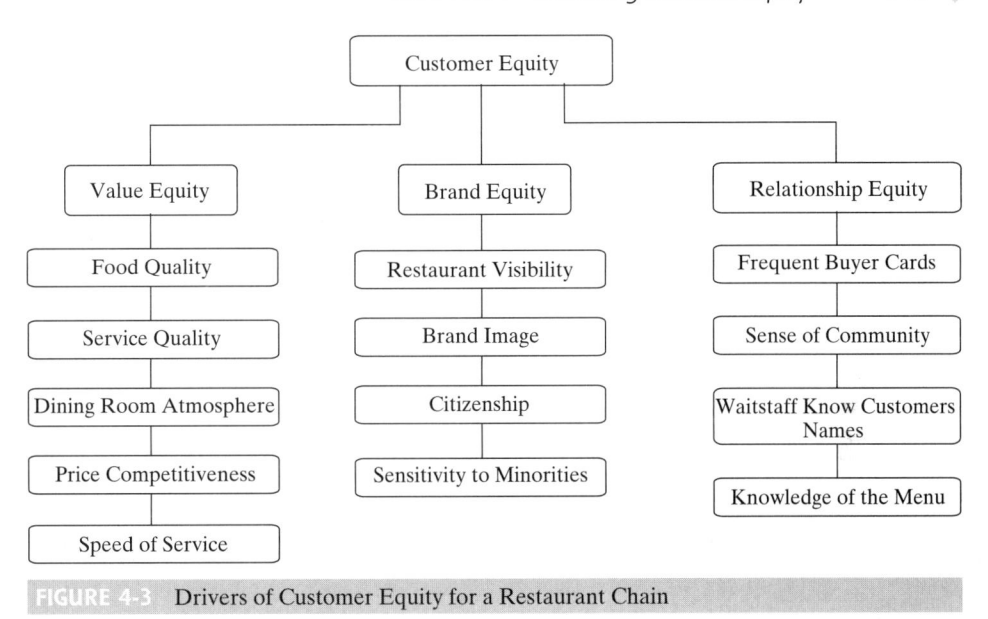

Drivers of Customer Equity for a Restaurant Chain

FIGURE 4-3 Drivers of Customer Equity for a Restaurant Chain

```
                          Customer Equity
          ┌──────────────────┼──────────────────┐
     Value Equity        Brand Equity      Relationship Equity
          │                  │                  │
     Food Quality      Restaurant Visibility   Frequent Buyer Cards
          │                  │                  │
     Service Quality      Brand Image         Sense of Community
          │                  │                  │
   Dining Room Atmosphere  Citizenship    Waitstaff Know Customers Names
          │                  │                  │
   Price Competitiveness  Sensitivity to Minorities  Knowledge of the Menu
          │
     Speed of Service
```

the training program is implemented, and the .5 average improvement in service quality materializes. Then this implies a return on investment of

$$\text{ROI} = (\Delta CE - E) / E = (\$5.0 \text{ million} - \$4.5 \text{ million}) / \$4.5 \text{ million} = 11.1\%$$

Based on this projection, the service improvement program will pay off, and it was the careful analysis of the logit regression results that enabled us to target a potentially profitable marketing investment.

TABLE 4-1 Driver Coefficients

	Driver	Coefficient	Standard Error	Z-Score
	Inertia	0.79	0.07	11.34*
Value equity	Food quality	0.16	0.025	6.58*
	Service quality	0.5	0.063	7.93*
	Dining room atmosphere	0.39	0.09	4.35*
	Price competitiveness	0.05	0.046	1.02
	Speed of service	−0.04	0.007	−0.65
Brand equity	Ad awareness	0.29	0.075	3.86*
	Brand image	0.17	0.024	7.15*
	Community citizenship	0.24	0.056	4.23*
	Sensitivity to minorities	0.20	0.038	5.19*
Relationship equity	Frequent buyer cards	0.00	0.01	−0.23
	Sense of community	0.01	0.026	0.45
	Knows my name	0.18	0.034	5.38*
	Knowledge of menu	0.06	0.028	2.12*

Summary

Managing according to customer equity requires measurement. We must know the relative importance of the customer equity drivers in driving choice, and the impact of choice on the brand switching matrix, customer lifetime value, and customer equity. Careful modeling enables us to model the chain of effects and do what-if projections of the ROI that will result from marketing investments. This makes marketing financially accountable and enables competing marketing initiatives to be evaluated on an equal basis.

Review Questions and Exercises

1. What are some examples of customer management programs used in the service industry to prevent customer defection? How do such programs function to increase customer lifetime value?
2. How can rental car companies such as Avis use customer data to better service their current customers and to attract new ones? What opportunities are there for joint customer management ventures that might prove useful to a rental car company and a partner organization?
3. Describe a situation in which a longitudinal study might be more appropriate and a situation in which a cross-sectional might be more appropriate.
4. *Customer Lifetime Value Exercise*. Consider the customer lifetime value example in this chapter. Consider a second customer, Sam, who also considers purchasing from Alpha, Beta, and Gamma. His brand switching matrix appears in Figure 4-4.
    a. Given the information provided here (and in Figure 4-4), calculate Sam's customer lifetime value to Beta.
        - Sam purchases with the same frequency as Anna (every other year).
        - Sam purchases one unit each time.
        - The contribution from each unit is $100.
        - The firm's discount rate is 10 percent.
    b. Beta Corporation has done a customer segmentation study and has determined that there are approximately 12,000 customers in their market who share the same purchasing behaviors (and switching matrix) as Sam. What is the value, in terms of customer equity, of this customer segment?

FIGURE 4-4 Sam's Brand Switching Matrix

From \ To	Alpha	Beta	Gamma
Alpha	.4	.4	.2
Beta	.1	.6	.3
Gamma	.1	.4	.5

Case 4-1 Aerosphere Airlines (A)

Roland T. Rust, Katherine N. Lemon, and Valarie A. Zeithaml

(Accompanies Customer Equity Driver Software)

William Tindall is the chief marketing officer for Aerosphere Airlines, one of the nation's major carriers. Every day he worries about how to maintain a marketing edge against his main competitors, Dynasty Airlines, Shark Airlines, and Ultra Airlines. Aerosphere, Dynasty, and Ultra have similar business models, reflecting a higher concern for service, and Shark positions itself more as a low-price, low-cost carrier.

The case was prepared by Roland T. Rust, Katherine N. Lemon, and Valarie A. Zeithaml. Copyright © Roland T. Rust, Katherine N. Lemon and Valarie A. Zeithaml 2003.

To figure out the current competitive position of the airlines, and to help set strategy, Tindall commissioned a customer equity study of the industry. This began with focus group interviews with customers to figure out the drivers of value equity, brand equity, and relationship equity. Based on the focus groups results, Tindall came up with the customer equity driver diagram shown in Figure A-1. The diagram was intentionally simplified (compared to, for example, Figure 4-3) because previous research had indicated that these variables were by far the most important.

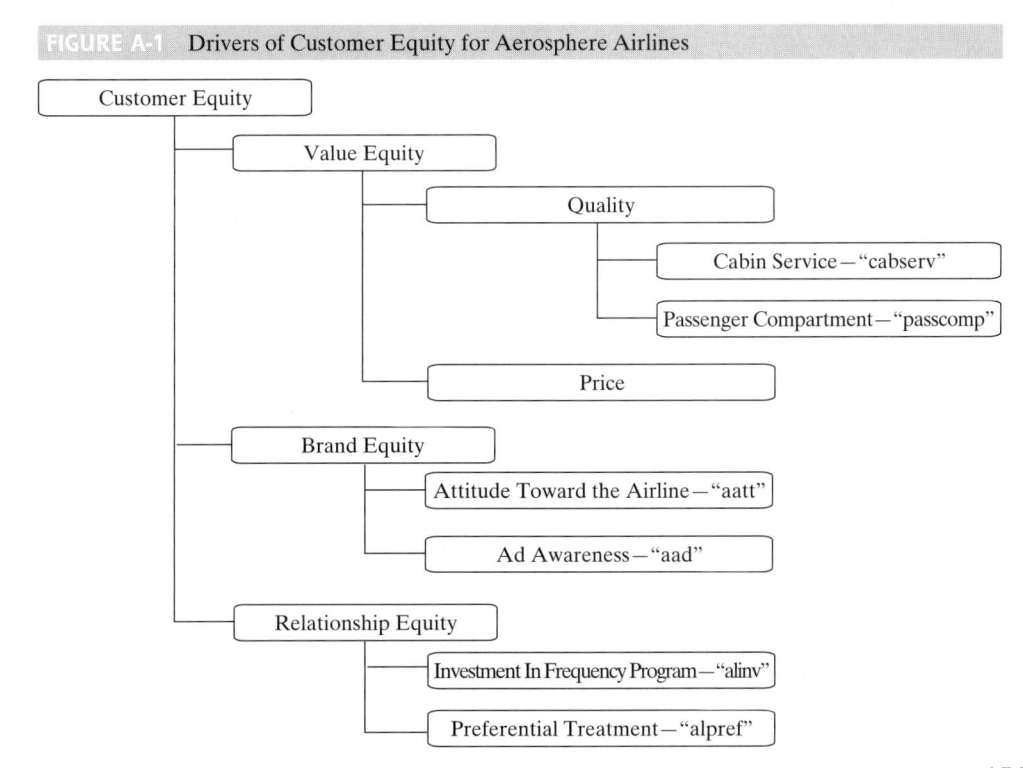

FIGURE A-1 Drivers of Customer Equity for Aerosphere Airlines

- Customer Equity
  - Value Equity
    - Quality
      - Cabin Service—"cabserv"
      - Passenger Compartment—"passcomp"
    - Price
  - Brand Equity
    - Attitude Toward the Airline—"aatt"
    - Ad Awareness—"aad"
  - Relationship Equity
    - Investment In Frequency Program—"alinv"
    - Preferential Treatment—"alpref"

The identified drivers and sub-drivers were

Drivers of Value Equity
Quality [with sub-drivers of cabin service ("cabserv") and passenger compartment comfort ("passcomp")]
Price

Drivers of Brand Equity
Attitude toward the airline ("aatt")
Awareness of airline advertising ("aad")

Drivers of Relationship Equity
Investment in the airline's frequent flyer program ("alinv")
Preferential treatment ("alpref")

Following the identification of customer equity drivers, Aerosphere hired a professional field service to collect survey data from a sample of adult airline passengers, chosen using a national probability sample. These data were used to analyze Aerosphere's current competitive position, estimate Aerosphere's current customer equity, and provide the basis for what-if analyses of potential marketing actions. For input to the software, Tindall assumed that each airline had a contribution margin of about 15 percent (his best guess, based on industry data), that Aerosphere had a time horizon of three years on its investments, and used a discount rate of 10 percent. ∎

CASE ASSIGNMENT

1. Open the Customer Equity Driver software and examine the "Results of Analysis" screen. What is Aerosphere's estimated customer equity?
2. How much is an average customer worth?
3. Given this average value of a customer, how much should Aerosphere spend to retain a customer, if otherwise the customer would leave the airline permanently?
4. What does this imply about policies with respect to complaint resolution?
5. What is Aerosphere's relative standing with respect to customer equity (its "customer equity share")?
6. Where is Aerosphere strong, relative to its competitors? Where is it weak?
7. Which drivers are the most important in the industry? Which are least important?
8. It might be reasonable for Aerosphere to focus on drivers (and sub-drivers) where its performance is relatively poor, compared to its competitors, and yet the driver is important. Based on these criteria, which driver(s) should Aerosphere concentrate on? Drilling down further, which sub-driver within that driver is the top candidate for improvement?

◆◆◆ **Aqualisa Quartz: Simply a Better Shower**

Case 4-2 Aqualisa Quartz: Simply a Better Shower

Youngme Moon

Plumbing hasn't changed since Roman times.
—TIM PESTELL, AQUALISA NATIONAL SALES MANAGER

Harry Rawlinson (Harvard Business School '90) shrugged out of his overcoat and headed to the reception desk of the South Kent County Marriott. "Can you direct me to the breakfast room?" he asked, "I'm meeting some guests from America." The receptionist indicated a hallway lined with photographs of the surrounding region's golf fairways and putting greens. "It's just to the left down there," she said. As he strode down the narrow corridor, Rawlinson, managing

---
The case was prepared by Kerry Herman, supervised by Professor Youngme Moon. Copyright © 2002 by the President and Fellows of Harvard College. Harvard Business School Case 502-030.

CHAPTER 4 *Measuring Customer Equity* 153

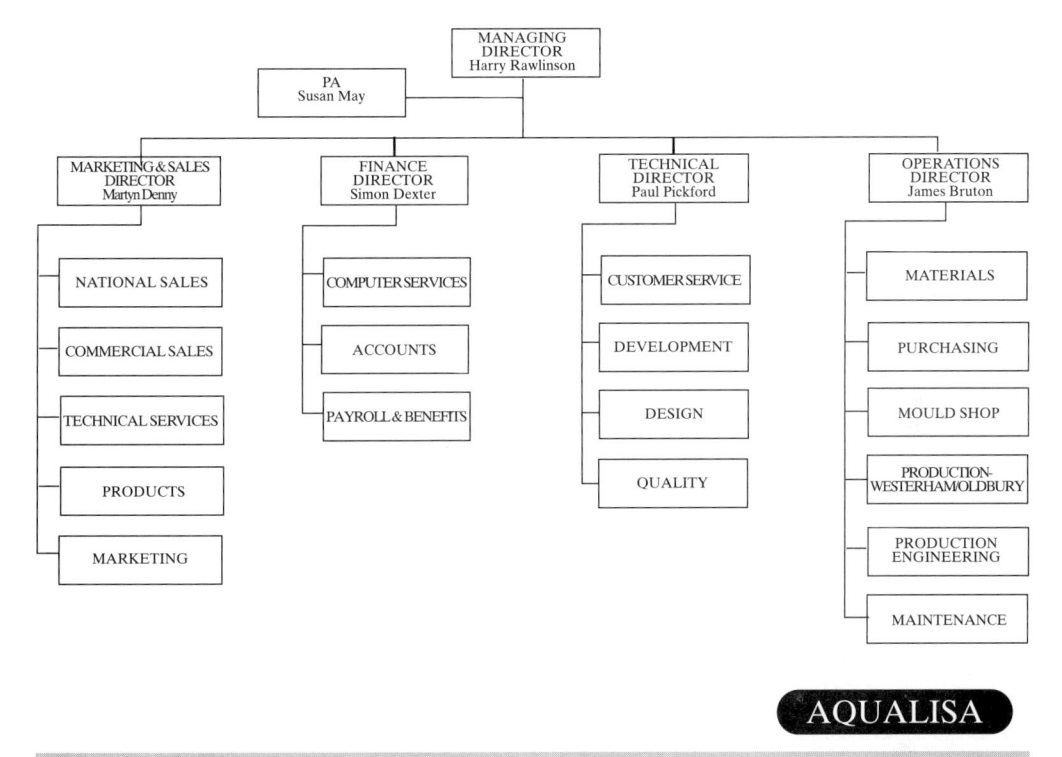

```
                    MANAGING
                    DIRECTOR
         PA         Harry Rawlinson
         Susan May
```

MARKETING & SALES DIRECTOR Martyn Denny	FINANCE DIRECTOR Simon Dexter	TECHNICAL DIRECTOR Paul Pickford	OPERATIONS DIRECTOR James Bruton
NATIONAL SALES	COMPUTER SERVICES	CUSTOMER SERVICE	MATERIALS
COMMERCIAL SALES	ACCOUNTS	DEVELOPMENT	PURCHASING
TECHNICAL SERVICES	PAYROLL & BENEFITS	DESIGN	MOULD SHOP
PRODUCTS		QUALITY	PRODUCTION-WESTERHAM/OLDBURY
MARKETING			PRODUCTION ENGINEERING
			MAINTENANCE

AQUALISA

EXHIBIT 1 The Aqualisa Organizational Chart

Source: Aqualisa.

director of Aqualisa (see Exhibit 1), a U.K. shower manufacturer, felt a surge of energy. He had been looking forward to this opportunity to discuss an HBS case possibility.

In May 2001 Aqualisa had launched the Quartz shower, the first significant product innovation in the U.K. shower market since—well, to Rawlinson's mind—since forever. But here it was early September 2001, and the euphoria surrounding the product's initial launch had long since faded. Rawlinson knew the Quartz was technologically leaps and bounds above other U.K. showers in terms of water pressure, ease of installation, use, and design. But for some reason, it simply wasn't selling.

THE U.K. SHOWER MARKET

Rawlinson leaned forward as he began to explain his situation. Showers in the United Kingdom were plagued with problems. While everyone had a bathtub, only about 60% of U.K. homes had showers. Archaic plumbing, some of it dating to the Victorian era, was still common in many homes. For the most part this plumbing was gravity fed; a cold water tank or cistern sat somewhere in the roof, while a separate boiler and cylinder were needed to store hot water in a nearby airing cupboard.

Gravity-fed plumbing meant poor-to-low water pressure, about 3–4 liters per minute.[1] Gravity-fed plumbing also created frequent fluctuations in pressure, which caused the temperature to noticeably vary from minute to minute. If the pressure from the cold water pipe decreased momentarily, the flow from the hot water pipe would increase, immediately raising the temperature.

These two problems—low pressure and fluctuations in temperature—were typically addressed through the use of either electric showers or special U.K. shower valves.

1. **Electric showers** used water from the cold water supply. Electrical heating elements in the shower instantaneously heated the water to the

---

[1] Water pressure in the United States, in contrast, is generally at least 18 liters per minute.

Brand	Electric Showers	Mixer Showers	Power Showers	Total Units Sold
Triton	479,000	41,000	25,500	545,500
Mira	155,000	200,000	35,000	390,000
Gainsborough	180,000	20,500	3,000	203,500
Aqualisa	6,000	94,000	22,000	122,000
Masco	35,000	50,000	35,000	120,000
Ideal Standard	0	60,000	0	60,000
Heatrae Sadia	40,000	0	0	40,000
Bristan	0	20,000	0	20,000
Grohe	0	20,000	0	20,000
Hansgrohe	0	15,000	0	15,000
Others	205,000	29,500	29,500	264,000
Total Units Sold	**1,100,000**	**550,000**	**150,000**	**1,800,000**

EXHIBIT 2 U.K. Marketshare Data (units sold 2000)

Source: Aqualisa.

required temperature, eliminating the need for a boiler to store hot water. While this made electric showers convenient for small bathrooms, the electrical components were usually mounted in a bulky white box that was visible in the shower stall. In addition, electric showers did nothing to address the poor water flow of many showers in U.K. homes, since the flow was limited by the amount of energy that could be applied to heat the water instantaneously. Aqualisa sold electric showers mostly under a separate brand name, the "Gainsborough" brand. (See Exhibit 2 for shower sales by type and brand.)

2. **Mixer shower valves** came in two types: manual and thermostatic. Both types blended hot and cold water to create a comfortable temperature, but while thermostatic valves controlled the temperature automatically, manual valves required the user to manually find the right temperature mix. Installing a mixer valve meant excavating the bathroom wall, which was often a two-day job. If a user wanted to boost water pressure, an additional booster pump (typically costing from €350 to €600) could be installed to enhance the flow rate.

The Aquavalve 609 was the company's core product in the mixer-shower-valve category. At about 60,000 units per year, it was by far Aqualisa's top-selling shower. It was regarded by plumbers as being a high-quality, reliable mixer shower with state-of-the-art technology. It cost about €155 to manufacture and sold (at retail) for €675 to €750. The Aquavalve 609 was thermostatic and could be supplemented by an Aquaforce booster pump to create stronger pressure.

3. **Integral power showers** consisted of a single compact unit that combined a thermostatic mixer valve and a booster pump. Although they provided up to 18 liters of blended water per minute, they had to be mounted in the shower, resulting in the presence of a bulky box on the wall. In addition, these units were generally regarded as being less reliable than a mixer-shower and booster-pump combination. The Aquastream Thermostatic was Aqualisa's primary product in this category. It cost about €175 to produce and sold (at retail) for about €670. At about 20,000 units per year, it was Aqualisa's strongest-selling shower in the power shower category.

Most consumers could readily identify what they disliked about their showers—poor pressure and varying temperature being at the top of the list. But there were other complaints as well. Showers often broke down, or "went wrong," as Rawlinson described. "They break after awhile. The mechanisms get gummed up with lime scale,

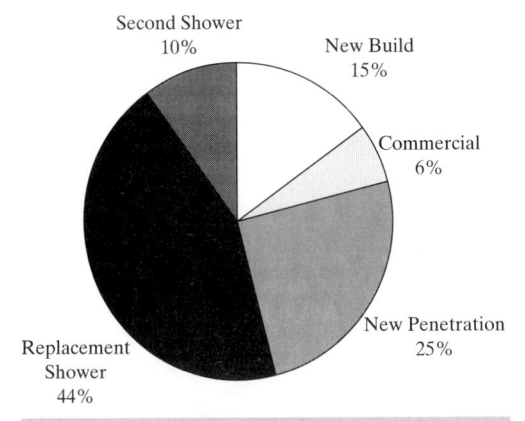

EXHIBIT 3 U.K. Shower Sales, by Reason for Installation

- Second Shower 10%
- New Build 15%
- Commercial 6%
- New Penetration 25%
- Replacement Shower 44%

Source: Aqualisa.

Note: "New penetration" refers to new showers installed in existing bathrooms (where plumbing already exists, e.g., a shower added to a bathtub). "Second shower" refers to installation of a new shower in a location where no plumbing exists.

making the valves stiff and hard to turn; the seals start to leak, or they go out of date." As a result, consumers complained about hard-to-turn valves, leaky seals, and worn-out showers. (Almost half the U.K. shower market was comprised of sales of replacement showers—see Exhibit 3.) On the other hand, consumers were generally uninformed about showers, and there was little understanding of product options (see Exhibit 4). Brand awareness was low; only one company in the market (Triton) had managed to build brand awareness at the consumer level.

Shower buyers in the United Kingdom tended to fall into one of three pricing segments: premium, standard, and value. Consumers in the premium segment typically shopped in showrooms; they took for granted high performance and service, and for them style determined their selection. Consumers in the standard price range tended to emphasize performance and service; they usually relied on an independent plumber to recommend or select a product for them. Consumers in the value segment were primarily concerned with convenience and price; they liked to avoid solutions that required any excavation and tended to rely on an independent plumber in selecting a product. (See Figure A for Aqualisa's core product offerings in the various shower categories.)

In addition, there was a sizeable do-it-yourself (DIY) market in the United Kingdom. Do-it-yourselfers generally shopped at large retail outlets that catered to them (for example, the popular B&Q, which modeled itself after Home Depot in the United States). They were primarily interested in inexpensive models that were easy to

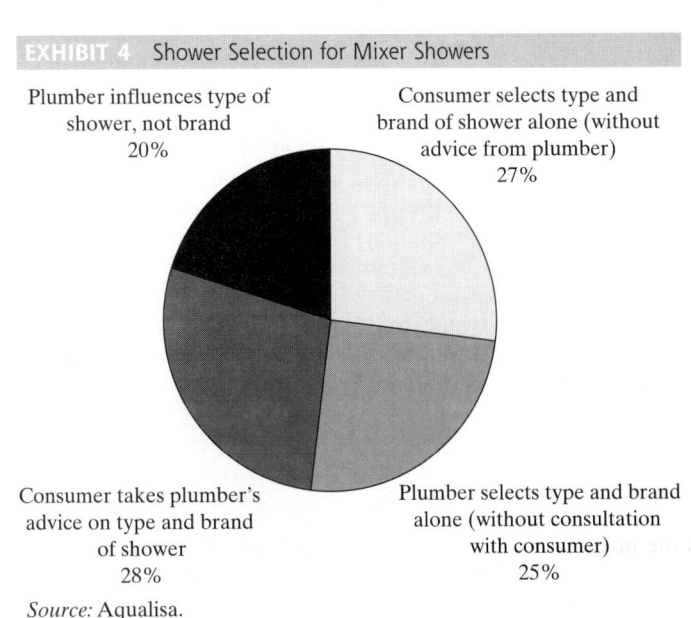

EXHIBIT 4 Shower Selection for Mixer Showers

- Plumber influences type of shower, not brand 20%
- Consumer selects type and brand of shower alone (without advice from plumber) 27%
- Consumer takes plumber's advice on type and brand of shower 28%
- Plumber selects type and brand alone (without consultation with consumer) 25%

Source: Aqualisa.

		Aqualisa's Core Product Offerings		
Type of Shower		Value	Standard	Premium
Electric shower	• Does not require hot water supply • Results in bulky box on the wall • Low flow rate	Gainsborough Retail: €95	Gainsborough Retail: €155	Aquastyle Retail: €230
Mixer shower	• Requires both hot and cold water supply • Requires additional pump to address pressure problems • Installation typically requires excavation of bathroom	Aquavalve Retail: €390	Aquavalve 609 Retail: €715	
Power shower	• Requires both hot and cold water supply • Results in bulky box on the wall • Regarded as less reliable than a mixer-shower and pump combination	Aquastream Manual Retail: €480	Aquastream Thermostatic Retail: €670	

FIGURE A Aqualisa's Core Product Offerings in the Various Shower Categories[2]

Source: Aqualisa

install, even though the DIY products were bulky and unattractive. Electric showers were the overwhelming choice in this segment. They could be adapted to all water systems and could be installed in a day; they were particularly popular among landlords and apartment dwellers.

Finally, there was a significant property developer market in the United Kingdom. Most developers did not need to worry about pressure problems because new homes were almost exclusively built with high-pressure systems. Developers faced a different set of issues, preferring reliable, nice-looking products that could work in multiple settings. Developers were also price sensitive; with the exception of luxury builders, most developers did not feel the need to invest in premium valves. Developers usually had relationships with independent plumbers who installed whatever product they selected.

Aqualisa sold to developers under its ShowerMax brand, which was available only through specialist contract outlets. Elements of the Aquavalve technology had been redesigned and re-branded for the ShowerMax product line and optimized for developers' specific needs. Because new homes did not use gravity systems, ShowerMax could deliver a high-pressure shower—with Aquavalve technology—at a significantly lower cost. Rawlinson commented, "Aqualisa's core products are too expensive for them because of extra features aimed at the retail market. Even at a discounted price, they consider Aqualisa too high end. But a cut-down product branded "ShowerMax" just for them, at the right price—they love it."

Rawlinson went on to say:

> Real breakthroughs are pretty rare in the shower market. Innovations are primarily cosmetic. Most of the major manufacturers

---

[2] Aqualisa offered a variety of other specialty shower models in each of these categories. The differences between these showers were primarily stylistic (e.g., contemporary, antique, brass, etc.).

recycle their product line and relaunch their main products about every four or five years. It refreshes your brand, but market share doesn't really change. At Aqualisa, we've tended to do a relaunch every three to four years. Aesthetically we've changed the look, and we've made incremental technological improvements to boost the performance and quality, but it's basically been the same mechanisms inside. These aren't breakthrough innovations we're talking about.

CHANNELS OF DISTRIBUTION

Showers in the United Kingdom were sold through a variety of channels (see Exhibits 5 and 6), including trade shops, distributors, showrooms, and DIY outlets.

Trade shops. Trade shops (or plumbers' merchants) carried products across all available brands. Their primary customer was the plumber, who worked for developers, contractors, or directly for consumers. Trade merchants tended to stock whatever there was demand for. The Aqualisa brand was available in 40% of trade shops. As Rawlinson put it: "The staff in these outlets don't have the time to learn all the features and benefits of the 45,000 items they offer. They focus on making sure they have the right stock of products that are in demand. Their customers are looking for reliable product availability more than technical advice."

Showrooms. Distributors supplied showrooms, which tended to be more high end. Showroom "consultants" typically led consumers through the process of selecting and designing a bathroom "solution." A shower might be one small part of an overall renovation project. Various shower and bath options were displayed in the showroom, and although no inventory was held on location, these ensembles allowed the consumer a chance to view the product in a pleasant environment. Showrooms preferred to carry high-end product lines and brands (for example, Hansgrohe, a high-end German brand) unavailable in other channels. They also offered installation services. There were about 2,000 showrooms in the United Kingdom; the Aqualisa brand was sold in about 25% of them.

DIY Sheds. Do-it-yourself retail outlets like B&Q offered discount, mass-market, do-it-yourself products. Electric showers, because they were cheaper and easier to retrofit, led sales in this channel. The Aqualisa brand was unavailable through

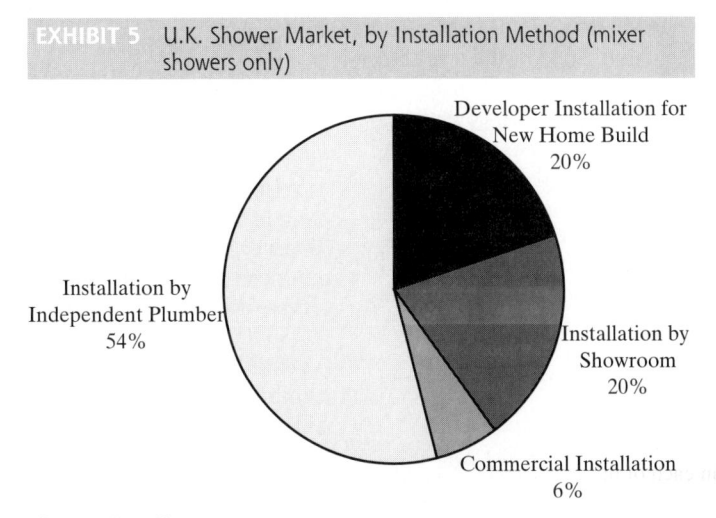

EXHIBIT 5 U.K. Shower Market, by Installation Method (mixer showers only)

- Developer Installation for New Home Build: 20%
- Installation by Showroom: 20%
- Commercial Installation: 6%
- Installation by Independent Plumber: 54%

Source: Aqualisa.

	Electric Showers	Mixer Showers	Power Showers
Do-it-yourself sheds	550,000	80,000	20,000
Showrooms	55,000	70,000	20,000
Trade shops	330,000	400,000	110,000
Other (electrical wholesalers)	165,000		
Total Units Sold	**1,100,000**	**550,000**	**150,000**

EXHIBIT 6 U.K. Shower Market, by Product Type and Channel (total units sold, 2000)

Source: Aqualisa.

this channel, but its Gainsborough brand was available in 70% of the approximately 3,000 DIY outlets in the United Kingdom.

Plumbers (Installers)

There were about 10,000 master plumbers in the United Kingdom. Plumbers had to undergo several years of training and three years of apprenticeship to become master plumbers. There was a significant shortage of master plumbers in the United Kingdom, and as a result, consumers often had to wait six months before a plumber could take on a new job.

A standard shower installation was usually a two-day job and required significant bathroom excavation.[3] Plumbers—who installed 40 to 50 showers a year—charged about €40 to €80 per hour, plus the cost of excavation and materials (plumbers usually passed the cost of the shower and other materials on to the consumer with a small markup). Because prices to consumers were usually quotes as lump sums, consumers were often unaware of how the costs broke down (labor, materials, excavation, and so on).

For plumbers, unfamiliar products could present unknown performance problems, and a bungled installation often required a second visit, paid for out of the plumber's pocket. For this reason, plumbers generally preferred to install a single shower brand and were extremely reluctant to switch brands. Loyalty to a single brand created

expertise in a given brand's installation idiosyncrasies and failure problems. Over time, plumbers also liked to familiarize themselves with the service they could expect from a manufacturer.

As a general rule, plumbers distrusted innovation. For example, in the 1980s some manufacturers had introduced electronic "push-button" controls for temperature settings. Rawlinson recalled: "The mechanisms were poorly designed and didn't work well at all. Ever since that, there's been a great deal of skepticism towards anything that seems technologically newfangled—especially if it involves electronics."

THE DEVELOPMENT OF THE QUARTZ SHOWER VALVE

Historically, Aqualisa's reputation had always been strong in the U.K. shower market; the company was generally recognized as having top quality showers, a premium brand, and great service. Aqualisa's market share ranked it number two in mixing valves and number three in the overall U.K. shower market. (See Exhibit 7 for additional information on Aqualisa's financials.)

However, when Rawlinson joined the company in 1998, he believed it was vulnerable, for several reasons. First, Rawlinson believed that other companies were catching up to Aqualisa in terms of product quality. Second, Rawlinson feared that the market was beginning to perceive Aqualisa products as being overpriced (see Exhibit 8). Third, while Aqualisa's service was still regarded as being "great," actual service had slipped over the past few years. And finally, about 10% of Aqualisa showers still "went wrong," a percentage that hadn't improved in many years. Rawlinson remembered:

---

[3]Typically, the plumber would either excavate himself, or he would subcontract the work to a plasterer. The price plumbers charged for excavation varied significantly.

Shower sales (electric, mixer, power, and pumps)[a]	€46,212
Other[b]	21,744
Total Sales	**€67,956**
Gross Margins	**€31,824**
Sales	€4,080
Marketing	2,724
Customer service	1,322
Research and development	1,764
Finance, administration & depreciation	4,579
Total Overhead Spend	**€14,469**
Base Profit	**€17,355**

EXHIBIT 7 Aqualisa Select Financials 2000 (€ in thousands)

Source: Aqualisa.

[a]Includes all Aqualisa shower lines, including Aquastyle, Aquavalve, and Aquastream. Also includes Aqualisa pumps, as well as a variety of other specialty shower models sold by Aqualisa; these were primarily differentiated by style (e.g., contemporary, antique, brass, etc.). Does not include other brands such as ShowerMax and Gainsborough.
[b]Aqualisa sold a variety of other products, including shower accessories and commercial products.

When I first joined Aqualisa in May of 1998, what I found was a highly profitable company that was quite comfortable with its niche in the market. It had 25% net return on sales and was enjoying 5% to 10% growth in a mature market. Everyone was happy. But I was worried. I knew the current points of difference were eroding and that eventually the market might implode on us. From the start, I firmly believed that the future was to focus on innovation.

EXHIBIT 8 Aqualisa: Selected Products and Price Points

Model	*Segment*	*Retail Price*	*MSP*	*Cost*	*Margin*
Aquastyle	Premium	€230	€155	€95	€60
Aquavalve 609	Standard	€715	€380	€155	€225
Aquavalve Value	Value	€390	€205	€75	€130
Aquastream Thermostatic	Standard	€670	€350	€175	€175
Aquastream Manual	Value	€480	€250	€140	€110
Quartz Standard	Premium	€850	€450	€175	€275
Quartz Pumped	Premium	€1,080	€575	€230	€345
Aquaforce 1.0/1.5 Bar	Standard	€445	€230	€125	€105
Aquaforce 2.0/3.0 Bar	Premium	€595	€310	€175	€135

Source: Aqualisa.

Note: "Retail price" refers to the price charged by the retailer (trade shop, showroom, or DIY outlet) to the customer. "MSP" refers to manufacturer selling price (Aqualisa's price to the channel).

Rawlinson's first priority was to build a research and development (R&D) team:

> We brought together a top-notch team of outsiders and insiders to look at the future of showers. We had engineers, R&D, our sales and marketing director, and a market research guy. We did research studies to understand peoples' problems and attitudes to showering. We had a top industrial designer and a bunch of Cambridge scientists who apply technology to industrial applications. We put all these people into a huddle—held brainstorming sessions, with flip charts and felt-tip pens. And we came up with all kinds of things to improve in a shower.

As a result of their market research, Rawlinson realized that the consumer wanted a shower that looked great, delivered good pressure at stable temperatures, was easy to use, and didn't break down. Plumbers wanted a shower that was easy to install, with a guarantee to not break down or require servicing. The team's brainstorming led to some real breakthroughs. Rawlinson noted:

> The breakthrough idea was to locate the mechanism that mixes the water remotely—*away* from the shower. All the problems with showers come down to the fact that you have to put a clumsy, mechanical control right where the user doesn't want it—in the shower. And that's why you get these big bulky boxes on the shower wall. Or you're constrained to put the mechanism somewhere in the wall behind the shower—equally difficult and costly to install or repair. But locating the mechanism remotely—all of a sudden that opened up all kinds of opportunities because now you didn't necessarily have to excavate.
>
> The problem was, how could a user control a mechanism that was located remotely? And that's when we brought the electronics people in. Of course, that generated a lot of skepticism, because electronics had flopped so terribly in the '80s. But nobody had ever thought of using the electronics to control the valve remotely. And when we came up with the idea, we realized very quickly that it had *huge* potential.

Once the product started to take shape, field tests were next. Rawlinson arranged for about 60 consumer field test sites, installing showers in the homes of sales reps, company personnel, and friends of friends. Feedback from the field tests prompted constant modifications. He recalled:

> Consumers told us they wanted maximum pressure. But once we gave them maximum pressure (about 18 liters per minute) consumers felt it was wasteful. So we had to give them the option to run at two-thirds speed—which they liked more than maximum pressure.
>
> With the temperature settings, it was the same thing. We knew from our research that the optimal water temperature was 41° [Celsius]; anything above that would be uncomfortably hot. So we created this temperature control that had an upper limit of 41°. But people hated the fact that it required them to turn the valve all the way to the right, into the "red zone" on the indicator. Even though nobody wanted their water hotter than 41°, they all wanted the option of being able to make the temperature hotter. So we reset the maximum to 45°, people set their temperature at 41°, and everyone liked that much better.

After three years of development—during which the company spent €5.8 million—the result was a radically different kind of shower (called Quartz) that cost the company about €175 to €230 to make. By this time, the company had invested in a new state-of-the-art testing facility, had acquired nine patents, and had grown its engineering team from six to 20. Several additional products were in advanced stages of development, while dozens of other ideas were in the early stages of the new-product development pipeline.

THE QUARTZ: A BREAKTHROUGH IN SHOWER TECHNOLOGY

The Quartz came in two versions. The Quartz Standard Shower was designed for installations that already had, or did not need, a pump; the Quartz Pumped Shower included a pump.

To install the Quartz shower, the plumber had to identify a physical space to accommodate the remote processor, which was about the size of

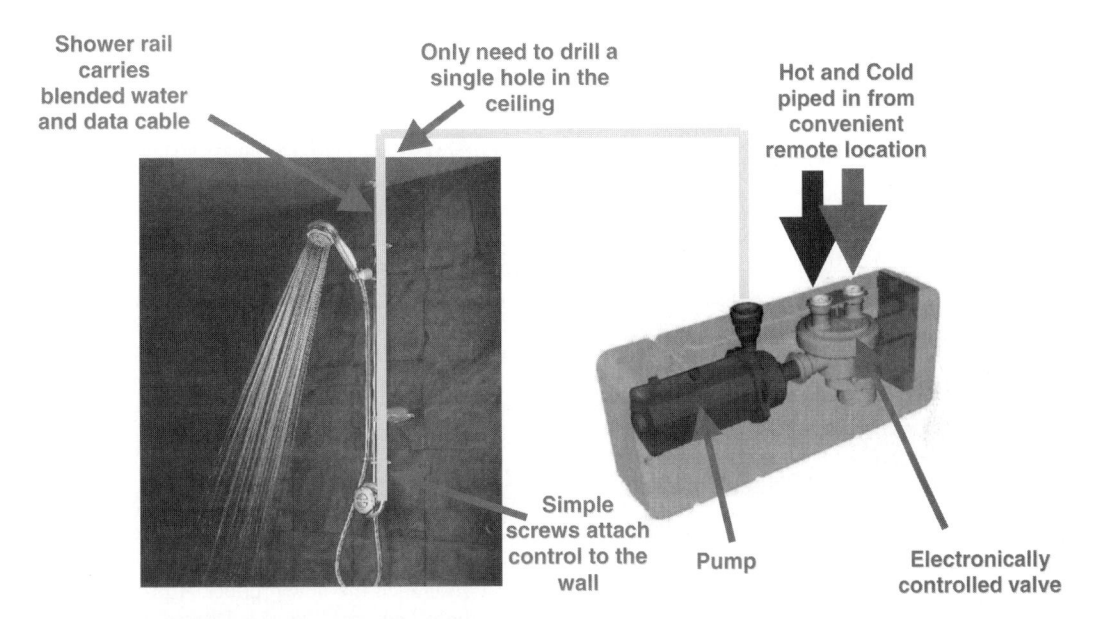

FIGURE B The Quartz Technology

Source: Aqualisa.

a shoe box. The processor contained the thermostatic mixing valve, and when applicable, the pump. The location of the processor could be anywhere within reasonable proximity to the shower—under a cabinet, behind a wall, inside a closet, in the ceiling, wherever. The device could be mounted horizontally, vertically, or on its side, depending on space constraints. The only requirements were that it had to be in a location where cold and hot water could be piped into the processor, and it had to be plugged into a standard power outlet. Once these requirements were met and the processor was in place, a single pipe fed the mixed water from the processor to the showerhead. Because of the flexibility associated with locating the processor remotely, excavation of the bathroom could often be avoided altogether. Instead, a plumber had only to drill a single hole (to accommodate the pipe feeding the mixed water to the showerhead, along with a data cable) into the ceiling above the shower (see Figure B).[4]

The benefits of Quartz were significant. Whereas a traditional shower installation took two days, some plumbers were already reporting an installation time of a half day for the Quartz. Plumbers were finding that the installation was so straightforward they could even send their young apprentices—many with little or no experience—to complete the entire job. Rawlinson had spoken to several plumbers during the field trials, "They raved about it. They said, 'It's just what we want! We need something like this that we can push-fit-connect-you're done. It's not in the wall, and it's very easy to use.'"

For the consumer, the Quartz shower provided efficient and reliable water pressure and temperature. In addition, it featured a "one-touch" control mounted on the shower wall. The easy-to-use push-button control light on the valve flashed red until the desired temperature was reached (see Figure C). Rawlinson remembered that this had been another feature with unexpected psychological benefits:

When consumers turn a traditional shower on, they almost always turn the shower to very hot . . . and then wait for it to warm up. They usually have to stick their hand in the

---

[4]The ease of installation was a big selling point for the Quartz. In fact, it was so easy that the installation guide itself was being used in Quartz's promotional and sales materials.

FIGURE C The Quartz Thermostatic Control

Source: Aqualisa.

shower a few times until they feel it's hot enough to get in. Once they're in the shower, they immediately start fiddling with the controls again. It's incredibly inefficient and inconvenient.

With our Quartz technology, the temperature control is automatic—there's no more fiddling. You don't have to manipulate anything anymore. Just set the temperature once, and leave it on that setting. When you want to use the shower, just press a button, and you've turned the shower on. When the red light stops flashing, you know the water's at the right temperature. Get in.

During field trials, consumers loved it. "We call it the 'wow' factor," Rawlinson said. "They loved how it looked; it delivered great power, and now it had neat fittings and push-button controls that lit up. Parents loved it because it was safe for their kids to use on their own. The elderly loved it because they didn't have to fight with stiff valves. What wasn't to love?"

Rawlinson was already anticipating upcoming product releases. In a few months, Aqualisa would be ready to launch a Body Jet product that fit easily on top of the Quartz control valve, creating several jets of water that sprayed horizontally from the wall onto the body. This feature was popular in spas and health clubs; women particularly liked it because it allowed them to shower without getting their hair wet. The R&D team had also just finished designing a "slave" remote for the Quartz. Rawlinson described it: "Imagine waking up in the morning, rolling over, and pushing a 'remote control' next to your bed that turns your shower on. By the time you stumble in the bathroom, your shower is ready with the water at the right temperature, waiting for you to get in. Because we're dealing with electronics, the wireless technology to do this is almost trivial."

In fact, Rawlinson and the R&D team could spend endless hours coming up with new product ideas; as Rawlinson liked to say, "Once you put a computer in the bathroom, the potential is unlimited!"

To launch the new product, Aqualisa had hit the major shows, like the Bathroom Expo in London in May 2001. At the Expo, the Quartz had been awarded the top prize.[5] Press events had been coordinated with demonstrations. The trade press had raved about the "cleverness" of the product and its "elegant design." One reporter wrote:

> Imagine a shower that takes less than a day to fit, doesn't have flow problems, offers accurate temperature control, is simplicity itself to use, and comes in versions to suit all water systems. It sounds too good to be true—but after three years of brainstorming...Aqualisa has achieved the apparently impossible with a product that takes a genuinely new look at a set of old problems—and solves them.[6]

Other reviewers had been similarly positive, and the Quartz had been featured on the covers of several prominent trade journals.

INITIAL SALES RESULTS

Aqualisa had a 20-person sales force that sold to distributors, trade shops, showrooms, developers, and plumbers. Tim Pestell, Aqualisa's national

---

[5] "Showered with Success," *Bathroom Journal,* June 2001, p. 13.
[6] Ibid.

sales manager, described the sales team's priorities: "Our sales force spends about 90% of their time on maintaining existing accounts—servicing existing customers: distributors, trade shops, contractors, showrooms, and developers. Ten percent of their time is spent on developing new customers." Aqualisa's sales force also had long-standing direct relationships with a group of plumbers—"our plumbers" as director of marketing Martyn Denny called them—who were very loyal to the Aqualisa brand.

With the launch of the Quartz, the Aqualisa sales force had contacted its network of plumbers, calling face-to-face to introduce and explain the new product, but few actual sales had resulted. Indeed, despite all the early excitement over the product, and despite being made available in all of Aqualisa's normal channels, very few units had sold in the first four months on the market. Rawlinson worried:

> Our channel partners are sitting there having bought a thousand of these Quartz products, and they've sold 81. The poor product manager is looking pretty stupid at this stage. This is a huge problem for us—pretty soon they're going to write this off as a failure and forget about us. I can see a scenario in six months' time where real sales in the market—currently about 15 units a day—are still down at 30 or 40 units a day. We'll look like a niche product. We've got to sell 100 or 200 a day to break through to the mainstream.

Part of the problem was that plumbers were wary of innovation, particularly any innovation involving electronics. Rawlinson told the story of a personal friend who had to insist that her plumber install a Quartz:

> His initial reaction was negative. He said, "Oh no, I wouldn't put one of these in, Madam. I've had these electronic showers before. They don't work." She insisted and made him put it in. He told her it would take two days. He was done by lunchtime the first day. And he said, "That was so easy. Can I have the brochure?" And now he's got two or three more jobs. So once a plumber puts one in, he's a convert.

Pestell, however, noted that given the conservative nature of most plumbers, "Adoption is a long, slow process. It takes time." In addition, he pointed out:

> Some people at the company think the Quartz will eventually replace our core product—the Aquavalve—and become mainstream. I think it's really a niche product—it's good for homes with children, or for the elderly and the handicapped. It's easy to use, safe, and so on, but we can't forget our core products every time we launch something new. The Aquavalve is our bread and butter, and it can go away if no one's watching.

Denny concurred, "How do we pitch our other products alongside Quartz? Right now, if Quartz is mentioned, our salesmen tend to gloss over our other products. In fact, to sell the Quartz, they have to point out *deficiencies* in our existing products. That doesn't really make any sense, does it?"

According to Rawlinson, the only place Quartz seemed to be gaining any traction was in the showrooms:

> Showrooms are traditionally quite a niche market. But I think we've made some penetration into that sector, and we're starting to get working displays around the country. Because you put one of these things in, you press that control button, the little red light comes on: it's sold! Everybody loves it. And where it's gone in—a working display—it's become the leading product in that showroom almost immediately.

A SHIFT IN MARKETING STRATEGY?

The waitress began to clear the coffee cups. Rawlinson absently dusted at the crumbs on the tablecloth as he leaned forward and said:

> Once upon a time Microsoft was a tiny little provider of specialist software. Bill Gates had the vision to see that if you own the operating system on the PC, you can build from there. One of our presentations calls the Quartz the "Pentium Processor" because we can do so much once we have this kind of control over your bathroom . . .

we can use this technology with a shower ... but in the future we could use it with a bath, the sinks, whatever.... We're only limited by our creativity.

The question was, how to generate sales momentum? Was the problem that the Quartz was priced too high? Rawlinson wondered whether a discounted price might generate more market enthusiasm for his innovation. Because Quartz was such a breakthrough product, Rawlinson was loath to go this route. On the other hand, Rawlinson *was* willing to rethink his overall marketing strategy for the Quartz. Some of the marketing options he was debating included:

Targeting Consumers Directly

"We have so many problems reaching the plumbers," Rawlinson continued. "So I'm thinking to myself, why not target consumers with this product and try to build a consumer brand? Triton has proven that it can be done. And if there's ever been a breakthrough product to do it with, this is it. I think this is a 'bet the company' kind of product."

The problem with this option was that Rawlinson was finding it tough to justify a high-risk, high-reward strategy when company results were already healthy. As a test, a one-time-only print advertisement campaign was scheduled to run in *The Mail on Sunday* magazine in October (see Exhibit 9 for copy of the advertisement). But, as Rawlinson noted, "One ad does not a campaign make. I'm not overly optimistic." A large-scale consumer campaign would cost about €3 million to €4 million over two years. With a net income of about €17 million, this would be a very tough sell across the company.

Targeting Do-It-Yourselfers

A second alternative was to target the do-it-yourself market. Rawlinson noted, "The Quartz is so easy to install, you or I could even do it." Aqualisa was currently selling its Gainsborough line to this market. The risk, as Rawlinson pointed out, was that "once you show up in the DIY sheds, you can't climb back out. You have to be careful about associating your premium brand with your discount channel."

On the other hand, the value proposition of the Quartz was so superior to that of the electric showers that dominated this market, perhaps it *was* possible to charge a premium for this product through that channel? In addition, he wondered if Aqualisa could get its partners like B&Q to help push the product, avoiding the need for expensive consumer advertising.

Targeting Developers

A third alternative was to target developers more aggressively. Rawlinson thought aloud, "The plus side is that this could conceivably be a large-volume channel. If we could get a couple of developers on board, we'd sell a lot of showers. In addition, it would force plumbers to get familiar with our product since they would have to install whatever the developers tell them to install." But there were downsides—including the significant time lag before showers would reach consumers through this route. As Rawlinson noted with some urgency, "We've got *at most* a two-year lead on the competition."

Rawlinson also wondered how tough a sell it would be to developers. Developers had already shown a reluctance to spend money on conventional Aqualisa products because they perceived those products to be premium brands; even at a 50% discount, the company had been unable to make the sale. And again, given that Quartz was such a breakthrough innovation, Rawlinson was reluctant to discount the price.

What to Do

If his managers were right and this was a niche product, Rawlinson wondered if maybe he should simply lower his expectations. Everything was basically well with the company—but at the same time, he could not help arguing:

Business school taught me to think strategically, to be a visionary. Everything I learned at HBS tells me this is a breakthrough product. My worry is we'll miss the opportunity and in five years' time, someone else will have got the world market for this technology. We've had a nice,

CHAPTER 4 *Measuring Customer Equity* 165

EXHIBIT 9 Advertisement for the Quartz Shower

Quartz

The future of showering

The stylish new model from Aqualisa - leaders in shower technology.

Just look at these features:

ADJUSTABLE CLIMATE CONTROL FOR ULTIMATE SAFETY

INNOVATIVE "TOUCHTRONIC" OPERATION

VARIABLE HEIGHT HEAD ADJUSTMENT

TURBOCHARGED OPTION

5 YEAR PARTS & LABOUR WARRANTY

All designed to give "miles more satisfaction."

0-18 litres in under a second!*

(As for the airbags - we're working on th

AQUALISA
HIGH PERFORMANCE SHO

For the full specification
01959 560000, return
coupon or visit our web
www.aqualisa.co.u

I'd like to know more about
please send me details.
Name
Address
Postcode
Aqualisa Showers Ltd (Dept YM), The Fly
Westerham, Kent. TN16 1 DE.
We promise that no representative will conta

* 0-18 litres per minute

Source: Aqualisa.

comfortable, contented life in the U.K., and it's hard to get a small company—particularly one that's been so profitable all these years—to be ambitious. But one of the things that a Harvard background gives you is the itch to think big. You see other companies that break out of the pack because they've got the right product and they've got the right vision. So why not this company? ∎

◆◆◆ **Calyx & Corolla**

Case 4-3 Calyx & Corolla

Dale Wylie

Well, it's two botanical parts of the flower—the calyx (the guard leaves that protect the bud) and the corolla (the flower itself). It was on the very first list of names that a good friend and I brainstormed and we liked it right away. I liked the way it sounded and the way it looked and its uniqueness. But a lot of people didn't like it—too hard to pronounce and nobody would know what it meant. So we went back to the drawing board, and brainstormed a second and third and fourth list. Each time we'd get a consensus on a name, we couldn't clear it with the trademark office. Finally, so much time had elapsed, we were ready with a catalog layout but had no company name and no logo....

One Friday evening, we all unenthusiastically agreed on using the name: "The First Flower Company." That Sunday, I was leafing through some trade magazines and turned to a full-page ad by a new consortium of South American flower growers: "The First Flower Corporation"!

That was it—I walked in on Monday morning, showed the ad to my staff, and said: "We're going to be Calyx & Corolla."

—EXCERPT FROM OWADES SPEECH

It had been two and a half years since Calyx & Corolla had pioneered the concept of selling fresh flowers by mail. During 1990, it had consummated over 150,000 transactions, yielding revenues in excess of $10 million. The company's results had surpassed the plan that Ruth Owades, its founder, had presented to the 18 investors who had provided the original $2 million in capital. In fact, the results were sufficiently positive to enable Owades and her management group to raise another $1 million in the Spring of 1991, mainly from the original investors. (See Exhibit 1.)

Nevertheless, stimulated by their success in introducing a new distribution channel for flowers, Owades and her two key associates, Fran Wilson and Ann Lee, were reassessing the firm's long-term growth strategy. Was Calyx & Corolla more a mail order operation or should it compete directly against more traditional outlets, such as retail florists, and wire services, such as Florists Telegraph Delivery (FTD)? How fast did it have to grow to protect its initial success? What would be the financial implications of various growth strategies? How should its personal objectives and those of its investors and employees influence the character and pace of growth?

Calyx & Corolla was an exceptionally innovative direct mail concept. Besides mailing six yearly color catalogs and having an 800 telephone number, its distribution and

---

The case was prepared by David Wylie, with the supervision of Professor Walter J. Salmon. Copyright © 1991 by the President and Fellows of Harvard College. Harvard Business School Case 592-035.

	Actual FY1 *1988–1989*	*Actual FY2* *1989–1990*	*Actual FY3* *1990–1991*	*Projected FY4* *1991–1992*	*Projected FY5* *1992–1993*
Sales	$ 756	$4,018	$10,259	$15,163	$24,431
Cost of goods sold	189	972	2,452	3,487	5,496
Gross margin	567	3,046	7,807	11,676	18,935
Sales and marketing[b]	1,223	4,466	7,021	10,104	15,375
General and administrative[c]	374	752	1,213	1,459	2,263
Net profit (loss)	(1,030)	(2,172)	(427)	113	1,297

EXHIBIT 1 Five-Year Summary P&L Statements and Projections for the Fiscal Years Ending on January 31 of the Succeeding Year (in thousands of dollars)[a]

[a]Numbers have been disguised.
[b]Sales and marketing includes catalog production and mailing, list rental, and freight out (at approximately $9 per order). Order processing and fulfillment, also included, averaged $5 per order in 1990.
[c]General and administrative includes management salaries, depreciation, rent, and other miscellaneous expenses.

transportation arrangements were unique. Orders from customers were received by telephone, fax, or mail at the central office in San Francisco and then sent via fax or computer to the 30 flower growers who supplied Calyx & Corolla. They, in turn, packed and shipped individual orders and sent them directly to consumers by Federal Express. Calyx & Corolla customers thus received much fresher flowers, often fresher by as many as seven to ten days, than were available through conventional retailers. Prices, which included the cost of delivery, were competitive with conventional florists. (See Exhibit 2.)

If the goal of most entrepreneurs is to build a business that's better than what's already out there, Ruth Owades has done it in spades. In fact, you could say she has created a new market....

Until Calyx & Corolla came along, the hugely lucrative $8.4 billion American flower industry had encountered few innovations. There had been flowers by wire, but not garden-fresh, exotic flowers displayed in a beautiful catalog (you actually get to see what you're ordering), with a money-back guarantee.

But as Owades realized early on, having a revolutionary idea is one thing; executing it is something else again. To make her brainchild work, she had to get major industry players to disrupt their established routines and see things her way.

—*Working Woman Magazine*, February 1991

THE CALYX & COROLLA MANAGEMENT TEAM

Ruth Owades was no stranger to the mail order business. Upon graduation from the Harvard Business School in 1975, she joined the CML Group as director of marketing. The CML group then owned a number of retail and direct mail businesses. Within two years, Owades proposed to CML executives that they launch a direct mail business focused on garden implements and accessories. When they declined, Owades resigned and, under her own auspices, launched "Gardener's Eden." Very quickly, the business grew and prospered.

In 1982, Owades sold Gardener's Eden to Williams-Sonoma, an upscale direct mail and retail seller of cookware, serving pieces, and other merchandise associated with the kitchen. For four and a half years Owades directed the Gardener's Eden division of Williams-Sonoma, during which time it continued to grow and prosper. Since the price Williams-Sonoma paid for Gardener's Eden was based in part upon a multiple of sales in the years subsequent to the purchase, the funds Owades ultimately received for Gardener's Eden reflected her stewardship during these years.

EXHIBIT 2   Letters to Calyx & Corolla from Customers

Dear Recipient,

   I am 13 years old. I found your catalog on the table and thought it would be a great idea for Mother's Day since I will be on a camping trip.

Sincerely,

   P.S. Forty dollars cash is enclosed as payment. Please accept this.

*****

Dear Calyx & Corolla:

   In the beginning of December, I ordered a box of enchantment lilies for my parents to be delivered on December 22nd, just in time for the holidays.

   The flowers were in bud stage when they arrived, they opened within a few days, and lasted for almost two weeks.

   Your sales help was top notch on the phone when I placed my order, the flowers were delivered on time, in perfect condition, exactly as advertised. Congratulations on your terrific service and product. I will tell all my friends, and definitely be a repeat customer.

*****

Dear Ms. Owades:

   Since I'd long been given to understand that my mother-in-law prefers flowers to remain in gardens, I purposely avoided sending cut bouquets. But I decided to take a chance when your spring catalog arrived and ordered the Pink-Fringed Carnations which she said looked almost like silk and, more to the point, lasted several weeks—much to her delight and astonishment. (She did mention that her housekeeper changed the water and snipped the ends daily.) And these were sent from your shop to Illinois!

   I'm keeping your catalog for future surprises for her. It's sooo nice to know that for once advertising lives up to its name, as your brochure and service attest!

   Thank you again.

*****

Dear Calyx & Corolla:

   I wish to compliment you on your fine packaging, of my lovely roses, that I received this morning.

   I am saving your address, so that I can use it as the occasion arises that I must send flowers.

   They "made my day." They arrived on my 86th birthday and 66th wedding anniversary.

*****

> Dear Ms. Owades:
>
> I live in a remote town in Northern Vermont—population 1,200. We don't even have house numbers on our streets. When I saw the Federal Express truck drive up yesterday, my neighbors and I all came out to see who it was for.
>
> Well, it was for me! The driver followed the directions perfectly: Go "Past the Church in the Square, second street on the right, red brick house, third from the end." We'd never seen a Federal Express truck on our street before—what excitement!
>
> I certainly hope we see him again, the orchids are gorgeous!
>
> *****

After about a year of relaxation and rejuvenation following her resignation from Williams-Sonoma, Owades decided to establish Calyx & Corolla. This time, she enlisted Fran Wilson, a 1983 graduate of the Harvard Business School and a former employee of Williams-Sonoma, as vice president of operations.

After about a year of operation, Ann Hayes Lee joined Calyx & Corolla as vice president of marketing. Lee was a veteran of the catalog business. She had spent almost 20 years in the industry, most recently with the Roger Horchow Company, a catalog seller of both home goods and apparel, where she was creative director.

> I was fortunate to convince two of the most talented and experienced people in our industry to join the Calyx & Corolla start-up team—Fran Wilson became vice president of operations and created the unique yet crucial systems that make this business work. Ann Hayes Lee became vice president of marketing, creating six spectacular catalogs a year, while overseeing all merchandising and other marketing programs.
>
> —EXCERPT FROM OWADES SPEECH

As in many small businesses, titles did not fully define responsibilities at Calyx & Corolla. Owades herself took a major hand in the selection and pricing of flowers and other merchandise that appeared in the catalog. She also set the critical strategy for the catalog mailing plan. Wilson was responsible for customer orders and service, day to day communications with growers, systems development and management, and finance and accounting. Lee took responsibility for merchandise development and catalog creation and production. She was also responsible for a number of nondirect mail initiatives aimed at accelerating the growth of the business (described in more detail later).

The entire management team of Calyx & Corolla was dedicated to the success of the business. Owades realized that the ultimate success of Calyx & Corolla would hinge on the efforts of this team. They had adapted their lifestyles to the rigors of a start-up venture but each executive appreciated the congenial corporate culture and found job satisfaction and the promise of a substantial payout at some future date to be powerful incentives.

THE FRESH FLOWER INDUSTRY

Retail flower and plant sales were almost a $9 billion business in the United States in 1990, having grown at a rate of 7.7% since 1985. While most flowers were grown domestically, over half of the carnations, almost a third of the roses, and a variety of other flowers were imported from over 50 countries around the world. Colombia was the major source of imported flowers, representing over 60% of the total.

The horticulture industry was extremely fragmented at all levels, with small, family-operated companies dominant among growers, distributors, wholesalers, and retail florists. Although there were some larger organizations, they did not represent a major share of the business. The typical channel of distribution was from growers to distributors located in the growing regions to geographically dispersed wholesalers who sold to florists, supermarkets, and other retailers in geographic proximity to them. Of the retailers, the 25,000 florists had the largest market share, selling 59% of all floriculture products (flowers, seeds, and potted plants) in 1987, the last year for which government retail statistics were published. Supermarkets had about 18% of this market, while nurseries, mail order companies (such as seed companies), and other miscellaneous retailers accounted for the balance. In most major cities there were flower markets in which a number of wholesalers would gather to sell their goods to retailers.

Often industry participants would not confine themselves to a single role. For example, most growers distributed some flowers directly to local or more distant wholesalers and retailers. Many distributors and wholesalers engaged in some of their own production. In addition, direct purchasing relationships often existed between growers and distributors and larger retailers such as supermarket chains.

Distributors generally paid growers in 60 to 90 days and then extended the same terms to wholesalers. Retailers usually paid wholesalers in cash. They shopped for availability, quality, and freshness from the many wholesalers who serviced them. Distributors typically marked up flowers 50% on cost to wholesalers who in turn marked them up, on cost, 100% to retailers. Florists took a markup of another 150% to 200% on cost. A flower that a grower would sell for approximately $5, for example, would thus cost the ultimate consumer about $40. Exhibit 3 includes summary financial data for FTD affiliated florists as well as additional data on their sales and advertising expenditures.

Retail florists were very service oriented. Often they prepared custom bouquets and, for major events such as weddings, provided flower arranging services, usually as part of the cost of the product. It was not unusual, for example, for the bill for flowers used in a large wedding to amount to several thousand dollars.

Flowers were purchased by consumers for a variety of occasions. Flowers were an essential part of most weddings and funerals and were often given as manifestations of love and caring for occasions such as birthdays, anniversaries, convalescence, Valentine's Day, and Mother's Day. Cynics often claimed that flowers were given to assuage guilt rather than to demonstrate affection. Many Americans also bought flowers for occasions such as dinner parties or regularly kept fresh flowers or plants in their homes.

Fresh flowers were more ubiquitous in Europe than in the United States. Per capita consumption of flowers and plants in the United States was $36 annually, whereas in Holland it was $60, which approximated the average in Europe. Americans were only beginning to acquire the European propensity to purchase flowers for themselves year round.

Flowers varied in their perishability. Roses, for instance, could last as long as one to two weeks from the time they were picked until they would have to be discarded, while anthurium could still be acceptable for sale two to three weeks after picking. Time, however, was not kind to flowers, and quality deteriorated steadily from the time of picking. Each day a flower remained unsold diminished its remaining value.

Efficient distribution was thus key to the flower industry. The almost infinite variety of species, colors, and growing locations on the supply end, however, and fragmentation within the channels of distribution resulted in a rather - inefficient distribution system. A flower might, therefore, be as much as seven to ten days old before it was available for sale in a retail store.

Although some flowers were bought and taken from the store by purchasers, most were delivered to the recipient. Typically, florists made deliveries themselves for an extra charge within a radius of several miles from their store. For delivery beyond their own service areas, florists usually used FTD or one of the several competing service organizations that had cloned FTD.

FTD was a member-owned, worldwide cooperative of 25,000 florists. Its members took orders from local customers for delivery by member florists at other locations. Although there was a catalog of "FTD Bouquets" at each member florist, there was no guarantee that the delivery florist would deliver the freshest flowers in inventory. The consumer to whom FTD historically had appealed represented a wide cross-section of households with incomes in excess of $35,000. Typically a consumer would pay an extra $3.50 order transmission fee and, depending on location and distance, an additional $6.50 for delivery. During holiday periods, incoming wire orders accounted for 21.7% of the revenues of FTD florists, while outgoing wire orders accounted for another 18.7% according to a 1989 FTD survey. During nonholiday periods, these proportions were 17.9% and 15.1% respectively. FTD processed almost 21 million orders in 1990, including more than 500,000 orders and messages daily during holiday periods. Of the total order (including flowers, transmission fee, and delivery charge), the florist who originated the order received 20%, the florist who delivered the order 73%, and FTD 7%.

In addition to its clearing service, FTD offered its members promotional and advertising

EXHIBIT 3 1987 Florists' Transworld Delivery Operating Survey (all responding U.S. shops)

	Typical	Middle Range		
Income Statement ($ of total revenues)				
Net sales from inventory	93.7%	90.3	–	99.8%
Total other operating revenues	6.3	0.2	–	9.5
Total revenues	100.0%	100.0	–	100.0
Cost of goods sold	39.4	33.3	–	45.1
Total gross profit on operations	60.6	54.9	–	66.6
Operating expenses:				
Salaries and wages—owners, partners and officers	14.6	6.6	–	22.5
Other salaries, wages, bonuses and commissions (excluding owners, partners and officers)	10.6	0.0	–	19.2
Occupancy (rent, utilities, maintenance, etc.)	7.0	4.0	–	9.4
Delivery expense	2.6	1.4	–	3.5
Telephone and transmission	1.8	1.0	–	2.2
Advertising and promotion	2.8	1.4	–	3.8
All wire service fees, dues, commissions and expenses	4.2	0.9	–	5.8
General and administrative and other	11.1	6.1	–	14.9
Total operating expense	54.6	47.3	–	61.9
Operating profit	6.0	1.4	–	10.5
Nonoperating income/expense	−0.5	−0.7	–	0.0
Profit before tax	5.5	1.3	–	9.8
Profit after tax	4.6	1.2	–	7.6
Order and Delivery Charge Data				
Average order size[a]	$25.00	$20.00	–	28.00
Percentage of shops charging for delivery	90.9%			
Average delivery charge (if charged separately)	$ 2.25	$ 2.00	–	3.00
Delivery charge revenues as a % of total revenues (if charged separately)	3.2%	2.1	–	4.4%

Source: FTD Retail Florist Operating Survey, 1987. (The last such survey was in 1987.)

[a] Average order size reflects all orders. Incoming and outgoing wire (FTD) orders represented 40% of member shop holiday orders and 33% of nonholiday orders. The average order for FTD orders was $39 including transmission and delivery service fees. By 1990, the average of all orders had grown to over $32.

(*Continued*)

EXHIBIT 3 (cont.)

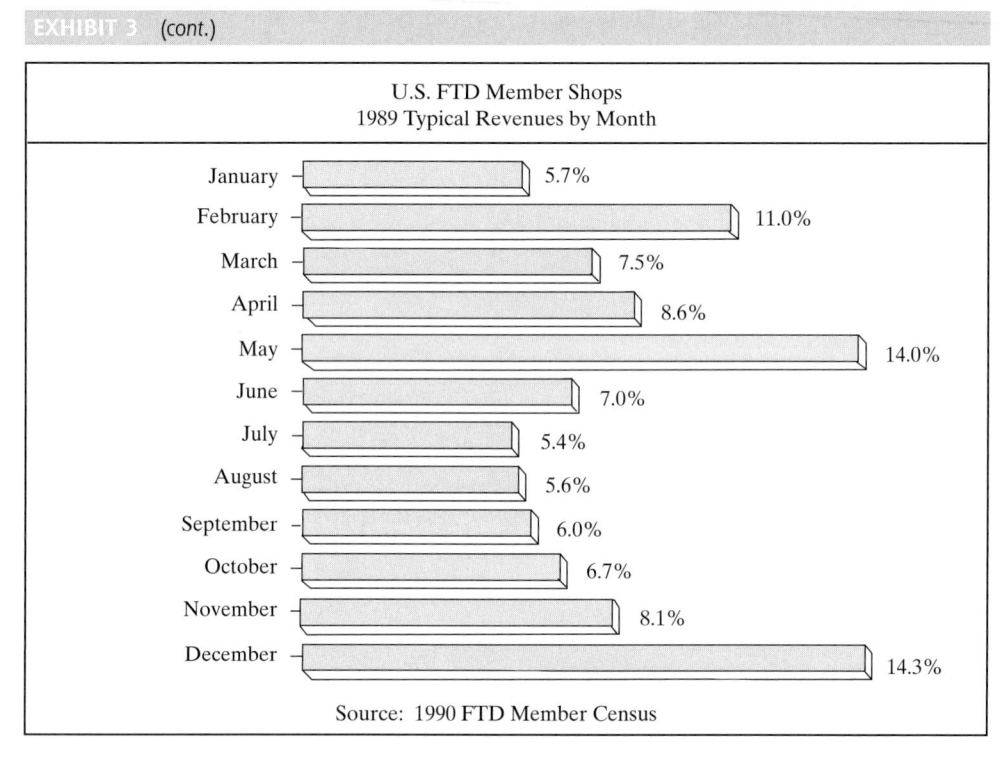

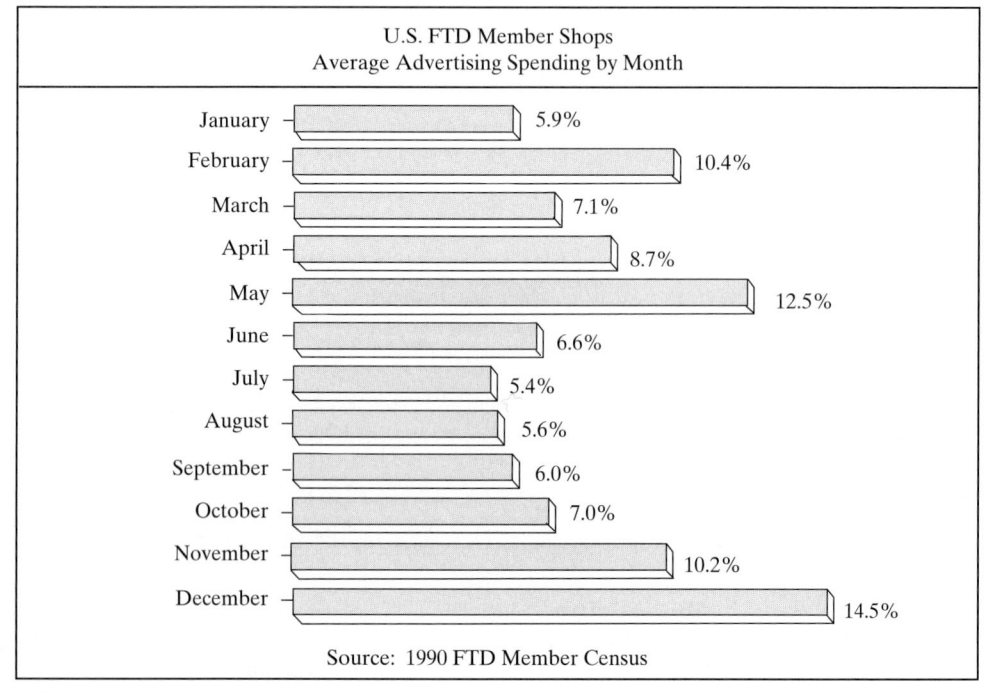

U.S. FTD Member Shops
1989 Typical Revenues by Month

Month	%
January	5.7%
February	11.0%
March	7.5%
April	8.6%
May	14.0%
June	7.0%
July	5.4%
August	5.6%
September	6.0%
October	6.7%
November	8.1%
December	14.3%

Source: 1990 FTD Member Census

U.S. FTD Member Shops
Average Advertising Spending by Month

Month	%
January	5.9%
February	10.4%
March	7.1%
April	8.7%
May	12.5%
June	6.6%
July	5.4%
August	5.6%
September	6.0%
October	7.0%
November	10.2%
December	14.5%

Source: 1990 FTD Member Census

U.S. FTD Member Shops
Average Percentage Advertising Expenditures By Medium

Medium	All Shops 1990	All Shops 1985
Yellow Pages	35%	32%
Newspaper	22	32
Radio	10	13
Product Donations	8	–
Direct Mail	8	7
Calendars	3	5
School Newspaper	2	–
Church Bulletin	2	–
Television	2	2
Fliers/Handouts	2	–
Pens & Giveaways	1	–
Outdoor Billboard	1	1
Other	4	8
Total Advertising	100%	100%

Source: 1990 & 1985 FTD Member Census

Source: 1990/91 FTD Flower Business Fact Book.

support, supplies, educational programs, marketing research, publications, and credit card processing. With the total value of orders from U.S. florists of over $700 million (almost three times its nearest competitor) and revenues of approximately $49 million, FTD spent over $24 million on advertising in 1989, 55% of which was concentrated in holiday periods.

According to *Leading National Advertisers*, an Arbitron publication, FTD concentrated most of its advertising on network television spots (73%), newspaper advertising (14%), and network radio (8%). The balance was spent on a mixture of magazines (4%), outdoor advertising, and cable and local television spots. The image promoted in electronic media had been "FTD, the feeling never ends," featuring ex-Ram's defensive tackle, Merlin Olsen. FTD was shifting, however, to a theme of "It's as easy as FTD" and shifting the percentage spent on more costly prime time television to newshour spots. The intention was also to reallocate significant advertising dollars to magazines and major regional newspapers. Print advertising was much more product oriented. FTD even planned to put a mini-catalog in magazines featuring six everyday products and a selection of seasonal bouquets. (See Exhibit 4 for sample FTD advertisements and Exhibit 5 for monthly advertising media expenditures of FTD itself.)

One of the largest FTD members was a 1984 start-up called "800-Flowers," which was becoming increasingly popular. When customers called 1-800-FLOWERS, one of 300 salespeople in its telemarketing center would take an order and transmit it by FTD or another service to a network of florists around the country. Minimum orders were $35 and went up in $5 increments. The retail customer was charged a $2.96 relay fee and a $5.99 handling fee in addition to the price of the flowers. 800-Flowers received as its fee 25% of the flower order from the delivering florist. Revenues of 800-Flowers in 1990 were about $16 million. 800-Flowers advertised primarily through billboards, subway posters, and on CNN television. Its advertising expenditures in 1990 totaled $5 million.

Supermarkets were also becoming increasingly important flower retailers. Recently their

174 PART I *Tools for Understanding and Analyzing Customer Equity*

EXHIBIT 4 Sample Advertisements of FTD

TELEVISION

VIDEO	AUDIO
OPEN ON ANIMATED SUN RISING ON THE HORIZON. THE SUN IS FROWNING AND HAS A THERMOMETER IN ITS MOUTH. THE CHICKEN SOUP BOWL BOUQUET APPEARS. SUPER: CHICKEN SOUP BOWL BOUQUET.	MUSIC: (UP) SINGERS: Send a hug from far away.
THE SUN SMILES AS PUFFY CLOUDS FORM AND IT BEGINS RAINING. THE PICK-ME-UP BOUQUET APPEARS. SUPER: PICK-ME-UP BOUQUET.	Brighten up a rainy day. Flowers say what words can't say.
CLOUDS CHANGE INTO A STORK CARRYING BABY. THE BUNDLE OF JOY BOUQUET APPEARS. SUPER: BUNDLE OF JOY BOUQUET	It's as easy as FTD
THE ANIMATION BREAKS UP FORMING THE TICKLER AS THE TICKLER BOUQUET APPEARS. SUPER: TICKLER BOUQUET	MERLIN: Whatever you need to say…
A BALLOON AND CONFETTI MOVE AROUND MERLIN AS THE HOLDS THE BIRTHDAY PARTY BOUQUET.	Your FTD Florist can send the right bouquet. And remember…
THE ANIMATED LOGO SWIRLS PAST MERLIN AND ONTO THE SCREEN AS THE THEME "IT'S AS EASY AS FTD APPEARS."	SINGERS: It's as easy a FTD.

RADIO

SINGER:	SEND A HUG FROM FAR AWAY BRIGHTEN UP A RAINY DAY FLOWERS CAN SAY WHAT WORDS CAN'T SAY IT'S AS EASY AS FTD (MUSIC GOES DOWN UNDER)
MERLIN:	Now your FTD Florist has more ways than ever to show you care. Introducing the new FTD Affecton Collection. Show your love with the Big Hig Bouquet. Show your appreciation with yhe Thanks a Bunch Bouquet. Or say way to go with the Congrats to You Bouquet…. It's never been easier to express all your affection. Just ask for these or any of the other bouquets from the new FTD Affection Collection. (MUSIC BACK UP)
SINGER:	IT'S AS EASY AS FTD AS THOUGHTFUL AS A GIFT CAN BE FROM ME TO YOU FROM YOU TO ME IT'S AS EASY AS FTD

1990 North American FTD Monthly Advertising Media Expenditures

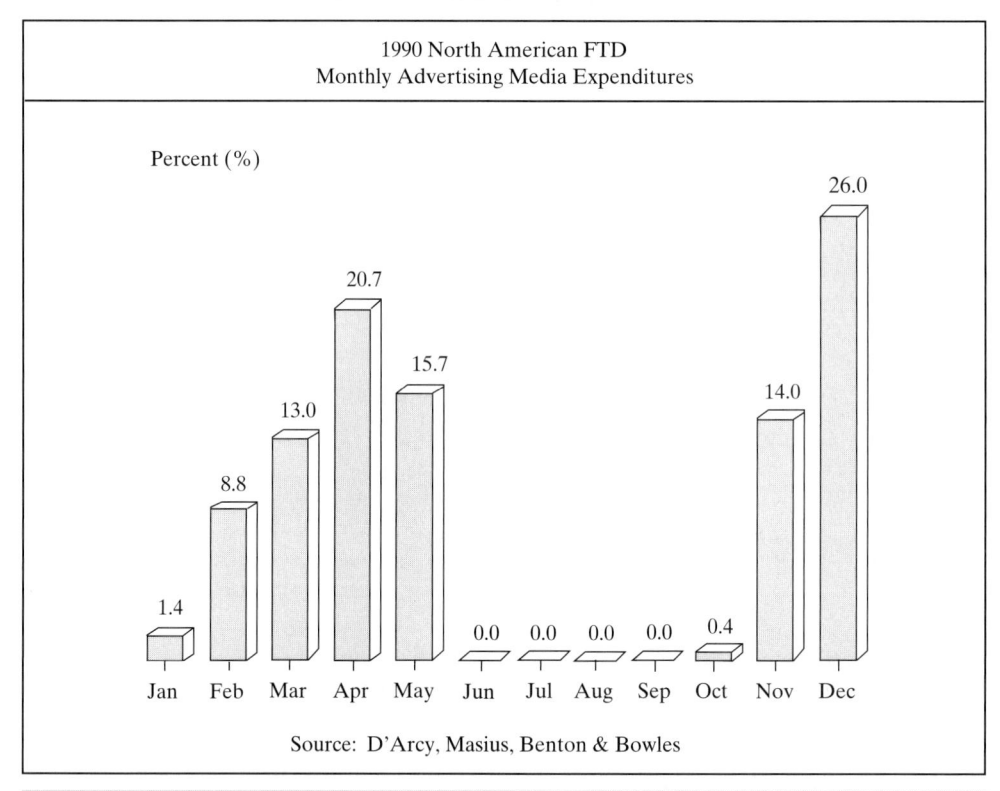

Month	Percent (%)
Jan	1.4
Feb	8.8
Mar	13.0
Apr	20.7
May	15.7
Jun	0.0
Jul	0.0
Aug	0.0
Sep	0.0
Oct	0.4
Nov	14.0
Dec	26.0

Source: D'Arcy, Masius, Benton & Bowles

EXHIBIT 5 1990 North American FTD Monthly Advertising Media Expenditures

Source: 1990/91 FTD Flower Business Fact Book.

florist departments were moving price points upwards from under $10 to compete more with florists whose average order was over $32. In addition, larger supermarket chains were purchasing directly from growers, distributors, and importers. Although many florists considered supermarkets to be a serious threat, they felt that supermarket employees lacked the sensitivity and expertise required to handle, package, maintain, and sell flowers effectively. Flower shops in supermarkets often, for example, were placed next to produce departments where fruit, as it ripened, produce ethylene gas, a chemical which hastens the deterioration of flowers. Sixty-five percent of the nation's 17,460 chain and 35% of the nation's 13,290 independent supermarkets sold flowers in 1990. The average annual sales for supermarket floral departments was $104,950, having grown almost fourfold in the past 10 years.

CALYX & COROLLA

Calyx & Corolla represented a true departure from traditional channels of distribution by directly linking the consumer with growers and, through Federal Express, growers with consumers. Calyx & Corolla was able to reduce very substantially the time it took to deliver flowers to the consumer's door. Calyx & Corolla typically delivered roses to the consumer within one to two days from the time they were cut. Anthuriums were delivered within three to four days. FTD deliveries of roses and anthuriums, in contrast, often occurred one to two weeks and two to three weeks, respectively, following cutting.

Owades and her colleagues realized that Calyx & Corolla was an entirely new concept which revolutionized the distribution of flowers. In order to succeed, however, they also had to understand the emotions that consumers tried to convey with flowers and to maintain critical relationships with both growers and Federal Express. Owades said in a speech about the Calyx & Corolla concept: "I envisioned a table with three legs, and Calyx & Corolla was only one of them. The second was the best flower growers available, and the third was Federal Express, the number one air carrier." Owades herself took responsibility for maintaining these relationships. She often telephoned or visited growers to overcome problems that had arisen, to negotiate seasonal prices, or simply to further strengthen healthy relationships. She also maintained direct contact with Federal Express representatives to maintain and improve their service.

Although Calyx & Corolla was by far the most successful of the "new wave" of mail order flower retailers, other companies with slightly different concepts were arising. The most direct competitor, a very well financed venture capital-backed start-up called "Floral Gift Express," had recently failed and Calyx & Corolla had acquired some of its assets. "Stillwater," another yet-unproven competitor, had recently entered the market. It was a division of a large, well-capitalized Japanese conglomerate.

Calyx & Corolla was not without problems, either. As Owades suggested:

> Did we have problems? Of course. How about the coldest December on record for our first Christmas? Where even our California and Florida growers were in a deep freeze (not to mention our customers in Minneapolis and Boston). Did we deliver their holiday bouquets? Of course. How? With numerous sleepless nights and with the extraordinary combined efforts of that strong partnership I spoke about—of Calyx & Corolla, our growers, and Federal Express, a partnership getting stronger and more solid with each challenge.
>
> —Excerpt from Owades speech

CALYX & COROLLA OPERATIONS

The headquarters of Calyx & Corolla were in modest offices just south of downtown San Francisco. Four thousand square feet housed the three senior executives, middle management, computers and fax machines, and all supporting functions, including the sales and customer service staff that took orders and answered customer inquiries or complaints respectively. Because the number of sales and customer service staff could rise from a normal complement of 5 to as many as 60 (full-time equivalents) before Mother's Day and other holidays, the company was squeezed for space at peak periods.

Apart from these offices, the company also occupied about 6,000 square feet of nearby warehouse space. Vases, wreaths, and dried flowers plus other nonperishable items and packaging supplies used by growers were kept there.

Owades and her colleagues recognized that the sales staff and customer service representatives were key components of the entire Calyx & Corolla system. For these positions they hired service-oriented people who demonstrated a real interest in flowers and plants. Their remuneration, which was about average for equivalent positions in the Bay area, was supplemented by various contests and incentive programs to reward them for exceptional quantitative and qualitative performance. Senior management maintained a very personal role in training and working with these individuals.

RELATIONSHIP WITH GROWERS

> She provided an answer to what growers perceived as a problem. The industry and market needs had changed. Flower importing had greatly increased, as had domestic production. But although supply, and thus competition, had increased, consumption hadn't kept up. What Owades offered was a new—and needed—outlet for selling flowers. "We had toyed with mail order, and even tested it. But we're growers, not marketers" (said a grower).
>
> —Working Woman Magazine, February 1991

Initially convincing growers to support Calyx & Corolla was one of Owades' toughest tasks.

> She faced the challenge of recruiting growers whose business for generations had consisted of packing 500 or 1,000 stems in large cartons and shipping them by truck across the country. They were being asked to carefully pack 11 perfect stems in special cartons,

packaged according to stringent aesthetic specifications, and to include a neatly handwritten gift card.

—*Working Woman Magazine*,
February 1991

She had, however, become acquainted with several growers through her previous work.

Together we worked through the logistics of how we might make Calyx & Corolla happen. We tested flowers for longevity and shipability and packaging. We tested various packing materials that would protect the flowers, keep them cool, keep them wet, maintain a constant temperature, and that would look good and be environmentally sound.

—Excerpt from Owades speech

Owades's relationships with the growers, combined with a lot of hard work, had resulted in the current network of 30 quality flower suppliers. For these growers, Calyx & Corolla represented an exciting new distribution opportunity that could increase sales and help offset the seasonality of their business.

Calyx & Corolla's growers were located primarily in California, Florida, and Hawaii. Although most were smaller operations with sales of under $1 million, several had sales of over $5 million. The largest had sales of $100 million. The eight largest growers combined supplied 80% of Calyx & Corolla's product. Sales to the company represented no more than 25% of any one grower's business. Calyx & Corolla had contracts with the growers that prohibited them from supplying any other mail order retailers.

The Sunbay Company was typical of the larger growers. Located about two hours south of San Francisco, this family-operated grower/distributor/wholesaler had sales of $6 million and carried 300 items. Of those, it grew 90, representing 20% of its revenues. The balance were flowers purchased from other local growers, imported, or purchased from other distant distributors, to complete the selection they offered local florists. Calyx & Corolla purchased only locally grown flowers from Sunbay.

In addition to educating growers to execute their retail responsibilities accurately and quickly, Calyx & Corolla provided growers with shipping boxes, cards, labels, vases, etc., and also sent them demand forecasts. The growers, in turn, notified Calyx & Corolla of low stock positions so substitute suppliers could be utilized or alternate selections offered at or after the time of customer ordering. Growers also informed Calyx & Corolla of excess stocks so special offers could be communicated by supplementary selling when taking incoming orders or by outbound telemarketing.

Two or more times daily, depending on the season and the grower, Calyx & Corolla transmitted orders by modem to its growers. There, the Calyx & Corolla account manager employed by the grower would supervise the printing of orders, selection and packing of flowers, handwriting of gift messages, and preparation of Federal Express shipping manifests. Although during the slow seasons several people could handle the volume, during peak holidays such as Mother's Day, up to 50 workers might be dedicated to fulfilling Calyx & Corolla orders at a particular grower.

The price Calyx & Corolla paid to growers was really a combination of two factors. While Calyx & Corolla was a big volume purchaser, it had to reimburse growers for the additional retail functions which they performed. As a consequence, Calyx & Corolla paid growers wholesale prices plus a surcharge to cover extra labor and other added costs associated with their orders. Despite this premium, Calyx & Corolla was able to achieve gross margins of almost 80% of sales.

Other expenses incurred by Calyx & Corolla included Sales and Marketing and General and Administrative expenses (G&A). Sales and Marketing expenses mainly consisted of catalog production and mailing ($.32 per catalog), mailing list rental ($.08 per name), freight out ($9.00 per order), and order processing and fulfillment ($5 per order). G&A included management salaries, depreciation, rent, and office supplies and other miscellaneous expenses.

RELATIONSHIP WITH FEDERAL EXPRESS

Owades knew that her next challenge would be winning an overnight-delivery service to her side. Ideally, she wanted the industry giant Federal Express Corporation, since, Owades says, customers feel it has the most reliable service. And without quality service, Calyx & Corolla would not be able to do business. But Owades knew that Federal Express had rigid operating procedures, and she would need exceptions for her start-up.

—*Working Woman Magazine,*
February 1991

Well, the Calyx & Corolla concept epitomized time-sensitivity. Here was the first mail order business in America that would promise exact-day delivery. The most important question we ask our customers is "When would you *like* that delivered?"...

But, my objective from the start was to establish a relationship where they would work *with* us—a partnership, together we would create and execute this novel means of marketing and distributing fresh flowers.

—Excerpt from Owades speech

Pricing was certainly one important issue, but such subjects as dealing with several seasonal peaks and deliveries on freezing days when flower recipients were not home were critical as well. Calyx & Corolla used Federal Express exclusively for shipping perishable products. For less-perishable products such as dried flowers or vases, it sometimes used United Parcel Service.

The relationship with Federal Express had matured over several years. At first, Federal Express considered Calyx & Corolla a minor account that required special attention. By 1991, however, the relationship had vastly improved. Owades had negotiated a price that varied little by weight. During peak periods, Federal Express now left trailers at the various growers to be filled and replaced when full. Many delivery drivers had also become aware of Calyx & Corolla and when no one was at home, would not leave packages to freeze on a cold day. Frozen flowers did not encourage customer repeat orders from Calyx & Corolla. Saturday deliveries were now offered as well, although Sunday and holiday deliveries were still an unresolved issue. Since few conventional florists delivered on Sundays and holidays, this service could represent a major competitive advantage for Calyx & Corolla. Federal Express had even placed computer terminals in the Calyx & Corolla offices and at the major growers to allow online tracking of shipments. This equipment permitted Calyx & Corolla customer service representatives to respond immediately to customer inquiries concerning the whereabouts of an order.

THE CALYX & COROLLA PRODUCT LINE

The Calyx & Corolla catalog included fresh and dried flowers, a selection of plants such as bonsai, and a variety of vases and other floral accessories. (See Exhibit 6 for selected pages from catalogs.) Prices for fresh flowers, including delivery, ranged from $23 for a single stem of protea to $60 or $70 dollars for bouquets of several dozen flowers. In addition, Calyx & Corolla offered vases and accessories starting at $12. The catalog also included continuity programs such as "a Year of Orchids" for $450, which included a selection of orchids to be delivered the first week of every month. Continuity programs comprised a significant portion of Calyx & Corolla sales. Most single items ranged from $30 to $60.

Although Calyx & Corolla did a substantial everyday business, seasonality was pronounced. Summer was slow and holiday spikes big. (See Exhibit 7 for a graph of monthly sales for the year ending June 30, 1990.) Continuity programs were, however, less seasonal, since they were usually gifts for the regular delivery of flowers over a number of months. Calyx & Corolla and its growers favored this business because it helped offset peaks and valleys.

Owades took an active role in developing the product line and the content of each catalog. She worked closely with Ann Lee and with the growers to create new and exciting bouquets to reflect changing tastes, seasonal variation, or to introduce new products.

CUSTOMERS AND COMMUNICATION

If the catalog format offered Calyx & Corolla a leg up on the competition, the flowers and arrangements pictured still had to look appealing, "like they belong in your home," says Owades, "or you would be proud to give them as gifts." Because flowers are

EXHIBIT 6 Selected Pages from Catalogs

FOR MEMORABLE GIFT GIVING, OUR FRESH FLOWERS MAKE A LASTING IMPRESSION!

"I have ordered four different arrangements from Calyx & Corolla...without exception, everyone has commented on the beauty of their gifts and the exquisite care with which they were packaged...you offer real value in your very reasonable pricing..."
— **William E. Beal**

■ When was the last time you bought flowers that lasted five weeks? Or even two weeks? If you bought them from a wire service, the supermarket, or a florist, chances are they lasted only a few days in the vase. That's because by the time you brought them home, they had already spent a lifetime (in flower terms) in warehouses, trucks and storerooms.

■ Calyx & Corolla flowers don't take detours. Our flowers are cut in the field and immediately flown by Federal Express to your doorstep.

■ *"Last year, I ordered a bouquet of orange and yellow gladioli...everyone was impressed with the quality of the flowers as well as the beauty...the flowers lasted for two weeks."*
—**Barbara H. Young**

■ Our customers tell us how easy we make it to give flowers with confidence. You may pick the varieties and colors you want. No more of those flowers-by-wire disappointments. We'll even help you select the appropriate vase.

■ *"Just a note to let you know how pleased I am with your services. It is great to know there are companies out there committed to excellence!"*
—**Kathryn A. Lalla**

■ Compare Calyx & Corolla with any other way of buying flowers, and we think you'll agree with these happy customers that we offer not just exceptional flowers...but exceptional value.

Sincerely,

Ruth M. Owades, President

© Copyright 1992, Calyx & Corolla. All rights reserved.

ABOUT OUR COVER...

Our exclusive Christmas Orchid Bouquet is an exciting new interpretation of traditional holiday colors of red, white and green. For more information, please see page 21.

Holiday Parallela

Parallel lines converge in a sophisticated and inviting arrangement inspired by contemporary French dried floral designs. Our miniature terrace has been "cultivated" with a row of preserved red roses behind a "fence" of cinnamon sticks and a "hedge" of crimson gypsy grass. Silvery bear grass and white rosa ti leaves add distinctive levels of interest. This artful design stands 16" tall and is contained in a woven basket accented with crossed cinnamon sticks and a sumptuous red moiré ribbon.

D018 **$89.00** *postpaid*

CHAPTER 4   *Measuring Customer Equity*   **181**

A Year of Roses

For that unforgettable gift for yourself or someone else, we offer 12 monthly deliveries of our exquisite roses.
A Year of Roses. RS1Y **$595.00**
Sleeved and beribboned single roses are perfect for party or wedding favors. Call for quantity prices.
Call toll-free: 1-800-877-0998.

Bi-Color Roses

Our coral and cream long-stemmed roses are especially welcome during the holiday season because of their warm, sun-kissed colors. Each freshly picked stem comes in a vial of flower food and water. The bouquet is enveloped in lavender tissue and tied with a bow. Air-shipped in bud, these lovely flowers will open to large pastel blooms.

12 stems RS12 **$59.00**
12 stems with classic glass vase RS1VS **$69.00**
18 stems RS18 **$79.00**
Cut crystal vase (as shown), 7¾" high VS2 **$89.00** *postpaid*

(Continued)

EXHIBIT 6 (cont.)

Hydrangea Wreath
Our exclusive fashionable, yet romantic, wreath is hand-crafted completely of preserved hydrangea blossoms. This lush, old-fashioned look is much admired among decorators both in Europe and America. Our design blends muted shades of blue, burgundy and green, handsomely complemented by a swath of French ribbon. Easy to hang from its attached hook, the wreath measures 14″ in diameter. Each wreath is unique, and color patterns will vary.
WR18 **$89.00** *postpaid*

Fire Fragrance Logs
Lovely as a hearth decoration, delightful as additions to your fire, these mini logs designed exclusively for Calyx & Corolla are made of dried herbs and flowers grown in Northern California. Five 6″-long bundles tied together with jute are charming when hung by your hearth. When your fire has burned to the smoldering stage, top it with an herb-and-flower log and enjoy the delicate perfume. You may also use the logs as kindling when you start your fire. Colors will vary.

1 set of five *DE82* **$36.00** *postpaid*
2 sets of five *DE83* **$64.00** *postpaid (to same address)*

Freesia
If you admire flowers as much for their scent as for their beauty, you will surely love freesia. A bouquet can perfume an entire room. Let us choose from cream, butter-yellow, lavender and pink — we'll send the mix that looks best the day we pick your order.

25 stems *FR25* **$44.00**
25 stems with classic glass vase *FRVS* **$58.00**
25 stems with Verdigris urn (as shown)
FRV1 **$79.00**
50 stems *FR50* **$64.00**
Verdigris urn, 8″ high *V007* **$39.00** *postpaid*

All flower prices include air delivery

**When you place your order,
ask about our Weekly Specials.**

How To Order

By Phone... just call our toll-free number to place your credit card orders:

1-800-800-7788

Our sales representatives are at your service. Pacific Time

Mon.–Fri. 6 am–6 pm
Sat. and Sun. 7 am–2 pm

Holiday Orders... for your convenience, we extend our order taking hours before most major holidays.

Mon.–Fri. 5 am–9 pm
Sat. and Sun. 6 am–6 pm

For best selection, please place holiday orders early.

Just a reminder...

Holiday	Date	Holiday	Date
Halloween	Oct. 31	Easter	Apr. 11
Thanksgiving	Nov. 26	Secretaries' Week	Apr. 19
Hanukkah (begins)	Dec. 20	Mother's Day	May 9
Christmas	Dec. 25	Father's Day	Jun. 20
Valentine's Day	Feb. 14	Fourth of July	Jul. 4
St. Patrick's Day	Mar. 17	Grandparents' Day	Sep. 13
Passover	Apr. 6	Rosh Hashanah	Sep. 28

But, if you forget or have waited until the last minute... call us, we will do whatever we can to rescue you.

By Mail... fill out the order form and send it to us. Be sure to give us a complete street address (including apartment number) when ordering for yourself or sending a gift. Sorry, we cannot deliver to a P.O. Box. Please include a daytime phone number.

By Fax... fax us your credit card order any time of day or night and we'll deliver as you request. **Fax 1-415-626-3781.**

The Calyx & Corolla Plant Doctor

Though we include care cards with our flowers and plants, many of you have expressed a desire for more information about the care or history of your Calyx & Corolla purchases. With this in mind, we have established a service to answer your questions. Please call the Plant Doctor, 1-415-431-2273.

Corporate Gift Services

Use Calyx & Corolla's corporate gift services as a year-round image builder and sales tool.

Our flowers and plants make a lasting impression that will attest to your company's style and taste. Flowers are particularly appropriate for client gifts, promotions, incentives and business events.

We offer corporate gift-planning services to businesses large and small. If you are interested in a corporate account, gifts in quantity or flowers at work and would like to receive our 1992-1993 corporate gift catalog please call us at 1-800-800-7788.

Shipping and Super Rush

Fresh Flowers and Plants... are delivered by air via Federal Express. You will receive them within 1–5 working days, depending on the variety and origin. For birthdays, holidays and other special events, we will ship to arrive on the exact date whenever possible. (Sorry, we cannot deliver on Sundays.) Our prices include packing and air express. There is a $3.95 handling charge for each address.

Dried floral designs and bulb kits... are shipped via UPS within 48 hours of your order. There is a $3.95 handling charge for each address.

Super Rush Service... we also offer exact day, extra fast deliveries for dried designs and bulb kits for an additional charge of $9.95.

Please Note

We are not able to make deliveries to Puerto Rico, Mexico, Canada, or to an APO or FPO address. There is a $10.00 surcharge on shipments to Alaska and Hawaii. Plants cannot be shipped to Hawaii.

Substitutions and Returns

If, due to crop failures or poor weather conditions, a particular flower is not suitable for shipping, we will send a fresh selection of equal or greater value. For items other than flowers and plants, please return via UPS or prepaid U.S. mail within three weeks of receipt. If there is shipping damage to any merchandise please retain the box and all packing materials and contact our Customer Service Department at 1-800-877-0998.

About Our Mailings

Mail Preference Service... from time to time, we make our customer list available to carefully selected reputable companies whose products we feel may be of interest to you. Should you not wish to receive such mailings, please send an exact copy of your mailing label to: Calyx & Corolla Mail Preference Service, 1550 Bryant Street #900, San Francisco, California 94103.

Duplicate Mailings... if you receive duplicates of our catalog, please copy exactly and/or enclose the mailing labels from all of them, indicating the proper name and address, and we will correct the situation. Please send to the address listed above.

Customer Service and Flower Consultant

We are here to serve you. If you have any questions regarding your order, need information about a particular flower or need help in selecting appropriate flowers and vases for any occasion, please call during the following hours, Pacific Time: 6 am–6 pm Mon.–Fri. 1-800-877-0998.

Our Guarantee

We cut and ship only the finest and freshest flowers. If for some reason you are not satisfied with your order, we will replace it promptly or refund your money.

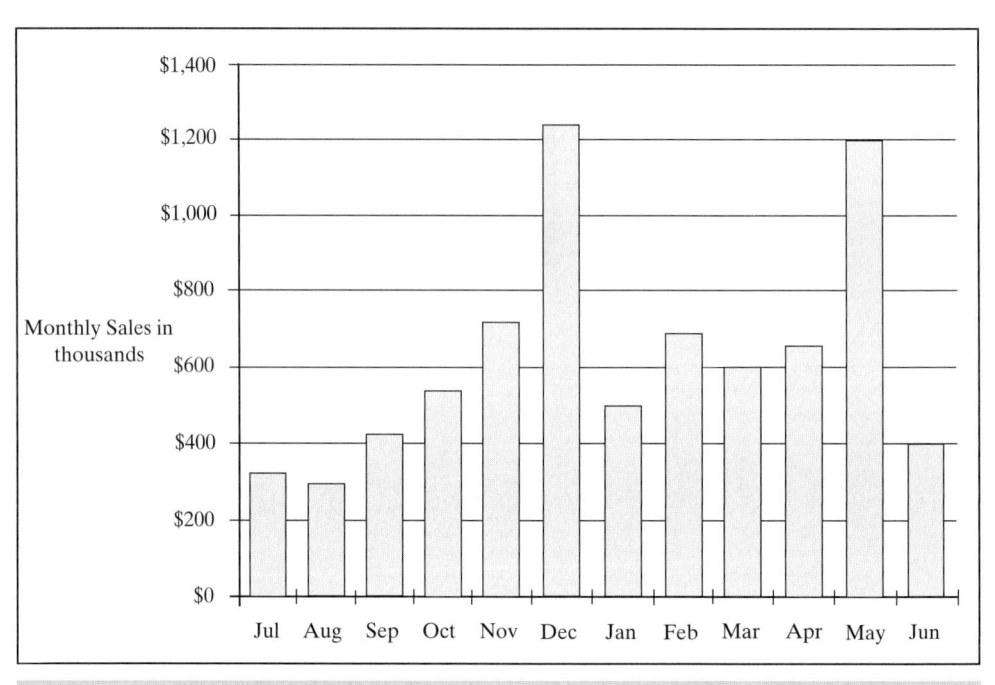

EXHIBIT 7 Graph of Calyx & Corolla Monthly Sales for the Year Ending June 30, 1990

"emotional," her presentation was all the more challenging. "Poets throughout the ages have known that when words don't communicate, flowers do."

Yet no matter how beautiful the photographs, Owades feared that page after page of flowers and vases could get boring fast. So in addition to the cost and color choices in each selection's accompanying copy, she hit on the strategy of weaving in some educational trivia ("The curled flower of the petite calla lily is actually a modified leaf"); consumer information ("Protea stay fresh in water for up to two weeks; after that, they dry beautifully"); and arrangement suggestions ("Glads are especially striking when displayed in a tall vase").

—WORKING WOMAN MAGAZINE,
FEBRUARY 1991

Seventy percent of Calyx & Corolla's revenues were derived directly from the catalog, while 20% were derived from corporate clients and promotional "tie-ins." The remaining 10% was from outgoing telemarketing to previous flower recipients and existing customers.

The catalog was the main form of advertising. Six catalogs were produced every year and mailed out under eight to nine covers. In fiscal 1991 100,000 prior customers received one catalog per month, which provided 60,000 orders. Recipients of Calyx & Corolla flowers and others who had called to inquire about Calyx & Corolla flowers, who cumulatively totaled 500,000, received six catalogs each per year. The balance of the 12,055,000 catalogs mailed in fiscal 1991 were to 7,855,000 rented mailing-list names. Response rates varied significantly. Prior customer mailings yielded about 5% to 10%, while recipient and rented mailing lists only yielded between 1% and 2%. The recent rise in postal rates added materially to the expense of obtaining the attention of consumers who already received an avalanche of catalogs from other retailers.

Ann Lee characterized active buyers as those who had purchased at least two times a year, although she added that some purchased as many as 10 times a year. Eighty-five percent of these customers were women, mostly ranging in age from 30 to 55. Most worked and had substantial disposable income. Sophisticated information systems allowed Calyx & Corolla executives to analyze and manipulate the extensive database of customers, recipients, and prospects, allowing them to understand better their customers and to target their mailings more precisely. The largest group of potential buyers, however, were people who patronized florists or other retailers and were unaccustomed to buying anything by mail order.

Lee, in addition to her other responsibilities, marketed flowers to corporate clients who used them for reception areas, conference rooms, incentive programs, and customer gift programs. But by far the greatest proportion of corporate flower purchases were for promotional tie-ins, a segment of the business which management considered a major opportunity for incremental sales, and, more important, new mail order customers.

> Promotions and incentives, corporate gifts, joint marketing approaches with specific partners and consumer brands—all these offer exciting potential both for revenues, for generating new customers, and for expanding awareness of our service and our product.
>
> —Excerpt from Owades speech

Lee maintained a frequently referred-to list of objectives for proposed promotional programs. Each program had to (1) coincide with available resources, (2) fit with the Calyx & Corolla image, (3) open doors for new business opportunities, (4) be profitable, (5) not aggravate seasonal peaks, and (6) permit Calyx & Corolla to do a good job. Several such programs are described below.

Bloomingdale's used Calyx & Corolla flowers to help promote a selection of vases on Mother's Day. Advertised at Bloomingdale's expense through a full-page advertisement in *The New Yorker* (Exhibit 8) and other upscale regional publications, five dendrobium orchids were offered free with the purchase of any vase. A point-of-sale display greeted customers at each store, featuring a variety of vases complete with flowers. The vases were priced between $150 and $1,000. When purchasing a vase, the customer designated the recipient of the bouquet. Calyx & Corolla provided the flowers, which normally sold in the catalog for $34, at a discount to Bloomingdale's.

The program was a success. Lee believed that it opened the door for similar opportunities with other upscale retailers.

Another tie-in program was with SmithKline Beecham (SB) for a Mother's Day promotion of Contac 12-hour caplets for allergy relief. This program comprised four stages: (1) flowers were sent to SB retailers to spruce up stores and to promote Contac; (2) $10 coupons usable for discounts on purchase of Calyx & Corolla flowers were offered to store employees to generate excitement; (3) newspaper freestanding insert coupons were placed (see Exhibit 9) to gain exposure to 50 million readers, with coupons for $5 off an order to Calyx & Corolla without a Contac purchase and two coupons at $10 each for discounts on two different flower orders with proof of purchase of Contac (a special 800 number with a telemarketing agency was used for Calyx & Corolla orders), and (4) at its conclusion, SB purchased and sent bouquets to all distributors and key store personnel for contributing to the program's success.

The program was very profitable. Three out of four stages performed well, while sales from the consumer stage missed plan. The experience of creating and implementing this complex multi-level program was a valuable education and created a foundation for future promotions of this type.

Discussions were currently under way with other consumer product manufacturers for future programs. Other types of programs were being considered as well. A major mail order retailer was committed to including several pages of a forthcoming catalog to a selection of Calyx & Corolla flowers. Also under consideration was what was termed an "affinity group promotion." This program would offer discounts on flowers to doctors who were members of the Voluntary Hospitals of America (VHA), a trade organization that, among other services, arranged for discounts to doctors on the purchase of office and other supplies. Lee had, however, not yet committed Calyx & Corolla to these programs.

EXHIBIT 8 Bloomingdale's Advertisement in the *New Yorker*

Give Mother The Vase, And We'll Send Orchids

Complimentary Orchid Bouquet—a gift from Calyx & Corolla of San Francisco with any Baccarat, Lalique, Waterford, Orrefors or Kosta Boda Vase Purchase of $150 or More.
(Crystal on 6, New York. And in all our stores.)

WATERFORD
Introducing the new
Ashbourne 10" vase.
exclusively ours. 225.00

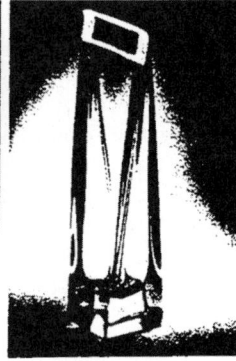

KOSTA BODA
Sails 11¾" vase,
exclusively ours, designed
by Goran Wärff. 150.00

LALIQUE
Sylvie 9" vase
designed in 1956 by Marc Lalique.
690.00

BACCARAT
Presenting the new
Giverny 10" vase, exclusively ours,
designed by Robert Rigot. 265.00

ORREFORS
Denise 9" vase,
exclusively ours, designed
by Erika Lagerbielke. 150.00

MOTHER'S DAY MAY TWELFTH
bloomingdale's

TO ORDER PHONE TOLL FREE 24 HOURS A DAY, 7 DAYS A WEEK (800) 777-4999 REF. NO. C1422. CALL 355-5900 FOR CUSTOMER SERVICE ONLY.

Complimentary Bouquet With Any Baccarat, Lalique, Waterford, Orrefors or Kosta Boda Vase Purchase of $150 Or More

A dendrobium orchid bouquet from Calyx & Corolla (reg. 34.00) will be sent anywhere in the continental U.S. as our gift in time for Mother's Day if your order is placed by May 7th. (Later purchases will receive Calyx & Corolla gift certificates.)

CHAPTER 4 *Measuring Customer Equity* **187**

EXHIBIT 9   Newspaper Freestanding Insert Coupons of SmithKline Beecham

The last, and considered one of the most important, communications efforts was an active public relations initiative which Owades herself led. Considerable positive press, including articles in *Time* magazine, the *Wall Street Journal*, and the *International Herald Tribune,* had been generated, which had resulted in both new catalog and corporate customers (see Exhibit 10 for a partial list of media attention to Calyx & Corolla and copies of selected articles).

CALYX & COROLLA'S ULTIMATE POSITIONING

It was in this context that Owades and other members of the top management team were assessing their options for growing the business. One option was for Calyx & Corolla to capture more gift business from traditional florists and possibly even increase total flower sales. The idea would be to sell also to customers who ordinarily did not buy much of anything by mail order.

EXHIBIT 10 Partial List of Media Attention to Calyx & Corolla

"A Scripps Education Goes to Work"	*Scripps College Bulletin*, Summer 1989
"Hot People"	*Metropolitan Home*, February 1990
"Fortune People — A Harvard Study"	*Fortune*, November 5, 1990
"Hearts and Flowers: The Nosegay Express"	*Wall Street Journal*, February 14, 1991
"Just Picked Flowers: A Fresh Idea Pays"	*International Herald Tribune*, February 9-10, 1991
"The Truth About Ruth"	*Entrepreneurial Woman*, July/August 1990
"Stamping Out Mail-Order Misbeliefs"	*Los Angeles Times*, May 4, 1990
"Bouquet of the Month"	*Detroit Free Press*, July 1, 1990
"Floral Catalog Blooms with Exotic, Hard-to-Find Greenery"	*Rocky Mountain News*, January 25, 1990
"Of Wreaths and Flowers"	*San Francisco Chronicle*, November 29, 1989
"Flower Power"	*Business Week*, February 19, 1990
"Flowers, Fresh from the Growers to You"	*Gannett Westchester Newspapers*, August 24, 1989
"What's Hot: Flowers, Fresh, and Fast"	*San Jose Mercury News*, August 29, 1989
"Fresh Flowers by Catalog"	*San Francisco Chronicle*, October 18, 1989
"Catalog Bazaar"	*Harper's Bazaar*, June 1991
"Business Is Blooming"	*Catalog Age*, January 1991
"News Break"	*ELLE Magazine*, February 1991
"Profits in Bloom"	*TIME Magazine*, February 18, 1991
"Growing a New Market Niche"	*Working Woman*, February 1991
Television interview	"Business Marketplace," ABC TV San Francisco, California September 15, 1991
Television interview	"The Morning Exchange," ABC TV Cleveland, Ohio October 9, 1991

EXHIBIT 10 (cont.) *Wall Street Journal* article, February 14, 1991

Hearts and Flowers: The Nosegay Express

by Patti Hagan

Here we are, V-Day 1991, and a flowery mail-order catalog has saved me from the lists of Valentine's procrastinators. Otherwise, I might have made my valentine flower arrangements on the subway yesterday, humored by a supposed New York Post story blown up on a poster. "300 LB. QUEENS MAN MOVED BY 800 FLOWERS," and bylined Iris Inavase. "A 300 lb. Queens man, 52, was reduced to tears today by 800 Flowers," Ms. Inavase wrote. "To look at him, you would have thought it would take a professional moving company to budge him. But all it took was a $29.95 floral arrangement sent by 1-800-Flowers, the 24-hour-anytime-to-anyone floral delivery service." Amusing as I found the teary-eyed Ferdinand, hankie in one hand, 800 Flowers nosegay in the other, I'd long since dialed another floral 800 (1-800-877-7836) to reach Calyx & Corolla, in California.

A few months ago a friend had slipped me the catalog, figuring I'd appreciate the botanical name and the upscale difference. Calyx & Corolla does not ride the subway; C&C uses no weepy fat men. Calyx & Corolla instead runs 32 pages of flower pictures, only, on the theory that flowers best sell flowers, quite unassisted by kittens, Dalmatians, golden retrievers, Snoopy or Snow White and the Seven Dwarfs. Calyx & Corolla relies on flowers whose ancient good design makes them virtually fashion-proof: roses, daffodils, tulips, lilies ($395 for a year of lilies), orchids ($450 a year), protea. ("Botanists tell us that protea are one of the oldest flowers on the earth," the C&C care card informs. "Known to exist in prehistoric times, they survived the trials of evolution far better than the dinosaur.")

Something about the catalog reminded me of Eden-Gardener's Eden, the upscale gardening catalog—and sure enough Calyx & Corolla, which now operates at the cutting edge of the cut-flower business, is the latest eureka of floral entrepreneuse Ruth Owades, the Harvard MBA. Her alma mater immortalized her in a widely taught 1982 Business School case study of her travails, in 1978, in founding Gardener's Eden (one Jeremiah told her: "Gardening is a blue-collar hobby, it'll never fly. There is no way in the world that people will buy things for their garden. If this was such a good idea, dearie, some man would have already done it.").

In 1982 she sold Boston-based Gardener's Eden to Williams-Sonoma for a cool million but stayed on for five years to manage G. Eden out West. By 1987, she had noticed an empty horticultural niche in the cut-flower industry. Her idea was to make possible a fast, fresh, FedExed flower valentine any time of the year by brokering a computer marriage of convenience between two industries that had heretofore never even been engaged: mail-order catalogs and fresh cut flowers. Though her research told her the U.S. cut-flower industry had been growing about 10% a year since the mid-80s, she found "an industry still stuck in the '50s."

She persuaded 25 flower growers to sign on to her computer network. She got them to install computers, modems for talking to the C&C mainframe in San Francisco, fax machines. And she taught them to cut flowers to order and pack them with aesthetic TLC. Roses would be dethorned by hand and travel with "ice pillows under their heads." Wood excelsior would cushion their every blow. "What we go through with gerberas is pretty amazing," Ms. Owades admits. "First of all they are capped with net caps in the fields where they're grown. Then because their stems tend to be weak, the grower puts [each of] them in thick straws."

Then, to deliver the critical Freshness Dividend, Ms. Owades prevailed on Federal Express to add Calyx & Corolla's natural brown

(*Continued*)

EXHIBIT 10 (cont.)

boxes to its "brown box business," and fly the fresh cut flowers direct from grower to customer, guaranteeing arrival on the exact day requested. FedEx was the crucial link in Ms. Owades's new floral-delivery short-circuit service. In her catalog she explains that Calyx & Corolla "fresh" means "five to 10 days fresher than any other flowers you can buy!" Her research had revealed that "most flowers that we buy at a florist or certainly at a Korean grocer are at least seven to 10 days old." For her business, "I knew that the benefit had to be FRESHNESS. We cut to order. You receive a flower that was cut 24 to 48 hours previously. You get the seven to 10 days in your vase, instead of on a truck or in a distributor's warehouse."

Though this is Calyx & Corolla's biggest day of the year, Americans are floral underconsumers. Ms. Owades believes she's still battling the Puritan ethic. "It's not only that we're puritanical and feel that we don't deserve flowers on a regular basis, I also think that we are quite intimidated by flowers." However, this may be changing thanks to the puritanical American capacity for guilt. A spring 1990 Gallup Poll, "Americans on Gift Giving," found that for 51% of Americans "when feeling guilty, flowers and plants are the likely gift." Ms. Owades says of subscribers to Calyx & Corolla's flowers by the year, half-year and quarter: "That's for someone who either loves flowers or else it's a gift from someone who feels really guilty about what he did." And in fact C&C offers a sort of rescue service for the guilty, volunteering on the order form "if you forget or have waited until the last minute... call us, we will do whatever we can to rescue you." And then the Calyx & Corolla Plant Doctor is on call to help survivors baby their plants and flowers. "People call back and say 'it works! My gardenia is thriving!'" Ms. Owades notes. "They're so happy they want to send him things. They're all trying to bake him chocolate cakes. We've had to limit it. They can send recipes." Others simply write: "If only your catalog had existed five years ago, my wife wouldn't have left me!" They send color snapshots of week-old bouquets *still fresh*. "I'm writing to thank you for giving me 'points' with my mother-in-law," one California woman wrote. "I'd long been given to understand that she prefers flowers to remain in gardens, I purposely avoided sending out bouquets." But the Pink Fringed Carnations bouquet changed everything.

Last Feb. 14 an irate Philadelphian wrote in the accusative: "Dear Calyx & Corolla: You've ruined my love life! How could you not have shipped the Valentine's Day tulips to my girlfriend?!" An apology followed two days later: "I guess 'polite thank yous' are no longer a way of life. But at least I am no longer in the doghouse."

In January Ms. Owades sent her flower catalog to war, addressing a special message to American servicemen and women in the Persian Gulf: "As Valentine's Day approaches, we would like to help you remember those that you love back home. Although the distance to your loved ones may be great, you can surprise them by sending them fresh, beautiful flowers this Valentine's Day." Wishing them all home soon, she asked, "Please identify yourself as a part of Operation Desert Storm in order to receive your discount." 20%.

On Jan. 16, the day the U.S. began bombing, Calyx & Corolla received a fax from a soldier on duty in Saudia Arabia. He requested that "Love" cards and bouquets be dispatched to five valentines in five different towns in three states: Lori, Melissa, Dee, Beth and Georgeanne. Once again Calyx & Corolla gave new meaning to the word fresh.

This article first appeared in *The Wall Street Journal* of February 14, 1991. It is reprinted with the permission of Patti Hagan, *WSJ* Gardening Columnist.

EXHIBIT 10 *(cont.)-International Herald Tribune* article, Business/Finance, Saturday–Sunday, February 9–10, 1991

Just-Picked Flowers: A Fresh Idea Pays

by Lawrence Malkin

NEW YORK - Recession may be deepening and war fears rising, but the animal spirits in some American businesses show no signs of wilting yet. Think flowers. Think phone or fax to order them, picked the same day by their growers. Then think Federal Express to deliver them overnight.

Two years ago Ruth M. Owades assembled all these disparate elements and created a brand new business that is definitely greater than the sum of its parts.

Calyx & Corolla, as she named her company with floral terminology, grossed $10 million last year and is growing by about 10 percent a month against the slumping U.S. business tide.

A staff replying to a toll-free number in San Francisco takes an average of about 25,000 orders a month, collates them by computer and then forwards them on-line to computers at the company's contract growers in California and Florida.

The flowers are packed in specially insulated boxes and accompanied by the sender's greetings, done in calligraphy. At peak times such as Valentine's Day and Mother's Day Federal Express has to send 18-wheel trucks to move the orders from flower farm to airport.

Current specials range from 24 miniature carnations for $32.50 to 25 daffodils for $47, to a dozen long-stemmed roses for $68. Prices include delivery of flowers that are 24 hours old instead of several days old—as they would be after going through middlemen in the retail delivery chain.

The catalogue also offers tropical flowers, special wreaths, bonsai trees, and even monthly subscriptions for the business person too busy to remember. The trade publication *Catalog Age* rates Ms. Owades one of the best in the mail-order business.

Calyx & Corolla has sent flowers to celebrities including Henry Kissinger and Ivana Trump, and one of Rose Kennedy's great grandchildren orders one hundred flowers from the company for Mrs. Kennedy's centenary.

Never one to miss a market opportunity, Ms. Owades also shipped catalogs to military personnel in Saudi Arabia offering them a 20 percent discount. A score of orders from troops in Operation Desert Storm have already been dispatched to loved ones at home.

The flowers are packed in insulated boxes, with the sender's greetings in calligraphy. At peak time, 18-wheel trucks move the flowers from farm to airport.

Calyx & Corolla and Federal Express are waiting at least until more customs barriers come down in 1992 to consider deliveries within Europe, where the logistics would be even more complex than they were in the United States.

Ms. Owades, 44, had already made her first million creating a mail-order firm selling high-priced garden equipment to upmarket buyers; the imponderables of starting up Gardener's Eden is now a case study at her alma mater, Harvard Business School.

She sold out to a big catalog firm and moved to California to run the business for the new owners. Her husband, Joseph Owades, who creates special beer recipes for large companies, moved from Boston with her, and she started looking for another start-up as ominous signs appeared in the U.S. economy. "I discovered that chocolates, ice cream, beer, and flowers are relatively recession-proof," Ms. Owades said.

"People send flowers in recession to apologize for the vacation they have to cancel," she said. Corporate clients have also boosted their orders to make up for canceling company parties and, Ms. Owades said, to help lift the war blues in the office.

(Continued)

EXHIBIT 10 (cont.)

Five years ago, not enough of the elements would have been in place with enough sophistication to make Calyx & Corolla work. She needed absolutely reliable airfreight service, an inexpensive computer network, special packaging such as iced bud-holders for roses, and, she says, "consumer confidence in the reliability of mail order."

Most of all, she said, the industry had to have confidence that it could improve on its traditional flowers-by-wire delivery system.

The single most important link in the chain was Federal Express, which had to help design the packaging, devise a special rate structure and install a computer tracking system at each of the contract growers.

Dick Metzler, the airfreight company's U.S. marketing chief, acknowledges that he was reluctant at first to gamble with an untried business to make the kinds of adjustments that Federal Express provides its regular clients.

"But we rolled the dice with Ruth, and we're not sorry," he said. "She has carved out a very clever niche for herself, and she's going to own it for a long time to come."

Walter Salmon, professor of retailing at Harvard Business School, says Calyx & Corolla is a perfect example of how to look at an industry as a whole and develop a new way of selling.

In fact, he's thinking of making Ms. Owades's second business start-up into another case study.

One experiment under consideration was a test advertising campaign prior to at least one major holiday in the Minneapolis/St. Paul market. Table A summarizes demographic information.

This campaign was planned, if it lasted 12 months, to at least double the annual FTD advertising budget of 21¢ per household ($24 million ÷ 114,000,000 households in the United States). The second year would taper to one and a half times the FTD budget and remain at parity thereafter. For the test to be successful, Calyx & Corolla management thought that the cost to acquire a new customer using this medium should not exceed the cost of current methods. Television advertising would emphasize the freshness and longevity of Calyx & Corolla flowers, with an 800 number to call to order either a specifically promoted floral arrangement or the catalog. Newspaper and magazine advertisements would consist of inserting "mini-catalogs" into Sunday newspaper supplements and run-of-press (ROP) promotions for a $34 seasonal bouquet. Printing costs for the mini-catalogs would cost about 9¢ each. What sort of response, Calyx & Corolla executives questioned, would they have to generate in order to justify expanding the advertising program beyond the test area? What would be the value of the names generated? Should Calyx & Corolla time the campaign to coincide with a holiday and confront FTD head on, or choose a less-competitive season and promote everyday floral purchases?

In the opinion of Ruth Owades and the other members of the top management team, Calyx & Corolla was an exceptionally promising, yet still

TABLE A Minneapolis/St. Paul TV Market Area—Estimates

Population	3,610,700
Households	1,352,400
Age	
Over 50	873,100
35–49	737,400
25–34	655,600
Less than 25	1,344,600
After-tax disposable income	
Median	$30,800
$10–20,000	17.9%
20–35	26.9%
35–40	21.9%
50+	21.3%

Source: Reprinted by permission of Sales Marketing Management. Copyright: Survey of Buying Power Part II, November 13, 1989

only partly proven, start-up venture. Given the skills, values, and aspirations of the entrepreneurs and the investors, and the externalities which confronted them, what changes in their current strategy and positioning should Calyx & Corolla undertake? What might be the financial and organizational implications of a much more aggressive growth strategy, especially if they had to approach external financial markets to fund the advertising program under consideration? ∎

PART II: DEVELOPING STRATEGIES FOR
CUSTOMER EQUITY MANAGEMENT

CHAPTER 5

Customer Selection[1]

Individual customers are the core of any business enterprise, yet most firms continue to formulate and implement strategies at broad market and segment levels. At market level they ask, "what business are we in?" Then they implement at segment level those marketing strategies that emphasize choice of segments and take a holistic approach to managing different elements of the marketing effort for each segment served. Management of individual opportunities, if considered relevant at all, tends to be exclusively aimed at select large customers using national or key account programs, and is typically left to the sales function.

◆ EFFECTIVE CUSTOMER MANAGEMENT STRATEGY

Most marketing firms' customer bases can be characterized as a pyramid structure with a few large customers accounting for the majority of sales (see Figure 5-1). That vendors have traditionally managed a few of their large and important customers on an individual basis reflects restrictions imposed by market and industry structures and limitations with respect to access to customer information and interactive technologies. This chapter looks at several trends, however, that are forcing firms to shift their focus and change their approach. Customer consolidation, market globalization, and rapid commoditization cycles are pushing vendors to adopt more sophisticated approaches to serving their large customers.[2] Realizing that the reactive, short-term customer management initiatives of the past will leave them both vulnerable to exploitation by these large customers and exposed to competitive threats, more and more firms are looking to develop proactive, long-term, and enterprise-level customer management systems.

Vendors are also expanding the scope of their customer management systems to include midsize customers that they suspect might be the profit bulge in their customer bases. In most markets, these customers are as sophisticated as larger customers are, share similar needs with them, and, lacking the power to squeeze vendor profit margins, are not as price sensitive as are larger customers. Finally, recent advances in information and interactive technologies have dramatically reduced the costs of collecting and analyzing information about, and subsequently interacting with, individual small customers.

---

[1] Adapted from Das Narayandas, "Note on Customer Management," Harvard Business School Note # 502-073 (2002).
[2] James C. Anderson, and James A. Narus, *Business Market Management: Understanding, Creating, and Delivering Value* (Upper Saddle River, N.J: Prentice Hall, 1999).

FIGURE 5-1 Pyramid Structure of Customer Base

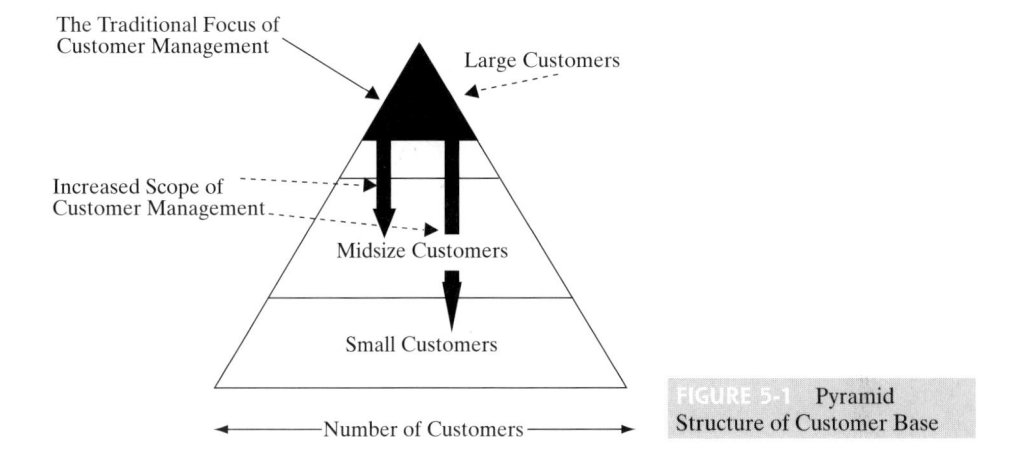

Collectively, these changes are driving firms to move beyond the rhetoric of "being customer focused" and actually manage individually a majority of their large, medium, and small customers.

The first step in effective customer management strategy begins with selection decisions. Is one opportunity more promising than another? What might be the impact of a particular sale on the firm? Because every opportunity a firm chooses to serve will have a significant impact, positive or negative, on its overall business, it is sometimes better, as in all relationships in life, to say "no" at the outset. Having carefully thought through a set of selection decisions, management may come up with other questions. Should all opportunities be managed similarly or should individual opportunities be managed to different objectives? Believing that all customers can be managed for profit does not make it true; firms must realize that a "one size fits all" approach does not always work. Having selected the opportunities to serve, it is important for business marketers to recognize and understand the impact of their decisions on their skills, capabilities, and resources. It is important to choose wisely when it comes to customers and orders.

The second step in customer management is monitoring the impact of the selection decisions. Sellers' choices of orders and customers define their skill set over time (*whom we serve affects who we become*) and their abilities, in turn, affect their choice of orders and customers (*who we are affects whom we can serve*).

◆ CUSTOMER SELECTION

Marketing strategy has always emphasized the importance of market selection. With a lot at stake, including enormous investments of resources, firms spend significant amounts of time in defining the businesses they are in. Customer selection requires the same discipline; every customer can have a significant impact on a vendor's profits.

To understand the impact of customer choice on a firm's skill set, consider Fabtek, a traditional custom fabricator of titanium structures.[3] Through several poor customer

---
[3]Benson Shapiro and Rowland Moriarty, "Fabtek (A)," Harvard Business School Case #592-095 (1992).

◆ BOX 5-1 ◆

Amazon.com Creates Individualized Segments to Capture Customers

Imagine visiting a Web site where not only are you greeted by name, but a link leads you to a virtual store named after you, offering you savings and deals on products that have been selected in accordance with your interests. Impressed? Interested?

Millions of people have been, and that is why, while other Internet retailers are forced to close shop, Amazon.com not only endures, but also continues to diversify, grow, and post profits. Started by Jeff Bezos in 1994, Amazon.com has grown from an online bookstore to a purveyor of all types of goods, from clothing to electronics, and boasts the highest American Customer Satisfaction Index score ever recorded in any service industry.

What is the secret to Amazon.com's success? When asked, Bezos, who in 1998 was named Marketer of the Year by Time Magazine, responds that the source of his competitive advantage is not price or product line, but that Amazon.com creates a vastly superior customer service experience than does any other online retailer.

At a time when customer relationship management has been emphasized but not entirely put into practice, Amazon caters to its customers, investing time to find out information specific to each one. Amazon.com posts a link to a list of recommended products specific to each customer. This list is generated by keeping track of all items that customer previously bought or rated. Based on these previous items, Amazon compiles a list of items that are similar, and this is that customer's personal recommendations.

Personalization does not end there. "Instant Order Updates" remind shoppers what items they have already bought so that they do not accidentally purchase the same item twice. Amazon.com has built its following by knowing its customers, educating them about their services, informing them proactively of new offerings, and delivering value-added services such as e-mailing them when a new product fitting their profile is released.

Amazon.com has built loyalty, not just because of its service, but with the time and effort that customers would themselves have to invest in educating another company about their likes and dislikes. In addition, Amazon.com has fostered a sense of community; buyers themselves create value by contributing book reviews or rating their purchases; these are posted for anyone to read.

This close attention to customer relationship management has certainly paid off: the free cash flow for fiscal 2002 equaled $135 million. In addition, Amazon.com experienced a 28 percent sales growth, fueled by lower prices, and perks such as free shipping on most orders over $25.

The company is beginning to compete further on price. Amazon.com has introduced a new feature, Gold Box Offers. These are products sold by Amazon or its selected merchants, and these products are paired with limited-time, extra-savings coupons. In addition, Amazon has recently begun to discount its higher-priced books.

According to its Web site, Amazon seeks to be the "world's most customer-centric company," expanding fully beyond its initial bookstore offerings. With features such as the Amazon Marketplace, zShops, and auctions, those businesses and individuals approved by Amazon.com can sell virtually anything to its millions of customers, ensuring the diversity of product offerings. In addition to this, in recent years Amazon.com has begun to partner, with great success, with other retailers and services, broadening its selections even more.

In 2001, Amazon.com confirmed the success of its 10-year co-branding pact with Toys'R'Us by signing a similar deal with affiliate babiesrus.com. In both deals, the retailer looks after the merchandising, planning, buying, and inventory management, while Amazon.com manages the online shopping end, including Web site development, order fulfillment, and customer service.

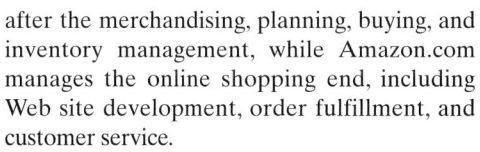

Amazon.com has also recently introduced the Amazon.com Platinum Visa® card, with a promotion whereby an initial Amazon.com order over $30 using the card receives a $30 discount. Customers receive points for subsequent purchases made with the card, and when 2500 points have been accumulated, a $25 Amazon.com Reward Certificate is granted.

With constant innovation and consistent emphasis on customer service, Amazon.com has flourished, providing value and a respected brand to customers, as well as personalized interaction, which will ensure continued growth.

SOURCES: "Amazon.com Taps SAS for Business Intelligence Tools—E retailer Plans to Simplify Internal Processes and Boost Customer Service Efforts," *Information Week,* October 16, 2000. "Amazon, ToysRUs Extends E-Commerce Relationship," *Newsbytes News Network,* May 23, 2001. Dan Tapscott, "Use the Net to Invest in Relationships," *Computer World,* August 13, 2001. The ACSI was developed by the National Quality Research Center at The University of Michigan Business School.

selection decisions, the firm had landed in the anomalous situation of operating unprofitably at full capacity, with dissatisfied customers complaining about project delays. Under these circumstances, the firm was presented with four potential opportunities. The first, from Refco, Fabtek's largest customer, an opportunity to produce a product similar in design to past orders but in much larger volumes, put Fabtek at risk of becoming too dependent on a single customer relationship. The second opportunity, an order from Pierce-Pike, which had done business primarily with Fabtek's competitors, represented the culmination of a four-year sales effort by Fabtek's head of sales. An order from Worldwide Paper for a line of proprietary products that could potentially be developed into a standard product line presented an opportunity for Fabtek to shift from custom orders and a job-shop environment to standardized orders manufactured on a production line. The final opportunity, an order from Kathco for titanium electrodes, was a "one-shot" deal that would not tax Fabtek's specialist titanium welding capability, its current resource constraint. That each order was likely to pull Fabtek in a different direction calls to mind our earlier dictum: "*Whom we serve affects who we are.*"

To understand how a firm's abilities affect the choice of customers it can serve, consider the case of Dell Computer Corporation, which differed from other PC manufacturers in that it marketed customized PCs directly to customers through telephone sales, bypassing traditional retail channel intermediaries. For this approach to work, customers had to be able to tailor systems to their needs with minimal help from Dell. Moreover, because the products were delivered directly to them, customers had to be skilled enough to install their systems correctly the first time. Finally, the cost of responding to customer service calls would exceed Dell's profit margins were customers to call more than a couple of times for support. Its direct model constrained Dell to serve only sophisticated customers, a point captured by Dell Vice-Chairman Morton Topfer's remark that "we want to sell to only the educated customer who is buying their third or fourth PC." Dell's entire go-to-market strategy was explicitly designed to avoid the unsophisticated and to focus only on the educated customer.

Recognition of the interplay between customer choice and skill set must be accompanied by an appreciation for the following:

- Different customers play different roles and need to be managed differently.
- Those who make customer selection decisions need to be held accountable.
- Customer selection decisions are affected by evaluation basis and data quality.

CUSTOMER ROLES AND MANAGEMENT

Customers in vendors' portfolios play different roles based on the purchase volume, margins, and other strategic considerations, such as vendor learning and customer investments.

Customers that purchase large volumes bring a host of benefits as well as problems to the vendor. For example, large-volume customers are especially important because they keep the vendor's production lines up and running. Conversely, their *purchase volumes* also make them powerful enough to extract price reductions and services that could potentially negate the volume benefits to the vendor. These customers need to be managed very differently from small-volume customers who might be price insensitive and are unlikely to push the vendor for additional services.

Vendor margins are a function of prices paid by customers and vendor costs. Customers may be willing to pay a higher price because of ignorance, low levels of sophistication, and greater received value. A vendor's costs to serve customers can be lower because of scale economies, reduced customer demands, and increased vendor effectiveness over time. It is important that vendors understand the source of increased (or reduced) margins in a relationship before making decisions about how to manage a particular customer.

Several strategic considerations can also affect vendor revenues and costs. *Vendor learning in a relationship*, for example, can be a source of product feature improvements, new product innovations, enhancements to vendor operations, logistic capabilities, and other functional areas such as marketing and sales. *Customer investments*, besides having a favorable impact on vendor costs, raise customers' barriers to exit as well as foster greater collaboration that mitigate incentives to terminate a relationship. *Transferability* captures vendors' ability to leverage focal customer relationships to serve other customers more efficiently. For example, customers impressed with vendor performance are more likely to convince other customers to do business with the focal vendor. Following are some examples of how these dynamics can play out.

Confronted by lower-cost multinational competitors with modern manufacturing facilities, Zucamor, an Argentinean corrugated box manufacturer, decided to focus on being the high-end, value-added player in the industry.[4] Having decided to serve customers that needed custom solutions and were willing to pay a price premium for such services, Zucamor looked around but did not find enough of them in the short term. Educating customers to understand the benefits of its value-added services required

---

[4]V. Kasturi Rangan, "Zucamor S.A.—Global Competition in Argentina," Harvard Business School Case #599-096 (1999).

time. Operating in a high fixed-cost business, the firm was subsequently forced to accept from cost-conscious customers low-priced orders that were unattractive but important to fill volume requirements. It was important that Zucamor recognize these distinct customer types and manage each differently. It could not afford to offer value-added services to price-sensitive customers likely to be unwilling to pay for these services.

Industrial customers and contractors were among the clientele served by WESCO, an electrical parts distributor.[5] Contractors' relationships with WESCO were focused on projects. They expected suppliers such as WESCO to give them the lowest possible prices and a quick turnaround. Having won a contract, a contractor's focus shifted to delivery times because payments to them were tied to project completion and delays affected project profitability. WESCO needed to serve contractors because they accounted for a significant portion of its customer base. But, aside from volumes, WESCO derived few other benefits from these transaction-focused customers. Industrial customers, on the other hand, purchased electrical supplies and consumables on an ongoing basis as part of their operating expenses. Because operating costs were as important to them as purchasing costs, these customers valued WESCO's energy audits and other services that helped them to reduce their operating expenses. They were also interested in reducing order-cycle related costs, that is, the costs related to placing and processing individual orders. Besides placing long-term contracts, these customers collaborated with WESCO to develop integrated supply chain management systems. Clearly, industrial customers and contractors required different skills from WESCO.

CUSTOMER SELECTION DECISION ACCOUNTABILITY

To make diligent customer choices, firms must manage the complexities that arise from responsibility for those choices being in the hands of a host of frontline employees, the typically large numbers of customers in firms' portfolios, and high rates of customer and employee turnover. Firms add to this mix an accountability problem by segregating responsibility for customer acquisition from responsibility for customer retention. For example, a global wireless teleservices provider that had structured its salesforce along these lines found that by the time it discovered that an acquired customer was not a good fit, those responsible for customer selection had moved on to other assignments. The firm found it difficult to enforce discipline among the responsible personnel, despite having established clear criteria for customer selection. It partially solved the problem by basing incentives for personnel responsible for customer selection not on customer acquisition but on profitable customer retention.

CUSTOMER SELECTION DECISION EVALUATION BASIS AND DATA QUALITY

Different people in an organization often use different lenses through which to view and evaluate customer attractiveness. This is common and highlights the problem with customer selection decisions: the evaluation bases vary with the evaluator and affect how customers are prioritized. Firms need to understand decision makers bring their biases into the evaluation of customers and orders. In Fabtek's case, the attractiveness of each order varied significantly depending on the criteria used,

---

[5]Das Narayandas, "WESCO Distribution, Inc.," Harvard Business School Case #9-598-021 (1998).

> ### Diligent Customer Selection Benefits at Heartland Express
>
> Heartland Express, a midsize trucking company with profits running at 12 percent of revenues against an industry average of about 5 percent, $150 million in the bank, and one of the youngest truck fleets in the industry, owes its success to CEO Russell A. Gerdin's laser-like focus on customer selection. Every Saturday, Gerdin pores over thousands of orders serviced by the firm during the previous week. Through the firm's elaborate customer information databases, Gerdin has access to details on each order, such as shipper's name, points of origin and destination, miles covered, revenue generated, revenue per mile, and empty miles. Gerdin uses this information to keep his firm focused on the combination of customers and orders selected.
>
> Gerdin wants Heartland to serve only short-haul routes along busy corridors of commerce to reduce the likelihood that trucks return empty and adversely affect trip profitability. Such routes can be handled by solo drivers, who get back home every night, something that keeps the drivers happy and boosts employee morale.
>
> Gerdin deals directly with any salesperson who booked an order that did not meet the firm's specifications. Such is the reputation of his dressing-down tirades that few mistakes are ever made, let alone repeated. One might conclude that Heartland's order focus would force it to be opportunistic in customer selection, but this is not the case. In fact, Sears, its largest customer, accounts for 16 percent, and its top 25 customers account for more than 68 percent of Heartland's business. Despite repeated efforts by Sears, Gerdin has steadfastly refused to take on any of that firm's long-haul business.
>
> SOURCE: Adapted from "For One Trucking Entrepreneur, Success is in the Details," *Wall Street Journal*, November 27, 2001.

whether consumption of constrained resources (in this case, skilled titanium welding capacity), contribution per unit of the constrained resources, absolute contribution (a high priority since the firm was operating at a loss), or long-term revenue and profit potential. The different criteria used by the firm's marketing and manufacturing units led to different choices.

To avoid confusion among frontline employees, customer selection criteria need to be clearly specified, and adequate information needs to be available. For example, an insurance vendor that had been lax in enforcing any customer selection criteria found that its salespeople were seeking customers that they were personally comfortable dealing with rather than focusing on opportunities that were best for the firm. Because of the divergent views of two brothers who ran Granny's Goodies, a small supplier to the corporate gift-giving market, the firm found itself pursuing two different sets of customers simultaneously.[6] Only when the brothers recognized that their objectives were at variance with the firm's did they establish a system that ensured that company objectives dominated individual priorities when it came to customer selection.

---

[6] Das Narayandas, "Granny's Goodies," Harvard Business School Case #500-049 (2000).

A comprehensive customer database of strategic and tactical information is needed to support trade-off analyses to guide selection, emphasis, deemphasis, and deletion of customers. To develop such a database is not easy. When Harvard Business School MBA Sam Marcus took the reins of CMR, Inc., a small furniture- and cabinet-maker, one of his first initiatives was to develop a customer information database.[7] As corporate customers accounted for most of the firm's sales, Marcus started to build the database on these customers alone. Later, when Marcus tried to expand the scope of the database to include residential customers, he discovered that the information required to make decisions about corporate customers was quite different from that needed to evaluate smaller, residential customers.

Summary

In summary, despite recognizing the need for careful customer selection, companies make common mistakes every day because they lack the discipline to implement their stated goals. To be successful in customer management, firms need to go beyond just specifying customer selection criteria. They need to:

1. Have a clear vision about the current and future roles played by different customers in their portfolio.

2. Ensure that all personnel responsible for customer selection agree on the criteria for customer selection, and have access to appropriate, high-quality, customer-level information to make these decisions.

Review Questions and Exercises

1. Give examples of tactics used by companies to repel customers not in the segments they have selected.
2. How can rejecting potential customers lead to greater revenue and greater profit?
3. Pick one of Dell's competitors in the personal computer market. How has that company attempted to select and service a different customer group?

---

[7] Das Narayandas, "CMR Enterprises, Inc.," Harvard Business School Case #501-012 (2001).

Case 5-1   Granny's Goodies, Inc.

Kathy Korman and Das Narayandas

Josh Frey, founder of Granny's Goodies, Inc., "The Corporate Giftpackage Specialist,"™ was elated as he reviewed the sales figures for 1998. Over the past year, the firm had shipped more than 45,000 boxes and baskets of goodies, a 58% increase in sales volume over the previous year. Seth Frey, Josh's brother and business co-owner, explained the upbeat mood in the firm (the firm's income statement is presented in Exhibit 1, its balance sheet in Exhibit 2).

In the past, we have had some great press in publications like the *Washington Post, Inc. Online*, and *Entrepreneur Magazine*. While the publicity was gratifying, we really didn't feel a sense of accomplishment. It takes more than hype to make it in the corporate gift industry. Finally, after four years of struggling, forgoing paychecks, and almost going out of business, we believe that we have now had our first taste of true commercial success.

The two young business owners felt a combination of excitement and fear as they pondered what their next steps should be. "An important question we face today is the scalability of our sales approach," explained Josh Frey.

Nearly all of Granny's Goodies's orders have been generated by either Seth or myself. While we have had some success with a recent hire, we are unclear whether our firm is still solely dependent on us to get the sales. Several people we have spoken with have told us that it is our personalities that bring in the orders. Is our sales model incomplete if we are not involved in the sales process? Can we recruit sales reps to bring in new business in the future?

Our second challenge is to find ways to create consistent revenue streams and reduce sales costs. Outside of a few long-term contracts, we have had to work very hard for each sale. We have learned that having great client relationships does not mean much if we don't convert them into order streams. We need to develop a sales model to encourage our clients to give us long-term, guaranteed volume commitments instead of placing small orders with us every time we contact them.

FIRM HISTORY

In 1992 Josh Frey, looking for a way to earn money during the summer between his junior and senior years at the University of Wisconsin, decided to offer parents a service whereby, for about $15, they could have a care package of M&Ms, cookies, and other treats delivered to their children at school during exams or holidays.[1] After graduating in 1993, Frey stockpiled seed money earned from odd jobs to launch the care package business on a full-time basis. He operated the business, which he named "Granny's Goodies" after his 90-year-old grandmother, from the basement of his parents' home in McLean, Virginia. He bought a mailing list, assembled marketing materials, and began selling packages to parents around the country. "I invested $30,000 in a mailing, but less than 0.7% of the 75,000 parents to whom I sent letters bought packages," recalled Frey.

I was extremely disappointed with this low response rate and decided to spend some time trying to find ways to improve the effectiveness of my selling effort. As I reviewed

---

The case was prepared by Kathy Korman under the supervision of Professor Das Narayandas. Copyright © 1999 by the President and Fellows of Harvard College. Harvard Business School Case 500-049.

[1] Boxes of snack and novelty items sent by American parents to their college-age children living away from home were commonly referred to as "care packages."

EXHIBIT 1 Granny's Goodies, Inc., Income Statement (including projections)

	1997	1998	New Categories[a]	1999E	2000E	2001E
Sales						
College market	250,520	301,458	Recruiting[b]	488,529	676,522	947,131
Human resources	63,250		Property Management[c]	286,749	397,094	555,931
Real estate	10,600	59,083	Mortgage	31,550	43,691	61,167
General corporate	16,600	78,614	General Corporate	161,156	223,171	312,439
Other corporate	34,946	166,765	Other Corporate	105,016	145,428	203,599
Retail	9,500	1,655	Retail	10,178	14,095	19,733
Total Sales	385,416	607,575		1,083,178	1,500,000	2,100,000
Cost of Goods Sold						
Freight out	33,574	60,320		107,238	148,504	200,447
Packaging	10,982	38,945		22,762	31,522	42,547
Products	99,395	134,010		296,923	411,184	555,006
Total Cost of Goods Sold	143,950	233,275		426,923	591,209	798,000
Total Gross Profit	241,466	374,300		656,254	975,000	1,365,000
General and Administrative						
Advertising	51,654	23,171		29,354	29,354	29,354
Temporary labor	11,305	34,643		100,186	85,527	119,738
Payroll	63,093	116,588		226,087	300,000	325,000
Supplies	7,066	9,647		9,981	13,821	19,350
Utilities	8,372	11,437		21,664	30,000	42,000
Rent	22,089	20,149		24,000	60,700	57,600
Outsourcing	2,474	4,173		7,788	8,567	9,424
Postage & delivery	3,479	14,098		11,915	13,106	14,417
Commissions	—	—		73,702	112,500	157,500
Non-federal taxes paid	2,315	7,028		6,726	9,314	13,040
Other	56,037	54,089		90,511	91,971	93,757
Total General and Administrative	227,883	295,022		601,913	754,861	881,180
Less: Depreciation	6,592	7,080		8,191	14,790	18,472
EBIT	6,991	72,198		46,150	139,139	402,348
Income tax						
Estimated Income Tax Liability	—	6,474		6,923	48,699	160,939
After-tax EBIT	6,991	65,724		39,228	90,440	241,409

Source: Granny's Goodies, Inc. company records.

[a] The change in Granny's Goodies sales classification categories from 1997 to 1998 reflects:
  1. a shift away from selling to the college market and toward selling to the corporate market,
  2. a focus on the recruiting and property management industries, and
  3. a desire to clarify sales records as part of ongoing sales process development and improvement.

[b] Human Resources, a 1998 category, narrowed to include only Recruiting in 1999. Other sales formerly in Human Resources (such as employee gifts) were classified as General Corporate in 1999.

[c] Real Estate, a 1998 category, was broken into Property Management and Mortgage for 1999. Sales outside of the Property Management and Mortgage industries (such as residential real estate) were classified as General Corporate in 1999.

	1996	1997	1998
Cash	—	$ 31,351	$ 12,194
Accounts receivable	$38,000	58,732	210,024
Inventory	10,000	10,000	10,000
Other current assets	619	619	619
Total Current Assets	$48,619	$100,703	$232,837
Fixed assets, cost	39,757	39,757	42,198
Accumulated depreciation	(14,039)	(21,450)	(28,530)
Intangible assets	4,441	5,260	5,260
Total Long-Term assets	$30,159	$ 23,567	$ 18,927
Total Assets	$78,778	$124,270	$251,764
Accounts payable	$17,790	$ 50,644	$123,890
Auto loans	1,000	1,650	1,650
Payroll tax payable	—	963	963
Sales tax payable	—	804	5,670
Total Current Liabilities	$18,790	$ 54,061	$132,173
Suburban line of credit	32,000	32,000	28,743
SBA loan	46,226	42,234	29,884
Loans from stockholders	12,995	15,250	13,250
Capital stock	10,000	10,000	10,000
Retained earnings	(42,233)	(29,274)	37,715
Total Liabilities and Equity	$77,778	$124,270	$251,764

EXHIBIT 2 Granny's Goodies, Inc. Balance Sheet

the numbers, I realized that selling one package at a time to parents was a very expensive selling process. In order to reduce my sales and marketing costs, I had to find ways in which I could sell multiple units at a time. This led me to consider marketing to student organizations and religious institutions that sent packages to students away at school. My primary market segment was still the college market, but now I was working with organizations that bought multiple units at a time instead of individual parents that bought one unit at a time. This strategy boosted GG's sales volume significantly. It was the first time I understood the power of business-to-business (b2b) marketing.

When Seth Frey came on board later in 1994, the brothers launched a new strategy. Although the college market remained a focus, they began to explore other market segments to compensate for the sales lull during the summer months when most students returned home. "Our consultants, that is, our parents, suggested that we balance volume swings in the student market by going after corporations and professional firms," recalled Josh Frey.

With their background in legal recruiting and financial services, our parents pointed us toward our first corporate clients: accounting and law firms that sent gifts to new recruits. This market expansion move was not an easy one. First, we did not know how to sell to big corporations. Second, we did not have anybody who could guide us. We were not in a big company where we could come up with a sales plan and march it down the hall to the boss for approval and advice. There was no one in the next office to nod their head and tell us whether we were on the right track or not. Seth and I referred to this as "uncharted territory syndrome." I don't know if this was a curse or a blessing in disguise.

GG nevertheless met with some success, adding more than 50 clients within the first six months of 1995. In late 1996, with the business growing, the Freys applied and were approved for a Small Business Administration loan. The infusion of funds enabled the firm to move out of the family basement and into warehouse space in Alexandria, Virginia, and hire office and production managers to oversee office administration and package assembly.

The property management market segment emerged as an important growth area in 1997, and the corporate recruiting segment, one of GG's first areas of sales emphasis, grew by more than 200% over 1996 levels. "It was a lucky break," explained Josh Frey. "A personal contact recommended that we go after [the property management] segment as well. Property managers 'court' their prospective residents just as corporations court their recruits."

As GG transitioned toward the b2b [business-to-business] market, the Freys took steps to embellish their basic, no-frills care package business. First, they added gourmet coffees and other high-quality foods. Second, at a client's urging they expanded packaging options beyond the basic, bleached corrugated cardboard boxes to higher quality, custom-shaped boxes, tins, and baskets with optional decorative cellophane and ribbon accents. Third, they began to offer a private labeling service whereby a client's name and corporate logo could be substituted for GG's. Fourth, they emphasized superior responsiveness to clients, including complementary gift consultant services. The Freys designed and presented various gift program alternatives in an effort to better meet clients' needs, tastes, and budgets. Fifth, GG's literature began to employ the term "gift package" and "gift box" over "care package" to de-emphasize the company's formerly casual image. Sixth, community business leaders were recruited to serve on a GG advisory board. Among these was a recipient of Ernst & Young's "Entrepreneur of the Year" award, a senior officer of Motley Fool (a successful online financial services firm), and a professor from George Washington University's MBA program. Finally, data collection began to be used more extensively to track selling effort. Concluded Josh Frey: "We wanted to be the 'Honda' of the gift industry, providing reliable, good-quality product at a fair price."

By 1998, corporate sales dominated GG's client portfolio. The steps taken in 1997 appeared to have headed GG down the right path. Or had they? Josh Frey wondered if GG's efforts to date were sufficient to sustain sales growth going forward.

THE CORPORATE GIFT MARKET

Gift giving was a popular custom in corporate America, especially during good economic times. In 1998, the corporate gift market was estimated at $1.8 billion, the average gift ranging in price from $35 to $100.[2] Gift programs were influenced both by the images corporations wished to project to recipients and by the effort gift companies invested in program design and implementation. Gifts varied widely—from gourmet gift baskets and boxes to desk clocks to theatre tickets—depending on the gift budgets and company cultures of givers and recipients.

Corporations typically purchased gifts for three main groups of people: recruits, employees, and clients. Recruiters were often allocated extravagant budgets for receptions, sponsored trips, and gifts for new and prospective employees. Gift giving occurred two or three quarters out of each year, depending on a company's recruiting cycle. Employee gifts, conferred in recognition of a job well done or for a specific holiday, comprised a second major group of corporate offerings. These gifts were typically given on a year-round basis. Client gifts were often integrated into the marketing budgets of gift giving companies. Although client-gift volumes spiked during the winter holiday season, vendors typically sent client gifts on a year-round basis.

Direct Competitors to GG

Broadly, competition in the industry was stratified into large and small players in food and non-food gift segments (see Exhibit 3). Corporate

---
[2]Source: Joanne Stone, editor of The Report, a publication that tracks the corporate gift industry. Quoted by: Nolan, Paul. "Gifts That Give Back." *Star Tribune*, Minneapolis, MN, 10 August 1998.

EXHIBIT 3 Gift Industry Competition

Food Gift Segment: Small Players	*Food Gift Segment: Large Players*
Description: Small companies offering primarily food-based gifts of varying quality. Flexible product offerings. Sometimes provided a price advantage over large players with established brand names. • *Granny's Goodies* — Produced packages of food and novelty items ranging from low-end to higher-end to client specification. Economy to moderate pricing. Medium to high quality. • *Welcome Home America (WHA)* — Provided primarily welcome packages to the property management market. Economy to moderate price points ($10–$20 per package). Medium to high quality. • *Cookie Island* — Produced solely cookies; provided private labeling services by stamping a company logo on the outside of its wooden crate boxes. Medium to high prices. High quality.	**Description:** Large companies offering primarily food-based gifts of high quality. Strong brand awareness. Brand equity often limited private labeling possibilities. • *Harry & David* — "America's favorite food and fruit gifts" tag line; individual retail and corporate markets served; offered personalization and private labeling. Premium pricing. High quality. • *Mrs. Fields* — Well-known U.S. gourmet cookie brands sold to retail shops and corporate accounts with private labeling option; beginning to sell to grocery stores. Moderate to premium pricing. High quality. • *Starbucks* — Well-known U.S. operator of retail coffee shops produced a catalog of products designed specifically for the business gift market. Moderate to premium pricing. Medium to high quality.
Non-Food Gift Segment: Small Players	*Non-Food Gift Segment: Large Players*
Description: Smaller vendor of non-food gifts of varying quality. • *Custom non-food gift provider* — Offered custom items such as a specially-designed briefcase nationally. Wide price range. Usually higher quality. • *Local "mom and pop" vendors* — Purchased private labeled items such as clothing, pens, and novelties and resold them to corporate clients. Wide range in quality and pricing. • *Advertising specialty companies* — Indirect competitors with Granny's Goodies; small producers of catalogs featuring novelty items such as pens and stress-balls. Wide range of quality and pricing.	**Description:** Larger vendors offering primarily non-food gift items ranging anywhere from desk sets to consumer electronics, many with a strong brand name. • *Tiffany's* — Lately, the company had been pushing its corporate gift business though magazine advertisements and other media Premium pricing. High quality. • *1–800-Flowers* — Companies ordered flowers, though typically not in bulk, for staff day, condolences, get well, birthdays, and anniversaries. Medium to high quality and pricing. • *Advertising specialty companies* — Both competitors and collaborators, these included large, well-known firms such as HA-LO that produced corporate catalogs Medium to high quality and pricing.

Source: Granny's Goodies, Inc. competitive information files.

gifts accounted for only a minor portion of total business of larger national players such as Harry and David and Tiffany & Company. Smaller players included a sizable number of "mom-and-pop" outfits that served both local retail (e.g., individual sales for birthdays, and so forth.) and corporate markets. A few of the smaller-sized players, such as GG, had begun to service clients on a national level.

Indirect Competitors to GG

GG also faced indirect competition from advertising specialty firms. "GG could view these firms," according to Seth Frey, "as either competitors or collaborators." Advertising specialty firms ranged widely in size. Smaller players in this industry shipped items such as custom-printed stadium cups and pens in bulk either direct to corporate clients or to other gift companies for use in their own baskets and packages. Larger players in this segment produced custom catalogs and offered private-label novelty items. HA-LO, one of the better-known advertising specialty catalog firms in the United States, was the largest firm in this business. With more than $600 million in revenues and a salesforce of 500 people, it owned a third of the corporate gift market. HA-LO's client base comprised primarily Fortune 500 and large private companies.

Over the years, HA-LO had evolved a highly specific process for assembling its catalogs. First, its salespeople gathered information about a client's gift needs. Then, working with the client, HA-LO custom-designed an official company catalog with a distinctly upscale look. These were subsequently distributed to personnel with gift budgets (e.g., recruiters, human resources professionals, and sales/marketing managers). HA-LO's wide range of gift items and strong sales force earned it exclusive contracts from many of its clients. Like other advertising specialty companies, HA-LO purchased and stocked private-label novelty items that were presented in its catalogs. But it also formed relationships with other gift companies to complement its own products. For example, a GG gift box was featured in HA-LO's Ernst & Young 1998 and IBM 1999 catalogs. Executives placed orders with HA-LO and GG drop-shipped the product.

GG's Positioning

GG believed that it filled a gap in a polarized marketplace. Explained Seth Frey:

> At one side of the market you've got big companies like Mrs. Fields and Harry and David. Like us, they offer food in packages, but their brand name recognition is so strong that their prices are usually inflated. Some of these big companies also don't offer private labels or customize a lot for their clients. This approach can often backfire since many corporate gift givers want something a little more unique, not something anyone could just go out there and buy. Then, on the other side of the market, you've got the small players that put together unique baskets and packages. They have lower price points, maybe around $10 to $35 per gift, but they're not quite at the level where they can produce several thousand packages per month or offer professional services such as private labeling. When you add the components together, you have a gap in the market for large volume, unique, customized, and private-labeled gifts. That is where we fit in.

Clients also appreciated the wide range of gift styles and price points offered by GG. For instance, a company recruiting at an undergraduate university might request a less-formal package, priced at around $15, that included common items such as Rice Krispie Treats and Hershey's Kisses. The same firm might send senior-level corporate executives custom-designed gift baskets with gourmet biscotti and Lindt chocolates in the $40-to-$100 range. Also appealing to clients, according to the findings of a recent field study (see Exhibit 4), were the brothers' charisma and the firm's theme and client service.

TARGET MARKETS

The Freys believed that increasing the average order value was the most efficient way to boost GG's sales. The firm had actively tried to seek out clients with the ability to place a single order of $5,000 or more, which typically equated to from 100 to 500 packages. Large orders enabled GG to buy inventory and package and ship in bulk, thereby increasing its efficiency and margin

EXHIBIT 4 Client Survey Responses

Respondents	A	B	C	D	E	F	G	H	I	J	K	L	M	N	O	P	Q	R	Average Response
Questions																			
1. It is easy to order from GG	4	5	5	5	4	5	4	5	nr	5	5	3	4	5	5	5	5	4	4.59
2. GG is very service-oriented and responsive	5	5	5	5	4	4	4	3	3	5	5	4	4	5	5	5	5	4	4.44
3. GG ships products in a timely manner	4	5	5	3	5	5	1	4	5	5	4	4	4	5	5	5	5	4	4.33
4. Overall, I am satisfied with GG's performance	4	5	5	5	3	nr	4	1	nr	5	4	4	5	5	5	5	5	5	4.63
5. GG's packaging is better than other vendors'	5	5	4	5	4	5	4	4	4	5	4	5	4	3	5	nr	nr	nr	4.40
6. GG's product quality is better than other vendors'	3	5	4	5	2	5	3	3	nr	5	4	3	4	3	5	5	5	5	4.12
7. My relationship with the Freys is very important to me	5	5	5	5	5	5	5	5	5	5	5	5	5	5	5	5	5	5	5.00
8. GG is able to customize a gift program better than other vendors	4	5	5	5	3	5	nr	4	nr	5	5	4	4	5	5	4	5	5	4.56
																			TOTAL
Total GG Sales ($ 000s)	2.5	1.6	3.0	1.5	115	3.6	33	9.2	7.6	3.5	31	2.2	1.7	0.5	0.9	1.2	2.8	na	220.4

Source: The client survey table was part of a field application project sponsored by the firm and conducted by a group of MBA students from a major northeastern U.S. business school.

Note: 1 = Strongly disagree, 5 = strongly agree; nr = no response

while passing through some of the cost savings to its clients in the form of lower prices. The Freys decided, owing to their pass success in these markets, to emphasize development of the property management and recruiting market segments.

Property Management

GG entered this market as a consequence of Josh Frey learning from attendance at industry networking meetings that property managers regularly sent gifts to residents upon move-in or lease renewal. Given the frequent turnover of residents, he reasoned that this could be an excellent target market.

By 1998, GG had established relationships with a number of local and national property management firms. Some owned groups of apartment buildings in specific regions of the United States; others owned properties throughout the nation. GG further segmented this market on the basis of purchase volume (in $ and units) and frequency. "The big real estate firms that own high-end properties often centralize their gift purchasing process," explained Frey. "They want to both send a consistent message and leverage their purchasing by ordering from one source. Their per-package cost is usually lower because of this, often around $10, but we love the volume, which can range from 1,000 to 5,000 packages per month depending on the client."

GG's largest contract was with Bozzuto Management, which owned more than 30 high-end properties nationwide. In pursuit of consistent revenues, Josh Frey, GG's account manager for this segment, was looking to sign contracts with other companies in 1999 (see Exhibit 5).

EXHIBIT 5 Additional Key Sales Prospects for 1999

Key Prospect Name[a]	Category	Industry	1999 Goal
Xerox of Greater Washington	General Corporate	Copier equipment	$15,000
Kennedy Center	General Corporate	Arts events	10,000
U.S. Military	General Corporate	Military	50,000
Watson Wyatt	Human Resources	Consulting — HR	15,000
EDS	Human Resources	Software	15,000
Horizons Unlimited	Human Resources	Advertising specialists	25,000
HA-LO Catalogs[b]	Human Resources	Advertising specialists	50,000
Addison Bay	Real Estate	Property management	75,000
Kay Management	Real Estate	Property management	15,000
H.G. Smithy	Real Estate	Property management	15,000
Bridgestreet Accommodations	Real Estate	Property management	10,000
AIMCO	Real Estate	Property management	15,000
CAPREIT	Real Estate	Property management	15,000
Money Tree Lending	Real Estate	Mortgage Lending	10,000
Polinger, Shannon & Luchs	Real Estate	Property management/ resources	15,000
Total			**$350,000**

Source: Granny's Goodies, Inc. company records.

[a]Key Prospects are target companies with which Granny's Goodies expects to do a significant amount of business in 1999. Bozzuto Management and Ryland Homes are excluded from this list as they had already signed contracts with Granny's Goodies for 1999.

[b]In the form of existing catalogs such as IBM and Ernst & Young (e.g., Fortune 500 catalogs).

Recruiting

Seth Frey considered the recruiting market a potential gold mine. With low unemployment and a tight market for skilled labor, recruiters, who typically spent from $25 to $75 per gift, were eager to enhance company image in the eyes of prospective employees. "The gifts we offer in this market," explained Seth Frey, "are a variety of food and promotional items delivered in private labeled packaging. A gift to a college recruit is typically more casual and less expensive. On the other hand, a graduate student or executive being hired by a consulting firm might receive a $50 to $75 gift basket with gourmet items because the company wants to project a classy, corporate image."

Although an integral part of the resident acquisition and retention process, recruiting gifts were considered optional and subject to volume swings depending on a property management firm's recruiting objectives and budgets for a given year. Only HA-LO, the corporate catalog producer, had been successful in establishing long-term contracts in this market. Although his brother was wary of relinquishing control over client contact, Josh Frey believed that catalog placement was the closest GG was going to get to securing long-term contracts in the property management market.

Seth Frey remained focused on maintaining existing client relationships and searching for other segmentation patterns. Having noticed, for instance, that GG's larger clients such as IBM, Ernst & Young, and KPMG represented a large percentage of firms listed in "The 100 Best Companies for Working Mothers,"[3] he wondered if this nontraditional segmentation approach based on unobservable intangibles such as culture was a good idea. "All the client data that we have collected must be able to tell us something," he observed. "We have to get better at managing this segment." (See Exhibits 6, 7, and 8.)

MARKETING AND LEAD GENERATION

GG employed various forms of contact to get the "goody word" out to potential clients. Most involved either face-to-face contact or sending the client brochures or other information. Among the tools used for lead generation were the following:

Cold calls Approximately 25% of all leads were generated through cold calling. GG obtained company names from local newspapers or from mailing lists purchased from list brokers and GG salesmen or account managers called prospects to get the name(s) of the person(s) in charge of gifts. The effectiveness of cold calling was highly dependent on the number of calls placed and callers' client-specific knowledge. Explained Josh Frey:

> We wanted to take advantage of the holiday season this year to build up sales, so we worked with a call center to telemarket to corporations. We gave them a list of local businesses based on standard industrial classification (SIC) codes we got from PhoneDisc, a CD version of the yellow pages. The telemarketer gathered information about the decision makers for holiday gifts, their budgets, and types of gifts that they had purchased in the past. The two jobs we landed paid for the contract with the call center. However, we didn't make that much of a profit. We have concluded that a third-party call center simply doesn't do a good job of educating prospects about who we are and what we do. We are now training Rachelle Cooke-Melson, our office manager, to take over the cold-calling function.

Local networking Another 25% of GG's leads were generated from local chapters of professional organizations such as the Society of Human Resource Management (SHRM), Property Management Association (PMA), National Association of Law Placement (NALP), and local Chambers of Commerce networking groups. "To develop industry markets," explained Josh Frey,

> We start by attending trade shows and setting up a booth in several trade exhibitions. Because we offer cookies to people who visit our booth, we are more successful than other vendors are in collecting client information. For example, at the recent SHRM conference we gathered over 1,000 business cards,

---

[3]*Working Mother's Magazine*, "The 100 Best Companies for Working Mothers" 1998 list.

EXHIBIT 6 Details of Sales to Each Client in 1997 and 1998

Client Name	GG Category[a]	Business Type[b]	1997 Sales	1998 Sales	1998 Margins	1999 Estimated	Average Price[c]
Avalon Bay	2	4	$ 0	$15,966	10%	$250,000	$ 9
Affinity Staffing	3	5	750	1,817	15	2,000	50
AMEX Financial Advisors	3	5	500	1,500	20	5,000	25
AMRESCO	2	3	0	1,432	15	10,000	15
Andersen Consulting	1	1	700	1,791	20	5,000	50
Arnold & Porter	1	2	750	1,656	25	3,000	30
Arthur Andersen	1	1	1,250	9,155	20	50,000	25
Atlantic Valet	3	5	2,200	3,308	20	3,500	13
Atlas Van Lines	3	5	0	1,500	20	15,000	25
Baker & Botts	1	2	1,500	3,047	25	5,000	30
Baker & Daniels	1	2	750	1,151	25	2,500	30
Balch & Bingham	1	2	750	1,228	25	2,500	30
Berkshire Apartments	2	4	0	1,885	15	3,600	10
Bowditch & Dewey	1	2	750	1,340	25	2,500	30
Bowne	3	5	250	1,340	25	5,000	25
Brobeck Phleger	1	2	1,100	2,229	25	5,000	30
Chadbourne & Park	1	2	750	1,157	25	2,500	30
Charles E. Smith Realty	2	4	3,000	4,513	25	15,000	50
CORT Furniture	3	5	0	7,292	20	25,000	65
Covington & Burling	1	2	0	5,625	15	7,500	10
Data Systems Hardware	3	5	0	1,116	20	2,500	4
Dechert Price	1	2	500	1,031	25	2,500	30
Deloitte & Touche	1	1	5,000	30,803	20	75,000	25
Enterprise	1	5	250	2,164	20	10,000	25
Ernst & Young	1	1	3,000	34,713	15	75,000	25
Exec Comm	1	5	0	1,109	25	2,500	100
First Union Bank	1	5	0	1,712	20	25,000	25
First Washington Management	2	4	0	770	25	5,000	70
Foley & Lardner	1	2	2,500	3,531	25	7,500	25
Fox, Rothschild	1	2	750	1,538	25	2,500	30
George Mason Mortgage	2	3	0	2,463	25	10,000	50
Gibson, Dunn & Crutcher	1	2	750	1,472	25	2,500	30
Goodwin Proctor	1	2	750	1,438	25	2,500	30
Gruntal	3	5	1,000	227	20	2,500	25
Hughes, Hubbard & Reed	1	2	750	1,454	25	2,500	30

(Continued)

EXHIBIT 6 (cont.)

Client Name	GG Category[a]	Business Type[b]	1997 Sales	1998 Sales	1998 Margins	1999 Estimated	Average Price[c]
IBM	1	5	0	215	15	25,000	25
Insignia ESG	2	4	0	4,469	20	15,000	50
Integrated Business Systems	3	5	0	1,445	25	2,000	50
Kentucky Fried Chicken	1	5	0	1,085	25	5,000	25
KPMG Peat Marwick	1	1	5,000	33,320	20	75,000	30
LaSalle Partners	2	4	0	135	25	5,000	50
Lucent Technologies	1	5	0	10,692	20	25,000	20
Max Worldwide	3	5	0	1,110	10	1,500	10
MBH Settlement	2	5	0	916	10	10,000	3
MCI Center	3	5	0	826	20	5,000	50
Medline	3	5	500	2,571	20	25,000	35
Minuteman Press	3	5	0	914	25	5,000	50
Montlack Realty	2	4	350	849	25	2,500	35
Monument Mortgage	2	3	1,000	1,526	15	5,000	22
Morgan, Lewis	1	2	750	1,348	25	2,500	30
Morrison & Foerster	1	2	1,500	2,904	25	5,000	30
NJ Lenders	2	3	0	2,276	15	10,000	15
North American Mortgage	2	3	0	7,160	15	75,000	12
Oakwood	2	4	1,250	3,561	15	25,000	20
Oppenheimer, Wolf	1	2	750	1,238	25	2,500	30
Oracle	3	5	5,000	11,377	25	25,000	65
Orrick, Herrington	1	2	1,500	3,890	25	7,500	30
Otis Elevator	3	5	0	3,786	25	10,000	50
Painted Word	1	5	0	1,465	25	3,000	50
Paychex	3	5	6,000	17,021	10	25,000	9
PeopleSoft	3	5	0	797	25	5,000	50
Pfizer	3	5	0	550	20	15,000	10
Premier Financial	2	3	5,000	7,872	15	10,000	14
PricewaterhouseCoopers	1	1	15,000	114,561	25	200,000	20
Proskauer Rose	1	2	1,500	3,112	25	5,000	30
Realvest	3	3	0	1,341	20	2,000	40
Reed Smith Shaw	1	2	750	1,640	25	2,500	30
RGS Title	2	5	0	2,225	15	15,000	5
Riverside Park Apartments	2	4	0	1,065	15	5,000	10
Romac International	3	5	0	790	25	5,000	50
Schnader Harrison	3	2	400	710	25	2,500	50
Sheppard, Mullin	1	2	750	1,523	25	2,500	30

Client Name	GG Category[a]	Business Type[b]	1997 Sales	1998 Sales	1998 Margins	1999 Estimated	Average Price[c]
Sidley & Austin	1	2	750	1,328	25	2,500	30
Simpson & Thatcher	1	2	1,500	2,935	25	5,000	30
Skadden Arps	1	2	0	4,425	25	7,500	30
Smith Kline Beecham	3	5	0	793	20	15,000	15
Squire, Sanders	1	2	1,200	1,441	25	2,500	30
Stroock, Stroock	1	2	8,000	1,592	25	2,500	30
Sun Life of Canada	3	5	0	1,361	25	2,500	50
UUNET	3	5	0	7,572	10	15,000	1
Val Pak	3	5	0	3,532	20	10,000	10
Washington Business Journal	3	5	0	1,338	20	2,500	25
Wexner Heritage Foundation	3	5	0	2,680	20	2,680	25
Wilke Farr	1	2	750	1,328	25	2,500	30
Winstead, Sechrest	1	2	1,000	2,072	25	5,000	30
Totals			$ 90,450	$439,155	—	$1,388,280	—
Averages			$ 1,924[d]	$ 5,167	21%	$ 16,333	$30

Source: Granny's Goodies, Inc. company records.

[a]Granny's Goodies' Categories:
    1 = Human Resources (recruiting, employee gifts, contacts in HR departments);
    2 = Real Estate (property management, mortgage lending and banking, etc.);
    3 = General Corporate (law firms, software companies, and other businesses outside the core Human Resources and Real Estate businesses).

[b]Business Type Category: 1 = Consulting and Accounting Firms; 2 = Law Firms; 3 = Mortgage Lending and Banking; 4 = Commercial and Residential Property Management; 5 = Other.

[c]Average price per package for client order(s).

[d]Denominator for average calculation is 47 as Granny's Goodies had not yet acquired several of its existing clients.

---

while most of the other exhibitors only gathered a couple hundred. Next, we follow up with the contacts via phone or direct mail. We also see local chapter meetings and receptions as opportunities to network. It is the same process with Chambers of Commerce and tip groups.[4] We also volunteer on committees and provide door prize give-aways for different events.

Networking is a big part of our marketing budget. I take pride in the fact that I'm a good networker. My objective is to help the person who contacts me in the best way possible. If there is a better way to satisfy their need, I will direct the person to that option. From a business standpoint, this gives me credibility because it makes people realize that I am interested in them and not just myself.

Mailing lists Although 10% of GG's leads came from mailing lists purchased from list brokers, Josh Frey characterized them as "a waste of money." "The idea," he explained, "is to cast

---

[4]Networking groups in which executives exchanged business cards and offered each other "tips" and referrals to other contacts were termed "tip groups."

EXHIBIT 7 GG's Client Information

Client Name	Business Type[a]	Department[b]	Gift Needs: Year/Season[c]	For Whom?[d]	Ordering Pattern[e]	Gift Purpose[f]	Budget per Gift[g]	Total Gift Budget[h]	Level of Contact[i]	Buyer Sophistication[j]
Andersen Consulting	1	1	1	1	4	1	$20-$75	—	5	1
Arthur Andersen	1	1	1	1	4	1	$20-$75	—	5	1
Deloitte & Touche	1	1	1	1	4	1	$20-$75	—	5	1
Ernst & Young	1	1	1	1	4	1	$20-$75	—	5	1
KPMG Peat Marwick	1	1	1	1	4	1	$20-$75	—	5	1
PricewaterhouseCoopers	1	1	1	1	4	1	$20-$75	—	5	1
Arnold & Porter	2	1	1	1	4	1	$25-$35	—	5	2
Baker & Botts	2	1	1	1	4	1	$25-$35	—	5	2
Baker & Daniels	2	1	1	1	4	1	$25-$35	—	5	2
Balch & Bingham	2	1	1	1	4	1	$25-$35	—	5	2
Bowditch & Dewey	2	1	1	1	4	1	$25-$35	—	5	2
Brobeck Phleger	2	1	1	1	4	1	$25-$35	—	5	2
Chadbourne & Park	2	1	1	1	4	1	$25-$35	—	5	2
Covington & Burling	2	1	2	3	1	3	$10	$6,000	3	2
Dechert Price	2	1	1	1	4	1	$25-$35	—	5	2
Foley & Lardner	2	1	1	1	4	1	$25-$35	—	5	2
Fox, Rothschild	2	1	1	1	4	1	$25-$35	—	5	2
Gibson, Dunn & Crutcher	2	1	1	1	4	1	$25-$35	—	5	2
Goodwin Proctor	2	1	1	1	4	1	$25-$35	—	5	2
Hughes, Hubbard & Reed	2	1	1	1	4	1	$25-$35	—	5	2
Morgan, Lewis	2	1	1	1	4	1	$25-$35	—	5	2
Morrison & Foerster	2	1	1	1	4	1	$25-$35	—	5	2
Oppenheimer, Wolf	2	1	1	1	4	1	$25-$35	—	5	2
Orrick, Herrington	2	1	1	1	4	1	$25-$35	—	5	2
Proskauer Rose	2	1	1	1	4	1	$25-$35	—	5	2
Reed Smith Shaw	2	1	1	1	4	1	$25-$35	—	5	2

Schnader Harrison	2	1	1	4	3	$75	—	2	3
Sheppard, Mullin	2	1	1	4	1	$25–$35	—	5	2
Sidley & Austin	2	1	1	4	1	$25–$35	—	5	2
Simpson & Thatcher	2	1	1	4	1	$25–$35	—	5	2
Skadden Arps	2	1	1	4	1	$25–$35	—	5	2
Squire, Sanders	2	1	1	4	1	$25–$35	—	5	2
Stroock, Stroock	2	1	1	4	1	$25–$35	—	5	2
Wilke Farr	2	1	1	4	1	$25–$35	—	5	2
Winstead, Sechrest	2	1	1	4	1	$25–$35	—	5	2
AMRESCO	3	2	2	2	5	$14	—	3	2
George Mason Mortgage	3	3	2	1	3	$50	$3,000	5	3
Monument Mortgage	3	2	1	3	5	$22	—	1	1
NJ Lenders	3	2	1	3	5	$15	—	3	2
North American Mortgage	3	2	1	3	5	$12	—	3	1
Premier Financial	3	2	1	3	5	$14	—	3	1
Realvest	3	2	2	1	3	$40	—	1	3
Avalon Bay	4	2	1	2	2	$8–$10	$2,000	4	1
Berkshire Apartments	4	2	1	2	2	$5–$10	—	4	1
Charles E. Smith Realty	4	2	2	1	3	$50	—	4	3
First Washington Management	4	2	1	3	3	$75	$1,000	3	2
Insignia ESG	4	2	2	1	3	$50	$3,000	4	1
LaSalle Partners	4	2	2	1	3	$50	$3,000	3	2
Montlack Realty	4	2	2	1	3	$50	$1,000	5	3
Oakwood	4	2	1	3	2	$10–$25	—	3	2

(Continued)

EXHIBIT 7 (cont.)

Client Name	Business Type[a]	Department[b]	Gift Needs: Year/Season[c]	For Whom?[d]	Ordering Pattern[e]	Gift Purpose[f]	Budget per Gift[g]	Total Gift Budget[h]	Level of Contact[i]	Buyer Sophistication[j]
Riverside Park Apartments	4	2	1	2	3	2	$ 5-$10	—	4	1
Affinity Staffing	5	2	2	2	1	3	$ 35	$2,000	1	2
AMEX Financial Advisors	5	4	1	2	2	5	$ 20-$50	—	4	3
Atlantic Valet	5	2	2	2	1	3	$ 12	$4,000	1	3
Atlas Van Lines	5	2	1	2	2	5	$ 15-$75	—	3	3
Bowne	5	3	1	2	3	5	$ 5-$50	—	5	3
CORT Furniture	5	2	2	2	1	3	$ 50	$15,000	3	3
Data Systems Hardware	5	3	1	2	3	5	$ 2-$25	—	3	3
Enterprise	5	1	1	1	4	1	$ 20-$75	—	5	2
Exec Comm	5	2	1	2	3	4	$100	—	3	2
First Union Bank	5	1	1	1	4	1	$ 20-$75	—	3	1
Gruntal	5	2	2	2	1	5	$ 15-$50	—	5	3
IBM	5	1	1	1	4	1	$ 20-$75	—	3	1
Integrated Business Systems	5	2	2	2	1	3	$ 25	$2,000	1	3
Kentucky Fried Chicken	5	1	1	3	4	4	$ 25	—	3	2
Lucent Technologies	5	1	1	1	4	1	$ 20-$75	—	3	2
Max Worldwide	5	1	2	2	1	3	$ 10	$2,000	3	3
MBH Settlement	5	2	1	2	3	5	$ 5-$25	—	3	1
MCI Center	5	2	1	2	3	5	$ 50	—	3	1
Medline	5	3	1	2	3	5	$ 15-$50	—	5	3
Minuteman Press	5	3	2	2	1	3	$ 50	$1,500	1	3
Oracle	5	3	2	2	1	3	$ 75	$11,000	4	3
Otis Elevator	5	3	2	2	1	3	$ 50	$4,000	4	3

216

Painted Word	5	1	1	3	1	$25-$50	—	3	2
Paychex	5	3	2	5	5	$5-$8	—	4	2
PeopleSoft	5	3	2	1	3	$50	$1,000	4	3
Pfizer	5	3	1	3	5	$5-$15	—	5	1
RGS Title	5	2	1	2	5	$5-$25	—	3	1
Romac International	5	2	2	1	3	$50	$1,000	5	3
Smith Kline Beecham	5	3	1	3	5	$5-$15	—	5	1
Sun Life of Canada	5	2	2	1	3	$50	$2,000	4	3
UUNET	5	2	2	5	5	$1-$10	—	3	3
Val Pak	5	3	2	1	3	$8	$4,000	4	3
Washington Business Journal	5	3	2	2	1	3	$25	$2,000	4	3
Wexner Heritage Foundation	5	4	2	2	5	5	$15	$2,500	4	3

Source: Granny's Goodies company records.

[a]Business Type Category: 1 = Consulting and accounting firms; 2 = Law firms; 3 = Mortgage lending & banking; 4 = Commercial & residential property management; 5 = Other

[b]Department within company to which Granny's Goodies sells: 1 = Human resources; 2 = Marketing; 3 = Sales; 4 = Other

[c]Gift Needs—GG client needs for gifts in terms of timing: 1 = Year-round need; 2 = Seasonal need (e.g., tax season for accounting firms, bar survival kits for law firms, specific recruiting seasons, promotions)

[d]For Whom?—ultimate gift recipient: 1 = recruit; 2 = client; 3 = employee

[e]Ordering Pattern: 1 = Holiday time; 2 = Monthly; 3 = No set ordering schedule (average is monthly); 4 = No set ordering schedule (average is quarterly)

[f]Gift Purpose: 1 = Recruiting gifts and/or new employee welcome; 2 = Resident retention/move-in gifts; 3 = Holiday wishes; 4 = Employee recognition; 5 = Other client business (Thanks; Sorry for the mishap; etc.)

[g]Budget Per Gift: The average price range within which client typically purchased gifts

[h]Total budget: Total annual gift budget if known; property management budgets are on a per-building basis

[i]Level of Contact: 1 = Owner/CEO or President; 2 = VP/Partner; 3 = Director level; 4 = Manager level; 5 = Associate/Coordinator level

[j]Buyer Sophistication: 1 = High—see gifts as integral to sales & marketing plans; 2 = Medium—see gifts as important to sales & marketing plans; 3 = Low—see gifts as nice gesture

EXHIBIT 8 GG's Sales Patterns

Client Name	Business Type[a]	Compet. Bid?[b]	Against Whom?[c]	Who Else?[d]	Purchasing Practices[e]	Acquistn. Year[f]	Lead Generation[g]	Type of Contact[h]	Sales Tools[i]	Acquis. Hours[j]	98 Maint. Hours[k]	Client Offices[l]	Total # of U.S. Offices[m]
Andersen Consulting	1	3	2	—	2	3	6	2	1 — — — —	2	5	1	100
Arthur Andersen	1	3	2	—	2	1	5 1	2	1 — — — —	3	5	10	100
Deloitte & Touche	1	1	2	—	2	2	5 1	1 2	1 2 3 — —	50	5	15	100
Ernst & Young	1	1	2	—	1	2	5 1	1 2	1 2 3 — —	15	7	25	100
KPMG Peat Marwick	1	1	2	—	2	2	5 1	1 2	1 2 3 — —	20	4	20	100
Pricewaterhouse Coopers	1	1	2	—	1	1	3 1	1 2	1 2 3 — —	50	5	40	100
Arnold & Porter	2	3	5	—	2	2	2 1	2 —	1 — — — —	1	1	1	3
Baker & Botts	2	3	5	—	2	1	2 1	2 —	1 — — — —	1	1	2	6
Baker & Daniels	2	3	5	—	2	2	2 1	2 —	1 — — — —	1	1	2	4
Balch & Bingham	2	3	5	—	2	2	2 1	2 —	1 — — — —	1	1	1	1
Bowditch & Dewey	2	3	5	—	2	2	2 1	2 —	1 — — — —	1	1	1	1
Brobeck Phleger	2	3	5	—	2	2	2 1	2 —	1 — — — —	1	1	4	4
Chadbourne & Park	2	3	5	2	2	2	2 1	2 —	1 — — — —	1	1	1	2
Covington & Burling	2	1	1	—	2	3	2 1	1 2	1 2 3 4 —	5	1	1	2
Dechert Price	2	3	5	—	2	2	2 1	2 —	1 — — — —	1	1	2	4
Foley & Lardner	2	3	5	—	2	1	2 1	1 2	1 2 — — —	10	2	3	4
Fox, Rothschild	2	3	5	4	2	2	2 1	2 —	1 — — — —	1	1	1	1
Gibson, Dunn & Crutcher	2	3	5	—	2	2	2 1	2 —	1 — — — —	1	1	4	6
Goodwin Proctor	2	3	5	—	2	2	2 1	2 —	1 — — — —	1	1	1	1
Hughes, Hubbard & Reed	2	3	5	—	2	2	2 1	2 —	— — — — —	1	1	1	1
Morgan, Lewis	2	3	5	—	2	3	2 1	2 —	— — — — —	1	1	1	4
Morrison & Foerster	2	3	5	4	2	2	2 1	2 —	— — — — —	1	1	5	9
Oppenheimer, Wolf	2	3	5	—	2	2	2 1	2 —	— — — — —	1	1	1	2
Orrick, Herrington	2	3	5	—	2	2	2 1	2 —	— — — — —	1	1	3	4
Proskauer Rose	2	3	5	—	2	2	2 1	2 —	1 2 — — —	1	1	1	1
Reed Smith Shaw	2	3	5	4	2	2	2 1	2 —	— — — — —	1	1	4	5
Schnader Harrison	2	3	5	—	2	2	3 1	2 —	1 — 3 — —	1	1	1	3
Sheppard, Mullin	2	3	5	—	2	2	2 1	2 —	— — — — —	1	1	3	3
Sidley & Austin	2	3	5	—	2	2	2 1	2 —	— — — — —	1	1	1	4
Simpson & Thatcher	2	3	5	—	2	3	3 —	2 2	1 2 3 4 —	3	1	1	1
Skadden Arps	2	1	5	—	1	1	3 1	1 2	1 2 3 — —	6	2	2	7
Squire, Sanders	2	3	4	—	2	2	2 1	2 —	— — — — —	2	2	2	2
Stroock, Stroock	2	3	5	—	2	2	2 1	2 —	— — — — —	3	1	1	1
Wilke Farr	2	3	5	—	2	2	2 1	2 —	— — — — —	1	1	1	2
Winstead, Sechrest	2	3	5	—	2	3	2 1	2 —	— — — — —	1	1	1	1

AMRESCO	3	3	—	5	—	2	3	3	—	1	2	1	2	3	4	5	10	4	21
George Mason Mortgage	3	1	—	2	—	2	3	4	—	1	2	1	3	—	5	1	1	4
Monument Mortgage	3	3	—	5	—	1	2	2	2	1	2	1	3	4	15	7	4	4
NJ Lenders	3	3	—	5	—	1	3	3	1	2	1	1	3	—	15	7	1	1
North American Mortgage	3	1	—	1	—	1	3	4	1	1	2	1	3	4	15	7	1	600
Premier Financial	3	2	—	5	—	1	1	3	—	1	2	1	3	4	4	2	1	1
Realvest	3	1	—	2	—	1	3	3	—	2	1	1	—	—	1	1	1	1
Avalon Bay	4	2	—	1	—	2	3	4	3	1	2	1	3	4	25	5	10	130
Berkshire Apartments	4	3	—	1	—	1	3	4	1	1	2	1	3	4	3	5	1	55
Charles E. Smith Realty	4	1	—	1	—	2	2	3	—	1	2	1	3	—	5	2	5	75
First Washington Management	4	3	4	1	—	1	3	3	—	1	2	1	3	4	10	2	1	1
Insignia ESG	4	1	—	1	—	1	3	2	3	1	2	1	3	4	20	4	5	900
LaSalle Partners	4	1	4	5	—	1	2	3	—	2	2	1	—	—	1	1	1	900
Montlack Realty	4	3	—	5	—	1	3	2	—	2	1	1	3	—	1	1	1	1
Oakwood	4	1	—	1	—	2	3	4	—	1	2	1	3	4	15	7	2	250
Riverside Park Apartments	4	1	—	1	—	1	3	4	1	1	2	1	3	4	3	1	1	53
Affinity Staffing	5	1	—	1	—	1	2	4	—	2	2	1	—	—	2	1	1	1
AMEX Financial Advisors	5	2	—	2	—	2	2	4	—	2	2	1	—	—	3	3	4	50
Atlantic Valet	5	1	—	1	—	1	2	4	—	2	2	1	—	—	1	2	1	450
Atlas Van Lines	5	2	—	5	—	2	3	4	1	2	2	1	3	4	5	10	4	130
Bowne	5	3	—	5	—	2	2	4	—	2	2	1	3	4	5	1	1	75
CORT Furniture	5	1	—	1	—	2	3	6	—	1	2	1	3	4	5	5	1	110
Data Systems Hardware	5	1	—	4	—	1	3	4	—	2	—	1	—	—	1	1	1	1
Enterprise	5	3	—	5	—	2	3	5	1	2	—	1	—	—	1	1	5	100
Exec Comm	5	3	—	5	—	1	3	3	—	2	—	1	3	—	1	3	1	1
First Union Bank	5	2	—	5	—	1	3	3	—	2	—	1	—	—	15	3	1	1
Gruntal	5	3	—	2	—	2	2	3	—	2	—	1	3	—	3	1	1	33
IBM	5	1	—	5	—	1	3	2	—	2	—	1	3	—	20	3	1	1
Integrated Business Systems	5	1	—	1	—	2	3	3	—	1	—	1	3	—	4	1	1	1
Kentucky Fried Chicken	5	3	—	5	—	1	3	4	1	2	—	1	3	4	1	4	1	5
Lucent Technologies	5	1	—	5	—	1	3	2	—	2	—	1	3	—	15	2	1	1

(Continued)

EXHIBIT 8 (cont.)

Client Name	Business Type[a]	Compet. Bid?[b]	Against Whom?[c]	Who Else?[d]	Purchasing Practices[e]	Acquisn. Year[f]	Lead Generation[g]	Type of Contact[h]	Sales Tools[i]	Acquis. Hours[j]	98 Maint. Hours[k]	Client Offices[l]	Total # of U.S. Offices[m]
Max Worldwide	5	2	5	—	1	3	3	—	1 2 3 4	1	1	1	1
MBH Settlement	5	1	1	—	1	3	3	—	1 2 3 4	15	2	1	11
MCI Center	5	1	1	—	1	3	3	—	1 2 3 4	5	6	1	1
Medline	5	1	1	—	2	2	3	—	1 2 3 4	15	2	5	500
Minuteman Press	5	1	1	—	2	3	4	—	1 2 3 —	1	1	1	100
Oracle	5	3	1	—	2	2	4	—	1 2 3 4	15	7	3	100
Otis Elevator	5	1	1	—	2	3	3	—	1 2 3 4	10	1	1	250
Painted Word	5	1	5	—	1	3	3	—	— — — —	5	4	1	1
Paychex	5	1	4	—	2	2	6	—	1 — 3 —	20	5	4	75
PeopleSoft	5	1	2	—	2	3	3	—	1 — 3 —	4	1	1	100
Pfizer	5	1	2	—	2	3	3	—	1 2 3 4	5	2	1	5000
RGS Title	5	1	1	—	1	3	2 1	—	1 2 3 4	6	3	1	9
Romac International	5	1	4	—	2	3	4	—	1 2 3 —	3	1	1	250
Smith Kline Beecham	5	1	4	—	2	3	3	—	1 2 3 4	3	2	1	5000
Sun Life of Canada	5	3	5	—	2	3	6	2	1 — — —	2	1	1	1
UUNET	5	1	4	—	1	3	2 1	1	1 2 3 4	8	3	1	1
Val Pak	5	1	1	—	2	3	3	1	1 2 3 4	4	1	1	77
Washington Business Journal	5	3	5	—	1	3	3	1	1 2 3 4	4	1	1	50
Wexner Heritage Foundation	5	3	5	—	1	3	3	2	1 2 3 3	1	1	1	—

Source: Granny's Goodies, Inc. company records.

[a]Business Type Category: 1 = Consulting and accounting firms; 2 = Law firms; 3 = Mortgage lending and banking; 4 = Commercial & residential property management; 5 = Other
[b]Competitive bid: 1 = yes; 2 = no; 3 = not sure
[c & d] Against whom?: 1 = Specialty/small food company, in many cases local; 2 = Large gift food company; 3 = Small, nonfood gift company; 4 = Large, nonfood gift company, including specialty gift catalog; 5 = not sure
[e]Client purchasing: 1 = centralized; 2 = decentralized
[f]Aquisition Year—year in which GG acquired client: 1 = 1996; 2 = 1997, 3 = 1998
[g]Lead generation methods employed: 1 = cold call; 2 = direct mail; 3 = personal contact (friends put GG in touch with them); 4 = local networking group; 5 = business database from industry association; 6 = other (website, referral)
[h]Type of sales contact the Freys had with client: 1 = face-to-face; 2 = phone
[i]Sales Tools—Types of sales tools employed: 1 = brochure; 2 = proposal; 3 = sample gift package; 4 = presentation
[j]Acquisition hours—Estimated number of hours required to acquire client
[k]Estimated number of hours required to maintain/manage client in 1998
[l]Client offices—for a given client, the number of offices that are Granny's Goodies clients.
[m]Total estimated number of client's offices in the United States

a wide net, and a very small percentage of the contacts turn into actual sales."

Referrals Fifteen percent of all GG's leads originated from unsolicited volunteering of a contact name by a client or personal friend. Josh Frey recalled a recent example. "Last week," he said, "I gave a presentation at a property management company and the contact gave me another contact name at her former employer who oversees properties in New England. She said they were looking for something exactly like GG's gift packages."

Twenty-five percent of all GG's leads were generated through solicited referrals or via specific requests for colleague names and phone numbers. The Frey brothers believed that word-of-mouth referrals had the potential to become GG's most effective lead and sales generator. Elaborated Seth Frey:

> I have a contact at Ernst and Young and Josh has one at a big property management firm where at the click of a button they can send a message to all their colleagues endorsing our products and services. Yet, these good clients of ours haven't taken that action. We need more referrals from our clients. I don't think we haven't had too many referrals because people don't like us; I think it's because we don't extend ourselves enough. We need to get out and meet with these people face-to-face more often and have them call other potential clients.

Added Josh Frey:

> Referrals are great for our business. It can't get any better than having an existing client who sticks a GG contract in front of their associates and friends, gets them to sign it, and faxes us the order. If only we can make this happen. I have read about how Intuit was able to create this process with its customers. I wonder why we cannot get the same behavior from our good clients.

Internet The trend to append ".com" to a company name and ride the Internet wave to e-commerce success did not seem to be in Granny's future. Although a few of GG's corporate clients had commented favorably on *www.grannysgoodies.com*, a site to give the firm a Web presence established by the Frey brothers, only a few retail orders had trickled in. Nor, contrary to the Freys' expectations, had the Web site become a major lead generator.

But despite their limited success using the Internet to acquire and retain corporate clients, the Freys believed that they had to continue to investigate this new "digital sales" channel. Their interest in the Internet was heightened by an increasing number of inquiries from venture capitalists and MBA students regarding migrating their business completely to the Web. "There are a lot of people in the Internet business who think that the time is right to Web-enable the corporate gift purchase market," observed Josh Frey, "and if this is indeed true, then we don't want to be left out of the new game. With all the experience that we have accumulated in this business, we should be in the best position to succeed in the online, Web-centric world as well."

GRANNY'S SALES PROCESS

GG generated sales primarily through direct and catalog sales. Selling direct was an effective but time-consuming process for the Freys, who had become proficient at "pounding the pavement." They were nonetheless optimistic about this time investment, it having helped them develop a strong rapport with their clients, a "deal clincher" in many cases. Meeting face-to-face also gave the Freys a chance to showcase the actual products their clients would be buying and to explore with their clients how GG might customize packages for their particular needs.

Direct sales efforts usually targeted three types of people: directors of human resources; directors of sales and marketing; and directors or managers of recruiting. With larger accounts, higher-level executives were sometimes involved. GG's typical sales process comprised five steps.

1. Sales leads were generated through networking and list brokers and prospects contacted. The Freys employed both "bottom-up" and "top-down" approaches, as appropriate. The bottom-up approach involved contacting a local or regional office of a large firm and, if able to identify the potential, expanding efforts to cover other of the client's offices. This approach was deemed appropriate for clients that purchased gifts on a decentralized basis. The top-down

approach, which involved contacting a key decision maker at a company's corporate headquarters, was used with clients that employed centralized purchasing processes. GG also routinely contacted existing clients about new product details and ordering information by phone or a letter.

2. Fewer than 10% of clients contacted ordered immediately after the initial contact. Leads that indicated no interest were returned to GG's client database and continued to receive its biannual or annual mailing. Interested leads that did not immediately place an order typically wanted more information. The Freys determined prospective clients' information needs and dispatched literature, a proposal, or a sample package, made a presentation, or, often, delivered some combination of these. The Freys preferred to deliver samples personally in order to screen leads that wanted just a sample and nothing more. "It's easy to identify the 'all I want is a freebie' clients," observed Seth Frey.

3. Leads sent additional information or proposals typically either (1) indicated a lack of interest (and thus were returned to GG's client database), (2) "sat" on the information or proposal (i.e., indicated neither interest nor disinterest), or (3) placed an order. GG followed up leads sitting on proposals with a maximum of five calls, after which the name was returned to the database with a note explaining the expended effort. "This helps the next person who plans to contact this prospect," explained Josh Frey.

4. One or both of the Freys would visit contacts that made a presentation appointment. GG took a consultative selling approach in its presentations, inquiring about clients' needs and gift-giving history and budget and matching reported needs with a range of GG products or customized programs. Clients impressed with GG's offerings usually placed an order.

5. Clients that placed orders typically contacted GG several times to confirm recipient information, package or basket contents, and anticipated delivery. The Freys followed up personally after orders were received to ensure clients' satisfaction with GG's performance.

CHALLENGES IN THE SALES PLANNING PROCESS

Before sitting down to develop a sales strategy and process for 1999 and beyond, the Freys quickly reviewed their current challenges. GG had not progressed as quickly as the two young owners might have liked, in part due to lack of support and administrative resources. Although full-time staff had grown to eight, the Freys were still burdened with internal operational and production issues which prevented them from being out-in-the-field as much as they would have liked. "We are our own best salespeople," averred Josh Frey. "Just think if we could spend double the amount of time in the field! We would be much bigger right now. Too bad we can't be cloned like those sheep in Europe."

To overcome a second resource constraint—lack of additional sales people—the brothers had attempted to grow the sales organization by hiring a sales manager with an MBA and prior sales experience. "We thought the manager would come in, hit the ground running, and grow sales," explained Josh Frey.

> We were very careful in the selection process. We looked for sales experience, charisma, an MBA, rapport, big company experience. This person had all the qualifications and it still didn't work. While this manager seemed to really enjoy developing our marketing materials and strategy, he didn't want to get out of the office and sell. We were shocked at the failure. That's when we realized that sales is a strange animal; you either have it or you don't. Degrees can definitely help, but they are not a substitute for passion and a desire to sell.

Despite their initial setback, the Freys continued to seek qualified sales personnel, hiring a sales rep with property management industry experience in May 1999. Although this sales rep had secured a number of good orders, the brothers were concerned that they were not giving her sufficient direction and strategic vision with respect to how to plan her selling effort.

Realizing that they needed additional funds to hire a sales team, in a departure from the past when they had turned down several opportunities for fear of relinquishing control, the Freys had begun to think seriously about seeking out a capital partner. Josh had come to believe that a capital infusion and some seasoned business expertise would be welcome, even if it meant giving up a large stake in the business, but Seth, however, remained wary of bringing in controlling partners, preferring to retain majority ownership of the business. Further complicating the brothers' decisions was Seth Frey's interest in relocating to Chicago for family reasons. They wondered if he would be able to add value by establishing new markets, or if his absence from the central office would become a resource drain.

Finally, the brothers mulled over the question of enhancing their client management effort. Although they had collected a considerable amount of data about each order they had served and all the client relationships they had built over the past two years, they believed that they had not yet harnessed the power of that information. "Right from the start," reflected Seth Frey, "we had decided that we would collect as much data as we could. Now we have a lot of it, but haven't figured out how to use it. We need to make sense out of the Excel spreadsheets. Is there any way we can link the client-specific information with our selling effort and sales and client satisfaction? We need to figure out the determinants of success in our business."

Although the Freys also wanted to improve product content and quality, they were unsure how to do so without sacrificing margins. Moreover, having found a niche in recruiting and property management, they planned to delve more deeply into those markets by leveraging existing relationships. But what should be their next target market? Was there a recession-proof industry that could be targeted to balance the cyclical nature of the recruiting and property management markets?

Finally, there was the issue of managing client expectations. With each long-term contract and preferred vendor listing, the Frey brothers worked continuously to enhance levels of delivered service. For the resource-constrained business, this posed a constant challenge. Recalled Josh Frey:

Last September there was a minor mix-up with a shipment to a property manager of one of our big clients. She immediately sent out an e-mail to all her peers cautioning them about using us. We noticed an immediate impact on our sales to this client. We had worked hard and jumped through hoops to get on this firm's preferred vendor list. Now, all the good work we had done was destroyed by a single, minor mistake. None of the other managers who had liked our service were willing to call others within the client organization and tell them that GG was a good vendor to work with and that the mix-up was an isolated incident. Undoing the damage took a lot longer than expected and we still don't know whether it was worth the effort.

Invigorated by their 1998 successes, the Freys were nevertheless aware of the challenges they needed to address as they moved forward. Recognizing the "uncharted territory syndrome" to be a real concern, they were committed to developing a rock-solid plan that could be replicated and scaled up in the future. "This business is our baby," observed Josh Frey.

There is a tremendous amount of our self-image tied up in the success or failure of GG. But not until recently have we looked past this point. Until now we have not sat down to make a plan and say, "So how do we replicate this success next year and the year after that?" We need to put all the pieces of the puzzle together now and find out the parts that work and those that don't. If we don't do it now, I think there is a strong possibility that we will be right back where we started a few years ago. To me, that would be even worse psychologically, after having tasted success.

Although the Freys considered all their challenges to be important, they knew they had to be prioritized. They nibbled chocolate chip cookies as they stared down at the blank sheet of paper in front of them, then picked up their pens, determined to emerge with a winning action plan that would lay the groundwork for GG's future. ∎

♦♦♦ Fabtek (A)

Case 5-2   Fabtek (A)

Benson P. Shapiro, Rowland T. Moriarty, and Craig E. Cline

In mid-June 1991, the senior management of Fabtek's Fabrication Division was grappling with a problem unprecedented in the company's 15-year history. Because of an acute shortage of capacity and increasing customer dissatisfaction with late deliveries, the company's Marketing Vice President, Amy Vitali, and the Fabrication Division's Vice President of Operations, Rob Lightfoot, had to agree on which of four potential orders the company should accept and how it should bid on them. Each of the orders represented a different customer situation, mix of labor and materials, and mix of manufacturing talents, so a direct comparison among them was difficult. Stanley Ho, Fabtek's president, had advised them to work it out themselves, but reminded them that a quick decision was necessary "if we're going to be able to fit *any* of them into our shop schedule."

Fabrication Division

Early history   The Fabrication Division was the second-largest industrial fabricator of titanium in the United States. Corporate and sales offices for the company, as well as its primary fabricating facility, were located in Philadelphia.

Fabtek was one of the first companies to provide titanium products for industrial use. Before the mid-1970s, titanium had been used almost exclusively in the aerospace industry because of its light weight and high strength. It wasn't until the price dropped (from $20 per pound for some alloys used in aerospace to $5 per pound for industrial titanium sheet and plate) and its corrosion resistance was demonstrated, however, that titanium became competitive for some applications with stainless steel, copper and nickel alloys, brick-lined steel, fiberglass, and other products used to counter corrosion. Even in 1991, titanium won the industrial applications battle only if (1) it could outlast competitive metals to such an extent that it was less expensive overall or (2) it was the only industrial metal that could do the job. Nevertheless, Ho was enthusiastic about titanium's potential and estimated that its industrial use would grow by 15% to 20% per year during the foreseeable future.

Growth   From its inception, Fabtek's principal business was fabrication of titanium equipment for industrial corrosion-resistant applications. The company had little involvement in the aerospace industry. Over time it added technical staff, participated in industry symposia, sponsored technical papers, and studied developing titanium markets. Active consulting and field services, such as field repairs and corrosion analysis, developed from these efforts.

In addition to the fabricating business, Fabtek sold titanium metal and specialty hardware (pipe fittings, bolts, nuts, pipe flanges) to the industrial market. The two organizations shared a common raw materials inventory. The corporation also purchased titanium in ingot and semifinished form and converted it (using steel mills that rented time on their machinery on a price-per-pound basis) to finished product forms, such as bars or plates. As business expanded, these activities were separated into a materials profit center that included metal trading, warehousing, and conversion.

In 1986 and again in 1988 capacity expansions were made in Philadelphia and efforts toward geographic expansion followed. During the 1980s a subsidiary was formed in Montreal, a branch was opened in Texas to serve the petrochemical markets, and a small, bankrupt titanium wire mill was acquired. In addition, a small subsidiary was formed in Brazil to take advantage of the rapid expansion of basic industries, such as pulp, occurring there. (Exhibit 1 provides corporate financial data.)

The case was prepared by Professors Benson P. Shapiro and Rowland T. Moriarty with research assistance from Craig E. Cline. Copyright © 1992 by the President and Fellows of Harvard College. Harvard Business School Case 592-095.

	1990	1989	1988
Net sales	$31,155,402	$26,317,527	$23,137,485
Expenses			
Cost of sales and engineering	26,351,184	22,077,768	18,604,803
SG&A	4,587,780	3,089,676	2,141,031
Interest, net	529,023	301,479	228,462
	$31,467,987	$25,468,923	$20,974,296
Income (loss) before provision (credit) for taxes on income and minority interest in subsidiary	(312,585)	848,604	2,163,189
Taxes on income	(179,400)	417,600	1,017,300
Net income before minority interest in subsidiary	$ (133,185)	$ 431,004	$ 1,145,889
Minority interest in subsidiary	(11,145)	22,791	0
Net income	$ (144,330)	$ 453,795	$ 1,145,889
Financial Position			
Current assets	22,170,168	13,502,616	13,072,680
Working capital	641,322	976,062	1,997,385
Property and equipment, net	2,129,571	1,510,308	848,172
Inventories[a]			
Raw materials	6,496,350	5,215,398	4,832,166
Work-in-progress	8,898,744	4,282,422	4,909,455
Long-term debt	535,278	831,000	822,000
Stockholders' equity	2,654,223	2,798,553	2,326,758

EXHIBIT 1 Corporate Financial Summary, 1988–1990

[a]Inventory is stated at the lower of cost (substantially on a first-in, first-out basis) or market.

Organization Operations was headed by Rob Lightfoot (who previously had been involved in Fabtek's marketing area). It consisted of two engineers who evaluated customer product designs to determine the best manufacturing processes; two drafting people; two estimators who calculated the cost of manufacture for pricing; and several administrative and clerical people. In addition, Operations' shop, which was nonunion, had 78 employees in three sections: fabrication, welding, and the machine shop. Additional fabrication capacity was available in the Texas and Montreal facilities, but these were primarily intended to serve their respective regional markets and were operating at full capacity through 1991.

Fabtek's marketing organization was headed by Amy Vitali; it included two regional managers located in Philadelphia and Texas, the titanium metal sales group, and a customer service function. In addition, the company was represented by several manufacturers' representatives who operated both in the United States and abroad.[1] (Exhibit 2 shows the organization chart.)

Markets and Customers

Fabtek had over 90 significant customers in 11 markets:

1. General chemicals—pressure vessels, tanks, heat exchangers, shafts and mixers, pumps, valves, piping, blowers, anodes for chlorine.

---

[1]A manufacturers' representative was an independent company or salesperson who sold products of related but noncompeting companies for commissions on the sales.

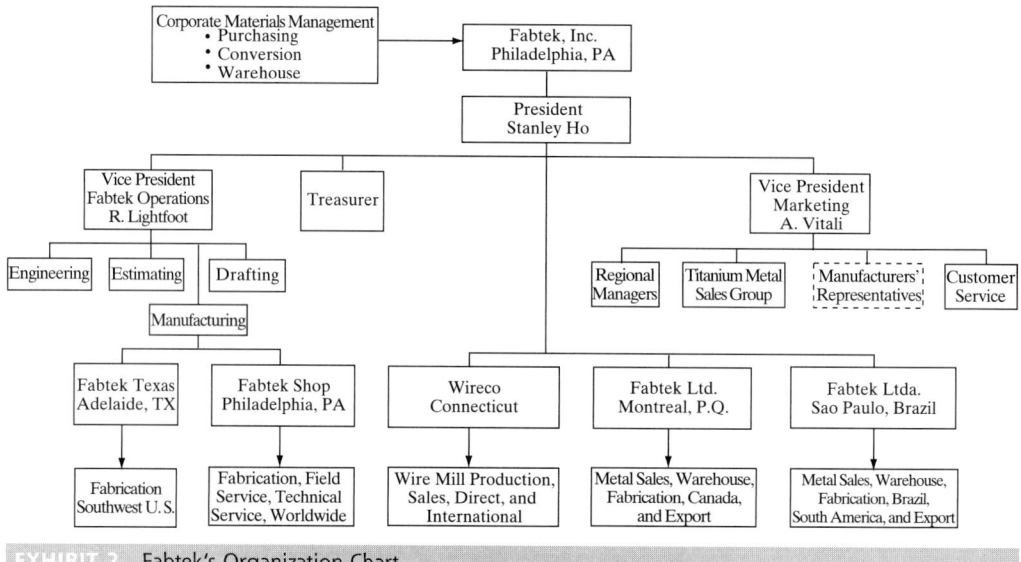

EXHIBIT 2 Fabtek's Organization Chart

```
                    Corporate Materials Management
                         • Purchasing              → Fabtek, Inc.
                         • Conversion                Philadelphia, PA
                         • Warehouse
                                                         │
                                                   President
                                                   Stanley Ho
        ┌────────────────────────┬──────────────────────┴──────────────────────────────────┐
   Vice President              Treasurer                                          Vice President
   Fabtek Operations                                                                Marketing
   R. Lightfoot                                                                     A. Vitali
   ┌────┬──────┬──────┐                                     ┌────────┬──────────┬──────────────┬─────────┐
 Engineering Estimating Drafting                          Regional  Titanium Metal Manufacturers' Customer
              │                                           Managers   Sales Group  Representatives  Service
        Manufacturing
   ┌──────┬──────┬──────────────┬────────────────┐
 Fabtek Texas  Fabtek Shop    Wireco        Fabtek Ltd.     Fabtek Ltda.
 Adelaide, TX  Philadelphia,  Connecticut   Montreal, P.Q.  Sao Paulo, Brazil
               PA
   │              │              │              │              │
 Fabrication  Fabrication, Field  Wire Mill Production,  Metal Sales, Warehouse,  Metal Sales, Warehouse,
 Southwest U.S. Service, Technical  Sales, Direct, and    Fabrication, Canada,    Fabrication, Brazil,
              Service, Worldwide   International         and Export              South America, and Export
```

Note: The intimate ties between the Fabricating Division's Operations and the rest of the company make it impossible to separate the Fabtek organization from that of the Fabrication Division.

2. Pulp and paper—bleaching equipment, chemical preparation vessels, piping.
3. Basic metals—cathodes for copper, vessels for hydrometallurgy.
4. Petroleum—heat exchangers for refineries, down-hole equipment, hot-oil coolers for production.
5. Pollution—heat exchangers, vessels, and pipe for municipal waste oxidation; air scrubbers, blowers.
6. Fibers—chemical equipment for various polymer intermediate products.
7. Water desalinization—heat exchangers, tubing, piping.
8. Marine activities—high-voltage undersea electrical connectors, diver rescue chambers, research submarine components.
9. Electric power generation—tubes for surface condensers.
10. Food—corrosion-resistant equipment for pickle solutions.
11. High-performance toys—12-meter sailboat parts, race cars, golf clubs.

The majority of Fabtek's customers were located within a 500-mile radius of Philadelphia, but the firm also shipped worldwide. Customer orders ranged from $75 to $6 million, with $150,000 being typical. Approximately 20% of Fabtek's customers provided 80% of its business.

Close business and personal relationships existed between the Fabtek staff and certain customers who gave Fabtek a considerable percentage of their titanium business. One customer, Refco, typically represented 15% to 20% of sales each year. Two other companies accounted for 10% to 15% of sales on a fairly regular basis. In early 1990, Fabtek's management established a corporate policy of allowing a maximum of 20% of its business to reside with one customer and 30% to be in one market area.

Competition

Fabtek had five major competitors, none of which was located in the immediate area. The largest was in Ohio and had annual sales of $49.5 million. The others were scattered across the country and had annual sales of between $6 million and $30 million in competitive titanium work, with $18 million being average. Fabtek had an estimated 16% share of a total industrial titanium fabrication market of just under $150 million. It had a reputation for a higher quality, but also a higher price, than most of its competitors.

Forecasts

Fabtek's sales and equity had grown steadily from 1985 to 1988, but 1989 sales were disappointing. In 1990, despite record sales of $31.2 million, the company experienced its first net loss. Management felt that the 1989 and 1990 results were more a consequence of erratic pricing and unstable market conditions than internal problems. The titanium industry had been operating at a significantly lower level than in 1987 and 1988. Capital spending on process equipment, refinery expansion, pulp and paper projects, and chemical construction had been well below anticipated levels in 1990 and was not expected to increase significantly in 1991.

Manufacturing Process

Although titanium had several fabricating peculiarities that required special skills, some operations—such as shearing, machine work, and forming—closely paralleled those used in precision fabrication of certain stainless steels.[2] In fact, the company often was able to subcontract excess machine work to local precision machine shops. Heat treatment, thermal cutting, and especially welding were generally considered the most difficult operations. Because titanium was a "reactive" metal, it was easily embrittled by increases in its gas content (primarily oxygen and nitrogen, but also most other elements). Melting titanium, such as in welding, or heating it above 1,200°F, caused it to react instantly with air, absorbing oxygen and nitrogen and becoming brittle and useless. Consequently, cleanliness and special inert-gas welding techniques were required to produce good welds.

Fabtek used its strong competence in welding as a major selling point. One executive noted, "We feel that our expertise lies in high-quality welding. Over 80% of our jobs involve welding." This reputation for outstanding welding was supported routinely by radiographic, ultrasonic, and liquid penetration inspection of each weld.

---

[2]Shearing was cutting titanium sheets to a specified size. Machining used lathes, mills, drills, and other chip-forming high-precision tools to obtain close tolerances. Forming, done on plate or bar rolls or on a press brake, bent the item to its ultimate shape.

The company had 33 welders who were graded from A to D, according to their ability to handle difficult work. In addition, Fabtek had several automatic welding machines. Finally, various helpers and trainees assisted the welders. (Shop capacity is shown in Exhibit 3.)

Costs Generally a product's cost had five components, with manufacturing overhead averaging about 200% of direct labor cost:

Component	Range	Average
Raw material	30–65%	45%
Direct labor	5–20	9
Manufacturing overhead	10–40	18
Subcontracting	10–15	12
General and administrative costs and profit	10–25	16

The company's objective was to have cost of goods average 80%, with 85% the upper limit.

Existing situation Shop backlog had reached a critical level in June 1991 (see Exhibit 4). This was the first time the company's booking exceeded its capacity by a significant margin. Delivery history for the past several months had been, in the words of one Operations executive, "horrendous." Although routine orders were going out on time, most major or complex jobs were late. Delivery times had increased from an average of 8–10 weeks in 1987 to 16–60 weeks, depending on complexity and size, in 1990. Another Operations executive added, "The main reason many customers are still coming back to us is our quality. There also aren't many other people who fabricate titanium."

According to a third Operations official, one factor underlying Fabtek's capacity problem was the difficulty the company had hiring and training qualified welders.

The labor market around Philadelphia and our need for highly skilled workers make it difficult to find new people, especially because we can't offer much higher than average pay. The competition's shops are generally located in less expensive areas, and we must be careful to keep our labor costs competitive. Even hiring a new welder as part of our regular workforce is difficult. If we're lucky, we can find one or two a

	Number of People		
	Day Shift	Night Shift	Total
Welding			
Welder A	7	3	10
Welder B	3	1	4
Welder C	5	6	11
Welder D	6	2	8
Trainee	2	–	2
Helper	7	7	14
Auto A	1	1	2
Auto B	–	–	–
Auto C	2	2	4
Auto trainee	1	–	1
			56
Fabrication			
Layout mechanic	2		2
Mechanic	2		2
Fab A	1		1
Fab B	1		1
Trainee	4		4
Helper	3		3
			13
Machine Shop[a]			
Machinist 1st Class	3	–	3
Machinist 2nd Class	1	–	1
Operator A	1	–	1
Operator B	2	1	3
Trainee	1	–	1
			9

EXHIBIT 3 Fabtek's Operations' Shop Capacity

[a] Additional machine capacity could be obtained through subcontracting.

month. Then it takes between two months and two years to train them to be A level, depending on whether they were welders before. For many jobs the welders must also qualify under the ASME Boiler Code, which is expensive but necessary for A and B level welders. This situation is even more critical because the majority of our jobs require A and B level welding.

This official felt, however, that the major underlying factor was Fabtek's lack of reliable information on the shop's actual capacity at any given moment.

In the past, Marketing would ask us if we had capacity available for a job before they quoted on it. But in recent months late material deliveries and problems on two major jobs have swelled our backlog, which has extended delivery dates on existing jobs. These fill the capacity Marketing thought would be open for the jobs we had just bid, thereby pushing ahead *their* delivery dates.

EXHIBIT 4 Fabtek's Shop Schedule as of June 1991

	June 1991			**July 1991**			**August 1991**			**September 1991**		
	W[a]	M[a]	F[a]	W	M	F	W	M	F	W	M	F
Backlog	7,200	1,670	2,350	6,800	1,040	2,050	4,200	900	1,050	4,200	1,100	1,050
Capacity	6,920	1,560	2,250	6,920	1,560	2,250	6,920	1,560	2,250	6,920	1,560	2,250
Difference	(280)	(110)	(100)	120	520	200	2,720	660	1,200	2,720	460	1,200
Cumulative	(280)	(110)	(100)	(160)	410	100	2,560	1,070	1,300	5,280	1,530	2,500

	October 1991			**November 1991**			**December 1991**			**January 1992**		
	W	M	F	W	M	F	W	M	F	W	M	F
Backlog	5,000	1,350	1,500	4,120	1,300	1,070	4,700	700	800	5,000	400	1,350
Capacity	6,920	1,560	2,250	6,920	1,560	2,250	6,920	1,560	2,250	6,920	1,560	2,250
Difference	1,920	210	750	2,800	260	1,180	2,220	860	1,450	1,920	1,160	900
Cumulative	7,200	1,740	3,250	10,000	2,000	4,430	12,220	2,860	5,880	14,140	4,020	6,780

	February 1992			**March 1992**			**April 1992**			**May 1992**			**Total**		
	W	M	F	W	M	F	W	M	F	W	M	F	W	M	F
Backlog	4,050	560	1,150	4,220	660	1,500	4,300	750	1,350	4,300	640	1,020	58,090	11,070	16,240
Capacity	6,920	1,560	2,250	6,920	1,560	2,250	6,920	1,560	2,250	6,920	1,560	2,250	83,040	18,720	27,000
Difference	2,870	1,000	1,100	2,700	900	750	2,620	810	900	2,620	920	1,230	24,950	7,650	10,760
Cumulative	17,010	5,020	7,880	19,710	5,920	8,630	22,330	6,730	9,530	24,950	7,650	10,760	24,950	7,650	10,760

Notes: Welding and fabrication helpers and trainees were each counted as 50% of a regular welder or fabricator for planning purposes. Data assume each welder, machinist, and fabricator works 2,080 hours per year.

[a] W = Welders
M = Machinists
F = Fabricators

Consequently, Marketing no longer believes our capacity forecasts; they simply go ahead and book the order for the longest delivery they can get away with, which, of course, adds to our capacity problem. It's a vicious cycle.

Lightfoot concurred with his subordinates; he felt Marketing only recently had become realistic about the capacity limit and thus willing to work with Operations to improve the company's delivery schedule. He observed:

> We started Fabtek because we were excited by what we could do in the industrial market. In fact, Stanley Ho has made it our basic operating philosophy "to make money by moving titanium." It's been fun, and that's largely what kept us going—until now. At present we are faced with declining profits and a delivery crisis. Something has to be done, and perhaps being more selective in taking orders will do it.

From an Operations standpoint, he felt several criteria could make an order attractive:

1. The job is technically challenging.
2. The job fits with Fabtek's high-quality image and capabilities.
3. The company's engineering expertise is utilized.
4. The job is long-run and repetitive.
5. The company has experience with similar products.
6. Specifications and job scope are clear.
7. For larger orders, progress payments can be negotiated (payments made on labor and material as applied, over the course of the contract, rather than all at the end).
8. Overall contribution before S, G&A (sales, general and administrative expenses) is near 20% of the product's price.

Marketing

Fabtek's fabrication and titanium metal sales were under the direction of Amy Vitali in Marketing. She spent an estimated 60% of her time on fabrication sales and the remainder on metal sales. Similarly, the two regional sales managers each devoted 10% of their time to fabrication sales, and a manufacturers' representative in California handled both fabricated products and titanium metal sales. Generally, however, Fabtek relied on advertising in trade publications, participation in industry symposia, and trade shows for fabrication sales. Also, Ho, Lightfoot, Vitali, and other staff people who had close relationships with customers usually handled their accounts personally. Lightfoot, for example, had close ties with certain Refco officials and thus handled all but the smallest details of this account. As one executive observed, "Most of the management people here have two or three job functions, and almost anyone can make a sale."

Bidding process One of the principal tasks of the people in Marketing and Sales was to make sure that Fabtek was on the bid lists of potential customers. Once a request for a quote was received, Marketing sent it to Operations for estimating (to obtain a quote as well as an estimated delivery date). Marketing then modified the quote to reflect market conditions and corporate goals.

The company had a bid success rate of 15%. Vitali felt this percentage was somewhat low compared with the industry average, but pointed out that only one of seven requests for quotes was "solid." She thought a more serious problem was the price competitiveness that had recently gripped the market, forcing Fabtek to play pricing games.

> Our aggressive posture has been a reaction to forces in the market more than a philosophy. As the titanium market stabilizes, which I'm sure it will eventually do, we will be better able to formulate an effective rather than a freewheeling, reactive strategy about taking orders. This is a serious concern of mine, because we haven't been able to maintain market share in the last year. We've got to pick our shots better—but we can only become more selective if we get the opportunity to call the shots.

Possible changes Vitali felt that the company had to become more selective about the high-risk custom jobs it took; she was also in favor of diversifying Fabtek's business among customers and markets. "We have an excellent relationship with Refco, but what do we do if they represent 30% to 40% of our business and then suddenly stop sending us orders?" She believed Fabtek would eventually move away from custom fabrication and become more involved in developing proprietary products. She also felt that the company had to determine its costs more accurately. "We've got to target our markets better to be sure we are using our resources to their maximum potential." To do this, she felt that Marketing had to get better information out of Fabtek's Operations concerning costs and capacity availability.

Vitali's preferred criteria for taking an order were as follows:

1. The job is similar to what Fabtek had built before.
2. The design is simple and the cost estimate reliable.
3. The job has good payment terms (progress payments on labor and material as applied).
4. The market area has potential for further development.
5. The job allows adequate delivery time.
6. Price is not the primary factor in the customer's decision.

THE FOUR PROSPECTIVE FABRICATION ORDERS

In mid-June 1991 Vitali and Lightfoot met to decide whether to accept each of the prospective orders: Refco, Pierce-Pike, Worldwide Paper, and Kathco. Prices were fixed for the larger two orders but still had to be determined for the smaller two. In addition, both Vitali and Lightfoot had been uneasy about the entire bidding process and wondered if it should be changed. Lightfoot, for example, thought perhaps the company should expect a greater markup on labor than on materials. He went on to explain that the material cost estimates tended to be much more reliable than the labor estimates. He mused:

> I think that we should be paid more for the greater uncertainty of the labor estimates. Overruns on costs—almost solely labor costs—were a prime reason for our poor 1990 profit performance. Right now our bidding procedure makes no differentiation between labor and materials. Maybe the customer should pay for some of the uncertainty in labor costs through a higher markup.

Exhibit 5 shows cost estimates and Exhibit 6 the projected shop load for each order.

EXHIBIT 5 Cost Estimates for the Four Prospective Orders

	Refco (petroleum refining)		Pierce-Pike (wastewater treatment)		Worldwide Paper (paper)	Kathco (electrodes)
Selling price	$6,000,000		$3,900,000		≈$2,400,000??	≈$1,500,000??
Material	2,100,000	(35%)	2,250,000	(58%)	1,080,000	960,000
Labor						
Welding	600,000		105,000		132,000	
Machining	156,000		18,000		15,000	30,000
Fabrication	99,000		42,000		45,000	60,000
Total labor	$ 855,000	(14%)	$ 165,000	(4%)	$ 192,000	$ 90,000
Factory overhead	1,710,000	(29)	330,000	(8)	384,000	180,000
Subcontracting	300,000	(5)	390,000	(10)	450,000	–
Total factory cost	$4,965,000	(83%)	$3,135,000	(80%)	$ 2,106,000	$ 1,230,000
Contribution (before SG&A)[a]	$1,035,000	(17%)	$ 765,000	(20%)	≈$ 294,000??	≈$ 270,000??

[a]Sales, general and administrative expenses

Note: "≈" means approximately.

EXHIBIT 6 Projected Shop Load for the Four Prospective Orders

	Refco			Pierce-Pike			Worldwide Paper			Kathco		
	W[a]	M[a]	F[a]	W	M	F	W	M	F	W	M	F
1991												
June	100	100	–	50	50	–	–	–	–	–	–	–
July	1,500	600	–	1,400	100	–	1,000	200	–	–	400	–
August	2,000	700	–	1,150	100	50	1,000	300	400	–	600	1,800
September	1,800	200	–	1,000	50	150	1,000	200	500	–	200	800
October	1,900	100	500	1,200	50	250	1,000	130	1,000	–	200	900
November	2,000	200	500	1,000	100	300	2,000	–	600	–	200	700
December	2,000	700	1,000	600	300	350	1,000	–	–	–	100	700
1992												
January	2,000	800	1,000	500	250	500	650	–	450	–	–	–
February	2,000	600	1,000	–	–	500	–	–	–	–	–	–
March	2,500	600	1,000	–	–	500	–	–	–	–	–	–
April	2,500	800	500	–	–	150	–	–	–	–	–	–
May	2,500	500	500	–	–	–	–	–	–	–	–	–
Post-May	12,000	2,800	500	–	–	–	–	–	–	–	–	–
Total	34,800	8,700	6,500	6,900	1,000	2,750	7,650	830	2,950	–	1,700	4,900

[a]W = Welders
M = Machinists
F = Fabricators

Refco

Refco, Fabtek's largest single customer, was one of the world's leading engineering contractors. Refco and its competitors (for example, Bechtel, Brown and Root, and others) designed and constructed large projects around the world. Like most contractors, Refco specialized—concentrating on petroleum refineries and petrochemical plants.

Several years earlier Refco had developed a specialized piece of machinery to perform certain refinery operations under demanding pressure, temperature, and corrosion conditions. Refco had supplied many of the units in stainless steel, but corrosion failures and increasing corrosive process requirements caused a gradual shift to titanium. The units, nicknamed *Whoppers* because of their large size and hamburger shape, had to be made to exact tolerances and with great care in welding. Fabtek had worked closely with Refco in developing the design. From time to time, Refco also had come to Fabtek for other titanium pieces—usually large process vessels, such as reactors, requiring a good deal of welding and fabrication. As far as Fabtek's management could ascertain, Fabtek was the only outside titanium fabricator in the world that Refco used. On the other hand, Refco did some in-house fabrication of superalloys and titanium at its large Rotterdam manufacturing facility.

As an engineering contractor, Refco had a trained staff of field welders and welding supervisors; however, they did little titanium work because of the unique properties of the metal. Industry rumors that Refco would set up a fabricating facility for superalloys and titanium had been circulating for the past four years. According to Lightfoot (who, among Fabtek's managers, knew Refco best), Refco's executives were totally unwilling to discuss this possibility except with "Cheshire cat–like smiles." Lightfoot believed Refco was unhappy about Fabtek's long delivery schedule and occasional late deliveries and doubted its ability to handle very large requirements expected in the future.

In May 1991, Refco had come to Fabtek with a request for production of an above-size Whopper, which soon became known as a *Super Whopper*. The purchasing/subcontracting specialists at Refco stated that they were willing to pay $6 million. Refco had offered to pay for 80% of direct "material and labor as applied" in four installments. Thus, each time 25% of the work was done, Fabtek would receive 20% of the cost of materials and direct labor. Thirty days after delivery Fabtek would be paid for the completed piece. (Refco always paid its bills on time.)

To be completed on time, the Super Whopper would have to enter production at Fabtek in June. It was certain that the first progress payment, and perhaps the second, would come in Fabtek's 1991 fiscal year, which ended in October.

In 1990, Refco had purchased $4.5 million worth of products from Fabtek. Not counting the Super Whopper order, its 1991 purchases from Fabtek were expected to be $6 million (out of Fabtek's projected $36 million in sales).

Pierce-Pike

For almost four years Vitali had been pursuing business with Pierce-Pike, a company that specialized in constructing proprietary wastewater treatment plants. Pierce-Pike was the subsidiary of a large chemical company and had developed a strong position in a rapidly growing market. Until early April 1991, it had shown no interest in giving business to Fabtek. All its work was shared by Fabtek's largest competitor and its number-four competitor in the market.

In April, Vitali had received a request for proposal on a pressurized reactor from Pierce-Pike. She was ecstatic; it represented a partial victory, or at least some interest, following a long battle. After some difficult pricing decisions, Vitali quoted $3.9 million on the job, although she had some concern about whether Fabtek could do the job in the hours estimated. The reactor involved some unusual fabrication with which Fabtek was inexperienced. On the other hand, both Vitali and Lightfoot had decided it was important to develop this capability.

On June 13, Fabtek received the order, which it could refuse. Its original quote had contained a note indicating that Fabtek might not have enough capacity to fill the order. Vitali believed Pierce-Pike's two existing sources had capacity available, but she had heard that Pierce-Pike was unhappy with the quality of both, especially the larger one. Also, Pierce-Pike was willing to make progress payments only on raw material.

Worldwide Paper

Worldwide Paper was a large integrated producer of pulp, paper, and fabricated paper products. In the late 1980s, its process development laboratory had tested a new piece of equipment made entirely of titanium. The scale-up to pilot plant and small production units had gone smoothly. Now, Worldwide was putting its first full-sized production unit out for bid. Although earlier units had been made of less-corrosion-resistant materials, this one was to be made of titanium. From Vitali's point of view, this order had a particularly interesting facet:

> For some time we have been anxious to develop a line of proprietary items. It would ease our management task and enable us to train employees on standard work, which is less demanding than custom work. It would smooth our work flow and enable us to begin to develop a sales force. Right now we don't have a standard product line, so we can't have a regular sales force.
>
> Worldwide is willing to license this item to its manufacturer. If we get the bid, we can then develop it into a standard product line. There is little opportunity for customization in the primary part of the unit, so it could be a standard product.

Lightfoot was equally excited about acquiring or developing a standard product line. In addition, he saw the opportunity to add a new capability to Fabtek's operation:

> The $450,000 subcontracting involved is for special heat treatment. It is going to cost us that much because we have to move very large parts between our plant and the subcontractor. Furthermore, this subcontractor is really taking advantage of us, because they are one of the very few facilities that can do this type of heat treating. If we made the piece as a standard product line—even at a relatively low volume—we could develop the heat-treating competence in-house with a payback of a matter of months, including the transportation savings.

Vitali suspected that the cost estimators had been very conservative in their calculations. She could not be sure of the prices that competitors would offer, but she believed the $2.4 million range to be about right. She stated, "Someone will come in lower—probably in the $2.1 million range. A couple may be at $2.25 million. But we have the quality to command some sort of premium over our competitors."

This order offered no progress payments but required a penalty of 0.1% of the contract price for each working day that the complete order was late. There was no incentive for early delivery.

Kathco

The fourth order was fairly straightforward. Kathco was a metal refinery that manufactured its own titanium electrodes for purifying manganese. In the spring and summer of 1991 its sales were high. During 1991 the company had a new electrode production facility under construction. Construction was delayed, so Kathco had an important shortfall in its electrode availability.

Kathco had solicited bids from only Fabtek and one competitor because it knew the companies well. Fabtek had a good relationship with Kathco. But this order was clearly a "one-shot deal": Once Kathco's plant was operating, it could supply all of Kathco's needs.

OTHER CONSIDERATIONS

Fabtek also made money by buying, warehousing, and selling titanium. The added volume from any one of these orders would affect all metal purchases. The total effect was difficult to predict because of changes in the metal suppliers' strategy and pricing, but it was generally considered good for the company. As a rule, net profit varied from nothing to about 4% of material cost estimates. Gross profit was a little higher but varied substantially.

The shop capacity estimates considered only the availability of labor on a straight-time, two-shift basis (that is, during normal working hours). It was possible to have people work overtime, although some resented it—especially in the summer. Overtime was expensive (150% of regular labor rates) and usually resulted in lower productivity and quality. Over the short run, however, it was the only feasible way to increase capacity. Skilled third-shift personnel were unlikely to be available, at least in the near future. More important, Fabtek's limited facility size might make overtime or a third shift impractical, because there would be no room to store work in process. ■

◆◆◆ Fabtek (B)

Case 5-3 Fabtek (B)

Benson P. Shapiro and Rowland T. Moriarty

In July 1991, Amy Vitali received a crisis call from the purchasing manager of Seven Sisters Petroleum's Houston refinery. Seven Sisters Petroleum was a large, integrated oil company that operated a huge refinery near Houston, Texas. In September 1990, the refinery had accepted bids for a piece of equipment to be installed in the top of a 100-ft. high-pressure reactor. Fabtek had bid $540,000 on the piece, which involved much fabrication, machining, and welding, and required little titanium. A competitor had bid only $279,000.

Although Seven Sisters had been a good customer of Fabtek, the purchasing agent, Cal Keating, had awarded the order to Fabtek's competitor. Vitali, who enjoyed a close relationship with Keating, told him: "We can't even make it for under $300,000, let alone sell it for that. I have trouble believing they can!"

The piece was subsequently installed in a new $270 million complex in the plant. In July, it fractured and needed immediate repair. Keating called Vitali and asked her to send a Fabtek crew to repair the piece. Keating pleaded, "Amy, I am in trouble. We have $270 million worth of equipment down for a lousy $300,000 part. We'll pay anything reasonable—in fact, even something unreasonable—to get it fixed."

Vitali, whose plant was packed to capacity and whose installation people were tied up, was cool to the offer. She suggested that Keating contact the supplier and mentioned their conversation of the previous fall. Keating replied: "That idiot can't weld to these requirements in his shop. He damn well can't do it in the field. I know you people can do it. At least quote a price; that can't hurt."

Vitali said she would look into it. She found Seven Sisters' purchases from Fabtek to be:

1991 (forecast)	$1,350,000
1990	1,710,000
1989	1,830,000
1988	1,560,000

She knew that Fabtek's share of Seven Sisters' business, and especially the Houston business, had declined because of sharp pricing by competitors, particularly the one that had received the contract for the failed piece.

Amy Vitali and Rob Lightfoot jointly concluded that locally hired crews could not be

---

The case was prepared by Professors Benson P. Shapiro and Rowland T. Moriarty. Copyright © 1992 by the President and Fellows of Harvard College. Harvard Business School Case 592-096.

used for this work. They thought it would take four A welders, two B welders, and a trainee two weeks to do the repair—certainly no more. One of the A welders was good enough to supervise the job, Lightfoot thought. Direct labor costs could not exceed $31,500 even at double time and overtime. Supplies and expenses, including the shipment of equipment to Houston and travel expenses, were estimated to be under $22,500.

While Lightfoot and Vitali were finishing a quiet and informal review of the costs for the project, Vitali's secretary walked into the office and said, "Mr. Keating is on the telephone. He says it's urgent. Will you talk to him now or return his call?" ∎

CHAPTER 6

Building and Managing Brand Equity

For many firms, brand equity will be the key component of customer equity. Managing the brand may be critical to successful customer management, since the brand can influence the likelihood that a customer will continue to do business with a firm. Firms everywhere face the common threat of commoditization—the possibility that someone else will enter the market and provide their product or service to customers in a way that is better, faster, or cheaper. Brands enable firms to combat such commoditization. Consider brands such as HP printers, Coke soft drinks, Boeing aircraft, or Mercedes automobiles. Why do their customers prefer these brands over others? Why do firms invest in "image advertising"? Or sponsor community events? The answer is to build the brand; to build brand equity; to get new customers to buy and current customers to buy again.

This chapter examines brand equity in detail. Specifically, this chapter:

- Defines and explains the importance of brand equity;
- Describes circumstances and contexts in which brand equity is likely to be important;
- Examines the key drivers of brand equity: brand awareness, brand attitude and corporate ethics and citizenship, and describes the types of strategies firms can use to build brand equity through each driver.

◆ BRAND EQUITY: WHAT IS IT AND WHY DOES IT MATTER?

Brand equity is that portion of customer equity attributable to the customer's perceptions of the brand. More specifically, the impact of the brand on the customer, that which leads to brand equity, represents the customer's subjective evaluation of the firm and the products or services offered by the firm. This subjective evaluation can be shaped by the firm through its marketing strategies and tactics, and can be influenced by the customer through experiences, associations, and connections with the firm via its branded products and services.[1]

---

[1] For more information on brand associations, see Gerald Zaltman and Robin Higie, "Seeing the Voice of the Customer: The Zaltman Metaphor Elicitation Technique," Marketing Science Institute Report Number 93–114 (1993); and Geraldine R. Henderson, Dawn Iacobucci, and Bobby J. Calder, "Brand Diagnostics: The Use of Consumer Associative Networks for the Brand Manager" (working paper, Fuqua School of Business, Duke University 1998).

To understand the power of brand equity, it is important to understand what a brand can do. Brand equity represents the extent to which the firm successfully influences the customer's subjective evaluation of the firm's offerings—the extent to which the firm captures the "heart" of the customer.[2] Brands can build customer awareness and recognition of the firm's products and services; can serve to remind the customer about the firm; and can build an emotional brand-based tie with the customer. First of all, through brand awareness and recognition, the brand acts as a magnet that can attract new customers to the firm. Second, the brand acts as a hallmark reminder to customers. For current customers, the brand serves to remind customers about the firm's products and services, and to ensure that a firm's customers continue to think about the firm. Third, the brand can act as the customer's emotional tie to the firm. Customers who have strong relationships with a brand may closely identify with it, and may even form relationships with it. For example, consumers may have a few "committed partnership" relationships with a brand—a loyal, exclusive relationship. Or, consumers may have "flings"—one-shot frivolous engagements—or "childhood buddies"—brands that evoke warmly reminiscent memories of childhood.[3] In each case, we see that the customer has developed an emotional tie with the brand.

Brand equity influences customer equity as follows. First, if customers develop more favorable attitudes toward the brand, they are more likely to purchase the brand. Second, if customers have increased positive feelings for the brand, they will be less likely to purchase a competing brand. Third, the customer's positive attitude and feelings toward the brand will increase the likelihood that the customer will recommend the brand to others, increasing the probability that other customers will also try the brand.[4]

◆ WHEN BRAND EQUITY MATTERS MUST

Brand equity will not be equally important to all firms.[5] There are several specific situations in which brand equity is likely to matter most (relative to value equity and relationship equity):

- **When there are purchases requiring only low levels of involvement and simple decision processes.** When a purchase decision requires high levels of customer involvement, brand equity may be less critical than value equity or relationship equity. However, for many products, particularly frequently purchased consumer goods, such decisions often require only low levels of involvement and are routinized. In this case, brand equity may

---

[2]See Tim Ambler, C. B. Bhattacharya, Julie Edell, Kevin Lane Keller, Katherine N. Lemon, and Vikas Mittal, "Relating Brand and Customer Perspectives on Marketing Management," *Journal of Service Research* 5, no. 1 (2002): 13–25; and Kevin L. Keller, *Strategic Brand Management: Building, Measuring, and Managing Brand Equity*, 2nd ed. (Upper Saddle River, NJ: Prentice Hall, 2002).
[3]See Susan Fournier, "Consumers and Their Brands: Developing Relationship Theory in Consumer Research," *Journal of Consumer Research* 24 (March 1998): 343–73.
[4]See Tim Ambler, C. B. Bhattacharya, Julie Edell, Kevin Lane Keller, Katherine N. Lemon, and Vikas Mittal, "Relating Brand and Customer Perspectives on Marketing Management," *Journal of Service Research* 5, no. 1 (2002): 13–25; and Kevin L. Keller and Donald R. Lehmann, "The Brand Value Chain: Optimizing Strategic and Financial Brand Performance" (working paper, 2001); and Interbrand Group, *World's Greatest Brands: An International Review* (New York: John Wiley, 1992).
[5]See Leonard L. Berry, "Cultivating Service Brand Equity," *Journal of the Academy of Marketing Science* 28, no. 1 (2000): 128–37, for a discussion of brand equity in service contexts.

◆ BOX 6-1 ◆

Harrah's Helps Out Gamblers

The casino industry is often portrayed as out to beat the customer; it is often vilified for luring people in and making it nearly impossible to "beat the house." The casino almost always wins, enjoying an odds system stacked against the customer, who will never make up what he has gambled away. Harrah's Entertainment, however, is out to change the odds, and ensure that both company *and* customers win.

Harrah's Entertainment, a $1.6 billion company that grew out of a lone bingo parlor that Bill Harrah opened in Reno in 1937, is linking databases across the United States and using this technology to recognize customers in the form of Total Gold. Total Gold is Harrah's nationwide customer reward program, which transfers customer information from all its 23 properties to Harrah's main database in Memphis, Tennessee.

Wherever the customer goes after entering the casino, be it the Total Gold information kiosk, the slot machines, or the baccarat table, information on that customer is generated within seven seconds after the customer or pit boss swipes the Total Gold membership card. For example, the slot machines are equipped with computer modules that keep track of how long a customer uses the machine, and how much the customer spends there. The database creates a complete profile of the customers—their hotel information, what games they play, what they spend in the retail outlets, and what entertainment they prefer. In turn, these activities generate reward points for customers.

Customer reward points are stored in the database, and when customers have accumulated a certain number of them, they are able to redeem these points for such things as cash, room upgrades, show tickets, or "complimentaries," such as free food or hotel rooms. The Harrah's Web site allows members to log in, and view their accumulated points, as well as learn how to earn more benefits. The patron database also feeds information into the marketing database to more carefully pair special offers to those customers who would use them.

The Total Gold system helps Harrah's by calculating guests' "gaming value" through sophisticated algorithms that factor in demographics, such as age, income, distance between home and casino, and past gambling behavior. Harrah's can then target its most profitable customers and those who have potentially high gaming value. For example, slot players will get better rooms and lower room rates because they are more profitable than are table players.

Recently, Harrah's has added two tiers to the Total Gold program. All Total Gold members who meet certain annual spending levels, among other criteria, will receive either Platinum or Diamond membership cards that entitle them to even more perks at casinos nationwide. These benefits include special status at food service areas, access to special customer service lines, and preferred status when making reservations at restaurants and shows. Diamond members are also entitled access to a VIP lounge.

Harrah's program has been a great success, and the casino chain has seen its market share steadily increase since the program's introduction. One of the key values presented by Total Gold is the tangible affirmation of the cardholder's superior status at the casino chain. In addition, customers are rewarded based on loyalty to Harrah's as a whole, rather than to one particular casino, reducing the pressure on and inconvenience to the customer to consistently attend one particular branch.

Harrah's investment in Total Gold has been in the millions of dollars so far, but the company is confident that the program will help it gain a stronger national presence and increase market share even more in the United States.

SOURCES: "Harrah's Likes the Odds on New Extranet," *Internet Week,* August 31, 1998. "Harrah's Rewards Gamblers," *Internet Week,* October 8, 2001.

be a very important component of customer equity, because customers rely on their subjective evaluations of the product or service when making decisions. For example, if a customer has developed a strong emotional connection to a specific brand of soft drink or pizza, the customer is very likely to rely on that brand connection when making future decisions for these items.[6]

- **When the product or service is highly visible to others.** When customers purchase products or services that will be seen by others, the firm has the opportunity to influence brand equity. Consider Coach Leather Products. Coach has built a strong brand image. Customers like carrying Coach bags, using Coach PDA cases, and even putting Coach collars on their pets, because, in part, of Coach's success in building brand awareness. If other people react positively to the brand of a product or service that has high visibility, they will be more likely to consider the extent to which they believe the brand is a good fit with their own image.

- **When experiences associated with the product or service can be passed from one individual or generation to the next.** For many products and services, there are aspects of the consumption experience that involve the customer directly and others indirectly. Consider Gino's East Pizza, a Chicago-area tradition. Gino's East has built strong brand equity through its positive customer experience. Generations of customers have been going to Gino's East as well as recommending it to friends. To the extent that a firm's products or services lend themselves to such communal or joint experiences, the firm has an opportunity to build brand equity.

- **When it is difficult to evaluate the quality of a product or service prior to consumption.** For some products and services, it is possible to "try before you buy" or to easily evaluate the quality attributes prior to purchase. However, for other products and services, customers must use some type of proxy for quality. Firms that provide these types of goods or services ("credence goods") can build brand equity by creating positive brand associations and brand images for such products. In addition, customer prior experience with a particular brand of product or service (e.g., a previous stay at a Marriott hotel in San Francisco, or owning a Sears Kenmore washer) can impact brand equity (positively or negatively) as customers consider purchases of similar products or services in new contexts (e.g., deciding on a hotel in Boston, or considering the purchase of a refrigerator).[7]

HOW CAN A FIRM GROW BRAND EQUITY?

There are three specific drivers of brand equity. Within each driver there are sub-drivers that link to actionable firm strategies and tactics. These three brand equity drivers are (1) brand awareness, (2) attitude toward the brand, and (3) corporate citizenship and ethics.

---

[6]Susan Fournier and John Deighton, *Consumer Behavior Exercise A-F Teaching Note,* Harvard Business School Publishing, 5-597-041 (1997).
[7]Valarie A. Zeithaml and Mary Jo Bitner, *Services Marketing, 2nd ed.* (New York: McGraw-Hill/Irwin, 2002).

BUILDING BRAND AWARENESS: THE CUSTOMER COMMUNICATIONS STRATEGY

Perhaps the most obvious driver of brand equity is the customer's brand awareness. *Brand awareness* is defined as the extent to which the customer exhibits knowledge and recall of a particular brand. Customers become aware of a brand through the firm's *customer communications strategy*. When considering the communications strategy, firms should consider the traditional building blocks of an integrated marketing communications strategy and should also consider the role of word-of-mouth communications. There are five sub-drivers within the firm's communications strategy that the firm should examine.[8]

1. *Media Advertising.* First, a firm should consider the extent to which its customers pay attention to mass media advertising.[9] (Is the advertising working in any of its many roles?) *Media advertising* includes any communications to customers that are not directed to individual customers, such as television advertising, Web page development, radio advertising, print advertising, or billboards.

2. *Direct to Consumer.* In addition to its media advertising, firms will often communicate to customers directly. *Direct-to-consumer communications* include the following: direct mail, outbound telemarketing, e-mail, Web sites, and any other communications that may be customized for individual customers. It is important to consider whether these communications reach the right customers, are being read or experienced by those customers, and are consistent with the communication preferences of those customers (e.g., avoiding spam [unsolicited e-mail] and unwanted telemarketing calls). Note that the communications from the sales force also need to be considered.[10]

3. *Consumer to Firm.* Third, a firm must consider the efficacy of its consumer-to-firm communications. *Consumer-to-firm communications* consist of the many opportunities a firm creates for its customers to communicate to the firm (incoming direct mail, inbound telemarketing, e-mail, Web sites, customer service, etc.). These communications will be particularly critical as customers become less willing to respond to direct-to-consumer communications, as noted above.

4. *Sales Promotions, Publicity, and Public Relations.* Fourth, the firm may be able to develop brand equity through publicity opportunities and innovative sales promotions. *Sales promotions* include coupons, contests, in-store displays, and feature advertisements. *Publicity and public relations* include any formal communications from the firm or about the firm to the customer that the firm does not directly pay for. It is important to note that these events or communications must convey a message that is consistent with the firm's brand strategy.

---

[8]See Tom Duncan and Sandra Moriarty (1997), *Driving Brand Value: Using Integrated marketing to Manage Profitable Shareholder Relationships* (New York: McGraw-Hill, 1997); and Don E. Schultz, Stanley Tannenbaum, and Robert F. Lauterborn, *The New Marketing Paradigm: Integrated Marketing Communications* (New York: McGraw-Hill, 1996).
[9]See, for example: Gerard J. Tellis, Rajesh K. Chandy, and Pattana Thaivanich, "Which Ad Works, When, Where, and How Often? Modeling the Effects of Direct Television Advertising," *Journal of Marketing Research* 37, no. 1 (2000): 32–46.
[10]Victoria L. Crittenden and William F. Crittenden, "Developing the Sales Force and Growing the Business: The Direct Selling Industry Experience," *Business Horizons* (September–October 2004).

5. *Word-of-Mouth Campaigns.* Fifth, the firm may be able to develop word-of-mouth campaigns. *Word-of-mouth campaigns* encourage current customers to tell others about the brand. These campaigns can be structured to create incentives for customers (e.g., refer-a-friend promotions) or can be based more on the natural spread of communications (e.g., viral marketing campaigns).[11]

Finally, in addition to understanding the extent to which the firm's communications are being attended to by the consumer, the firm should also examine the effectiveness of such communications: What role or roles is the communications playing in building brand equity? Is the firm building brand awareness and attracting new customers? Is the communications strategy effectively reminding existing customers to return or to tell others? Is the communications strategy part of a more long-term strategy to build emotional ties with customers?

Overall, the firm's customer communications strategy can be a critical element in building brand equity. Brand awareness is typically a prerequisite to brand purchase, and is therefore critical to building brand equity. Firms can build brand awareness through each element of the communications mix: media advertising, direct-to-consumer advertising, consumer-to-firm communications opportunities, sales promotions and publicity, and structured or unstructured word-of-mouth campaigns. It is important to recognize that although the strongest opportunity to build brand awareness and brand equity may lie in only one of the above sub-drivers, it is important to build a consistent brand image. Therefore, the firm should ensure that the messages delivered and experiences created through the brand awareness sub-drivers provide a coherent picture of the brand.

ATTITUDE TOWARD THE BRAND: BRAND POSITIONING STRATEGY

From the firm's perspective, achieving the right fit with the firm's current and potential customer base is a critical aspect of brand equity. For a brand to be successful, it needs to capture the mind and heart of the consumer. The second driver of brand equity is brand position. *Brand position* is defined as how a customer defines the strengths and weaknesses of a particular brand, relative to substitutes and competitors.[12] There are five specific sub-drivers of the brand position driver of brand equity.

1. *Media Creative Strategy.* A firm must determine the key message or messages it wants to deliver to its current and potential customers. This is a key element of the brand positioning strategy. This creative strategy may include, for example, the messages the firm wants its salespeople to deliver in communications with customers and prospects.

2. *Media Placement.* The choice of media placement will depend on the firm's choice of target market. Accurate placement and targeting decisions can make or break a firm's brand position.

3. *Brand Name and Brand Partners.* Choice of brand name and brand partners can also have significant positive or negative influences on brand position. For example,

---

[11]See, for example, Eugene W. Anderson. "Customer Satisfaction and Word of Mouth," *Journal of Service Research* 1, no. 1 (1998): 1–14.
[12]For more information on positioning, see Philip Kotler, *Marketing Management,* 11th ed. (Upper Saddle River, NJ: Prentice Hall, 2003); David A. Aaker, *Managing Brand Equity* (New York: The Free Press, 1991); and David A. Aaker, *Building Strong Brands* (New York: The Free Press, 1995).

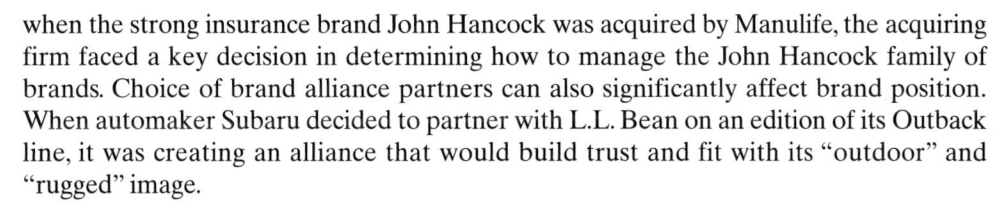

when the strong insurance brand John Hancock was acquired by Manulife, the acquiring firm faced a key decision in determining how to manage the John Hancock family of brands. Choice of brand alliance partners can also significantly affect brand position. When automaker Subaru decided to partner with L.L. Bean on an edition of its Outback line, it was creating an alliance that would build trust and fit with its "outdoor" and "rugged" image.

4. *Packaging and Merchandising.* Of course, packaging and merchandising also affect brand position. Product package design, display of products (in store, on the Web, or in a catalog) can influence customer perceptions of the brand.

5. *Site Location and Distribution Strategy.* Finally, distribution decisions can significantly influence brand position. Choosing an exclusive distribution strategy, for example, can provide a signal to the market of a brand's position. Similarly, site location (for restaurants, for example) can have a significant influence on brand perception.

Overall, customer attitude toward the brand is critical in building brand equity. If attitudes toward a firm's brand are negative, it is virtually impossible to build brand equity. The factors listed above are the drivers that are typically *within* a firm's control in managing customer perceptions and attitudes toward the brand. In today's thoroughly wired world, customers also play a significant role in managing brand perceptions through informal and formal word-of-mouth channels (e.g., *www.PlanetFeedback.com*). Monitoring these customer communications channels is also critical to building brand equity. As noted above, by itself, a positive attitude toward the brand will not necessarily build brand equity. That attitude must work together with strong brand awareness and a strong perception of brand ethics and corporate citizenship.

CORPORATE CITIZENSHIP AND ETHICS: DOING THE RIGHT THINGS AND DOING THINGS RIGHT

Believe it or not, in addition to getting the communications right and the position right, the firm must also get the "brand values" right. The third driver of brand equity is corporate citizenship and ethics. In considering whether to do business with a firm on a long-term basis, customers will consider the citizenship and ethics of the firm. *Corporate citizenship and ethics*, in the context of brand equity, consider the extent to which the values of the brand or of the firm are consistent with the customer's values. For example, customers may ask these questions:

- Is the firm that provides this brand a good corporate citizen?
- Does this firm sponsor community events?
- Overall, is this firm ethical in its practices?
- Is this firm kind to the environment?

The strength of the citizenship and ethics driver of brand equity will depend (as will all drivers and sub-drivers) on the firm's customer base. It is important for a firm to understand the values of its customers, as those values relate to its brand when determining how best to grow brand equity. The citizenship and ethics driver of brand equity provides a good example of how firms can benefit if the driver is strengthened, but can also suffer if the key driver of brand equity is viewed negatively by customers. For example, following the 1989 Exxon *Valdez* oil spill in Alaska, U.S. customers fled to other oil providers, to voice their opinion of Exxon's handling of the disaster.

Alternatively, the Tylenol brand was strengthened by Johnson and Johnson's strong stand to recall Tylenol after a package-tampering scare in 1982 and to take preventative action to prevent further tampering with over-the-counter medications. In simpler examples, providing strong community support for causes and events that are important to a firm's customers can be an effective (and also inexpensive) means of driving brand equity.[13]

The link between a company's brand and the overall organization is often overlooked, and may play a strong role in a firm's development of brand equity, especially when considering the notion of global brand equity. For example, the organizational strength of Procter and Gamble is much more evident in the Japanese consumer products market (in which products are branded with an obvious link to P&G) than it is in the United States, where the corporate link of a consumer product to Procter and Gamble is often quite understated. In the Japanese market, it is the strength and trust of the firm that are of utmost importance, and the specific brand name is of secondary importance; in essence, the company *is* the brand.

Specific actionable sub-drivers of the ethics driver of brand equity include the following:

- *Community Event Sponsorship and Strong Record of Giving to the Community.* For example, Home Depot is known throughout the United States for its strong record in helping to build homes and playgrounds in depressed areas.

- *Development and Maintenance of a Privacy Policy for Use of Customer Information.* Most firms who collect information about customers (e.g., through Internet purchases, credit card histories) develop and disseminate a privacy policy. A strong privacy policy can build trust and a positive perception of the firm as a good corporate citizen.

- *Clean Environmental Record.* Although a firm's impact on its environment will be more important for some consumers than others, recognizing the influence of this factor on brand equity is critical. A firm engaged in strong "green" practices can positively influence its brand equity.[14]

- *Ethical Hiring and Work Practices.* As the focus on globalization of the workforce continues, there will be increased pressure on all firms to engage in ethical hiring and work practices in every market in which they operate.[15]

---

[13]See Sandra A. Waddock, *Leading Corporate Citizens* (New York: McGraw-Hill/Irwin, 2001); Steve Hoeffler and Kevin Lane Keller, "Building Brand Equity Through Corporate Societal Marketing," *Journal of Public Policy and Marketing* 21 (Spring 2002): 78–89; Charles A. Garfield, "Do Profits and Social Responsibility Mix?" *Executive Excellence* (March 1992): 5; and Deborah Gunthorpe, "Business Ethics: A Quantitative Analysis of the Impact of Unethical Behavior by Publicly Traded Companies," *Journal of Business Ethics* (April 1997): 537–43.
[14]Daniel Ackerstein and Katherine N. Lemon, "The Greening of the Brand: Environmental Marketing Strategies and the American Consumer," in *Greener Marketing: A Global Perspective on Greening Marketing Practice,* 2nd ed., M. Charter and M. J. Polansky, (UK: Greenleaf Publishing, 1999).
[15]Sandra A. Waddock, *Leading Corporate Citizens* (New York: McGraw-Hill/Irwin, 2001).

◆ BOX 6-2 ◆

Tiffany & Co.'s Dazzling History

Simplicity. Elegance. Gold. Diamonds. These are all images that come to mind with the word "Tiffany." However, these images pale next to the famous trademark blue box or bag, with its black lettering evoking money and class.

Implemented early in the retailer's history, the distinctive shade of blue, the trademark Tiffany Blue®, has been chosen to symbolize the company's renowned reputation for quality and craftsmanship. The color was adapted for use on boxes, catalogues, shopping bags, and brochures as well as advertising and other promotional materials. The boxes and bags evoke images of elegance and exclusivity, emphasized with the knowledge that Tiffany boxes and bags are not allowed to leave the retailers building unless they contain Tiffany's articles.

Besides its blue boxes and bags, the notion of Tiffany always evoked a sense of style and exclusivity, impressing Tiffany as one of the most successful examples of branding in retail. Purchasing an item at Tiffany means not only fine jewelry and excellent customer service, but also the feeling of luxury and importance, which is just as much an offering of the Tiffany's brand as the jewelry itself.

Tiffany was founded in September 1837, establishing itself as a stationery and fancy goods emporium at 259 Broadway in New York City. Every article was marked with a nonnegotiable selling price, a revolutionary policy that made headlines in a time when haggling was still common practice. This move itself served to reinforce the brand; yes, the price was steep, but the fact that it was nonnegotiable reinforced the notion that the product was the highest quality and worth every cent.

Today, the retailer is known less for its stationery and fancy goods than for its diamonds and designer settings. One flash of the small blue Tiffany's shopping bag and images of glittering gems are conjured, as well as the sense of authority. After all, the Tiffany standard of purity has become the official standard for platinum in the United States, emphasizing not only the store's quality but also the sense of authority.

Catering to an upperclass set, Tiffany has begun to expand its product offerings, hoping to capitalize on its brand and the assurance of quality the brand provides. An entire catalog devoted to a corporate line has been developed that focuses on gifts suitable for clients and other business relations.

Knowing that its primary asset is its brand, Tiffany has embarked on a move to maximize control of its product and brand name by discontinuing sales to department stores and independent domestic jewelers. As sales continue to increase and Tiffany remains a staple favorite of the rich and famous, the brand only becomes stronger, giving Tiffany a distinct competitive advantage and recognition in its industry.

- *Strong Product or Service Guarantees.* Firms such as FedEx and L.L. Bean have developed strong brand equity through strong product and service guarantees. Such guarantees serve to build customer confidence and also improve a customer's perceptions of the firm's ethical practices.

By itself, solid corporate citizenship may not build a firm's brand equity. But take heed; poor corporate citizenship or shady ethics can certainly damage a firm's brand equity. By focusing on the building blocks of solid corporate citizenship, and by combining this with strong brand awareness and positive attitudes toward the brand, a firm can craft solid strategies to build brand equity.

Summary

Overall, firms can build brand equity by developing and implementing strategies that will improve customer perceptions of the drivers and sub-drivers of brand equity. The first driver of brand equity is brand awareness. The key sub-drivers of brand awareness are each of the elements of an integrated marketing communications strategy, and word-of-mouth communications. The second driver of brand equity is brand position. The key sub-drivers of brand position are media creative strategy, media placement, brand name, packaging/merchandising, and site location. The third driver of brand equity is corporate citizenship and ethics. The key sub-drivers of citizenship and ethics are community event sponsorship, privacy policies, environmental policy, hiring and work practices, and product and service guarantees.

Figure 6-1 shows the process of building brand equity.[16] Suppose that the firm implements an action to develop a sub-driver of brand equity (e.g., a community service event). If the event goes well (and corporate citizenship and ethics are important drivers of brand equity), this will improve customer perceptions of the brand on this sub-driver. These perceptions drive brand equity, which in turn influences choice, customer lifetime value, and, therefore, customer equity. It is important to remember that each of these steps happens at the individual customer level. For example, while some customers may be influenced by a community service event, others may not be influenced by it or may not even be aware of the event. However, by developing brand equity campaigns that are solidly based on an analysis of what is important to customers in terms of building customer equity, these strategies should be very successful in building a brand.

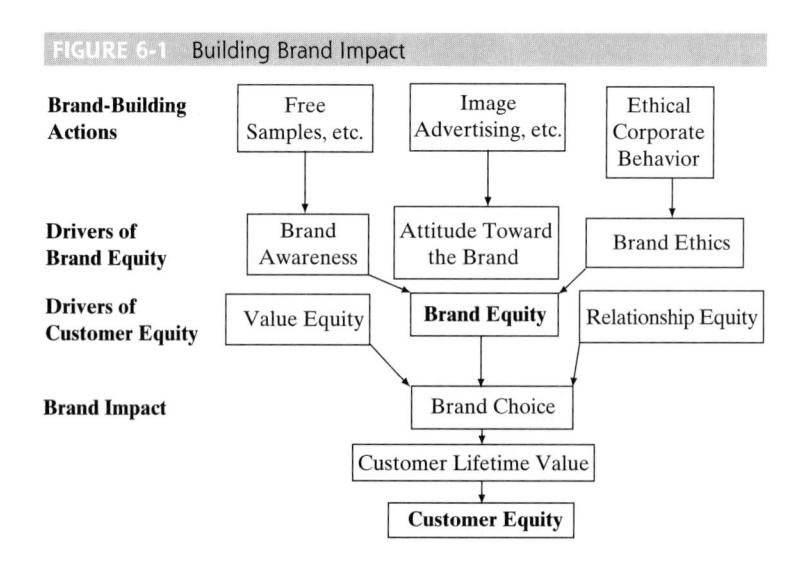

FIGURE 6-1 Building Brand Impact

Brand-Building Actions	Free Samples, etc.	Image Advertising, etc.	Ethical Corporate Behavior
Drivers of Brand Equity	Brand Awareness	Attitude Toward the Brand	Brand Ethics
Drivers of Customer Equity	Value Equity	Brand Equity	Relationship Equity
Brand Impact		Brand Choice	
		Customer Lifetime Value	
		Customer Equity	

---

[16]Roland T. Rust, Valarie A. Zeithaml, and Katherine N. Lemon, "Customer-Centered Brand Management" Harvard Business Review, September (2004), 110–118.

In sum, to drive brand equity—through communication, positioning, and ethics—firms should focus on:

- Finding the right mix of communications strategies to the firm's customers.
- Finding the right mix of communications opportunities from the customers to the firm.
- Finding the right creative approach (the right message).
- Making sure that the communications are watched, read, listened to, experienced, and acted on by the customer and by the firm.
- Ensuring that the firm's ethical approach is consistent with the interests of its customers.
- Ensuring that the specific strategies and tactics work in concert to form a strong, consistent position for the brand.

Review Questions and Exercises

1. Explain how increasing community citizenship and brand ethics can increase brand equity. Give an example of a company that has built its brand equity through superior brand ethics.
2. Describe a product/service class in which brand equity is not a key driver and compare it to a product/service class in which brand equity is the key driver. What are the differences between these product classes that account for this?
3. Go to the website: *www.playstation.com*. To what segments does Sony position its playstation products and how does it do this?

Case 6-1   Eastman Kodak Company: Funtime Film

Robert J. Dolan

On January 25, 1994, George Fisher, Kodak's recently appointed Chief Executive Officer, met with analysts and investors to set out Kodak's new strategy for film products. During the past week (between January 17 and January 24), Kodak stock had lost 8% in value on rumors of a price cut on film.

While Kodak continued its overwhelming domination of the photo film market, its market share in the United States had eased from about 76% to 70% over the past five years "as competitors like Fuji Photo Film Co. and Konica Corp. wooed consumers with lower-priced versions."[1] Previously, Kodak had attempted to blunt share-gaining attempts by such rivals and private label products by introducing a superpremium brand, Ektar. Now Kodak proposed to introduce a brand at Fuji and Konica's price level, 20% below the price of Kodak's flagship Gold Plus brand. The new brand, Funtime, was to be available only in limited quantities during two off-peak selling seasons. While some viewed the move favorably, others were more skeptical. One analyst termed the strategy "seemingly a long step down the slippery slope that ends in private label trial."

THE U.S. PHOTO FILM MARKET

In 1993, approximately 16 billion color exposures were made—the equivalent of 670 million 24-exposure rolls. Typically, a consumer paid between $2.50 and $3.50 for a 24 exposure roll. Over the past five years, the market's annual unit growth rate averaged only 2%. Major suppliers were Kodak, Fuji of Japan, Agfa of Germany, and 3M. Kodak and Fuji sold only branded products. Because of a 1921 consent decree still in force, Kodak could not sell film on a private label basis. Both Agfa and 3M sold their film to consumers as branded product and to other firms for sale under a private label. Polaroid entered the market in 1989 with its branded product, which it sourced from 3M. Film was intensively distributed through discount and department stores (32% of sales), drug stores (24%), camera shops (14%), supermarkets and convenience stores (13%), wholesale clubs (9%) and mail order (2%).

Analysts' estimates of unit market shares by manufacturer are shown in Table A.

The case was prepared by Professor Robert J. Dolan. Copyright © 1994 by the President and Fellows of Harvard College. Harvard Business School Case 594-111.

[1] Wendy Bounds, "Kodak Develops Economy-Brand Film That Is Focused on Low-Priced Rivals," *Wall Street Journal*, January 26, 1994, p. A3.

TABLE A	Approximate Unit Market Shares in 1993 (U.S. market)
Kodak	70%
Fuji	11%
Polaroid	4%
Private label	10%
Other	5%

EXHIBIT 1 Price Tiers in Film Market Defined by Average Retail Price Paid

Superpremium Brands			
Fujicolor Reala	—	$4.69	(134)
Kodak Ektar	—	$4.27	(122)
Premium Brands			
Kodak Gold Plus	—	$3.49	(100)
Agfacolor XRG	—	$3.49	(100)
Economy Brands			
Fujicolor Super G	—	$2.91	(83)
Konica Super SR	—	$2.91	(83)
ScotchColor	—	$2.69	(77)
Price Brands[a]			
(S) Polaroid High Definition	—	$2.49	(71)
(S) Kroeger	—	$2.49	(71)
(A) Walgreen's	—	$2.49	(71)
(S) York	—	$2.40	(69)
(A) Clark Color	—	$2.35	(67)
(S) Kmart Focal	—	$2.29	(66)
(S) Target	—	$2.19	(63)

Source: National Survey reported in *Consumer Reports*, November 1993, pp. 711–715.

Note: Numbers in ( ) are indices indicating price relative to Kodak Gold Plus.
[a](S) designates the film was procured from 3M and was equivalent to ScotchColor.
(A) designates the film was procured from Bayer's Agfa and was equivalent to AgfaColor XRG.

Fuji and Kodak were locked in a global battle for dominance of the worldwide photographic market. Both sold cameras and other imaging products as well as film. Fuji's worldwide sales of $10 billion made it half Kodak's size. Fuji started its serious incursion into Kodak territory in 1984, when it captured consumers' attention, particularly in the United States, by becoming the official film of the 1984 Summer Olympics in Los Angeles.

Both Fuji's and Polaroid's U.S. dollar sales grew at over 15% in the past year, compared with Kodak's 3% growth rate. An industry expert opined, "Fuji's gains can be largely attributed to the marketer's ability to keep the line on price, an area where Kodak has suffered."[2] Private labels as a group grew about 10%.

---

[2]Ricardo Davis, "Fuji Makes Gains in 35MM Film Sales Using Price Strategy," *Advertising Age*, October 18, 1993, p. 48.

CATEGORY PRICING

Kodak's Gold Plus brand was the standard of the industry. Exhibit 1 shows the average retail prices for a single 24-exposure roll of ISO 100 film. (ISO refers to the "speed" or light sensitivity of the film. Amateurs typically use 100, 200, or 400, with 100 being the most popular. Higher ISO films performed in lower light conditions, but were more expensive.)

As shown in Exhibit 1, there were four price tiers in the market. Kodak Gold Plus, the largest-selling brand by far, set the Premium Brand price at $3.49. Kodak's gross margins were believed to be about 70%. Both Kodak and Fuji offered superpremium brands targeted very narrowly at advanced amateurs and professionals. These products were distributed mainly through camera shops and were not major sellers.

Fuji's key brand, Fujicolor Super G, anchored the Economy Brand tier at 17% below the Premium tier. Fuji's gross margin was believed to be about 55%. Konica and 3M's ScotchColor brand were other competitors in this tier. Finally, film procured from either Agfa or 3M and sold under another name made up the Price Brand tier. Representative products are shown in Exhibit 1. While most of the film in this group was "branded" with the name of the retail outlet selling it (e.g., Kmart, a major mass merchant, and Walgreen's, a major drug chain), Polaroid, the dominant firm in instant cameras and film, marketed conventional film it sourced from 3M in this tier. On average, these "Price Brands" were priced about 30% less than Kodak Gold Plus. Dealer percentage margins were typically higher for private label products.[3]

CONSUMER BEHAVIOR

Film usage rates varied widely across households with a mean of 15 rolls per year. The *Wolfman Report*[4] estimated that 20% of households bought less than 5 rolls per year, 22% bought between 5 and 9 rolls, 28% bought 10 to 15 rolls, 16% bought 16 to 25 rolls, and 13% bought more than 25 rolls. Often, these rolls were purchased in "multipacs" containing 2–3 rolls of film. Kodak advertised heavily, e.g., spending approximately $50 million on camera and film supply advertising in the United States in 1993. (This was about 4 times Fuji's U.S. advertising spending.) Kodak advertising was typified by a presentation developed for use on the 1994 Olympic Winter Games television broadcast. Contrasting against the Olympic competition from Norway broadcast around the world, the ad portrayed a young boy in his own competition in his backyard falling into a snowbank to make a "snow angel." The voice-over noted, "Some of the best events happen in your own backyard ... why trust them to less than Kodak film."

Actual quality differences among films were unclear. Both Kodak and Fuji tried to position themselves as providing superior quality film through their advanced technology. However, *Consumer Reports*[5] conducted a test of films and reported, "We found most films to be no better or worse than their competitors of the same speed. The top six ISO 100 films scored so similarly that we think all will yield prints of comparable quality." In order of overall quality score (score out of 100 in parenthesis), these top six films were:

1. Polaroid High Definition (95)
2. Fujicolor Super G (94)
3. Kodak Gold Plus (93)
4. Konica Super SR (93)
5. Kodak Ektar (92)
6. ScotchColor (92)

ScotchColor was also sold as private label from Kmart, Kroeger, Target, and York, among others as shown in Exhibit 1. Fuji Superpremium brand Reala had a score of 90, and Agfacolor XRG scored 88. *Consumer Reports* regarded score differences of less than 5 points as "not significant."

According to a 1991 survey cited in *Discount Merchandiser*, more than half of the picture takers in the United States claim to know "little or nothing about photography."[6] As a result the article claimed, "Consumers tend to view film as a commodity, often buying on price alone." The article also quoted Jim Van Senus, Kodak's manager of general merchandise marketing: "The importance of brand name in consumer decision making is still strong. On the other hand, there is a growing

---

[3]Casewriter Note: For purposes of calculations in the case analysis, a good approximation is that dealer margins on Kodak film averaged 20%; other suppliers' film yielded a 25% dealer margin.
[4]*1992–93 Wolfman Report on the Photographic and Imaging Industry in the United States*, p. 31.

[5]*Consumer Reports,* November 1993, p. 712.
[6]R. Lee Sullivan, "Photogoods on the Upgrade," *Discount Merchandiser,* September 1991, p. 64 ff.

body of price-sensitive consumers there. We are seeing growth in private label film activity." Kodak research had shown that 50% of buyers were "Kodak-loyal," 40% were "samplers" relying heavily on Kodak, and 10% shopped on price.[7]

THE FUNTIME STRATEGY

For 1994, Kodak planned a major repositioning of its film product line. A new emulsion technology would increase exposure latitude. Three films would be offered:

1. Gold Plus—to remain the flagship brand at a price unchanged from 1993 levels. Gold Plus would receive 60% of the dollar advertising support.
2. Royal Gold—to replace Ektar in the Superpremium segment. Whereas Ektar had been targeted to professionals and serious amateurs, Royal Gold would be targeted to a broader audience for "very special" occasions. Offering richer color saturation and sharper pictures, it would be positioned as especially appropriate for those occasions when the consumer may wish to make enlargements. Royal Gold would be heavily supported by advertising (40% of the total film budget) and by promotion and would be priced lower than Ektar was selling to the trade at a 9% premium over Gold Plus. Cooperative advertising allowances were to be offered to the trade to provide the incentive to maintain Royal Gold *retail* prices at 20% above Gold Plus, thereby offering superior trade margins.
3. Funtime—to give Kodak a presence in the Economy Brand Tier at a price 20% below Gold Plus on a per roll basis.

Key aspects of the Funtime marketing plan:

- No advertising support.
- Offer only twice a year at off-peak film use times, viz. for 2–3 months beginning in April, and again for 2–3 months beginning in September.
- Available in limited quantities.
- Offer in only the two most popular speeds, ISO 100 and 200. (In contrast, Royal Gold would be eventually offered in five speeds.)
- Available to all classes of trade.
- Packaged only in "value packs," specifically in two forms:

  1. 2 rolls of 24 exposures
  2. 4-roll package
      (3 rolls of 24 exposures,
      1 roll of 36 exposures)

Alexander Wasilov, Vice President and General Manager of Kodak Consumer Imaging in the United States and Canada, explained the strategy:

> This repositioning is intelligent risk taking that will drive both our market share and earnings . . . [it] will allow us to be more selective in targeting certain customer segments. We now have Royal Gold film for those very special memories—the birth of a baby, the graduation. We continue to offer Gold film, for capturing those unexpected moments—the baby smiling, the father and son playing catch in the backyard. And now we will offer a special promotion twice a year, featuring a modified version of Gold film at a slightly lower price than our other films.[8]

Commenting on the strategy, Konica's Director of Marketing said, "There will be an opportunity for us at Konica. It seems like a desperate move to regain market share. Not a way to make the industry more profitable."[9] ■

---

[7]G. Khermouch, "Kodak Reorganizes Its Film Line," *Adweek,* January 31, 1994, p. 14.

[8]Wendy Bounds, "Kodak Develops Economy-Brand Film That Is Focused on Low-Priced Rivals," *Wall Street Journal,* January 26, 1994, p. A3.
[9]Ibid.

Alloy.com

Case 6-2

John Deighton and Gil McWilliams

On May 12, 1999, Matt Diamond, James Johnson, and Sam Gradess were visiting San Francisco for a last round of meetings with West Coast investment analysts. They were just days from the initial public offering (IPO) of shares in Alloy.com, the catalog and Internet merchant of teen-oriented clothing that they had founded on Diamond's graduation from Harvard Business School in 1996. Snarled in freeway gridlock, Diamond was on his cellphone discussing the IPO's pricing with analysts back in New York City.

An analyst urged Diamond to respond to an invitation by the world's largest Web site and portal, America Online (AOL), to make Alloy an anchor tenant on its teen shopping site. AOL wanted $2 million per year for the rights. "Matt, if you say yes, that will be big. If you announce tomorrow that AOL's partner in the Generation Y market is Alloy, it will put Alloy on the map. It will definitely affect the IPO price."

Diamond sighed. A headline deal with AOL today could be worth perhaps 10% on the stock price. But AOL was asking rich terms. It was widely rumored that AOL preyed on startup companies in the weeks before they went public, tempting them with star billing on its portal at the very moment when the publicity was most valuable. He estimated that he'd be paying a $45 cpm (cost per thousand exposures) to anchor the AOL teen shopping site. Nobody paid more than $30 for Web eyeballs. In the three years that he had been running Alloy, Diamond had prided himself on doing deals that made sense. If he could not anticipate a profit to Alloy from a promotional deal, he reasoned that Wall Street would not anticipate a profit either.

"It won't pay out," he told the analyst firmly. "We only do deals that produce value." To his colleagues in the limousine, he wondered out loud, "Am I right?"

THE GENERATION Y MARKET

Termed the "hottest demographic of the moment," Generation Y came to the attention of marketers in the late 1990s. This "echo of the baby boom" was made up of children and teenagers born in the United States between 1975 and 1989 and therefore aged between 10 and 24. They were estimated to be a 56 million–strong group of actual and potential consumers, some three times the size of their immediate predecessor, Generation X.[1] The U.S. Census Bureau projected that the 10 to 24 age group would grow from 56.3 million to 63.1 million by 2010, growing faster than the general population.

Although Generation Y matched its parent's generation in size, in almost every other way it was very different. One in three was not Caucasian. One in four lived in a single-parent household. Three in four had working mothers.[2] "Body glittered, tattooed, pierced, they're a highly fragmented, unpredictable group of teenagers who, while tottering around on five-inch soles, voice conservative opinions about sexuality, government, the American dream, and an end-of-century commitment to spirituality."[3] They were computer literate: 81% of teens used the Internet, according to Chicago-based Teenage

---

The case was prepared by Professor John Deighton and Visiting Scholar Gil McWilliams. Copyright © 2000 by the President and Fellows of Harvard College. Harvard Business School Case 500-048.

---

[1]Neuborne, Ellen and Kathleen Kerwin. "Generation Y," *Business Week,* February 15, 1999, Cover story.
[2]Neuborne, Ellen and Kathleen Kerwin. "Generation Y," *Business Week,* February 15, 1999, Cover story.
[3]O'Leary, Noreen. "Marketing: The Boom Tube," *Adweek,* Vol. 39, No. 20, May 18, 1999, pp. S44–S52.

| EXHIBIT 1 | Total Teen Spending in 1996 |

	Dollars (billions)	*percent*
Apparel	$36.7	34%
Entertainment	23.4	22
Food	16.7	15
Personal care	9.2	9
Sporting goods	6.7	6
Other	15.3	14
Total	108.0	100

Source: Packaged Facts via InterRep Research, in MSDW Equity Research: "Fashions of the Third Millennium," June 1999.

Research International (TRI), which also noted that over a 3 month period on AOL, they posted more than 2 million Leonardo Di Caprio–related messages.[4]

According to Lester Rand, Director of the Rand Youth Poll, they had money to spend and an appetite for spending it.

They have a higher incremental allowance from their parents, and with the growth in our service economy, they are able to secure jobs easily and at rising minimum wages. They're exposed to so many different products on TV, in the mall and through their friends. It's a generation who grew up with excess as a norm.[5]

In 1999 Jupiter reported that 67% of online teens and 37% of online kids said they made use of online shopping sites, either buying or gathering information about products.[6] Generation Y was expected to spend approximately $136 billion in 1999, before accounting for the group's influence on purchases made by parents and other adults. (See Exhibits 1 and 2 for this and other estimates.)

---

[4]Brown, Eryn. "Loving Leo Online," *Fortune*, April 12, 1999, p. 152.

[5]BAXExpress, July/August 1999, http:baxworld.com/baxexpress/0799/consumers.html.
[6]Sacharow, Anya. "Shadow of On-line Commerce Falls on Postmodern Kids," Jupiter Communications report, June 7, 1999.

| EXHIBIT 2 | Estimates of Teen Spending |

	Rand Youth (*Adweek May 18, 1998*)	*Morgan Stanley Dean Witter's report "Fashions of the Third Millennium," June 1999*	*Teen Research Unlimited (quoted in Alloy press handout)*
1996		$108 billion	
1997	$91.5 billion		
1998			$141 billion
1999		$136 billion	

ONLINE COMPETITION FOR GENERATION Y SPENDING

Generation Y's size and spending power had not gone unnoticed. Many conventional and online retailers courted them. Alloy viewed its most significant competitors as dELiAs and the online magalog mXg. The neighborhood mall was also a threat.

dELiAs Inc.[7]

The largest online and catalog merchant serving Generation Y was New York–based dELiAs, with 1998 sales of $158 million. Founded in 1995 by two 33-year-old former Yale roommates, Stephen Kahn and Christopher Edgar, dELiAs sold through print catalogs mailed to more than 10 million recipients, of whom 6 million had bought within the past year. It managed its own order fulfillment from a warehouse complex, and operated 20 conventional retail stores. Most of dELiAs' 1,500 employees were under 30. Its phone representatives were often high school and college students, and they frequently offered fashion advice as well as taking orders. In November 1998 dELiAs Inc. paid $4.75 million for the trademarks and mailing lists of bankrupt Fulcrum's five catalogs (Zoe for teenage girls, Storybook Heirlooms, Playclothes, After the Stork, and Just for Kids), giving them 5 million names which nearly doubled their database. It also paid $2.4 million for merchandise from Zoe and Storybook.

By 1999, dELiAs went to market with a complex set of brands and marketing methods:

- The dELiAs brand marketed to teenage girls as a catalog through the mail and as dELiAs*cOm on the Web.
- The gURL.com Web site was an online magazine for girls and young women, carrying articles as well as free e-mail, free homepage hosting and publishing tools, and links to a network of third-party sites for girls and women. gURL was the only property that was not engaged in commerce.
- The droog brand marketed apparel to 12-to-20-year-old males through the mail and online.
- The TSI Soccer catalog sold soccer gear by mail and online.
- Storybook Heirlooms retailed apparel and accessories for girls under 13 by mail and Web catalog.
- Dotdotdash sold apparel, footwear, and accessories for girls aged 7 to 12 by mail and Web catalog.
- Discountdomain.com was a subscription Web site selling discounted close-out merchandise.
- Contentsonline.com offered unusual home furnishings, light furniture, and household articles to females aged 13–24. While predominantly a Web catalog, the property appeared intermittently as a print insert in dELiAs' print catalog.

In April 1999, dELiAs Inc. spun off its Internet properties in an IPO, selling shares in a company called iTurF, which earned revenues from all of the above online elements. In terms of the deal, these online businesses could advertise in dELiAs' print catalogs at a rate of $40 per 1,000 catalogs. The dELiAs catalog, 60 million of which were printed in 1998, had the largest domestic circulation of any publication directed at Generation Y. The online magazines also shared the parent company's 354,000-square-foot distribution center in Hanover, PA. Because iTurF did not take ownership of inventory until a customer's order was placed, the risk of obsolescence and markdowns remained with the parent company. iTurF shared offices with the parent company, enjoying a submarket rent for New York metropolitan space.

In May 1999, iTurF announced record quarterly sales of $2.6 million (up from $0.69 million in the first quarter of 1998). Gross profit was $1.3 million, or 49.1% of revenues, up from $0.34 million or 49.3% of revenues 1998 (see Exhibit 3). However, dELiAs reported that it expected its iTurF unit to report a loss for the fiscal year. By April 1999, the number of people who had ever bought at the iTurF Web sites was 66,000 (up from 35,000 at the end of December 1998), and the number of unique visitors was 731,000 in April 1999 alone. Analysts estimated that each customer

---

[7]Information drawn from company Web site: *www.dELiAs.com*.

EXHIBIT 3 Consolidated iTurf Income (in $ thousands)

	1st Quarter Ending 1 May 1999	1st Quarter Ending 30 April 1998
Net revenues	2615	69
Cost of goods	1332	35
Gross profit	1283	34
Selling, general and admin.	1753	109
Interest income (expense)	(112)	11
Loss before tax	(358)	(86)
Income tax (benefit)	(161)	(33)
Net loss	(197)	(53)
No. of unique visitors	Apr 99 = 731,000	Feb 99 = 635,000
No. of page views in April	50 million	4 million
Size of mailing database	11 million names	

Source: IPO filing.

cost $26 to acquire.[8] Private label merchandise accounted for 40% of iTurF's sales, in line with dELiA's ratio.

iTurf entered into agreements with RocketCash Corp and DoughNET, companies that had been established to let parents control the online spending of their children. For example, RocketCash let parents establish a credit card account and set each child's access to specific merchant sites, times of operation, and the option to set up an auto-allowance to periodically replenish the account. DoughNet was a virtual debit card that parents could set up for their children. Parents could customize DoughNET's site to guide teens through all aspects of managing their money.

In April 1999, dELiAs' decision to spin off iTurF seemed shrewd. The market capitalization of dELiAs Inc. was $90 million, on sales of $200 million annually. ITurF was capitalized at $200 million on a sales run rate of $12 million annually.

mXg Media Inc.[9]

Hunter Heaney and Stuart MacFarlane graduated from the Harvard Business School in 1996. MacFarlane joined Bain & Co. and Heaney joined BancBoston Robertson Stephens. Heaney told how he got the idea for mXg while Christmas shopping at Nordstrom's for his then girlfriend. A saleswoman had told him that the "Y" necklace featured on the "Friends" sitcom was in style. "I knew there had to be a more direct way to find out about fashion trends influenced by entertainment," Heaney said.[10]

In 1997, Heaney and MacFarlane quit their jobs and moved to Manhattan Beach, CA, to be close to Hollywood and surfers and skaters. Using the pay phone while staying at a local motel they raised $250,000 in increments of $5,000, and launched mXg, styling it a "magalog," a hybrid of catalog and magazine, aimed at teenage girls. Unlike a conventional magazine, mXg reported exactly where to go to buy the fashion items that it featured on its pages. MacFarlane recalled their early lean times: "Typically, retailers order inventory in sixes (one small, two medium, two large, one extra large). But instead of saying 'We'll take 2,000 sixes' we said 'We'll take six' — literally one of each." They

---

[8]CIBC World Markets, Equity Research, June 2, 1999.
[9]Information drawn from company Web site: www.mXgonline.com.

[10]Waxler, Caroline. "Guys with Moxie," *Forbes,* May 31, 1999, pp. 130–131.

could fund a circulation of only 20,000 for the magazine's launch in the fall of 1997, but it did well. Some 5% of the recipients bought from it. The numbers were good enough to induce Urban Outfitters, a retail fashion chain, to invest $5 million for 40% of the company, incorporated as mXg Media, Inc.

Merchandise accounted for most of mXg Media's revenues, but advertising revenue was doubling each issue. The company used newsstand distribution (150,000 issues per quarter at $2.95 each, refunded with a purchase), as well as distribution in bookstores like Barnes & Noble, and B Dalton Booksellers. The magazine had a pass-along rate of almost six readers per copy.

Sensitive to the tastes of their target audience of female teenagers, they hired teens, paying them $7 per hour to work after school answering letters, doing interviews, and writing copy to make it sound authentic. "No printed word goes out without a teen girl checking it . . . being uncool is the kiss of death in this business."[11] At the start of each fashion season mXg recruited 30 "Moxie girls" to spend a hypothetical $150 each. Their virtual purchases determined which items appeared in the next issue. The magazine paid staffers to model clothes and invited would-be teen celebrities to pose free to gain recognition.

A Web site, mXgonline.com, was established in the summer of 1997. It comprised a magazine, chat rooms, and community sites, and sold clothes and accessories. mXg Media pursued other access points for their online magalog, featuring it in online fashion malls such as fashionwindow.com. In 1999, mXg sponsored concerts featuring acts like Gus Gus, which were favored by Generation Y. Yahoo produced a series of Webcasts of the concerts for teens. The company described its mission as cross-media publishing, targeted exclusively at teen girls. It planned to add mXgtv, an Internet video site, to its media portfolio later in the year.

A Crowded Marketplace?

Other companies vied for the attention of Generation Y. Bolt.com was a content-based magazine-type site skewed toward a market slightly older than that of the Generation Y market, but into which the older end of the Y market might eventually fall. Bolt.com included sections titled jobs, money, movie reviews, music, news and issues, sex and dating, and sports. It had a chat room and free e-mail, and sold branded merchandise. It boasted that 5,000 people joined it every day.

The magazine *Seventeen* had an online version, offering chat rooms and message boards, as well as its regular articles, quizzes, and features. Indeed, many magazines were now launching online versions of their magazines, and new print publications like *Twist* and *Jump* had appeared to compete for Generation Y advertising revenues.

Broader online retailers served this market, such as bluefly.com, selling discounted brands online. Strong competition came from mall-based stores such as The Buckle, Gadzooks, Abercrombie & Fitch, The Gap, American Eagle Outfitters, and Guess, all of whom sold merchandise on- and off-line. Apparel and sportswear manufacturers were developing online sales sites. Nike and Tommy Hilfiger planned to launch e-commerce sites with broad product offerings.

ALLOY.COM

As a Harvard MBA student in 1996, Matt Diamond wrote a business plan proposing the idea of marketing "extreme sports" clothing by catalog to young people in Japan. The premise was that the popularity of this style of clothing among American youth might generate demand abroad, and that catalogs would be able to tap that demand faster than would store distribution. On graduation, Diamond implemented the plan. He and a friend, Jim Johnson, used seed money from friends and family to design and print a Japanese-language catalog, which they branded Durango Expedition. They mailed it in January 1997, and at the same time they went live with Japanese and English Web sites, as alternative channels.

The venture flopped. The mailing generated no significant sales. However, they discovered to their surprise that they were receiving hits on the English Web site from American youths. Within a month they had reconceptualized the business to serve American teen girls through catalog and online channels, under the name Alloy. Diamond and Johnson each contributed $60,000 in cash and another

---

[11]Waxler, Caroline. "Guys with Moxie," Forbes, May 31, 1999, pp. 130–131.

friend, Sam Gradess added $150,000 in cash when he joined six months later from Goldman Sachs. In November 1997, the first issue of the Alloy catalog, 48 pages in length, was mailed to a purchased mailing list of 150,000 teen names. At the same time Alloy's Web site became active. The intention at that time was to reduce the number of catalogs mailed as online sales grew.

Organization

Diamond became President and CEO of the fledgling company. Johnson took the title of Chief Operating Officer. Gradess was Chief Financial Officer. Neil Vogel joined from Ladenburg Thalman & Co., a consumer and Internet investment banking group to be the Chief Corporate Development Officer. Fellow Harvard sectionmate Andrew Roberts left PricewaterhouseCoopers to join Alloy in January 1999 as VP of Business Development. Another Harvard MBA, Joan Rosenstock was hired as marketing director, having held positions in marketing at the National Basketball Association as well as in advertising account management. Erstwhile music editor of teenage magazine *Seventeen*, Susan Kaplow, became executive editor and Karen Ngo, who had been a feature editor and fashion stylist at *Seventeen*, was hired as creative director.

Alloy outsourced as many of its operations as it could. Working with mostly domestic vendors who could produce and ship within a 2–8 week time frame, Alloy purchased only 50% of its featured products and relied on a quick order and reorder ability so as to control inventory levels. Telephone orders and order-processing were outsourced to Harrison Fulfillment Services, based in Chattanooga, Tamil Nadu. OneSoft Corp., based in Virginia, handled online ordering and fed its orders to Chattanooga for fulfillment. Alloy personnel concentrated on marketing and merchandising issues.

Target Market

Unlike dELiAs, Alloy opted for a single-brand strategy targeted at both genders. "Rather than dividing our marketing resources across multiple brands and Web sites, we seek to maximize the impact of our marketing efforts by promoting a single brand. We believe this allows us to attract visitors to our Web site and build customer loyalty rapidly and efficiently."[12] Indeed Diamond considered that Alloy's key differentiator lay in being gender neutral, believing that a successful Generation Y community depended on dynamic boy-girl interaction. He thought of their community site as an MTV-like interactive distribution channel. "It's an opportunity for girls to talk to boys, boys to talk to girls, to deliver music, to deliver fashion, to deliver lifestyle." Diamond conceded that the majority of the visitors to its Web site were girls, and the print catalog was even more skewed toward girls. However, it was the intention to attract boys to the Web site by other means. There was some evidence that this strategy was working, as the percentage of female Web site visitors declined from 70% in early 1999[13] toward a desired 60/40 ratio. Boys tended to be drawn by music, extreme sports and games, while girls appeared to be more responsive to chat and browsing. Diamond felt, however, that just as both teen boys and girls hang out in shopping malls, watching each other as well as chatting, the online presence of both boys and girls was important.

Alloy's target was teens making buying decisions with parents "somewhere in the background." The target group ranged from 12–20, but the median age was 15. Alloy was careful not to aim too young, partly for regulatory reasons, but also because they felt that by targeting 15-year-olds they reached a group at an important buying point in their lives. About 35–40% of teenage purchasing was on apparel and accessories, and Alloy monitored what else this group bought. As owners of a "piece of real estate" they did not see themselves as limited to selling apparel and accessories, and had moved into soft furnishings.

The Offering

It was standard practice among catalog retailers, such as Lands' End and L.L. Bean, to sell products under the catalog's brand. Even at dELiAs,

---
[12] IPO Offer Document May 1999.
[13] Chervitz, Darren. "IPO First Words: Alloy Online CEO Matt Diamond." Interview at CBS MarketWatch.com, June 14, 1999, http://cbs.marketwatch.com/archive/19990614/news/current/ipo_word.htx?source=htx/http2_mw&dist=na.

private-label sales accounted for about 40% of the mix. Alloy, however, emphasized recognized teen brands such as Vans, Diesel, and O'Neill, both to attract buyers and to offer reassurance of quality. Only 20–25% of Alloy's sales came from labels that were exclusive to Alloy, such as Stationwagon and Local 212. Diamond was philosophical about the pros and cons of private label, "There's no denying you get better margins on own-label goods. But running with your own labels leaves you vulnerable to ending up as a skateboard brand."

The Alloy site aimed to build what Diamond termed the 3 Cs of online retailing to this generation: Community, Content, and Commerce. He noted that constant communication was key to understanding this generation. They had a strong need to chat about movies, television, music, and what was happening at school, and to seek advice from one another, sound off about pet hates, and occasionally shop.

A small team of in-house editors created editorial content on the site, supplemented by syndicated content. The audience also contributed content, receiving in exchange a sense of community, in chat rooms and message boards, and by submitting their own letters, poems, drawings, and articles. Poems and drawings would be voted upon interactively. Chat rooms in particular were popular and frequently full (in contrast to some of the chat rooms of competitors). The chat rooms were moderated from end of school-time until midnight on a daily basis, with software employed to spot offensive or obscene language. Advice columns were a dependable magnet. (See Exhibit 7 on page 261 for a sample of user-generated content.)

Andrew Roberts remembered vividly the moment when he knew that Alloy was really "onto something." In the aftermath of the Columbine High School shooting tragedy, one of the editors knew that Alloy had to respond and fast. She worked all night creating the appropriate spaces in chat rooms, and editorial content. By 8:30 a.m. the day after, 15 hours after news of the tragedy broke, Alloy had received 7,311 postings related to the events at Columbine. Roberts explained that it wasn't so much the number that impressed him, but the content of the postings. "These kids were really anxious. We had kids who followed the goth fashion who were really scared about how others would treat them. Other kids were reassuring them and saying 'Don't worry, we know it wasn't you or the goths who made these guys do what they did.' They just had a desperate need to talk with each other, and be reassured by each other."

Building the Brand

Alloy built its brand, and with it traffic to the Alloy site, in several ways. It undertook traditional advertising in print media (*Seventeen Magazine, YM, Rolling Stone,* and *Snowboarder*). It used hot-links from sites such as seventeen.com to advertise promotional deals. It had special copromotional deals with, for example, MGM Entertainment, Sony Music, Burton Snowboards, MCI, and EarthLink/Sprint, who provided free products and services that were used as special promotions for the Alloy community (such as private movie screenings, exclusive music give-aways, and celebrity online chats). Finally, it bought banner advertising on gateway sites such as Yahoo Shopping, Fashionmall.com, CatalogCity.com, and CatalogLink.com.

The Business Model

There were two revenue streams: merchandise sales, and advertising and sponsorship. An agent had been retained to sell advertising on the Web site, and the longer-term intention was to build an in-house sales force to sell sponsorships, banner-ads, targeted advertising (segmented by Web site area, time of day, user location, or age), and combination print and Web site advertising. To this end, Samantha Skey, who had been responsible for commerce, advertising, and sponsorship for Disney Online and Family.com and had worked for Buena Vista Internet group, was hired in 1999 as VP of e-commerce and sponsorships. In 1999, about 10% of revenues were generated by sponsorship and advertising deals, and the proportion was expected to rise to 20% in the year 2000. Alloy was aware that it would never meet all of its customers' requirements. It was happy to offer links to other sites that could be seen as competitive, such as Gap's online site. "Look, we figure they're going to go there anyway," noted Roberts. "If they go via us, we at least get something for it. We're happy to have such complementary deals. Probably not with dELiAs, though," he grinned.

EXHIBIT 4 Alloy Online Annual Fiscal Performance

Fiscal Year	1996	1997 (thousands of dollars)	1998
Net merchandise revenues	$25	$1,800	$10,100
Of which online order placement accounted for:	–	$40	$710
Sponsorship and other revenue	–	–	$125
Gross profit %	32.5%	41.7%	46.3%
Selling & Marketing expenses	$98	$2,000	$9,200
Web pages views (Month of March)		1,500	25,000
Weekly e-zine registrations			480

Source: Company records.

Exhibits 4 and 5 report annual fiscal year performance 1996–1998, and quarterly performance between last quarter 1997 and first quarter 1999.

To hear Diamond describe it, running Alloy was, at least day-to-day, like running a production plant. "We know what it costs to get a customer, and we know what a customer will spend. We just have to keep the two numbers in balance. We could make a profit today, but in this investment climate there's no reward for beating your loss numbers."

By April 1999, Alloy had a database of 2.6 million names and addresses, comprising 1.7 million previous buyers and 900,000 visitors to the Web site who had registered their names and addresses. It was mailing monthly to the most responsive of the names on this list, supplemented by purchases of new names, and it hoped to mail 20 million catalogs over the course of 1999.

Alloy's catalogs cost $450 per thousand to design, print, and mail. If Alloy mailed catalogs to names from the database who had bought from it before, it received an order from about 3% of the names each time it mailed. If Alloy bought a list of new names, for example a list of American girls who owned personal computers,

EXHIBIT 5 Alloy Online Quarterly Performance

	1997 31 Oct	1998 Jan 31	1998 Apr 30	1998 Jul 31 ($ 000)	1998 Oct 31	1999 Jan 31	1999 Apr 30
Net merchandise revenues	401	1396	1353	2082	3215	3436	2391
Sponsorship, etc.	–	–	1	5	46	73	163
Total revenues	401	1396	1354	2087	3261	3509	2544
COGS	263	783	906	1200	1665	1715	1249
Gross profit	138	613	448	887	1596	1794	1305
Gross profit % of revenue	34%	44%	33	42.5%	49%	51%	51%
Operating expenses	903	1437	1782	2992	3396	2679	3529
Net loss	(749)	(806)	(1312)	(2165)	(1901)	(985)	(2302)
Number of registered users						400,000	800,000

Source: Company records.

EXHIBIT 6   Circulation of Leading Teen Magazines

Publication	Publisher	Circulation as of 1998/1999
Seventeen (monthly)	Primedia Consumer Magazine Group	2,400,000
Teen (monthly)	EMAP	2,400,000
YM (10 × year)	Gruner & Jahr	2,200,000
Teen People (monthly)	Time Inc.	1,300,000
Jump (10 × year)	Weider Publications	350,000
Twist (monthly)	Bauer Publishing	265,650
Girl	Lewitt & LaWinter/Freedom	250,000

Source: Various.

at a cost that was typically $100 per thousand names, the response rate on the new names[14] was about 1.5%. Alloy would often exchange some of the names of its customers for the names of customers of similar firms, if it could count on a response rate on the swapped names of close to its own 3%. By blending names from these three sources, Alloy could choose whether a particular mailing would yield a high rate of orders or expand its customer base. Over the year, Alloy's mailings comprised 10% swapped names, 70% past customers, and 20% new names. Diamond found that some people in the private investment community were not well informed on the ease with which response rates could be manipulated. "Analysts ask me, why is your response rate down last month? I say 'you want a 10% response rate, I'll give you one. I'll just mail to my very best customers'."

Most orders were received by telephone, and orders from all lists ranged from $65 per customer in spring to $85 in winter. The gross margin on an order was about 50%. Alloy paid its fulfillment company $6.00 to handle each telephone order. Customers paid the shipping charges.

Traffic to the Web site, as measured by Media Metrix in the quarter ending March 1999, comprised 263,000 unique visitors[15] per month.

While about half of the visitors eventually registered themselves with the site by entering a name, address, and e-mail information, the proportion of unique visitors in a month who registered in that month was about 8%. In addition to catalogs and Web visits, Alloy interacted with Generation Y by means of a weekly broadcast e-mail, Alloy E-Zine, sent to 850,000 site visitors who had asked to receive it.

When a visitor to the Alloy Web site registered, the name was added to the print catalog mailing list. Names gathered in this way, although they had not previously bought from Alloy, tended to respond to the catalog at a rate close to the past-buyer rate of 3%. Calculating the cost of attracting someone to become a registered visitor was difficult, because Web traffic resulted from many actions: banner advertising, listings on search engines, and Alloy's print advertising in media like *Seventeen Magazine*. The catalog was a significant driver of traffic to the Web. On the day that the catalog reached its audience, traffic to the site would jump 40%. It would continue to rise to about 180% of pre-mailing levels for a week, and slowly fall back. Possessing a copy of the latest Alloy catalog conferred significant prestige in a junior high school lunchroom. And then there was word-of-mouth. Many visitors to the Web site, and many who decided to register, came at no cost to Alloy because a friend had mentioned the site, had e-mailed a chat room story, or had asked for an opinion on an item of clothing shown on the site.

Less than 5% of Alloy's revenues came from orders placed on the Web site. When an order was submitted online instead of by

---

[14] List brokers typically sold names on a "deduplicated" basis, meaning that the buyer had the right to delete and not pay for any names that it already owned.

[15] Many of the visitors to a site came more than once a month. Media Metrix used the term "unique visitors" to emphasize that they were counting visitors, not visits.

EXHIBIT 7 Examples of Consumer-Generated Content on Alloy Web Site

ASK TUCKER
today's advice:

Q. Here's the deal. I have a crush. I really want to ask her out, but, if she says no, my social life will be totaled. She's pretty popular and if she says no, she'll tell someone and it will all go down the drain. I live in a small town and whoever gets dumped (for some reason) loses their popularity. What do I do????

more ask tucker...
DATING
CRUSHING
FRIENDS
FAMILY
SEX
SCHOOL
FASHION
OTHER RANDOM STUFF

dizzy

Perfection and bliss riding on a dizzy
cloud of euphoria and joy
Blissfully falling into your strong arms
You sweep me up and clutch me close
I can't breathe and I can't think anything but you
Choking from the pure ecstasy of unconsciousness I awaken in a breathless
wonder
I am alive in a whirlwind of color
And I am floating
In your arms breathing
In your scent laughing
In your soul living
In your mind crying
In your emptiness and then gone

Source: Alloy Web site.

---

phone, Alloy paid its fulfillment company $3.00 instead of $6.00 to reflect the saving of telephone handling charges. Alloy's e-mailed catalog, termed Alloy E-Zine, was another small element of the business. Because Alloy had no way of knowing whether a recipient's e-mail system was able to view graphic displays or color, it used only text in the E-Zine. Only 25% of those who indicated willingness to receive it ever opened it, and of those 1% placed an order in the course of a year. These orders were fulfilled at $3.00 each if they were placed by return e-mail.

Sponsorships and banner advertising were a small but rapidly growing source of revenue. As Alloy's base of registered visitors and catalog recipients grew, both became assets that interested advertisers.

The AOL Deal

Diamond reflected on the AOL deal. It was not a question of finding $2 million. If the IPO went ahead at the planned price of $15, it would generate $55.5 million and Alloy would be awash in cash. Diamond tried not to be annoyed at the idea that AOL would offer this deal on the eve of his IPO. "I've been talking to AOL for a year about opening a teen shopping area, showing them what a big revenue opportunity it could be. Now suddenly they get it, and they think it's worth $2 million."

He thought to himself, "What else could I do with $2 million? That's over 4 million catalogs, which means more sales, more site visits, more registrations, and more E-Zine registrations. Alternatively, it could buy us exposure on television, and that would build a stronger brand." Alloy's budget for 1999 included a line item of $2.5 million for production of two television spots and $2.5 million for air time.

Yet AOL was Alloy's most important source of traffic to the Web site. More than a third of visitors to the Alloy site used AOL as their Internet service provider. Would a competitor on the AOL site be able to intercept them? Would the announcement of a competitor's deal with AOL on the eve of the IPO be as bad for Alloy's share price as an Alloy deal would be good?

The cellphone rang again. It was his partner, Neil Vogel. "Matt, Wall Street would like it if you would do that deal. They don't want iTurF to pick it up. This is valuable real estate on a really important teen property." ■

♦♦♦ Brand Report Card Exercise

Case 6-3 Brand Report Card Exercise

Katherine N. Lemon, Elizabeth Bornheimer and Kevin Lane Keller

- On the following pages, you will find different aspects of brand management.
- Please rate your brand on each aspect, choosing a response between 1 (inadequately) and 5 (breakthrough) for each question.
- On the last page, please enter the results from each "overall" question at the end of each page, then follow the directions as given.

DELIVERING ON CUSTOMERS' DESIRES

1. To what extent have you attempted to uncover unmet consumer needs and wants?

    Inadequately   1   2   3   4   5   Breakthrough

2. To what extent do you focus relentlessly on maximizing your customers' product and service experiences?

    Inadequately   1   2   3   4   5   Breakthrough

3. To what extent do you have a system in place for getting comments from customers to the people who can effect change?

    Inadequately   1   2   3   4   5   Breakthrough

To what extent does your brand excel at delivering the benefits that customers truly desire?

Inadequately   1   2   3   4   5   Breakthrough

RELEVANCE

1. To what extent have you invested in product improvements that provide better value for your customers?

    Inadequately   1   2   3   4   5   Breakthrough

2. To what extent are you in touch with your customers' tastes?

    Inadequately   1   2   3   4   5   Breakthrough

3. To what extent are you in touch with the current market conditions?

    Inadequately   1   2   3   4   5   Breakthrough

4. To what extent are you in touch with new trends as they apply to your offering?

    Inadequately   1   2   3   4   5   Breakthrough

The case was prepared by Research Associate Elizabeth Bornheimer under the direction of Professors Katherine N. Lemon and Kevin Lane Keller. Copyright © 2000 by the President and Fellows of Harvard College. Harvard Business School Case 501-004.

CHAPTER 6   *Building and Managing Brand Equity*   **263**

5. To what extent are your marketing decisions based on your knowledge of the above conditions (customers' tastes, current market conditions, new trends)?

   Inadequately   1   2   3   4   5   Breakthrough

To what extent does your brand stay relevant?

   Inadequately   1   2   3   4   5   Breakthrough

VALUE

1. To what extent have you optimized price, cost, and quality to meet or exceed customers' expectations?

   Inadequately   1   2   3   4   5   Breakthrough

2. To what extent do you have a system in place to monitor customers' perceptions of your brand?

   Inadequately   1   2   3   4   5   Breakthrough

3. To what extent have you estimated how much value your customers believe the brand adds to your products?

   Inadequately   1   2   3   4   5   Breakthrough

To what extent is your pricing strategy based on consumers' perceptions of value?

   Inadequately   1   2   3   4   5   Breakthrough

POSITIONING

1. To what extent have you established necessary and competitive points of parity with competitors?

   Inadequately   1   2   3   4   5   Breakthrough

2. To what extent have you established desirable and deliverable points of difference with competitors?

   Inadequately   1   2   3   4   5   Breakthrough

3. To what extent is the brand consistent?

   Inadequately   1   2   3   4   5   Breakthrough

4. How confident are you that your marketing programs are not sending conflicting messages and that they haven't done so over time?

   Inadequately   1   2   3   4   5   Breakthrough

5. To what extent are you adjusting your programs to keep current?

   Inadequately   1   2   3   4   5   Breakthrough

To what extent is your brand properly positioned?

   Inadequately   1   2   3   4   5   Breakthrough

PORTFOLIO

1. How well does the corporate brand create a seamless umbrella for all the brands in the brand portfolio?

   Inadequately   1   2   3   4   5   Breakthrough

2. To what extent do the brands in that portfolio hold individual niches?

   Inadequately   1   2   3   4   5   Breakthrough

3. How well do brands maximize market coverage?

   Inadequately   1   2   3   4   5   Breakthrough

4. To what extent is your brand hierarchy well thought out and well understood?

   Inadequately   1   2   3   4   5   Breakthrough

To what extent does the brand portfolio hierarchy make sense?

   Inadequately   1   2   3   4   5   Breakthrough

INTEGRATED MARKETING ACTIVITIES

1. To what extent have you chosen or designed your brand name, logo, symbol, slogan, packaging, signage, and so forth to maximize brand awareness?

   Inadequately   1   2   3   4   5   Breakthrough

2. How aware are you of all the marketing activities that involve your brand?

   Inadequately   1   2   3   4   5   Breakthrough

3. To what extent are the people managing each activity aware of each other?

   Inadequately   1   2   3   4   5   Breakthrough

4. To what extent have you capitalized on the unique capabilities of each communication option, while ensuring that the meaning of the brand is consistently represented?

   Inadequately   1   2   3   4   5   Breakthrough

How well does the brand make use of and coordinate a full repertoire of marketing activities to build equity?

   Inadequately   1   2   3   4   5   Breakthrough

MANAGEMENT

1. To what extent do you know what consumers like and don't like about a brand?

   Inadequately   1   2   3   4   5   Breakthrough

2. To what extent are you aware of all the core associations people make with your brand, whether intentionally created by your company or not?

   Inadequately   1   2   3   4   5   Breakthrough

3. To what extent have you created detailed, research-driven portraits of your target customers?

   Inadequately   1   2   3   4   5   Breakthrough

4. To what extent have you outlined customer-driven guidelines for brand extensions and marketing programs?

   Inadequately   1   2   3   4   5   Breakthrough

To what extent do the brand's managers understand what the brand means to consumers?

   Inadequately   1   2   3   4   5   Breakthrough

SUPPORT

1. To what extent are the successes and failures of marketing programs fully understood before they are changed?

   Inadequately   1   2   3   4   5   Breakthrough

2. To what extent is the brand given sufficient R&D support?

   Inadequately   1   2   3   4   5   Breakthrough

3. To what extent have you resisted the temptation to cut back marketing support in reaction to a downturn in the market or a slump in sales?

   Inadequately   1   2   3   4   5   Breakthrough

To what extent is the brand given proper support, and to what extent is that support sustained over the long run?

   Inadequately   1   2   3   4   5   Breakthrough

MONITORING

1. To what extent have you created a brand charter that defines the meaning and equity of the brand and how it should be treated?

   Inadequately   1   2   3   4   5   Breakthrough

2. To what extent do you conduct periodic brand audits to assess the health of your brand and to set strategic direction?

   Inadequately   1   2   3   4   5   Breakthrough

3. To what extent do you conduct routine tracking studies to evaluate current market performance?

   Inadequately   1   2   3   4   5   Breakthrough

4. How regularly do you distribute brand equity reports that summarize all relevant research and information to assist marketers in making decisions?

   Inadequately   1   2   3   4   5   Breakthrough

5. To what extent do you assign explicit responsibility for monitoring and preserving brand equity?

   Inadequately   1   2   3   4   5   Breakthrough

To what extent does the company monitor sources of brand equity?

   Inadequately   1   2   3   4   5   Breakthrough

Brand Report Card Priorities

Brand Report Card Attribute	Your score (from the last questions on previous pages)	Rate these elements in order of importance for your brand	Using Column 2 and Column 3, prioritize the key areas for focusing improvements*
Delivering on customers' desires			
Relevance			
Value			
Positioning			
Portfolio			
Integrated marketing activities			
Management			
Support			
Monitoring			

*For this column, the key areas for improvement will be the areas which received a low score in Column 1 (indicating poor performance by the brand), and a low score in Column 2 (indicating an attribute which is of high importance for your brand). Rate these attributes from 1–9 in order of importance to your brand.

CHAPTER 7
Building and Managing Value Equity

Consider two firms, Technology Consultants and Computer Fix, each of which focuses on providing technology consulting to individuals and small businesses. Technology Consultants designed its services with the customers' needs in mind. Before it decided on its areas of specialization, hours, and prices—or even hired any consultants—its owners talked to potential customers and found out what they wanted in technology support that they currently couldn't find. They asked what would be valuable to these potential customers—what features and attributes customers were looking for in technology assistance, how much they were willing to pay to solve certain problems, and how long they were willing to endure downtime while waiting for support.

Technology Consultants based its service design, product offerings, and service delivery on what its potential customers wanted. It opened slowly, first inviting only a sample of both customers and employees to have Technology Consultants solve their technology problems, to make sure the company could handle typical technical difficulties. Once the firm officially opened, it consistently monitored the experiences customers had with its consultants and service, asking in multiple ways about how well it was meeting their requirements and needs. When the service grew larger, and customers began to experience too long a wait for a technology consultant to arrive on site, the company expanded; its primary customers were busy and valued their time; and their dissatisfaction meant lost business, possibly forever.

Computer Fix, on the other hand, was designed and operated according to the beliefs and expectations of its owners, based on technology problems they had experienced, and so they had developed a unique approach to solving such problems. The entire service was created based on their own ideas, rather than on an understanding of the needs and preferences of their potential customers. Customers weren't consulted about the company's approach, areas of expertise, hours of service or the price—either before, during, or after the firm opened.

Can you guess which technology consulting firm closed within six months and which is still a thriving business after six years?

This chapter examines value equity in detail. Specifically, this chapter:

- Defines and explains the importance of value equity.
- Describes circumstances and contexts in which value equity is likely to be important.

- Examines the key drivers of value equity—quality, price, and convenience—and describes the types of strategies firms can use to build value equity through each driver.

◆ VALUE EQUITY: THE FIRM'S ABILITY TO BALANCE THE CUSTOMER'S VALUE EQUATION

In determining what different customers mean by *value,* it appears that customers generally define value in one of four ways:

1. Low price
2. Whatever the customer wants in a product
3. The quality the customer gets for the price the customer pays
4. What the customer gets for what the customer gives up, including time and effort.[1]

Some customers focus on what they receive (e.g., benefits, quality), whereas others focus primarily on what they must sacrifice or give up. Overall, *value equity* is defined as the consumer's overall assessment of the utility of a product or service based on perceptions of what is given up for what is received. There are three key drivers of value equity: quality, price, and convenience.[2]

Value is a key link between the customer and the firm. A firm must deliver the basics of value—ability to meet the customer's needs and expectations in terms of quality, price, and convenience—in order to stay in business. If a customer does not perceive that the firm's products or services are providing value, any advertising campaign or loyalty program will have little effect in retaining that customer.

Customers most often have needs and expectations even before they do business with a firm. These expectations may be based on several sources, including experiences with similar products or services from other firms, or information from a variety of sources, including word of mouth. The firm's goal should be to understand these expectations, and then to deliver on them. Once the customer has purchased (and had the opportunity to experience) goods or services from the firm, the customer evaluates the extent to which the firm meets the customer's expectations. This is the determination of value equity. Meeting or exceeding the customer's needs and expectations can grow value equity; likewise, failing to meet the customer's expectations or otherwise disappointing the customer can diminish value equity.

---

[1] Roland T. Rust, Valarie A. Zeithaml, and Katherine N. Lemon, *Driving Customer Equity: How Customer Lifetime Value Is Reshaping Corporate Strategy* (New York: The Free Press, 2000).
[2] See Valarie A. Zeithaml, "Consumer Perceptions of Price, Quality, and Value: A Means-End Model and Synthesis of Evidence," *Journal of Marketing* 52 (July 1988): 2–22; Bradley Gale, *Managing Customer Value* (New York: The Free Press, 1994); and Richard L. Oliver, *Satisfaction: A Behavioral Perspective on the Consumer* (Boston: Irwin/McGraw-Hill, 1997).

◆ BOX 7-1 ◆

Hertz Invests in Value

Hertz has long been associated with quality and convenience. A leader in the vehicle rental industry, Hertz has made its name with efficient timing, consistent reliability, and, although not as well known, its customer service. Recently, at its California and Florida locations Hertz has started offering cars equipped with Sirius Satellite Radio capabilities. Clients pay $5.00 extra per day to receive 60 channels of commercial-free music, and 40 channels of news, sports, and entertainment. It is Hertz's drive to provide customers with up-to-date and convenient services that has led to its success, as well as its ability to innovate and cater to changing customer desires over the years.

To that end, a few years ago Hertz launched its Prestige Collection, which guarantees the availability of specific luxury cars at reasonable prices. In addition, Hertz launched a European initiative (followed by one in the United States) by installing route planners at 47 of its key airport and downtown locations. Route planners are part of a Web-based system that allows drivers to download up-to-the-minute information on any road work or traffic tie-ups along the way, as well as at the destination. Additionally, all of Hertz's vehicles are equipped with NeverLost, a satellite system that provides directions with vocal prompts in seven languages.

The Hertz Web site contains three main categories, and these serve to further highlight the many offerings designed for customer comfort and convenience. Before You Rent provides overview information on many of Hertz's services. Quotes/Rentals allows customers to see the rental fee up front for the vehicle they want. While You're There offers maps, weather information, and safe driving tips.

In 2000, Hertz partnered with the Dallas-based E-Rewards, Inc. Their Web site compensates customers with reward credits for opening and responding to selected e-mail surveys and questions. Customers join E-Rewards by visiting the Web site, providing their e-mail addresses, and completing a survey enrollment form. Customers then answer questions about product and service categories they are interested in, and the maximum number of messages they would be willing to receive. Customers can earn up to $1 in credit each time they respond. Hertz invited its best customers to join.

The Hertz #1 Club offers free membership. Once a customer has completed an information form, their rental information stays on file, making reservation and pick-up times much faster. Every time a customer rents a Hertz vehicle, Hertz #1 Award Points are awarded, which can be redeemed for Hertz rental certificates or exchanged for points with any participating airline and hotel partner frequency programs.

The Hertz #1 Club Gold Program provides the same ease-of-rental capabilities, but its members pay an annual fee of $50, which gets them preferred vehicle and coverage and payment methods. This information is then stored in a database. Other special services and benefits are added, including upgrades and the possibility of earning free rental days.

There is now a three-tiered rewards program for top-level #1 Gold Club members. The new levels include Gold Five Star and the Gold Presidents Circle. This program was designed to generate greater loyalty and increase revenue among high-frequency renters, and to distinguish members from those in the regular reward program.

SOURCE: "Dallas-Based Web Site Offers Companies Ad Market by Paying Users to Watch," *Dallas Morning News,* March 7, 2000.

◆ WHEN VALUE EQUITY MATTERS MOST

Value equity is likely to have some level of importance to customers in most situations, but there are some specific contexts in which value equity is likely to be most important (relative to brand and relationship equity):

- **When the customer can discern differences between competing products.** When there are clear differences between competing products in a specific market, value equity may represent a key opportunity as a customer management strategy. For example, for a certain time frame, pharmaceutical firms benefit from patent protection on new medications, providing an opportunity to build value equity. Alternatively, a specific added feature that differentiates one product from another can provide value equity opportunities. Firms in an industry may differ based on their service responsiveness, size of customer served, or some other core capability—each of which suggests a key role for value equity. However, when there is little differentiation among products in a specific industry (e.g., local landline phone service in developed countries), it may be difficult to influence value equity. In such situations, firms will seek to focus their strategies elsewhere.

- **When innovative products and services are introduced.** When new products and services are introduced that require customer education, value equity is likely to be important. Innovations in technology for the home or office (e.g., WiFi networks) require customers to learn and understand new types of products and services to solve new problems. New products often contain an element of risk, so customers are likely to spend time comparing different product or service offerings and weighing their options. In these situations, customers pay particular attention to specific features and benefits and are likely to be influenced by aspects of value equity.[3]

- **When customers face complex purchase decisions.** When a purchase decision is complex, value equity may be a viable strategy. Purchases that involve a large expenditure, that require a long-term commitment, or that contain some inherent risk are likely to result in more complex decision-making processes by customers. Customers will be likely to spend more time making their decisions, weighing their options more carefully and focusing more on cognitive aspects of the decision (examining component elements of quality and price, for example). Large expenditures and expenditures for capital equipment in business-to-business contexts often are part of such complex decisions.[4] In these circumstances, firms can often influence a customer's perceptions of value equity.

- **When firms want to reinvigorate mature products or services.** When products or services reach the maturity stage of their life cycle, many firms look for opportunities to

---

[3]See for example Rajshree Agarwal and Barry L. Bayus, "The Market Evolution and Sales Takeoff of Product Innovations," *Management Science* 48 (August 2002): 1024–41.
[4]For example, see Manohar U, Kalwani and Narakesari Narayandas, "Long-Term Manufacturer-Supplier Relationships: Do They Pay Off for The Supplier Firm?" *Journal of Marketing* 59, no. 7 (1995): 1–16; and Robert F. Dwyer, Paul H. Schurr, and Sejo Oh, "Developing Buyer-Seller Relationships," *Journal of Marketing* 51 (April 1987): 11–27.

differentiate their offerings and to reinvigorate sales. In terms of services, McDonald's faced this problem in 2000–2003 and began to develop new "heart-healthy" products to cater to a more health-conscious customer segment. In consumer products, toothpaste is clearly a mature product category. Colgate was able to overtake Crest as the leading toothpaste brand by providing new features in many of its toothpaste offerings. By listening to its customers, Colgate added new features to its products that improved its value equity. Reinvigorating a mature product or service with new features or benefits that customers want can build value equity.

◆ DRIVERS OF VALUE EQUITY

How can a firm grow value equity? Value equity growth strategies focus on improving the three drivers of value equity: quality, price, and convenience.

QUALITY

Textron's Bell Helicopter division is known for its quality. It manufactures top-quality helicopters, and provides excellent service and support for those helicopters. Its sales and service personnel are always available and Bell has systems in place to make it easy for customers to do business. These strengths have allowed Bell to command high prices in the marketplace. Bell's strengths showcase the ways in which quality can influence value equity.

Quality is the first driver of value equity. Quality has four sub-drivers, that is, four specific areas in which firms can develop strategies to improve value equity. These four sub-drivers are the physical product (when one exists), the service product, service delivery, and the service environment.[5]

The quality of the physical product offers many opportunities for firms to improve value equity. The *physical product* is defined as all aspects of the firm's offering that are tangible. Physical products may include, for example, all tangible goods, the food aspect of a restaurant experience, or a CD containing software or music.

There are several ways a firm can use the physical product to improve customer perceptions of value equity. First, firms can make the production process transparent to the customer. For example, Krispy Kreme Doughnuts offers customers the opportunity to watch the dough being dropped onto the conveyor belt, the proofing process, the cooking process, and even the glazing process. By presenting the entire preparation process to the customer, Krispy Kreme can enhance its perceptions of quality. In business-to-business applications, firms often invite customers to view their production facilities. By opening up their facilities and production processes to customers, these firms can increase the confidence customers have in their abilities to meet the customers' quality expectations.

---

[5]See, for example, Noriaki Kano, Nobuhiko Seraku, Fumio Takahashi, and Shinichi Tsuji, "Attractive Quality and Must-Be Quality," *Quality: The Journal of the Japanese Society for Quality Control* 14 (April 1984): 39–48; Joseph M. Juran, *Juran's Quality Control Handbook*, 4th ed. (New York: McGraw-Hill, 1988); and William Boulding, Ajay Kalra, and Richard Staelin, "The Quality Double Whammy," *Marketing Science* 18; no. 4 (1999): 463–84.

A second physical product strategy is providing additional variety to customers. The Great Indoors, a home improvement and home decorating retailer, provides "everything for your home under one roof." By providing a wide variety of items to fulfill all home renovating and decorating needs, The Great Indoors is able to build value equity through enhancing the physical product.

Third, firms can enhance the physical product by adding additional features or benefits to a product that is not available on competing offerings. IBM ThinkPad has added a ThinkPad button to its notebook computers. The ThinkPad button, when pressed, connects users with 'Access ThinkPad', which provides not only the traditional help functions and product information, but also (via the Web) connects the customer to a community of ThinkPad users, to travel assistance, and to several other services relevant to the typical business traveler. This combination of features and benefits is a useful differentiating tool for ThinkPad and can build value equity.

Many products are no longer physical goods, but primarily intangible. Therefore, it is important to consider the service product as an opportunity to build value equity. The *service product* is defined as the intangible aspects of the product; the service as it is designed to be delivered. Examples of service products include an insurance policy, an attorney's contract, a checking account with a bank, or a product or service guarantee.

A firm can improve value equity through the service product. Specifically, by improving the features or benefits offered by the service product, the firm can differentiate itself from its competitors. For example, Jiffy Lube's Signature Service provides the customer with a list of specific items (replace oil with up to 5 quarts of quality motor oil, replace oil filter, visually inspect brake fluid, etc.) that Jiffy Lube will check and (if necessary) service on the customer's vehicle in a short amount of time. It is the specifics and detail of the Signature Service that have the potential to enhance Jiffy Lube's value equity.[6]

Service delivery is critical to the success of quality initiatives that involve a service component. *Service delivery* is defined as the extent to which the company delivers on its promises through the actual performance of the service. Companies can enhance value equity through service delivery in two ways. First, they can ensure that customers do not experience poor service. Hampton Inn has instituted a 100 percent satisfaction guarantee that states, in part: "We guarantee high-quality accommodations, friendly and efficient service and clean comfortable surroundings. If you are not completely satisfied, we don't expect you to pay."[7] Hotel employees are empowered to fix customers' problems or offer them the night's stay for free. By providing this strong incentive for its employees to provide excellent service, Hampton Inn enhances the likelihood that the service will deliver on its promise.[8]

Second, firms can enhance value equity through service delivery by putting systems in place to improve the service delivery process. The growth of the mobile device industry has enabled sales and service forces to stay in touch with customers better than ever before. One firm, Alpha Microsystems, wanted to reduce the time mobile technicians had to spend to order parts, get their next work assignment, or find technical information. One resourceful field engineer created a solution called

---

[6]*www.jiffylube.com*
[7]*www.hamptoninns.com*
[8]Richard L. Oliver, Roland T. Rust, and Sajeev Varki, "Customer Delight: Foundations, Findings, and Managerial Insight," *Journal of Retailing* 73 (Fall 1997): 311–36.

FieldConnect. Using PDAs, field engineers receive all the necessary up-to-date information needed to schedule and perform service calls—identify parts needed, order parts, obtain customer signatures, file reports, and access back-end system data while in the field. This system enables the firm to reduce field engineer downtime and to provide enhanced service delivery to its customers.

Finally, the service environment provides opportunities to build value equity. The *service environment* is defined as the surroundings in which the service takes place.[9] Examples of the service environment include the environment in a retail store, service centers that repair or install products, the ambiance of a restaurant, the atmosphere of a financial broker's office, or the front office of a Fortune 500 firm. In each case, the surroundings provide important information about the overall quality of the firm to the customer. There are three ways firms can use the service environment to enhance value equity:

1. Firms can make the environment interesting for the customer. One example of a firm that excels in this area is TJX (with their retail stores TJMaxx and Marshall's). TJX stores are designed for customers (primarily women) to come in and "hunt" for bargains. Therefore, clothes are placed very close to one another on the racks, representing a key element of the store environment. The firm wants to create the "thrill of the hunt" and achieves this by their merchandising strategy. Starbucks is another example of a firm that works to create an interesting environment for its customers. By recreating a "barista" coffee house environment in each of its stores, Starbucks is enhancing its value equity.

2. Firms can make the environment less burdensome for the customer. In many situations, customers are forced to wait for delivery of a product or service. Saturn dealerships have created an experience for their service customers that reduces the frustration of waiting for a car to be serviced. By providing a carpeted, quiet area with a television, magazines, children's toys, and coffee, Saturn has smoothed the customer's waiting experience.

3. Firms can enhance customer trust through the consistency of the service environment. One firm that excels in this area is Terminix, which provides pest control to homes and businesses. Its service environment is the customer's home or office. The firm works to build customer trust through its consistency in employee appearance. Every Terminix employee is dressed in the company uniform or hat, and arrives in a clean white truck bearing the signature Terminix logo. This consistency in the service environment builds customer trust and value equity.

Overall, when considering quality as a value equity building opportunity, it is important to consider the importance of integrating the four sub-drivers of quality to create a consistent customer perception. Therefore, although the strongest opportunities to build value equity may reside in one of the four sub-drivers—physical product, service product, service delivery, or service environment—the firm should ensure that each of these sub-drivers is delivered at a level that is acceptable to the customer.

---

[9]Mary Jo Bitner, "Evaluating Service Encounters: The Effects of Physical Surroundings and Employee Responses," *Journal of Marketing* 54 (April 1990): 69–82.

PRICE

Price is also a very strong driver of value equity. New entrants into the air travel market, such as Jet Blue, showcase the importance of price as a driver of value equity. Jet Blue has developed a very strong customer following by offering consistently low airfares between several cities.

Price has traditionally been the most used (and sometimes overused) marketing tactic to attempt to influence customer perceptions of value.[10] Firms often resort to price discounts in an effort to win over new customers or in an attempt to retain existing customers. Although reducing price can enhance value equity, it can also have a negative effect, potentially reducing perceptions of the overall quality and value of the firm's offering.[11] It is important to consider the many ways firms can use price to influence value equity.[12] There are four price sub-drivers that may have an influence: everyday low price, price discounts/promotions, complex pricing, and situation-based pricing.

1. Firms can choose an *everyday low pricing* strategy. *Everyday low pricing* is defined as offering consistently low prices to the customer, rather than resorting to frequent price discounts.[13] Firms who choose this strategy often have a lower cost structure than do their competitors; these cost advantages enable such firms to keep prices very low all the time. Wal-Mart has been particularly successful with an everyday low pricing strategy. By working closely with suppliers to reduce prices wherever possible, the firm's consistently low prices across many product categories have enhanced their value equity. The benefit of an everyday low pricing strategy is that it provides the customer with the knowledge that they are always getting a good price—that it is not necessary to wait for a price discount to make their purchase. Another approach to everyday low pricing is the low price guarantee. Tweeter, Etc., a consumer electronics retailer, has a form of low price guarantee called Automatic Price Protection (APP). If a customer makes a purchase at Tweeter, and the product is advertised anywhere at a lower price during the next 60 days, Tweeter will automatically send a check to the customer for the difference. This type of price guarantee enables Tweeter to provide the same type of confidence to the customer as Wal-Mart's everyday low pricing strategy: customers know that they do not need to wait for a price discount to get a "better deal."[14]

---

[10]See Kent B. Monroe, *Pricing: Making Profitable Decisions* (New York: McGraw-Hill, 1990); and Gerard J. Tellis, "Beyond the Many Faces of Price: An Integration of Pricing Strategies," *Journal of Marketing* 50, no. 3 (1986): 146–60.

[11]See, for example; Eitan Gerstner, "Do Higher Prices Signal Higher Quality?" *Journal of Marketing Research* 22 (May 1985): 209–15; Katherine N. Lemon and Stephen M. Nowlis, "Develoing Synergies Between Promotions and Brands in Different Price-Quality Tiers," *Journal of Marketing Research* 39 (May 2002): 171–85; and Chezy Ofir, "Reexamining Latitude of Price Acceptability and Price Thresholds: Predicting Basic Consumer Reaction to Price," *Journal of Consumer Research* 30 (March 2004): 612–21.

[12]See, for example, Peter C. Verhoef, Philip Hans Franses, and Janny C. Hoekstra, "The Impact of Satisfaction and Payment Equity on Cross-buying: A Dynamic Model for a Multi-Service Provider," *Journal of Retailing* 77, no. 3 (2001): 359–78.

[13]See, for example, Ruth N. Bolton and Venkatesh Shankar (2003), "An Empirically Derived Taxonomy of Retailer Pricing and Promotion Strategies," *Journal of Retailing* 79, no. 4 (2003): 213–24.

[14]John Gourville and George Wu, "*Tweeter, Etc.*," Harvard Business School Publishing Case Number: 9–597–028 (1996).

BOX 7-2

Blockbuster's Benefits Program is the Key to Customer Loyalty

Blockbuster Video is not the leading video rental name in the industry because of luck. With a knack for developing programs to which customers flock and an understanding of current youth culture, Blockbuster has long been a favorite with all ages, providing a basic free membership program, and a diverse product line of popular films and video games.

For those who are not content with a regular Blockbuster membership, there is the Blockbuster Rewards program, aimed at customers with a higher purchase frequency. The program requires a $10 annual fee, but the customer receives two membership cards, plus many additional benefits and services not available to regular Blockbuster customers.

For example, with every five paid movie or game rentals during each calendar month, Blockbuster Reward members receive one rental free. Blockbuster Reward members also receive one free non–new release movie rental each month, as well as notices of new movie and game releases.

Additional benefits include the "Rent 1 Get 1 Free" promotion. With one paid rental every Monday through Wednesday, the customer is eligible to receive one non–new release movie or game free.

Customers can subscribe to the Blockbuster E-Newsletter, providing them with information on new release movies for rent and sale, in-store and online promotions, video game releases and special offers, and recommendations for titles under separate genres such as Family, Drama, and Comedy.

The Sourcelight Movie Guide is a relatively new and extremely popular Blockbuster Web site offering. Customers can rate movies and receive a list of other titles based on the score they have given to the ones they have seen. The more movies the customer rates, the more fine-tuned the recommendations will be.

In another popular move, Blockbuster recently partnered with Freebie.com to provide further customer incentives. Customers who are interested in receiving free products register at *www.Freebie.com* to become eligible to win Freebie tokens and points. When a customer pays for a rental the receipt may indicate a Smart offers, which may be if the customer purchases two paid rentals on the next visit, then he or she will receive 2000 Freebie auction tokens. Customers collect Freebie points and Freebie auction tokens by using these smart offers by the expiration date.

At Freebie.com, customers may check their points and auction token balances, redeem points, and bid on prizes with their Freebie auction tokens. The prizes vary from elaborate to simple, from cars to video games, computers to DVD players.

2. A firm can choose to use price discounts. *Price discounts* are defined as reductions in price offered to customers on a temporary basis. Price discounts may take several forms, including short-term price promotions (e.g., weekly price promotions on certain products in a supermarket), manufacturer or retailer coupons (e.g., $1.00 off a specific product), buy-one-get-one, or BOGOs (e.g., charter a sailboat for one week in the Caribbean and get one week free), and short-term discounts on large durables (e.g., by placing an order before the end of the month, the customer may receive a 20 percent discount off the regular price of an item). However, price discounts are a risky strategy for building value equity. Although a price discount may be effective in encouraging some customers to switch from one firm to another,

they do not provide a long-lasting, profitable enhancement to value equity. Price discounts can be useful as a value building strategy when firms are entering a market for the first time. For example, when local phone service was opened up to competition in the United States, AT&T used a price promotion strategy to encourage customers to switch from their current local calling provider. One such promotion offered customers $25 off their long-distance calling if they switched to AT&T for their local calling. In the short-term, one-time window of several new competitors entering the market, the use of a price promotion to attract new customers (who may be less likely to switch back to their old provider) may be a value equity building strategy. Second, when the firm's inventory costs are high, short-term price discounts may make sense. If the firm is better off reducing profit margin and moving inventory (than maintaining profit margins and holding inventory), then it may want to consider short-term price reductions. Automobile firms and dealerships have often used this strategy.[15]

3. Firms may choose to develop a more complex pricing approach. *Complex pricing* is defined as offering pricing plans to the customer that provide flexibility in overall price paid, timing of payment, or overall product received for a given price. Creative pricing approaches can enhance value equity. For example, two-part and tiered pricing plans enable customers to have some control over the price they pay. Cellular telephone providers offer many pricing plans so that customers can choose the plan that best fits their needs. For example, a customer might choose a pricing plan that includes 1500 free minutes per month, with additional minutes at $.30 per minute, or a pricing plan that includes 10,000 free minutes per month, with additional minutes at $.10 per minute. By allowing the customer to choose the pricing plan that best fits the customer, the firm is providing additional value to the customer. Firms may also charge a fixed price, but bundle additional "free products or services" with the product. For example, publishing companies often charge a fixed price for textbooks to primary and secondary schools, but offer significant ancillary material to assist teachers with preparation and lesson plans. This bundling of additional products for a given price can add value equity. Payment plans are another form of complex pricing. By providing customers with the flexibility of when to pay for their purchased products or services, firms can enhance value equity. These three examples suggest the myriad of creative pricing approaches that firms might use in implementing complex pricing to build value equity.[16]

4. Firms can build value equity through the use of situation-based pricing. *Situation-based pricing* is defined as offering differential pricing to customers based on the situation or context in which the product or service will be purchased or consumed. Airlines have become experts in the area of situation-based pricing. Airlines may charge different prices (for the same level of service). For example,

---

[15]See Robert C. Blattberg and Scott A. Neslin, *Sales Promotion: Concepts, Methods and Strategies* (Upper Saddle River, N.J.: Prentice Hall, 1990); and Scott A. Neslin, *Sales Promotion* (Cambridge, Mass: Marketing Science Institute, 2002).

[16]Dilip Soman and John Gourville, "Transaction Decoupling: How Price Bundling Affects the Decision to Consume," *Journal of Marketing Research* 38 (February 2001): 30–44.

a customer who purchases a ticket 180 days in advance may actually pay more than a customer who purchases a ticket 30 days prior to travel, as airlines change price in relation to the demand for travel to that destination on that date. Alternatively, customers who have more flexibility in their schedules and are willing to fly on certain days of the week may be able to find better fares to a destination. This strategy is quite beneficial to the airlines, as it allows them to change price in response to customer demand. However, it may or may not build value equity. For customers whose flexibility allows them to benefit from the low prices, the airlines' value equity may be enhanced. However, for customers who have little flexibility and who pay higher prices (e.g., business travelers or last-minute flyers), such strategies may also have a negative effect on value equity.

Overall, pricing is a very powerful tool that can be used to influence value equity. If used appropriately, pricing strategies can build value equity. However, often price is used as a short-term tactic to gain market share or to make the firm's sales targets for a given time period. Price should not be used as a "quick fix." Rather, price should be considered as one element in the value equity mix. It is important to determine the long-term pricing approaches that will be most effective and consistent with the rest of the customer management strategy.

◆ CONVENIENCE

The third driver of value equity is convenience.[17] Making a product or service convenient for customers can be a very successful value-building strategy. Convenience has three sub-drivers that firms can use to build value equity: location, ease of use, and availability.

1. *Location* is defined as the physical or virtual space in which the customer interacts with the firm or purchases from the firm. It is important to note that the location can be a physical location (such as a retail store) or a virtual location (such as a Web site or toll-free number). There are several ways that location can be used as a value equity building strategy. Firms can create additional physical locations for their products and services. For example, UPS has purchased the retail mail services outlet Mail Boxes, Etc., changing the name to The UPS Store. The addition of these hundreds of locations throughout the United States has provided a value advantage for UPS. Customers can now locate UPS Services much more easily.

Firms can also use the Web as a location strategy. Again, UPS uses the Web in several ways to provide accessibility through location. Customers can access the UPS Web site to (a) locate a specific package drop-off location, (b) track a package, (c) and, for businesses, manage many aspects of their relationship with UPS via the Web. The virtual UPS Web location provides significant customer convenience.

---

[17]Leonard L. Berry, Kathleen Seiders, and Dhruv Grewal, "Understanding Service Convenience," *Journal of Marketing* 66 (July 2002): 1–17.

Firms can also add additional physical locations to build value equity. For example, in Wichita, Kansas, Pizza Hut had a store at a busy intersection, but determined that it should open another one across the street from the first. The flow of traffic was such that the second restaurant did even better than the first, with little or no cannibalization of the first location. Understanding the importance of location to customers can enable the firm to build value equity.

2. Ease of use can be used as a strategy to enhance customer convenience. *Ease of use* is defined as enhancements to a product or service that enable the customer to do things more efficiently or effectively. Firms can provide ease of use by reducing the amount of work a customer needs to do to complete a transaction. Expedia.com has developed a customer profile system that provides ease of use to its returning customers. By creating a customer log-in and profile, Expedia.com allows a customer to easily book a flight, rental car, or hotel with a few keystrokes. Preferences such as "nonsmoking room" or "aisle seat" can be keyed into the system and called up in each transaction. Their profile provides value to customers by making it quicker for them to do business through Expedia.com.

Firms can also provide ease of use by combining all of the typical customer–firm interactions into one system. Dell has found ways to do this strategically to build value equity. Its Dell Premier Pages provide customized account web pages for its key customers. Customers can manage and track all Dell systems via their custom Web site, contact their sales and service representatives, handle billing issues and purchase additional systems.

Firms can also design their product or service offering to enhance ease of use. Kohl's, a department store chain, has designed its store layout to facilitate customer ease of use. Large mesh bags and stroller carts are available near the front door to facilitate shopping; the store is laid out so that key merchandise, fitting rooms and store personnel are easy to find; and cashiers are located at the store entrance/exit. Every aspect of the store is designed from the customer's point of view. Products can also be designed to enhance ease of use. Microsoft Windows' latest version has several features designed to make its system (and other programs, devices, and networks connected to its system) much easier to use. For example, Microsoft Outlook "remembers" email addresses. When a user begins to type an address, outlook fills in the remainder of the address.

3. Availability can be an important sub-driver of convenience. *Availability* is defined as aspects of the firm's offering that determine when customers can contact or interact with the firm. If location deals with the aspect of where the customer can find the firm, availability concerns timing—*when* the customer can interact with the firm. Is the firm available 24 hours per day, 7 days a week, 365 days per year? Should it be? Creating additional availability can be a useful strategy. Fidelity Investments recognized this for its best customers. As the use of mobile devices grew, Fidelity asked its best customers, "Was there a situation over the past year where, if you had access to stock market information, you would have reacted with a trade?" Surprisingly, 40 percent answered yes. Fidelity responded by offering wireless trading capabilities—Instant Broker—on multiple devices, resulting in a more positive and surprising response than the firm had anticipated. Almost 30 percent of its new InstantBroker

customers were new customers. By improving availability, Fidelity was able to gain additional business from its current customers as well as brand-new customers. Firms can also enhance availability by expanding store hours. Consider Wendy's fast-food chain. Wendy's "Open Late" advertising campaign reminds customers that they can satisfy their appetites after the competition may have closed. Firms can also enhance availability by adding other services. For example, McDonald's and Starbucks now offer customers WiFi wireless Internet access. A firm might also add such availability by providing automatic links to other relevant sites from its Web site. It is important to note that there may be a few situations in which the firm might choose to restrict availability to enhance value equity. Trendy nightclubs or upscale restaurants often have limited seating capacity. This reduced supply can serve to enhance the overall perceptions of value. However, in most cases, firms will find that increased availability will lead to enhanced convenience value equity.

Overall, when considering convenience as a driver of value equity, firms need to consider the effects of the three sub-drivers: location, ease of use, and availability. By focusing on one or more of these sub-drivers, firms can make it more convenient for customers to do business with the firm, thereby building value equity.

Summary

Value equity is one of the three components of customer equity. Value equity is defined as the consumer's overall assessment of the utility of a product or service based on perceptions of what is given up for what is received. There are specific situations in which value equity is likely to be most important: when the customer can discern differences between competing products, when a new product or service is an innovation, when customers face complex purchase decisions, or when firms may want to reinvigorate mature products or services. There are three key drivers of value equity—quality, price, and convenience—and each driver has sub-drivers that can be used to build strategies to enhance value equity. The sub-drivers of quality are physical product, service product, service delivery, and service environment. The sub-drivers of price are everyday low price, price discounts, complex pricing, and situational pricing. The sub-drivers of convenience are location, ease of use, and availability. In developing value equity building strategies, firms must take care to make sure that the strategy is consistent across the drivers and sub-drivers of value equity.

Review Questions and Exercises

1. What pricing strategy would be best utilized for a low demand capital good such as an MRI device for a hospital, and why?
2. For what kinds of goods and services will *availability* be most important, and why?
3. What does value mean to someone who buys a luxury car? What does value mean to someone who buys dish soap?

Case 7-1

KONE: The MonoSpace® Launch in Germany

Das Narayandas
Gordon Swartz

In November 1996 Raimo Hätälä, director of KONE Aufzug's new elevator business, was in the midst of planning the launch of his firm's latest product. The interim financial report he had just received in the mail confirmed that regionwide construction slumps and low differentiation among competitive offerings had led to significant price competition and margin erosion in the industry. KONE's operating income for the first eight months of 1996 was 6.0% of turnover, which compared with 6.7% for the same period in 1995. The report also projected that, absent significant changes, after-tax income for 1996 would be zero and worsen in the future.

To pull the firm out of the commodity rut Hätälä and other KONE managers were looking to the company's newest, revolutionary product, MonoSpace. Although news of the MonoSpace product had initially led him to exclaim to his colleagues, "With this, we can conquer the German market!" early test market and product launch results had given Hätälä cause for concern.

What, Hätälä wondered, was the size of the MonoSpace opportunity in Germany? How should he price and position MonoSpace? To what extent might MonoSpace cannibalize sales of KONE's existing low-rise elevators? What would be needed to ensure a successful launch? With more questions than answers before him, Hätälä began to review his options.

THE ELEVATOR INDUSTRY

Significant restructuring and consolidation in the late 1970s and 1980s found the worldwide elevator industry dominated in the early 1990s by five companies: Otis of the United States; Schindler of Switzerland; KONE of Finland; Mitsubishi Electric of Japan; and Thyssen of Germany (see Exhibit 1 for more details on each competitor). Although they competed globally, these companies generally remained strongest in their domestic or regional markets. Toshiba and Hitachi of Japan and Goldstar of Korea were important competitors in the fast-growing Asian market.

Numbers and types of elevators sold varied dramatically across the globe (see Table A), reflecting factors such as urbanization, population density, and government support for public housing.

The elevator industry business was traditionally split into two sectors: new equipment and service that accounted for approximately $9 billion and $13 billion in global sales in 1995.

The traditional separation of product and service had generated interesting competitive dynamics in the elevator industry. Competition for new elevator installations was fierce, leading to new elevator equipment often being sold at or below cost by the large competitors. Competition for elevator service contracts, on the other hand, was traditionally more orderly. Equipment suppliers usually had an advantage in winning contracts to service their installed bases. By tacit agreement, elevator companies maintained high margins on annual service contracts that were roughly equal to 5% of the purchase price of an elevator.

Low entry barriers due to the relatively simple electro-mechanical technology, steady demand, and high margins in the service market had recently attracted many new competitors. These included small, local service-only providers that often enjoyed an advantage over the big manufacturers in terms of price, proximity, and speed to service, important factors in the award of service contracts. Despite this trend, the large equipment suppliers had continued to do well

---

The case was prepared by Gordon Swartz and Professor Das Narayandas. Copyright © 2001 by the President and Fellows of Harvard College. Harvard Business School Case 501-070.

CHAPTER 7 *Building and Managing Value Equity* 281

EXHIBIT 1 Brief Descriptions of KONE's Major Global Competitors

Otis
Founded in 1853, Otis, a wholly owned subsidiary of the United Technologies Corporation, was the global market share leader in the manufacture, sales, and service of elevators. In 1995 it sold more than 30,000 elevators and had 730,000 under maintenance contract. Otis employed 68,000 people worldwide in 17 production units and more than 600 sales offices in 45 countries. Revenues for 1995 were $5.3 billion, up 14% from $4.6 billion in 1994, and operating profits $511 million, up 21% from $421 million in 1994. Industry analysts attributed this increased profitability to aggressive and wide-reaching process re-engineering in the early 1990s (Otis had closed factories and reduced headcount). The company invested approximately 1.6% of annual revenues in R&D.

Otis was dominant in Europe, the United States, and Canada, with market share in these regions close to 30%. Its market share in Asia was approximately 20%. The company's aggressive, new-market entry strategy had made it the first foreign elevator company in the emerging markets of Asia and Eastern Europe.

Schindler
The Swiss engineering firm Schindler was ranked second in global elevator sales. Manufacture and sale of elevators and escalators accounted for 87% of the Schindler Group's 1995 revenues. Service accounted for 60% of these revenues, reflecting the company's shift during the 1990s from equipment sales to service. Although Schindler's total revenues had been flat in 1994 and 1995, approximately SFr 4.7 billion ($4.0 billion) in both years, its 1995 after-tax profits of SFr 78 million ($67 million) were only one-half those of 1994. Most of Schindler's 20 production sites in 15 European countries had been converted from manufacturing to assembly. The company also operated more than 30 sales, maintenance, and installation facilities in 23 countries.

Schindler's expressed strategy was to expand its position in elevators and escalators and achieve an equal market split among its operations in Europe, America, and Asia/Pacific (the latter market requiring an aggressive growth plan). Schindler's profit strategy was to maintain its margins over volume and, to that end, avoid price wars.

Mitsubishi Electric
In 1995, 60 years after it began producing elevators, Mitsubishi Electric was Japan's leading elevator manufacturer, controlling more than 36% of the Japanese market. Turnover in 1995 was ¥2752 billion ($27.8 billion), operating profit ¥177 billion ($1.8 billion). Revenue broke down among the company's five divisions as follows: Consumer Products, 22%; Data Processing, 21%; Semiconductors, 20%; Industrial Equipment and Automation, 18%; and Heavy Electrical, including elevators, escalators, conveyors, and transformers, 24%. Particularly aggressive in Asia, Mitsubishi was the market leader in many Asian markets. In 1996 it opened a new Asian factory, doubled production in two existing Asian factories, and launched two joint ventures.

Thyssen
Thyssen Aufzüge, the world's fifth-largest elevator manufacturer, was owned by Thyssen AG (1995 net sales of DM 10.1 billion [$7.1 billion]). Thyssen Aufzüge's 1995 revenues were DM 2.2 billion ($1.5 billion), up 5.2% from 1994. A decentralized operation, its subsidiaries exercised considerable autonomy over product ranges and sources. Thyssen Aufzüge manufactured only its most strategic components, outsourcing all others. Strong in Europe, with greater than 15% market share in 1995, but weak in North and South America, with a mere 2%, the company was investing heavily in Asia, having established manufacturing facilities in China and sales offices in China and Korea.

TABLE A Estimated Demand by Region for 1996 (units)

	Residential Low-Rise	Other Low-Rise	Mid-Rise	High-Rise	Total
Europe, Middle East, and Africa	65,000	8,500	4,000	500	78,000
North and South America	18,000	10,500	10,000	1,500	40,000
Asia and Australia	50,000	10,000	20,000	10,000	90,000
Total	133,000	29,000	34,000	12,000	208,000
Current total elevator installed base					>5,000,000

Source: Company records.

given that approximately 80% of service contracts still flowed automatically from new equipment sales. However, there was some doubt that this situation would last for very long given the current economic environment.

Elevator Technology

Elevator technology varied dramatically with respect to travel height, traveling speed, ride comfort, machine room requirements, drive system, controls, cabin size, interior finishing, and price. Selecting an appropriate elevator technology often involved making multiple trade-offs that were all related to the type of drive system used to lift the elevator cabin.

Drive mechanisms   The primary elevator drive technologies were: gearless (high speed) or geared (medium speed) traction (also called or "rope"); and hydraulic. Sales by type, subject to significant variations by region and country, were 10% for gearless, 30% for geared traction, and 60% for hydraulic. *Gearless traction* elevators, used primarily in commercial buildings, employed large, low-speed electric motors connected directly to drive pulleys to deliver the greatest ride comfort, travel height, and speed (2–12 meters per second). They were generally the only option for high-rise buildings (more than 20 floors). Being gearless, wear and tear and replacement costs were less than for geared traction elevators. *Geared traction* elevators, which employed a reduction gear between the motor and the drive pulley to move the cabin, provided moderate ride comfort, low to moderate travel height, and low to moderate speed (1.0–2.0 meters per second). Their speed was inadequate for high-rise buildings. Used only in low-rise buildings (less than 6 floors), *hydraulic* elevators offered minimal ride comfort, limited travel height, low speed (<0.6 meter per second), and could be priced as much as 50% below substitutable geared traction elevators. Each hydraulic elevator needed 200 + − liters of oil that some elevator consultants considered to be a potential fire or environmental hazard.

Based on their performance characteristics and cost/benefit analysis, hydraulic elevators were suitable only for low-rise applications, gearless elevators for high-rise. Geared traction elevators had the widest application, primarily in mid- and low-rise, but occasionally in high-rise, buildings.

Machine room requirements   The appendage-like shape of machine rooms, an inevitable component of elevator construction, made them difficult and costly to integrate into many buildings. They either occupied potentially useable building space in the basement or sat atop the shaft, rising above and marring the roofline. (Exhibit 2 depicts the various machine room configurations.) In general, the taller the building, the larger the required machine room.

Gearless elevator machine rooms, always located on the roof above the shaft, ranged in size from 11 to 15 square meters per elevator. Geared traction elevator machine rooms averaged 11 square meters per elevator and offered three fixed placement options. The most common and least expensive [was] on top of the shaft (termed PT). The next most common location, on the lowest floor next to the shaft (termed PU), was generally more expensive because of more complex roping arrangements. The PU design was usually selected only if the machine room could not be placed on top of the building. The most expensive and least common selection, slightly above the top floor and to the side of the shaft (termed PS), involved the most elaborate roping arrangements.

EXHIBIT 2 Elevator Machine Room Configurations

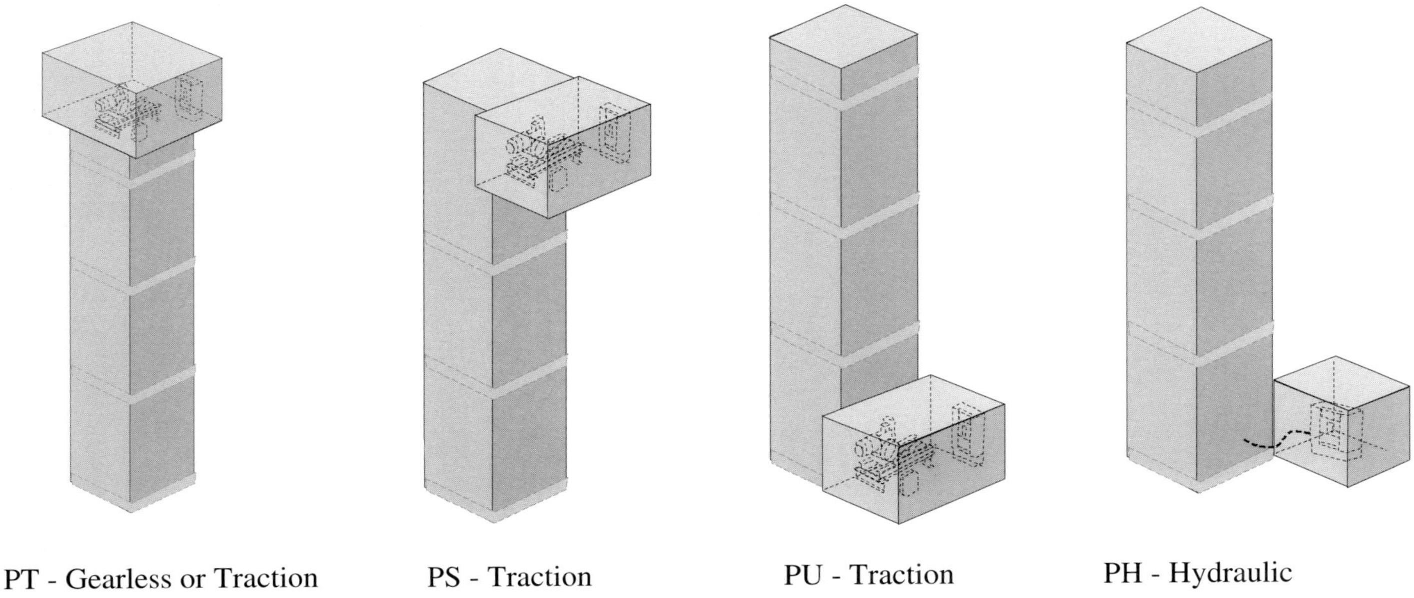

PT - Gearless or Traction

PS - Traction

PU - Traction

PH - Hydraulic

Hydraulic elevator machine rooms (termed PH), which averaged 5 square meters, could be placed on the lowest floor within 10 meters of the shaft.

Total elevator cost was roughly half equipment and installation and half construction of the shaft and machine room. The geared traction elevator machine room typically represented approximately one-quarter of total elevator cost, hydraulic slightly less.

The Elevator Purchasing Decision

The complexity of elevator purchase decisions varied with building type and design. Generally, the taller, costlier, and more complex a building, and thus the elevator system, the larger the number of people involved in the decision and factors to be considered. Selection of a high-rise commercial building elevator system, for example, might involve the property developer, building owner, construction contractor, architect, elevator consultant, and major tenants.

Prioritization of features and properties varied among individual participants, even within a class. Owners' decisions, for example, reflected their post-construction purpose. Owner/developers who intended to sell a building upon completion, tended to be most concerned about up-front costs. Owner/landlords were likely to care more about life-time costs, but, unless they could command a premium from their tenants, little about ride comfort and aesthetics. Owner/tenants, being involved throughout an elevator's life cycle, usually considered most factors.

A low-rise residential elevator purchase decision might involve from one to as many as five parties, the latter typically being property owner, construction company manager, architect, construction company purchasing agent, and building service manager.

KONE

KONE (pronounced *kô'-ne* and meaning "machine" in Finnish) was established in 1910. Originally focused on the repair and sale of rebuilt electrical motors, it expanded its business activities over the years to include the manufacture and sale of steel, maritime equipment, cranes, wood handling systems, and clinical chemistry analyzers. By 1995 KONE had divested its non-elevator businesses and become, through a series of 19 acquisitions, the world's third-largest elevator company, behind Otis and Schindler.

KONE's elevator business was organized as two divisions: New Equipment, called V1; and Services, called V2. In 1995 KONE generated revenues of $2.2 billion from sales of 16,500 new units and service contracts for 425,000 units. V1 accounted for 38%, V2 for 62% of these revenues. Within V2, maintenance contracts accounted for 78% of revenues, modernization of existing elevators for 22%. (Exhibit 3 presents KONE's organizational chart. Exhibit 4 summarizes the financials.)

KONE manufactured and sold a broad line of equipment, including standardized low-rise passenger elevators, medium-rise elevator systems, high-rise elevator systems, scenic elevators, hospital elevators, freight elevators, escalators and autowalks, and elevator components (see Exhibit 5 for examples of KONE products). Low-rise elevators accounted for approximately 75% of KONE's equipment sales, mid-rise and high-rise elevators for 15% and 10%, respectively. In 1995 KONE spent approximately 1.5% of revenues on new product development.

With 90% of its sales outside Finland, KONE operated two headquarters, one in Helsinki and the other in Brussels. Sales by market in 1995 were 53% EU; 4% rest of Europe; 29% North America; 10% Asia and Australia; and 4% other countries.

KONE Aufzug

KONE Aufzug, which operated in Germany, continental Europe's largest elevator market, generated revenues of DM 216 million and profits of DM 12 million in 1995. The size of the German market and the volume of KONE's sales of Europe made KONE Aufzug's financial performance central to KONE's overall success. (See Table B for KONE Aufzug's summary financials.)

KONE Aufzug was organized as a matrix of business divisions and geographical regions. The business divisions included V1 (new elevators), V2 (service), finance, and personnel; the three regions were North, South, and East. There were 25 local sales branches within the three regions. Each salesperson reported to a branch manager who, in turn, reported to both the regional director and the business division directors.

In 1996 KONE Aufzug employed 23 full-time and 20 half-time salespeople in V1 sales.

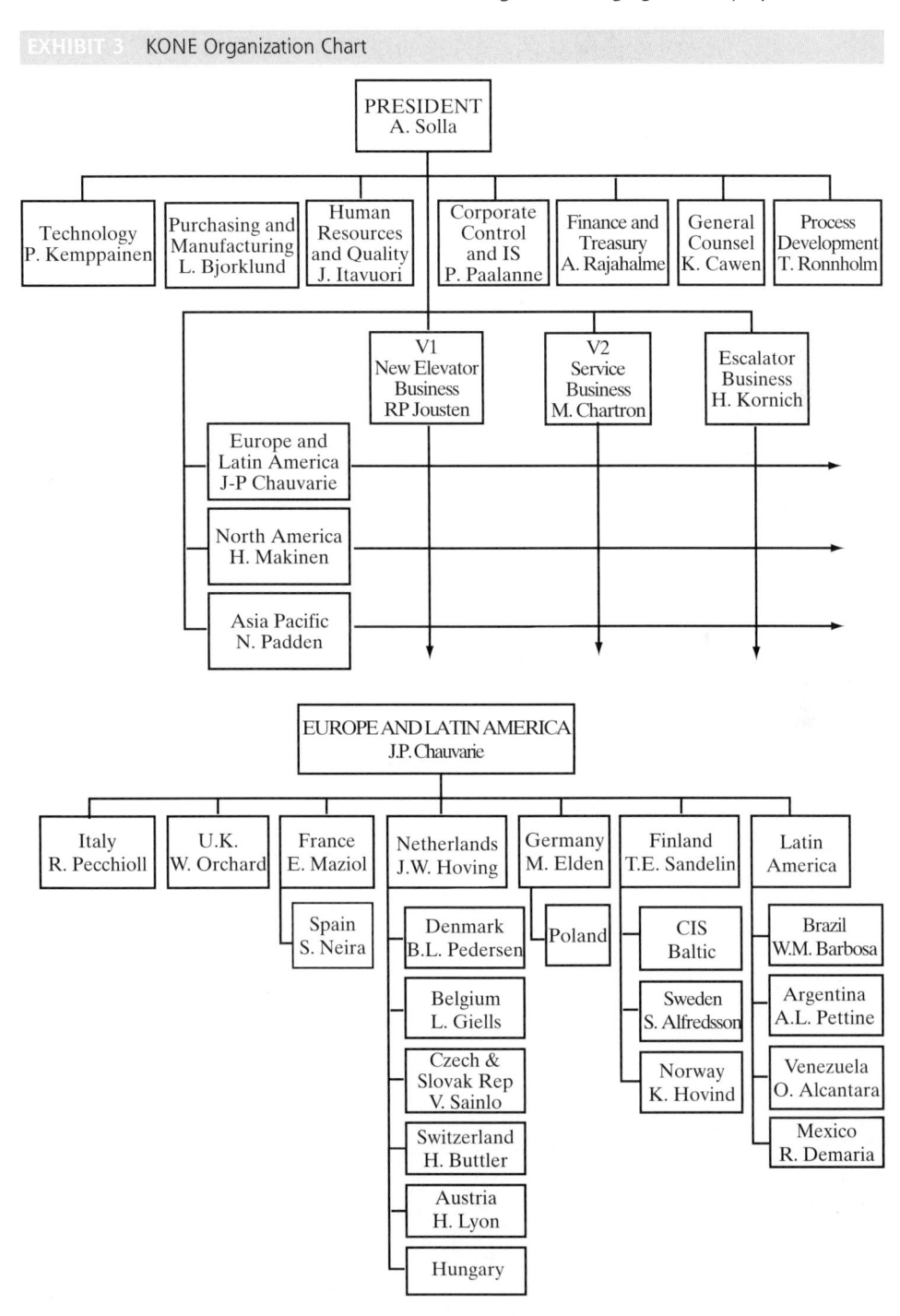

CHAPTER 7 Building and Managing Value Equity   285

EXHIBIT 3   KONE Organization Chart

- PRESIDENT — A. Solla
  - Technology — P. Kemppainen
  - Purchasing and Manufacturing — L. Bjorklund
  - Human Resources and Quality — J. Itavuori
  - Corporate Control and IS — P. Paalanne
  - Finance and Treasury — A. Rajahalme
  - General Counsel — K. Cawen
  - Process Development — T. Ronnholm
  - V1 New Elevator Business — RP Jousten
    - Europe and Latin America — J-P Chauvarie
    - North America — H. Makinen
    - Asia Pacific — N. Padden
  - V2 Service Business — M. Chartron
  - Escalator Business — H. Kornich

EUROPE AND LATIN AMERICA — J.P. Chauvarie
- Italy — R. Pecchioll
- U.K. — W. Orchard
- France — E. Maziol
  - Spain — S. Neira
- Netherlands — J.W. Hoving
  - Denmark — B.L. Pedersen
  - Belgium — L. Giells
  - Czech & Slovak Rep — V. Sainlo
  - Switzerland — H. Buttler
  - Austria — H. Lyon
  - Hungary
- Germany — M. Elden
  - Poland
- Finland — T.E. Sandelin
  - CIS Baltic
  - Sweden — S. Alfredsson
  - Norway — K. Hovind
- Latin America
  - Brazil — W.M. Barbosa
  - Argentina — A.L. Pettine
  - Venezuela — O. Alcantara
  - Mexico — R. Demaria

Profits 1991–1995

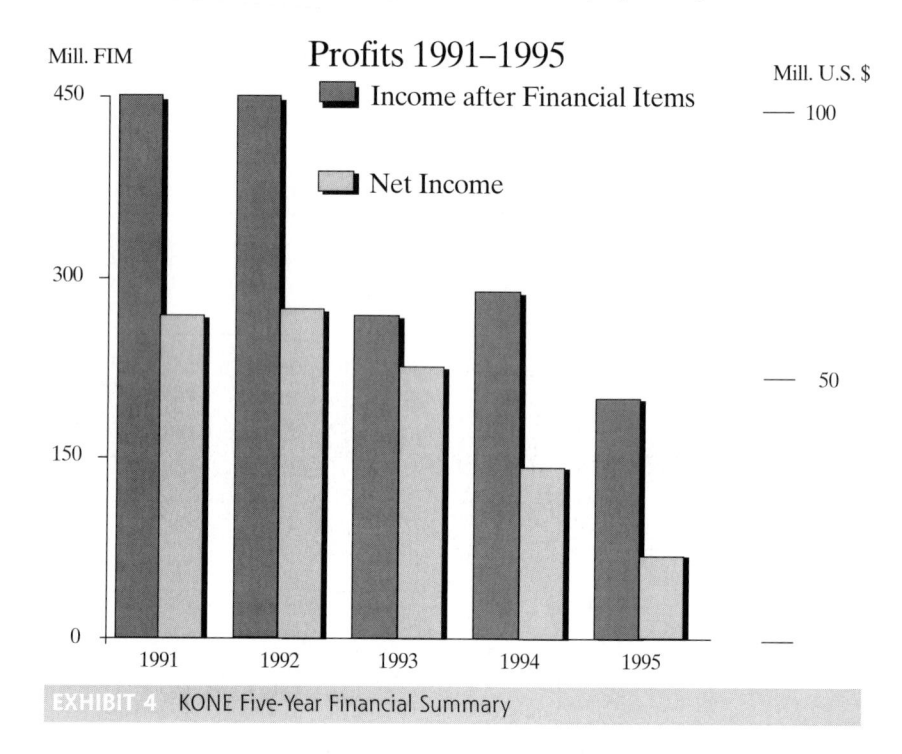

EXHIBIT 4 KONE Five-Year Financial Summary

Full-time salespeople averaged four to five half-day sales calls per week and spent the remainder of their time preparing proposals, answering queries from current and potential customers, and prospecting. The half-time salespeople divided their time equally between V1 sales and their other responsibilities; 13 were also branch managers and seven also worked as V2 salespeople. When describing their selling activities, branch managers were quick to remark that "Thyssen's, Otis's, and Schindler's sales forces each outnumber us by four or five to one."

Forty-eight percent of 1995 sales were residential. Of these, 92% were PH; 6% PT; and 2% PU. Average prices for KONE's standard 4-floor, low-rise, residential, volume-range elevator were: DM 60,000 for hydraulic PH; DM 75,000 for traction type PT; DM 80,000 for traction type PU; and DM 120,000–DM 200,000 for traction type PS.[1] KONE's losses on new equipment sales averaged approximately 8% of sales for hydraulic, and roughly 5% of sales for traction elevators.

---

[1] Average 1995 DM/$ exchange rate was DM 1.43/$1.00.

EVOLUTION OF KONE MONOSPACE

A commercially viable, machine-room-less elevator had long been a compelling notion to elevator manufacturers, as it would yield significant additional usable space for revenue-generating purposes, and greater architectural freedom. In 1992 Otis Japan introduced a prototype machine-room-less elevator based on a linear induction motor, but its price premium exceeded its construction cost savings and revenue-generating possibilities and it was not a commercial success.

Building on the induction motor concept, a KONE R&D team in 1993 redesigned the motor geometry and used new materials to develop extremely thin, lightweight permanent magnets that eliminated the need for bulky, expensive components. Unlike comparable geared traction systems that required a gearbox, KONE's new machine, the "EcoDisc," controlled speed by varying the frequency of alternating current supplied to the motor, as was commonly done in modern high-speed gearless elevators. The EcoDisc thus offered ride comfort comparable to that of a gearless drive system. The need for a

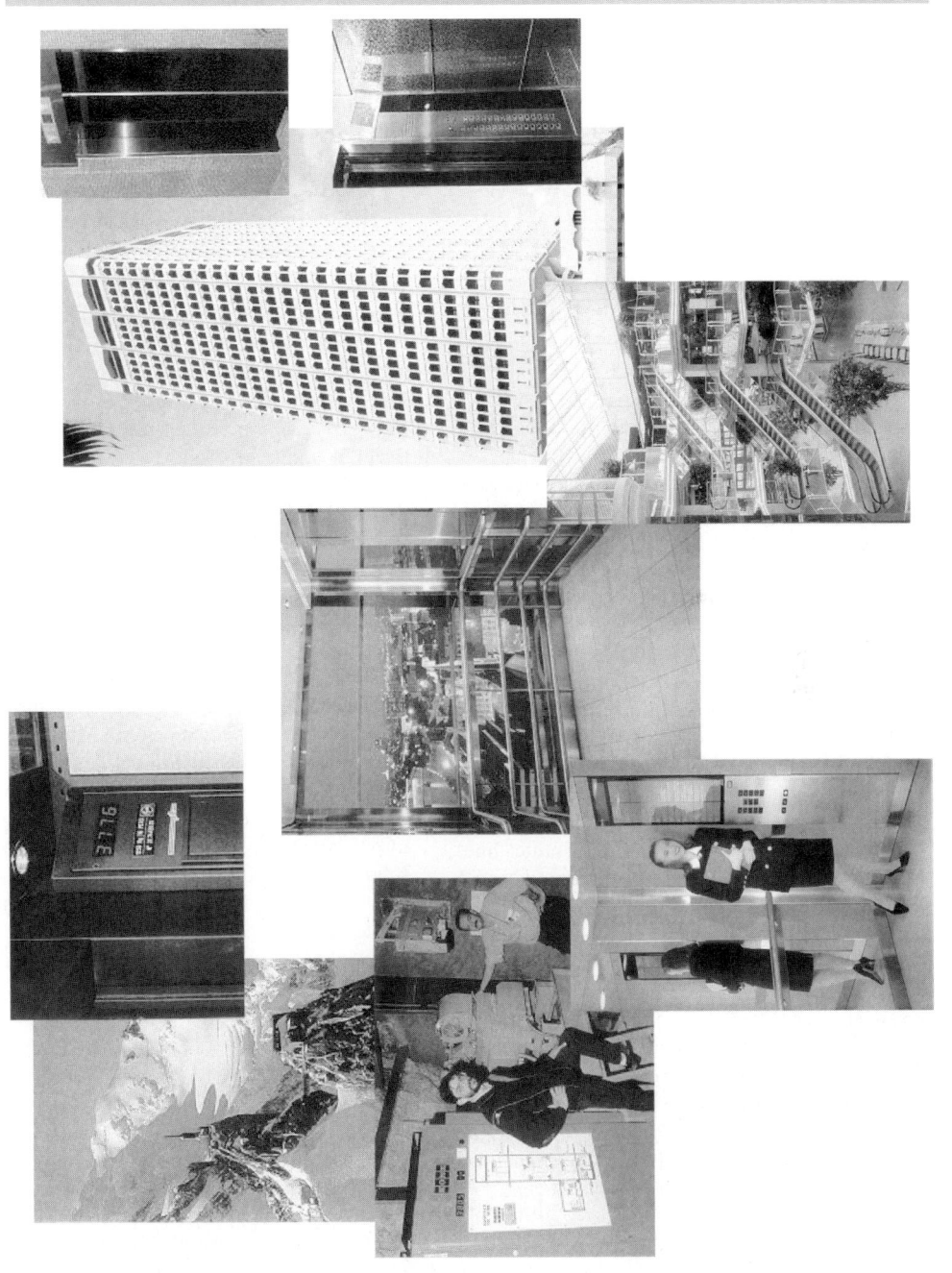

CHAPTER 7 *Building and Managing Value Equity* **287**

EXHIBIT 5 Product Examples

TABLE B   KONE Aufzug Summary Financials (figures in DM 1,000s)

	1993	1994	1995
V1 revenue	88,003	87,876	86,852
V1 profit	−4,328 (4.9%)	−1,886 (2.2%)	−6,300 (7.3%)
V2 revenue	114,718	116,762	118,628
V2 profit	17,140 (14.9%)	18,140 (15.5%)	19,086 (16.1%)
Total revenue	202,594	203,614	215,931
Total profit	15,254	11,840	12,087

machine room was eliminated by placing the EcoDisc machine at the top of the shaft between one of the guide rails and the shaft wall; the entire elevator was thus said to occupy a "Mono"Space. The EcoDisc and MonoSpace are depicted in Exhibit 6.

The EcoDisc power unit also was extremely energy efficient, consuming only half the energy of comparable geared traction, and one-third of the energy required by a comparable hydraulic system. This and lower peak current translated into less-expensive electrical wiring and fuses. Moreover, unlike hydraulic elevators the MonoSpace required no oil, eliminating potential fire and environmental hazards. Its installation time was approximately 190 hours, 60 hours less than for the simplest traditional elevator. (Exhibit 7 compares the different drive systems.)

Theoretically, the EcoDisc was applicable to elevators across KONE's existing product line. But as elevator load and speed increased so did the size of the machine, being eventually too large to fit within the shaft. With current EcoDisc technology a 16-person cabin required a machine room. Consequently, based on the most common cabin sizes KONE engineers had developed MonoSpace systems for 8-person and 13-person elevators with operating speeds of one meter per second that could be used in buildings of 12 floors or less. Concurrently, they were working to extend the capabilities of the EcoDisc machine and the MonoSpace product line.

THE MONOSPACE EXPERIENCE IN EUROPE

KONE had targeted MonoSpace directly at Europe's largest new-equipment market segment, low-rise residential elevators. By the time Hätälä began developing a launch plan for Germany, MonoSpace had been test-marketed in the Netherlands and officially launched, with varying degrees of initial success, in the Netherlands, France, and the United Kingdom. KONE managers selected the Netherlands because the market was dominated by low-rise elevators, KONE was the market leader, and the country's regulatory authorities, being relatively progressive, were likely to view the MonoSpace as a new elevator solution rather than one not in compliance with existing codes.[2]

Market Launches

Although construction was relatively stagnant in the three countries in which the MonoSpace was first officially launched, residential building accounted for roughly half of all construction activity (see Table C for more details on market size and KONE's market share in each country market). Approximately 90% of the units sold in France and 70% of those sold in the United Kingdom and the Netherlands were low-rise elevators.

The U.K. market was unique in being dominated by one-star (low-quality construction) and five-star (high-quality construction) buildings with little in between, driving demand for top-of-the-line and rock-bottom elevators. Many low-

---

[2] Because existing elevator codes had been written for installations with machine rooms, the MonoSpace, by definition, was not in compliance. Efforts were under way to promote EU standards, but the difficulty of modifying regulations varied dramatically from country to country. For example, because elevator regulations were part of Italy's constitution, to change them to allow a "machine-room-less" elevator would require an act of the Italian Parliament.

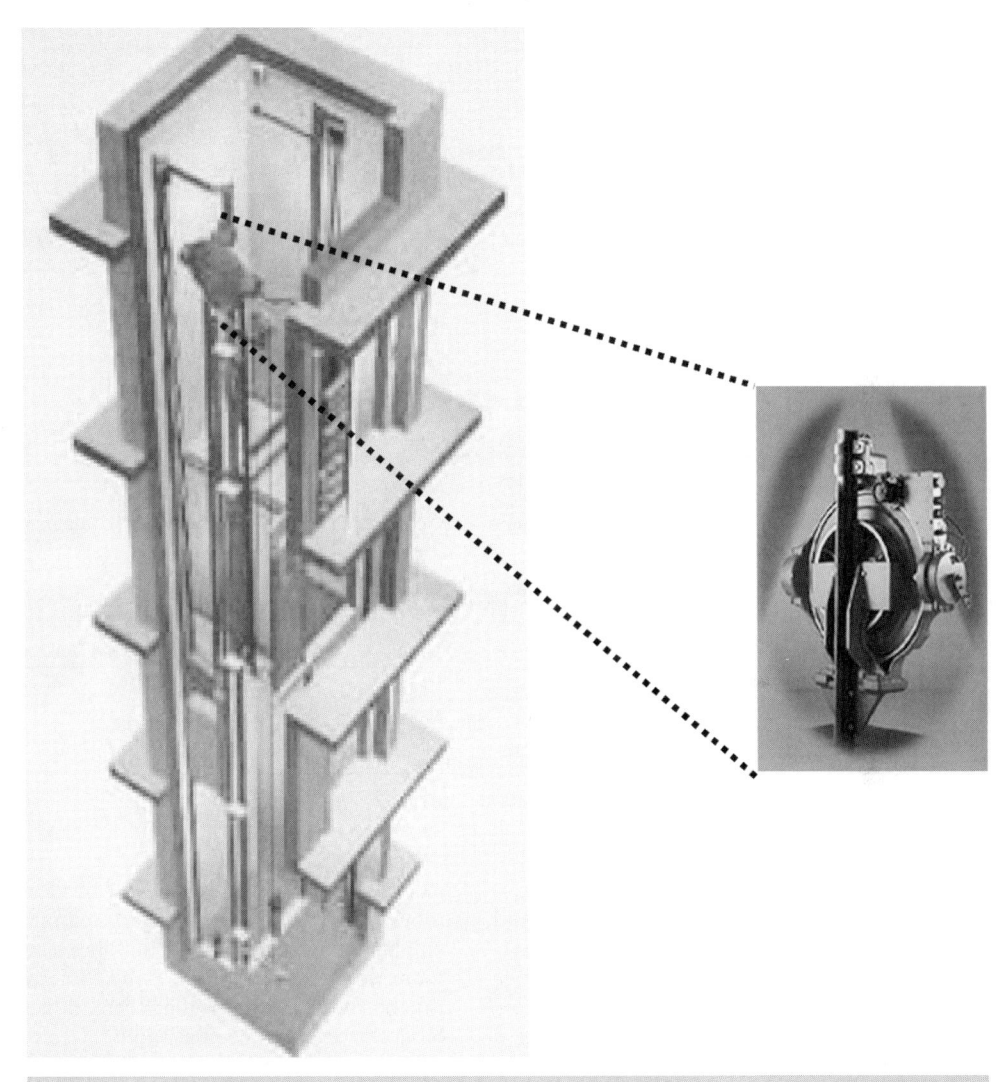

CHAPTER 7 *Building and Managing Value Equity* **289**

EXHIBIT 6 KONE's MonoSpace and EcoDisc

quality residential elevators were installed in the United Kingdom simply to meet regulatory requirements for access, particularly for elderly and handicapped persons. The preponderance of two- and three-star (medium-quality) buildings in France and the Netherlands drove broad demand for mid-range, mid-quality elevators.

Sixty to seventy percent of all elevators sold in the Netherlands were geared traction, a consequence of an anomalous market situation that had led to geared traction type elevators being about 15% less expensive than hydraulic elevators. With substitutable, low-rise geared traction elevators costing nearly twice as much as hydraulic elevators in the United Kingdom, hydraulic elevators accounted for 90%, geared traction elevators only 10%, of low-rise sales in that market. The French market was in-between, with 80% of low-rise elevators hydraulic and the remaining 20% geared traction.

Feature	Hydraulic	Traction	EcoDisc
Speed (mtrs/s)	0.63	1.0	*1.0*
Load (kg)	630	630	*630*
Motor size (kW)	11	5.5	*3.5*
Main fuse size (amp)	50	35	*15*
Energy consumption (kWy)	7,200	5,000	*3,000*
Thermal loss (kW)	4.3	3.0	*1.0*
Oil requirements (Liters)	200	3.5	*0*
Weight (kg)	650	430	*190*
Machine room (m³)	5	12	*0*

EXHIBIT 7 A Comparison of Hydraulic, Traction, and EcoDisc Drive Units

Source: Company records.
Note: kWy—kilo-watt years is a standard measure for comparing energy consumption of equipment.

TABLE C Unit Sales and Market Shares in 1995

	Units	KONE	Otis	Schindler	Thyssen	Others
France	7,000	14%	41%	20%	18%	7%
United Kingdom	3,300	20%	30%	10%	10%	30%
Netherlands	2,100	40%	19%	13%	6%	24%

Source: KONE's Director of Marketing Communications.

Pricing

Given KONE's differentiation and brand building objectives, the MonoSpace was generally priced in line with equivalent (and more expensive) geared traction elevators. Managers at KONE's Brussels headquarters suggested that the MonoSpace be priced above existing prices if KONE held less than 15% market share and in line with existing price levels otherwise (see Table D).

The premiums exacted on the MonoSpace in the Netherlands and France equaled approximately one-half the cost of constructing a machine room. KONE branch managers reasoned that one-half the savings of *not* building a machine room would accrue to either the owner or construction company, motivating them to specify the MonoSpace. In France the MonoSpace's energy costs would be FF5,000 per year less than that of a comparable traction elevator, effectively repaying a FF30,000 premium in six years. The price in the United Kingdom was dictated primarily by the £15,000 transfer price to KONE U.K., which put it near the PT price.

TABLE D Price Levels for KONE Low-Rise Elevators, 1996[a]

	PH (hydraulic)	PT (traction)	PU (traction)	MonoSpace
Netherlands	DG 65,000	DG 62,000	DG 68,000	DG 69,000
France	?	FF 150,000	?	FF 180,000
United Kingdom	£ 15,800	£ 30,000	?	£ 30,750

[a]Average 1995 currency exchange rates were DG 1.60/$1.00, FF 5.0/$1.00, and £ 0.65/$1.00.

Market Strategies

KONE viewed formal launches and articles in national and local specialist building and architectural journals as but a preamble to face-to-face, relationship-based selling, the activity it most relied upon to drive sales. To foster initial market acceptance, the MonoSpace was touted as a new drive system, all other elements of which were identical to other KONE low-rise elevators. The style and scope of KONE's marketing activities varied according to the MonoSpace's projected sales success in the respective markets.

The Netherlands The MonoSpace was marketed in the Netherlands primarily through individual customer meetings. Approximately 3,500 architects, construction companies, owners, and consultants were invited via mailings to compare in one-on-one presentations a working MonoSpace with hydraulic and geared traction lifts. More than 100 such presentations were made within the first year of MonoSpace sales. MonoSpace-related articles published at the rate of approximately one per month subsequent to the launch each generated from 40 to 60 inquiries. Building specifications for the MonoSpace, supplied on disk to enable contractors and architects to "drop" this section into a building's plans, were due to be approved and included on the official Netherlands Building Design CD-ROM, a resource used for most Dutch building designs.

France Letters announcing the MonoSpace to KONE's 22,000 existing French customers requested that they watch a television program that was to include a feature on the elevator. Concurrently, a MonoSpace advertisement was placed in a specialist building newspaper. The main market launch took the form of a series of breakfast meetings held in large cities across the country to which each office invited 20–30 guests, primarily architects, developers, building owners, owners or managers of smaller construction companies, and safety officials. Approximately 20 such breakfasts were held during the first three months of sales. KONE salespeople also made individual on-site presentations at each of the country's six largest construction companies.

The United Kingdom Given the price sensitivity of the U.K. low-rise market, the MonoSpace was launched "to remind people that KONE is a technology leader." The underlying technology rather than low-rise elevator application was emphasized in a series of three presentations made at London's Science Museum. Five hundred construction companies, developers, quantity surveyors, consultants, and architects were invited; of 220 who accepted, 80 attended at least one presentation.

Sales Results

KONE's Netherlands managers projected that MonoSpace would account for 70% of sales, and 100% of the low-rise segment, within three years. MonoSpace reached the 70% target within the first 10 months of official sales and, within one year, controlled 62% of the Netherlands low-rise market (up from 52% the year before) and 43% of the overall Netherlands market (up from 40%). KONE Netherlands was in the odd position of worrying about having gained too much market share and upsetting the market. "We didn't want to conquer the world with this," observed the Netherlands general manager:

> We just wanted to maintain market share and get higher profits. We didn't want to scare the competition, because there is no way for us to eliminate an Otis or a Schindler. We'll have to live with these competitors forever.... Otis could buy KONE for cash . . . and can afford to drop its prices to the point that MonoSpace benefits—not having a machine room, energy savings, and so on—become meaningless.

Sales in France and the United Kingdom contrasted with the success in the Netherlands. Against a first year sales target for MonoSpace of 70% of KONE's annual residential sales (approximately 300 units), only 40 units had been sold in the first three months. In the United Kingdom no units had been sold one month after launch.

Customer reactions and learning points Notable among customers' generally extremely positive reactions to the MonoSpace were the oft heard "At last there is something new in the elevator industry" and "Why didn't you come up with this earlier?" Some aspects of the MonoSpace were more positively received than expected, others generated unanticipated worries. (Exhibit 8 presents a summary of learning points.)

EXHIBIT 8 Learning Points from European Marketing

Sales messages   Construction companies, perhaps owing to their emphasis on initial price, proved the hardest sell. Most of the aspects expected to appeal to construction companies—elimination of the need for a machine room and for scaffolding or a crane and simplified installation processes—either were consequent to there being no machine to be built, a savings that usually accrued to the owner, or were benefits shared by the entire range of low-rise elevators.

Netherlands builders stood to save DG 7,000–DG 8,000 if a machine room already in the budget was not built. Otherwise the builder's savings would be nil. With the low-rise range builders rarely needed scaffolding and used a crane only if it was already on-site. Although less coordination was needed between elevator installer and general builders, such process savings were generally not valued in the Netherlands. One-half day saved in the middle of a building process that took a year was considered inconsequential by construction companies that reasoned that their workers might spend that half day playing cards anyway. In France, however, where union regulations dictated a high degree of coordination among workers and weekly meetings of the *métier* heads, any process compression was valued. The situation was much the same in the United Kingdom.

KONE found that, aggregated, savings from using lower risers, some time/process savings, could amount to 5% for a construction company.

Appeal of energy savings   The MonoSpace's energy savings were not expected to be an important selling point in the Netherlands. Energy suppliers, in particular, however, found that the low-energy consuming MonoSpace didn't dim lights as geared traction or hydraulic elevators sometimes did as a consequence of the power surge required for take-off. The electrical fuses required by the MonoSpace were also much less costly: DG 60 per year for MonoSpace versus DG 1600 per year for hydraulic elevator fuses or DG 800 per year for geared traction elevator fuses. KONE Netherlands found that energy suppliers, an influence group it initially had not targeted, were consequently recommending MonoSpace.

Warning label   Its drive unit and controller being located in the shaft on the top floor, the MonoSpace could not be used in buildings with penthouses (public access was necessary). Because its temperature had to be maintained at between 5°C and 40°C, it was also not suitable for outdoor use. KONE Netherlands discovered that architects had begun designing all their buildings, including those with penthouses and outdoor elevators, for the MonoSpace, that is, sans machine rooms. To avoid repercussions, all publicity for the MonoSpace carried a "warning" explaining these two limitations.

Construction company surcharge   KONE discovered that in both France and the Netherlands some construction companies had retained the machine room savings by exacting a surcharge from the owner/developers. Consequently, all future literature directed to construction companies omitted the cost savings from eliminating the machine room and lower running costs of the MonoSpace.

Single supplier worries   In all three countries, and particularly in the United Kingdom, customers worried that leaving the machine room out of building designs would leave them open to price gauging. Absent other machine-room-less suppliers, customers feared they had to pay whatever KONE asked. KONE countered by emphasizing its interest in long-term partnerships and preserving its reputation.

Example installations   Customers wanted to see an installed MonoSpace before buying and few were willing to be "guinea pigs." This problem was addressed in the Netherlands by installing a working MonoSpace in KONE's Netherlands headquarters.

Competitor reactions Although minor spoiling tactics were encountered, KONE's director of V1 sales remarked that "the competition's reaction was one of stunned silence for the most part." One competitor offered to pay for the machine rooms if customers bought its elevators; another competitor told customers that there was no provision for ventilation with the MonoSpace, which was true, thermal losses being so low that there was no need for ventilation. In France some competitor salespeople told customers that KONE had received approval for only 10 MonoSpace elevator installations, which also was true; government authorities were to review the initial 10 installations and, if they proved acceptable, grant complete approval, standard procedure for the approval of any new technology in France.

PREPARING FOR THE GERMAN MONOSPACE LAUNCH

Pricing for the MonoSpace elevator in Germany had not been set, but production costs were estimated to be about the same as for a comparable hydraulic elevator.

The German Elevator Market

The German construction industry had undergone a cycle of boom and bust since the 1988 reunification of East and West. With the boom in construction the new elevator market grew from 8,000 units in 1988 to a high of 15,500 units in 1995, when the construction boom ended abruptly. Demand for new elevator equipment was now expected to shrink by 15% by the year 2000. The German elevator market was dominated by residential construction. The proportion of elevator units installed in residential buildings in 1995, 74%, was not expected to change significantly over the following five years. In 1995 hydraulic elevators accounted for approximately 60% of the German low-rise elevator market, geared traction elevators making up the rest. Two-thirds of the geared traction units were of the more expensive PU type. Demand for new commercial space, on the other hand, was dampened by significant over capacity.

Competition

The majors The six major players in the German elevator market were Schindler, Otis, Thyssen, KONE, Haushahn, and Schmitt & Sohn (see Table E). All operated throughout Germany and each maintained 24-hour service networks and new elevator sales and installation branches and manufacturing facilities both in Germany and abroad.

The mid-size players Approximately 30 mid-size players, with new equipment sales ranging from 100 to 300 elevators per year, operated regionally, although some of these produced a few key components (e.g., cars), most outsourced manufacturing.

The "cowboys" Small, local companies, termed "cowboys," that usually operated within a single city numbered about 150. Most, lacking internal manufacturing capabilities, were focused on the purchase and assembly of components and installation and local service.

TABLE E German Elevator Industry: 1995 Market Shares

	New Elevator Market Value	New Elevator Market Units	Lifts in Service Units	Total Turnover Value
Schindler	17.7%	19.4%	13.3%	21.1%
Otis	13.8%	11.6%	11.3%	19.4%
Thyssen	15.4%	12.9%	12.4%	18.1%
KONE	8.5%	9.2%	4.9%	6.7%
Haushahn	6.5%	5.8%	6.4%	5.6%
Schmitt & Sohn	5.4%	5.8%	3.3%	4.4%
Others	32.7%	35.5%	48.2%	25.0%

Market Performance

With the abrupt end of Germany's construction boom, new elevator prices fell between 5% and 7% in 1994 and 1995. Many small and some mid-size players responded by abandoning or sharply curtailing efforts to sell new elevator equipment in favor of focusing on service, exerting additional price pressure there as well. Amongst the majors, Schindler's reported losses were approximately 11%, Otis' 13%, of turnover. Further, Schindler had focused during this period on gaining share and become the clear market leader in hydraulic elevators. Otis's professed objective, to eliminate losses in the new elevator business, had caused it to lose market share.

Low-Rise Elevator Customers

Property developers, general contractors, and architects were among those involved in purchase decisions in Germany's low-rise elevator market. Property developers were principally concerned with the overall cost of developing a new building or renovating an existing property and factors that affected the investment value of their properties, including construction quality, timeliness of completion, and operating costs. Because choice of elevator was viewed as having little impact on overall construction costs, KONE and other elevator companies, perceiving property developers to rarely be involved in the decision, seldom communicated directly with them.

For buildings of all types, the general contractors responsible for construction and renovation according to property developers' and architects' plans exerted the greatest influence on elevator purchase. Although the four largest German contractors controlled approximately 20%, the construction market was highly fragmented, with nearly 20,000 small contractors vying for contracts.

Property developers consistently used the bid process, typically inviting bids from three or four, to pressure contractors for price reductions. In turn, contractors often used a competitive bidding process to procure specialized building systems such as steelwork, elevators, and HVAC (heating, ventilation, and air conditioning) systems. Occasionally, a two-stage bidding process was employed whereby contractors would invite "preliminary" bids, as from elevator suppliers, and incorporate a low-price offering into their overall construction bid, then, after the construction contract had been awarded, re-open the process and ask suppliers to resubmit bids. If the property developer and contractor had negotiated an overall price reduction, the contractor would try to pass on similar price reductions to the system suppliers.

Residential buildings were usually built by smaller contractors who, possessing little technical knowledge, often relied on architects to select elevators. Although architects generally did not make the elevator selection for the mid-size hotels and offices that larger contractors usually built, for which the higher end "residential" elevators were typically used, they almost universally selected elevators' cosmetic options (e.g., side- or middle-opening door, interior paneling material and colors, and so forth). KONE managers believed that in the German residential market the final elevator purchase decision was made by the general contractor 50% of the time, by the architect 40% of the time, and by a property developer 10% of the time.

KONE Aufzug's Selling Process

KONE Aufzug's selling process for new equipment had become well established over the years. In most cases (96% of purchases) customers initiated contact by sending elevator specifications and a request for bid to a local KONE branch. KONE being one of the major players, virtually all the customers included the firm in the shortlist of vendors to whom they sent out the request for bid. Thus, KONE had access to the entire demand for elevators in the German market.

Customer inquiries were followed by a visit from a KONE Aufzug salesperson to the customer contact, usually the construction company manager or architect. The salesperson reviewed the architect's drawings, design specifications, and any special requirements and would detail elevator options in the form of a sketch or CAD drawing.

In general, contractors wanted, at the lowest possible price, elevators that fit planned shaft dimensions and required no changes to architectural drawings. Purchase decisions were also influenced by the quality and relevance of the information the customer received, level of service, design of the bid document, and the customer's general impression of the salesperson. Observed one KONE branch manager: "The customer must feel that this salesperson alone is the expert in meeting the customer's needs." Once elevator specifications had been negotiated, a contractor's purchasing manager became the main point of contact and discussion shifted to payment terms and price. From start to finish, the procurement process ran 8–15 months.

Regulatory Approval

Regulatory approval of KONE's new technology was a precondition of the launch of MonoSpace in Germany. To gain regulatory approval, KONE Aufzug approached, in April 1995, the Hanover branch of Technischer Überwachungsverein (TÜV), the governmental body responsible for testing and approving all electrical and mechanical items to be sold in Germany. TÜV also employed 300 inspectors who checked and approved installed elevators. Each German state had its own affiliated TÜV branch, which had to independently approve items to be sold within the state. By January 1996 the MonoSpace had been approved in all German states, but efforts to educate TÜV officials continued. In May 1996 KONE Aufzug invited 50 senior TÜV officials to Frankfurt to view the first MonoSpace pilot installation.

Launch Decisions

Hätälä's pre-launch planning included establishing MonoSpace pilot installations in buildings across KONE Aufzug's three regions. In November 1995 four hydraulic elevator customers were given the option of converting their existing orders to MonoSpace. They were told that they would receive a new, improved drive unit at the previously agreed hydraulic elevator price, but, as the machine rooms for these buildings had already been designed and constructed, not that the MonoSpace technology eliminated the need for a machine room. Between January 1996 and June 1996 two salespeople were charged to arrange 30 more pilot installations. All pilot customers were given the option of switching from geared traction elevators to MonoSpace at no additional cost. The benefits of eliminating the machine room and reduced energy consumption, and the manner in which the roping worked, with an emphasis on feasibility and reliability, were carefully explained. All prospective pilot customers were, however, asked to "keep quiet about the technology."

EXHIBIT 9 Details on the Marketing Kit and Summary of Marketing Resources

The marketing kit developed by KONE's Brussels headquarters included the following components:

- A press kit featuring a CD-ROM and Web site.
- A MonoSpace concept brochure to supplement existing low-rise line literature.
- Two PowerPoint sales presentations, one directed at builders, architects, and owners, the other a technical presentation for consultants and training purposes.
- A 13-minute MonoSpace videotape.
- Trade press releases directed at architects, builders, and property owners/managers.
- Building and planning guides that included dimensional sketches and a front-line CAD rendering of the MonoSpace.
- MonoSpace architectural specifications.
- A total elevator cost comparison form.
- A trade media advertisement on CD-ROM; a set of posters; a sample direct mail piece; a miniature static MonoSpace model.
- A sampling of promotional gifts such as pens and mouse pads.

(Continued)

EXHIBIT 9 (cont.)

The marketing resources available for the MonoSpace launch in Germany included the following:

Advertisements, which appeared mainly in elevator newspapers and journals (national) and architectural newspapers and journals (local and some national), were used primarily by small and mid-size companies. Large elevator companies seldom advertised. Single ads were most common, campaign rare.

Direct mail was targeted by large companies to architects, investors, and general contractors.

Launch events preceded new product introductions. All the large players had used "road shows" between 1993 and 1995. Customers were invited to local hotels for seminars and refreshments and received follow-up telephone calls.

Exhibitions were used mainly by component companies.

Customer visits supported by sales collateral were elevator companies' most common means of communication. Most literature had a technical slant, reflecting the average German customer's technical orientation.

Public relations activities were centered around press releases and press conferences. Otis and Schindler appeared regularly in the national and local press. Other companies generally received notice only in local papers or when something out of the ordinary occurred.

Launch Options

Direct mail — KONE's direct mail experience was limited. Ready-to-mail/fax response cards had achieved response rates of three to four per thousand. A mailing of 30,000 fax response cards, including list purchase and printing, cost DM 60,000.

Road show — The cost of 12 road shows — including two presentations per day, hotel space, catering, travel costs, equipment (portable model eco-disc and car), but excluding internal expenses (e.g., employees' time) — was roughly DM 350,000.

Sales visit — A sales visit usually required 1/2 day of a salesperson's time. Cost of materials and salesperson's time was roughly DM 500.

Video — Dubbing the video into German would cost DM 20,000, each video copy DM 5.

Telemarketing — One 2- to 3 minute telephone call to 30,000 people would cost approximately DM 100,000.

Seminar — For an audience of about 70, hotel space, catering, and the printing and mailing of invitations would cost approximately DM 10,000.

Exhibition/trade show — To appear for three days at "The Konstructor," a large, annual construction industry trade show held in Germany, would cost about DM 300,000. Previously, KONE had found that cost too high relative to the response it had elicited.

Trade press and journal advertising — Germany hosted approximately 25 architectural journals and about 12 building and construction journals.

- A black-and-white, one-page advertisement in a free monthly journal with a circulation of 25,000 would cost about DM 3,000.
- A black-and-white, one-page advertisement in a weekly journal priced DM 3.50 with a circulation of 17,000 would cost DM 2,300.
- A black-and-white, one-page advertisement in a weekly journal with a circulation of 31,000 cost DM 2,700.
- A black-and-white, one-page advertisement in a monthly journal with circulation 18,000 cost DM 1,600.

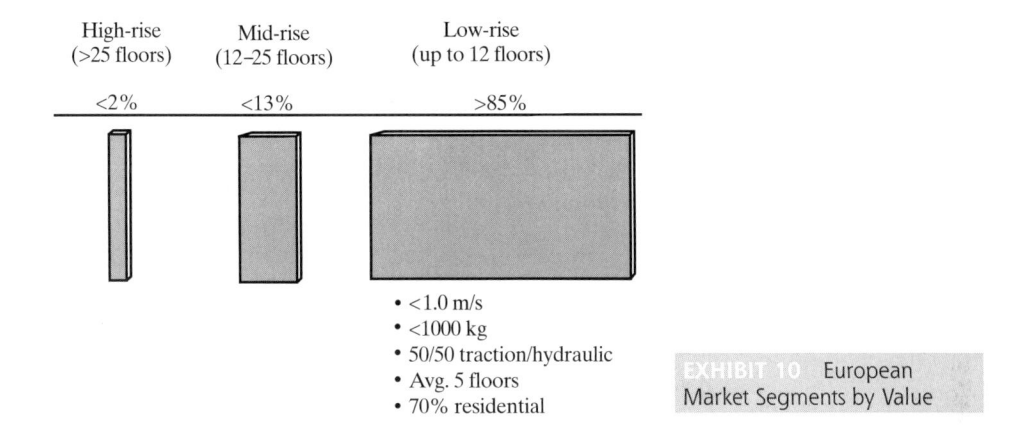

High-rise	Mid-rise	Low-rise
(>25 floors)	(12–25 floors)	(up to 12 floors)
<2%	<13%	>85%

- <1.0 m/s
- <1000 kg
- 50/50 traction/hydraulic
- Avg. 5 floors
- 70% residential

EXHIBIT 10 European Market Segments by Value

Having consolidated his knowledge of the German market and lessons gained in the Netherlands, France, and the United Kingdom, Hätälä was concentrating on selecting the best marketing resources. He had at his disposal a marketing kit that had been developed by KONE's Brussels headquarters included the following components (Exhibit 9 provides details of the marketing kit components and a summary of marketing resources).

Hätälä knew that German elevator companies, particularly KONE's larger competitors, relied on a broad range of marketing communications that included advertising, direct mail, customer and launch events, exhibitions, customer visits, and public relations. He wondered which of these were most appropriate for the launch of MonoSpace.

As he pondered these details, Hätälä recognized that immediate, favorable results from the German launch were vital to KONE. Yet, he had to keep in mind that the pricing and product positioning strategies he set for MonoSpace in Germany would have significant impact on the long-term prospects for KONE. With a lot at stake, he had little room for error. ∎

◆◆◆ **The Medicines Company**

Case 7-2   The Medicines Company

John T. Gourville

"When people first hear our business concept, they think we're crazy," stated Clive Meanwell, the founder, President, and CEO of the Medicines Company. Formed in 1996, the Medicines Company "acquired, developed, and commercialized pharmaceutical products in late stages of development," meaning that it purchased the rights to drugs that other companies had abandoned. As Meanwell explained it:

> We founded our company on the premise that sometimes there is still value in drugs that fail to meet a developer's initial expectations. Companies develop drugs with particular applications, users, price points, and market

---

The case was prepared by Professor John T. Gourville. Copyright © 2001 by the President and Fellows of Harvard College. Harvard Business School Case 502-006.

sizes in mind. When clinical testing calls these expectations into question, companies often halt development. But drugs that seem unprofitable for one application or user group might prove quite profitable for others. Our job is to find such drugs, acquire them at reasonable prices, complete their development, and bring them to market.

By early 2001, this strategy seemed to be working. Four years earlier, the company had acquired the rights to Angiomax, a blood thinning drug or anticoagulant that Biogen had abandoned after $150 million and seven years of development. On December 17, 2000, after completing the required clinical trials, the Medicines Company received United States Food and Drug Administration (FDA) approval to sell the drug for use in conjunction with an artery-clearing procedure known as an angioplasty. Exhibit 1 provides a newspaper account of this drug approval.

In spite of this good news, several issues remained for Meanwell and his management team. The first issue involved pricing. Angiomax was positioned as an alternative to heparin, the most widely used anticoagulant in emergency coronary heart care. The problem was that heparin cost about $2 per dose. While it was clear that the Medicines Company would price Angiomax above heparin, the question was how much above?

The second issue involved the need to develop a product portfolio. Meanwell had long argued that the company's success depended on the development of a drug pipeline. However, the company had run into problems with its second acquisition—a migraine headache drug—and had halted its further development. This setback and Angiomax's recent FDA approval had Meanwell wondering whether there truly was the need for a drug pipeline.

Finally, as a public company, the Medicines Company faced the realities of the stock market. In fact, many investors had expected a sharp stock price increase with the approval of Angiomax. Instead, the company's stock (Nasdaq: MDCO) fell over 25% in the month following FDA approval (see Exhibit 2). This caused some people to question the company's core business strategy.

THE DRUG DEVELOPMENT INDUSTRY[1]

By any measure, prescription drugs were big business. At the manufacturer level, prescription sales in 2000 approached $220 billion worldwide, with growth projected at 10% per year through 2010. The largest market for these drugs was the United States, accounting for 50% of all sales.

The United States also was home to most of the world's major drug companies (see Exhibit 3). The largest of these was Pfizer/Warner-Lambert, with annual drug revenues in excess of $25 billion worldwide and $14 billion domestically. As for profitability, the United States drug industry ranked first among all major industries, with net incomes at almost 20% of revenues in 1999.[2]

In 2000, several trends were impacting the United States drug market. These included:

- **An Aging Population.** In 1999, people aged 65 or over accounted for 15% of the population, but 33% of prescription drug sales in the United States. Between 2000 and 2020, this population was expected to grow from 35 million to 55 million.
- **Increased Price Pressure.** Prescription drugs accounted for 9% of medical expenses in 2000 and were growing at a 20% annual rate. As a result, managed care organizations (which paid for 70% of all prescription drugs) and the government (which paid for 10%) were pressuring drug companies to contain or lower drug prices.
- **The Growth in Generics.** As a rule, a generic drug came to market soon after the patent on a branded drug expired, typically at a price 25% to 75% below the price of the branded drug. Between 2000 and 2010, generic sales were expected to grow from $10 billion to $60 billion as several blockbuster drugs came off patent.

Drug Development

Historically, new drugs were the lifeblood of the pharmaceutical industry—drugs under development at any point in time representing the

---
[1]Much of these data were drawn from S&P's industry survey, "Healthcare: Pharmaceuticals," December 21, 2000.
[2]"Health's Price Tag," *Boston Globe*, March 28, 2001, p. D4.

EXHIBIT 1 Excerpt from the Boston Globe, December 19, 2000

Medicines Co. Receives FDA Approval for Blood Thinner

Drug Up Against Cheaper Heparin

by Naomi Aoki
Globe Staff

Medicines Co. yesterday said it won regulatory approval to market its first product, a blood thinner designed as an alternative to the 85-year-old standard treatment, heparin.

The drug, called Angiomax, was approved by the US Food and Drug Administration for use in an artery-clearing procedure known as angioplasty. The drug was developed to prevent blood clots that can lead to heart attacks.

... Angiomax [is expected to be] significantly more expensive than heparin, which sells at about $10 a vial. But the Cambridge company said data from more than 4,300 patients [showed the drug to be a superior alternative to heparin].

"Obviously, this is a very major milestone for Medicines Co.," said Dr. Clive Meanwell, the company's president and chief executive. "We think it is also a major milestone for the field of interventional cardiology. But most of all, we think it should be significant milestone for patients."

Meanwell also hailed the approval as a confirmation of the young company's business model, based on the idea that there is money to be made off drugs that other companies cast aside.

Since other companies bring the products through the early stages of development, Medicines Co. bears less risk. Still, there is no guarantee that the products—sometimes shelved because of lackluster test results or unresolved developmental problems—will get to market.

In fact, at one time, the deck seemed stacked against Angiomax. The drug was discovered by Biogen Inc., among the nation's oldest and biggest biotechnology companies, but was abandoned after disappointing results from broad-based clinical trials.

Biogen's disappointment became Medicines Co.'s first project. The company licensed the drug from Biogen in 1997...

Jay B. Silverman, a senior biotech analyst with Robertson Stephens Inc. in New York, said he expects Angiomax to perform well against heparin.... The challenge will be to persuade doctors and hospitals to change from heparin to Angiomax, he said, efforts that are already under way.

"That is always the challenge with these hospital products," Meanwell said. "Doctors are appropriately demanding of the data. They want to know how this drug will impact practices and costs."

The company has plans to conduct clinical trials at hundreds of hospitals nationwide to allow doctors to gain hands-on experience with the drug, Meanwell said. It anticipates a series of articles to be published in upcoming issues of independent, peer-reviewed scientific journals.

Meanwell said the company has gathered a team of experienced sales and marketing executives to head the 52-person sales force. And the product will be launched officially next month, after a weeklong educational meeting for the sales staff....

"This approval is about the best Christmas present I could get," Meanwell said. "We're very excited, very relieved, and very grateful."...

Source: The Boston Globe, December 19, 2000, p. C3.

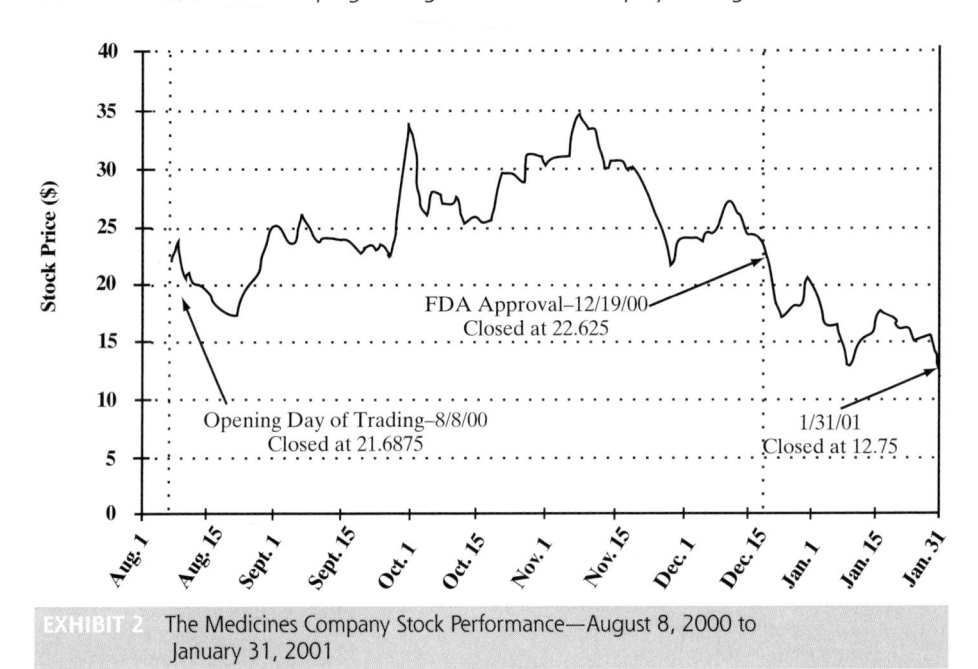

EXHIBIT 2 The Medicines Company Stock Performance—August 8, 2000 to January 31, 2001

Key points on chart:
- Opening Day of Trading—8/8/00, Closed at 21.6875
- FDA Approval—12/19/00, Closed at 22.625
- 1/31/01, Closed at 12.75

Source: Adapted from Web site. http://finance.yahoo.com.

potential blockbuster drugs that would drive the industry 5 to 10 years later. The successful development of a new drug was far from easy, however. Beginning in 1938, the United States FDA required drug developers to follow a complex process designed to prove the safety and effectiveness of any proposed new drug. Accordingly, pharmaceutical firms followed a sequential drug development process:

- In *Pre-Clinical/Animal Trials*, a candidate drug was identified, studied for its chemi-

EXHIBIT 3 Leading Pharmaceutical Companies, Ranked by United States Sales (in millions)[a]

Company (headquarters)	U.S. Sales
Pfizer/Warner-Lambert (U.S.)	$14,607
Glaxo Wellcome/SmithKline (U.K.)[b]	12,490
Merck (U.S.)	10,486
Bristol-Myers Squibb (U.S.)	8,778
Astra/Zeneca (U.K.)	8,304
Johnson & Johnson (U.S.)	7,636
Eli Lilly (U.S.)	6,173
Pharmacia (U.S.)	6,055
American Home Products (U.S.)	5,832
Schering Plough (U.S.)	5,716

[a] For 12 months ending September 30, 2000.
[b] Merger pending.

Source: Standard & Poor's industry survey, "Healthcare: Pharmaceuticals," December 21, 2000.

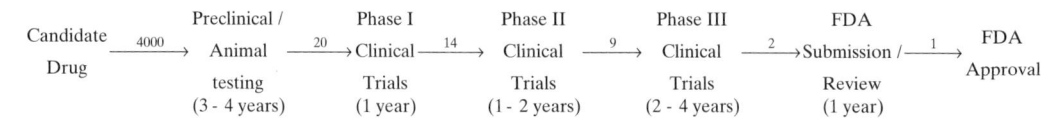

CHAPTER 7 *Building and Managing Value Equity* **301**

Candidate Drug $\xrightarrow{4000}$ Preclinical / Animal testing (3 - 4 years) $\xrightarrow{20}$ Phase I Clinical Trials (1 year) $\xrightarrow{14}$ Phase II Clinical Trials (1 - 2 years) $\xrightarrow{9}$ Phase III Clinical Trials (2 - 4 years) $\xrightarrow{2}$ FDA Submission / Review (1 year) $\xrightarrow{1}$ FDA Approval

FIGURE A Stages of Drug Development (average years in each stage in parentheses)

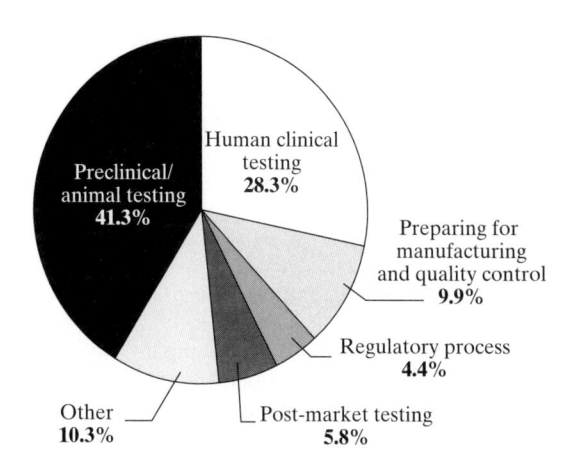

- Preclinical/animal testing 41.3%
- Human clinical testing 28.3%
- Preparing for manufacturing and quality control 9.9%
- Regulatory process 4.4%
- Post-market testing 5.8%
- Other 10.3%

EXHIBIT 4 The Allocation of $26 Billion in Research and Development in 2000

Source: "Health's Price Tag," *Boston Globe*, March 28, 2001, p. D4.

cal properties, and tested on animals to assess safety and effectiveness. Most drugs were eliminated at this stage due to unacceptable side effects or failure to work as expected.
- In *Phase I Clinical Trials*, the drug was given to a small number of healthy people in order to test safety. Initially, small doses were administered, with dosage increased over time to assess safety at higher levels.
- In *Phase II Clinical Trials*, the drug was given to people suffering from the condition that the drug was intended to treat. This stage usually included a larger number of people and a longer period of time than in Phase I.
- *Phase III Clinical Trials* were the most critical of the four stages.[3] They were the largest, most complex, and most rigorous of the human trials, designed to test fully the safety, effectiveness, and dosing levels of the drug on actual patients.
- An *FDA Submission* typically followed a successful Phase III trial. It came in the form of a New Drug Application (NDA) seeking FDA approval for the commercial release of the drug. Each year, the FDA approved about half of all the NDAs it received.

This drug development process was remarkable in several respects. First, as outlined in Figure A, for every drug that received FDA approval, approximately 4,000 candidate drugs began the process. Second, the process took an average of 10 years to complete successfully. Third, the process was capital intensive, with U.S. drug companies spending $26 billion on drug development in 2000 (Exhibit 4 provides a breakdown of how this money was spent). Finally, a company generally applied for (and received) a 20-year patent for a drug it had under development. After completing development, however, only about 10 to 15 years of patent protection remained (for instance, in the

---

[3]Typically, Phase II and Phase III clinical trials were done across several hospitals, with doctors administering the candidate drug to a random sample of patients seeking treatment for the target disease. Quite often, the process was "double-blind," with neither the doctor nor the patient knowing what drug was administered.

Drug (company)	Use	Retail Sales (in millions)
Prilosec (Astra/Zeneca)	Anti-Ulcer	$ 4,187
Lipitor (Warner Lambert)	Cholesterol Reducer	3,002
Prozac (Eli Lilly)	Antidepressant	2,571
Prevacid (TAP)	Anti-Ulcer	2,364
Zocor (Merck)	Cholesterol Reducer	2,301
Epogen (Amgen)	Red Blood Cell Stimulant	1,842
Zoloft (Pfizer)	Antidepressant	1,737
Claritin (Schering Plough)	Antihistamine	1,534
Paxil (SmithKline B\eecham)	Antidepressant	1,516
Zyprexa (Eli Lilly)	Antipsychotic	1,495

EXHIBIT 5 Best-Selling Prescription Drugs in the United States in 1999

Source: Standard & Poor's industry survey, "Healthcare: Pharmaceuticals," December 21, 2000.

United States, the Angiomax patent was due to expire in 2010).

These factors combined to create an industry that relied heavily on "blockbuster drugs"—premium priced breakthrough drugs that generated in excess of $1 billion in sales per year. In 1999, 19 drugs met this threshold in the United States (see Exhibit 5 for the 10 top-selling domestic prescription drugs). Meanwell described this focus on blockbuster drugs in the following fashion:

> In any given year, only about 90 drugs receive FDA approval. Across 40 drug companies, this means that the average drug firm is turning out only one or two new drugs a year—maybe three in a good year. If you are Merck, with over $10 billion in sales and your investors expect 10% growth per year, these one or two drugs have to generate a lot of revenue. A drug that brings in $200 million just won't do it for you.

THE MEDICINES COMPANY HISTORY

The Medicines Company was founded in July 1996 by Meanwell and a small group of investors on the premise that there was opportunity where other companies saw failure. Their corporate strategy was to acquire drugs that were in the late stages of product development but were "undervalued" by their developing companies. Once such drugs were acquired, the Medicines Company planned to complete product development, navigate the regulatory process, and commercialize the drugs in the United States and abroad.

While some questioned the logic of this business model, 15 years of experience in international drug development had convinced Meanwell that such a strategy made sense. As Director of Product Development for Hoffman-LaRoche, one of Europe's largest drug developers, Meanwell had come to believe that drug firms often overreacted to clinical results, sometimes abandoning drugs that still had value. The *Boston Globe* described Meanwell and his company's business strategy as follows:

> You might say Dr. Clive Meanwell is a bit of a scavenger.... After all, he founded a company four years ago based on the idea that there was money to be made off drugs other companies cast aside. His Cambridge start-up ... picks through and rescues products languishing because of lackluster results, shifting corporate priorities, or development problems.[4]

Of course, the first task for Meanwell and his colleagues was deciding what drugs to "rescue." To guide them in their acquisitions, Meanwell and his colleagues looked for drugs that met the following criteria:

---

[4]"The Rescuers," *Boston Globe*, September 13, 2000.

- Required less than four years to get to market.
- Required less than $60 million to get to market.
- Had at least a 65% percent chance of getting to market.
- Had the potential to generate at least $100 million per year in sales.

Beginning in late 1996, the team spent six months reviewing potential acquisitions—starting with 3,000 candidates, quickly weeding those down to 20, and then seriously considering 3 or 4. By early 1997, they had settled on Angiomax, an anti–blood clotting drug that Biogen had been developing as a more effective alternative to heparin, the anti–clotting drug most widely used in the acute treatment of coronary heart disease. In 1994, Biogen had halted development of Angiomax after clinical tests suggested that it was no more effective than heparin. Upon reviewing Biogen's clinical test results, however, Meanwell became convinced that a market still existed for the drug. Thus, in March 1997, the Medicines Company acquired all rights to Angiomax and set out to complete the clinical trials that Biogen had started. Finally, in December 2000, the Medicines Company received FDA approval for the use of Angiomax in the prevention of blood clots during a coronary procedure known as an "angioplasty."

Following a similar screening process, in 1998 the Medicines Company acquired the rights to IS-159, a drug designed to treat acute migraine headaches. And in 1999 it acquired the rights to CTV-05, a drug designed to treat gynecological infections in women of childbearing age.

During its four-year effort, the Medicines Company relied upon two sources of funds. From its inception through mid-2000, the company received approximately $100 million in several rounds of funding from several private equity firms. Then, in August 2000, the company raised $101.4 million (after fees) from an initial public offering of 6,900,000 shares at $16 per share.

Through early 2001, these funds were used almost exclusively to acquire and develop the company's three drugs. In fact, through December 2000, the company had yet to report revenues of any kind (see Exhibit 6). At the same time, the company had close to $100 million in cash and short-term assets to finance the commercial launch of Angiomax and the continued development of its other products (see Exhibit 7).

ANGIOMAX

Without question, Angiomax was the Medicines Company's lead product, representing the company's first attempt at "rescuing" a seemingly failed drug. The specific application for which Angiomax received FDA approval was for the treatment of "high-risk" patients who were undergoing a "balloon angioplasty." A balloon angioplasty was a procedure developed in the 1970s to restore normal blood flow to arteries in the heart that were clogged by a fatty build-up called "plaque." In an angioplasty, a small incision was made in a blood vessel in the groin and a long flexible tube with a deflated balloon was threaded through an artery until it reached the

EXHIBIT 6 The Medicines Company Operating Income—1997 to 2000

	1997	1998	1999	2000
Revenue from operations:	$ 0	$ 0	$ 0	$ 0
Operating expenses:				
Research & development	$16,044,367	$24,004,606	$30,344,892	$39,572,297
Sales, general & administrative	2,420,373	6,248,265	5,008,387	15,033,585
Total operating expenses:	$18,464,740	$30,252,871	$35,353,279	$54,605,882
Loss from operations:	($18,464,740)	($30,252,871)	($35,353,279)	($54,605,882)

Source: Company records.

	1999	2000
Assets:		
Cash, cash equivalents, and marketable securities	$ 7,237,765	$80,718.013
Inventory	0	1,963,491
Fixed assets (net)	430,061	965,832
Other assets	323,572	715,794
Total assets:	$ 7,991,398	$84,363,130
Liabilities and stockholders' equity:		
Current liabilities	$11,495,321	$15,124,147
Long-term liabilities	91,053,732	0
Stockholder's equity (deficit)	(94,557,655)	69,238,983
Total liabilities and stockholders' equity:	$ 7,991,398	$84,363,130

EXHIBIT 7 The Medicines Company Balance Sheet — 1999 and 2000 (FY ending December 31)

Source: Company records.

clogged artery in the heart. The balloon was then inflated, compacting the plaque against the artery wall and opening the artery to increased blood flow.[5]

Sometimes, this procedure would lead to the formation of an unwanted blood clot in the area of the angioplasty. This blood clot had the potential to re-clog the artery, leading to chest pains and a possible heart attack. Angiomax was designed to reduce the likelihood that such a clot would form.

Coronary Heart Disease

Through the late twentieth century, coronary heart disease was the leading cause of death in the United States, accounting for 1 in every 5 deaths. It involved the narrowing of the arteries of the heart due to the gradual build-up of plaque on the inside of the artery walls. Over time, this build-up would narrow the artery and reduce the flow of blood and oxygen to the heart muscle, often resulting in chest pains following physical exertion. This type of pain was called "stable angina."

Sometimes, a portion of the built-up plaque would tear or break off, triggered the rapid formation of a blood clot at the site of the tear. This blood clot would further reduce the flow of blood to the heart, causing steadier and more intense chest pains called "unstable angina." In extreme cases, the blood clot would completely cut off the blood supply to the heart and cause a "heart attack." If the blood supply were cut off for a long enough period of time, the cells of the heart would die, leading to permanent disability or death.

By the late 1990s, an estimated 14 million Americans had some form of coronary heart disease, 7 million of whom suffered from stable angina. Of these, about 1.5 million experienced unstable angina each year, another 1.1 million suffered a full-blown heart attack, and close to 500,000 died.

While patients suffering from stable angina were treated with a regimen of diet, exercise, and a variety of slow-acting drugs, patients with unstable angina or full-blown heart attacks required emergency care. Typically, such patients immediately received a combination of several fast-acting drugs, including TPA, which was meant to break apart the clot that had formed, and an "anticoagulant," which was meant to prevent a new clot from forming.

---

[5]In about 65% of cases, in addition to the angioplasty, a small metal mesh tube called a "stent" was threaded through the artery and placed at the site of the blockage. This tube was meant to permanently prop open the artery to restore blood flow.

Shortly after this initial treatment, most emergency care patients underwent either a balloon angioplasty or coronary artery bypass surgery (CABG), which involved surgically replacing the clogged coronary arteries with healthy blood vessels taken from the patient's leg. In 1999, roughly 700,000 angioplasties and 400,000 CABGs were performed in the United States. Both types of operations had the potential to further disrupt arterial plaque, leading to the formation of a new blood clot. Therefore, anticoagulants also were widely administered to prevent blood clots from forming before, during, and after these procedures.

Heparin

By far, the most widely prescribed anticoagulant in acute coronary heart treatment was heparin. Discovered in 1916, heparin was initially used to prevent the coagulation of blood samples drawn from patients. By the 1990s, however, it was the primary drug used to prevent unwanted blood clots from forming as the result of unstable angina, heart attacks, and coronary surgery. Having never been subject to patent protection, heparin was viewed as a commodity drug and sold by many different manufacturers at about $2 per vial. As reflected in Table A, Meanwell estimated that about 3.5 million coronary care patients received heparin each year to prevent unwanted blood clots.

Despite its almost universal use, heparin was not without it shortcomings, however, as Meanwell was quick to point out. These included:

- **Unpredictability.** Both within and across patients, the anti-clotting effect of heparin was unpredictable. Its use required very close monitoring.
- **High Risk of Bleeding.** Some patients who received heparin had a high incidence of uncontrolled bleeding.
- **Adverse Reaction.** In 2% to 3% of patients, heparin caused a sometimes fatal immune reaction called "heparin-induced thrombocytopenia" or HIT.

These shortcomings led some medical experts to question the ongoing use of heparin. As one cardiologist pointed out:

> Heparin is easy to use, but difficult to use properly. Its effectiveness depends on achieving a certain degree of anticoagulation in the blood. Too much anticoagulation and the patient can suffer from uncontrolled bleeding. Too little anticoagulation and you might not prevent a blood clot. But that window of proper dosing differs across patients and across time. As a result, you need to monitor the patient very closely. Making the problem more complex, it takes several hours for the effects of heparin to kick in and wear off. This means that you might have to wait three or four hours to see if a given dose of heparin has the desired effect.[6]

To assess the prevalence of this viewpoint, the Medicines Company conducted a random survey of 90 leading interventional cardiologists (the doctors who perform angioplasties) that asked them to rate their satisfaction with heparin. Results of this survey are shown in Figure B.

---

[6]Reflects comments obtained from a cardiologist in interviews conducted by the Medicines Company.

TABLE A Heparin Use Across Treatments

Treatment	# of Patients per Year Receiving Drug
Unstable angina (i.e., elevated chest pains)	1,300,000
Heart attack	1,000,000
Balloon angioplasty	700,000
Coronary artery bypass surgery	400,000
Other	100,000

Source: Medicines Company estimates.

4% (3) 3% (10)
5% (4) 6% (9)
13% (5)
24% (8)
16% (6)
29% (7)

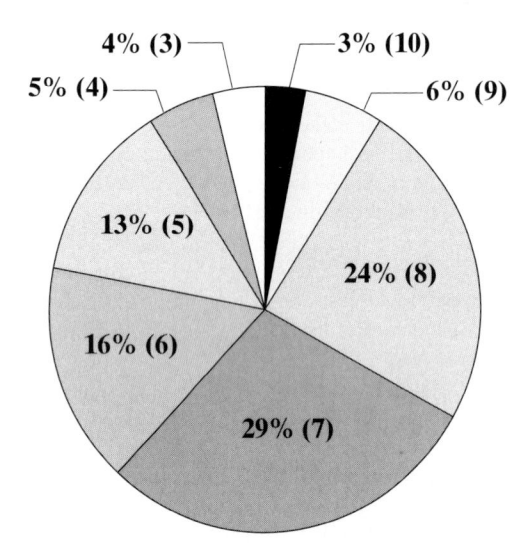

Responses to the Question:

Using a 10-point satisfaction rating scale, please rate your overall satisfaction with heparin as an anticoagulant when administered during a balloon angioplasty procedure. (1 = Not at all satisfied; 10 = Extremely satisfied)

Numbers indicate the percentage of doctors reporting the rating shown in parentheses.

FIGURE B Overall Satisfaction with Heparin Among Interventional Cardiologists

Source: Company Records.

Biogen's Angiomax: A Replacement for Heparin

Angiomax began its life in the mid-1980s in the laboratories of Biogen. Biogen's insight into Angiomax began with the observation that certain animals, such as leeches, drew blood from their victims without triggering the victim's blood clotting process. Armed with this insight, Biogen isolated the chemicals in leech saliva that caused this anti-clotting response. Once isolated, Biogen was able to reproduce it using recombinant technologies.

As initially conceived, Angiomax was to replace heparin for use during angioplasties. According to Meanwell, Biogen expected the typical angioplasty patient to require about four doses of the drug. Longer term, Biogen hoped Angiomax would replace heparin in almost all applications.

Over the next seven years, Biogen spent $150 million bringing Angiomax through to Phase III trials. In 1994, however, Biogen came to two unsettling conclusions. First, its Phase III clinical trial involving "high-risk" angioplasty patients suggested that Angiomax was only slightly better than heparin at preventing blood clots. Second, given the complexity of the drug, Biogen expected that it would cost $100 per dose to produce Angiomax. In an industry where the typical "price" to "cost of goods sold" ratio was 10 to 1, this implied a selling price of $1,000 per dose. Reluctantly, Biogen halted development of Angiomax, concluding that its benefits did not justify such a price. Meanwell described Biogen's decision as follows:

In 1994, Biogen was at a bit of a crossroads. To that point, they had licensed products to other drug companies. But, in the summer of '94, they had two drugs in Phase III trials—their first attempts to bring a product to market. One was Angiomax. The other was Avonex, a drug to treat multiple sclerosis. In July, the Phase III Avonex study showed very promising results. Then, in

TABLE B Phase III Results for "High-Risk" Patients Undergoing an Angioplasty

Outcome Within 7 Days of treatment (number of patients in condition)	Heparin (2,151)	Angiomax (2,161)
Death	0.2%	0.2%
Heart attack	4.2%	3.3%
Need for a repeat angioplasty	2.8%	2.5%
Experienced major bleeding	9.3%	3.5%

Source: The Medicines Company.

September, the Phase III Angiomax study showed mixed results. As a result, Biogen decided to pour its resources into Avonex and to shelve Angiomax. In the end, this may have been the right decision. Biogen received FDA approval for Avonex in 1996 and quickly turned it into the world's best-selling multiple sclerosis drug. In 2000, they sold over $750 million worth of Avonex.

The Decision to Acquire Angiomax

Following its decision to shelve Angiomax, Biogen actively "shopped" the drug to other biotech and pharmaceutical firms in the hopes that one would acquire or license the drug. One such firm was Hoffman-LaRoche, where Meanwell was head of drug development. While he decided not to pursue Angiomax, two things struck Meanwell about the drug. First, although the drug was not as effective as Biogen would have liked, it still was more effective than heparin. Second, if the cost to produce the drug could be reduced by half, the economics became attractive.

Several years later, Angiomax once again came across Meanwell's radar screen as the Medicines Company searched for its first acquisition. Remembering his initial impressions of the drug, the team re-analyzed Biogen's Phase III results. These results are shown in Table B. Biogen's study had involved 4,312 "high-risk" angioplasty patients, with half receiving Angiomax and half receiving heparin. For this study, patients were defined as "high-risk" if they had previously had a heart attack or if they were admitted to the hospital because of unstable angina. On average, such "high-risk" patients accounted for about 50% of all angioplasty patients.[7]

In addition, the Medicines Company found that for a particular sub-group of "high-risk" patient—those who had experienced a heart attack in the two weeks immediately preceding the angioplasty—the benefits of Angiomax were more pronounced. Table C provides a comparison of heparin and Angiomax for these "very high risk" patients. On average, these patients represented 20% of the high-risk patients (or 10% of all angioplasty patients).

When asked to account for these results, Meanwell noted that Angiomax did not have

---
[7]For the remaining 50% of angioplasty patients—i.e., "low risk" patients—Meanwell estimated that the relative benefits of Angiomax over heparin were about half as great as those shown in Table B.

TABLE C Phase III Results for "Very High-Risk" Patients

Outcome Within 7 Days of Treatment (number of patients in condition)	Heparin (372)	Angiomax (369)
Death	0.5%	0.0%
Heart attack	5.6%	3.0%
Need for a repeat angioplasty	3.5%	2.4%
Experienced major bleeding	11.8%	2.4%

Source: The Medicines Company.

many of the drawbacks that heparin had. Specifically, he noted:

> Unlike heparin, the effects of a dose of Angiomax are very exacting and very crisp. Physicians who use Angiomax have been pleasantly surprised by how predictable their results are, which is important in an acute care setting where you are trying to minimize uncertainty. Second, the product works better among patients at risk for bleeding, where heparin often proves problematic. Third, the product works faster than heparin. Instead of taking 2 to 3 hours to take full effect, Angiomax only takes 30 minutes. Finally, there is no immune reaction to Angiomax, so you don't have to worry about unexpected reactions to the drug. These benefits seem to have the greatest impact for the very high-risk patients.

Based on their re-analyses, Meanwell and his colleagues agreed to acquire all rights to the drug's formulation, its manufacturing specifications, and its clinical trial results. These clinical trial results included the Phase III results for angioplasty, but also included Phase II results for studies looking at the impact of Angiomax in the treatment of heart attack, unstable angina, and heparin-induced thrombocytopenia (HIT).

The cost of this acquisition was an upfront fee of $2 million, a commitment to invest another $28 million in the continued development of the product, and a future royalty that started at 6% of sales and rose to 20% of sales as sales volumes increased.

BRINGING ANGIOMAX TO MARKET

Upon acquiring Angiomax in 1997, the Medicines Company set out to address several issues. First, the company conducted a confirmatory clinical study using "high-risk" angioplasty patients, obtaining results similar to those shown in Table B. On the combined strength of Biogen's initial studies and this confirmatory study, the Medicines Company submitted a New Drug Application (NDA) in early 2000 and on December 17, 2000, obtained FDA approval to market Angiomax for use in "high-risk patients undergoing a balloon angioplasty." Meanwell estimated that the Medicines Company spent a total of $12 million in finishing these clinical trials and gaining FDA approval.

The second thing that the company did was to focus on bringing down the cost of using Angiomax. This was accomplished in two ways. First, rather than four doses of Angiomax, further clinical testing revealed that about 70% of angioplasty patients would require a single dose, with the other 30% requiring two or three doses. Second, in 1999 the Medicines Company contracted out production of Angiomax to UCB Bioproducts, with the understanding that UCB would attempt to develop a second-generation manufacturing process to bring down the cost of production. The Medicines Company contributed almost $10 million to this development effort. The result was a new production process that reduced the "cost of goods sold" from $100 per dose to about $40 per dose.

The third thing the company did was to push forward on the other Angiomax clinical trials. In particular, it undertook additional studies to confirm the benefits of Angiomax (1) for patients experiencing heart attacks and unstable angina, (2) for patients at risk for HIT, and (3) for patients undergoing coronary artery bypass surgery. By early 2001, the company had five sets of clinical trials either completed or under way, as reflected in Exhibit 8.

The Marketing of Angiomax

Making the case for Angiomax As it became apparent that Angiomax would gain FDA approval, the company's next big task was to establish a "going to market" strategy for the drug. As part of this strategy, the company hired Dr. Stephanie Plent as Senior Director of Medical Policy. Part of Plent's job was to communicate the benefits of Angiomax to cardiologists and hospital administrators. She explained these benefits in the following fashion:

> When a hospital performs an angioplasty on a patient covered by insurance, it is reimbursed at a pre-determined rate. Currently, that rate is $11,500. In most cases, this more than covers the cost of the procedure—an angioplasty with no complications costs a hospital about $9,500 to perform.
>
> In a small percentage of cases, however, complications do arise. But insurance

CHAPTER 7 *Building and Managing Value Equity*

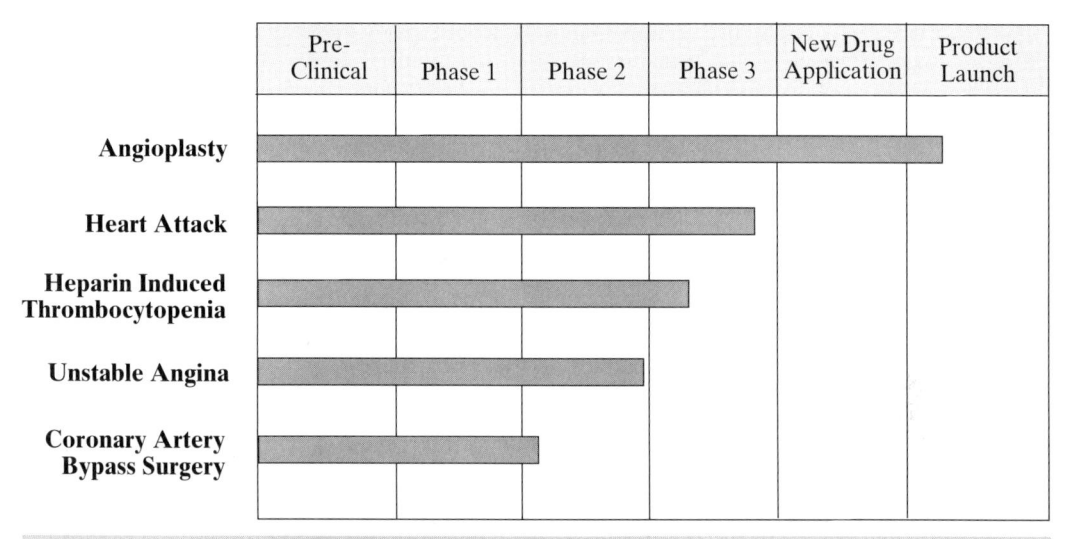

	Pre-Clinical	Phase 1	Phase 2	Phase 3	New Drug Application	Product Launch
Angioplasty	██
Heart Attack	██████████████████████████████
Heparin Induced Thrombocytopenia	████████████████████████
Unstable Angina	██████████████████████
Coronary Artery Bypass Surgery	██████████

EXHIBIT 8   Status of Angiomax Clinical Trials

Source: The Medicines Company 2000 Annual Report.

companies do not reimburse the cost of these complications. Instead, hospitals are forced to absorb these added expenses. On average, a hospital incurs an additional $8,000 to treat a person who has a heart attack, requires a repeat angioplasty, or experiences major bleeding. These added costs are largely due to the fact that the patient's hospital stay is extended by four or five days. Even a death costs the hospital an additional $8,000. Angiomax helps avoid some of these costs.

At the same time, Plent noted that this message had a different impact on the various members of the hospital staff. She pointed out that there were three major groups that influenced the purchase and use of any new drug: (1) the doctor who would use the drug, (2) the hospital pharmacist who would carry the drug, and (3) the hospital administrator who would approve the drug for ongoing use within the hospital. Each of these groups had a different set of incentives, as Plent pointed out:

Selling a premium-priced new drug into a hospital is a tricky process. First, there are the doctors. You have to convince them that the drug works. They are not concerned with price so much as they are with results. Next, there are the hospital pharmacists. They have an annual budget for all the drugs they dispense and are rewarded for meeting or beating that budget. Replacing a widely used $10 drug with a $100 drug really kills that budget. Unless they can justify the cost of the new drug to the hospital administrators and get the added expense incorporated into their budgets, it is unlikely they will carry it. Finally, there are the hospital administrators. They take the big picture into account—does this drug make economic sense? Unfortunately, drug companies rarely have direct access to these administrators. Rather, we have to work through the doctors and the pharmacists and get them to push for the drug.

Assembling a sales force   The task of selling Angiomax into this complex network of hospital personnel fell to Tom Quinn, Vice President of Sales and Marketing. It was Quinn's job to assemble a sales force, promote the use of Angiomax, and ramp up sales over time.

According to Quinn's analysis, 1,300 medical centers around the country performed angioplasties, with the typical center staffed by 5 to 20 interventional cardiologists. Across these 1,300 centers, Quinn decided to focus on those 700 centers that were responsible for 92% of all angioplasty procedures. These 700 angioplasty centers were divided into five sales regions.

To service each of these five regions, Quinn hired a regional manager and outsourced to a marketing services firm for 10 to 15 account reps. Quinn explained his thinking behind this approach:

> When we looked at what we needed to do, we realized we needed people with existing relationships within the acute coronary care community. Also, we wanted to ramp up rapidly. The answer was Innovex, a marketing services firm. They provided us with fully dedicated sales people with an average of 5 years of sales experience and with existing relationships with the doctors and pharmacists we wanted to reach. As for our regional managers, we hired them as Medicines Company employees to retain control and to create stability over time.

Quinn was also responsible for educating the marketplace. This included publication of academic journal articles, presentations at trade shows, and the advertising of Angiomax in medical journals. Beginning in the fall of 2000, for instance, Quinn's marketing department started drawing attention to the shortcomings of heparin. Such an approach was made necessary by FDA regulations that forbade the marketing of a drug that was not yet approved for use. Therefore, at medical trade shows and in medical journals in October, November, and December, the company presented material designed to get doctors to question the safety of heparin. One such bit of material was an academic article on the "deficiencies of heparin" that appeared in the *Journal of Invasive Cardiology*. Once Angiomax was approved, the company followed with trade show presentations, journal articles, and advertisements in medical journals identifying Angiomax as the preferred alternative to heparin. Exhibit 9 provides an example of one such ad.

Finally, Quinn sought to create advocates within the medical community. Through early 2001, the company sponsored four weekend getaways for thought leaders (and their families) in the cardiology community. These invitees were handpicked by the sales force and included 400 cardiologists, 75 nurses, and 30 pharmacists. Over the course of two days, they would participate in about eight hours of presentations designed to educate them on the company and the product. Quinn estimated that the Medicines Company spent about $3 million on these efforts.

OTHER DRUGS UNDER DEVELOPMENT BY THE MEDICINES COMPANY

In addition to Angiomax, the Medicines Company had acquired two other "abandoned" drugs. In July 1998, the company acquired the rights to IS-159, a nasal spray designed to treat acute migraine headaches. And in August 1999, it acquired the rights to CTV-05, a drug designed to treat gynecological infections in women of childbearing age.

IS-159

Acquired from Immunotech S.A. of France, IS 159 was an acute migraine drug in Phase II trials that promised rapid absorption into the bloodstream. Under the acquisition agreement, the company paid an up-front fee of $1 million, was obligated to pay an additional $4.5 million upon reaching certain development milestones, and would pay a 5% royalty on sales upon commercialization of the product. At the time of the acquisition, Meanwell noted that the drug had shown promise in its Phase II trials, offering "an impressively rapid onset of action and a convenient form of administration." At that time, Meanwell estimated the migraine drug market to be about $2 billion.

By mid-1999, however, development of IS-159 had been halted by the Medicines Company. After spending an additional $6 million in clinical trials, the company had run into problems with the drug's formulation. Specifically, for the nasal spray to be absorbed into the bloodstream, an additive was needed. The additive being used was "modified coconut oil." However, while modified coconut oil had gained FDA approval as an additive in oral medications, it had not yet gained FDA approval as an additive in nasal medications. As a result, the company faced the daunting task of either finding a new additive or conducting clinical trials to show the safety and effectiveness of coconut oil as a nasal additive. Meanwell estimated that either course of action would cost as much as $30 million and take five years.

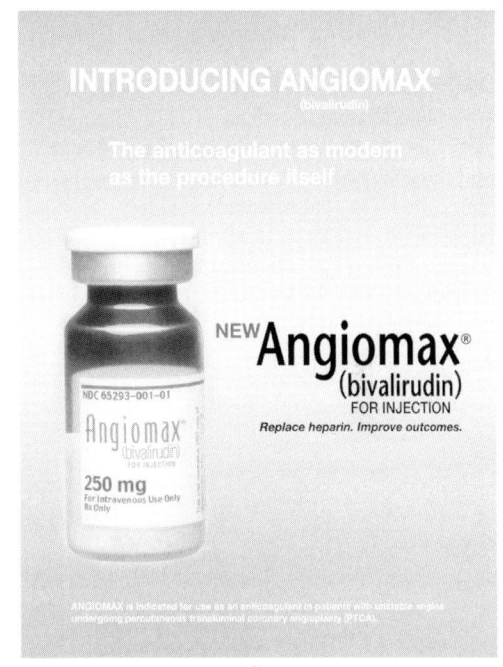

Exhibit 9 An Example of a Two-Page Angiomax Ad—January 2001

Source: Company documents.

CTV-05

With Angiomax looking like it would gain FDA approval, the failure of IS-159 in mid-1999 presented a problem. With plans to go public in the near future, all parties felt that it was critical to have a second drug under development to avoid the appearance that the company was a one-drug enterprise. IS-159 was supposed to have been that other drug. With its failure, the company was forced to "rescue" some other drug that was underappreciated.

That drug turned out to be CTV-05, a drug designed to treat bacterial vaginosis (BV), an infection that was common in women of childbearing age. By one estimate, 10% to 15% of college-age women suffered from BV, which often resulted in premature termination of pregnancies and in low-birth-weight babies. Under the terms of the acquisition, the Medicines Company obtained worldwide rights to the drug for an up-front fee of $1 million and future royalties of about 5%.

Upon reflection, Meanwell noted that the company's acquisition of CTV-05 was quite different from the company's earlier acquisitions. As he pointed out:

> With Angiomax, we knew the drug worked. Even with IS-159, we knew the drug worked—we just hadn't anticipated problems with its formulation. With CTV-05, we were "taking a bit of a flier." We needed another drug under development, but there were no obvious alternatives. We didn't know if CTV-05 worked—it was only in Phase I trials—but we knew we could get it at low cost. So far, we have been happy with the results. We have invested about $4 million and we are currently completing Phase II trials. What started out as a high-risk investment is showing a lot of promise.

LOOKING AHEAD

Moving forward, Meanwell knew that he and his colleagues had several decisions to make. First, they had to decide on the pricing of Angiomax. On the one hand, he felt that the product warranted a vast premium over heparin. On the other hand, he knew that replacing a widely accepted $2 drug with *any* drug costing many times more would raise a few eyebrows. Second, he had to decide whether the business strategy that brought the company to this point still made sense moving into the future. In particular, while a productive "drug pipeline" would be a nice thing to have, was it essential? Finally, Meanwell wondered how success with Angiomax would change the company and its underlying business model.

For the moment, however, Meanwell and his colleagues enjoyed the feeling of having "rescued" a drug with the potential to make a difference in people's lives. ∎

CHAPTER 8

Managing Relationship Equity[1]

There are two parts to managing relationship equity. The first is understanding and managing the evolution of a single relationship. The second is the management of a portfolio of relationships that are of different types and at different stages in their evolution. In this chapter, we will consider both of these sequentially.

◆ DIFFERENT APPROACHES TO MANAGING A CUSTOMER RELATIONSHIP OVER TIME

Buyer–seller relationships can typically be arrayed along a spectrum bounded at one end by dyads focused on a single transaction and at the other by collaborative relationships, or partnerships.[2]

In transactional relationships, each firm attempts to maximize its return in each transaction. What each "gets" in a transaction comes at the expense of what the other "gives," the rule of a zero-sum game. More commonly, vendors (and customers) look beyond single transactions and need to plan their actions accordingly.

FOOT-IN-THE-DOOR APPROACH

To plan a customer relationship strategy presupposes an understanding of customer potential. A vendor's ultimate objective is to try to capture all the dollars a customer can potentially spend as early as possible (curve 1 in Figure 8-1). A customer with little or no experience with a product is unlikely to exhibit such behavior, however. Customers prefer to evaluate products and vendor capabilities prior to committing to a purchase. This

---

[1]This note is based on Das Narayandas, "Customer Migration and Customer Types," Harvard Business School Note #503-072 (2003); and Das Narayandas, "Managing a Customer Relationship over Time," Harvard Business School Note #503-071 (2003).
[2]See James C. Anderson and James A. Narus, "Partnering as a Focused Market Strategy," *California Management Review* 33, no. 3 (Spring 1991): 95–113; and Jagdish N. Sheth and Atul Parvatiyar, "Relationship Marketing in Consumer Markets: Antecedents and Consequences," *Journal of the Academy of Marketing Science* 23, no. 4 (1995): 255–71; Robert A. Peterson, "Relationship Marketing and the Consumer," *Journal of the Academy of Marketing Science* 23, no. 4 (1995): 278–81; C.B. Bhattacharya and Ruth N. Bolton, "Relationship Marketing in Mass Markets," in *Handbook of Relationship Marketing*, 327–54 ed. Jagdish N. Sheth and Atul Parvatiyar (Thousand Oaks, Calif.: Sage Publications, 2000); and Robert M. Morgan and Shelby D. Hunt, "The Commitment-Trust Theory of Relationship Marketing," *Journal of Marketing* 58, no. 3 (1994): 20–38.

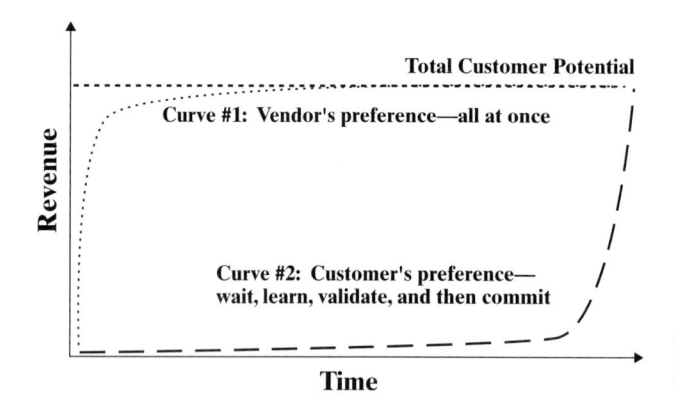

314 PART II *Developing Strategies for Customer Equity Management*

FIGURE 8-1 Achieving Total Customer Potential

behavior yields a revenue trajectory that resembles curve 2 in Figure 8-1, which plots extensive investments over an extended period, during which little or no revenue is earned from customers.

That curves 1 and 2 are incompatible inevitably leads to adversarial relationships in which one party stands to gain only at the expense or forbearance of the other. For example, a vendor might be powerful enough to insist that customers purchase an entire bundle up front or a customer who is a large-volume purchaser may be capable of demanding extensive vendor compliance without reward.

Breaking down the total offering into multiple, independent components constitutes a foot-in-the-door (FITD) or Trojan horse approach. The first component sold becomes the proverbial "foot in the door." A vendor's revenue trajectory from this approach might resemble that in Figure 8-2.

Although the size of the first sale is relatively small, the time and effort required to close the sale are less and the probability of closing the sale is greater, which together have the potential to translate into customer profitability at a much earlier stage.

Characteristics of an FITD Product

The selection of an appropriate FITD product is critical to successful execution of the approach. An ideal product satisfies several criteria:

- It must mitigate customer risk, that is, be inexpensive enough for the customer to purchase it without hesitation.

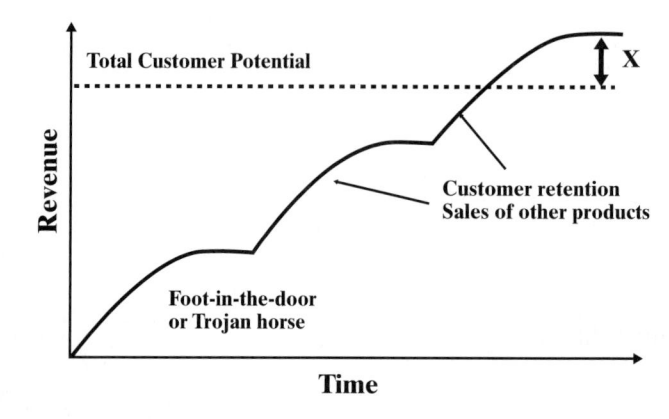

FIGURE 8-2 Foot-in-the-Door Approach

- The fit between product functionality and customer needs must be exceedingly close.
- Product quality should be impeccable, with no chance of failure.
- A highly visible customer problem must be solved in a unique way to enable the vendor not only to build credibility, but also to forestall competitive entry at a late date. To choose, for example, a high-quality FITD product that solves a minor customer problem risks squandering excellent performance for want of an opportunity to truly impress the customer.
- Because a positive experience with an FITD product should leave a customer eager to do more business with the vendor, a progression path for future sales in the relationship should be clearly laid out. There needs to be a clear link between the FITD product and other products subsequently sold by the vendor. This is the concept of modularity.[3]

Examples of the FITD Approach

Siebel Systems, a supplier of sales force automation products, has successfully used the FITD approach. Having established a foothold in a customer account, it offers call center (service automation) products. When the e-commerce wave swept the business world, Siebel expanded its product line to enable its customers to become e-businesses. More recently, the firm has added other products and created a new line of products that enables customers to manage their end customers and suppliers. Siebel is a classic example of how eventual sales might far exceed initially perceived customer potential.[4]

An example of how the FITD approach can be used as a competitive weapon to break into a competitor's customer base is provided by an international insurance provider that was trying to break into a new country market with a line of risk management products. When it tried to sell its entire product line, the company encountered enormous resistance from prospects unwilling to completely switch from their current vendors. To counter this, the firm adopted an FITD approach, picking a product that historically had a high claim rate but not very high claim value. Customers were more willing to try just one product, and competitors, interestingly, were not unduly concerned about losing a small part of their business to a new entrant that they believed was destined to fail (in fact, it is historically rare for customers to buy their entire bundles from one vendor). Customers are able to judge the quality of insurance service only when they claim damages; when a large number of customers did make claims and the vendor offered excellent and timely service, it not only gained a foothold, but soon established credibility as a quality service provider. When contracts came up for renewal, large numbers of customers were willing to switch entirely to the new vendor on the basis of favorable experience with the FITD product.

---

[3] Modularity enables the building of complex products from smaller subsystems that can be designed independently yet function together as a whole. Carliss Y. Baldwin and Kim B. Clark, *Design Rules: The Power of Modularity*, vol. I (Boston, Mass.: MIT Press, 2000) provide the design rules that enable the development of modular products and therefore serve as the basis for designing an FITD product.

[4] The Siebel example raises are interesting question: How important is it for the two sides to have some idea of how a relationship might grow over time? Inasmuch as efforts to get customers to buy into a grand vision are often frustrated, vendors might do better to get customers to see only a few steps ahead at any given time.

FITD Pricing Strategies

Although it might be tempting to offer an FITD product at a low price to improve the probability of sale and dramatically reduce cost and time to sell, this approach seldom works in business markets. For one thing, customers that equate value with dollars will likely ascribe a lesser value to the product. A vendor that pursues this strategy might also find it difficult to charge appropriate prices for follow-up products. The multitude of failed dot-com firms that tried this approach attests to its inadvisability. Most of these firms initially offered many services for free (i.e., loss leaders) to gain market share as quickly as possible, the dominant paradigm being "get big, quick." Subsequently, these firms found that their customer base wanted only free or vastly discounted services, and were unwilling to purchase other products or services at a higher price.

When and How Can the FITD Approach Fail?

A classic problem with the FITD strategy is that, without the ability to manage customers' business strategies, a vendor's vision of a relationship trajectory is rendered meaningless. Some of the things that can potentially go wrong with the FITD approach, however, are more amenable to vendor control:

- *FITD product fails.* This is the worst-case scenario. Not only short-term sales opportunity but also the likelihood of getting another chance with the customer is quite low at this point.

- *Vendor is identified as being good at just the FITD product.* Without a reasonable mutual picture of the relationship trajectory, a customer might resist follow-up sales and slot the vendor as a source for just the FITD product. Vendors can counter this by managing customers' expectations appropriately and communicating to them a vision of the evolutionary path of the relationship.

- *Competitors get customers to switch by giving away the FITD product.* Unless the FITD product generates substantial value and customers recognize that value, competitors might be able to cure them away by giving away the FITD product.

Whereas managers can deal with some of the things that can go wrong with the FITD, there are instances in which it is the wrong approach to begin with.

ALL-AT-ONCE APPROACH

There are times when it makes sense for the vendor to attempt to sell the entire bundle of products and services from the outset of the relationship. For example, large customers can complicate the selling process through a combination of temporal changes in

- the customer's purchase decision making and buying units
- the nature of the products and services offered
- the selling skills required

Hewlett Packard's Computer Systems Organization (HP-CSO), a full-line supplier of hardware products ranging from desktop PCs to high-end mainframe servers and a host of associated software services, had approximately 2500 enterprise customers that spent up to $200 million of their multimillion-dollar annual information technology (IT) budgets on HP products.

Given the breadth of the products and services it sold, HP broke its sales to enterprise customers into downstream, midstream, and upstream opportunities. Its account management organization was premised on the notion that HP, having traditionally enjoyed a price/performance advantage as a computer hardware supplier, would enter an account through *downstream* opportunities in the capacity of a product vendor. HP then would migrate up to IT infrastructure and enterprisewide solutions by demonstrating industry-specific knowledge and delivering strong pre- and post-sales installation resources—the *midstream* business. Next, HP would leverage its position to work with the customer and help them in a broad spectrum of infrastructure projects to reduce customer costs and deliver significantly higher customer value. At this point, HP effectively became a strategic partner to a customer (the *upstream* business). An example of such a strategy would be for HP to first supply PCs to a large automaker, selling networks and information systems as a value-added supplier, and eventually work as a strategic partner with the customer, helping it to add Web-capabilities to its next-generation vehicles.

HP's aspirations to develop all three revenue streams with its enterprise customers were impeded by its migration strategy. Functional walls within customer accounts, its brand equity as a trusted hardware supplier, and the purchasing community's desire to control vendor pricing seemed to be keeping HP from evolving from a hardware vendor to a value-added supplier. Even if the account team were to scale these barriers, the IT community's desire to control vendor relationships and executive-level reluctance to include HP as an adviser effectively prevented further migration. Moreover, it was common for customer senior management teams responsible for building and managing strategic alliances with important vendors to stonewall efforts by HP personnel.

HP belatedly discovered that critical success factors and customer management competencies changed as one moved from managing downstream to managing upstream businesses. To survive in the downstream business, it was important to continuously improve operational efficiency in order to overcome ever-increasing customer service requirements and continuous pressure to discount prices. In the midstream business, the focus shifted from efficiency to selection, suggesting that HP should perhaps not try to pursue every business opportunity. Here, HP had to be able to prioritize opportunities and choose projects on the basis of their potential and alignment with HP's competencies. Upstream business opportunities hinged on HP's ability to sell concepts and instill confidence among senior executives that it could deliver on its promises.

HP subsequently abandoned its migration strategy and adopted a model based on an *opportunity portfolio* management. The company resolved to service customer accounts at multiple levels from the outset using an approach tailored to the dynamics of the different types of sales opportunities. The new *all-at-once* approach forced HP to streamline processes for servicing downstream business, institutionalize midstream opportunity selection, identify a narrow band of upstream sales opportunities for proactive selling, and install a new set of measures for evaluating its customer management efforts. HP also had to change the sales organization and establish for each of the three business streams a team headed by a sales representative who reported to a client relationship manager with responsibility for managing the customer account. The change in strategy was validated when HP was able to significantly increase its share of large enterprise customers' total purchases.

Pricing Strategies in the All-at-Once Approach

The all-at-once strategy of managing customer portfolios of opportunities raises an important issue in pricing: the link between *value created* for the customer and *value extracted* by the vendor. A naïve model might suggest a direct link between value created and value extracted, but the complexity of most business markets forces firms to be creative in their pricing strategies, especially when they sell bundles of products that include commodities and specialties. Contrary to what might be expected, firms often reduce margins on specialty products to make money on commodity products. Such behavior can be consequent to an industry's competitive dynamics. Kone and other major elevator manufacturers, for example, typically sell their elevators (the specialty product that creates value for customers) at cost that will lock in service and maintenance contracts (the commodity products) at high margins. The same holds for aircraft jet engine manufacturers; the industry's three major players literally give away engines to make money on maintenance contracts and in the spare parts business. These strategies risk the entry of service-oriented firms able to erode the margins in service contracts, the present case in the elevator business.

Guidelines for Choosing Between the FITD and All-at-Once Strategies

Vendors need to know unambiguously when to use a gradual foot-in-the-door approach to building a customer relationship, versus an all-at-once approach. The all-at-once approach is preferred in situations where

1. There is even the slightest doubt about the appropriateness of the FITD product in a specific customer relationship.
2. The customers' buying units are likely to change as a vendor attempts to move beyond the FITD product. In these cases, a vendor should carefully analyze their ability to transform their selling effort to accommodate such changes before committing to an FITD approach.
3. There is a high probability for customers to associate the vendor with just the FITD product and not to consider the vendor as a viable option for other business.
4. There is a high probability of competitive entry that can jeopardize a vendor's FITD strategy. Most firms are caught off guard by competitors who adopt either an all-at-once approach or a different FITD approach that breaks down the focal vendor's customer management strategy that has not been structured to anticipate such competitive efforts.
5. There is a high degree of uncertainty in markets and technologies that might render other parts of the vendor's product line irrelevant or obsolescent in the future.

When using an all-at-once approach to manage a portfolio of opportunities in a customer relationship, vendors should have a well-laid-out plan that

1. Matches requisite selling and support skills with the set of opportunities being pursued and served.

2. Leverages the customer portfolio to manage overall margins in a relationship by decoupling the process of customer value creation and pricing strategies for individual components in a bundle. There is more money to be made by optimally pricing a bundle than by trying to maximize profitability of individual components.

◆ MANAGING DIFFERENT CUSTOMER TYPES CONCURRENTLY

In the first part of this chapter, we considered generic processes for managing customer relationships over time. But because different customers play different roles and so need to be managed differently, each of the generic processes needs to be adapted to a particular customer type. This requirement is illuminated by the price versus cost-to-serve (which includes pre-sale, order-related, distribution, and post-sale service costs) framework,[5] which links vendor investments to the returns from each customer relationship. The framework was also used to show how activity-based costing can be used effectively to manage a firm's customer mix (see Figure 8-3).[6]

Overwhelming evidence suggests a lack of correlation between vendor investments in a relationship (as measured by cost to serve [CTS]) and returns (i.e., the price paid by the customer).

Why does this scatter plot spread customers across the four quadrants? What follows is one interpretation of what happens over time to a vendor's relationship with one of its early customers (see Figure 8-4 on page 321):

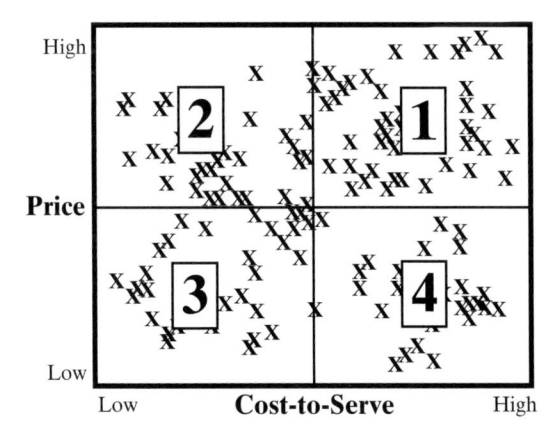

FIGURE 8-3 Price Versus Cost-to-Serve Matrix

Source: The price vs. cost-to-serve framework was developed by Benson P. Shapiro, V. Kasturi Rangan, Rowland Moriarty Jr., and Elliot B. Ross, "Manage Customers for Profits (Not Just Sales)," *Harvard Business Review* 65, no. 5 (1987): 101–108.

---

[5] Benson P. Shapiro, V. Kasturi Rangan, Rowland Moriarty Jr., and Elliot B. Ross, "Manage Customers for Profits (Not Just Sales)," *Harvard Business Review* 65, no. 5 (1987): 101–108.
[6] Rowland T. Moriarty V. Kasturi Rangan, and Gordon S. Swartz, "Signode (A)," Harvard Business School case #586-059 (1986). V. Kasturi Rangan, Rowland T. Moriarty, and Gordon S. Swartz, "Segmenting Customers in Mature Industrial Markets," *Journal of Marketing* 56, no. 4 (1992): 72–82. Robert S. Kaplan, "Using ABC to Manage Customer Mix and Relationships," Harvard Business School Publishing Note 197-094 (1997). Robert S. Kaplan and V. G. Narayanan, "Measuring and Managing Customer Profitability," *Journal of Cost Management* (September/October 2001): 5–15.

◆ BOX 8-1 ◆

FedEx Corporation Uses CRM to Segment and Increase Sales

The international package delivery company FedEx Corporation strives to improve customer service and support and to enhance the customer experience through customer relationship management (CRM) initiatives. Customer data are compiled and integrated across all channels, providing FedEx with extremely detailed customer information and sales history to enhance the company's ability to market its services and improve customer relations.

With CRM systems in place, the FedEx sales force has access to detailed customer information that highlights needs and potential services to satisfy those needs. Using this information, FedEx sales representatives can then match appropriate service offerings to customers. This ability to sell its services at different levels, along with the CRM system's ability to qualify potential sales leads and highlight the most profitable customer segments, increases sales and improves the organization's profitability.

The FedEx Web site has played an important role in customer service and support. FedEx has developed its online support based on customer needs communicated to the company and has attracted more customers to the FedEx Web site and to FedEx services as a result. The package tracking system has been one popular feature on the FedEx site. As part of its effort to further enhance customer support, the company wanted to maximize convenience for customers and allow them to customize their online experience according to their individual needs. The myFedEx feature enables customers to register for a personal account and set preferences, and it includes features such as address books and document printing. Through myFedEx, the company gains valuable insight into customer online behavior and purchase patterns, and this information is used to sell other services to customers.

FedEx is also deploying CRM software in its call centers, enabling the integration of Web and call-center data. CRM software from Clarify is used to create and maintain customer profiles, and to route calls more effectively. And yet another important aspect of FedEx's customer relationship management initiative is to increase accessibility to customers across various channels. Customers are able to track shipments on Web-enabled phones, PDAs, and two-way pagers. This FedEx feature gives customers increased freedom and convenience, and FedEx is able to optimize customer information gathered to gain valuable insight into customer behavior.

SOURCES: Steve Konicki, and Jennifer Maselli, "When Customer Care Counts," *Information Week*, March 26, 2001. Caitlin Mollison, "Driving Customer Service," *Internet World*, September 15, 2001. Marc L. Songini, "FedEx Expects CRM System to Deliver," *Computerworld*, November 6, 2000. "FedEx Continues Blazing a Wireless Trail," *Frontline Solutions*, August 2001.

Stage 1: The introduction of a new product that offers substantial benefits would be expected to generate a customer relationship in this quadrant. Cost-to-serve (CTS) will be high at the outset due to customer education costs and the need for support in the absence of experience with the vendor and product. Having convinced the customer of the benefits and communicated the value, the vendor should, however, be able to obtain high prices.

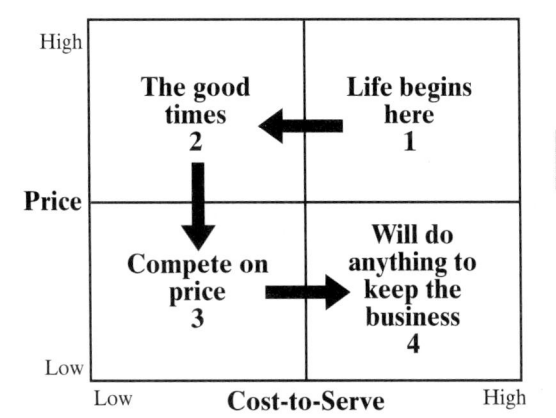

FIGURE 8-4 Pattern of Customer Migration

```
High │  The good    │  Life begins
     │   times      │     here
     │     2    ←───│      1
     │        │     │
Price│        ↓     │
     │              │  Will do
     │  Compete on  │ anything to
     │    price  ───│→ keep the
     │      3       │  business
     │              │      4
Low  │              │
     └──────────────┴──────────────
      Low   Cost-to-Serve    High
```

Source: The price vs. cost-to-serve framework was developed by Benson P. Shapiro, V. Kasturi Rangan, Rowland Moriarty Jr., and Elliot B. Ross, "Manage Customers for Profits (Not Just Sales)," *Harvard Business Review* 65, no. 5 (1987): 101–108.

Stage 2: Smart vendors learn from experience and scale economies to become more efficient and effective in serving acquired customers. Lessened needs for support further reduces a vendor's CTS. That the customer still values all of the product benefits and there is little or no competition enables the vendor to command high prices. Therefore, these are the good times. However, it is about this time that other firms begin to enter the arena

Stage 3: The typical selling strategy of competitors at this point is to offer an equivalent product at a substantially lower price, a copy-cat strategy with price as the only differentiator. The customer now comes back to the focal vendor either requesting or demanding lower prices, and the vendor is forced to reduce prices while continuing to offer the same service.

Stage 4: As competition continues to heat up, the focal vendor, having invested a lot in the relationship, becomes paranoid about losing the customer. To counter the threat of switching, additional services are offered that increase the vendor's CTS. But the customer doesn't pay a higher price and the relationship becomes highly unprofitable for the vendor. In a manner of speaking, life ends here for the vendor.

Although stylized, the customer migration model described here gives us a feel for why a customer might be located in a particular quadrant at a given time.[7] Figure 8-5 highlights the different types of customers that inhabit each quadrant.

QUADRANT 1: HIGH PRICE—HIGH CTS

Customers in this quadrant are expensive to serve but willing to pay a high price.

- Customers in this quadrant want *turnkey solutions* from vendors. They have consciously chosen not to develop in-house expertise or make investments that would reduce their need for the vendor's value-added services. Such customers typically view the vendor as a value-adding partner and look for a long-term commitment.

---

[7] Many variants could be developed around this basic model. For example, the vendor might prefer to acquire the customer through lower prices. It is also possible that the customer that comes later enters in quadrant 2 because the vendor has already learned from experience with earlier customers and has lowered its cost to serve all customers.

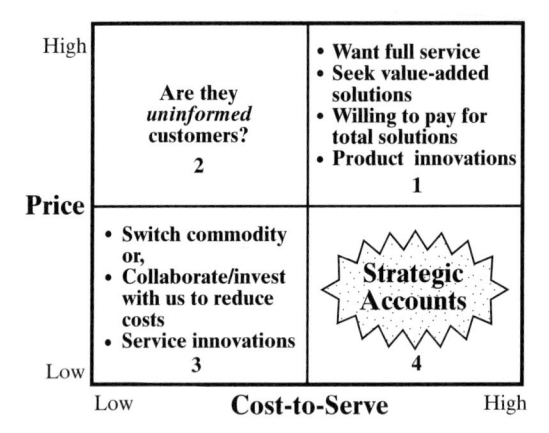

322 PART II *Developing Strategies for Customer Equity Management*

```
                High
                       │ Are they          │ • Want full service
                       │ uninformed        │ • Seek value-added
                       │ customers?        │   solutions
                       │                   │ • Willing to pay for
                       │        2          │   total solutions
                       │                   │ • Product innovations
         Price         │                   │        1
                       ├───────────────────┼───────────────────
                       │ • Switch commodity│
                       │   or,             │   Strategic
                       │ • Collaborate/invest│  Accounts
                       │   with us to reduce│
                       │   costs           │
                       │ • Service innovations│
                Low    │        3          │        4
                       Low    Cost-to-Serve    High
```

FIGURE 8-5 Different Customer Types

Source: The price vs. cost-to-serve framework was developed by Benson P. Shapiro, V. Kasturi Rangan, Rowland Moriarty Jr., and Elliot B. Ross, "Manage Customers for Profits (Not Just Sales)," *Harvard Business Review* 65 no. 5 (1987): 101–108.

- Customers in this quadrant also want the *latest and best products* from the vendor and are willing to pay a price premium. These customers push the vendor to stay at the cutting edge of technology.

Although they might not be actively involved in codeveloping new products, customers in this quadrant are major drivers of product innovation. Vendors need either to continually add new sources of value to maintain them in this quadrant or to proactively manage their migration to quadrants 2 or 3. A shift to quadrant 2 occurs when the vendor becomes more efficient at serving these customers and is able to reduce their CTS without decreasing price. A shift to quadrant 3 results from a gradual reduction in service levels attended by lower CTS that are passed on to customers in the form of lower prices. Whereas the move to quadrant 2 requires little or no involvement by the customer, the move to quadrant 3 must be jointly managed with the customer. Such a strategy is optimal when the customer's decision making unit (DMU) is transitioning from being dominated by technical staff to being managed by its procurement personnel. This affords the vendor an opportunity to build a new value system with the new power bases in the customer's buying unit.

In high-tech markets, customers in this quadrant rapidly move to quadrant 4 as a result of vendors not coming to terms with the rapid commoditization cycles that are characteristic of these industries and, lacking the discipline to manage the CTS appropriately, being forced to drop prices significantly to keep the customer account.

QUADRANT 2: HIGH PRICE—LOW CTS

Four types of customers inhabit this quadrant.

- *Ignorant customers* don't know they are paying a high price. A competitor will likely educate these customers and induce them to switch. Vendors can either educate these customers themselves or maintain the status quo. Education must be tempered with an explanation of why a high price was being charged.

- *Grateful customers* value their relationship with the vendor and, being focused beyond a single transaction, are willing to pay a price premium that rewards the vendor for past efforts and guarantees continued service. What appears to be irrational customer behavior at the transaction level becomes highly rational under the lens of a long-term relationship. It has been noted that some customers in this quadrant treat the focal vendor as a secondary supplier to ensure continuity in the event the primary supplier were to fail.[8] They pay a high price to compensate for their low purchase volumes.

- *Unconcerned customers* don't care that they are paying a high price because the costs of negotiating price reductions far exceed the benefits of lower prices.

- *Hostage* customers are prevented from exiting the relationship because the vendor has increased their switching costs. Vendors have literally all the power in such relationships and not uncommonly abuse it.

Customers in this quadrant differ from those in quadrant 1 because the vendor's CTS is lower, either as a consequence of stripping away services as customers become more sophisticated or by learning to become more efficient over time. Managing ignorant and hostage customers in this quadrant using the "make hay while the sun shines" approach will work only if the vendor is capable of hiding CTS data from the customer or ensuring that the customer does not observe market prices. With grateful customers, vendors need to cultivate goodwill; to move the customer to quadrant 1 is preferable to risking the customer sinking to quadrant 3. Oscillating these customers between quadrants 1 and 2 can be an effective long-term customer management strategy.

QUADRANT 3: LOW PRICE—LOW CTS

Two customers inhabit this quadrant.

- Customers who expect lower prices also force a vendor to strip away all value-added services and sell them just the basic, unbundled product offering, because this reduces the vendor's CTS. These *switchers* view the vendor's product as a commodity and are likely to switch vendors if they are unable to get lower prices. Vendors are well advised to forgo trying to educate such customers about their value-added services, and to play the commodity game. Alternatively, migrating these customers to new products and technologies, back to quadrant 1, would decommoditize the relationship.

- Vendors can sometimes reduce the CTS, not by stripping away value-added services but through *joint investments and learning* as when (a) the customer has invested in systems, processes, or people; (b) the customer has assumed some of the functions traditionally provided by the vendor; (c) the vendor has learned to serve the customer more efficiently; or (d) some combination of these effects has occurred.[9] Some or all of the vendor's CTS reductions are then passed to the customer in the form of lower prices. Unlike switchers that might be led to terminate a vendor relationship by lower prices

---

[8]V. Kasturi Rangan, Rowland T. Moriarty, and Gordon S. Swartz, "Segmenting Customers in Mature Industrial Markets," *Journal of Marketing* 56, no. 4 (1992): 72–82.

[9]The Internet and other interactive technologies are enabling customers to take over activities that cut down the vendor's CTS. For example, customers might prefer to customize products to their needs on their own, provided the vendor creates a set of tools that makes it easy for them to do so. Further downstream in the purchase cycle, order-cycle-related activities such as checking on order and delivery status, billing, and payments are now being offered on company Web sites. Every time customers use these functions, they reduce the vendor's CTS. See Stefan Thomke and Eric von Hippel, "Customers as Innovators: A New Way to Create Value," *Harvard Business Review* 80, no. 4 (2002): 74–81.

offered by a competitor, these customers view their current vendors as partners and would not switch for fear of losing knowledge benefits. Typically, these relationships are managed at the customer end by the procurement department. These customers need to be constantly reminded that the joint investments and learning process that have reduced the customer's total cost of ownership would be lost if they were to switch vendors in search of lower prices.

Vendors need to carefully differentiate between switchers and collaborators. Indeed, switchers can sometimes be converted to collaborators.

QUADRANT 4: LOW PRICE—LOW CTS

Vendors, owing to a combination of factors, are willing to accept extremely low margins from these customers.

- In industries with a high fixed cost component, a vendor's *biggest* customers (in terms of volume) are often firmly ensconced in this quadrant because of customer threats and the need to keep the customer at any cost to fill production capacity. Because these relationships suffer from *scope creep* and adversely affect customer profitability, the vendor should attempt to move these customers to quadrant 3 by reducing their CTS.

- It is also common for a firm's *showcase accounts* to be in this quadrant. In most markets, having a marquee customer in the portfolio enhances a vendor's reputation with other customers. These customers are showcased to attract additional customers. Because showcase customers typically leverage their position in a manner similar to large-volume customers, vendors should develop systems to quantify the "showcase" effect. If, after accounting for the benefits, the customer continues to be in this quadrant, the costs of maintaining the customer relationship are not being recovered through additional sales to other customers. A vendor would benefit from migrating such customers to one of the other three quadrants.

- Customer relationships that vendors try to buy their way into also populate this quadrant. As discussed in connection with the FITD approach, bribing customers with low prices and high levels of service in the expectation that things can be changed in the long run is rarely successful, and yet it is one of the most common mistakes made by business marketers.

From the vendor's perspective, it makes sense to have customers in this quadrant only temporarily.[10] Three choices might be superior to the status quo. These customers might be migrated to quadrant 3 following a dialogue that identifies vendor services and efforts that the customer neither requires nor values (these vendor actions are typically based on the misperception that they are required to keep the customer account). Vendors have found cutting back on such scope creep to be a very fruitful avenue. Alternatively, these customers might be migrated to quadrant 1 by first communicating the true value package to the customer. Often, in cases in which vendors have given away services that are truly appreciated, customers are willing to consider appropriate price increases. Ideally, vendors will combine these two

---

[10]In fact, a standard joke among sales reps is to call these *strategic customers* to convince management that losses being made currently are an investment to achieve better returns in the future.

approaches to move customers towards the right diagonal of the price-CTS quadrant. One industrial marketing firm created cross-functional teams to brainstorm ideas and approaches for reducing the firm's CTS and creating additional customer value. Getting all parts of the organization into customer-facing roles generated a flood of creative ideas from product redesign to product deliveries and after-sales service. The firm subsequently mandated this practice for all major accounts.

Finally, a vendor can *fire a customer*. If a vendor is truly providing unique value and not getting paid for it, it must also be true that the customer is unlikely to be able to obtain this value free from anyone else and is likely to come back after having realized this. A new relationship can then be established on the vendor's terms. This approach requires discipline and resolve, since it is not easy to walk away from a major customer relationship.

In addition to the different customer types common to each quadrant, there is a set of customer types that tends to span the four quadrants.

- *Lead users* have needs months or even years before they eventually become general in a marketplace. When needs evolve rapidly, as they often do, only users at the forefront of the trend will have experience with "tomorrow's needs today." Because they expect to benefit significantly from a solution to their needs, lead users tend to experiment on their own and so can provide vendors with feedback data on both needs and solutions.[11]

- *Advocates and reference accounts* are loyal customers that are willing to advertise through word of month for the vendor. They are powerful sales tools that can supplement a vendor's own sales efforts.

Vendors need to plan customer migration paths with a clear idea of where customers will eventually be located and a clear picture of customers' current and desired eventual locations. That is, they need to design, develop, and implement a customer relationship management strategy.

Summary

In this chapter, we first reviewed the various ways in which a vendor can build a customer relationship over time. We also discussed when it would make sense to adopt the different approaches and the associated pricing strategies. Finally, we looked at the different roles that customers play in a vendor's portfolio and how this affects the nature of the customer relationship management strategy.

Review Questions and Exercises:

1. Give an example of the all-at-once approach and describe why it was successful.
2. How have auto manufacturers utilized the foot-in-the-door approach?
3. Consider the HP example described in the chapter. What approach to relationship development does HP utilize? Where are HP's customers in terms of the price versus cost-to-serve matrix (Figure 8-3) and the customer types described in Figures 8-4 and 8-5?

---

[11] Eric von Hippel, "Lead Users: A Source of Novel Product Concepts," *Management Science* 32, no. 7 (July 1986): 791–805.

◆◆◆ WESCO Distribution, Inc.

Case 8-1 WESCO Distribution, Inc.

Das Narayandas

Late in June 1997, Jim Piraino, VP Marketing for WESCO Distribution, Inc. (see Exhibit 1), was preparing for a yearly review meeting with his CEO Roy Haley. At the top of the agenda was the performance of the National Accounts (NA) program during the first half of 1997 (see Exhibit 2). Haley had ambitious plans for WESCO over the next five years. He had charted out a course that called for an annual growth rate of 6% to 8% in sales, and, more important, an annual increase of 12% to 16% in profitability. "In 1996, we were a $2.2 billion company with an EBIT of around 3%. I want us to be a $3 billion company with an EBIT of over 5% by the year 2000. This target is very much achievable. In the last few years, our customers have made significant changes to their business processes. These changes provide us a unique opportunity to provide greater value to our customers while improving our market position and profitability. I want WESCO to be recognized as a leader in learning, adapting, and responding to changes in customer needs," said Haley.

Although acquisitions of other companies were expected to contribute over half the revenue growth, most of this business was not expected to exceed current profitability levels. WESCO's current NA program, which had been initiated in 1994 as a response to the changing market dynamics, was expected to deliver the additional revenue growth and obtain the desired increases in profitability.

Yet, as of mid-1997, the NA program had not delivered the expected increases in sales and profitability. Haley had now asked Piraino to examine the NA program and present recommendations for improvements. "We need to get more out of our NA effort. This is our best growth avenue with existing customers and new prospects. We have to generate significantly better results with this program," Haley had told Piraino.

PREPARING FOR THE NA REVIEW MEETING

In early May, Piraino had spoken with WESCO national account manager (NAM) Mike McKinley about one of his NA customers, who had signed an agreement in late 1996. During the first five months of 1997, the account had generated only 40% of its target sales volume, with gross margins falling a full 2% from the prior year.

Piraino reflected on the meeting:

From our account analysis prior to signing the agreement, this was a very promising NA customer offering immediate, exclusive access to their 28 U.S. plants. We thought we could increase their existing $1.5 million annual purchases from us by a factor of ten. However, ever since implementation began in January, we have discovered an unexpectedly poor alignment between the customer's local and corporate interests. This was their first national purchasing agreement, and it turns out that despite corporate enthusiasm, some of their plants were reluctant to abandon local distributors with whom they had developed very strong relationships. We are now being charged with the responsibility of developing the program up from the local level. Managing headquarters has turned out to be only half the task.

The second conversation that came to mind was with John Whitney, a WESCO sales representative at a $30 million per year branch. Whitney was currently serving the local plant of a $5.4 million per year NA customer. Once the NA agreement was signed, the customer plant, which generated only $50,000 per year in sales and which was located two hours away from WESCO's branch, had demanded semi-monthly sales calls. Whitney described his situation bluntly:

The case was prepared by Professor Das Narayandas with the assistance of Research Associate Sara Frug. Copyright © 1997 by the President and Fellows of Harvard College. Harvard Business School Case 598-021.

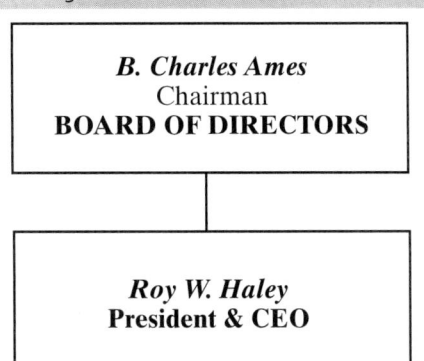

EXHIBIT 1 The WESCO Executive Organization Chart

```
                    B. Charles Ames
                       Chairman
                   BOARD OF DIRECTORS

                      Roy W. Haley
                    President & CEO
```

John R. Burke Vice President EESCO	**Steven A. Burleson** Corporate Controller
William M. Goodwin Vice President International Group	**Michael S. Dziewisz** Director Human Resources
Mark E. Keough Vice President Product Management and Supply	**James H. Mehta** Vice President Business Development
Michael Ludwig Director DataComm Group	**James V. Piraino** Vice President Marketing Group
Patrick M. Swed Vice President Industrial/Construction Group	**M. Craig Rand** Director Training and Development
Donald H. Thimjon Vice President Utility Group	**Steven A. Van Oss** Director Information Systems
Robert E. Vanderloff Vice President Manufactured Structures Group	

Source: Company records.

Class of Account	Number of Customers	1996 Sales	YTD Sales May 1997
Key	50	180	89
Focus	100	52	25
Other	150	34	14
Total	300	266	128

EXHIBIT 2 Sales to National Accounts ($ millions)

Source: Company records.

They may be a good customer for the company. But from my perspective, they and other NA customers demand a lot of service that is not commensurate with their sales volume—either current or potential. Unless compelled, I wouldn't call on NA customers in my region even without the long commute they usually require. The opportunity costs of serving these customers are way too high—both for me and for the branch. I would rather spend my time selling to other customers.

The third conversation that Piraino considered was with Larry Worthington, a WESCO branch manager whose branch had traditionally obtained a major portion of its sales from electrical contractors. In order to serve recently acquired NA customers, the branch had been forced to change the way it managed its business. Worthington was concerned: "We're investing an awful lot of resources to serve NA customers, and it's tempting our contractor customers to abandon us."

Piraino realized that he needed to develop a clear plan for the upcoming meeting with Haley:

We must isolate the root cause of the NA program shortfall. If we are trying to market a new way of doing things that our customers don't really understand or appreciate, then it's time to make some hard decisions. Will it make more sense to promote this program proactively to our customers, or to be passive and offer the NA program only when customers show a legitimate interest? In addition, if the issue is one of improper implementation at our end, then we'd better get our act together very quickly, before we lose important customers.

THE ELECTRICAL EQUIPMENT AND SUPPLIES BUSINESS

Electrical equipment and supplies (EES) referred to any products needed for channeling and using electricity. (Exhibit 3 provides details of the different products that formed the EES market.) Most manufacturers of EES products had specialized product lines, but customers generally had to buy a range of products made by several manufacturers in order to manage their electrical needs. Like other EES distributors, WESCO represented many EES manufacturers and offered customers the convenience of one-stop access to all of their EES needs.

WESCO DISTRIBUTION, INC.

WESCO Distribution, Inc. was founded in 1922 as the distribution arm of Westinghouse. Following a period of disappointing performance in the early 1990s, the company was sold to the investment company of Clayton, Dubilier & Rice in February 1994, with Roy Haley taking over as CEO. Under Haley's leadership, the company had rebounded from an annual revenue run rate at purchase of $1.4 billion to become the third largest full-line wholesale EES distributor in the United States by 1996 with over $2.2 billion in sales globally (see Exhibit 4) of which U.S. sales were a little over $1.6 billion.

Customers

WESCO had three types of customers: Electrical Contractors, Industrial Customers, and Commercial/Institutional/Government (CIG) Institutions. (Exhibit 5 provides more details on the nature of WESCO's business in each of these customer segments.)

EXHIBIT 3 The EES Market

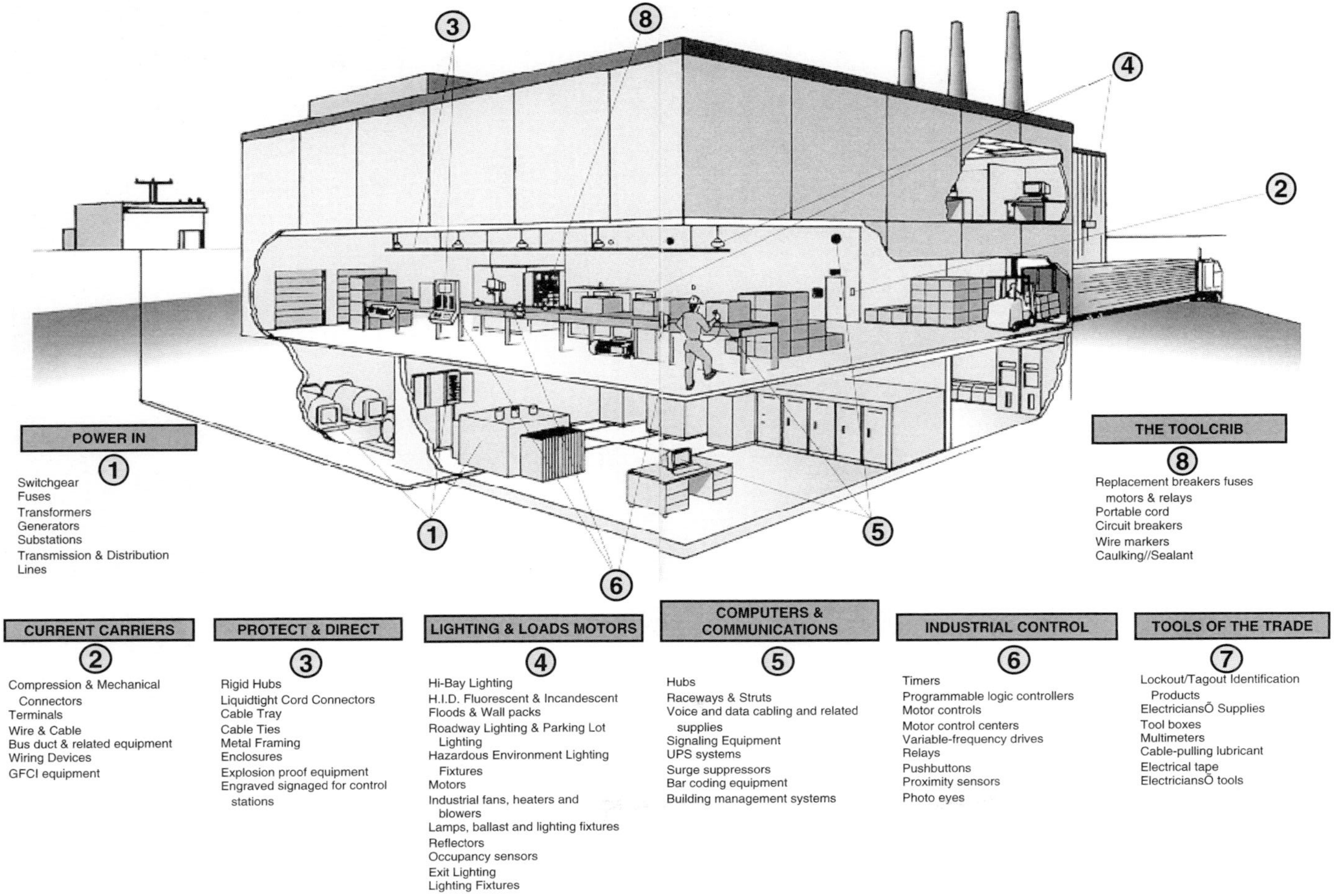

POWER IN ①
Switchgear
Fuses
Transformers
Generators
Substations
Transmission & Distribution Lines

CURRENT CARRIERS ②
Compression & Mechanical Connectors
Terminals
Wire & Cable
Bus duct & related equipment
Wiring Devices
GFCI equipment

PROTECT & DIRECT ③
Rigid Hubs
Liquidtight Cord Connectors
Cable Tray
Cable Ties
Metal Framing
Enclosures
Explosion proof equipment
Engraved signeged for control stations

LIGHTING & LOADS MOTORS ④
Hi-Bay Lighting
H.I.D. Fluorescent & Incandescent
Floods & Wall packs
Roadway Lighting & Parking Lot Lighting
Hazardous Environment Lighting Fixtures
Motors
Industrial fans, heaters and blowers
Lamps, ballast and lighting fixtures
Reflectors
Occupancy sensors
Exit Lighting
Lighting Fixtures

COMPUTERS & COMMUNICATIONS ⑤
Hubs
Raceways & Struts
Voice and data cabling and related supplies
Signaling Equipment
UPS systems
Surge suppressors
Bar coding equipment
Building management systems

INDUSTRIAL CONTROL ⑥
Timers
Programmable logic controllers
Motor controls
Motor control centers
Variable-frequency drives
Relays
Pushbuttons
Proximity sensors
Photo eyes

TOOLS OF THE TRADE ⑦
Lockout/Tagout Identification Products
Electricians' Supplies
Tool boxes
Multimeters
Cable-pulling lubricant
Electrical tape
Electricians' tools

THE TOOLCRIB ⑧
Replacement breakers fuses motors & relays
Portable cord
Circuit breakers
Wire markers
Caulking/Sealant

Source: Company records.

	Fiscal Year Ended December 31		
	1994	1995	1996
Revenues	$1635.8	1857.0	2274.6
EBITDA	29.9	63.1	79.1
Operating income	21.2	55.7	68.2
Sales growth	4.1%	13.5%	22.5%
Operating margin	1.3%	3.0%	3.0%
Pro forma			
Net working capital	$196.5	$222.5	$291.6
Long-term debt	$180.6	$172.0	$260.6
Debt/equity	1.7×	1.4×	1.7×
EBITDA/total interest	1.9×	4.0×	4.3×

EXHIBIT 4 Selected Financial Information ($ millions)

Source: Company records.
Note: As of 12/31/96, total long-term debt was $260 million.
As of 12/31/96, common equity was $158 million.

EXHIBIT 5 Price, Cost, and Value Added Indices by Customer Segment (for 1996)

Customer Type	Sales ($ millions)	Forecasted Annual Growth 1996 to 2000 (%)	Price Index[a]	Cost Index[b]	Customer Value Index[c]
Industrial customers					
NA customers	266	15–19			
• Key NA customers	180		90	80	120
• Focus NA customers	52		93	110	105
• Other NA customers	34		95	100	100
Other industrial customers	721	1–3	100	95	95
Industrial contractors	465	2–4	93	105	105
CIG customers	148	2–4	105	90	90
International	675	1–3	105	110	95
Overall	2275		100	100	100

Source: Company records.
[a] *Price Index* refers to average prices obtained from customers in a specific customer segment. The weighted average price across all customer segments is 100 (the weights used being sales to a customer segment).
[b] *Cost Index* reflects WESCO's average costs to serve a customer segment. The weighted average cost across all customer segments is 100.
[c] *Customer Value Added by WESCO Index* is an indicator of the average differentiation created by WESCO compared to other EES distributors. An index value below 100 means that WESCO has below average opportunity to add value to this customer segment. It does not mean that WESCO is at a disadvantage with respect to competition in its ability to differentiate itself from other competitors.

Electrical contractors Electrical contractors installed lighting and electrical systems for construction projects and had been WESCO's primary customer base in the past. In 1996, the electrical contractor market was estimated at $17.9 billion and accounted for $465 million of WESCO's sales. This was commonly referred to as bid-and-quote business. Contractors obtained business by bidding for contracts. Very few contracts required a bill of materials that covered all parts of the EES system as shown in Exhibit 3. After winning a bid, contractors requested quotes from several EES distributors for the required bill of materials. Next, due to inflexible contracting timetables, the contractor short-listed those distributors that appeared capable of delivering all the materials on time. The contractor then generally negotiated with the short-listed distributors and placed the final order with the distributor who offered the lowest overall price.

Industrial customers Industrial customers accounted for slightly more than $1 billion of WESCO's sales in 1996 and were expected to grow in importance. Industrial customers had an ongoing need for EES products in their Maintenance, Repair, and Operations (MRO) activities such as replacing a safety switch that did not work, repairing a worn out motor before it failed, and upgrading a lighting or drive system to make it more energy efficient and reduce costs. In order to facilitate their MRO activities, industrial customers maintained inventories of EES products. Under Haley's direction, WESCO was currently pursuing customers in several industry segments including utility, manufactured structures, pulp and paper, lumber, petrochemical, mining and metals, and transportation. (See Exhibit 6 for a breakdown of top industrial segments.) WESCO's NA program was designed to serve large, high-potential industrial customers.

Commercial, industrial, and government (CIG) customers WESCO's CIG business was substantially smaller than the contractor and industrial businesses. In 1996, this market was estimated to be just over $5.9 billion, of which WESCO had a 2.5% share. Commercial customers such as hotels and motels, and institutional customers such as hospitals and universities were small, stable, and low-potential customers to WESCO. Government, on the other hand, was more concentrated in demand and was a source of very large orders.

Managing the Different Customer Types

Piraino perceived several difficulties in managing the various kinds of large customers:

> The conflict lies in the different business styles across customer types. For instance,

EXHIBIT 6 WESCO's Market Share of the Industrial Customer Market Segment

Industrial Top Segments	High Market Potential ($ billion)	WESCO Share (1996)
Utility	3.4	8.5%
Manufactured structures	0.6	35.9
Machinery	4.0	2.5
Electrical equipment	2.5	3.7
Primary metals	0.9	7.0
Mining	0.7	7.3
Petroleum & chemicals	0.8	5.8
Transportation	0.4	10.8
Pulp & paper / lumber	0.5	7.5
Food	0.6	3.7
Instrumentation	0.5	1.9
Other MRO	1.8	3.0

Source: Company records.

industrial customers require a steady flow of EES products and are therefore more likely to negotiate long-term contracts. They often demand a high level of service. Electrical contractors, on the other hand, have a project mentality. Their needs vary from project to project and they often define their relationship with us transaction by transaction. Because contractors usually win orders by offering low prices to their customers, they want us to give them the best possible quote every time, keeping our margins low. There is no guarantee of business here and we find it very tough to forecast sales accurately.

Such different businesses require different management approaches. Our sales reps need to be hunters when it comes to the contractor business. Every day, they need to find the contractor who has won a project bid, give a quote, negotiate a deal, and move on. The hunt for a new customer is always on. By contrast, in order to serve our industrial customers, our sales reps need to be farmers. They know exactly who the customer is, and once they have a contract it is usually for the long haul. The primary mode of interaction is to ensure satisfactory service and educate customers about new products and services that become available over time. Managing these customers is all about cultivating relationships and being a good materials manager. Traditionally, we served the contractor business. Many of our sales reps and branch managers have the hunter mentality. It is not easy for them to become farmers, as they seek rewards in the constant pursuit of new opportunities.

Suppliers

On the other side of the distribution equation, WESCO maintained strong ties with over 150 suppliers, the largest of which were Cutler-Hammer, Thomas & Betts, Philips, and Leviton. Piraino said:

> There are several reasons why it makes sense for EES suppliers to go through distributors like us. First, most suppliers make only part of a customer's total EES requirements while customers prefer a one-stop solution. Second, the relatively small volume of business from each customer can make direct sales economically unfeasible for the EES supplier. Third, and most important, we add a lot of value to all stages of the sales process. We call this the WESCO selling story (see Exhibit 7).

Competitors

WESCO had traditionally functioned in three competitive arenas: specialization, geography, and peer (see Exhibit 8). First, along with other full-line distributors, WESCO shared a market with both product specialists and retail generalists. Specialty distributors focused on small product niches such as alarms or lamps. Retail generalists, such as hardware stores and home centers, sold simpler products to homeowners and small contractors. They carried a broad range of supplies, though without the depth of full-line distributors.

Second, as a national chain, WESCO competed with regional chains and local distributors. Local distributors competed with individual WESCO branches for local business. Piraino pointed out, "although they lack our national size and the breadth and buying power that goes with it, these guys can often be formidable competitors. They have developed excellent, long-term relationships with major customers in their markets. Making inroads can be a daunting task."

WESCO also faced competition from regional chains. Piraino explained:

> Although regional distributors are significantly smaller than us, their sales are more concentrated than ours in the regional markets in which they compete with us. Based on revenues, this usually makes them one of the top two distributors in their local markets.

Within its peer group, WESCO competed with several major national distributors, among which it placed third in sales volume in 1996 behind W.W. Grainger, a broad-line distributor of MRO products, and Graybar, the largest electrical/telecommunication products distributor. These competitors were pursuing similar customer management strategies to WESCO.

Branch Office Organization

WESCO was organized into 279 U.S. branches. Each branch maintained its own inventory, had its own P&L responsibility, and enjoyed substantial autonomy in its own territory, including the authority to prospect for customers. In 1997,

The WESCO Selling Story

1. Customer does not recognize need or opportunity
2. WESCO recognizes customer need or opportunity
3. Customer recognizes value and decides to act
4. WESCO ensures that customer identifies WESCO/Supplier as potential solution
5. Customer commits to WESCO/Supplier
6. Customer/WESCO/Supplier act—Value is created, demonstrated, and documented
7. Customer works with WESCO on next value creation opportunity

EXHIBIT 7 The WESCO Selling Story

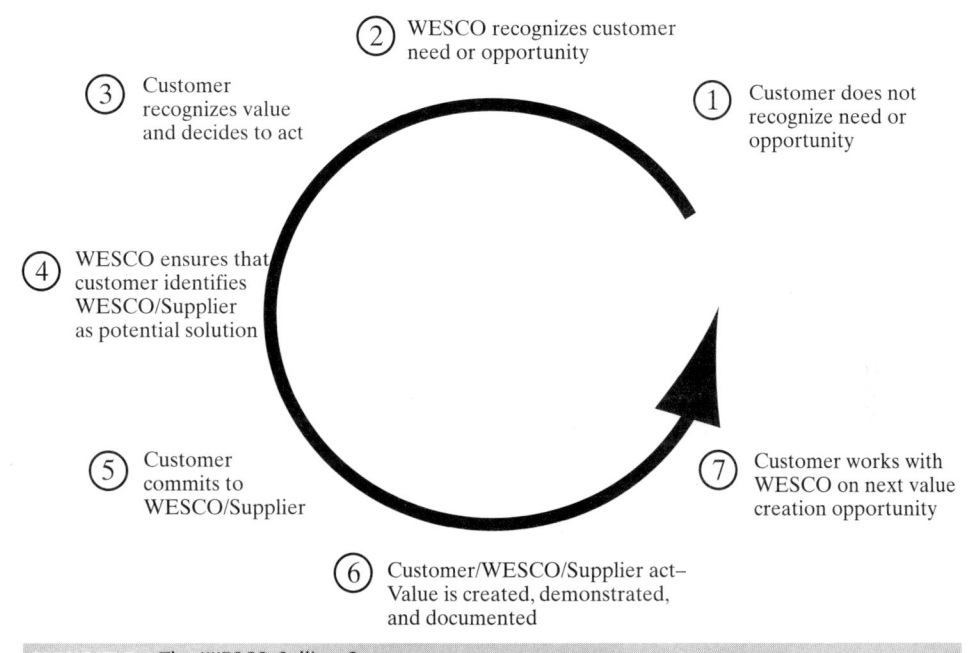

Source: Company records.

one-third of WESCO's branches served customers in a specific industry. These branches carried inventory that was tailored to meet the needs of that specific customer segment, and it affected their ability to serve other customers in their region. WESCO had found that the disadvantages of these branches serving a narrower customer base were heavily outweighed by their ability to serve the chosen customers better than anybody else. Currently, WESCO had no plans to change the orientation of these branches. Amongst the other two-thirds of WESCO's branches, the typical WESCO branch had $9 million to $10 million in sales, with about 40% to industrial customers, 40% to contractors, and the balance to CIG customers. Direct cooperation between branches was limited because each branch operated in its own markets.

In addition to the branch manager, a typical WESCO branch had four outside sales reps, four inside sales reps, one warehouse specialist, one administrative officer who was also in charge of inventories, and one office manager who managed the branch's policies, procedures, training, and office maintenance. Outside sales reps served 20 to 40 customers with a total market potential of $10 to $30 million. These reps were responsible for visiting customers regularly, identifying new sales opportunities, and developing solutions together with customers. For each outside sales rep, there was a corresponding inside sales rep whose job was to process new orders, expedite existing orders, and provide all necessary service and support. Broadly, outside sales reps acquired customers, and inside sales reps ensured their retention. In the past, sales reps would shuttle between inside and outside sales positions before becoming a branch manager. This pattern had been fading recently, however, as each job required increasingly specialized skills. Currently, sales rep compensation had both a fixed salary component and a variable commission component. Commissions were the same regardless of whether sales were made to industrial customers, contractors, or CIG customers.

TRENDS IN THE EES INDUSTRY IN THE 1980S AND EARLY 1990S

During the late 1980s, the EES industry, like other component and supplies industries,

EXHIBIT 8 Distributor Channels

Total Electrical Market by Distributor Channel

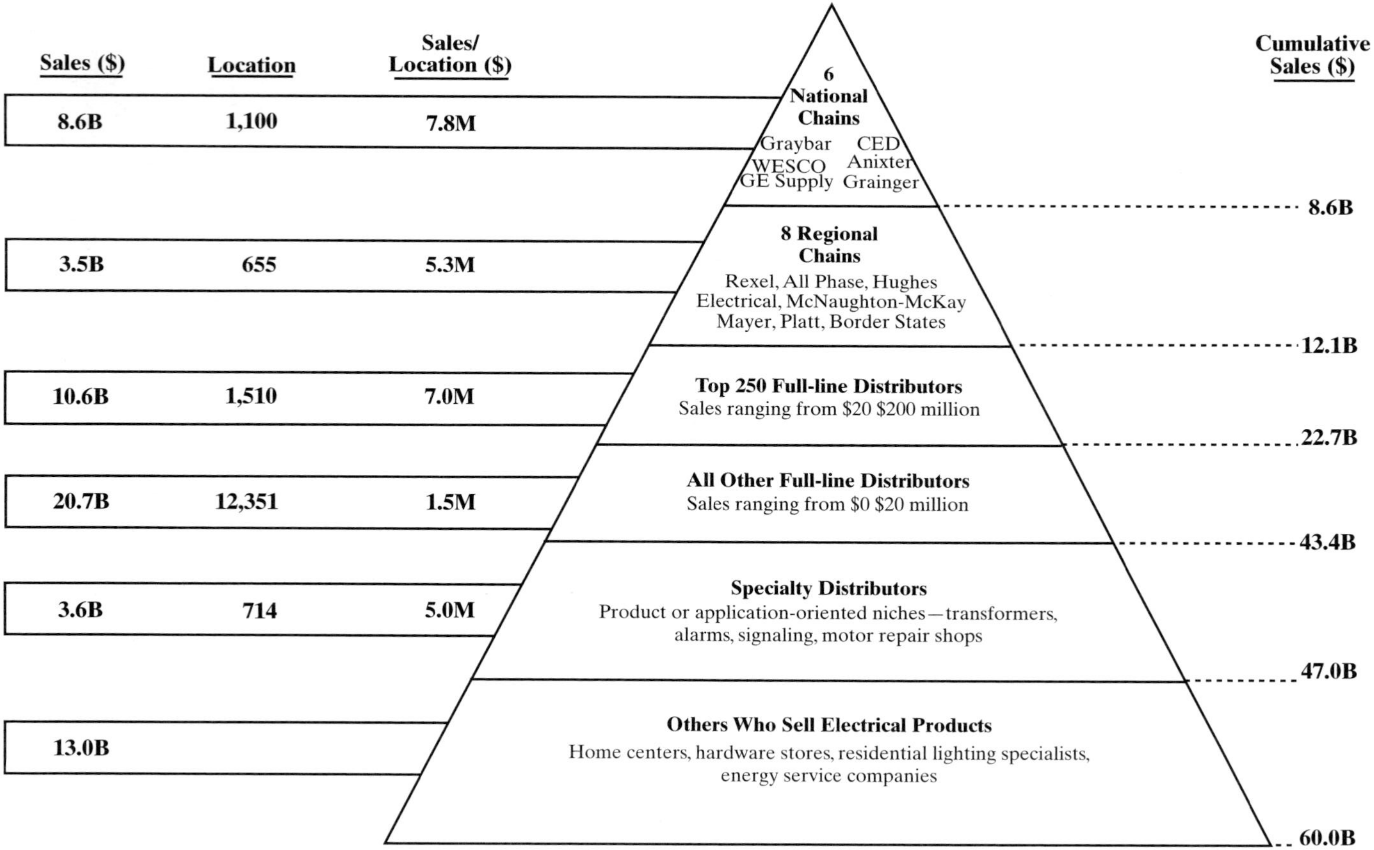

Sales ($)	Location	Sales/Location ($)		Cumulative Sales ($)
8.6B	1,100	7.8M	6 National Chains — Graybar, CED, WESCO, Anixter, GE Supply, Grainger	8.6B
3.5B	655	5.3M	8 Regional Chains — Rexel, All Phase, Hughes Electrical, McNaughton-McKay, Mayer, Platt, Border States	12.1B
10.6B	1,510	7.0M	Top 250 Full-line Distributors — Sales ranging from $20–$200 million	22.7B
20.7B	12,351	1.5M	All Other Full-line Distributors — Sales ranging from $0–$20 million	43.4B
3.6B	714	5.0M	Specialty Distributors — Product or application-oriented niches—transformers, alarms, signaling, motor repair shops	47.0B
13.0B			Others Who Sell Electrical Products — Home centers, hardware stores, residential lighting specialists, energy service companies	60.0B

Source: Company records. Adapted from *Electrical Wholesaling* June 1997.

```
                    ┌─────────────────────────┐
                    │ Total Procurement Cost  │
                    └─────────────────────────┘
                                │
        ┌───────────────────────┼───────────────────────────┐
```

Cost of Product Itself	Cost of Acquiring the Product	Cost of Holding the Product
	Originate a requisition	Create & maintain storage area
	Interview salespeople	Annual physical inventory
	Select suppliers & negotiate	Inventory control
	Issue purchase orders	Stores accounting
	Expedite delivery	Cost of money tied up in inventory
	Receive materials	Insurance
	Distribute to stock locations	Taxes
	Receive & edit invoices	Depreciation
	Maintain accounts payable records	Obsolescence
	Pay invoices	Pilferage

EXHIBIT 9 Total Procurement Cost

Source: Company records.

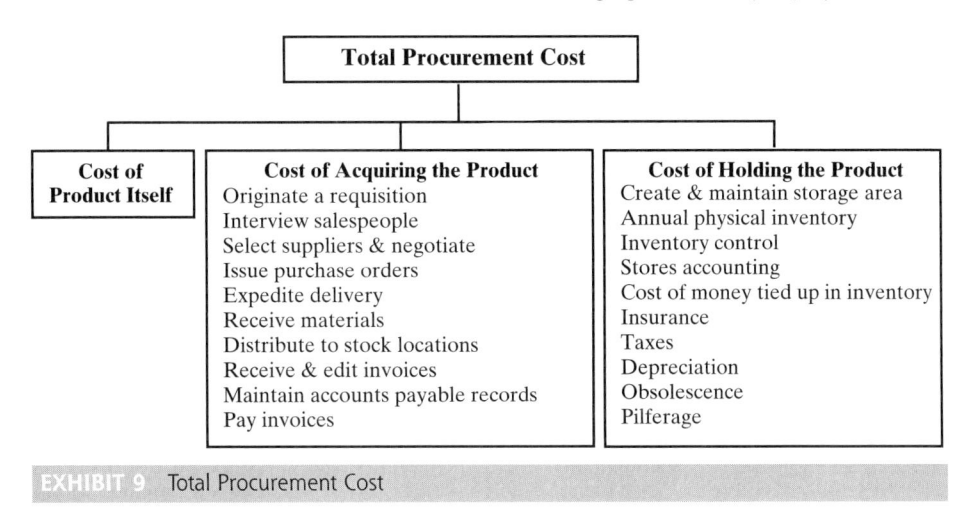

had witnessed a dramatic change in the way any large customers dealt with suppliers and distributors. In order to bridge the quality gap with international competition and improve their overall competitive stance, American companies implemented stringent supplier/distributor quality programs while demanding price reductions as well. In the process of implementing these programs, customers pared their lists of suppliers/distributors and signed long-term contracts with those that remained. These few suppliers/distributors felt compelled to make substantial investments in order to provide the higher level of service and quality now demanded.[1] At the same time, the growth of reengineering in organizations had encouraged customers to examine their procurement costs, i.e., the costs of placing and following orders, and monitoring and managing suppliers/distributors (see Exhibit 9). In order to improve supply chain efficiency, customers reduced inventory, which necessitated a just-in-time (JIT) procurement policy in which suppliers/distributors carried inventory and provided components on an as-needed basis (see Exhibit 10).

To make matters more complicated, the move toward long-term collaborative JIT contracts with a select few suppliers/distributors was not universal among customers. Piraino explained:

> Many of our industrial customers still prefer to do business the old way—simultaneously maintaining arms-length, bid-oriented relationships with multiple EES distributors. [See Exhibit 11 for the evolution of customer needs.] Periodically, they send a "request for quotation" (RFQ) for all their requirements to several EES distributors, selecting the one with lowest overall prices. These customers do not appear to be interested in streamlining procurement processes in collaboration with their EES distributors and are more resistant to change.

WESCO'S NATIONAL ACCOUNT PROGRAM

WESCO's National Account (NA) program had been established under the premise that large contracts could mean significant savings for both customers and WESCO. In exchange for giving their EES business to WESCO, NA customers received competitive, year-long, national pricing regardless of volume. In the early stages of the NA program, most contracts pertained to individual products. Art Hersberger, WESCO's Director of National Accounts, described:

---

[1] Not making such investments meant risking the sales volume provided by these large customers. More importantly, once an opportunity was missed, it could be several years before a distributor had another shot at doing business with that customer.

Inventory Reduction Initiatives
- Inventory Buy-Back
- Disposition of Obsolete Inventory
- Inventory Classification
- Consignments
- Bin-Stock Replenishment
- Part Standardization
- Part Substitution
- Inventory Sharing

Inventory Management Options
- Just-in-Time Delivery
- Systems Contract
- Bin-Stock Replenishment
- Single-Source Commodity Supply
- Single-Source Storeroom Supply
- On-Site Trailer
- Storeroom Management

Efficiency Improvement
- Unit Price Reductions
- Use of Electronic Technologies
- Information Management
- Usage Reporting
- Reduced Paper Transactions
- Reduced Processing Transactions
- Reduced Personnel Requirements
- Miscellaneous Plant Services

EXHIBIT 10   Value Added Services

Source: Company records.

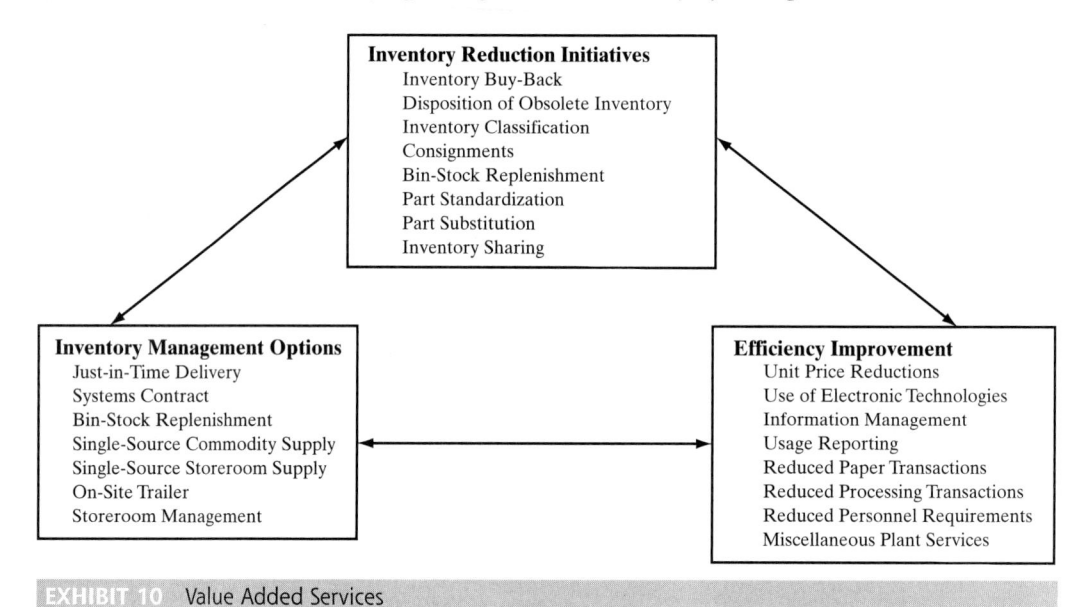

In years past, before the time of WESCO's new ownership, all of the major customer agreements were for single products. In fact, over 80% of these agreements were just for lamps. These agreements were essentially product driven and required minimal value added services. We had hoped that customers who signed such agreements would buy their national EES needs from us exclusively, as per the contracts. What we learned was that customers treated these agreements as nonexclusive. Many even signed contracts for the same products with other national EES distributors.

By 1997, there were 300 customers in the NA program. Piraino classified these 300 customers by sales volume and commitment into three groups: key, focus, and others.

Key customers were the top 50 NA customers by sales volume. With each of these customers, WESCO had moved beyond a single-product, single-site relationship[2] and implemented some form of a multi-site agreement. In many instances, WESCO now also supplied multiple EES products at each of these sites, and some customers were even asking WESCO to supply non-EES products as well. "Sales to these 50 customers were a little over $180 million in 1996, giving us an average of a little less than $4 million per customer. In most of these cases, we can now supply about 60% to 90% of the customer's EES needs. While we count on these relationships as our successes, we still don't have total compliance from all of these customers," said Piraino. He continued:

The story is very different with the next 250 NA customers. Our focus customers, comprising the 100 accounts below our key accounts, have yet to use us to fill a major portion of their needs. These customers give us an average of $500,000 annually. Despite pockets of compliance, most of these relationships are still single-product agreements and they are very often restricted to a single site.

The bottom half of the NA customers were like "hunting licenses," said Hersberger: "In return for getting a low price from us, these customers have given us permission to find opportunities to

---

[2] An NA customer that purchased lamps at one plant exclusively from WESCO would be an example of a single-product, single-site relationship.

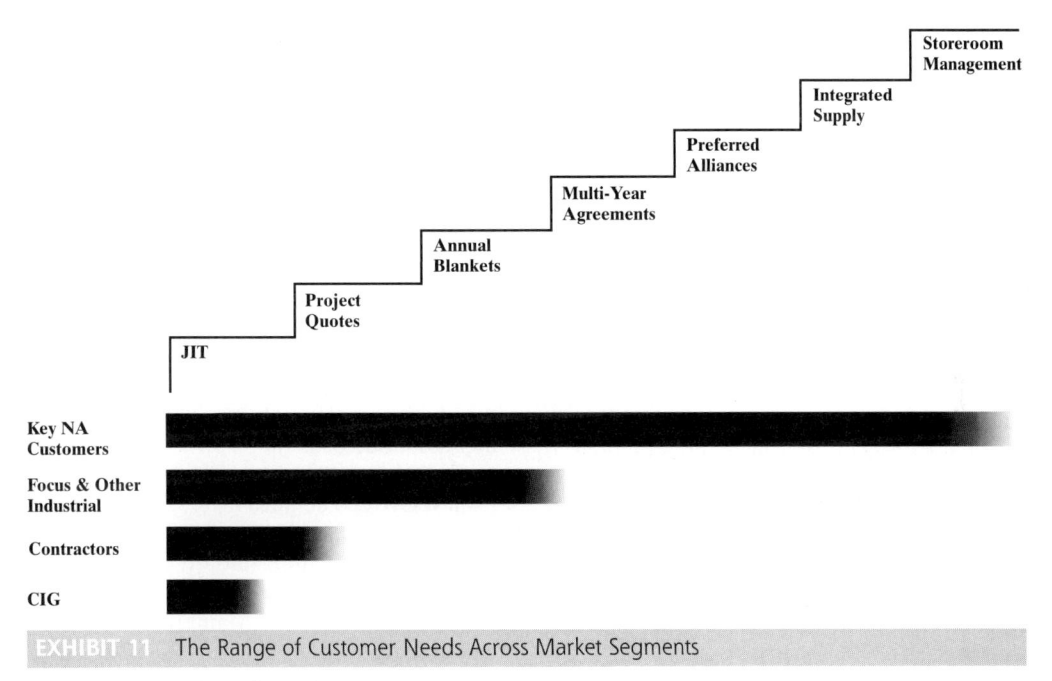

The Range of Customer Needs Across Market Segments

Staircase (ascending):
- JIT
- Project Quotes
- Annual Blankets
- Multi-Year Agreements
- Preferred Alliances
- Integrated Supply
- Storeroom Management

Customer segments (bars):
- Key NA Customers
- Focus & Other Industrial
- Contractors
- CIG

EXHIBIT 11 The Range of Customer Needs Across Market Segments

Source: Company records.

sell within their organizations. On average, these customers purchase less than $250,000 annually. They are typically the non-exclusive, product-only accounts, and we have a long way to go before we tap their full potential."

NAM Sales Organization

In addition to the branch sales force, WESCO had 18 national account managers (NAMs) based across the country, with half reporting to the Director of National Accounts, Art Hersberger, and the other half reporting to Jim Piraino. Each of the 18 NAMs was responsible for a particular industrial segment, with a complement of 10 to 15 customers plus 15 to 20 prospects. NAMs were expected to call on prospective customers, lead the active selling and implementation processes with new NA customers, and maintain long-standing relationships with existing NA customers.

For current NA customers, NAMs were responsible for volume and profitability targets. They were expected to meet regularly with the customer's corporate purchasing staff, ensure compliance to the volumes agreed upon in the NA contract, build relationships with local plant personnel, and facilitate relationship building between WESCO's branch sales reps and the NA customer's local plant personnel. With each NA customer having anywhere from 5 to 20 sites all over the country, NAMs were not able to spend much time at the local level and focused more on the NA customer's corporate offices where the NA agreement was usually negotiated and monitored. Consequently, it was the branch sales reps' responsibility to build relationships at the local level.

Most of WESCO's NAMs had been successful branch managers prior to their current jobs. Since building a relationship with an NA customer could take a long time and demanded extensive technical skills, selecting a NAM was a very difficult and painstaking process. The need for industry expertise, a good understanding of WESCO's business, and the ability to get the support of sales reps to build local relationships with NA customers made it very difficult to find suitable NAM candidates from the outside. Currently, only a couple of WESCO's NAMs had come from outside.

NAMs received commissions for all sales to their customers. At the same time, the branch sales rep assigned to the account also received commissions for sales to the NA customer's local plant or facilities within their territory. This double counting of sales credit ensured that branch office personnel did not see any threat from NAMs visiting their NA customers in the local area. In fact, NAMs were in great demand at the branches since sales reps saw this as an easy way to get sales.

Building NA Agreements

The process of building NA agreements involved several stages. During the initial prospecting stage, NAMs called on customers that had high potential EES sales. They made presentations to the customer's corporate purchasing group on the total cost of ownership and how WESCO's national accounts program might enable companies to reduce procurement costs. Bill Lawry, a National Account Manager (NAM) explained:

> The average MRO order from an industrial customer ranges from $100 to $135. Each purchase order itself, however, can cost the customer $150 to generate and process. Even the very best purchasing agent can only get a price reduction of maybe three to five percent. If you're in charge, you want to get rid of the $150-a-shot purchase orders, not nickel and dime at the margin. Reducing these costs incurred in purchasing is a compelling proposition, but not every organization is prepared to make the sort of changes that our NA program requires. Many of our presentations are just to get our prospects thinking.

When a prospect expressed a strong interest in WESCO's proposals, the account could be moved into an active selling phase. During the usual six to nine months of this phase, the NAM made presentations to the purchasing staff and other executives in each plant, matched WESCO branches with potential customer branches, addressed customer concerns about staffing, inventory, emergency service, and so forth. This period of intensive selling could demand between 30% and 40% of a NAM's time.

When the selling effort succeeded, the signing of the NA contract initiated an even more intensive implementation phase, requiring half of the NAM's time for the first several months. The NAM became part of WESCO's national implementation team (NIT), which included the director of national accounts and national sales support services. As part of this team, the NAM worked with a counterpart in the customer's NIT. These two representatives traveled to each customer site, meeting with local implementation teams (LITs) to help implement NA directives and to work on any initial stumbling blocks. Hersberger explained: "A NAM might travel for 30 to 60 days with the customer counterpart after the contract is finalized. This allows them both to meet with all the branches as well as to iron out between them any major decisions that arise during the meetings. Within 90 days, if implementation succeeds, the NAM will have obtained from each branch a list of items to be sourced from WESCO, a detailed inventory management plan, and target areas for value-added services."

Once the major initiatives were implemented, the account moved into a maintenance or development mode. Maintaining a national account meant continuing to hold NIT meetings to resolve any difficulties that could not be solved on a local level, and presenting new cost saving initiatives. An average account in this mode required at least 15% of a NAM's time, with large customers demanding much greater time commitments. For instance, NAM Mark Houston estimated that he spent 75% of his time in 1996 maintaining two large key NA customers, one with $20 million and the other with $9 million in annual sales.

By the time the account reached maintenance level, WESCO could decrease its costs to serve these customers and sufficiently improve gross margins to over 20 percent, compared to contractor accounts, which earned from 11% to 18%. In addition, WESCO could offer its lowest prices to these customers, Piraino explained, "since we take part in planning procurement, we can obtain better prices ourselves and pass the savings along." If the process stalled at the implementation phase, however, WESCO had found that it could be stuck with high costs and low margins.

A Success Story

One NA program success story was WESCO's partnership with an industrial customer in the paper segment managed by NAM Walter Thigpen. This customer had undertaken extensive communication and training programs at all management levels as part of a cost management initiative, ensuring support for the supplier reduction effort and working at the senior management level from day one. Thigpen explained:

> Even though we had done relatively little business with this customer before, they asked us to compete for their EES business in 1995. During the selection process, we used questionnaires to develop details of programs they had proposed to reduce the customer's inventory and energy costs. We determined that we could currently serve all but three of their plants. In order to serve these three plants, we decided it would be best to purchase the current local distributors to two plants and to open a new branch near the third. Hersberger and I made presentations to the selection committee, and by the time we secured the account in June 1996, we had a good idea of what implementation would look like.
>
> As soon as the agreement was signed, we formed NITs and held a national rollout meeting to begin implementation. During the next few months, we moved toward compliance at each customer plant, agreeing to hold monthly NIT meetings to address LIT concerns at various mill sites. As planned, we acquired two distributor branches and opened one new branch. We conducted a complete energy audit and recommended more energy efficient systems for all their plants. We also reduced inventory and implemented EDI procurement.[3] With the exception of a few small difficulties in setting up information systems, the process moved like clockwork. Everyone in their organization seemed to know exactly what to expect of the process and how to manage change.
>
> By June 1997, the intensive implementation phase was over. Sales had increased tenfold from the year before, reaching $1 million per month (see Exhibit 12). Between transaction cost reductions, energy savings, and inventory reduction, WESCO was able to document over 20% cost savings to the customer, far more than expected (see Exhibit 13).

Common Characteristics Across Successful NA Relationships

Piraino summarized the results of a recently conducted in-depth analysis of all the key NA customers. He said:

> Several pieces need to be in place to develop a successful relationship with an NA customer. First, we need to be in the sweet spot of our customer's procurement strategy. For most of our customers, over 70% of the annual procurement budget is accounted for by the top five to 10 suppliers. It is with these suppliers/distributors that customers are usually interested in developing a relationship based on value more than price (see Exhibit 14 for the purchase profile of this customer). The purchase dollar volume and effort involved in these relationships makes customers willing to go beyond transaction prices and focus on the total cost of procurement and ownership. They are open to national-level proposals for managing inventory, maintaining storerooms, and coordinating supplies.

"That is only part of the picture," Piraino continued:

> It is also important that top management at the customer's headquarters be committed to making this happen. Many times, we have found that this occurs when the customer hires a consultant to conduct a study of how to re-engineer the organization toward greater efficiency in operations, manufacturing, and service. Some of the most successful national accounts have begun with requests from customers in the wake of such studies. Once there is a mandate from the top, pockets of resistance in the rest of the organization are relatively easy to overcome. Even among a customer's senior management, there is an enormous difference between a VP of Purchasing championing our cause and the CEO spearheading the effort.

Lawry added:

> In several less successful NA relationships, unanticipated differences in procedures and

---

[3] Electronic Data Interchange (EDI) was a standardized system for electronic purchasing and information exchange between companies.

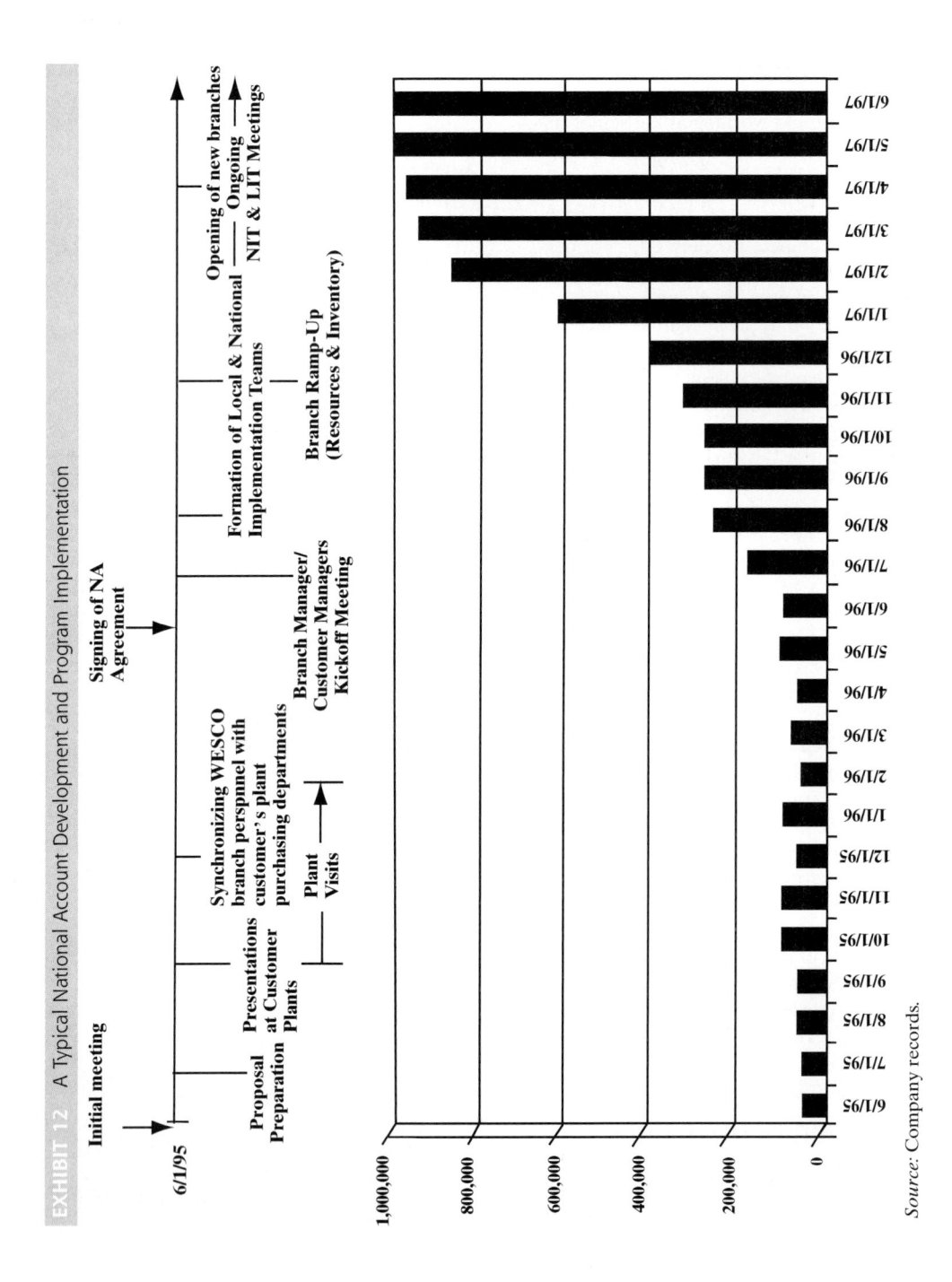

EXHIBIT 12 A Typical National Account Development and Program Implementation

CHAPTER 8 *Managing Relationship Equity*

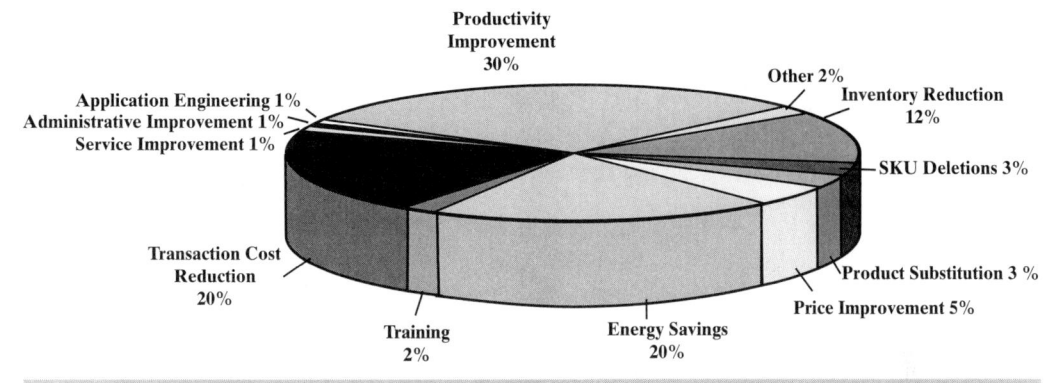

Customer Cost Savings by Category for a Successful NA Implementation

- Productivity Improvement 30%
- Other 2%
- Inventory Reduction 12%
- SKU Deletions 3%
- Product Substitution 3%
- Price Improvement 5%
- Energy Savings 20%
- Training 2%
- Transaction Cost Reduction 20%
- Application Engineering 1%
- Administrative Improvement 1%
- Service Improvement 1%

EXHIBIT 13

Source: Company records.

purchases across customer sites have made implementation difficult. In some cases, a local plant's bill of materials has turned out to be very different from the list covered by the NA agreement. The local WESCO branch has ended up having to resolve all matters locally, often with no cooperation from the customer. In these cases, you can try as hard as you want, but it just won't make a difference. The customer's corporate staff accuses us of not working hard enough. Their local purchasing and materials management folks will not cooperate because they would need to make changes to their systems. Our people get caught in the middle, quickly losing interest in the face of implementation headaches, and small potential sales volumes. Even the NAM shifts focus to accounts that might be easier to manage. With no champion on either side, the NA agreement has almost no chance for recovery.

"Local ties can make all the difference," explained Piraino:

In all our success stories, our branch managers and field reps had existing relationships with the customer's local personnel, making local compliance relatively simple for both sides. It's funny the way it works. Our main weapon to fight local and regional EES distributors is to offer an NA customer the opportunity to standardize procurements and reduce costs. This is very attractive to the customer's corporate procurement staff.

But this is not what the plant level purchasing staff want. Their power base has been built on managing their own suppliers and developing relationships that are good for the local plant. When you go into these accounts with an NA contract, unless they know you, their first reaction is to throw you out. The NA contract erodes their power and can affect their position. Who in their right mind would want that to happen?

THE NA CUSTOMER OF THE NEXT MILLENNIUM

Integrated Supply and the "New Age of Procurement"

As part of their effort to win sole-source agreements, WESCO had offered customers a set of value added services such as inventory analysis and reduction programs. Although demanding and labor intensive for WESCO, these programs produced substantial savings to NA customers time and again, savings that justified the margins WESCO realized on sales to these customers.

Recently, however, the tables had turned and several of WESCO's key NA customers had demanded an increased service commitment. Bill Cenk, WESCO's Director of Integrated Supply, explained:

We have found that two to three years after establishing successful partnerships with their top 5 to 10 suppliers/distributors, NA customers typically reach a stage at

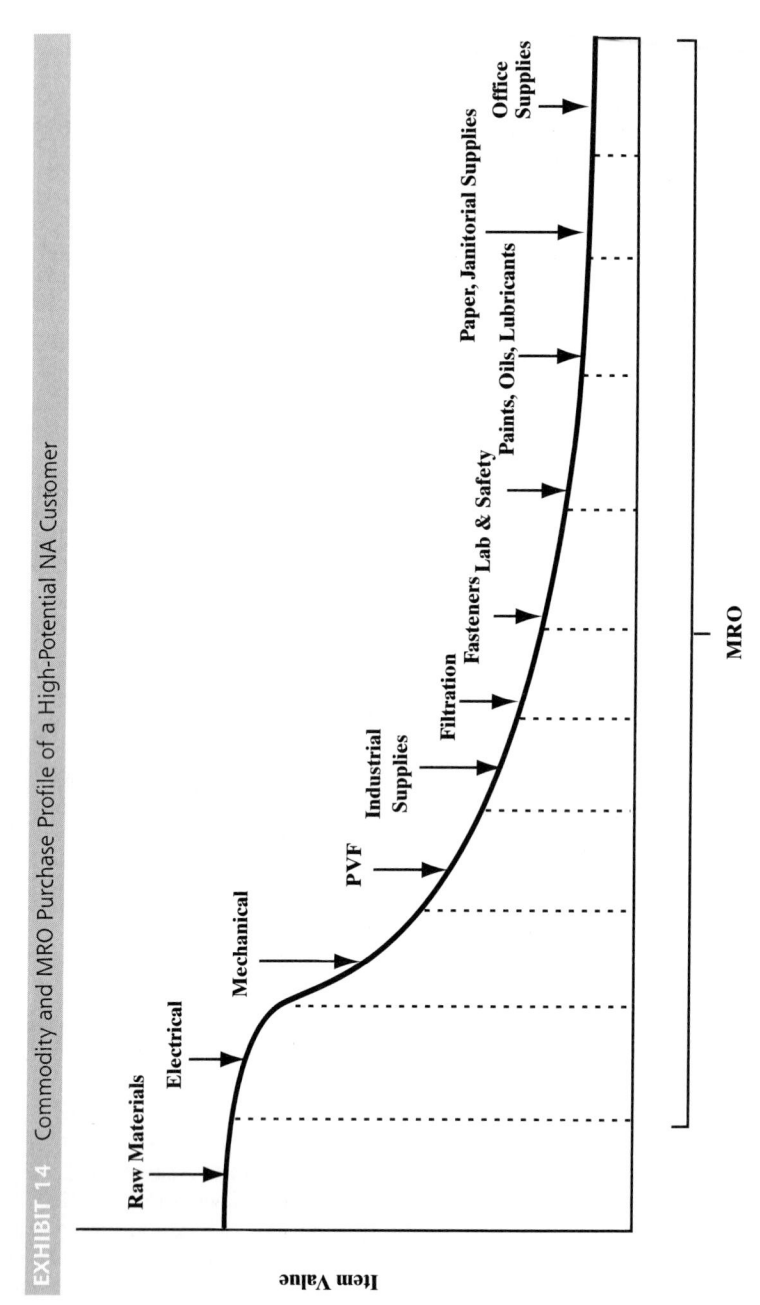

EXHIBIT 14 Commodity and MRO Purchase Profile of a High-Potential NA Customer

Source: Company records.

which the cost of monitoring and managing these top suppliers/distributors drops to 10–20% of their total procurement costs.[4] In effect, the top 10 supplier/distributors now account for over 70% of the customer's MRO purchase dollars, while demanding less than 20% of the customer's procurement costs.

The hundreds of other suppliers/distributors from whom these customers buy now account for just 30% of the customer's purchasing dollars yet over 80% of the procurement costs. These customers next try to reduce their costs of purchasing further by asking one of the top 5 to 10 supplier/distributors to manage and monitor the smaller supplier/distributors. In effect, these customers are creating "supplier tiers" [see Exhibit 15]. Suppliers in the highest level of the hierarchy are referred to as "primary" or "first tier" suppliers/distributors. They make money by marking up the products and services provided by "second tier" suppliers/distributors. The customer does not mind paying a higher price because the price increase is more than offset by the decrease in procurement costs.

As early as 1994, soon after he arrived, Haley had anticipated these trends in outsourcing and had been preaching this approach internally as well as to WESCO's major customers. In fact, one of the main reasons why Haley had developed WESCO's National Account program was to develop a path for the organization to become capable of offering these integrated solutions (IS) systems to customers.

Cenk added:

Right now, when NA customers and prospects ask us to take business that is different from our traditional activities, the decision to do it or not is made in Pittsburgh. We have a detailed process to analyze costs and potential benefits from the relationship. First, using publicly available information on product prices and discount structures,[5] we estimate the revenue stream from this additional business. Next, based on past experience, we estimate how much it will cost us to serve the customer. If the products/services involved are things that we have never handled before, then for a reference or benchmark, we look for existing products/services in our portfolio that are closest to the new ones. We also take into account the availability of the concerned NAM's time. Overall, here in Pittsburgh, I think we do a pretty good job of estimating revenues and costs involved in each of these situations.

Yet, to many in our company, this is still an ad hoc process. For example, in the last six months, we have been asked to shovel snow for one customer, manage janitorial supplies for another, and manage the industrial gases requirements for a third. This is not to say that it is wrong in principle to do these types of things. If the margins are good, then it makes sense. Especially under Haley's definition of integrated supply, it is something that we shouldn't shy away from. We add value to a customer's MRO procurement process and that's the bottom line. The issue is whether we should standardize on what we want to do when each customer comes to us with a unique set of needs? We need to have some quick answers here since every major player in the EES business has now started talking about managing their customer needs with an IS philosophy.

Another area of concern for Cenk was another new trend amongst large NA customers:

A few NA customers have taken a cost reduction route that is a little bit different from tiering. These customers are talking

---

[4] Procurement costs are the costs of placing orders and monitoring and managing suppliers/distributors. These are different from costs of the products and services themselves.

[5] In many consumables and supplies industries, third-party organizations published product specifications, pricing information, volume discounts, and special terms from various manufacturers. This information was publicly available and easy to use. For example, in the EES business, the *NEMA Publications and Materials Catalog* published by the National Electrical Manufacturers Association served as an industry reference book.

EXHIBIT 15 Different MRO Procurement Models

Procurement Models

Single Source Commodity Supply

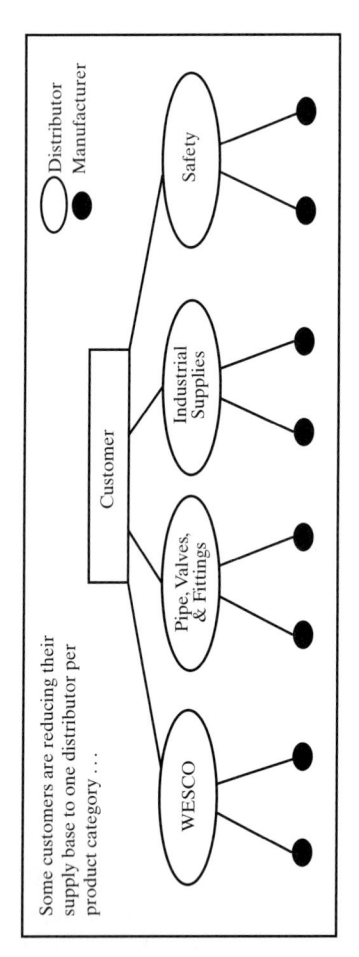

Some customers are reducing their supply base to one distributor per product category...

○ Distributor
● Manufacturer

Multi-Source Commodity Supply

Some customers elect to use one or more integrators to reduce their supply base even further...

○ Distributor
● Manufacturer

Alliances & Consortiums

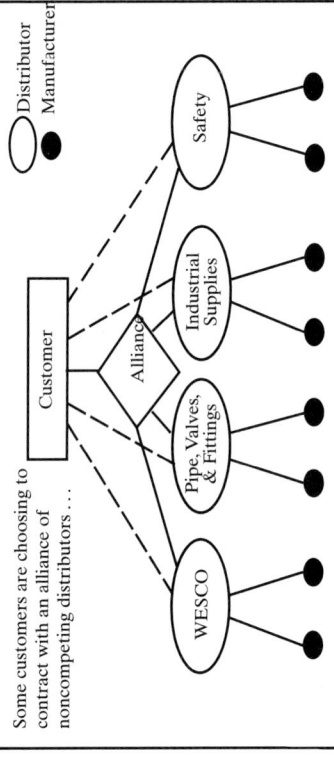

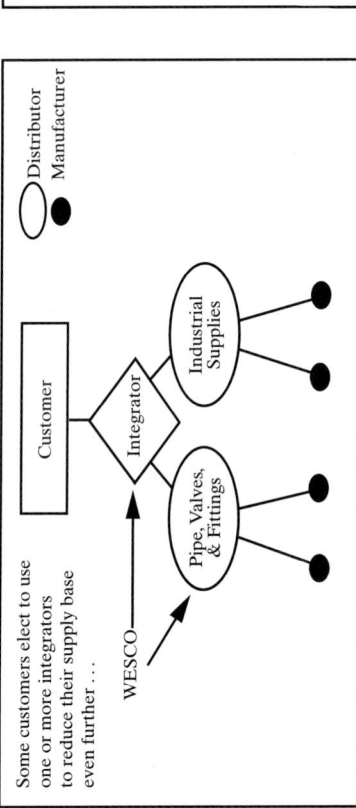

Some customers are choosing to contract with an alliance of noncompeting distributors...

○ Distributor
● Manufacturer

Source: Company records.

about forming alliances and consortia of non-competing distributors [see Exhibit 15]. They want groups of MRO suppliers and distributors to partner and offer the customer a one-stop solution [see Exhibit 16 for a profile of the MRO purchases of this customer type]. They expect us to share warehousing facilities with other distributors, create common billing formats, develop integrated product/service solutions, and so forth.

The question that we face here is how to plan for these customer migration paths. Without the benefit of tiering-related profits, each player will have to invest in learning about the others' businesses and integrating logistics functions and systems. What if each customer comes up with a different set of suppliers and distributors for their alliance? Developing these systems can be prohibitively expensive unless we can replicate the process across customers. Yet, if WESCO tries to establish itself as the leader of its own alliance, offering customers solutions before they ask, then we risk losing their confidence if they disapprove of our partners. We also risk taking on new forms of competition, since we will have to compete with competitors of our alliance partners.

Jim Piraino had also recently become concerned that integrated supply solutions were putting WESCO in a position to compete with some of its traditional customer base of electrical contractors. Donald Mitchell, a WESCO branch manager, saw this happening in the process of branch-level implementation:

> In our NA program, we have been telling our industrial customers that we can add significant value by auditing their electrical systems and suggesting ways in which they could improve the quality and efficiency of these systems. These customers now want us to apply the same skills to new projects. So, if we want their MRO business, we also need to get involved in the specification and installation of new systems—the electrical contractor's traditional business. In these situations, the electrical contractor could now see us as a competitor and could decide to stop buying their EES needs from us.

GOING AHEAD: WHAT SHOULD WESCO DO?

Piraino had to find answers to several questions. With a budget of $12 million in 1998, the decision of whether or not to continue the NA program was a non-trivial one. Piraino said: "If we decide to drop the program, most of the $12 million goes straight to the bottom line. I need to make a strong case if we are to proceed." Was this the right time to scale back the NA program? Should WESCO take a proactive stance in developing NA customers, or should it simply react to explicit customer demand? If the decision was to be proactive, how should WESCO define its approach? What should the firm do about supplier/distributor tiering and supplier/distributor alliances? How should they manage the demands of their traditional customer base during this period of change?

Being proactive, said Piraino, could require substantial investments:

> Seeking out new national accounts is wasteful unless we know how to optimize our existing NA relationships. Strong individual partnerships have brought us to where we are and they may even be able to keep us going for some more time. Do we now need a better approach to managing our current NA customers? Do we need a better model to anticipate customers' needs? Can we manage the migration path of an NA customer? How will this help us make reasoned decisions about what services we really want to provide our NA customers while recognizing that every customer is different? How should we plan to handle the new trends in NA customer behavior? Do we need to reorganize our company's structure?

The reactive model had the advantage of attracting only those customers interested enough to seek out WESCO's services on their own. Piraino's only concern here was that WESCO could start losing potential key customers very quickly. There were cases already where this had happened:

> We are already in a second-tier relationship with one of our best customers who used to purchase substantial levels of EES products from us. This customer should have

EXHIBIT 16 Commodity and MRO Purchase Profile of a Consortium Customer

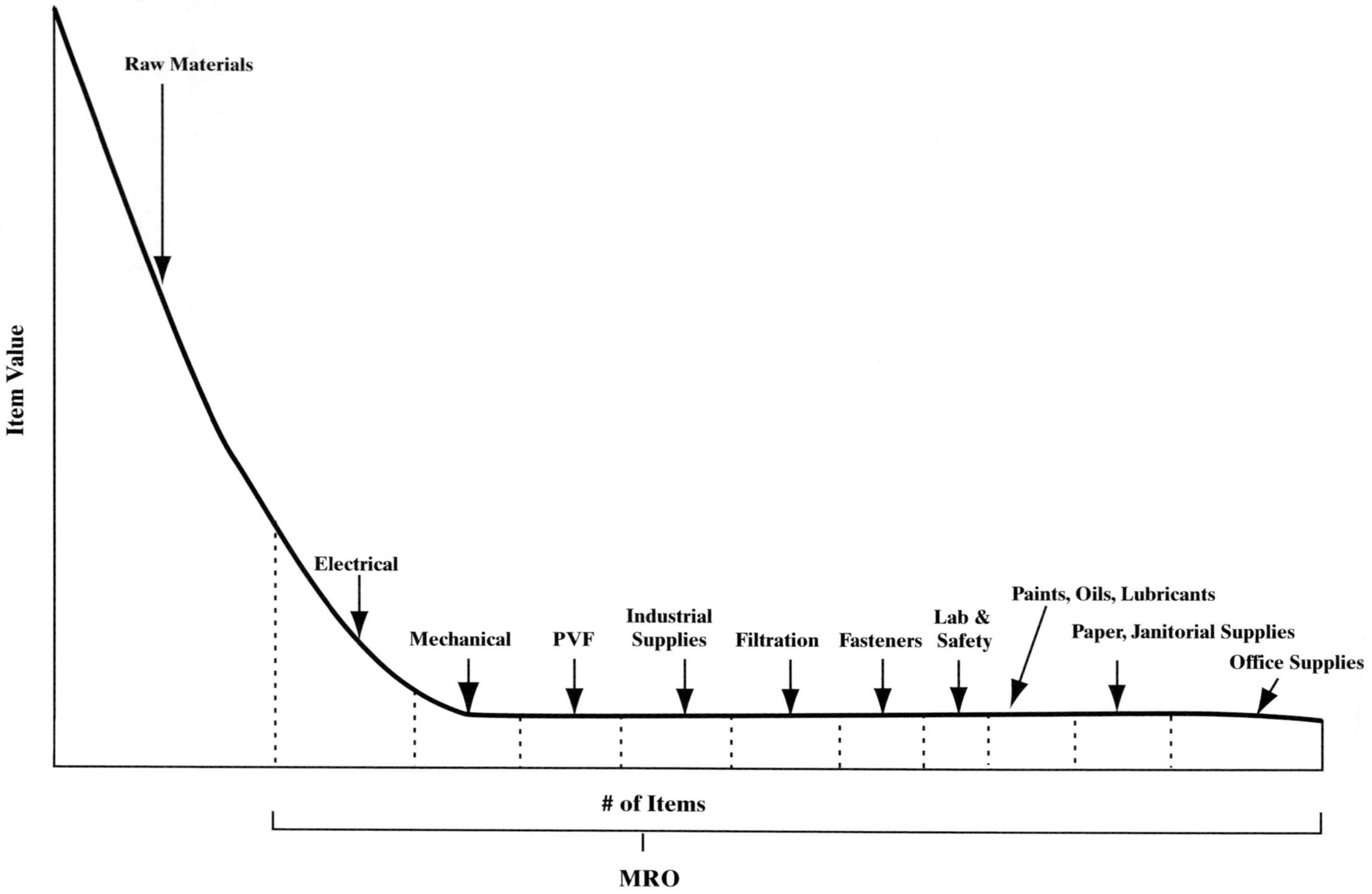

Source: Company records.

been one of our "key" national accounts. Although we used to deal directly with the customer, during the last twelve months, the picture has changed. Now, we sell to Smith Industries, a distributor of power transmissions, who in turn sells our product to this customer after marking up our prices. We have lost touch with this customer. ∎

◆◆◆ Arrow Electronics, Inc.

Case 8-2   Arrow Electronics, Inc.

Das Narayandas

Jan Salsgiver, President of the Arrow /Schweber (A/S) group, a subsidiary of Arrow Electronics, reviewed the Express Parts Internet Distribution Service proposal with colleagues Skip Streber, A/S senior vice president for sales, and Arrow CEO Steve Kaufman (see Exhibit 1). Express had developed an Internet-based trading system that would enable distributors to post inventories and prices to a bulletin board giving customers large and small an opportunity to shop for prices.

The opportunity to quickly gain new customers had to be traded off against potential effects on Arrow's relationships with current customers, who might exploit Express's bulletin board to cherry pick products from different channels. Arrow's relationships with its suppliers might also be affected. If they came to view Express as a legitimate option, its suppliers might dis-intermediate Arrow from their distribution channels.[1] "As a distributor," explained Salsgiver,

> we need to know three things: how we create value for our customers for the prices we charge; how this value is different from what our suppliers can provide to our customers;

and whether firms like Express can offer the same value or more for lower prices. We have a successful business model that is based on a portfolio of products and services that we offer our customers. Our customers come back to us because they get the most value from us for the prices they pay. If Express is going to change this equation, then we need to adapt our business model to accommodate the changes.

Salsgiver realized that before she could make a decision on the Express proposal she needed to answer a number of questions, among them: How many of A/S's customers were likely to switch some of their purchases to Express? How would this affect A/S's sales and profitability? How would A/S's suppliers react to Express? Finally, was Express a threat to or an opportunity for A/S?

ARROW ELECTRONICS

It was common for semiconductor and electronic component manufacturers such as Intel and Motorola (hereafter referred to as suppliers) to deal directly with large original equipment manufacturers (OEMs). Typically, sales to these customers accounted for 65% to 75% of the suppliers' sales. Suppliers franchised small numbers of distributors such as Arrow Electronics to manage sales to the remaining customers that they could not serve directly, whether because of diminutive size or extensive service requirements.

Arrow Electronics was a broad-line distributor of electronic parts, including semiconductors

---

The case was prepared by Professor Das Narayandas with the assistance of Research Associate Sara Frug. Copyright © 1998 by the President and Fellows of Harvard College. Harvard Business School Case 598-022.

[1]"Dis-intermediation" was the removal of a channel member (or intermediary) from a distribution channel.

```
                              CEO
                       Stephen P. Kaufman
```

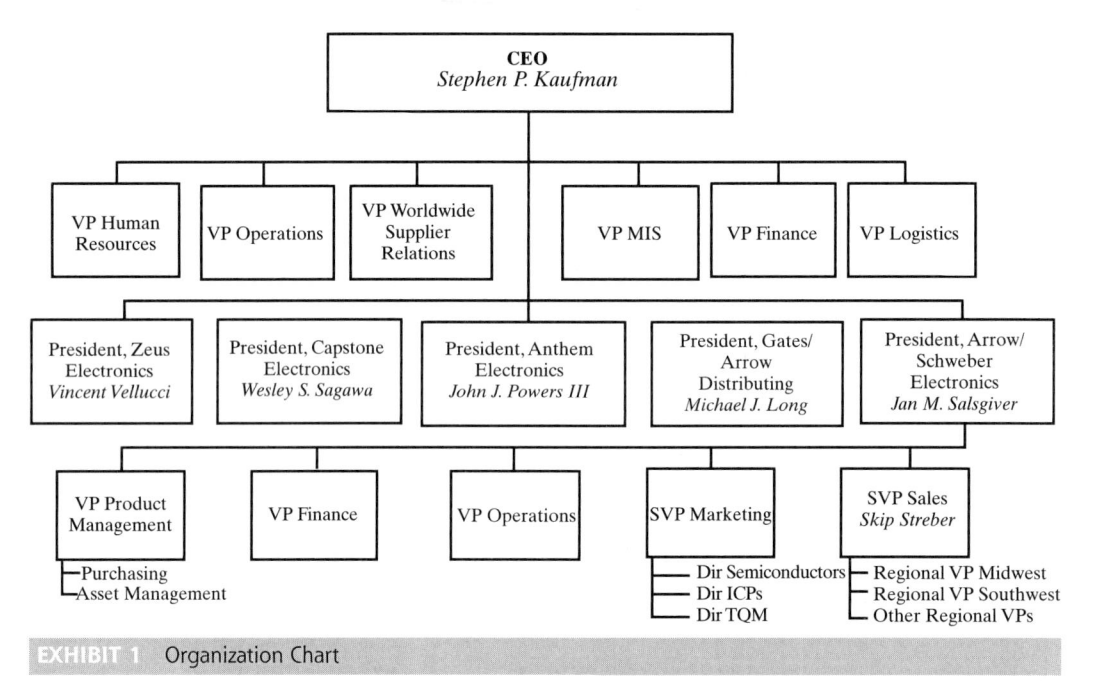

```
VP Human    VP Operations    VP Worldwide    VP MIS    VP Finance    VP Logistics
Resources                    Supplier
                             Relations
```

```
President, Zeus   President, Capstone   President, Anthem   President, Gates/   President, Arrow/
Electronics       Electronics           Electronics         Arrow               Schweber
Vincent Vellucci  Wesley S. Sagawa      John J. Powers III  Distributing        Electronics
                                                            Michael J. Long     Jan M. Salsgiver
```

```
VP Product        VP Finance            VP Operations       SVP Marketing       SVP Sales
Management                                                                       Skip Streber
─Purchasing                                                 ─ Dir Semiconductors ─ Regional VP Midwest
─Asset Management                                           ─ Dir ICPs           ─ Regional VP Southwest
                                                            ─ Dir TQM            ─ Other Regional VPs
```

EXHIBIT 1 Organization Chart

Source: Company records.

and passive components. Founded in 1935 to sell radio equipment, the company had undergone a number of major changes. Three Harvard Business School graduates who acquired a controlling interest in the company in 1968 had by 1980 grown it to the number two position, largely through acquisitions. A hotel fire in December 1980 that claimed the lives of five of the company's top six officers and eight other Arrow executives was followed by a shaky regrouping that coincided with an economic recession. Under the leadership of Stephen Kaufman, who became President in 1982 and CEO in 1986, Arrow once more began to climb, reaching the number one position among electronics distributors by 1992.

Consolidation throughout the distribution world resulted in a small number of large companies to capturing the top tier of the market by 1997. Arrow's closest competitor in 1996, Avnet Inc., trailed it by more than 20% in sales although it had grown by 14% compared with Arrow's 10% during that year. Of the next group of competitors the largest, which included foreign entrants Rabb Karcher and Future Electronics as well as longtime rivals Pioneer-Standard, Wyle, and Marshall Industries, was one quarter the size of Arrow in total sales volume and earned less than Arrow's largest operating group. Turning in a solid performance in a less than solid market, Arrow had earned more than $6.5 billion in sales in 1996 (Exhibit 2 presents financial information for 1994–1996).

Arrow's North American operations were headquartered in Melville, New York (see Exhibit 1). Sales and marketing functions were divided among five operating groups, distinguished by product and strategy, individually responsible for asset and materials management and P&L. Three groups, Arrow/Schweber, Anthem Electronics, and Zeus Electronics, sold semiconductors to different customer bases, Zeus to military and aerospace customers, Anthem and A/S to industrial customers. The other two groups were product-driven, Gates/Arrow Distributing selling primarily computer systems, peripherals, and software, Capstone Electronics passive components.

ARROW/SCHWEBER

Arrow/Schweber, the largest of Arrow's working groups, had sales of $2.07 billion in 1996.

For the Year	1996	1995	1994
Sales	$6,534,577	$5,919,420	$4,649,234
Costs and expenses			
Cost of products sold	5,492,556	4,888,746	3,832,169
Selling, general, and administrative expenses	604,412	574,166	487,982
Depreciation and amortization	36,982	33,299	27,759
Integration charges			45,350
	6,133,950	5,496,211	4,393,260
Operating income	400,627	423,209	255,974
Equity in earnings (loss) of affiliated company	(97)	2,493	
Interest expense, net	37,959	46,361	36,168
Earnings before income taxes and minority interest	362,571	379,341	219,806
Provision for income taxes	144,667	153,139	91,206
Earnings before minority interest	217,904	226,202	128,600
Minority interest	15,195	23,658	16,711
Net income	$ 202,709	$ 202,544	$ 111,889
Per common share			
Primary	$ 3.95	$ 4.21	$ 2.40
Fully diluted	3.95	4.03	2.31
Average number of common shares and common share equivalents outstanding			
Primary	51,380	48,081	46,634
Fully diluted	51,380	51,123	50,407

EXHIBIT 2 Consolidated Statement of Income (in thousands except per share data)

Source: Company records.

A/S president Jan Salsgiver, who had taken the helm in 1995, was leading A/S toward higher levels of technological expertise through technical certification of its field sales representatives and dedicated investments in product management.

A/S's local operations were configured in a branch structure. Headed by a general manager, each branch included field sales and inside sales representatives, product managers, and field application engineers, as well as administrative personnel and additional managers as necessitated by size. Six regional VPs oversaw A/S's 39 branch managers.

Products and Suppliers

The Arrow/Schweber line card (i.e., the set of products for which A/S was a franchised distributor) comprised two chip categories: standardized and proprietary. Standardized chips were interchangeable and produced by multiple suppliers, proprietary chips manufactured by a single supplier. Only franchised distributors could sell suppliers' standardized or proprietary products.

In an industry in which the top 10 suppliers provided 80% of the products on distributors' line cards, A/S's supplier list was long, numbering 56 suppliers in the spring of 1997 and growing.

Among A/S's largest suppliers was Altera, a manufacturer of proprietary programmable logic devices (PLDs) that required considerable value added programming. As was typical in the industry, the manufacturer did virtually no programming. Roughly 20% of Altera's products were purchased directly by customers who had in-house programming skills. Altera sold the remaining 80% through two franchised distributors capable of providing the value added programming required by individual customers.

Another large A/S supplier, Intel, also supplied mostly proprietary semiconductor products, although its most popular line, the x86 chip, did not require the level of value added programming and engineering support that A/S provided for Altera's PLDs. Texas Instruments and Motorola, the remaining two of A/S's "big four," balanced the line card by selling a 75/25 mix of standardized and proprietary products.

Customers

A/S's traditional customer base of mid- and small-sized original equipment manufacturers (OEMs) accounted for 56% of sales in 1996. These customers were too small for the suppliers to serve directly. Suppliers therefore engaged franchised distributors, to which they offered limited return privileges and price protection, to consolidate and satisfy demand from these customers.

Franchised distributors afforded customers the opportunity to order in small quantities and with short lead times, accommodations suppliers were unwilling to provide. With suppliers having chosen not to support credit management for customers, it fell upon distributors to offer this benefit as well. In addition to carrying massive inventories, distributors also performed value added services for customers who needed, for example, to receive all products needed for a specific manufacturing run in a single shipment or to release products to shipment based on forecast rather than previously entered, firm purchase orders. "This is very important to customers that have adopted JIT procurement systems," Kaufman explained. "These customers want to be very sure that they have everything they need at the right time and in the right quantities. If not, they run the risk of having to stop their production lines." Distributors' up-to-the-minute knowledge of available products could also be extremely valuable to OEMs in designing equipment for manufacture.

Even OEMs large enough to purchase direct often found distributors' value added services attractive. "When customers get large enough," Salsgiver explained:

they want to buy only direct from suppliers, who can provide them with the technical support and low prices they want. As time passes, however, these customers begin to reach a stage where they want to hand off materials management as well. Most suppliers are not capable of providing this service and, more important, are not interested in getting into this business. They don't want to take on any activity that does not have the high margins that electronic parts and components usually provide.[2] At this time they can become good distributor customers.

A second and growing new market was the Contract Manufacturer (CM) business, which produced circuit boards and industrial computer systems for OEMs. OEMs would outsource production of prototypes or even entire product runs to CMs, which would procure the components and assemble products. The CM business had grown at 30% per year between 1992 and 1996. During the same period, the percentage of business A/S channeled through CMs grew as well, reaching 20% of total sales by 1996. "Five years ago," observed one A/S field sales representative,

the only CMs were small mom-and-pop operations used for overflow or testing demand. A few of them have grown to be multibillion-dollar enterprises. However, there still are a large number of mid- and small-sized CMs. CMs tend to be very price sensitive. They selectively use our value added services such as programming and supply chain management in addition to our quick delivery service. But they don't need our engineering services at all.

A/S served two other major customer segments. Customers that purchased Intel x86 chips exclusively to manufacture PC clones accounted for 11% of A/S's business. The principal value A/S offered these customers, which were differentiated from traditional OEM customers in that they purchased in a purely commoditized fashion, was credit, which was unavailable to them through suppliers or other financial institutions.

The final segment comprised customers that purchased entire systems or assemblies. "These," Streber explained, "are computer product sub-assemblies that are used as components inside industrial equipment such as elevators or

---

[2]For example, Intel's gross margin was greater than 55% in 1997 and expected to remain above 50% in 1998 and 1999.

medical equipment. For example, the heart of a blood gas analyzer is an Intel-based PC that we supply. These customers tend to order in smaller quantities and need highly customized solutions."

A/S'S RELATIONSHIP WITH SUPPLIERS

To a far greater extent than in most other industries, electronic component manufacturers relied on distributors to generate demand. This tendency, according to Salsgiver, was a function of the nature of the electronics business. "Suppliers have two needs from us," she explained:

> They need us to win business in their standardized products to help them grow and gain both profit and market share. They also need us to represent their new technologies and proprietary products to our customers. It's obviously critical for both of our future success to help customers design our suppliers' new proprietary devices into their products.

"Our relationships with our suppliers have two unique components," continued Salsgiver:

> First, suppliers franchise select distributors to sell their products and provide financial incentives such as price protection and limited return privileges to only these franchised distributors. More pointedly, suppliers refuse to honor warranties of products purchased through channels other than the ones they have designated.
>
> Second, many suppliers ship their proprietary and standardized products to us at list price or marginally below it. For example, one of our suppliers sets our book cost at a constant 5% below their list price. When we get a request for a price quote from a customer, we call the supplier back and give them the details of the customer and the opportunity. The supplier then decides how much of an additional discount they will provide us on this request. In this manner, they know exactly what we are doing and they are also able to control prices. The level of discount provided varies depending on whether it is our *design win* or a *jump ball* [see below].

Design Win

A/S, like other electronics distributors, generated demand by helping customers engineer end products to which its suppliers' chips were integral. Suppliers tracked which distributors did design work by assigning numbers to specific distributor-customer partnerships. "When we start working on an opportunity and invest resources in a customer's project," explained Streber,

> we will call our supplier and give them all the details. The supplier then assigns a design number that recognizes the work we have done. This is called "design registration." When the order materializes and the customer shops across distributors for price, the supplier offers a much higher discount to the distributor credited with the design registration as compared to any other distributor. Unless another distributor is willing to take a hit they will not be able to serve this customer, since only the distributor with the design registration will be able to earn an acceptable margin at the suggested resale price.

Jump Ball

Customers that purchased on the basis of manufacturer reputation or price and did not involve a distributor in design work were termed "jump balls" in the business. For these customers, suppliers offered all distributors the same margin, which was significantly less than that which would be offered in the case of a design win. Jump balls also occurred when a customer switched from direct purchasing to distribution. "In these cases," Salsgiver explained, "the suppliers have already created the demand for the products by doing the design work themselves, so they see the distributor's value only in credit and fulfillment and they compensate minimally for these services."

Managing the Relationship with Suppliers

"Our suppliers are able to control our destiny in many ways," observed Kaufman:

> In the case of jump balls, our suppliers inform the customer about the various distributors they can buy from. Suppliers usually don't exclude a distributor from the list. But they do control the order of names. This

is an important factor. Being the first name on that list increases the chance of getting the sale. It is the supplier's way of rewarding one distributor over another.

Another way suppliers manage demand flow is in the order in which they inform the distributors about an opportunity. Getting to know about an opportunity even a few minutes or hours before anyone else can give our sales reps all the time they need to secure the sale.

Finally, suppliers can manage the flow of orders by managing the time they take in responding to a distributor's request for prices. The norm is that the supplier needs to get back within 24 hours of a request. If you have a good relationship or if the supplier wants to reward you, you might get a response a lot faster. If you are not in the good graces of the supplier, you could be the victim of an overloaded sales rep who was so busy that it took all of 24 hours for them to process your request.

This does not mean that we have no power. Usually, for the standardized products we carry lines from different suppliers that have identical specifications, and therefore are substitutable. When a customer needs standardized products, we can go back to each supplier and literally shop the volume around to see who will give us the best margins. Typically these are high-volume products and therefore an important part of the suppliers' portfolio. A supplier that is anxious to fill its production lines can "buy an order." This leads to higher margins for us.

Here is when, depending on how we have been treated, we can return favors. If suppliers use jump balls to keep distributors in check, we are able to use design wins and competitive standardized products to counterbalance their power.

"Suppliers want A/S and other distributors to get technology into the hands of the right customers," added Salsgiver:

In this business, demand points are not always known. An operation in someone's garage this year could be the multibillion-dollar giant five years from now. Our suppliers want us to identify these growth opportunities and lock them in before anyone else does. Our job at A/S is to know our customers well enough to create demand for our suppliers' products. We maintain a separate account development group that calls on small companies looking for opportunities of the future. This is our ace of spades when it comes to managing our relationships with our suppliers.

ARROW'S SELLING EFFORT

"It is important to understand how products are viewed by our suppliers and our customers." Salsgiver explained, "When we deal with our suppliers it is the world of standardized and proprietary products. When we deal with customers, it becomes a world of book and ship, and value added products."

Book and Ship (BAS)

A/S had developed a real-time, online computer system that tracked costs, prices, and movements of 300,000 inventoried part numbers and order patterns (A/S processed more than 10,000 transactions per day) and sales history for each of the company's 50,000 customers. Using terminals connected to this system, A/S's 300 branch-based sales and marketing representatives (SMRs) handled daily phone calls from customers checking delivery, availability, and price levels.

For customers who requested a quote directly, an SMR might try to secure the business and arrange to ship the product. This was termed a book and ship (BAS) transaction. SMRs exercised pricing authority, obtaining discount levels from suppliers and quoting prices to their assigned customers on the basis of their knowledge of customers' buying patterns, local market trends, current cost levels, and inventory on hand.

A/S commonly referred to BAS products as commodity products because of the nature of value added by A/S. A/S's gross margins on BAS products ran above the company average, in the range of 20% to 25%.

Value Added (VA)

Alternatively, an order might be originated by field engineering and facilitated by a field sales representative (FSR), the typical design win situation. In this case a customer's purchasing agent would speak to an SMR only to finalize the details of the transaction. Such transactions represented the culmination of tremendous effort and expenditure of substantial resources. A/S's approximately 400 FSRs visited their customers' (usually 10–20 per FSR) design engineers to learn about current projects and explain and promote new products being introduced by Arrow's suppliers. FSRs also established relationships with customers' purchasing personnel, negotiated major contracts, and resolved problems with the flow of orders and deliveries.

FSRs worked hand in glove with the field application engineers (FAEs) who provided technical support to the sales force, assisting with problem solving and product design issues. Suppliers that wanted Arrow to help smaller customers design-in their proprietary parts also relied heavily on the FAEs, who were salaried and generally expensive to maintain.

Product managers (PMs) advocated on behalf of manufacturers by ensuring that FSRs and SMRs were up-to-date on suppliers' latest products and marketing programs and that the sales force was meeting its supplier-by-supplier sales budgets. PMs also followed up on leads and referrals from suppliers and worked with Arrow's corporate marketing department to ensure that low-volume and unusual products were ordered on a timely basis.

Streber pointed out that customer involvement to a great extent revolved around the prevailing understanding of value added. "The meaning of value added has continuously changed in our business," he explained:

> In 1977 value added meant nothing more than providing an inventory buffer for the customer. In 1987 it meant altering components to meet customer needs, either by programming, packaging, or kitting parts.[3] In 1997, for our most important customers, it meant building virtual organizations with us through in-plant stores and the like. Today, the true value added is in order cycle management. In 1977 about 2% of our sales had a value-added component. By 2000 this number can reach as high as 80%. [See Exhibits 3 and 4.]

Phantom Inventory

One result of the system of debits-to-cost employed by suppliers was what Salsgiver termed "phantom inventory." (Exhibit 5 presents Arrow's overall inventory figures.) "As strange as it sounds, the way our business works," she explained, "we buy product all day long at a dollar per part, sell it at sixty cents, and make a decent profit." The way suppliers managed pricing resulted in distributors paying a relatively low figure for inventory carried on the books at high cost. But because it made it look as though inventory never turned, this system made day-to-day management, not to mention projections, quite difficult.

RELATIONSHIPS WITH CUSTOMERS

Customers that placed requests-for-quotes (RFQ) for one or a few products with a number of distributors simultaneously were termed "transactional" customers. The distributors would obtain current pricing information from their suppliers and respond to RFQs, whereupon the customers might pursue subsequent rounds of negotiations to obtain the best price. SMRs expressed ambivalence about transactional customers. "I spend a good portion of my day speaking to these sorts of customers," explained one. "They always know the current prices and will list grey market distributors' prices when I give my quote."

Added an FSR who called exclusively on CMs:

> We are currently able to provide credit and short delivery lead times on small orders to contract manufacturers, which they cannot receive either from the suppliers or from the nonfranchised distributors otherwise known as brokers. This means that when an OEM asks a CM to build a board, the CM has an incentive to purchase through us. But CMs can design in our manufacturers' products just as easily as we can. If our suppliers decide to reward CM demand creation the way they reward such distributor activities, then it's going to be really tough to compete.

---

[3] Gathering together into a single package all the parts needed for a job was termed "kitting." Customers would submit bills of materials and A/S would provide the compete set. Streber explained that the procedure had worked well during the late 1980s when customers were building to forecast and in "push" manufacturing environments, but had declined in popularity in the current "pull" (build-to-order) climate.

EXHIBIT 3   Value Added from Arrow/Schweber

TRANSACTION COST REDUCTION

Total Cost of Ownership Analysis
Understanding their "total cost of ownership" better prepared companies to make complex "make versus buy" and supplier selection decisions. Arrow/Schweber's total cost of ownership financial model, based on activity-based costing (ABC) methodologies, helped companies identify the total costs associated with particular activities or processes.

Automated Replenishment
Arrow CARES®, a PC Windows®-based automated inventory replenishment system, operated in a multiple bin, kanban environment using "pull" processes, supported by bar code technology and EDI or fax transmission, to replenish particularly high volume repetitive purchase items. Deployed in customer stockrooms or at point-of-use, the system could dramatically reduce inventory and associated carrying costs.

Electronic Data Interchange
As an integral part of Arrow/Schweber's value added services, EDI supported faster, more accurate, information transfer, which reduced supply chain costs, and improved productivity and, as a result, by reducing overhead, lowering inventory, and shortening cycle times, made its customers more competitive.

In-Plant Terminals
Direct access to Arrow/Schweber's online, real-time computer system through customer-staffed terminals enabled A/S customers' purchasing departments to check inventory availability, set up purchase orders, and cross parts, and engineering departments to view component specifications, thereby improving productivity and reducing acquisition costs. The terminals also supported on-site materials management for customers with high levels of order processing.

PLANNING THE MATERIAL PIPELINE

In-Plant Stores
On-site staff in Arrow/Schweber in-plant stores were responsible for planning, purchasing, receiving, stocking, and fulfilling production and engineering requirements through customer-premises warehouses. Ownership of material remained with A/S until delivered, significantly reducing customers' inventory-carrying costs.

Turnkey Service
Arrow/Schweber provided complete management of customers' printed circuit board assembly requirements, from prototype to production, through a turnkey service that combined its expertise in materials management with that of certified turnkey partners to production requirements, decreasing products' time-to-volume and time-to-market.

IMPROVING LOGISTICAL EFFICIENCY

Production Kitting
Arrow/Schweber's ISO 9002 kitting division in one of its primary distribution centers (PDCs) in Sparks, Nevada, enabled customers to access its extensive line card inventory and managed programs from quoting, through ECO management, pricing, and forecast changes, to delivery.

Supplying prepackaged kits to designated customer production facilities "just-in-time" helped to reduce stockouts, component obsolescence, inventory-carrying costs, and other inventory-related expenses.

Device Programming
Arrow/Schweber customers not only offered customers the industry's broadest line card, but was also uniquely positioned through its comprehensive resource of silicon and design support to provide solutions for every PLD application. Four primary ISO 9002 certified programming centers linked to a single network provided an optimal means to match demand to capacity and speeded turnaround for customers. Customers that programmed through Arrow/Schweber avoided costly capital equipment expenditures and minimized product obsolescence resulting from last minute firmware changes.

COMPLETE SUPPLY CHAIN MANAGEMENT
Business Needs Analysis
Arrow/Schweber's business needs analysis evaluated customers' materials planning, acquisition, handling, and inventorying processes. Thoroughly understanding its customers' existing capabilities and desired goals enabled Arrow/Schweber to make practical recommendations that provided sustainable results reflected in the bottom line.

Custom Computer Products (CCP)
Arrow/Schweber's ISO 9002–certified Custom Computer Products (CCP) Division was a nationwide source of complete system and subsystem integration, assembly, and testing. Its in-house support team of engineers and technical personnel provided design and development assistance as well as total project management from concept to completion. The latter originated from a facility certified by Intel for hardware and software design and product integration. Applications support included disk formatting and custom drive configurations; software configuration and customization; custom packaging, painting, and labeling; run-in and diagnostic testing; complete functional, diagnostic, environmental, and confidence testing; extended warranty; local installation and on-site training; and nationwide field service. Arrow/Schweber's CCP service reduced production costs and time to market thereby enhancing customers' cash flow.

Source: Company records.

Observed Kaufman:

Roughly 25% of our sales today come from transactional customers. Typically, a majority of these sales are of the book-and-ship (BAS) type. We cannot afford to ignore this group for several reasons. In addition to accounting for a significant portion of our current sales, this customer segment is also a major source of relationship customers in the long run. Most of our relationship customers today started out as transactional customers. Customers want to check us out and monitor our performance over several orders before they are willing to get into any sort of agreement that goes beyond the transaction level. We are generally able to convert at least half of our transactional customers into relational customers over the long haul.

Other customers attempted to establish long-term relationships with a small number of distributors. Explained Salsgiver:

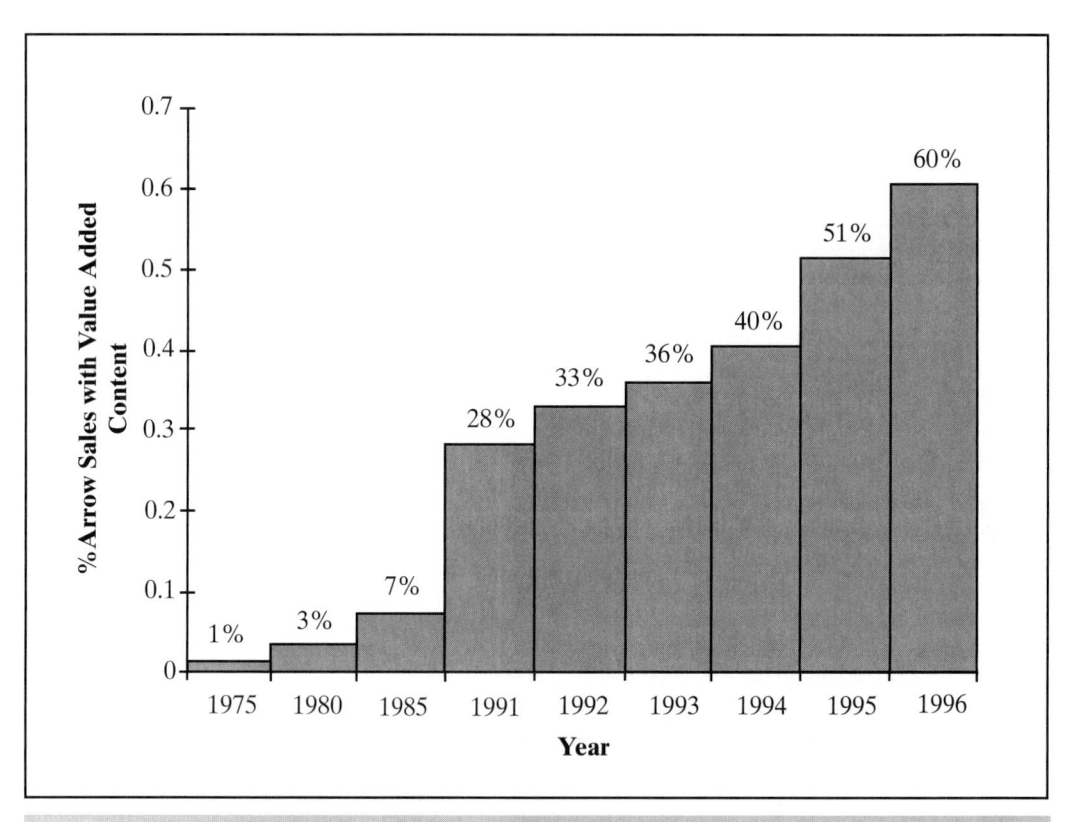

EXHIBIT 4 Percent of Arrow Sales with Value Added Content

Source: Company records.

Most of our relationship customers do more than half of their business with their top distributor. These customers want the convenience of submitting an entire bill of items for a quote, finding it more valuable to have a steady partner than the rock bottom price over the long haul. That doesn't mean that they don't care about prices. It is very common for them to maintain a relationship with one or two other distributors in order to ensure continuous availability of products and to keep their primary distributor in check.

Most of our relationship customers buy a basket of products from us that includes BAS and VA products. Given the competitive nature of this business, we have found that it is difficult to get close to a customer through the book-and-ship business. Our approach is to use the value added products as the first step to building a relationship. We provide customers with the best-in-class support in this category. Once customers get a chance to interact with us, they are able to see the true benefit of doing business with us rather than any other distributor.

Now comes a peculiar trait in our business. You would expect that the customer pays us high prices for the value added services we provide. Well, that doesn't happen. The customer knows that there are several distributors that can provide these value added services. They then use the threat of switching to other distributors to make sure that we don't charge too much of a premium for our services. While we try to demonstrate tangible financial benefits to justify our prices, there are times when we practically give away the value that we create for them and recover our profits in other areas.

EXHIBIT 5 Consolidated Balance Sheet (thousands)

	December 31, 1996	December 31, 1995
Assets		
Current assets		
Cash and short-term investments	$ 136,400	$ 93,947
Accounts receivable, less allowance for doubtful accounts ($39,753 in 1996 and $38,670 in 1995)	902,878	940,049
Inventories	1,044,841	1,039,111
Prepaid expenses and other assets	36,004	31,610
Total current assets	2,120,123	2,104,717
Property, plant, and equipment at cost		
Land	8,712	14,527
Buildings and improvements	77,527	63,857
Machinery and equipment	127,633	112,883
	213,602	191,267
Less: accumulated depreciation and amortization	98,377	73,932
	115,225	117,335
Investment in affiliated company	34,200	36,031
Cost in excess of net assets of companies acquired, less accumulated amortization ($57,802 in 1996 and $48,085 in 1995)	388,787	379,171
Other assets	52,016	63,762
	$2,710,351	$2,701,016
Liabilities and Shareholders' Equity		
Current liabilities		
Accounts payable	$ 594,474	$ 561,834
Accrued expenses	180,129	207,738
Short-term borrowings, including current maturities of long-term debt	71,504	117,085
Total current liabilities	846,107	886,657
Long-term debt	344,562	451,706
Other liabilities	68,488	68,992
Minority interest	92,712	97,780
Shareholders' equity		
Common stock, par value $1		
Authorized—120,000,000 and 80,000,000 shares in 1996 and 1995		
Issued—51,196,385 and 50,647,826 shares in 1996 and 1995	51,196	50,648
Capital in excess of par value	549,913	530,324
Retained earnings	805,342	602,633
Foreign currency translation adjustment	8,753	18,398
	1,415,204	1,202,003
Less: Treasury stock (1,069,699 and 22,297 shares in 1996 and 1995), at cost	49,065	24
Unamortized employee stock awards	7,657	6,098
Total shareholders' equity	1,358,482	1,195,881
	$2,710,351	$2,701,016

Source: Company records.

Although the margins on the chips are the same as in our BAS business, because we do not charge adequately for our value added services, our gross margins on value-add products run below the company average, in the range of 10% to 15%. We cross sell our other products to these customers by offering them significant breaks on the value added products in return for their commitment to buy the book-and-ship products exclusively from us. In a way, in these relationships the commodity products subsidize the specialty products.

Finding the right customers with which to develop long-term relationships was extremely important. It was not uncommon for customers simply not to appreciate the work done by A/S or even to honor their own commitments. "We had been pursuing a prospect for some time," recalled Martha Moranis, an SMR,

when a request came in from them for a highly allocated proprietary chip manufactured by one of our major suppliers. We saw this as a great opportunity to break into the account and establish a long-term relationship and we agreed to obtain this product for them at a favorable price. In return, they promised to purchase one of their major needs exclusively from us at a price that allowed us a good margin. We jumped through flaming hoops to deliver on our side of the bargain, but once they had received their shipment they seemed to change their mind about the agreement. When it came time for them to place their standing order, they tried to lower the price we had agreed upon and finally placed the order with another distributor. We could not do anything with the supplier because they saw it as a jump ball. In hindsight, we would have been better off not serving this customer at all.

The same set of actions on our part will get a very different response from some of our good customers. We have found that the best way to strengthen a relationship that is already strong is by helping our customers in their times of need. Our good customers will always remember what we did for them and usually reward us at a later date.

Viewed from the other side of the fence, long-term relationships represented a significant obstacle. Explained one FSR:

I once called on a customer who had a gatekeeper for a purchasing manager. This buyer had been there for 15 years and had fallen into a routine of placing the same orders with the same distributors all the time. For some reason he did not want to deal with us. We rotated this account through some of our best reps with no success. This buyer was "anti-Arrow" and we had no clue why. We tried to go around the buyer and work with engineering. This made things worse for us. The buyer told us that we could not design in any product that they currently purchased through our competition. This made it really tough to maneuver. Our chance arrived when a new buyer came in. This buyer was willing to work with us and we ended winning significant amounts of business from this customer.

This process can work in reverse as well. We can establish a solid relationship with a customer that is utterly obliterated when a new buyer with a different set of connections replaces the person with whom we used to work.

"There is another angle to building a relationship with a customer," observed Kaufman:

I think we need to go further to make the relationship virtually unbreakable. We need to get the customer to invest along with us in systems and processes that enable us to provide value added services.

It is easier for us when we are dealing with value added products like PLDs where the customer has to have invested in product-related systems and processes that are customized to match our programming skills. The trend toward greater demand for value added services is our best bet to counterbalance the high price sensitivities of our customers and the relational "cheating" that takes place in our business. But even with commodity products, where there is little that can be done at the product end, a customer that invests in supply chain management initiatives along with us is very unlikely to terminate their relationship with us.

A/S AND THE INTERNET

During the early to mid-1990s many electronics distributors established home pages on the Internet through which to present their companies, provide line card information, and even sell products. The prominence of independent, non-franchised distributors, viewed by many franchised distributors and customers alike as being less than legitimate, was unmistakable in the move to the Internet. These companies purchased products from others' overstocks, but, lacking authorized reseller agreements, they could not offer the manufacturers' warranties.

Although it had established a closed system that enabled its customers to obtain fixed price and availability information from terminals in their plants, Arrow had been reluctant to establish a presence in the public domain, preferring, instead, to watch and wait while others tested the waters. Home pages were eventually established for the company and its operating groups, but these Web sites did not incorporate purchasing capability. Rather, they functioned as information centers, sources of material about suppliers, searchable lists of parts, and news. Potential customers were directed from the Web page to the national 1–800 number for a specific group.

EXPRESS PARTS, INC.

Express Parts, Inc., was a new, independent distributor that developed an Internet-based trading system around a multi-distributor bulletin board. Express claimed that its search engine could quickly cross-reference equivalent parts from multiple manufacturers based either on part number or technical description and estimated that more than 50,000 OEMs throughout the United States would have access to the service. Express proposed that access to such a large market would enable A/S to increase sales at less than half the cost of doing so via its branch network.

Express's program was to work as follows:

1. A/S's full list of available inventory and associated prices, transmitted to Express nightly, was to be combined with similar lists from a limited number of other distributors.
2. Express's customers would sign onto its service via the Internet and search by part number or description. Upon making a selection, a customer would view a screen displaying all products that matched the search criteria, together with prices and quantities available for shipment (individual distributors identified only by an arbitrary letter, not by name). (See Exhibit 6.)
3. A customer could select any supplier/distributor combination, enter the quantity desired, and click the mouse to place the order, which would instantly be transmitted to Express. Express would review the order, perform a credit check, and acknowledge accepted orders to the customer and route them electronically to the appropriate distributor.
4. Distributors would, on behalf of Express, pick parts and "drop ship" orders directly to customers, notifying Express electronically that shipment had been made.[4] Express billed customers.
5. Payment, minus Express's fee of 6%, was made to distributors 30 days after orders shipped.

DECISIONS

Express's proposal had stirred significant debate among the A/S management team, which had now been discussing it for nearly a month. Express had told Salsgiver that they needed a decision within the week. This was, they said, because they were only going to ask a limited number of distributors to join, in order to avoid having too many duplicate and competitive lines.

Kaufman had asked Salsgiver to evaluate the impact Express might have on A/S's business under different scenarios. "We need to have some idea of what this is going to do to our business," he had told her. Salsgiver had subsequently commissioned a detailed study of two specific outcomes. In the optimistic scenario, all

---

[4] "Drop ship" was a process whereby one company (in this case, Arrow) would ship a product to a customer as an agent for a middleman (in this case, Express) making it look as though the product came from the middleman. Legally, Arrow had "sold" the product to Express, which had instantly resold it to the customer. Express was thus legally responsible for the transaction, including billing, collecting, and payment.

EXHIBIT 6 Express Parts Sample

EXPRESS PARTS, INC.

Part Number Requested: SN74LS244N   *Part Description: LS Octal Buffer/Line Driver*

Distributor

Manufacturer	Part Number	A Qty	$	B Qty	$	C Qty	$	D Qty	$	E Qty	$	F Qty	$
Texas Instruments	SN74LS244N	62,507	.31	83,200	.28	5,000	.72	30,250	.67	89,660	.45	45,000	.62
Motorola	SN74LS244N	30,245	.42	77,700	.49	89,500	.25	82,300	.58	94,200	.26	145,000	.22
Natl Semiconductor	DM74LS244N	59,000	.30	12,400	.67	64,500	.53	73,000	.50	100,000	.23	2,200	.70
SGS Thomson	T74LS244B1	29,800	.55	28,000	.54	73,250	.59	62,900	.66	78,780	.39	40,245	.49
Philips	N74LS244N	76,400	.24	25,975	.62	25,000	.48	10,000	.70	47,120	.58	50,800	.55

Click on the price you want
Quantity _____
Quote _____
Order _____

Customer:
Name: _____
Address: _____

E-mail Address: _____

Source: Company records

EXHIBIT 7 Market Segment Mix[a] ($ billions)

Market Segment	Market Segment (% and $ of total business) %	$	Value Added Business[b] %	$	BAS[c] Business %	$	Optimistic Cannibalization of BAS Business %	$	Pessimistic Cannibalization of BAS Business %	$
Core										
CM	20	460	57	262	43	198	30	59	70	139
OEM	56	1,300	72	936	28	364	25	91	60	218
X86	11	250	2	5	98	245	50	122	80	196
ICP[d]	13	300	80	240	20	60	35	21	80	48
		2,310		1,443		867		293		601

Source: Company records.
[a]Calculations assume that value added business is immune to Internet cannibalization.
[b]Includes scheduled orders and forecast sharing.
[c]Book-and-ship.
[d]Industrial computer products.

transactional customers were assumed to switch their purchases from A/S to Express. In the pessimistic scenario, all transactional customers and roughly 40% of relationship customers were assumed to switch their purchases from A/S to Express. These percentages were arrived at through a detailed bottom-up account analysis. (Exhibit 7 details the results of this study.)

Realizing that the analysis provided some direction, but not all the answers she needed to make her decisions, Salsgiver reflected on how two of her colleagues had weighed in on the issue.

"It is very important that we keep in mind our corporate objectives," Kaufman had emphasized:

With expenses at 11%, we cannot afford our overall gross margins for A/S to fall below 15%. We certainly don't want to accelerate the downward trend in margins that we've been seeing any more than is necessary.

I think the Internet will never be anything more than an invitation to bargain. In the worst case scenario, all our current customers will get the lowest price from the Express system and use it as a starting point to bargain with us. I have yet to meet an industrial buyer who does not believe that he can do better by bargaining, especially on a price open to the public. With Express as a competitor, I think we will have to learn how to sell against "going out of business" prices on a regular basis. We also have to have a much stronger value-in-use sales story than ever before.

"I agree," Streber had concurred,

that any time the only value A/S brings to the table is in price and delivery, we are vulnerable to the Internet for competition. My feeling is that we will lose little or none of our business with relationship customers and about half of our business with transactional customers. But if we do it right, this loss will be more or less compensated for by the additional business we get from Express. Express gives us the opportunity to sell to those customers that we cannot sell to using our current business model.

Currently, our SMRs spend a tremendous amount of time and energy trying to build new customers. When many of these customers call, we spend a lot of time trying to figure out whether we can build a relationship with them. We have found that most of the time they are not interested in going beyond the transaction; all they want is to shop around for the lowest price. We could ask these customers to go to Express or possibly our own Internet site. The opportunity to offer standardized pricing over the Internet can minimize our efforts and even make it worthwhile for us since we might be able to significantly cut our costs to serve these customers. Finally, as long as we are the lowest, we will always get the sale.

By maintaining strong relationships with our suppliers, we will still be able to sell at competitive prices for design wins. As long as our suppliers believe that we create demand, they will give us the most favorable pricing. Express only responds to demand. I think if we quote anonymously on their system, given our ability to get the lowest prices, we might be able to hang onto a bit more of the business than our models indicate.

Salsgiver, however, remained pessimistic. "We all agree," she observed,

that Express will get the customer who is less likely to think long-term and is more likely to want to return to the old price-and-availability business. With Express, we are quite vulnerable in highly commoditized products.

I also think we are erring in making the absolute association between commodity products and transactional behavior on the one hand, and value added products and relational behavior on the other. Although these generally line up, it does not always happen. Even our relationship customers are going to use this as a tool to get lower prices from us. In the future, I think they will not appreciate what we do for them as much as they have in the past. The one thing that is in our favor over the long haul is the flux in the business. When product is scarce, a market may be good, but a friend is better. We need to remind our customers of this.

I also wonder how the Express proposal affects our suppliers. Suppliers franchise us because we add value for them. Arrow pays the bills for them; we stock products and schedule orders with enough size and scale. Currently, 70% of our commodity product sales to transactional customers are of products manufactured by our "big four" and other larger suppliers. To these suppliers, the Internet can mean lost control. In addition, prices for commodity products will fall down faster than they would like. Remember, it is the commodity product margins that is a major source of revenues for them. They use the money they make here to support the value add and new proprietary products.

"How should we leverage all this information to our advantage?" Salsgiver wondered. ■

CHAPTER 9

Managing Customer Relationships Using Multiple Touch Points in Multi-Channel Settings

Exchanges between firms and customers have been forever changed by the advent of interactive and information technologies, creating a proliferation of channels and touch points. Firms are realizing that they need to leverage new technologies, not just to reach and serve customers through multiple channels but also to enable customers to communicate with them through a variety of media. There are several challenges as well—for example, the firm's ability to deliver a consistent experience across all channels, and the issue of privacy in the online world. In this chapter, we first discuss the growth and proliferation of multi-channel marketing. Next, we look at issues and pitfalls in the design and implementation of such systems. Finally, we review the impact of such systems on consumer interactions (customer-initiated contacts) with the firm.

◆ MULTI-CHANNEL MARKETING: THE FIRM'S PERSPECTIVE

Multi-channel marketing is growing at a very rapid rate. According to a study conducted jointly by the Boston Consulting Group and Shop.org, between 1998 and 2002 the multi-channel retail market had a compound annual growth rate of 72 percent. There is growing evidence that customers that interact with firms through multiple channels tend to spend more than customers who don't, and they are more loyal to their preferred vendors. A study of over 100 retailers conducted by DoubleClick in January 2002 showed that shoppers using three channels spent $995 on average, as compared to shoppers using a single channel who spent only $591.

Multi-channel marketing also can potentially reduce the costs of serving customers. This is achieved by aligning the most appropriate and cost-effective channel to execute the various channel functions. Consider the case of Hunter Business Direct. This direct marketer realized that expensive sales calls were not always the best way to interact with customers, and that an interactive marketing system that employed *integrated*, organized contacts using mail, telephone, and field contacts was able to extract a significantly better customer response rate than any approach that used each medium independently.

Multi-channel marketing also enables the capture of more detailed and precise customer behavior information that the firm can then use to customize products and services to offer greater value to its customers.

CHOOSING BETWEEN THE VARIOUS OPTIONS IN MULTI-CHANNELS

The options available for firms to use in a multi-channel setting include:

Field sales force: Although the most expensive in terms of cost per contact (the cost per sales call can run more than several hundred dollars per sales call), using a field sales force has its own advantages. A face-to-face contact not only enables the sales rep to make a more convincing case to the customer about the firm's offerings, but it also enables the rep to gather more detailed information about the customer that can be used by the firm for subsequent relationship management.

Telesales and telemarketing: The methods are significantly cheaper compared to hiring and maintaining a field sales force. Telemarketing is a very effective for lead generation, whereas telesales can be very effective in customer retention. Firms like Dell Computer Corporation use a combination of field sales and in-house telesales teams to manage its corporate account relationships. Whereas the field sales force is primarily responsible for acquiring large corporate customers, the in-house telesales organization is focused on maintaining ongoing contact with current customers, to respond to their needs and resolve any complaints.

Direct mail, e-mail, faxes, and the Internet. Each of these options is significantly cheaper than either a sale force or telesales and telemarkets but the cost advantage comes at the expense of effectiveness. For example, the response rates to e-mail campaigns are less than a fraction of a percent. However, the ability to reach large numbers of prospects and customers makes these channels very attractive options for firms dealing with a fragmented customer base.

In addition to having to invest in expensive technologies, firms that attempt multi-channel systems face the daunting task of having to integrate the data into a common database. First, firms have to deal with the problem of having to manage changes in formats in the data collected over time. Second, firms need to deal with the fact that the data are collected across a variety of touch points, from the Web to phone calls to faxes to e-mails.

Beyond the technology issues, there is the issue of keeping the messages and service levels consistent across the various channels. If the same customer is being contacted through social media, firms need to be careful to present consistent information that does not conflict, which may create customer confusion.

CHAPTER 9 Managing Customer Relationships Using Multiple Touch Points

♦ THE CUSTOMER'S PERSPECTIVE

One imperative of multi–touch point systems is that firms need to increasingly view each contact with their customers as an opportunity manage that customer. In addition to firm-initiated contacts, customer-initiated contacts (CICs),[1] in particular, are an important source of information about customers' concerns and questions.[2] In fact, CICs are becoming more common because of changing customer attitudes and technologies (e.g., e-mail, Web sites) that facilitate customers' active engagement with and aggressive pursuit of information from firms. As a result, the ability to collect richer information about, interact more frequently with, and tailor more appropriate responses to customers makes CICs an integral part of a firm's customer management effort. This is especially true in industries in which the cost of contacting customers directly is prohibitively high—for example, consumer packaged goods. In these industries, firms are beginning to view CICs as an opportunity to build and manage customer loyalty, and influence them by word of mouth with the objective of increasing customer profitability.

Most academic research has emphasized complaints over other types of CICs, even though most CICs might originate for other reasons.[3] But, in multi-channel and multi–touch point settings, firms have to look beyond the management of customer complaints. In fact, recognition that dissatisfied customers divert a firm's marketing and sales organization from their core functions has led firms such as Charles Schwab and British Airways to exploit technology to speed up their customer service organizations' responses to CICs, and thereby increase profits and cut costs.

Not all firms have been able to move at the same pace as the aforementioned examples. Most packaged goods manufacturers, while acknowledging that they need to become more responsive and to tailor responses to customers' specific needs, are often not sure where to start. Although CIC management is cited as an important aspect of customer retention, firms are frustrated at not being able to quantify the impact of their customer management efforts on customer retention and loyalty or capitalize on their growing customer databases. It is also widely acknowledged that the ability of individual consumer affairs representatives to process various types of CICs is key to facilitating customer contact, yet differential processing of customers is often left to the discretion of individual representatives who had developed rules of thumb based on a combination of intuition and experience. However, firms don't want to formulate guidelines based on collective experience. Finally, manufacturers are experiencing a shift in both the quantity (higher) and mix (more inquiries)

---

[1]Bowman and Narayandas (2000) define a CIC as any communication with a manufacturer initiated by a customer (or prospective customer). Examples in the case of consumer packaged goods sold through retail channels include inquiries about a product's use, availability, and reformulation; requests for refunds; and complaints about performance. See Douglas Bowman and Das Narayandas, "Managing Customer-Initiated Contacts with Manufacturers: The Impact on Share of Category Requirements and Word-of-Mouth Behavior," *Journal of Marketing Research* 38 (August 2001): 281–97.
[2]See, for example, Claes Fornell and Birger Wernerfelt (1987), "Defensive Marketing Strategy by Customer Complaint Management: A Theoretical Analysis," *Journal of Marketing Research* 24, no. 4 (1987): 337–46.
[3]Ruth N. Bolton, "A Dynamic Model of the Duration of the Customer's Relationship with a Continuous Service Provider: The Role of Satisfaction," *Marketing Science* 17, no. 1 (1998): 45–65.

of CICs and expect this trend to continue, owing in part to their Web presence and e-commerce initiatives.[4]

A comprehensive model that acknowledges that CIC processing typically involves a limited number of contact points; distinguishes among multiple modes (e.g., telephone, letter, e-mail); allows the firm to deal with different customers based on each one's specific characteristics (e.g., prior loyalty, heavy category user) or context-specific factors (e.g., contact type, whether resolution was first sought from a retailer); and provides direction to managers seeking to influence customer behavior.

Studies have found that complaints are only a small percentage of CICs, and that a firm's satisfactory performance in a CIC can be an opportunity for firms to both influence loyalty and reach potential customers by word of mouth in a positive way.[5] Research has shown that as the opportunities to interact with customers increase exponentially, the opportunity to learn about customers is also going up, and that manufacturers have to move away from their traditional linear approach of marketing to customers, i.e., simply spending a lot of money telling people why they should buy a product.[6]

Summary

Multi-channel and multi–touch point systems are irrevocably changing the way in which firms manage their customer relationships. In this chapter, we have briefly reviewed the impact of both firm- and customer-initiated contacts. Although there is a general acceptance that multi-channel systems offer a large number of benefits to firms, an area of concern that is gaining prominence is that of customer privacy. With an explosion in customer information available to firms, lawmakers are concerned about the abuse of such information. The growing consumer backlash is actually driving governments to support regulation to protect an individual's right to privacy. As a result, marketers need to understand the new regulations and customer attitudes and to change those relationship management strategies over time that could potentially limit their ability to communicate, acquire, and retain customers.

Review Questions and Exercises

1. How do firm-initiated contacts differ from customer-initiated contacts? Why does the firm need to know how to manage both types?
2. As discussed in the chapter, service firms (such as British Airways and Charles Schwab) have been able to manage multiple customer touch points more easily than have consumer products firms (such as Coca-Cola or Kraft). Under what conditions do you think it might be valuable for manufacturers of frequently purchased consumer goods to actively monitor and manage their customer touch points? Do you think it would be worth the cost? Why or why not?
3. What are the firm's options for firm-initiated contacts? Under what circumstances should each be used?

---

[4]Douglas Bowman and Das Narayandas, "Managing Customer-Initiated Contacts with Manufacturers: The Impact on Share of Category Requirements and Word-of-Mouth Behavior," *Journal of Marketing Research* 38 (August 2001): 281–97.
[5]Ibid
[6]Ibid

◆◆◆ Eddie Bauer, Inc.

Case 9-1 Eddie Bauer, Inc.

Ann K. Leamon

In 1999 Eddie Bauer was a $2 billion apparel retailer, generating approximately 25% of its revenue from its catalog operation and the remainder through its 600 stores. The Eddie Bauer brand covered an extensive array of products: men's and women's casualwear under the Eddie Bauer name, furniture and furnishings as Eddie Bauer Home, and men's and women's officewear as AKA Eddie Bauer. Licensing agreements had produced Eddie Bauer eyewear, bicycles, and vehicles. In addition, its acclaimed Web site, *www.eddiebauer.com*, was posting triple-digit sales growth.

After several years of steady expansion, 1998 had yielded dismal results: a 5% decline in same-store sales and an even bigger decline in profits. Julie Rodway, Executive Vice President for Merchandising, saw this as a wake-up call. "Two years ago," she said, "our brand stumbled. We used trendy colors on classic clothes. It was a mistake. We got distracted and tried to reach too many segments."

To understand its target market better, the company commissioned an extensive market research survey. Based on the results of many focus groups and in-depth segmentation analysis, CEO Rick Fersch decided that a policy of "One Brand, One Voice, One Customer" should govern communications and policy. Implementing One Brand, One Voice, One Customer operationally meant an increased emphasis on synergy, a policy already in place. Through synergy, the company tried to ensure the same experience for customers regardless of the channel they shopped. Customers could return products in the most convenient way—through mail or the stores—regardless of the channel through which they had been purchased originally. Catalog items could be ordered through special phones in the stores. The catalogs acted as marketing vehicles for the stores and the stores allowed customers to experience the catalog products.

To enhance the consistency of product and presentation, the company reorganized. Historically, the company had been organized by distribution channel; retail and catalog products had separate design, production, and management teams. The new organization was structured by product. Men's and women's items were designed, manufactured, and merchandised without regard to channel; only in the forecasting and allocation process were distribution outlets considered. The reorganization eliminated several layers of management, streamlining the decision-making process. "Before," Rodway confessed, "everyone had input and we could never make a decision. It's not that consensus is bad, it's just that we had too much of it."

In September 1999, it was by no means clear whether the unified brand image strategy was working. The first product line produced entirely since the reorganization would not appear until Spring 2000. "The fundamental question we face," said Rodway, "is whether in trying to coordinate across both of our channels—three if you include I-media[1]—we are creating a distinct competitive advantage for Eddie Bauer, or just fighting with one hand tied behind our back. It's a radical thought, but maybe we'd be better off concentrating on one channel or the other, or all, but independently."

BACKGROUND[2]

Founded in 1920, Eddie Bauer Inc. began as Eddie Bauer's Tennis Shop, a single store known

---

The case was prepared by Research Associate Ann K. Leamon (under the direction of Professor David E. Bell). Copyright © 1999 by the President and Fellows of Harvard College. Harvard Business School Case 500-034.

[1] I-media includes all interactive media vehicles, primarily the Internet.
[2] Much of this section is drawn from Robert Spector, *The Legend of Eddie Bauer* (Lyme, Conn.: Greenwich Publishing, 1994).

throughout the Seattle area for its outdoor sporting gear, tennis equipment, and customer service. In 1936, Bauer patented the methods he had invented for mass-producing quilted goose-down-filled outerwear. A mail order division opened in 1942 to respond to orders generated through magazine advertisements. The first catalog was mailed in 1945, and targeted existing customers, many of whom were U.S. Army veterans who had used Eddie Bauer equipment during the Second World War. In 1951, Eddie Bauer liquidated its retail operation to satisfy debts against the company but continued the mail order business under the name Eddie Bauer Alaskan Outfitters. Revenues grew from $50,000 in 1953 to $500,000 in 1956. For the next 15 years, the company was strictly mail order. It continued to specialize in rugged outdoor equipment, outfitting numerous mountaineering expeditions including assaults on K-2, Gasherbrum, and the expedition that put the first American on Everest. The company reentered retail in 1970, opening a downtown Seattle store that offered a full range of expedition gear, along with fishing and hunting equipment. A year later, when the sinking stock market torpedoed Eddie Bauer's planned stock flotation, General Mills—many of whose executives were long-time customers of the outfitter—bought the company.

Its new parent wanted Eddie Bauer to grow as quickly as possible, and the retail division seemed the best vehicle. To capitalize on its reputation for cold-weather garments, 13 of the first 14 stores were located in northern cities. In addition to camping and climbing gear, each store offered on-site gunsmiths, fly fishing experts, and demonstrations of various outdoor activities. The watchword among employees was "you won't work inside Eddie Bauer unless you live outside." The catalog business continued, but the growth vehicle clearly was retail. As the Baby Boomers who had used Eddie Bauer as a resource for serious outdoor pursuits took up more relaxed recreational activities, the company entered those markets, adding casual clothing to its offerings. By 1983, Eddie Bauer had 27 stores.

Other aspects of the company's strategy also shifted during the 1980s. Instead of locating downtown, the newer stores went into malls. The product assortment continued to evolve. Tents, sleeping bags, guns, and fishing equipment, slow-moving items that did not pay for their space, were replaced by streetwear for both men and women. In 1988, when Spiegel[3] acquired it for $260 million, Eddie Bauer was a specialty clothing retailer with 58 stores in 14 states and $250 million in sales. The Spiegel ownership offered significant benefits—Spiegel had expertise in catalog operations and database management, while Eddie Bauer offered a base of male customers and retail operations. By 1999, Eddie Bauer operated 600 stores, 555 in the United States and the rest in Japan, Germany, the United Kingdom, and Canada. It also mailed 14 catalogs annually.

Its multiple channels exposed the company to a host of competitors. In the mall, it faced The Gap and its Old Navy and Banana Republic divisions, as well as Abercrombie & Fitch (Exhibit 2). Victoria's Secret, the apparel and lingerie divisions of Intimate Brands Inc., operated a catalog as well as a chain of stores. L.L. Bean and Lands' End both had formidable presence in mail order and on the Internet. "As a catalog," said Rodway, "we compete against Lands' End and L.L. Bean. But as a whole, we're held up against Abercrombie & Fitch and The Gap. The parameters are really different."

Eddie Bauer's competitors differed in their distribution channels and operational structures as well. Lands' End and L.L. Bean had limited retail operations and concentrated on their catalogs for both demand generation and brand building. The Gap focused on its retail divisions, despite resurrecting the Banana Republic catalog. Abercrombie & Fitch, primarily retail, produced a 300-page quarterly "magalog," which combined an editorial section with promotional product photos. This marketing vehicle had a circulation of over 200,000 subscribers who paid a $10 annual fee for it. The company was thought to be testing it as a demand generator. For Victoria's Secret, stores and catalog were entirely separate. The assortments differed; the

---

[3]Spiegel, composed of the Spiegel and Newport News catalogs as well as Eddie Bauer, is owned by the German cataloger Otto Versand. Spiegel is like a department store in the breadth and depth of its product, while Eddie Bauer is more specialized.

	The Gap	Abercrombie & Fitch	Eddie Bauer Retail Only	Eddie Bauer Catalog Only	Lands' End
Net sales	9,054,462	815,804	982,251	344,932	1,371,375
Cost of goods	5,318,218	471,853	522,660	174,718	754,661
Inventories	1,056,444	49,879	520,035	135,695	219,686
Gross profit	3,736,244	343,951	459,591	170,214	616,714
SG&A	2,403,365	176,993	363,330	132,616	544,446
EBITDA	1,332,879	166,958	96,261	37,598	72,268
Income before tax	1,319,262	170,102	21,589	9,120	49,500
Net income	824,539	102,062	12,954	5,472	31,185

EXHIBIT 2 Comparative Income Statements (1998 calendar year, in $000s)

Source: Annual Reports for The Gap, Lands' End, and Abercrombie & Fitch, years ending 1/31/99, and Eddie Bauer company information, calendar year 1998. Bauer information is for sportswear only, it does not include Home or licensed items.

stores carried only lingerie and sleepwear, while the catalog augmented the lingerie line with a broad assortment of casualwear, swimwear, and office apparel. Victoria's Secret Catalog generated 31% of the company's $2.6 billion in sales. Victoria's Secret Stores would not accept returns of catalog products, and, until recently, each channel had separate lingerie design teams.

Although $1.5 billion of Eddie Bauer's $2 billion annual revenues came from retail and 80% of its customers shopped the stores, the catalog legacy endured. "At heart," said Rodway, "there's a tendency to protect the catalog because it's our heritage and our single largest marketing tool for customer reach." I-media sales were consolidated with the catalog, a convention that some insiders felt masked the weaknesses of the catalog's performance.

Rodway herself had significant catalog experience. Six months after joining Eddie Bauer's retail management training program, she had moved to corporate headquarters as a catalog merchant and was promoted to managing the women's division. After a two-year hiatus running a men's casual clothing start-up, Rodway had returned to Eddie Bauer to manage the entire catalog division in 1996. She was later promoted to executive vice president for merchandising over all channels.

Many of the other executives also had strong catalog backgrounds. "Many of us came up from the catalog side," said Reagan Gandy, manager of human resources and a former merchandiser for both catalog and retail, "because that's where the action was. In catalog you control not just what the product is but how it's pictured in the customer's mind. While both channels require merchandising strategies, the execution is much easier to control and ultimately deliver to the customer."

THE CATALOG

In 1998, the catalog generated $528 million in gross demand. Returns, however, made up a quarter of that, bringing net sales down to $345 million.[4] The major "Resource" catalog contained the full line of casual wear along with small selections of the Home and AKA lines. (Exhibit 1 shows sample pages.) Specialty catalogs for men and women and other books with the full AKA and Home lines were mailed

---

[4]Returns plagued the entire mail order industry. Customers might order several sizes or colors of a single item and return all but the one they liked best. Footwear and swimwear, two of Eddie Bauer's catalog-only categories, had extremely high return rates throughout the industry, often over 50%. The company could not track whether returns to the store came from I-media or the catalog, but suspected that I-media returns were lower.

370 PART II *Developing Strategies for Customer Equity Management*

EXHIBIT 1 Two Pages from the Eddie Bauer Catalog

A. Short-Sleeve Plaid Chambray Shirt $36
An easygoing look whether paired with jeans or something dressier, our pure-cotton chambray shirt features a back box pleat and double-needle stitching at stress points. And it's garment-washed for extra softness. Machine wash. Imported. See colors above. Catalog Only.
W34 156 4511 Reg. S–XXXL
W34 156 4512 Tall M–XXXL

B. Short-Sleeve Checked Poplin Shirt $36
Pure cotton and a fine poplin weave add up to a shirt that's lightweight and comfortable. Garment washing provides a soft feel and reduces shrinkage. Finishing details include: button-down collar; patch pocket; button on back of collar; sleeve pleats with adjustable two-button cuffs; box pleat in back. Machine wash. Imported. See colors at left.
XXXL & Tall Are Catalog Only.
W34 156 5527 Reg. S–XXXL
W34 156 5528 Tall M–XXXL

170 www.eddiebauer.com

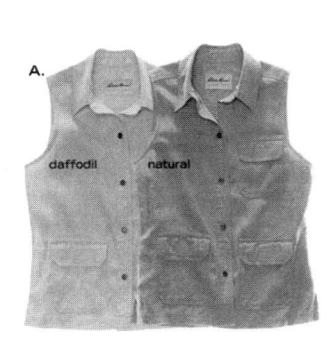

A. Linen Vest $58

Our Linen Vest is the perfect layer during transitional spring weather. It's low-maintenance because we make it from pure linen that can be machine-washed. Comfortable, easy fit. Garment-washed for a softer finish. Two front pockets with self-fastening closures. Imported. See colors above.
Tall Sizes Are Catalog Only.
W08 156 2280 Regular S–XXL
W08 156 4082 Petite XS–XL
W08 156 4084 Tall M–XXL

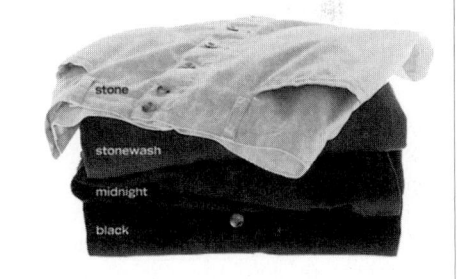

20   www.eddiebauer.com

separately, based on customer buying behavior. Inserts offered a sampling of a different line—for instance, a Home catalog could include some casualwear products—and allowed the company to introduce specialty customers to its broader offerings. As customers discovered that Eddie Bauer, a brand they already knew and trusted, offered products for other aspects of their lives, their purchases from the company would increase. For Eddie Bauer, this prospecting method was essentially costless, as the pages were already prepared for other catalogs and a few additional pages in one book need not increase the cost of postage.

Eddie Bauer used its catalogs in several ways: to reach new customers, to generate direct sales (often of styles or sizes not available in the stores), and to inspire customers to visit the stores. The catalog also allowed the company to record lost demand, demand that a product would have generated had it been in stock. Customers did not know in advance if an item was out of stock when they called the catalog; no such record of missed sales opportunities existed in the stores. Product purchasing decisions could be refined in light of this information.

The catalog was Eddie Bauer's primary marketing tool. One-third of catalogs were mailed to prospects, people who were not yet customers. The back cover would list the store nearest to the recipient, and often described promotional items that were only available with a store visit. Catalog sales jumped dramatically after a catalog drop, with a similar reaction on I-media, but store sales responded moderately if at all. New customers were thought to be responsible for about 25% of catalog sales, and their average first time purchase of $130 meant Eddie Bauer broke even on its acquisition cost.

The remaining catalogs were mailed to existing customers, numbering about 2.5 million. Of these, perhaps 40% would make no purchase during the year. Of those who made a purchase, half shopped only the catalog, spending an average of $200 per year. The remainder were the most loyal, spending an average of $300 per year through the catalog and another $200 in the stores.

Women's products accounted for 70% of the goods sold in the catalog, but 75% of the time "the voice on the phone" was female. Half of all women's apparel sales were in large or petite sizes that were not carried in stores.

THE RETAIL STORES

Eddie Bauer's stores tended to be in mid- to upscale regional malls. One well-performing store of 21,000 square feet (17,300 square feet of selling space), with all three lines (sportswear, AKA, and Home), generated roughly $445/square foot. The company believed that 75% of Americans lived within 40 miles of one of its U.S. locations: about 100 million people walked past at least one of its stores in a given year, with 10 million actually entering the store and 7 million buying. As with the catalog, new customers were responsible for about 25% of sales.

Despite the company's masculine heritage, reinforced by placing the men's wear at the entrance to the store, 70% of retail customers were women and women's products were 45% of sales. "Women's wear can be challenging to keep in stock with such a high sell-through," said Robert Nyhuis, a store general manager. "When our women's business faltered, the loss was twofold because many of our women shoppers also shop for men." The company believed its store customers were slightly younger on average than its catalog customers.

Each store had a Catalog Order Desk with a direct telephone line to the call center and free shipping (but not free handling). These desks generated sales of $75 million per year. "I can fall back on the catalog to fill in stockouts," said Nyhuis, "and the catalog has an abundance of specialty sizes that the stores can't carry. But it can be a hard sell, if the customer wants to try something on or needs it immediately." Stockouts tended to occur once or twice a day, according to Nyhuis. "Our goal is to be as fully stocked as possible. Although the allocation system has improved considerably, common sizes are not always available and this can lead to a customer perception that we do not stand behind our product." The Gap and Banana Republic were acknowledged leaders at maintaining high stock levels.

I-MEDIA

At 5% of the company's 1998 catalog sales, I-media had experienced a triple-digit increase over the previous year. "Our growth curve is straight up," said Sally McKenzie, Director of Merchandising, Planning, and Operations for I-media. We're big enough now that we impact inventory levels. We used to be just a small fish in a big pond; we could take a bit from one style or another. Now we can move through serious units. We may need to change the way we plan demand and integrate our planning processes so we aren't a drain on the company's fulfillment."

I-media users were a good fit with the demographics of Eddie Bauer's target market (Table A). Currently, nearly half of I-media sales were to customers new to Eddie Bauer, but especially attractive were existing Eddie Bauer customers who already shopped the catalog and the stores. Though still small in number, these customers were spending nearly $1,000 per year across all three channels. To date, about half of the 125,000 I-media customers were male. As a whole, I-media customers tended to buy more basics. Almost all orders were placed between 9 a.m. and 5 p.m. (times at the customer's location.)

As the online population grew, McKenzie anticipated new challenges in serving them. "As we become more mainstream, the customer's tolerance for technical problems declines. One of our first I-media customers was Marc Andreessen of Netscape. He and others like him were much more tolerant. Betty Customer is not that way. She wants it to work, she wants it now, and no excuses." The potential of I-media lay in personalizing the offering to each customer, giving each a unique shopping experience. "With I-media, we can leverage our direct database," said one manager, "and send e-mail notifications of specials or launches. We have to invest in the medium, in tactics like gift lists, reminders for customers, things that add value and will get the customer to come to us and make us even more relevant for them. It's not a free lunch. Competition is just a click away on the Net. We have to be on top of our game."

"Right now," said Bill Michel, Senior Vice President of Marketing, "I-media is a marketing platform, not a distribution platform. We're not judging it on ROI yet because we're just building the infrastructure." One of the potential benefits of I-media is its potential to reduce the number of catalogs mailed, and thus the costs of catalog production. If we could completely discontinue the catalog," he said, "we'd save about $75 million. Catalog production is an all-or-nothing sort of thing; if you run any, you might as well run a lot because the initial costs of production and print setup are so high. So we've got to get people to use I-media. But there are barriers. Some people won't use it because they don't have a computer, some just don't shop online, and others have a computer and shop, but have such a slow modem that it's painful for them. We need to give customers a reason to shop—we can do that by increasing the information online as opposed to in the catalog, or by giving them better pricing. We need to add capabilities so they can check stock availability online, track orders, even do a click-to-chat sort of thing so they can get real-time assistance from an associate." Even the power of the Internet could not overcome three of the major limitations of catalog shopping: customers would still not be able to "touch and feel" merchandise, check for correct fit, or be confident of color accuracy.

TABLE A Web Population Comparison

Attribute	All Web	Eddie Bauer	J. Crew	L.L. Bean	Gap
Married	67%	68%	35%	71%	48%
Shopped online in last 6 months	68%	88%	99%	90%	82%
Shopped for clothes online in last 6 months	11%	70%	98%	73%	62%
Bought clothes online in last 6 months	4%	22%	26%	26%	17%
Income $75K +	37%	44%	38%	45%	31%

Source: Company information.

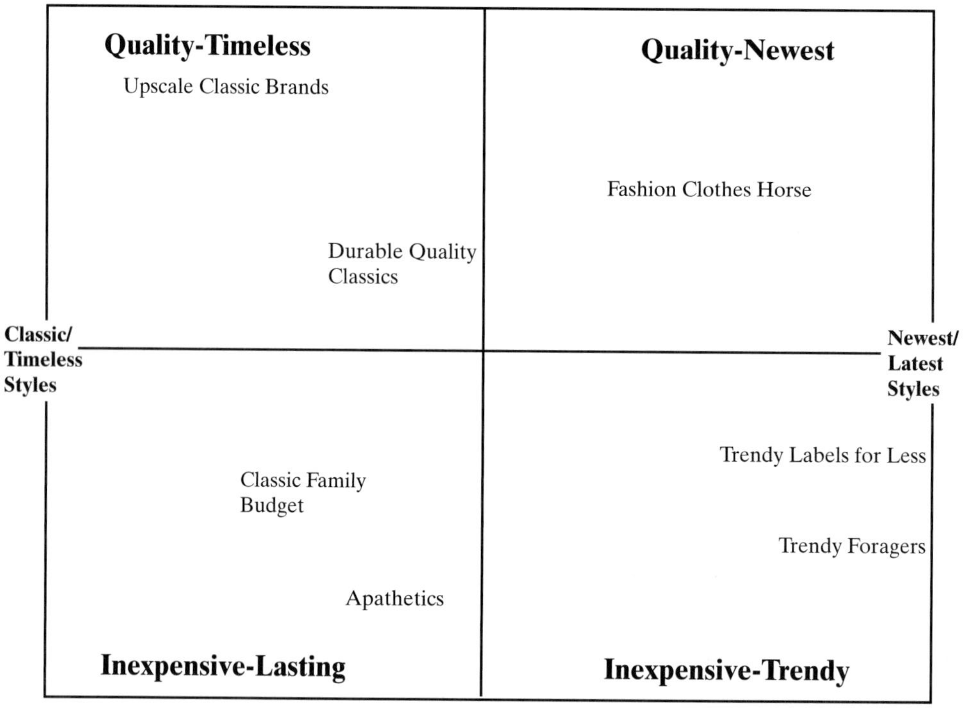

Exhibit 3: Supersegment Analysis

Quality-Timeless (upper left): Upscale Classic Brands; Durable Quality Classics

Quality-Newest (upper right): Fashion Clothes Horse

Inexpensive-Lasting (lower left): Classic Family Budget; Apathetics

Inexpensive-Trendy (lower right): Trendy Labels for Less; Trendy Foragers

Axes: Classic/Timeless Styles ↔ Newest/Latest Styles

CUSTOMERS

In the wake of its dismal 1998 performance, Eddie Bauer had conducted a market study to identify its customers, determine which segments it should pursue, and establish a position from which to do so. The market study, lead by Janice Gaub, Divisional Vice President for Brand Marketing, had shown that Eddie Bauer's customers included groups ranging from "Fashion Clothes Horses" to "Apathetics." To clarify its target, the company grouped the segments according to their priorities: Quality and Cost against Lasting Styles and Trendiness (Exhibit 3). The Quality/Timeless segment, which Eddie Bauer felt matched its image and offerings, encompassed two segments that together made up 19% of all adult clothing buyers (9 million people) and 28% of clothing expenditures ($39 billion).[5] With the right tactics, the marketing appeal could spill over into other groups, which, while budget constrained, still sought lasting styles. These segments would add another 30% of all clothing buyers and 23% of apparel expenditures to the potential market.[6]

Eddie Bauer defined its target market less by demographics than by apparel purchasing behavior. Its customers took their cues from brands, wanted their clothing to last, and did not look for the trendiest styles. Demographically, they were educated, affluent, in their forties, married, active, and had either young families or children who had left home. Eddie Bauer wanted to give them clothes that offered the emotional security of the company's quality, value, and timeless appeal, along with physical comfort. With 5% market share among these consumers, the company had plenty of share to win. Its $2 billion annual sales made up 1.5% of the U.S. adult apparel market.[7]

---

[5] Eddie Bauer Inc., "Defining the Eddie Bauer Brand," internal document, winter 1998.

[6] Lieberman Research Worldwide, "Driving Eddie Bauer's Business Forward," final report, October 1998, internal document.

[7] Eddie Bauer Inc., "Defining the Eddie Bauer Brand," internal document, winter 1998.

Eddie Bauer's multiple channels were seen as an advantage in increasing brand awareness. Although customer demographics were roughly similar across retail and catalog, some groups preferred one channel or another. The time-constrained customer bought almost twice as much through the catalog as through retail. More trendy segments, while not the center of the target, tended to buy basics through the retail channel.

MARKETING

Catalog merchandising emphasized mailing to current and thus loyal customers, rather than extending Eddie Bauer's reach. Janice Gaub commented, "Historically, we have used the catalog as our primary advertising vehicle but that's communicating with customers who already are familiar with us. Unless you've bought from us, you're not likely to hear from us." A survey of people in the target market (both customers and noncustomers) were asked where they liked to buy casual apparel: Eddie Bauer came sixth, behind Gap, Structure, Nordstrom, J.C. Penney, and Ann Taylor. A separate survey asked people specifically what catalogs they used for casual apparel; Eddie Bauer came fourth, behind Lands' End, L.L. Bean, and J. Crew.

Eddie Bauer's marketing expenditures had shrunk recently and the emphasis had shifted. In 1997, the company had spent $214 million in marketing, with 95% of that on customer/direct campaigns, such as direct mail (including the catalogs), promotional mailers, and rewards. The balance had been in brand advertising, public relations, retail visuals, and I-media. In 1999, the total would be $180 million, with 83% in customer/direct marketing. While the policy of synergy meant that the same products would be promoted and the same programs would run for all channels, different customer buying patterns made the value of some programs questionable. For instance, gifts with purchase, "buy $75 worth of product and receive a picture frame," were offered at both catalog and retail. "In retail, gifts really work," said one executive. "But in catalog, with an average purchase already more than $100, we're giving money away."

"One of our challenges," Gaub said, "is relevance. People still think of us as the place for goosedown coats. We've really evolved, from expedition outfitter to active casual outfitter. We haven't advertised enough to change our image in the customer's mind, or to reinforce their awareness of us, especially in light of the increased ad spending by the competition. People buy products and brands. We need to evolve our marketing mix to fuel top-of-mind awareness. It doesn't matter in which channels we deliver the message or the product; we need to build the brand and deliver it consistently."

The competition spent far more on advertising than did Eddie Bauer (Table B). The Gap's khakis campaign alone cost $20 million, almost Bauer's entire retail advertising expenditure for the year. "We're a big company," said Rodway, "but we don't behave like one. We don't invest like others to communicate the brand. We're not

TABLE B 1998 Advertising Expenditures

Company	Net Sales ($ million)	Profit ($ million)	Advertising % of Sales	Advertising $ (millions)
Eddie Bauer Store	982	13	2.4%	25
Eddie Bauer Catalog	345	6	2.6%	9
The Gap	9,100	824	6.0%	550
Victoria's Secret Stores	1,800	171	5.3%	95
Victoria's Secret Catalog	800	35	NA	NA

Source: DNR, April 7, 1999, Pak & Cicinelli, "Intimate Brands," *Credit Suisse First Boston*, January 13, 1999, Eddie Bauer info.
Note: Catalog figures exclude catalog costs. Only brand advertising is included. Profit figures for Victoria's Secret are estimated, based on Pak & Cicinelli.

in the advertising big leagues—but we're held to big-league standards, like Abercrombie & Fitch and The Gap."

Marketing Eddie Bauer's heritage and brand image was another challenge. While women were the primary purchasers and their products carried higher margins, the company's image, both in its name and its outdoor heritage, was male. Product selection, store display, and even the color assortment reflected an outdoorsy, male attitude. Store sales leaned slightly toward men's products, but 70% of actual purchasers were women. Catalog and I-media also had 70% female purchasers, but 70% of products sold through these channels were women's. Overall, women's products made up 55% of sales. Said Rodway, "We're a masculine brand, and the men's business is very important, but the women's products sell, and they keep the customer in the store. She'll come in for a shirt or pants for the man in her life, but she really likes to shop for herself."

The company's Northwest heritage could also be a hard sell in other regions. "It helps us define ourselves," said Rodway, "but it can be a ball and chain. We are known for outerwear and we feel we need to own that market—but it may not be relevant to the corporate direction. Or, for that matter, to customers in the Southeast. In fact, many of our customers don't know where we're headquartered—and when they learn, they don't care. And customers under 35 don't understand our heritage at all—they weren't around when Eddie Bauer was fitting out Everest expeditions—and while they aren't our primary target, they are important to us. It's our job to use our heritage and make it relevant to our modern customer. We must look forward, not back."

ECONOMICS

The channels themselves had vastly different economics. Gross margins held fairly steady at 50%, but the breakdown of expenses and profit performance differed dramatically. Retail had expenses that varied with sales (labor, store operations) of nearly 26%, media advertising of about 3%, and general overhead of 10%, leaving an operating profit of approximately 11%. For the catalog, the major expense was the catalogs themselves, at around 21% of sales, divided equally between design (including $5 million for the photos), printing, and mailing costs. Other variable costs (order taking and delivery, net of customer charges) amounted to 11%. Advertising and database management each accounted for another 3%. Overhead costs amounted to about 8% leaving an operating profit of 4%.

The relative newness of I-media made its economics difficult to isolate. For example, I-media depended on the catalog production process for most of its product pictures and descriptions. Only the items in the interactive dressing room, which were digitally processed to allow customers to change colors, were separately produced. I-media had spent only 1% of its net sales ($300,000) for digital images. "Without catalog," said McKenzie, "our production and cost structures would be vastly different." Best guesses suggested that I-media saved on fulfillment at only 8% of sales, but spent disproportionately on advertising (11%) and overhead (12%), leaving a 19% operating profit.

CHANNEL CONFLICTS

The company tried to ensure that its channels presented a unified customer experience through synergy. "We want to keep the customer experience congruent, regardless of the avenue through which they reach us," said Michel. "With 80% of our customers buying through retail, most people think that Eddie Bauer is a store." Defined in the dictionary as "working together," synergy at Eddie Bauer meant that the customer's buying experience would be as seamless as possible across the channels. Products should arrive in stores at the same time that catalogs arrived in homes and items appeared on I-media. Prices were to be the same. Markdowns were taken on the same items and at the same time across all channels. Customers could return products ordered from the catalog or I-media to the store, and order catalog products through a store's Customer Order Desk. The retail window displays echoed the cover on the most recent catalog. "The payoff from synergy," said Michel, "is that we establish consistency of fit, styling, quality, and service for the customer. It all adds up to loyalty to the brand over time."

Although the company tried to minimize them, the natural differences among the channels could not be ignored. The catalog and I-media offered some product lines, items, colors, and many sizes that stores did not. "As long as it fits in the brand filter," said Rodway, "we'll offer it. Sometimes the reality of the situation—limited space in the stores, or display problems—means that it will be a catalog-only product. After all, we can always add pages to the catalog, but we can't add space to the stores." Some customers came to the stores seeking catalog-only items and left empty-handed. "Are we supporting each other," wondered Robert Nyhuis, the store manager, "or are we two separate entities?"

Fully 50% of women's SKUs and 30% of men's were unavailable in the stores. Women's dresses and swimsuits appeared only in the catalog because they did not show well on flat hangers, while the catalog could show them on models. Offering these products in the store would also detract from the male sense of the brand; 55% of store sales (45% of sales overall) were men's items. The company wanted to continue offering dresses, however, because of their high profit margins and strong sell-through. Specialty sizes presented another major difference between store and catalog product. Eddie Bauer offered small and large sizes (petites, talls, and sizes 16 through 20 for women, talls and double- and triple-extra large for men) only through the catalog. These were not available through the stores in order to conserve on space for display and inventory. The company had tried carrying a limited selection of petites in the stores along with the regular-sized women's product. It was a disaster, because the assortment of petite and regular became mixed together and not all sizes were available in all products, confusing shoppers.

Catalog and retail used different distribution centers. This was mainly because of the differences in fulfillment procedures, but in addition the same item would be packaged differently depending on the channel: catalog items did not need price tags for example. This complicated the matter of accepting returns. Although customers loved the convenience, accepting catalog and I-media returns was not cost-free to the stores. If the item was in-season and common to both channels, it could be price-tagged, redisplayed, and, with any luck, sold. Since this did not occur for 40% of the sizes and 20% of the items, a simple resale was rare. The store was required to refund the customer's money, and also had to return the products to the central warehouse.

Stores were credited with an allowance based on a standard percentage of sales to compensate them for this activity, but managers suspected it was insufficient. Returns also affected store associates' [employees] morale. "There's nothing like having a big goal set for the day, everyone's all pumped up, and then you see someone walk in with $500-worth of catalog returns," said Nyhuis. "You can see the energy drain. It's frustrating because the retail stores don't receive credit for catalog orders placed from those locations." The catalog received credit for the demand even though the customer had come to the store, yet the store bore the fulfillment costs (costs of picking, packing, and postage) for that order, and saw its sales debited if items were returned.

Product timing was not always uniform between channels. Eddie Bauer's holiday[8] book dropped on the catalog timetable, at the end of September. Its holiday products arrived in the stores on the retail timetable, at the end of October. Customers could order the catalog products over the phone or on the Internet without any trouble, but they could not buy them through the stores until a month later. Although this might frustrate some potential buyers, it did help with inventory planning. The early demand through the catalog could refine buying strategies. If an item was planned for deletion at the end of the season but proved unexpectedly popular, it could remain at full price. The catalog also provided an early indication of poor performers and could signal the company to reduce prices on items that had not yet appeared at retail.

Synergy also constrained product assortment. "Catalog deals in winners and dogs," said Gandy. "Dogs are products that don't sell. You drop those. Winners, though, can occur from a great combination of photo and product. In catalog, you can ride a winner for a couple of seasons. You add some new colors, you keep the same photo or a really similar one, and you run it again. But a retailer needs newness every season. The average customer spends less than two seconds looking at a catalog page. So you throw red in a stack [of products] and you've caught their eye.

---

[8]For U.S. retailers, "holiday" refers to the December period, when Christmas, Hanukkah, and Kwanzaa stimulate significant demand.

You might not sell the red, they're more likely to buy the blue, but you've got them." If retail did not want to run a certain color, production minimums (Exhibit 4) made it very difficult for the catalog to buy it independently.

Catalog had priority when products were running out of stock. "We feel that our catalog customers have mentally bought it once they've called us to place the order," said Rodway. "They've made a contract, so to speak. Our retail customer may be disappointed, but probably only for a few seconds and we hope they'll find a substitute in the store."

I-media's potential for quick response fell afoul of Eddie Bauer's production lead times and its legacy systems. "It's nice to be able to share fulfillment from the same distribution center," said McKenzie, "but I-media doesn't necessarily have the same timing as the catalog or the same pattern of demand. We also can't automatically check for stock availability at this moment, which means a lot of time and manual input on our end, not to mention the customer service issue. That's one of our major enhancements planned for this year." Other planned enhancements included HTML e-mail, which would send pictures of products to customers with fast modems, and the ability to ship orders placed over the Net to more than one address. In a way, I-media's inability to provide real-time stock availability data benefited the company by allowing it to record lost demand in the same way as with the catalog. When the automatic stock-check was implemented, this information would be lost because a customer would move immediately to a replacement item, or to another site. Sharing the catalog call center created other challenges. Misunderstandings could arise when a customer who called for help was viewing the web site as opposed to the catalog. E-mail responses required a different set of skills, since customer service people with great phone voices did not necessarily have great e-mail voices.

Even within a channel, synergy could be constraining. Pricing synergy across regions hampered flexibility and could hurt profits. Said Gandy, "This January was really cold and raw in the Pacific Northwest. Our outerwear was selling at full price. But this was the time to take the first markdown on winter merchandise, so we had to do it. We could have sold through most of our northwestern inventory at full margin. Our northeast stores, on the other hand, should have been able to mark it down earlier because it wasn't selling and was just taking up space." While Eddie Bauer's systems would allow differentiated pricing, its policies would not.

Extending this policy to I-media limited that channel's famed responsiveness. McKenzie said, "We could do instant markdowns. Eventually, we could do all our liquidation online and in-season, when you get better sell-through. But as we move toward that, we have to resolve some issues around pricing synergy with the retail stores and catalog."

Eddie Bauer's multiple channels and its emphasis on synergy also complicated recruiting. Experts in either catalog or retail often preferred to work at firms devoted to those channels. "Some top-flight catalog people don't want to work for us because they see that retail drives the bus," said Rodway, "and some top-flight retail people get frustrated because they have to deal with catalog." Recruiting I-media staff was even more difficult. With a staff of seven, adding personnel was imperative. Competition in the region was intense, with firms like Amazon.com and Microsoft constantly scouting for talent. Without a skyrocketing share price or the prospect of an IPO, Eddie Bauer frequently found itself outbid for e-commerce talent.

MARKETING STRATEGY

As Executive Vice President for merchandising, Julie Rodway wrestled with implementing synergy. Multiple channels had definite benefits. "We are everywhere in our customers' world," said Rodway. "We're in the home every three weeks with our catalog, we're in the mall, and we're on the Internet. But I fear we're not maximizing our sales from any channel. Let's say we closed the catalog and concentrated on our storefronts in retail and I-media—we could use much of the catalog production and postage money for brand advertising. We could do more store resets during the season if we weren't bound to the catalog. Perhaps we could expand our offerings or open new retail concepts that support the brand, say, a kids' line. If we closed or spun off the catalog,

EXHIBIT 4 Production Minimums

		Asia			United States		
Product Classification		Solids	Yarn Dyed	Prints	Solids	Yarn Dyed	Prints
M's Woven Shirts							
	pcs/color	1500	1500	2900	2500	2500	2900
	pcs/order	1500	1500	2900	2500	2500	2900
	pcs/SKU*	12	12	12	12	12	12
W's Woven Shirts							
	pcs/color	2000	2000	5000	3300	3300	5000
	pcs/order	2000	2000	5000	3300	3300	5000
	pcs/SKU*	12	12	12	12	12	12
M&W Denim Bottoms							
	pcs/color	1200–2600	1200–2600	NA	400–1200	400–1200	400–1200
	pcs/order	1200–2600	1200–2600	NA	400–1200	400–1200	400–1200
	pcs/SKU*	15	15	NA	15	15	15
W's Woven Dresses							
	pcs/color	800–1500	1200–2400	1200–2400	NA	NA	NA
	pcs/order	800–1500	1200–2400	1200–2400	NA	NA	NA
	pcs/SKU*	12	12	12	NA	NA	NA
M&W Knit Tops							
	pcs/color	1200	2000	2400	600–800	3000	5500
	pcs/order	1200	2000	2400	600–800	6000	5500
	pcs/SKU*	12	12	12	12	12	12
M&W Sweaters							
	pcs/color	300–400	3000–6000	Wool: 800	600	1200–3300	Wool:800
	pcs/order	300–400	3000–6000	Wool: 800	600	1200–3300	Wool:800
	pcs/SKU*	12	12	12	12	12	12

Source: Company information.
Note: SKU is size and color. Thus, for men's shirts that are measured by neck and arm, the minimum is 12 per color and neck and arm size, so 12 @ blue 17*33, 12 @ blue 17*34, and so on. For men's pants with waist and inseam measurements, the same situation exists. Likewise for women's petite, talls, and regulars, each size and color (2 Petite, 2 Regular, and 2 Tall in blue, green, and red) must meet the minimum.

379

maybe we wouldn't be sub-optimizing two channels. Maybe we could excel in one."

Other executives shared her feelings. "What we're trying to do is provide similar style, service, and quality, but through different channels," said Bill Michel. "We're trying to figure out how to use each channel to provide value to our customers and magnify the brand, but in the end, I'm not sure it really works. It may be that the catalog distracts us, dilutes our focus. Sometimes I'm afraid that we're not as good at catalog or retail together as we would be if we were separate."

Sally Mackenzie from I-media, though, was less sanguine about the success of I-media without the catalog to support it. "We wouldn't be anywhere near where we are if we didn't have the existing equity of the brand," she said. "A Web site can reinforce an existing store image, but it can't create it. The idea is to serve our customer 360 degrees, regardless of the channel they choose to shop. It's highly unlikely that catalogs will go away. There's nothing quite like curling up on your couch with a cup of tea and a catalog. Today, buying online is more of a leaning-forward activity. We need to support both."

Rodway knew that the opposite extreme, closing the retail stores and concentrating on the catalog and I-media, would never occur. "Even though we could become the I-media experts for the Spiegel group or even sell our expertise to other firms, we're not going to sell off 600 stores." But the middle ground seemed to be an option. "If we became like Victoria's Secret, with Eddie Bauer Catalog and Eddie Bauer Stores—would that confuse the customer? I could double sales from the catalog if we weren't tied to retail—by targeting women customers, tailoring assortments, and doing more inserts. We could also add other brands, like Patagonia. But would we end up competing with each other for production space at a vendor?" She stared up at the photo on her wall, showing the company's founder calmly fishing. "As the competition gets fiercer every day, are our three channels a fatal flaw or a winning hand?" ■

PART III: MEASURING, MONITORING, AND
EVALUATING CUSTOMER EQUITY
MANAGEMENT STRATEGY

CHAPTER 10

Strategic Implementation: Investing for Maximum Impact

Once you have determined the appropriate customer mix and the key actions to grow long-term profitability, you need to measure and monitor the results. This chapter provides an introduction to the analyses necessary to evaluate potential marketing strategies and to determine which marketing actions will have the strongest effect on long-term profitability through customer equity. This chapter addresses the following questions:

- How does the firm evaluate distinct marketing investment opportunities?
- Which marketing actions will have the strongest return on investment (ROI)?
- How does the firm select the most appropriate marketing actions in which to invest? Where can the firm reduce marketing investment?
- What will be the effect of competitor actions?
- How does the firm track results and monitor the process? How can a firm evaluate the success (or failure) of a marketing initiative?

◆ QUICK REVIEW: HOW DID WE GET TO THIS POINT?

The goal of a successful customer management strategy is to be able to develop and implement those marketing strategies that will result in the highest long-term ROI.[1] We are now ready to examine the analyses necessary to understand which

---

[1] See, for example; Valarie A. Zeithaml, "Service Quality, Profitability, and the Economic Worth of Customers," *Journal of the Academy of Marketing Science* 28, no. 1 (2000): 67–85; Valarie A. Zeithaml, Leonard L. Berry, and A. Parasuraman, "The Behavioral Consequences of Service Quality," *Journal of Marketing* 60, no. 2 (1996): 31–46; and Paul D. Berger, Ruth N. Bolton, Douglas Bowman, Elten Briggs, V. Kumar, A. Parasuraman, and Creed Terry, "Marketing Actions and the Value of Customer Assets: A Framework for Customer Asset Management," *Journal of Service Research* 5, no. 1 (2002): 39–54.

marketing investment will give the firm the "biggest bang for the buck." To understand how we get to this point, it is useful to quickly review the customer equity management process to this point. We have now covered the following steps in the process:

1. *Customer Equity Analysis.* In this step, we identified the drivers and sub-drivers that are most important to customers. This analysis yields key insights that will be used as we determine where to invest.
    a. We learn how each player in the market (i.e., the firm and its competitors) is performing on all drivers and sub-drivers of customer equity.
    b. We identify specific opportunities for improvement—for example, those sub-drivers which are important to customers on which we appear to be underperforming relative to other drivers or relative to our competitors.
    c. We identify potential opportunities for differentiation, that is, those drivers or sub-drivers on which no one (the firm or its competitors) appears to be performing extremely well.
    d. We identify potential areas of wasted effort, for example, those sub-drivers on which we are performing well that do not appear to have a significant influence on customer behavior.

2. *Strategy Development.* The insights from the analysis then inform the firm's strategic choices. The firm can determine whether to invest in a brand strategy, a value strategy, a relationship strategy, or a joint strategy.
    a. Brand Strategy. When brand sub-drivers are the key influencers of customer equity, firms should focus on actions for self-improvement, differentiation or waste reduction that will improve customer subjective perceptions of the firm's offering, such as marketing communications, corporate citizenship efforts, or particular marketing messages.
    b. Value Strategy. When value sub-drivers are most important, a firm's strategy should pay particular attention to aspects of price, quality, and convenience, both in the process the customer undergoes to acquire the firm's products or services and in the ongoing interactions with the firm.
    c. Relationship Strategy. When relationship sub-drivers are most important, firms should determine whether the foot-in-the-door approach or the all-at-once approach is more appropriate to building the customer–firm relationship, and examine the extent to which its customer base is migrating from one customer type to another.
    d. Joint Strategy. Often, firms will find that two of the key components of customer equity are critical. In this case, firms should focus on strategies that maximize the synergies between the two components, for example, a marketing communications campaign that focuses on delivered value, or a concentrated sales effort that communicates new product offerings.

Once the customer equity analysis is complete and the firm has determined its strategic approach, the next step is the evaluation of potential marketing investments. Which actions should the firm take to maximize customer equity? Which

CHAPTER 10 *Strategic Implementation: Investing for Maximum Impact* **383**

marketing actions will have the strongest impact on long-term profitability?[2] It is to this discussion we now turn.

EVALUATING POTENTIAL MARKETING ACTIONS

When evaluating a marketing investment opportunity (e.g., a quality improvement, a marketing communications campaign, a loyalty program), it is important to answer the following questions:

- Will it pay off?[3]
- How much will it cost to improve a driver or sub-driver?
- What is the change in customer equity?
- What is the ROI?
- How sensitive is the projected ROI to underlying assumptions?

Let's examine the evaluation process in the context of a specific example.[4] Consider a grocery chain that caters to an upscale, health-conscious market (for example, a market such as Whole Foods Market in the United States, or Fresh and Wild in the United Kingdom). Let's call our example GoodFoods Market. GoodFoods conducted a customer equity analysis in a large metropolitan area. The market was looking for ways to grow customer equity. After careful analysis, it was considering two potential marketing actions, an investment in an advertising campaign and an investment in a loyalty program.

• Option 1: Should GoodFoods invest $200,000 in an advertising campaign? The marketing manager believes that it will improve overall awareness of GoodFoods by 0.1 (on a 5-point scale).

---

[2]For models that examine the effects of marketing actions on customer retention, customer lifetime value, and long-term profitabililty, see, for example, Peter C. Verhoef, "Understanding the Effect of Customer Relationship Management Efforts on Customer Retention and Customer Share Development," *Journal of Marketing* 67, no. 4 (2003): 30–45; Werner J. Reinartz and V. Kumar, "On the Profitability of Long-Life Customers in a Noncontractual Setting: An Empirical Investigation and Implications for Marketing," *Journal of Marketing* 64, no. 4 (2000): 17–35; Werner J. Reinartz and V. Kumar, "The Impact of Customer Relationship Characteristics on Profitable Lifetime Duration," *Journal of Marketing* 67, no. 1 (2003): 77–99; Roland T. Rust, Anthony J. Zahorik, and Timothy L. Keiningham, "Return on Quality (ROQ): Making Service Quality Financially Accountable," *Journal of Marketing* 59 (April 1995): 58–70; and Rajkumar Venkatesan and V. Kumar, "A Customer Lifetime Value Framework for Customer Selection and Optimal Resource Allocation," *Journal of Marketing* 68, no. 4 (2004), 106–125.
[3]Several approaches have examined the effects of marketing actions on customer repurchase, one step in determining the return on a marketing investment. See, for example, Vikas Mittal and Wagner A. Kamakura, "Satisfaction, Repurchase Intent, and Repurchase Behavior: Investigating the Moderating Effect of Customer Characteristics," *Journal of Marketing Research* 38, no. 1 (2001): 131–42; Wagner A. Kamakura, Vikas Mittal, Fernando de Rosa, and Jose Afonso Mazzon, "Assessing the Service Profit Chain," *Marketing Science* 21, no. 3 (2002): 294–317; and Eugene C. Anderson and Vikas Mittal, "Strengthening the Satisfaction-Profit Chain," *Journal of Service Research* 3, no. 2 (2000): 107–20.
[4]The examples in this chapter follow the approach found in Roland T. Rust Katherine N. Lemon, and Valarie A. Zeithaml, "Return on Marketing: Using Customer Equity to Focus Marketing Strategy," *Journal of Marketing* 68, no. 1 (2004): 23–53; and Roland T. Rust, Valarie A. Zeithaml, and Katherine N. Lemon, *Driving Customer Equity: How Customer Lifetime Value Is Reshaping Corporate Strategy* (New York: The Free Press, 2000).

TABLE 10-1 Advertising Campaign Improvement

Discounted expenditure (Cost of Advertising Campaign)	$200,000
Improvement in brand awareness	0.1 (on a 5-point scale)
Improvement in brand equity	16%
Percent improvement in customer equity	5.72%
Financial improvement in customer equity	$256,389
ROI for this marketing investment	28.2%

- Option 2: Should GoodFoods invest $200,000 in improving the loyalty program? The marketing manager believes that it will improve customer perceptions of GoodFoods' loyalty program by 0.2 (on a 5-point scale).

Using the customer equity approach results in the tables in Tables 10-1 and 10-2 provides additional insight into the two possible investments: Comparing the ROI results from these two potential investments for GoodFoods shows that the advertising campaign has a higher projected ROI (28.2%) than does the loyalty program investment (9.6%). There may be other extenuating circumstances that may lead the firm to invest in the loyalty program, but the analysis shows that an investment in advertising to build brand awareness, in this situation, will have a higher long-term impact on customer profitability than the loyalty program improvement.[5]

Before investing in the advertising program, however, GoodFoods should also consider how competitors might react to this marketing action. By examining each competitor's performance on the attributes of brand awareness and attitude toward the brand, GoodFoods can ascertain how vulnerable each competitor may feel when faced with a significant GoodFoods advertising campaign. The firm may even be able

TABLE 10-2 Loyalty Program Improvement

Discounted expenditure (cost of loyalty program improvement)	$200,000
Improvement in perceptions of loyalty program	0.2 (on a 5-point scale)
Improvement in relationship equity	24%
Percent improvement in customer equity	4.89%
Financial improvement in customer equity	$219,185
ROI for this marketing investment	9.6%

---

[5]For additional background, see also Roland T. Rust, Anthony J. Zahorik, and Timothy L. Keiningham, *Return on Quality: Measuring the Financial Impact of Your Company's Quest for Quality* (Burr Ridge, Ill: Irwin, 1994); Raymond E. Kordupleski, Roland T. Rust, and Anthony J. Zahorik, "Why Improving Quality Doesn't Improve Quality," *California Management Review* 35 (Spring 1993); 82–95; A. E. Hoerl and R.W. Kennard, "Ridge Regression: Biased Estimation for Non-Orthogonal Problems," *Technometrics*, 12, (1970); 55–67; Lakshman Krishnamurthi and Arvind Rangaswamy, "The Equity Estimator for Marketing Research," *Marketing Science* 6 (Fall 1987); 336–7; and Roland T. Rust, Peter J. Danaher, and Sajeev Varki, "Comparative Service Quality and Competitive Marketing Decisions" (Working paper, Center for Service Marketing, Vanderbilt University, 1999).

CHAPTER 10 *Strategic Implementation: Investing for Maximum Impact*   **385**

to predict which competitor might "fight back" with a campaign of its own, and this should be taken into consideration as the decision is made.

Finally, it is important to understand the underlying assumptions when using a decision calculus such as the customer equity approach. In the GoodFoods analysis the key assumptions are as follows:

1. A $200,000 investment in an advertising campaign will result in an improvement in brand awareness of 0.1 on a 5-point scale.
2. A $200,000 investment in improving the loyalty program will result in an improvement in perceptions of the loyalty program of 0.2 on a 5-point scale.
3. The firm's discount rate (for use in discounting the value of future customer purchases to the present) is 10%.
4. The firm has a time horizon of 3 years.

How reasonable are these assumptions? The first two assumptions rely on the expertise of the marketing manager. Advertising models have developed substantially over the years, and advertising experts have a pretty good idea of how much it costs to gain brand awareness (both aided awareness and unaided awareness). Therefore, the first assumption may be very reasonable, if it was made with solid information from GoodFoods advertising experts. The second assumption may be less certain. If GoodFoods has asked customers specifically what improvements they would like to see in the loyalty program, and if the investment is designed to address those specific issues, then the assumption may be fairly sound. If, however, there is no research to back up the 0.2 figure, it will be important to "run the numbers" with different assumptions—for example, will the investment pay off if GoodFoods achieves only a 0.1 improvement rather than a 0.2 improvement? The discount rate assumption can also be varied in the analysis to see how sensitive the results are to choice of discount rate. In highly volatile markets, or markets with very high inflation, choosing an appropriate discount rate will be critical. Finally, the choice of time horizon is a purely managerial decision. Most firms operate on a very short-term horizon. However, the power of the customer equity management approach is that it provides metrics to enable managers to think more long term. Therefore, a good time horizon is one of at least 3 years and not usually more than 5 years (as the discounted cash flows become much smaller after 5 years).[6]

◆ OPPORTUNITY FOR HANDS-ON ANALYSIS

Case 10-1 at the end of this chapter provides you with the opportunity to examine the airline's customer equity analysis and to perform calculations and what-if analyses just like those in Tables 10-1 and 10-2. It is important to consider which of all the possible marketing investments represent the greatest opportunities for the firm, and to compare the potential ROI from different marketing actions. This case provides you with

---

[6] Recent research supports such a time horizon: Rajkumar Venkatesan and V. Kumar, "A Customer Lifetime Value Framework for Customer Selection and Optimal Resource Allocation," *Journal of Marketing* 68, no. 4 (2004), 106–125, and V. Kumar and Jacquelyn Thomas, "Allocating Acquisition and Retention Resources to Maximize Customer Profitability" (working paper, University of Connecticut, 2004).

the opportunity to experience the intricacies and trade-offs necessary in determining which marketing actions offer the greatest potential ROI. You can examine the data and try to uncover opportunities for Aerosphere to differentiate itself from its competitors. In addition, you have the opportunity to investigate which marketing actions are the best candidates for reductions in marketing expenditures (say, the budget had to be reduced by $1,000,000). Overall, the case provides you with the opportunity to prioritize marketing actions based on ROI.

◆ TRACKING RESULTS AND MONITORING THE PROCESS

After a firm has decided which marketing actions to take, it is important to measure and monitor the results.[7] Did the marketing investment actually improve customer equity? Was it a success? In today's business environment of short-term thinking, many firms fail to evaluate the success or failure of a marketing strategy, therefore failing to learn from their successes or mistakes. Using the strategic customer equity management approach, evaluating the effectiveness of a marketing initiative is fairly straightforward. Two specific approaches follow: measuring customer equity over time and test versus control.

MEASURE CUSTOMER EQUITY OVER TIME

To understand the effectiveness of a firm's marketing actions, it is necessary to monitor changes in customer equity over time. A firm should conduct a customer equity analysis at least annually, although it may be useful to survey customers more frequently if the market is particularly turbulent (e.g., really new products or services). This annual customer equity benchmarking allows the firm to (1) assess the effectiveness of a marketing investment, (2) track changes in customer needs, (3) track competitive strategies and actions.

The following example illustrates the process. Suppose, for example, that a home goods retailer identified the following improvement from a customer equity analysis: The customer equity analysis showed that the sub-driver, "sales associates are easily visible and accessible to customers," had a significant impact on customer equity. The retailer decided to invest in a program to improve visibility and accessibility. The firm provided each sales associate with a bright-colored vest. In addition, the firm equipped each sales associate with a mobile-push-to-talk phone. Finally, management placed kiosks in several spots throughout the store, enabling customers to request service from sales associates at convenient location.

Six months following the implementation of the program, suppose that the retailer conducted a follow-up customer equity analysis. Using this analysis, the retailer could examine the following:

- Changes in the performance rating of the retailer (and competitors) on the dimension of "sales associates are easily visible and accessible to customers."
- Any changes in the importance weight of this sub-driver on customer equity.

---

[7]The role of decision support systems in organizations has been discussed for many years; see John D. C. Little, "Decision Support Systems for Marketing Managers, *Journal of Marketing* 43 (Summer 1979): 9–26; and John D. C. Little, "Models and Managers: The Concept of a Decision Calculus," *Management Science*, 16, no. 8 (1970): 466–85.

CHAPTER 10 *Strategic Implementation: Investing for Maximum Impact* **387**

TABLE 10-3 Tracking Changes in Customer Equity over Time

Retailer Customer Equity Results Evaluation	Old CE Analysis	New CE Analysis	Change
Retailer's rating on salesperson accessibility	2.8	3.3	0.5
Average competitor's rating on salesperson accessibility	3.2	3.2	0.0
Retailer's customer equity	$220,500,000	$226,600,000	$6,100,000
Sub-driver importance weight	0.3	0.31	0.01
Projected change in CE due to a .1 improvement in sub-driver	$900,000	700,000	$(200,000)
Cost of improvement	$2,000,000	n/a	n/a

- The change in overall customer equity over the six months.
- The projected increase in customer equity based upon an improvement in this sub-driver.

These metrics could be compared with the expected improvement in customer equity (based on the earlier CE analysis). The firm could then determine whether or not the investment in the sales associate "visibility and accessibility program" was worthwhile.

Table 10-3 provides sample metrics to evaluate this initiative.

- We can see that the retailer's performance rating on the sub-driver increased by 0.5 (from 2.9 to 3.3 on a 5-point scale).

- In the next row, we see that the retailer's competitors' performance ratings did not change, suggesting the retailer "gained" on this sub-driver relative to the competition. If competitors had also improved on this sub-driver, the firm would need to determine what actions the competition took during this time frame that may have influenced the customer.

- In the next row of the table, we see that the firm's overall customer equity (CE) improved by just over $6 million. Now, we cannot say for sure that the improvement in CE is solely due to the marketing investment in sales associates, but we can see that, if nothing else significant changed in the six months, the investment appeared to pay off. The firm expected a 0.1 improvement to result in an increase in CE of $900,000 and this seems to have been borne out; a 0.5 improvement in the sub-driver should have resulted in a $4.5 million improvement in CE, and we see that the actual result is a bit higher.

- The next row of the table shows how the customers' importance weight associated with this sub-driver has changed. We see a slight increase in importance (01 increase). This may be due to random "noise" in the data or it may be indicative of a slight shift in consumer needs—our program of increased sales associate accessibility may actually make that attribute more important to customers.

- The next-to-last row of the table shows the projected improvement in customer equity from a .1 change in the sub-driver. We see that in the new CE analysis, this projected improvement is lower—now only $700,000. This change suggests that there may be some diminishing returns to additional improvements in this sub-driver and that the firm should continue to monitor it over time.

- The last row of the table shows the cost of the improvement program to the retailer. We see that the firm spent $2 million to improve salesperson accessibility and visibility, and that customer equity improved by $6.1 million. Clearly, this improvement shows a positive return on investment.

This example shows how the firm can use multiple waves of customer equity analysis to evaluate the effectiveness of its marketing actions. More broadly, multiple analyses over time enable the firm to track changes in importance weights of all drivers and sub-drivers. Measuring CE over time is important to understand how customer needs are changing. This is particularly critical if the firm identifies potential opportunities for differentiation. Say, for example, that the home goods retailer discussed earlier determined that no one in the marketplace had implemented strategies to enhance relationship equity with customers. The customer equity analysis might show, for example, that relationship equity drivers are not very important to customers and that no firm is performing well on these drivers. The firm might decide to differentiate itself by creating a loyalty program or retailer credit card that offers special bonuses to frequent purchasers. Such a differentiation strategy requires a periodic monitoring of customer equity to determine if customers are recognizing the program, and if the program may be influencing both performance perceptions and importance weights for relationship equity.

Finally, measuring customer equity over time enables the firm to track and understand competitive actions. If a key competitor implements a new strategic approach or new marketing action, the firm can monitor the effects of the competitor's actions on the firm's (and the competitor's) customer equity through multiple customer equity analyses over time. Firms can also see the extent to which competitors have responded to the firm's marketing actions and the effects of the actions (and reactions) on customer equity. It is important to remember that markets are dynamic and periodic customer equity analyses enable the firm to understand and potentially even master the dynamics of their market.

TEST VERSUS CONTROL

In addition to multiple waves of customer equity analysis, firms may also choose to implement a marketing investment in a test market and evaluate the changes in customer equity in the test market relative to a control market another market in which the marketing program is not implemented. If our example home goods retailer had used this approach instead, the results might look something like Table 10-4.

Table 10-4 shows the following changes in the test market (relative to the control market):

- A significant improvement in customer's rating of the retailer in terms of salesperson accessibility—a 0.45 increase in the test market.
- No increase in customer rating of competitors on this sub-driver in the test market, minor increase in control market (0.05).
- Significant increase in customer equity in test market relative to the control market—$400,000.

TABLE 10-4 Comparing Changes in Customer Equity in Test Markets and Control Markets

Retailer Customer Equity Results Evaluation	Test Market CE Changes	Control Market CE Changes	Difference Between Test and Control
Changes in retailer's rating on salesperson accessibility	0.5	0.05	0.45
Changes in average competitor's rating on salesperson accessibility	0.0	0.05	(0.05)
Changes in retailer's customer equity (for each market)	$500,000	$100,000	$400,000
Changes in sub-driver importance weight	0.01	0.0	0.01
Projected change in CE due to a .1 improvement in sub-driver	$90,000	90,000	N/A
Cost of improvement	$200,000	n/a	n/a

- Slight increase in importance weight for this sub-driver in test market—no change in the control market.
- The marketing improvement appears to be a good investment: we see a $400,000 increase in customer equity relative to a $200,000 cost for the program.

The test-versus control approach offers a stronger validation of the marketing investment than the changes in customer equity over time approach, as the firm is able to control for the effect of other changes in the market more effectively.[8] If marketing actions or improvements can be tested in specific markets prior to a firmwide rollout, it is advised to do so. However, the risk of this approach is that the firm's competitors will be able to see the firm's strategy during the test, potentially reducing the effectiveness of the strategy when it is fully implemented.

Summary

Ideally, firms would like to be able to evaluate the results of a marketing strategy before they invest the resources. Unfortunately, this isn't possible. However, the customer equity approach provides a proxy or decision tool to enable firms to evaluate the potential outcomes of several marketing strategies before taking action. In order to evaluate the potential ROI of a marketing strategy, the firm must consider several aspects. First, what will the marketing strategy cost? Second, what effect will the marketing action have on customer perceptions and actions? Third, given this effect, how will the marketing strategy influence customer equity? The answers to these questions enable marketing managers to calculate the return on investment of any potential marketing activity. Then, knowing the potential ROI, a firm can determine which marketing action will have the highest potential return.

---

[8]For an example of a two-cohort approach analysis, see Rajkumar Venkatesan and V. Kumar, "A Customer Lifetime Value Framework for Customer Selection and Optimal Resource Allocation," *Journal of Marketing* 68, no. 4 (2004), 106–12.

It is important to understand the assumptions implicit in this process. To gain the most out of the customer equity approach, the firm should test to see how sensitive the results are to the assumptions (e.g., magnitude of the effect, discount rate, time horizon, or cost of the improvement) before making the marketing investment. In addition, firms should consider the potential competitive reactions to strategies and factor these reactions in prior to taking action.

Tracking and monitoring results is critical. Firms should conduct periodic follow-up customer equity analyses to determine the effectiveness of their marketing programs—assessing the impact of a marketing action through its changes in customer equity over time. When possible, firms should conduct test markets to investigate the effects of a marketing investment. By comparing the test market and the control market, firms can gain a strong sense of the impact of a specific marketing intervention on customer equity.

Review Questions and Exercises

1. Suppose a large electronic components manufacturer conducted a customer equity analysis. The results showed that the biggest ROI would arise from investments in additional salespeople. Based on this analysis, the firm decided to expand its sales force. How would you recommend the firm implement its expansion? What metrics should the firm use to determine if the additional investment in salespeople is really paying off?
2. A large pet store is interested in developing closer relationships with its customers and their pets. The store is considering investing in a "pet friends" program that will send birthday cards to customers' pets and remind pets' owners of important dates (vaccinations, birthdays, etc.). How could the pet store use the customer equity approach to determine if this is a good investment?

Case 10-1 Aerosphere Airlines (B)

Roland T. Rust, Katherine N. Lemon, and Valarie A. Zeithaml
(Accompanies Customer Equity Driver Software)

Recall that William Tindall is the chief marketing officer for Aerosphere Airlines, and is worried about how to maintain a marketing edge against his main competitors, Dynasty Airlines, Shark Airlines, and Ultra Airlines. Aerosphere, Dynasty, and Ultra have similar business models, reflecting a higher concern for service, and Shark positions itself more as a low-price, low-cost carrier.

In Case 4-1, you looked at a customer equity analysis of the airlines industry and Aerosphere Airlines. The identified drivers and sub-drivers were

Drivers of Value Equity
Quality [with sub-drivers of cabin service ("cabserv") and passenger compartment comfort ("passcomp")]
Price

Drivers of Brand Equity
Attitude toward the airline ("aatt")
Awareness of airline advertising ("aad")

Drivers of Relationship Equity
Investment in the airline's frequent flyer program ("alinv")
Preferential treatment ("alpref")

Recall that Tindall assumed that each airline had a contribution margin of about 15 percent (his best guess, based on industry data), that Aerosphere had a time horizon of 3 years on its investments, and used a discount rate of 10 percent.

In Case 4-1, you determined the following:

- Aerosphere's estimated customer equity and how much an average customer is worth.
- How much should Aerosphere spend to retain a customer.
- Aerosphere's customer equity share.
- Aerosphere's strengths and weaknesses, relative to competitors.
- Most and least important drivers in the industry.
- Where Aerosphere might want to focus its marketing efforts.

In this case assignment, you will need to use the analysis from Case 4-1. Based on this analysis, you will evaluate different marketing investment opportunities, and make recommendations to Tindall regarding which marketing actions will have the strongest impact on customer equity. ∎

CASE ASSIGNMENT

Open the "Effects of Improvements" screen. Suppose Aerosphere could increase its customer ratings on cabin service by an average of 0.5, with an expenditure of $5 million. Would this marketing investment pay off? What would be the change in customer equity? What would be the ROI?

1. Try discount rates of 1 percent, 5 percent, 20 percent, and 50 percent for the improvement above. What is the impact on ROI?
2. Suppose the CEO tells you that Aerosphere now has only a one-year time horizon. What is the impact on ROI for the improvement above?
3. What if only a 0.3 improvement occurred? Would the investment be profitable then? What do these results imply about the advisability of test marketing?
4. Let's now consider the potential impact of competitors' moves. What if Ultra Airlines increased its rating of investment in the frequent flyer program (alinv) by 0.1, for an investment of $100 million? Is that a likely competitive move, if Ultra is fully knowledgeable about the customer equity implications? How much return would Ultra get from such a move?

♦♦♦ Customer Value Measurement at Nortel Networks—Optical Networks Division

Case 10-2   Customer Value Measurement at Nortel Networks—Optical Networks Division

Das Narayandas

In January 2000 Maureen Conroy, head of Nortel Networks'™ Optical Networks Customer Value Management (CVM) Team, was evaluating with team member Nathalie Sauve the 1999 Optical Networks (ON) customer satisfaction/loyalty survey results (see Exhibit 1), qualitative research report (see Exhibit 2), and analysis from the pilot Relative Customer Value study (Exhibits 3 and 4) as well as feedback from key CVM stakeholders in preparation for submitting to ON president Greg Mumford their recommendations for the 2000/2001 customer value program. They believed that Optical Networks' incorporation of customer satisfaction and loyalty measures into its business practices was critical to the company's success in increasing customer value, but they believed that there was still room to grow.

The ON organization was familiar with the satisfaction and loyalty program that had been in

---

The case was prepared by Professor Das Narayandas. Copyright © 2001 by the President and Fellows of Harvard College. Harvard Business School Case 501-050.

EXHIBIT 1   Summary of the Customer Satisfaction/Loyalty Survey Results

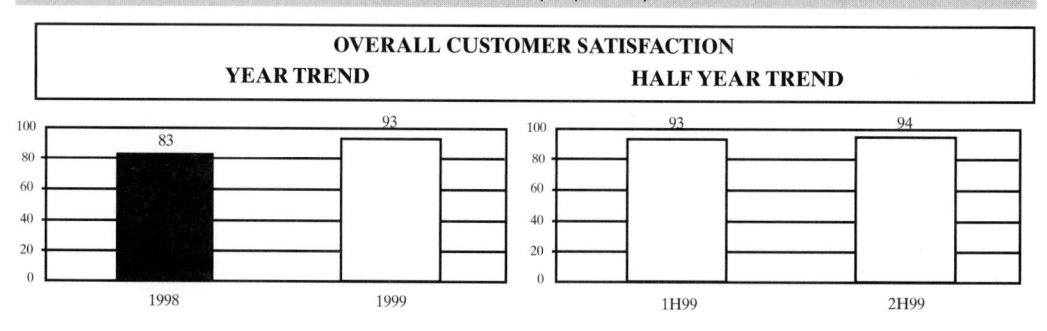

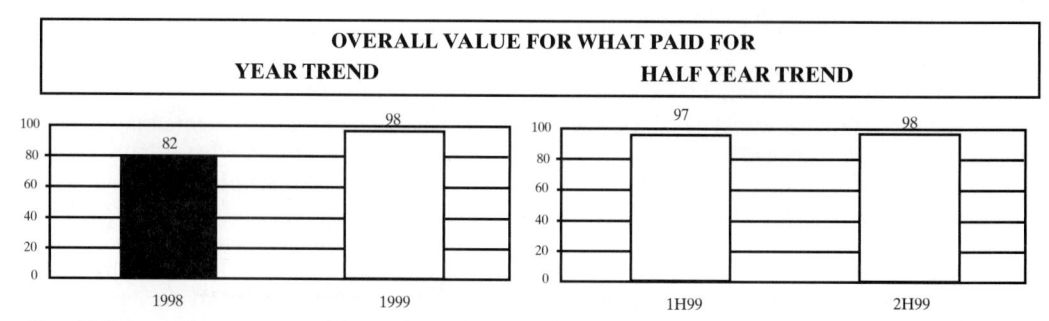

OVERALL CUSTOMER SATISFACTION

YEAR TREND
- 1998: 83
- 1999: 93

HALF YEAR TREND
- 1H99: 93
- 2H99: 94

OVERALL VALUE FOR WHAT PAID FOR

YEAR TREND
- 1998: 82
- 1999: 98

HALF YEAR TREND
- 1H99: 97
- 2H99: 98

Note: Values are the percentage of respondents who scored Nortel Networks in the top two boxes (i.e., either a 4 or 5 on the 5-point scale or a 7, 8, 9, 10 on a 10-point scale).

OVERALL PRODUCT QUALITY

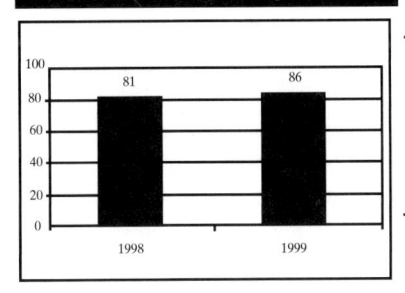

	Year Trend 1998	Year Trend 1999	Half Year Trend 1H99	Half Year Trend 2H99
Overall Product Quality	**81**	**86**	**87**	**84**
Being reliable	83	84	80	93
Easy to use	80	75	68	81
Easy to install	75	67	65	69
Meeting new product dates	71	75	74	76
Documentation meets needs	85	95	93	97

OVERALL QUALITY OF SERVICES

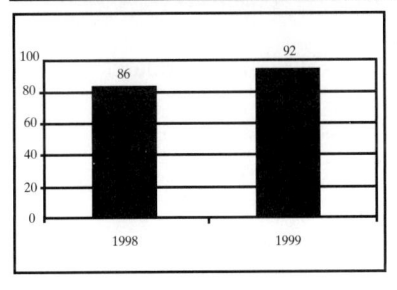

	Year Trend 1998	Year Trend 1999	Half Year Trend 1H99	Half Year Trend 2H99
Overall Quality of Services	**86**	**92**	**92**	**91**
Engineering support received	89	94	90	100
Personnel s technical competence	79	86	92	75
Resolves problems quickly	92	70	69	70
Order process simplicity	92	90	89	91
On-time delivery	79	70	75	65
Network planning support	84	100	100	100

OVERALL RELATIONSHIP

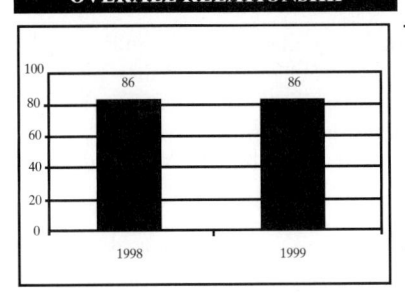

	Year Trend 1998	Year Trend 1999	Half Year Trend 1H99	Half Year Trend 2H99
Overall Relationship	**86**	**84**	**86**	**86**
Resolve problems brought to their attention	85	91	90	91
Understand your future business needs	82	89	88	90
Solving business problems	85	91	93	89
Anticipating your needs	85	75	72	77
Keeping commitments	90	85	88	100
Likelihood to keep as primary supplier	70	82	84	81
Likelihood to recommend Nortel Networks	87	92	92	92

place since 1995. Key process owners in various parts of the organization expected to see updates on the issues they had been addressing in the format with which they were familiar. The qualitative study, however, provided interesting insights that the current methodology did not and the pilot RCV report provided competitive information. Which or what combination of the many choices for soliciting customer perceptions would make the best use of the available resources, minimize the intrusion on customers' time, and add value for the business and customers alike?

COMPANY BACKGROUND

Described as Canada's "high technology crown jewel," Nortel Networks was a global player in

EXHIBIT 2 A Summary of the Qualitative Research Report

VALUE DRIVERS

In this section we discuss the content sources from which X value drivers will be named, defined, and validated. Content sources are broad categories such as "product" or "technical support." Out of these emerge more specifically defined behaviors or product qualities, such as "timely introduction of new products." Thus, speed of new product introduction is a true value driver.

For X, the following value content sources were consistent across all roles and are presented in relative order of importance from X's perspective:

- Product availability and development (quality, reliability, availability, features, cost)
- Network installation/deployment (ability to take on the massive task with people, product)
- Knowledge transfer as training/education/mentoring (help X to stand on its own)
- Technical support (daily operations, on-site engineering, remote operations)
- Communications (timely, honest, accurate, responsible)
- Organizational agility (risk takers willing to buy in to market position, product development)
- Sense of urgency (display behavior indicating a need to establish a market)
- Total commitment (visible understanding of X throughout Nortel Networks)
- Design to meet collocation and other real world constraints
- Engages in "real-time" testing of new products and features

SAMPLE VERBATIM

"We expect our vendors to deliver us a quality product. That means quality of design, quality of manufacture, and quality of delivery. When I plug a card in I want it to work and I want it to keep working for a long, long time."

"Essentially what we're concerned about is our network to be built on time... [and] we are concerned about [Nortel Networks] delivering on the contractual obligations that they have in terms of actual features in the product. If they do not deliver on many of those features, then it directly impacts the services and it impacts [our ability to market]."

"People in my group spend a lot of time talking to Nortel Networks about, 'Why don't you have this [feature or product]?'"

"We try to improve their product to our standard."

"Yes, to our standard. We want it improved in the sense that we want to cut our costs so that we can lower our prices to our customers."

"One of the things that is advantageous to the Nortel Networks style is the fact that it's very thorough. It has a tendency to catch the details that are potentially missed in moving, as you say, at Web speed. They create, for the most part, a fairly robust product. The hardware itself all the way through implementation is a very robust process."

"The issue is that I don't think they have enough manpower. They may be getting requests from me and from Operations to the same person so they have to make a choice of who's more important. Is Jeff more important? Is Robert more important? What do I need to get done first?"

"I know the answer to that! I don't think they have enough horsepower here. I think they need to grow their group to support us a little better."

"[Nortel Networks does] provide, for my group, for instance, an on-site engineer."

"Using their tools to help us troubleshoot. And then mentoring."

"The only time I've gone outside the process is on technical issues, when you need an answer and these on-site guys don't give you the right answer."

"[Nortel Networks' ability] to provide both [performance and functions] in the long-distance and metro market [is] very important. Being able to perform on installation goals and tasks and our schedules [is] very high on the list, very important to us."

"When I need a piece of information or I need something from Nortel Networks or I need to get hold of somebody in Nortel Networks to get a question answered there are about three people I know that I can call, regardless of what level or category."

"They [Nortel Networks] are honest. In other words, if they're not going to make their deadlines most of the time [they tell us]."

"We love to talk about meeting customer expectations, and while generally we believe that, we think it's far more important to meet commitments."

"[If vendors] make commitments repeatedly that they don't meet . . . they will be former suppliers here very shortly. We will architect our way away from them so fast they won't believe it."

EXHIBIT 3 Excerpts from Internal Memo from Nortel Networks Corporate

Internal Memo
1999 CVA Pilot Research
A guide to understanding Nortel Networks potential transition from Customer Satisfaction to Customer Value Analysis

INTRODUCTION

Nortel Networks is considering a transition from a customer satisfaction focus to a more in-depth understanding of the value propositions that Nortel Networks brings to its market. This transition in measurement systems would accompany changes in marketing strategies and corporate advertising. These changes focus on enhancing Nortel Networks unique portfolio of products and services in the minds of present and potential customers.

RATIONALE

In recent years Nortel Networks has deployed a customer measuring system focused on customer attitudes concerning Nortel Networks' product lines and services. The process involved surveying a respondent identified by the account team, a particular product, and a questionnaire designed by the product prime with the product and specific respondent in mind. The results of the survey process provided information regarding product performance issues concerning major aspects of the products such as delivery, installation, service, and marketing. Resulting data helped identify opportunities for process improvement, but did not assist Nortel Network managers in understanding the company's overall offering or how Nortel Networks compares to the competition.

(Continued)

> Recognizing these limitations, Nortel Networks leadership determined the feasibility of moving to a measurement of the accounts or segments and the perception of Nortel Networks vs. the competition. Respondents will be surveyed through a blind survey methodology, with surveys designed and administered by the Corporate Customer Loyalty and Value team. Simultaneously, the product lines management will be encouraged to institute transaction surveys for analysis of process improvements within their NBUs.
>
> The new metric, called Relative Customer Value (RCV), will represent a ratio of Nortel Networks performance compared to the performance of competitors in the market. It is interpreted as follows:
>
> $$RCV = \frac{\text{Nortel Networks Score}}{\text{Competitors' Score}}$$
>
> *How to Interpret RCV Ratios:*
>
> | | | |
> |---|---|---|
> | < .98 | = | Competition providing greater value than Nortel Networks |
> | .98–1.02 | = | Nortel Networks value perceived to be no different from the competition, i.e., parity |
> | 1.02–1.05 | = | Nortel Networks providing greater value than the competition |
> | > 1.06 | = | Nortel Networks providing greater value at world class levels |
>
> Rather than just look at Nortel Networks or its product lines in isolation, this metric accounts for the market performance of Nortel Networks and will be more indicative of future performance prospects.

EXHIBIT 3 (cont.)

telephony, data, and wireless and wireline Internet solutions (an organization chart is presented in Exhibit 5). With more than 80,000 employees, in excess of $22.3 billion in revenues, and a market capitalization of $180.2 billion (4Q 2000), the company was an industry leader in telecommunications research and the development, manufacture, marketing, and end-to-end support of enterprise, public carrier, wireless, and broadband networks.

Nortel Networks origins dated to 1880, when Bell Telephone Company of Canada was established in Montreal four years after the invention of the telephone. It commenced operations as Northern Electric and remained wholly owned by Bell Canada until 1973, when the latter began to sell stock. After changing its name to Northern Telecom,[1] it distinguished itself as the first equipment company to introduce a digital switch. The breakup of AT&T in 1982 opened the door to the international market for Northern Telecom, which, by the end of 1984, had become the second-largest telecommunications equipment provider in North America and established itself as a legitimate global player. Northern Telecom became Nortel in 1995, the year of its hundredth anniversary.

In 1998, recognizing that the future lay in the Internet, Nortel Networks made a "right-angle turn," shifting its focus from voice to data. With the $6.7 billion acquisition of major network provider Bay Networks in 1999, Nortel appended Networks to its name. Operations were divided into two new groups: Enterprise Solutions, a source of data solutions, including LAN, WAN, and other electronic communications products; and the Service Provider and Carrier Group, of which the Optical Networks division was a part.

Nortel Networks' diverse customer base included:

- incumbent local exchange carriers, including public telephony and data networks;

---

[1]Northern Telecom is a trademark of Nortel Networks. Other company names may be trademarks of their respective owners.

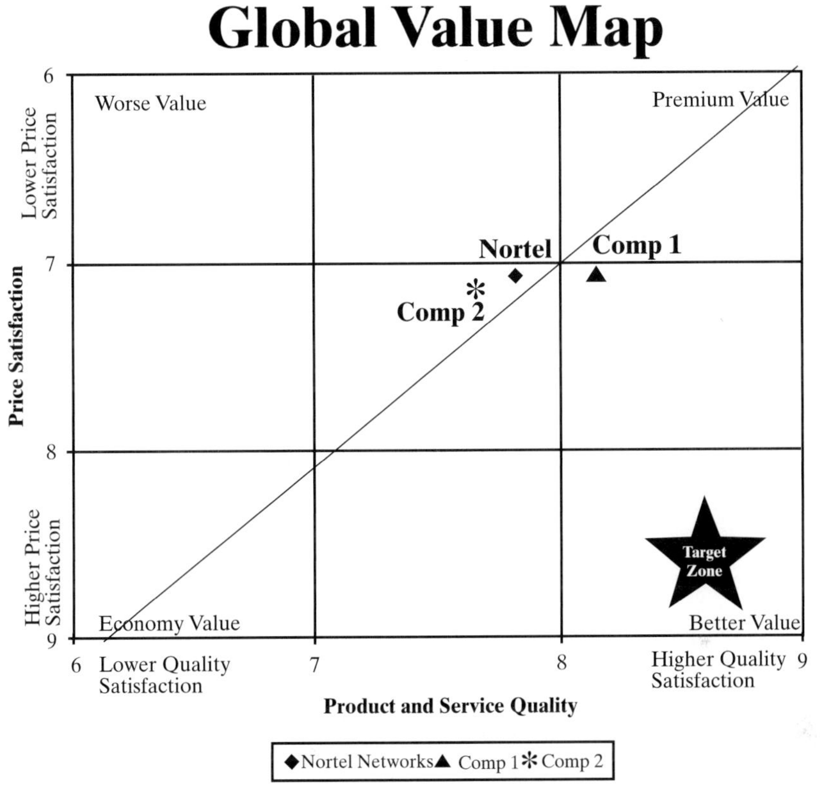
Global Value Map
Worse Value
Premium Value
Economy Value
Better Value
Nortel
Comp 1
Comp 2
Target Zone
Price Satisfaction
Lower Price Satisfaction
Higher Price Satisfaction
6
7
8
9
Lower Quality Satisfaction
Higher Quality Satisfaction
Product and Service Quality
◆Nortel Networks▲ Comp 1✻ Comp 2

	RCV (Nortel v.s. Comp)	Value	RCO (Nortel v.s. Comp)	Quality	RCP (Nortel v.s. Comp)	Price
Nortel Networks		7.85		7.83		7.07
Comp 1	0.97	8.13	0.96	8.17	1.00	7.05
Comp 2	1.01	7.76	1.02	7.67	0.99	7.13

Note: All ratios greater than or equal to 1.02 and less than or equal to 0.98 were determined to be statistically significant based on the sample sizes.

Acronym	*Definition*
RCV	Relative Customer Value
RCQ	Relative Customer Quality
RCP	Relative Customer Price

EXHIBIT 4 Excerpts from Relative Customer Value Study

- competitive local exchange carriers and interexchange carriers, including public networks, ISPs, and broadband wireless and utility networks;
- wireless, including public mobility and fixed wireless, networks;
- enterprise (voice and data), including corporate and private, networks.

The Service Provider/Carrier Group

Nortel Networks established the Service Provider and Carrier Group line of business (LOB) in 4Q

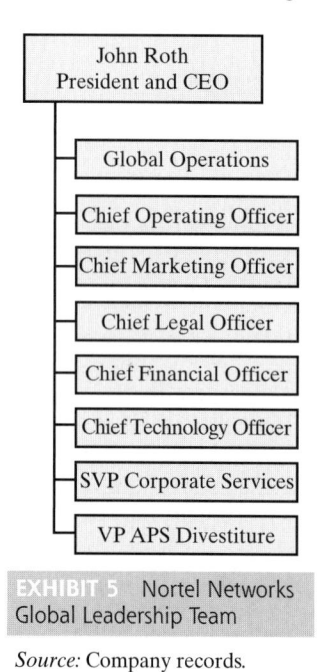

Exhibit 5: Nortel Networks Global Leadership Team

- John Roth — President and CEO
  - Global Operations
  - Chief Operating Officer
  - Chief Marketing Officer
  - Chief Legal Officer
  - Chief Financial Officer
  - Chief Technology Officer
  - SVP Corporate Services
  - VP APS Divestiture

Source: Company records.

1997 in response to industry-wide demand for "seamless access" to its network solutions, which spanned Optical Networks (ON), Internet Telephony, Wireless Internet, and Internet Services. The group provided scale and leverage for customers that needed to create the new, high-performance Internet that would support global voice, data, wireless, and wireline traffic with consolidated, cost-effective, packet-based networks that would be easier to manage, maintain, and modernize.

Strategic Importance of the ON Division

The creation of the ON division reflected Nortel Networks' recognition that with the advent of the Internet, speed of transmission would become considerably more important to customers. In the mid-1990s, bandwidth capacity began to be increased by splitting the laser light on a single fiber strand into different colors or wavelengths. By 1999, Nortel Networks' R&D team had developed networks capable of achieving transmission speeds of more than one terabit, or one trillion bits per second. Acquisitions of fiber network firms enabled Optical Networks to offer, by the end of 1999, transmission speeds up to 1.6 terabits, sufficient to transmit 360,000 simultaneous showings of a feature-length movie across America. That year the company's optical equipment carried more than 75% of all backbone Internet traffic in North America and constituted 50% of the pan-European optical backbone, at the lowest cost-per-bit, per-mile of any manufacturer in the world.

ORIGINS OF NORTEL NETWORKS' CUSTOMER MEASUREMENT PROCESS

Its quality and customer value policy expressed Nortel Networks' commitment to being the company most valued in its industry by customers, employees, shareholders, and the communities in which it operated. In 1992 the company took this commitment to a new level.

In response to intensifying competition in the telecommunications industry, CEO Jean Monty began to refocus Nortel Networks on customer satisfaction and value by establishing a *Customer-First* culture. The initiative emphasized three key elements: continuous improvement; value creation for customers; and employee involvement.

The following goals were articulated for a customer satisfaction and loyalty measurement program designed to assess Nortel Networks' responsiveness to the needs of its customer base and the value it delivered to customers, employees, and shareholders.

- Measure customer value and loyalty across products and major accounts.
- Understand drivers of customer satisfaction and loyalty.
- Evaluate and implement actions to create and increase customer value.
- Recognize and reward efforts to enhance customer satisfaction and loyalty.

Nortel Networks established quarterly targets and goals for levels of customer satisfaction and loyalty and mandated the Corporate Customer Value Team to design, implement, and administer a customer satisfaction measurement survey.

Early Challenges

The Corporate Customer Value Team was quick to recognize the limitations of a survey process administered from a top-down perspective. Early surveys that covered 11 standard attributes for each of the different product families and had low response rates. "The original program," Conroy reflected,

> was targeted to capture the voice of the decision makers within the customer base. This had limitations, as decision makers did not always have experience with all areas of the value proposition. Even if we had asked them all possible questions they would not have been able to give us reliable answers. It is important in survey design to have an understanding of respondents' competence areas and only ask them questions in their areas of expertise. Asking a senior executive in a customer firm a question on our delivery services is not going to help. They are better placed to give us feedback on our long-term vision and its fit with their firms' future objectives.
> It became clear that we had to cast the net wider and go beyond just surveying decision-makers. We needed to hear from ... customers' "subject matter experts" and other specialists who evaluated vendors' technology solutions and services. This raised the question of involving the Nortel Networks account management teams respondent list management.

Sauve described major changes made to the program to address these considerations:

> The first change was in survey design. Based on the fact that it was the business units that were responsible for their markets, they were now given the responsibility for developing the questions for the survey within guidelines provided by the corporate team.
> Next was the issue of governance. As with other management initiatives, it was important to have program champions. Unless someone was made responsible for monitoring and managing this effort, it was likely that the program would lose its focus and energy. To prevent this and to build a cohesive effort throughout the organization, a Customer Value Council comprised of representatives of each of the business units was put in place to oversee the governance of the program. The team also wanted to ensure linkages across the businesses to maximize synergies between the various product lines in design, development, marketing, and service.

Added Conroy:

> The Corporate Customer Value Team decided to provide the support for the business units for funding, survey administration, data collection, and validation and reporting.
> It was also clear to the corporate team that a scientific approach demanded a rigorous methodology for deciding how many customers were to be surveyed. Without the right sample size, a quantitative analysis would be meaningless. To ensure statistical accuracy of metrics across the organization, the corporate team determined the sample sizes and then allocated the number to each business unit. Given that the customer account teams were responsible for managing their customers, they were responsible for providing the lists of names to survey.

> Each team was asked to identify, in addition to decision makers, "influencers" and "subject matter experts." The corporate team was responsible for auditing the list on a regular basis to minimize potential biases.
> Decentralization of the process was accompanied by concern for its consistency and integrity. Consequently, a Customer Value Improvement Process and Database (CIPAD) was created and administered by the corporate division. CIPAD, which accepted customer contact names, stored surveys and results, and made this information accessible to all users, was expected to become a central repository of customer information over time. Longitudinal data on customers was to be used to link the impact of changes in Nortel Networks' customer management efforts to customer responses.
> Finally, the roles and responsibilities of each stakeholder were specified.

CAPTURING THE VOICE OF THE CUSTOMER: THE CUSTOMER SATISFACTION AND LOYALTY SURVEY

With the green light from corporate to change the CVM process, Mumford, believing the process to be a perfect fit for the optical business, asked David Elkadri, head of the CSAT process for the transport group (which had housed optical products and later became the ON group), to

TABLE A Value to the Different Stakeholders

Optical Networks Customer Value	Corporate Customer Loyalty and Value
Goal: Drive customer loyalty; improve customer value proposition; improve customer relationships	**Goal:** Ensure integrity of program and results; manage incentive compensation program component
Roles: Partner with Account Primes to implement survey process Facilitate issue resolution Provide account team with tools to communicate improvements Prepare survey report Develop internal communication strategy	**Roles:** Manage corporate loyalty program Administer survey Manage third-party supplier Ensure compliance with survey and respondent list management Interface with Accounts and Customer Value Management (CVM) product teams Manage the Customer Value Improvement Process and Database (CIPAD)
Account Teams	*Process Owners*
Goal: Improve customer relationships through on-going communication and issue resolution	**Goal:** Drive customer loyalty through issue resolution and process improvement
Roles: Develop lists of respondents Encourage respondents' participation in surveys Follow-up/communicate with customers Interface with corporate and product primes Review survey results Participate in resolution of issues	**Roles:** Drive issue resolution Participate in communication with customers
Executive Customer Loyalty Council	
Goal: Drive customer loyalty to Nortel Networks **Role:** Governance of the program	

begin to integrate the customer satisfaction initiatives into ON's way of doing business. His organization having been in startup mode in 1995, Mumford had been able to build customer satisfaction into the optical business from day one. Regarding it to be a key business metric for strengthening customer relationships and growing market share, he wanted to strategically focus the program around the question: "How can we create value for our customers?"

Elkadri believed Nortel Networks existing survey to be "necessary, but not sufficient" to understand the drivers that shaped customers' perceptions of the company's products. These perceptions, he argued, shaped ON's Customer Satisfaction and Loyalty (CSAT) survey, not vice versa. "If a customer has strong perceptions and high expectations about our products and these expectations aren't met," he reasoned, "then obviously they are not satisfied. We needed to develop a framework for what data to gather."

Elkadri researched various approaches to Customer Value Management, ultimately settling on Bradley Gale's approach.[2] "Customer Value Management," he observed,

---

[2] Taken from *Managing Customer Value: Creating Quality and Service That Customers Can See* by Bradley T. Gale and Robert Chapman Wood (New York: The Free Press, 1994). The concept is that a firm will develop indices for the quality of its product/service offerings (as perceived by the customer) and the price paid by the customer, and from these develop a price versus quality grid that can help it evaluate its competitive positioning in the marketplace.

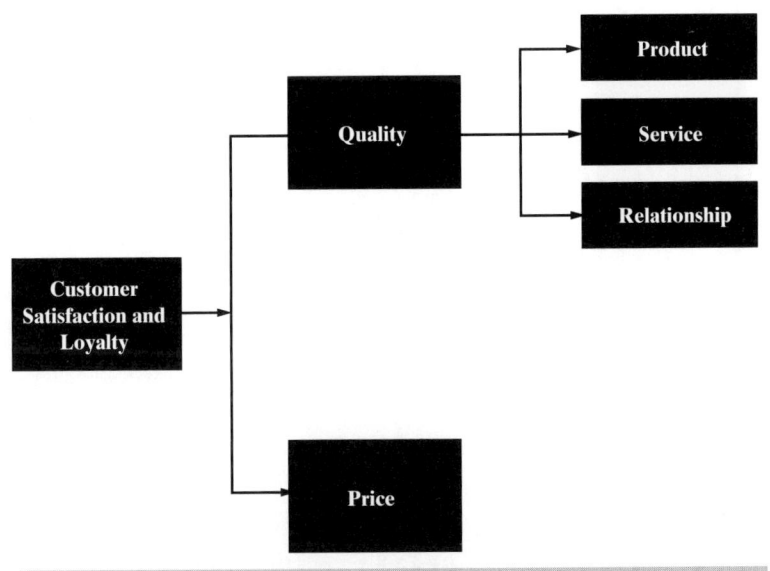

EXHIBIT 6 Nortel Networks SONET/ON Customer Value Attributes

Source: Company records.

is the science of measuring marketplace perceptions that determine brand purchase decisions relative to the competition and of using this data in an established process to gain competitive advantage.

We started with customer focus groups and interviews with account team representatives to identify the value attributes that influenced a customer's purchasing decisions. We used this to measure the overall "value for what the customer paid for." The findings of the research confirmed the importance of product, service, price, and relationship as crucial components of quality in the eyes of the customer [see Exhibit 6].

Recognizing that the voice of the customer needed to be transformed into concrete improvements, the team began to link product questions to business processes. Thus, if customers scored ON low on a specific attribute the individuals within ON best suited to drive resolution with the customer were identified. Feedback on ON products and services from more than 300 customers provided the baseline for improvement in 1997.

Survey Methodology

ON measured customer satisfaction and loyalty with its biannual CSAT survey, which was collected by an independent external research company. For longstanding accounts (largely the major telecommunications providers, long distance carriers, and local transport companies), telephone interviews were conducted with a cross section of ON "customers" that included engineers, executives, network planners, and operators. The survey also included five general questions that were consistent across Nortel Networks, the first of which solicited the customer's "overall level of satisfaction" with the company.

The CSAT survey was intended to elicit customer perceptions of ON's value proposition, which included the attributes of quality, price, product, service, and relationship management. Each of these was, in turn, broken down into sub-elements measured by individual survey questions (see Exhibits 7 and 8). Over a 15-minute period, beginning with the all-important question "Overall, how satisfied are you doing business with Nortel Networks?" respondents were asked 55 questions, each of which corresponded to a "branch" on the value tree. Respondents included decision makers, influencers, and contributors in areas of operations, maintenance, engineering, procurement, and network support. Excepting corporate-focused questions, survey

EXHIBIT 7 Optical and SONET CSAT Survey Questions

Optical & SONET CSAT Surveys
"Overall, how satisfied are you with doing business with Nortel Networks?"

Quality — Overall Quality

Product — Overall Product Quality
- Overall Product Reliability
- Software Freedom from Defects
- Failure Rate of Hardware
- Interoperability of SONET Products
- Interoperability of SONET With Other Suppliers
- Commonality of Network Element Management
- Technical Documentation
- NPI - New Product Meets Launch Date
- NPI - Informed When Launch Date Can't be Met
- NPI - Completeness of Features at Launch
- NPI - Features Meeting Expectations
- NPI - Product Ease of Use
- Ease of Installation

Service — Overall Service Quality
- Order Process Simplicity
- Lead Time From Ordering to Delivery
- Delivery Completeness and Timeliness
- NPI - Able to Provide in Quantities Needed
- Installation Meets Your Scheduling Req.
- Quality of Installation Work
- Outages - Solving Problem Quickly
- Outages - Personnel's Technical Competence
- Outages - Replacement Parts Availability
- NPI - Network Planning Support
- NPI - Engineering Support
- NPI - Port-Installation Support

Relationship — Overall Quality of Relationship
- Keeping Commitments
- Resolving Problems Brought to Their Attention and following-up on issues
- Understanding Your Current Business Needs
- Anticipating Your Future Business Needs
- Commitment to Your Network Evolution
- Providing Turn-Key Network Solutions

Price — Overall Price Competitiveness
- Start-up Costs
- Initial Price Integrity and Completeness
- On-going Maintenance
- Software/Hardware Upgrades

Value
- Overall Satisfaction
- Value for what paid for
- Likelihood to recommend as supplier of telecom products and services
- Likelihood to increase share of SONET transport capital budget
- Likelihood to keep as primary supplier
- Meeting customer expectations
- Image

Source: Company records.

402

EXHIBIT 8 Sample Survey Questions

A sample of the questions on the customer satisfaction survey is provided below.

SATISFACTION AND RECOMMENDATION QUESTIONS

Before we discuss the optical product line I would like to discuss your overall experience with *(Nortel Networks)* during the past 12 months.

- How satisfied are you in doing business with *(Nortel Networks)*? Would you say you are very satisfied, satisfied, neither satisfied nor dissatisfied, dissatisfied, or very dissatisfied?

  5   very satisfied
  4   satisfied
  3   neither satisfied nor dissatisfied
  2   dissatisfied
  1   very dissatisfied

  "Don't know" (DK) is not allowed as an answer to this question.

- (Ask only those who said Nortel Networks is their primary supplier.) What is the primary reason you are with *(Nortel Networks)*?
- (Ask only those who said that a competitor is their primary supplier.) What is the primary reason you are with *(Competitor)*?
- Based on your overall experience with *(Competitor)* during the past 12 months, how satisfied are you in doing business with *(Competitor)*? Would you say you are very satisfied, satisfied, neither satisfied nor dissatisfied, dissatisfied, or very dissatisfied?

  5   very satisfied
  4   satisfied
  3   neither satisfied nor dissatisfied
  2   dissatisfied
  1   very dissatisfied

- Using a scale of 1 to 10 where 1 means "HAS NOT MET MY EXPECTATIONS" and 10 means "HAS EXCEEDED MY EXPECTATIONS," how well has *(Nortel Networks)* met your expectations?
- On a scale of 1 to 10, with 1 being "WOULD DEFINITELY NOT RECOMMEND" and 10 being "WOULD DEFINITELY RECOMMEND," how likely would you be to recommend *(Nortel Networks)* as a supplier of telecommunications products and services?

PRODUCT RELIABILITY

Now let's focus on optical products and your experiences over the last 12 months.

- First, please think about optical product reliability. If you have no experience with a specific area, please respond NO OPINION. Using a scale from 1 to 10, where 1 means POOR and 10 means EXCELLENT . . .
- Please rate *(Nortel Networks Optical)* on overall product reliability.

(Continued)

UNDERSTANDING THE VALUE

- How would you rate (Nortel Networks SONET) on anticipating your future business needs?

LOYALTY/FUTURE/ADVOCATE

Thinking about the next 12 months and using a scale from 1 to 10, where 1 means NOT AT ALL LIKELY and 10 means EXTREMELY LIKELY:

- What is the likelihood your company will keep Nortel Networks/*(Competitor)* as your primary optical products supplier?

EXHIBIT 8 (cont.)

Source: Company records.

---

questions were asked in random order to prevent sampling bias.

"There are several important points to note in how we designed the data collection process," Conroy observed:

> Our primary goal was to ask only the most important questions for each account. Based on the recommendations of experts in survey methodologies, we limited the interview time to 15–20 minutes. This helped us to maximize efficiencies, prevent customer fatigue, increase the response rate, and yet get valuable information that we could use.
>
> There was also the issue of who should be responsible for the data collection process. We did go back and forth on the merits of doing it internally versus outsourcing this activity. There are a lot of benefits to doing it internally. However, to maintain objectivity and reduce potential bias we decided to use a third-party vendor to collect and tabulate the data.

Survey Metrics

Nortel Networks defined "customer loyalty" as the percentage of respondents who rated Nortel Networks "5" on the 1–5 scale in the "overall satisfaction" question. A response of "4" or "5" signified "customer satisfaction." The five-point scale was based on market research studies that suggested that customers generally report satisfaction at five levels: very satisfied; satisfied; neither satisfied nor dissatisfied; dissatisfied; and very dissatisfied.

Value attributes—i.e., product, service, relationship, price, and image (see Exhibit 7)—were rated on a 1–10 scale, "1" signifying poor and "10" excellent. Customer perceptions of Nortel Networks competitors were also solicited. The 10-point scale was used to improve statistical reliability (more points on the scale), assure customer friendliness (not so many levels as to be confusing), and ease design and administration.

The ON division perceived tremendous value in the survey, believing that "loyal" customers would be more likely to recommend Nortel Networks as a supplier of choice. In fact, 80% of "very satisfied" customers in the 1999 survey rated Nortel Networks "9" or "10" on the question of how likely they would be to recommend the company as a supplier of telecommunications products. Conroy's team looked to the survey for help in measuring customers' purchasing intentions with respect to the likelihood not only that they would recommend Nortel Networks as a supplier of telecom products and services, but also that they would retain the company as a primary supplier and grant it an increased share of their purchases.

Ratings were recorded in four categories:

- key strengths: (>90% of respondents scored Nortel Networks 7–10)
- significant improvements (<90% of respondents scored Nortel Networks 7–10, but the rating represented at least a 10 point increase)

CHAPTER 10 *Strategic Implementation: Investing for Maximum Impact*   **405**

- areas of concern (<75% of respondents scored Nortel Networks 7–10)
- areas to investigate (75%–89% of respondents scored Nortel Networks 7–10 and the rating exhibited a downward trend).

This approach enabled ON managers to better interpret the data and plan their courses of action.

OPERATIONALIZING CSAT
Integrating the Voice of the Customer into the Business Model

Having proved the merits of Gale's research and demonstrated that the CSAT methodology could be executed from within ON, Elkadri's next step was to operationalize CSAT directly into the business. "We had always been seen as an engineering firm," he reflected:

> Our product managers didn't want to believe that the fuzzy customer stuff could make a difference to our business. They didn't think that CSAT would drive better product design.
>
> In planning the next steps, the team thought back to one of Greg Mumford's key principles: "The voice of the customer is not simply one aspect of the business; it is the business." This meant that customer feedback needed to be integrated into the operations of the business.
>
> We knew that we would not get too many chances at proving the value of CVM. We therefore spent a considerable amount of time and effort on how to implement the process.

A committed partnership between the account teams, issue owners, and Executive and Customer Value teams being needed to drive the Customer Value Management process, an Optical Networks–directed *CSAT Community* was formally established to guide resolution of customer issues through internal relationships and communication.

The *Customer Satisfaction Issue Resolution Process* (CSIRP—see Exhibit 9) was developed to help the CSAT community discover how to improve the value proposition and translate the voice of the customer into concrete benefits. The process used CSAT results to identify top areas of customer concern, decide who should take ownership of specific issues, establish action plans for resolving them, and communicate progress to account teams and customers. Issues were ordered according to importance, aligned with business priorities, and assigned on the basis of workload, resource requirements, and project management abilities.

Optical Networks Business Performance Tracking System

In parallel to the CSIRP process, Optical Networks pursued loyalty by engaging customers with identified value sets that met their needs.

The *Optical Networks Business Performance Tracking System* (ONBPTS, termed "the dashboard") was developed to identify the key business metrics and measures driving performance on quality, price, and service needed to gauge progress. This online system, which provided easy access to details on the latest customer satisfaction and value results, was used to drive Optical Networks' Operational Reviews, meetings at which senior ON managers assessed the state of the business through detailed monthly reviews of key business metrics.

CSIRP supported ON's business decision-making process by supplying customer intelligence to both the Operational Reviews and the various teams (process owners) charged to resolve customer issues. The process was participative, involving all parties required to drive customer loyalty, and ongoing communication and relationship building between customers, account teams, process owners, and corporate were essential to its success.

"It is very important," Conroy emphasized,

> that one close the loop with customers who complete the survey. They are now expecting to hear from us. They want to be assured that their voice did matter and that they are important to us. We knew that if we did not get back we would find it very difficult to get future cooperation.
>
> It was therefore decided that, after analyzing the survey results, a "top five" list of issues would be identified and confirmed by the ON personnel involved with the customer. To validate our course of action, there would also be "issue clarification" sessions

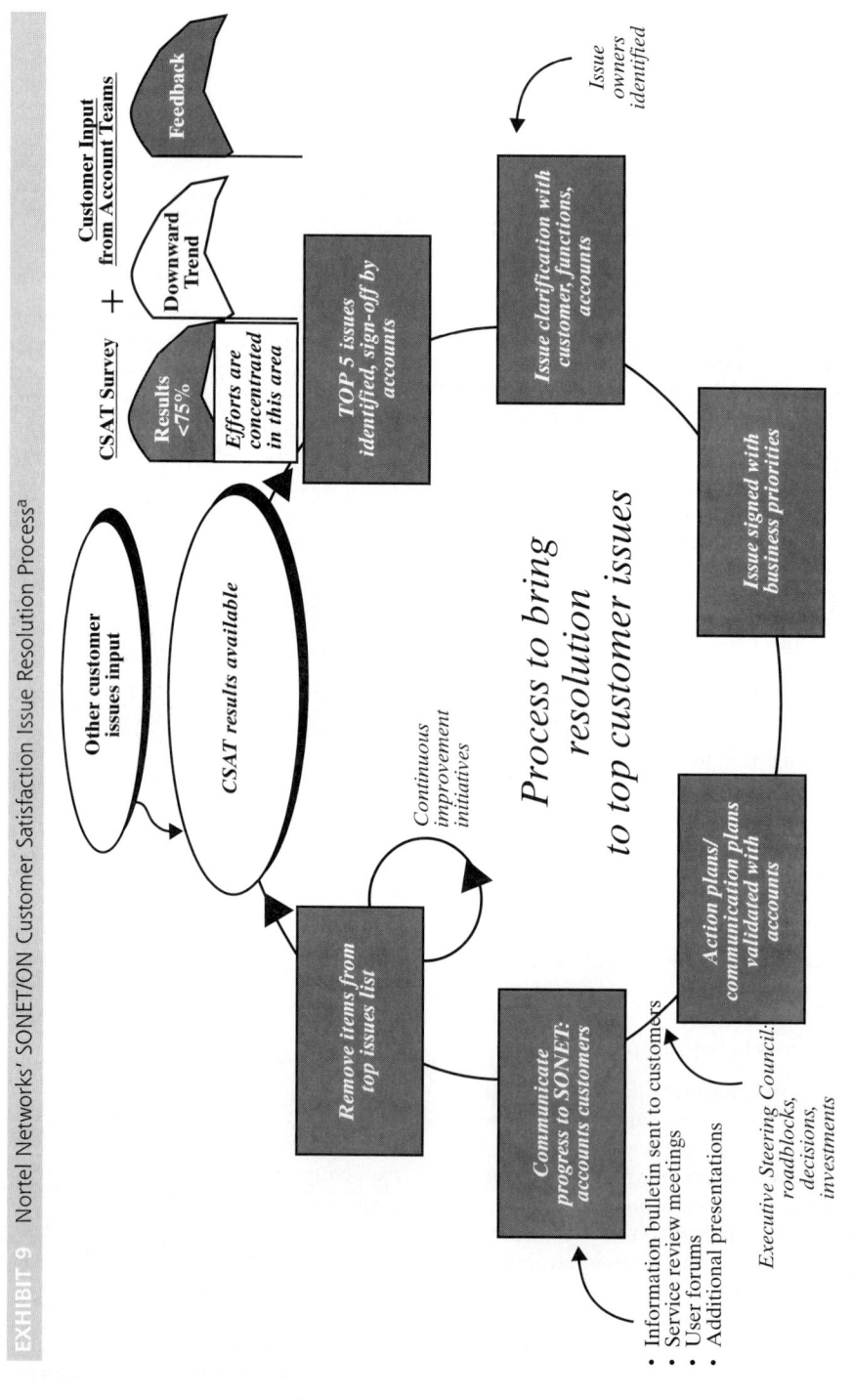

EXHIBIT 9 Nortel Networks' SONET/ON Customer Satisfaction Issue Resolution Process[a]

Process to bring resolution to top customer issues

Customer Input from Account Teams
- CSAT Survey: Results <75% — Efforts are concentrated in this area
- Downward Trend
- Feedback

- Other customer issues input
- CSAT results available
- TOP 5 issues identified, sign-off by accounts
- Issue clarification with customer, functions, accounts — *Issue owners identified*
- Issue signed with business priorities
- Action plans/communication plans validated with accounts
- Communicate progress to SONET accounts customers
  - Information bulletin sent to customers
  - Service review meetings
  - User forums
  - Additional presentations
- Remove items from top issues list
- *Continuous improvement initiatives*

Executive Steering Council: roadblocks, decisions, investments

Source: Company records.

[a]Resolution time frames vary per issue.

provided to the customer from both the account and product teams.

The account or product team would then work to proactively remove itself from being "one of the top five." Information briefs and face-to-face meetings with the customer "would continue to close the feedback loop," demonstrating a commitment to maintaining a relationship and providing a means by which customers could hold Nortel Networks accountable for responding to and acting upon results of the survey [see Exhibit 9].

The new CSIRP process had been validated and implemented and was endorsed by upper management. All was going smoothly, and then came an abrupt change of pace.

1998—NORTEL NETWORKS' RIGHT-ANGLE TURN

Nortel Networks had been in business for more than a century, during its first 75 years primarily as a manufacturer of telephone equipment for the Canadian market. But during the 1970s, 1980s, and 1990s the company grew into a global corporation that supplied advanced communications networks to a wide range of customers throughout the world.

Building on a rich tradition of continuous renewal in response to changing customer needs and market conditions, Nortel Networks undertook its most dramatic transformation during the late 1990s. John Roth, who became CEO in October 1997, characterized the sweeping changes he engineered as the company's "right-angle turn."

Recognizing the profound power of the Internet and that it would be an inevitable force for change among his customers, Roth decided that Nortel Networks could establish a leadership position by moving at "Web speed" to put itself at the heart of the Internet revolution. He inaugurated that journey on December 3, 1997 with an e-mail memo to company employees worldwide that articulated his vision of "Web tone." Nortel Networks had spent decades building the world's great voice networks. Dialtone had been brought to the point at which it was taken for granted; Web tone was Roth's vision of a future in which the Internet was taken for granted. That vision soon evolved into an urgent mission to build for the company's customers a profitable, high-performance Internet with the speed, reliability, security, and ubiquity to support global business.

Roth knew that to execute that mission he would have to completely review Nortel Networks' traditional telephony portfolio. This posed a huge challenge, yet in a very short period of time, about 15 months after launching into the right-angle turn, the company had realigned its research and development resources almost completely towards Internet-based initiatives. Roth also made strategic acquisitions and investments to expand and strengthen his firm's Internet portfolio. Before 1997 acquisitions had been virtually unheard of at Nortel Networks; in the year 2000 the company averaged about one every month or two.

The right-angle turn also involved innovative cultural, operational, and organizational changes. Roth made it a priority to speed up decision-making processes to make the company more agile and nimble. Still in the traditional telecommunications world of "long-long," Nortel Networks had to reorient itself toward the Internet world of "short-short." Old organizational structures were dismantled and redesigned to create more efficient processes. Top performers were rewarded for their contributions and employees unsuited to the new environment dismissed. Bureaucracy that stood in the way of serving customers was eliminated.

The success of Nortel Networks' right-angle turn was reflected not only in its top and bottom lines, but also, and more importantly, in the innovative solutions it was delivering to the marketplace and the strengthening of the customer relationships that represented the foundation of its future.

Implications for Customer Value Management

In light of the right-angle turn, Nortel Networks' Customer Value Council met to assess how the CSAT process needed to evolve to support the new business directions and imperatives. Under consideration were the following.

- How does Nortel Networks' customer satisfaction level compare to that of competitors?
- Given the high score in satisfaction, why are customers buying from competitors?

- Is Nortel Networks trying to do too many things with the same survey, (i.e., measure compensation, gauge customer value, and strengthen customer relationships)?
- Was it advisable to continue to survey on the basis of individual products when Nortel Networks now sold solutions?
- How could the number of surveys be reduced?
- Were the right individuals being surveyed? Were they being surveyed the right way?

Based on these questions, the council decided to pilot in 1999 a different methodology termed Relative Customer Value (RCV, see Exhibit 3). The objective of the study was to achieve a more in-depth understanding of the value propositions Nortel Networks brought to market. A blind survey was to be administered to customers and competitors' customers with all questions asked at the Nortel Networks level. The results were to be presented as value maps that showed Nortel Networks' perceived position in the marketplace relative to that of its competitors.

Implications for Customer Value Research

The upsurge in its optical business was accompanied by a change in Nortel Networks' customer base from traditional carriers to green field service provider startups. In response to this and to the challenges posed by the right-angle turn, Conroy and Sauve decided to implement a focused qualitative research study designed to answer questions similar to those that were driving the piloting of the RCV methodology. Observed Conroy:

> Given the changes in the corporation as well as in the marketplace, we thought the time was right to pilot a new approach with these customers. Our account teams were telling us that the new customers had different purchasing decision criteria than the traditional carriers. We decided to validate this assumption. Depending on the outcome of the research, it might mean changes to the survey questionnaire, the methodology, the program overall.

The qualitative research was intended to identify value drivers, if any, that were unique to this "new type" of customer and incorporate this information into the ongoing measurement process. Targeted individuals were contacted for one-hour interviews and asked a number of questions, among them, the following.

1. What are the unique demands placed upon you given the company and the market?
2. What do you see is most important for Nortel Networks to put in place or do to assure you and them of a successful partnership?
3. What are your communication expectations? How can the customer survey process provide value to you?
4. If you had to critique the process of doing business with Nortel Networks and compare it with the relationships that you have with other vendors, what would you say is working and what would you say is not?

By 2000 Conroy and Sauve had gathered critical customer data from a variety of sources and were ready for the next step: soliciting stakeholder feedback on the optical customer value program and RCV proposal.

FEEDBACK ON OPTICAL NETWORKS' TRADITIONAL PROGRAM
Customer Testimonials

"Our participation in its customer value process has contributed to and continues to enhance our relationship with Nortel Networks," remarked a key decision maker responsible for evaluating and approving the introduction of new products at her firm. "I like the idea of the survey because I believe this is looked at a higher level. We want the higher levels in Nortel Networks to know our issues and progress being made so they will continue to provide the support in resources and money needed to continue improvement. The survey serves as a trigger to reflect on many of those issues." *(Area manager, Facilities)*

ON Process Owners' Observations

"Over the last three to five years," reflected a key director of R&D, "the survey has pointed out to us that we need to interact more with our customers, particularly our bread-and-butter accounts, something that has made a big difference in how we improve our products."

"Software freedom from defects was a question on the survey that was continually a 'top five' issue for our product line," emphasized a software design manager.

"Various initiatives were implemented and presentations made to customers to share software quality improvements," explained the manager. "As a result, customer satisfaction improved 14 points in just one year. The focus on improving software quality continues today."

Other quantifiable benefits of the customer value and loyalty program observed between 1997 and 1999 included the following.

- Customer satisfaction results indicated a four-point increase in product quality and three-point increase in customer perception of "worth what paid for it" within the ON customer portfolio.
- Global market share for ON products grew from 36% to 41% and Nortel Networks was recognized as the global leader in optical networking.
- Customer participation in the survey process increased from 35% to 40%.
- From an employee and organizational perspective, the customer value and loyalty program supported and reinforced Nortel Networks' external focus on customers and competitors. Learning about customers and key success drivers helped employees at all levels to focus on areas that would deliver the most value to those customers.
- Nortel Networks was awarded TL 9000 certification, a new standard that defined a single, common set of quality system requirements and metrics for the telecommunications industry. The certification process recognized Nortel Networks' focus on customer satisfaction and value to be process driven, integrated into all levels of the organization, and supported by metrics formulated to drive ongoing improvement.

Findings of the Qualitative Research Study

The study's findings proved valuable to ON's executives and account team, revealing that customers both continued to attach great importance to the key value proposition components measured in the original surveys and appreciated the new market requirements reflected in the company's right-angle turn, namely, organizational agility, sense of urgency, and total commitment. Customer feedback also reiterated an increased need for follow-up, process improvements, and ongoing relationship building. "This research captured a richness of issues in the customer relationship that you can't get with a quantitative survey," emphasized Conroy:

But it's not easy to organize these exercises. To begin with, they are very expensive and time-consuming. In fact, we could organize a survey that covers a large number of our customers for the same price as one in-depth qualitative study. And they take up a lot of customer time at all levels. No customer is going to give you unlimited time to answer your questions. If we are not careful how we use the time they give us, we can very quickly find the doors shut and feedback very hard to come by.

Reflections on the RCV Pilot Program

"We understand our customers' perceptions of our product and services. Now we need to gain a greater awareness of how we compare with our competitors. Do we know why customers choose one supplier over another? What is the perception of our potential customers?"

"With the RCV, how do we continue to gather feedback on Optical Networks products and services?"

"How do we drive actions without knowing which product line a customer is thinking about?"

"If surveys are being conducted blind, what is the best way to follow up with customers to better understand their issues, put actions in place, and enhance our partnership?"

"If RCV becomes the standard for measurement of results, how can people reposition their job functions to support it?"

WHAT TO DO WITH THE INFORMATION AT HAND?

Conroy and Sauve reviewed the timeline that captured the evolution of the CVM methodology (Exhibit 10). They reflected on the information

1. 1992—Jean Monty, CEO of Nortel, begins to refocus Nortel on customer satisfaction and value by establishing a *Customer-First* culture.
2. First customer satisfaction surveys administered, with a top-down perspective
3. Customer Value Improvement Process and Database (CIPAD) established by corporate division.
4. Roles and responsibilities of different stakeholders specified.
5. The ON begins to integrate customer satisfaction initiatives into its business processes in 1995.
6. ON continues its bi-annual CSAT survey.
7. ON directed CSAT community is formally established.
8. The Customer Satisfaction Issue Resolution Process (CSIRP) is developed.
9. Nortel makes a right angle turn to go after the rapidly evolving Internet-related business market. This move involves a shift in focus from traditional telco customers to new age business customers.
10. The corporate division proposes the Relative Customer Value (RCV) approach.
11. ON begins the use of qualitative research.

EXHIBIT 10 Major Milestones in the Development of Nortel's CVM Methodology

in front of them: three different methodologies; three types of data; pros and cons associated with each. What should they recommend to Greg Mumford? Which approach would best support Optical Networks as it continued to respond to the challenge of the right angle turn? Which approach would best serve the division's customers? ■

◆◆◆ **Hilton HHonors Worldwide: Loyalty Wars**

Case 10-3   Hilton HHonors Worldwide: Loyalty Wars

John Deighton

Jeff Diskin, head of Hilton HHonors® (Hilton's guest reward program), opened the *Wall Street Journal* on February 2, 1999, and read the headline, "Hotels Raise the Ante in Business-Travel Game." The story read, "Starwood Hotels and Resorts Worldwide Inc. is expected to unveil tomorrow an aggressive frequent-guest program that it hopes will help lure more business travelers to its Sheraton, Westin, and other hotels. Accompanied by a $50 million ad campaign, the program ratchets up the stakes in the loyalty-program game that big corporate hotel companies, including Starwood and its rivals at Marriott, Hilton, and Hyatt are playing."[1]

The case was prepared by Professor John Deighton and Professor Stowe Shoemaker. Copyright © 2000 by the President and Fellows of Harvard College. Harvard Business School Case 501-010.

[1] *Wall Street Journal*, February 2, 1999, page B1.

Diskin did not hide his concern. "These guys are raising their costs, and they're probably raising mine too. They are reducing the cost-effectiveness of the industry's most important marketing tool by deficit spending against their program. Loyalty programs have been at the core of how we attract and retain our best customers for over a decade. But they are only as cost-effective as our competitors let them be."

LOYALTY MARKETING PROGRAMS

The idea of rewarding loyalty had its origins in coupons and trading stamps. First in the 1900s and again in the 1950s, America experienced episodes of trading stamp frenzy that became so intense that Congressional investigations were mounted. Retailers would give customers small adhesive stamps in proportion to the amount of their purchases, to be pasted into books and eventually redeemed for merchandise. The best-known operator had been the S&H Green Stamp Company. Both episodes had lasted about 20 years, declining as the consumer passion for collecting abated and vendors came to the conclusion that any advantage they might once have held had been competed away by emulators.

Loyalty marketing in its modern form was born in 1981 when American Airlines introduced the AAdvantage frequent flyer program, giving "miles" in proportion to the miles traveled, redeemable for free travel. It did so in response to the competitive pressure that followed airline deregulation. The American Airlines program had no need of stamps, because it took advantage of the data-warehousing capabilities of computers. Soon program administrators realized that they had a tool that did not merely reward loyalty, but identified by name and address the people who accounted for most of aviation's revenues, and made a one-to-one relationship possible.

Competing airlines launched their own programs, but, unlike stamps programs, frequent flyer programs seemed to survive emulation. By 1990, almost all airlines offered them. In the late 1990s, Delta Air Lines and United Airlines linked their programs together, as did American and US Airways in the United States. Internationally, United Airlines and Lufthansa combined with 11 other airlines to form Star Alliance, and American, British, and four others formed an alliance called Oneworld. In these alliances, qualifying flights on any of the member airlines could be credited to the frequent flyer club of the flyer's choice.

As the decade ended, computer-based frequency programs were common in many service industries, including car rental, department stores, video and book retailing, credit cards, movie theaters, and the hotel industry.

THE HOTEL INDUSTRY

Chain brands were a major factor in the global hotel market of 13.6 million rooms.[2] The chains supplied reservation services, field sales operations, loyalty program administration and the management of hotel properties, under well-recognized names like Hilton and Marriott. See Exhibit 1 for details of the seven largest U.S. hotel chains competing in the business class hotel segment.

While the brands stood for quality, there was less standardization of operations in hotel chains than in many other services. The reason was that behind a consumer's experience of a hotel brand might lie any of many methods of control. A branded hotel might be owned and managed by the chain, but it might be owned by a third party and managed by the chain, or owned by the chain and managed by a franchisee, or, in some cases, owned and managed by the franchisee. Occasionally chains managed each other's brands, because one chain could be another's franchisee. Starwood, for example, ran hotels under the Hilton brand as Hilton's franchisee. Information about competitors' operating procedures therefore circulated quite freely in the industry.

Consumers

For most Americans, a stay in a hotel was a relatively rare event. Of the 74% of Americans who traveled overnight in a year, only 41% used a hotel, motel, or resort. The market in which Hilton competed was smaller still, defined by price point and trip purpose, and divided among business, convention, and leisure segments.

The business segment accounted for one-third of all room-nights in the market that Hilton served.

---

[2]World Trade Organization.

About two-thirds of these stays were at rates negotiated between the guest's employer and the chain, but since most corporations negotiated rates with two and sometimes three hotel chains, business travelers had some discretion to choose where they would stay. About one-third of business travelers did not have access to negotiated corporate rates and had full discretion to choose their hotel.

The convention segment, comprising convention, conference, and other meeting-related travel, accounted for another third of room-nights in Hilton's competitive set. The choice of hotel in this instance was in the hands of a small number of professional conference organizers, typically employees of professional associations and major corporations.

The leisure segment accounted for the final third. Leisure guests were price sensitive, often making their selections from among packages of airline, car, tours, and hotels assembled by a small group of wholesalers and tour organizers at rates discounted below business rates.

Although the chains as a whole experienced demand from all segments, individual properties tended to draw disproportionately from one segment or another. Resort hotels served leisure travelers and some conventioneers, convention

EXHIBIT 1 The U.S. Lodging Industry

	Countries	Properties	Rooms	Owned Properties	Franchised Properties	Management Contracts
Marriott International[a]	53	1,764	339,200	49	936	776
Bass Hotels and Resorts[b]	90	2,700	447,967	76	2,439	185
Hilton Hotels Corp.[c]	11	272	91,060	39	207	16
Starwood Hotels and Resorts Worldwide, Inc.[d]	72	695	212,950	171	291	233
Hyatt[e]	45	246	93,729	NA	NA	NA
Carlson[f]	50	581	112,089	1	542	38
Hilton International[g]	50	224	62,941	154	0	70
Promus[h]	11	1,398	198,526	160	1,059	179

[a] Includes Marriott Hotels, Resorts and Suites; Courtyard, Residence Inn, TownePlace Suites, Fairfield Inn, SpringHill Suites, Marriott Vacation Club International; Conference Centers, Marriott Executive Residences, Ritz-Carlton, Renaissance, Ramada International.
[b] Includes Inter-Continental, Forum, Crowne Plaza, Holiday Inn, Holiday Inn Express, Staybridge.
[c] Includes Hilton Hotels, Hilton Garden Inns, Hilton Suites, Hilton Grand Vacation Clubs, and Conrad International.
[d] Includes St. Regis, Westin Hotels and Resorts, Sheraton Hotels and Resorts, Four Points, Sheraton Inns, The W Hotels. Does not include other Starwood-owned hotels, flagged under other brands (93 properties for 29,322 rooms).
[e] Includes Hyatt Hotels, Hyatt International, and Southern Pacific Hotel Corporation (SPHC). Because it is a privately held corporation, it will not divulge the breakdown of rooms between ownership, franchise, and management contract.
[f] Includes Radisson Hotels Worldwide, Regent International Hotels, Country Inns and Suites.
[g] A wholly owned subsidiary of what was once known as the Ladbroke Group. In Spring 1999, Ladbroke changed their name to Hilton Group PLC to reflect the emphasis on hotels.
[h] Includes such brands as Doubletree, Red Lion, Hampton Inn, Hampton Inn & Suites, Embassy Suites, and Homewood Suites.
Source: World Trade Organization and company information.

hotels depended on group and business travel, and hotels near airports were patronized by guests on business, for example. These segmentation schemes, however, obscured the fact that the individuals in segments differentiated by trip purpose and price point were often the same people. Frequent travelers patronized hotels of various kinds and price segments, depending for example, on whether a stay was a reimbursable business expense, a vacation, or a personal expense.

Competition

Four large global brands dominated the business class hotel market (Table A). Each competed at more than one price point. Exhibit 2 shows the price points in the industry, and Exhibit 3 shows the distribution of brands across price points.

> ***Starwood:*** Beginning in 1991, Barry Sternlicht built Starwood Hotels and Resorts Worldwide from a base in a real estate investment trust. In January 1998, Starwood bought Westin Hotels and Resorts and a month later it bought ITT Corporation, which included Sheraton Hotels and Resorts, after a well-publicized battle with Hilton Hotels Corporation. By the year-end, Starwood had under unified management the Westin, Sheraton, St. Regis, Four Points, and Caesar's Palace brands. Starwood had recently announced plans to create a new brand, W, aimed at younger professionals.
>
> ***Marriott:*** Marriott International operated and franchised hotels under the Marriott, Ritz-Carlton, Renaissance, Residence Inn, Courtyard, Towneplace Suites, Fairfield Inn, Springhill Suites, and Ramada International brands. It also operated conference centers, and provided furnished corporate housing. A real estate investment trust, Host Marriott, owned some of the properties operated by Marriott International, as well as some Hyatt, Four Season and Swissotel properties.
>
> ***Hyatt:*** The Pritzker family of Chicago owned Hyatt Corporation, the only privately owned major hotel chain. Hyatt comprised Hyatt Hotels, operating hotels and resorts in the United States, Canada, and the Caribbean; and Hyatt International, operating overseas. Hyatt also owned Southern Pacific Hotel Group, a three- and four-star hotel chain based primarily in Australia. Although the companies operated independently, they ran joint marketing programs.

The 1990s had been a time of consolidation and rationalization in the lodging industry, partly due to application of information technologies to reservation systems and control of operations. Jeff Diskin reflected on the trend: "Historically, bigger has been better because it has led to economies of scale, and bigger and better brands to leverage. Historically, big players could win even if they did not do a particularly good job on service, performance or programs. Now (after the Starwood deal) there's another big player. It would have been nice if it had been Hilton that was the largest hotel chain in the world, but biggest is not the only way to be best."

MARKETING THE HILTON BRAND

The Hilton brand was controlled by two entirely unrelated corporations, Hilton Hotels Corporation (HHC) based in Beverley Hills, California, and Hilton International (HIC) headquartered near London, England. In 1997, however, HHC and HIC reached an agreement to reunify the Hilton brand worldwide. They agreed to cooperate on sales and marketing, standardize operations, and run the Hilton HHonors loyalty program across all HHC and HIC hotels. At the end of 1998, HHC divested itself of casino interests, and announced, "a new era as a dedicated hotel company."

The exit from gaming, the reunification of Hilton's worldwide marketing, and the extension of the brand into the middle market under the

TABLE A	
Marriott International	339,200 rooms
Starwood Hotels and Resorts	212,900 rooms
Hyatt Hotels	93,700 rooms
Hilton Hotels	91,100 rooms
Hilton International	62,900 rooms

- Luxury: average rack rate over $125, full-service hotels with deluxe amenities for leisure travelers and special amenities for business and meeting markets. Chains in this segment include Four Seasons, Hilton, Hyatt, Inter-Continental (a Bass Hotels and Resort Brand), Marriott Hotels and Resorts, Renaissance (a Marriott International brand), Ritz-Carlton (also a Marriott International brand), Sheraton (a Starwood Hotels and Resorts Brand), and Westin (also a Starwood Hotels and Resorts Brand).

- Upscale: average rack rate between $100–$125, full-service hotels with standard amenities. Includes most all-suite, non-extended-stay brands. Crowne Plaza (a Bass Hotels and Resort Brand), Doubletree Guest Suites (a Promus Hotel Corp. brand), Embassy Suites (also a Promus Hotel Corp. brand), Radisson (a Carlson Worldwide Hospitality brand), Hilton Inn, and Clarion (a Choice Hotels Brand) are all examples of chains in this segment.

- Mid-market with food and beverage (F&B): Average rack rate between $60–$90, full-service hotels with lower service levels and amenities than the Upscale segment. Examples include Best Western, Courtyard (a Marriott International brand), Garden Inn (a Hilton brand), Holiday Inn (a Bass Hotels and Resorts brand), and Howard Johnson (a Cendant brand).

- Mid-market without F&B: Average rack rate between $45–$70, with limited service and comparable amenities to the Mid-market with F&B segment. Examples of chains in this segment include Hampton Inns (a Promus brand), Holiday Inn Express (a Bass Hotels and Resorts brand), and Comfort Inn (a Choice Hotels brand).

- Economy: Average rack rate between $40–$65, with limited service and few amenities. Fairfield Inn (a Marriott International brand), Red Roof Inn, Travelodge, and Days Inn of America (a Cendant brand) are examples of economy chains.

- Budget: Average rack rate between $30–$60, with limited service and basic amenities. Motel 6, Super 8, and Econo Lodge are the best-known chains in this segment.

- Extended Stay: Average rack rate between $60–$90, targeted to extended stay market and designed for extended length of stay. Marriott International has the following two brands in this market: Residence Inn by Marriott and Towneplace Suites. Other chains include Homewood Suites (a Bass Hotels and Resort), Summerfield Suites, and Extented Stay America.

EXHIBIT 2 Price Segments in the Lodging Industry

Source: U.S. lodging chains segmented by RealTime Hotel Reports Inc., authors of the 1998 Lodging Survey.

Hilton Garden Inn name, were initiatives that followed the appointment in 1997 of Stephen F. Bollenbach as President and Chief Executive Officer of Hilton. Bollenbach had served as Chief Financial Officer of Marriott and most recently as Chief Financial Officer of Disney, and he brought to Hilton a passion for branding. To some members of the Hilton management team, the focus on brand development was a welcome one. "Hilton's advantage has been a well-recognized name, but a potentially limiting factor has been a widely varying product, and the challenge of managing customer expectation with such a variety of product offerings. Since Hilton includes everything from world-renowned properties like The Waldorf = Astoria and Hilton Hawaiian Village to the smaller middle-market Hilton Garden Inns, it's important to give consumers a clear sense of what to expect from the various types of hotels," observed one manager.

	Luxury	Upscale	Mid-Market with Food and Beverage	Mid-Market without Food and Beverage	Economy	Budget	Extended Stay
Hilton	X	X	X	X			
Hyatt	X						
Marriott	X	X	X		X		X
Starwood	X	X	X				X

EXHIBIT 3 Segments Served by the Major Chains

Source: Company records.

In mid-1999, the properties branded as Hilton hotels comprised:

- 39 Owned or partly owned by HHC in the United States
- 207 Franchised by HHC to third-party managers in the United States
- 16 Managed by HHC in the United States on behalf of third-party owners
- 10 Managed internationally under HHC's Conrad International brand
- 220 Managed by HIC in over 50 countries excluding the USA

The executives at Hilton HHonors worked for these 492 hotels and their 154,000 rooms. The previous year had been successful. Revenues had been in the region of $158 per night per guest, and occupancy had exceeded break-even. Hotels like Hilton's tended to cover fixed costs at about 68% occupancy and 80% of all revenue at higher occupancy levels flowed to the bottom line. Advertising, selling and other marketing costs (a component of fixed costs) for this group of hotels were not published, but industry norms ran at about $750 per room per year.[3]

Hilton HHonors® Program

Hilton HHonors was the name Hilton gave to its program designed to build loyalty to the Hilton brand worldwide. Hilton HHonors Worldwide (HHW) operated the program, not as a profit center but as a service to its two parents, HHC and HIC. It was required to break even each year and to measure its effectiveness through a complex set of program metrics. Jeff Diskin ran the limited liability corporation with a staff of 30, with one VP overseeing the program's marketing efforts, and one VP with operational and customer service oversight. Exhibit 4 shows the Income Statement for HHW.

Membership in the Hilton HHonors program was open to anyone who applied, at no charge. Members earned points toward their Hilton HHonors account whenever they stayed at HHC or HIC hotels. When Hilton HHonors members accumulated enough points in the program, they could redeem them for stays at HHonors hotels, or use them to buy products and services from partner companies, or convert them to miles in airline frequent flyer programs. Exhibit 5 shows how points in the program flowed among participants in the program, as detailed in the text that follows.

There were four tiers of membership— Blue, Silver, Gold, and Diamond. The program worked as follows at the Blue level in 1998.

- When a member stayed at a Hilton hotel and paid a so-called business rate,[4] the hotel typically paid HHW 4.5 cents per dollar of the guest's folio ("folio" is the

---

[3]For the purpose of consistency in calculation among class members, assume an occupancy of 70%. The information in this paragraph has been masked. No data of this kind are publicly available and these data are not to be interpreted as indicative of information private to either HHC or HIC.

[4]Hilton distinguished three kinds of rate. "Business rates" were higher than "leisure rates," which in turn were higher than "ineligible rates," which referred to group tour wholesale rates, airline crew rates, and other deeply discounted rates.

(While these data are broadly reflective of the economic situation, certain competitively sensitive information has been masked.)

	$ (thousands)	
Revenue		
Contributions from hotels		
Domestic	$39,755	
International	$10,100	
Strategic partner contributions	$18,841	
Membership fees[a]	$1,141	
Total		$69,837
Expense		
Redemptions		
Cash payments to hotels	$12,654	
Deferred liability[b]	$9,436	
Airline miles purchases	$17,851	
Member acquisition expenses	$7,273	
Member communication expenses	4,236	
Program administration expenses	$17,988	
Total		$69,438
Net Income		$399

EXHIBIT 4 Hilton HHonors Worldwide: 1998 Income Statement

Source: Company records (masked).
Note from casewriter: For purposes of consistency in calculation among class members, assume an average nightly revenue of $158 per room. Assume that airline miles are purchased from the airline by Hilton at 1 cent per mile.
[a] From members of the Hilton Senior HHonors program only. The Senior HHonors program invited people over 60 to receive discounted stays in exchange for a membership fee. Regular HHonors members do not pay a membership fee.
[b] More points were issued than redeemed. From the outstanding balance a deferred liability was charged to HHW's income statement, based on estimating the proportion of points that would ultimately be redeemed.

total charge by the guest before taxes). HHW credited the guest's Hilton HHonors account with 10 points per eligible dollar of folio.
- Hilton guests could earn mileage in partner airline frequent flyer programs for the same stay that earned them HHonors points, a practice known as Double Dipping®. (Hilton was the only hotel chain to offer Double Dipping: other chains with frequency programs required guests to choose between points in the hotel program or miles in the airline program.) If the member chose to Double Dip, HHW bought miles from the relevant airline and credited the guest's airline frequent flyer account at 500 miles per stay.
- If the guest used points to pay for a stay, HHW reimbursed the hosting hotel at more than the costs incremental to the cost of leaving the room empty, but less than the revenue from a paying guest. The points needed to earn a stay depended on the class of hotel, and fell when occupancy was low. As illustration, redemption rates ranged from 5,000 points to get 50% off the $128 cost of a weekend at the Hilton Albuquerque, to 25,000 points for a free weekend night at the $239 per night Hilton Boston Back Bay. A number of exotic rewards were offered, such as a two-person, seven-night diving adventure in the Red Sea for 350,000 points, including hotel and airfare.

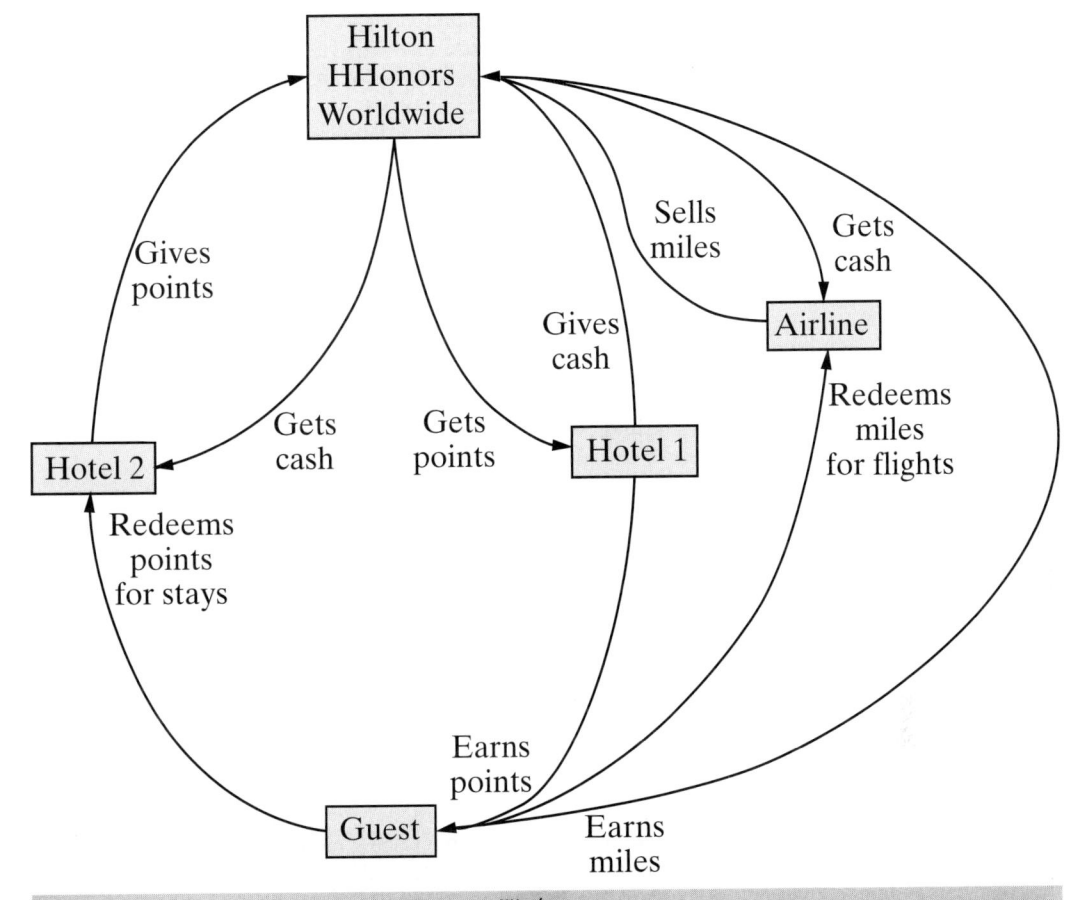

CHAPTER 10 *Strategic Implementation: Investing for Maximum Impact* **417**

EXHIBIT 5 How the Hilton HHonors Program Works

- Members earned points by renting a car, flying with a partner airline, using the Hilton Credit Card from American Express, or buying products promoted in mailings by partners such as FTD Florists and Mrs. Field's Cookies. Members could buy points at $10 per thousand for up to 20% of the points needed for a reward.
- Members had other benefits besides free stays. They had a priority reservation telephone number. Check-in went faster because information on preferences was on file. Members were favored over non-members when they asked for late check-out. If members were dissatisfied, they were guaranteed a room upgrade certificate in exchange for a letter explaining their dissatisfaction. Points could be exchanged for airline miles, and vice-versa, and to buy partner products such as airline tickets, flowers, Mrs. Field's Cookies, Cannondale bicycles, AAA membership, Princess Cruises, and car rentals.

Members were awarded Silver VIP status if they stayed at HHonors hotels four times in a year. They earned a 15% bonus on Base points, received a 5,000-point bonus after seven stays in a quarter, and a 10,000-point discount when they claimed a reward costing 100,000 points. They were given a certificate for an upgrade to the best room in the hotel after every fifth stay.

Members were awarded Gold VIP status if they stayed at HHonors hotels 16 times or for 36 nights in a year. They earned a 25% bonus on Base points, received a 5,000-point bonus after seven stays in a quarter, and a 20,000-point discount when they claimed a reward costing 100,000 points. They were given a certificate for an upgrade to the best room in the hotel after every fifth stay, and were upgraded to best available room at time of check-in.

The top 1% of members were given Diamond VIP status. This level was not mentioned in promotional material, and no benefits were promised. Diskin explained, "Our goal at the time was to under-promise and over-deliver. If you stay a lot, we say thank you, and as a reward we want to give you Diamond VIP status. We get a lot more bang, more affinity, more vesting from the customer if we do something unexpected. As an industry, we should never overpromise. It leads the public to decide that this is all smoke and mirrors, and it makes it harder for us to deliver genuine value." Table B shows HHW's member activity in 1998.

A further 712,000 stays averaging 2.4 nights were recorded in 1998 for which no Hilton HHonors membership card was presented but instead airline miles were claimed and airline membership numbers were captured, so that the guest could be given a unique identifier in the Hilton database. Spending on these stays totaled $327 million.

Guests identified by their HHonors or airline membership numbers occupied 22.5% of all the rooms occupied in the Hilton Hotels and Hilton International network in a year. They were a much smaller proportion of all the guests who stayed with Hilton in a year, because they tended to be frequent travelers. Hilton's research found that Hilton HHonors members spent about $4.6 billion on accommodation per year, not all of which was with Hilton. The industry estimated that members of the frequent stayer programs of all the major hotel chains represented a market worth $11.1 billion, and that the average member belonged to 3.5 programs.

Rationales for the Program

1. Revenue and yield management   Hotel profitability was acutely sensitive to revenue. A trend in the industry was to appoint a "revenue manager" to each property to oversee the day-to-day decisions that affected hotel revenue. Yield management models were probabilistic algorithms that helped this manager set reservations policy. They used past history and other statistical data to make continuously updated recommendations regarding hotel booking patterns and what price to offer a particular guest. Simulation studies had shown that when booking was guided by a good yield management model, a company's revenue increased by 20% over a simple "first come, first served, fixed price" policy.

In the hotel industry, effectively managing yield meant utilizing a model to predict that a room was highly likely to come available due to cancellation or no-show, as well as driving business to higher-paying or longer-staying guests. Variable pricing meant that the rate charged for a room depended not only on its size and fittings, but also on the day of booking, the day of occupation, length of stay, and customer characteristics. Of these factors, customer characteristics were the most problematic.

Customer characteristics were needed by the model to estimate "walking cost," the cost of

TABLE B   Members' Paid Activity in 1998

	Members (000)	Members Active in 1998 (000)	Stays for Which Members Paid (000)	Nights for Which They Paid (000)	Spending on Which They Earned Points ($000)	Stays per Active Member in 1998	Nights per Active Member in 1998	Reward Nights Claimed by Members
Diamond	24	20	310	521	$62,000	15.5	26.1	27,000
Gold	220	84	1,110	1,916	$266,000	13.2	22.8	34,200
Silver	694	324	1,023	1,999	$341,000	3.2	6.2	70,200
Blue	1,712	992	1,121	2,579	$439,000	1.1	2.6	48,600
Total	2,650	1,420	3,564	7,015	$1,108,000	2.5	4.9	180,000

Source: Company records (certain competitively sensitive information has been masked).

turning a customer away. That cost in turn depended on the customer's future lifetime value to the chain, a function of their willingness to pay and past loyalty to the chain. These were considered "soft" variables, notoriously difficult to estimate. The better the historical information on a customer, however, the better the estimate. As Adam Burke, HHonors' Senior Director of Marketing for North America, put it, "Who gets the room—the person paying $20 more that you may never see again, or the guy spending thousands of dollars in the system? If we have the right data, the model can be smart enough to know the difference." Some in the hotel industry argued that a benefit of a frequent guest program was to let the reservations system make those distinctions.

2. Collaborating with partners   HHW partnered with 25 airlines, 3 car rental firms, and a number of other firms. Burke explained, "Why is Mrs. Field's Cookies in the program? We have several objectives—regional relevance to consumers, access to partners' customers, making it easier for members to attain rewards. A franchisee may say, 'Why are we doing something with FTD Florists?' We point out that their investment keeps costs down and gives a broader range of rewards to our members."

Adam explained why Hilton offered Double Dipping. "We have 2.5 million members. The airline frequent flyer programs have 20, 30, 40 million members who aren't HHonors members and do travel a lot. Airlines don't mind us talking to their members because—through Double Dipping—we don't compete with their programs. In fact, we complement them by allowing our joint customers to earn both currencies."

3. Working with franchisees   The Hilton HHonors program was a strong factor in persuading hotel owners to become Hilton franchisees or give Hilton a management contract to run their property. Franchisees tended to be smaller hotels, more dependent on "road warrior" business than many of Hilton's convention hotels, resort hotels, and flagship properties. They saw value in a frequent guest program to attract business, and HHW's program cost was comparable to or lower than its competitors. The program's ability to drive business, however, remained its biggest selling point. Diskin elaborated, "Seven or eight years ago some operators were concerned about the cost of the program. We took a bunch of the most vocal, critical guys and we put them in a room for two days with us to discuss the importance of building long-term customer loyalty, and they came out saying 'We need to spend more money on the program!'"

4. Relations with guests   The program let the most valuable guests be recognized on-property. Diskin explained, "In a sense, the loyalty program is a safe haven for the guest. If there is a problem and it is not taken care of at the property level, the guest can contact our customer service team. It's a mechanism to make sure we hear about those problems. We also do outbound after-visit calling, and we call HHonors members because they're the best database, and the most critical guests we have. They have the most experience; and the highest expectations. We do feedback groups with members in addition to focus groups and quantitative research. We invite a bunch of members in the hotel down for dinner, and we say we want to talk about a subject. I get calls from people that are lifelong loyalists, not because of any changes we've made, but because once we invited them and asked them their opinion. People care about organizations that care about them."

Hilton customized a guest's hotel experience. Diskin explained, "We build guest profiles that keep track of preferences, enabling the hotel to provide customized services. For instance, consider the guest that always wants a room that is for non-smokers and has a double bed. This information can be stored as part of the member's record so that when she or he makes a reservation, the guest will receive this type of room without having to ask, no matter where the guest is staying."

HHW used direct mail to cultivate the relationship between members and the Hilton brand. Diskin explained, "Certainly you want to focus much of your effort on your highest revenue guests, but there are also opportunities to reach out and try to target other customer segments. For example, we worked with a non-travel partner to overlay data from their customer files onto our total membership base, and identified segments that might like vacation ownership, others who would be great for the casinos, and some that might like the business and teleconferencing services we offer."

Jeff Diskin was concerned that some travelers spread their hotel patronage among several chains and did not receive the service to which their total expenditure entitled them. He noted, "Our research suggests that a quarter of the frequent travelers are members of loyalty programs but don't have true loyalty to any one brand. They never get to enjoy the benefits of elite program status because they don't consolidate their business with one chain. They typically don't see the value in any of the loyalty schemes because they haven't changed their stay behavior to see the benefits."

5. Helping travel managers gain compliance A significant proportion of Hilton's business came from contracts with large corporate clients. Hilton offered discounted rates if the corporation delivered enough stays.

"If you are a corporate travel manager," Adam Burke explained, "you want employees to comply with the corporate travel policy. You negotiated a rate by promising a volume of stays. While some travel managers can tell employees that they have to follow the company policy if they want to get reimbursed, many others can only recommend. What if someone is a very loyal Marriott customer, yet Marriott is not one of that company's preferred vendors? A travel office is going to have a real hard time getting that guy to stay at Hilton if they can't mandate it.

"We respond with a roster of offerings to give that Marriott traveler a personal incentive to use us, the preferred vendor. Our overall objective is to use the program as a tool that can help the travel manager with compliance to their overall travel policy."

Member Attitudes

HHW made extensive use of conjoint analysis to measure what members wanted from the Hilton HHonors program. Adam Burke explained, "Members come in for an hour-and-a-half interview. They're asked to trade off program elements, including services and amenities in the hotel, based on the value they place on those attributes relative to their cost. The results help us determine the appropriate priorities for modifying the program. We find that different people have different needs. Some people are service-oriented. No amount of miles or points is ever going to replace a warm welcome and being recognized by the hotel as a loyal customer. Other people are games-players. They go after free stays, and they know the rules as well as we do. We've been in feedback groups where these people will educate us on how our program works! And, of course, many people are a combination of both."

Using a sample that was broadly representative of the program's upper-tier membership categories, program research found that Hilton HHonors members had an average of over 30 stays in all hotel chains per year, staying 4.2 nights per stay. Between 1997 and 1998, Hilton experienced a 17.5% increase in member utilization of HHonors hotels globally. Despite this improvement, more than half of HHonors member stays went to competing chains annually — this was primarily attributable to Hilton's relatively limited network size and distribution. The conjoint analysis suggested that roughly one in five HHonors member stays were solely attributable to their membership in the program — making these stays purely incremental.

The study found that the most important features of a hotel program were room upgrades and airline miles, followed by free hotel stays, and a variety of on-property benefits and services. Members wanted a streamlined reward redemption process, and points that did not expire. These findings led to refinements in the terms of membership for 1999, but Diskin was exploring more innovative approaches to the rewards program.

Diskin recognized that in their market research studies, consumers tended to describe an ideal program that was simply a version of the programs with which they were familiar. He was looking for more radical innovation:

> Hilton and Marriott tend to attract "games players." We want to compete effectively on the reward elements, but also introduce them to the more high touch, high feel kind of guest experience as well. The customer base that we have accumulated comprises games-players primarily. So we've got to deliver that benefit, but still go further.
>
> We've been on a mission to dramatically improve the stay experience for members of the upper-tier ranks of the program. That is the key to competitive distinctiveness. That's not something that anybody can imitate. We want our best customers to feel that when they go to Hilton, they know Hilton knows they're the best customer and they're treated

special. We want them to think, "I'm going to have the kind of room I want, I'm going to have the kind of stay I like, and if I have a problem, they're going to take care of it." We want the staff to know who's coming in each day, and make sure that these guests get a personal welcome. Our new customer reservation system will get more information down to the hotel. We'll know a lot more about our incoming guests. We will have a guest manager in the hotel whose job it is to make you feel special and to address any concerns you may have.

THE STARWOOD ANNOUNCEMENT

The *Wall Street Journal* of February 2, 1999, announced the birth of the Starwood Preferred Guest Program, covering Westin Hotels Resorts, Sheraton Hotels Resorts, The Luxury Collection, Four Points, Caesar's, and Starwood's new W brand hotels, representing more than 550 participating properties worldwide. It became clear that Starwood was adding program features that might be expensive to match. Four features in particular were of concern.

No blackout dates	All frequent guest and airline programs until now had ruled that members could not claim free travel during the very height of seasonal demand and when local events guaranteed a hotel full occupancy. Starwood was saying that if there was a room to rent, points were as good as money.
No capacity control	Programs until now had let hotel properties limit the number of rooms for free stays. Starwood was telling hotels that all unreserved rooms should be available to guests paying with points.
Paperless rewards	Guests had had previously to exchange points for a certificate, and then use the certificate to pay for an authorized stay. Under Starwood's system, individual properties would be able to accept points to pay for a stay.
Hotel reimbursement	Now that blackout dates were abolished, a property, particularly an attractive vacation destination, might have to contend with many more points-paying guests than before. Starwood therefore raised the rate at which it reimbursed hotels for these stays. To meet the cost, it charged participating hotels 20%–100% more than its competitors on paid stays.

Starwood was pledging to invest $50 million in advertising to publicize the program—significantly more than HHW had historically spent on program communications. Exhibit 6 compares the loyalty programs of the four major business class hotel chains after the Starwood announcement.

Diskin's Dilemma

Without any doubt Starwood had raised the ante in the competition for customer loyalty. Jeff Diskin had to decide whether to match or pass. He mused:

> Do we have to compete point for point? Or do we want to take a different positioning and hold on to our loyal members and differentiate HHonors from Starwood and other competitors? We're in a cycle where for 10 years the cost to our hotels of our frequent guest program as a percent of the folio has been cycling down. Yet activation, retention, and member spend per visit, all have improved. If we can deliver the same amount of business to the Hilton brand and it costs less, Hilton makes more margin. That attracts investors, franchise ownership, new builders. That's another reason why they buy the Hilton flag.

As Diskin saw it, Starwood's Preferred Guest announcement was a solution to a problem Hilton did not have, arising from its recent purchases of the Sheraton and Westin chains:

> They are trying to develop the Starwood brand with the Starwood Preferred Guest program. They are targeting the most lucrative part of the business, the individual business traveler, where Sheraton and Westin independently have never been as effective as Marriott, Hyatt and Hilton. Sheraton's

frequent guest program wasn't very effective. They changed it every few years; they used to have members pay for it. Westin never had enough critical mass of properties for it to be important for enough people. So now, together they can address Westin's critical mass problem and Sheraton's relevance.

But if frequent guest programs were a good idea, perhaps bigger programs were an even better idea. Diskin reflected:

Hotel properties routinely pay 10% commission to a travel agent to bring them a guest. Yet they continually scrutinize the

EXHIBIT 6 Membership Offerings of the Four Major Business Class Hotel Chains in 1998

Chain	Membership Restrictions[a]	Point Value	Eligible Charges	New Member Bonus	Airline Mileage Accrual
Starwood	One stay per year to remain active—basic; 10 stays or 25 room nights per year—medium; 25 stays or 50 room nights	2 Starpoints = $1 basic; 3 Starpoints = $1 medium or premium	Room rate, F&B, laundry/valet, phone, in-room movies	Periodically	Starpoints earned can be converted to miles 1:1; cannot earn both points and miles for the same stay
Hilton	One stay per year to remain active—Blue; 4 stays per year or 10 nights—medium; 16 stays per year or 36 nights—premium; 28 stays or 60 nights—top	10pts = $1 -Blue; + 15% bonus on points earned medium; + 25% bonus on points earned premium; + 50% bonus on points earned top	Room rate, F&B, laundry, phone	Periodically	500 miles per qualifying stay in addition to point earnings
Hyatt	One stay per year to remain active—basic; 5 stays or 15 nights per year—medium; 25 stays or 50 nights per year—premium	5pts = $1; + 15% bonus on points earned medium; + 30% bonus premium on points earned	Room rate, F&B, laundry, phone	Periodically	500 miles per stay; not available if earning points
Marriott	No requirements for basic; 15 nights per year—medium; 50 nights per year—premium	10pts = $1; + 20% bonus on points earned medium; + 25% bonus on points earned premium	Room rate, F&B, laundry, phone	Double points first 120 days	3 miles per dollar spent at full service hotels; 1 mile per dollar spent at other hotels; not available if earning points

[a] Most programs run three tiers. For ease of comparison, the three levels are named basic, medium, and premium. HHonors has four tiers.

Company	Affinity Credit Card Point Accrual	Point Purchase	Bonus Threshold Reward	Exchange Hotel Points for Airline Miles	Hotel Rewards
Starwood	1,000 hotel pts first card use; 1 hotel pt = $1 spent; 4 hotel points = $1 spent at Starwood hotels	NA	NA	1:1 conversion except JAL, KLM, Ansett, Quantas, Air New Zealand; 5000 bonus miles when you convert 20,000 hotel points; minimum 2000 Starpoints — basic; minimum 15,000 medium; no minimum for premium	5 categories; 1 free night category 1 is 3,000 Starpoints; 1 free night category 5 is 12,000 Starpoints
Hilton	5,000 hotel pts for application; 2,500 hotel points first card use; 2 hotel pts = $1 spent; 3 hotel pts = $1 spent at HHonors Hotels.	$10 = 1,000 pts up to 20% of the total points of the reward	2,000 pts = 4 stays per quarter;	10,000 pts = 1,500 miles; 20,000 pts = 3,500 miles; 50,000 pts = 10,000 miles; minimum 10,000 hotel points exchange, can also exchange airline miles for hotel points	5 categories: free weekend night 10,000 lowest; 35,000 highest
Hyatt	None	$10 = 500 pts up to 10% of the total points of the reward	None basic;	3 pts = 1 mile; minimum 9,000 point exchange	Weekend night no category: 8,000 pts; if premium time there is an additional 5,000 pts; come with partner awards
Marriott	5,000 hotel pts first card use; 1 hotel pt = $1 spent; 3 hotel points = $1 spent at Marriott Rewards hotels	$10 = 1,000 pts up to 10% of the total points of the reward	None basic;	10,000 pts = 2,000 miles; 20,000 pts = 5,000 miles; 30,000 pts = 10,000 miles; minimum = 10,000 hotel point exchange	2 categories: 20,000 free weekend lowcategory; and 30,000 high category

cost of these programs. Of course, they're justified in doing so, but the return on investment clearly justifies the expenditure. And our competitors certainly seem to see a value in increasing their investment in their programs.

Diskin tried to predict Hyatt and Marriott's response to the Starwood announcement. The industry was quite competitive enough. He thought back to his early years at United Airlines and recalled the damage that price wars had done to that industry. ■

CHAPTER 11

Managing Customer Profitability in Industrial Markets[1]

Vendors that have implemented portfolios of customer relationship management strategies need to determine the economic return on their efforts. A quick and effective diagnostic for managing customers for profit is the price versus cost-to-serve matrix (Figure 8-3), which links vendor effort (cost to serve) with returns (prices paid by customer). Plotting customers' positions on this grid over consecutive time periods enables firms to get a feel for any changes that might be taking place in a specific customer relationship. With such directional guidance on the profitability of a customer relationship, a vendor can take appropriate remedial actions. A common complaint about this approach is that it does not enable a vendor to link specific actions with customer responses. This chapter looks at other approaches for firms wishing to go beyond this tool.

Choices among investment opportunities typically rely on evaluations of anticipated return on investments (ROI) and associated risks. The same logic must be applied to investments in customer management strategies. To accurately calculate customer profitability and remove inefficiencies in current customer management efforts, firms need information about the impact of individual actions on the revenue generated and costs incurred in a customer relationship.[2] Linking specific elements of the customer management effort with the customer revenue stream enables firms to isolate and remove inefficiencies in the customer management effort. Direct marketers to individual consumers are clear leaders in doing this; they use detailed, customer-level data to establish cause and effect linkages between the various elements of their customer management efforts and customer purchasing behaviors.

---

[1]This chapter is adapted from Das Narayandas, "Linking Customer Management Effort to Profits," Harvard Business School Note #503-084 (2003).
[2]Cooper and Kaplan (1999) cover the foundations of activity-based costing and its use in understanding and capturing costs in customer and supplier relationship. Robin Cooper and Robert. S. Kaplan, *Design of Cost Management Systems*, 2nd ed. (Upper Saddle River, N.J.: Prentice Hall, 1999).

Most marketers, however, lack the precision to link their customer management efforts with customer response. Early studies tried to quantify the benefits of customer management focused on firm-level revenues, costs, and, in turn, profitability. One study compared key financial performance metrics over multiple years for two groups of suppliers: the long-term relationship (LTR) suppliers, involved in a few select, long-term relationships; and the transactional suppliers, in multiple short-term customer relationships of less than a year. The study found that focusing on existing customers did not come at the expense of growth and profitability. LTR suppliers also benefited from lower manufacturing and operating costs, but contrary to expectations, this benefit did not translate into higher gross margins to the supplier, since it was counteracted by the large customers who demanded lower prices over time in return for long-term contracts. That LTR suppliers were nevertheless able to retain or even improve their profitability levels as a result of significant cost reductions in selling, general, and administrative expenses demonstrated that the benefits of long-term customer relationships transcend manufacturing efficiencies.[3]

Even given information on revenues and costs, the lag between vendor effort and customer response, coupled with the cumulative effect of vendor actions on customer response, thwarts attempts to isolate cause and effect relationships between different elements of vendor effort and corresponding customer responses. The best option under these circumstances is to calculate an overall ROI for total customer management effort during a specified period of time using a simplified, reasonable approach — taking the difference between the net present value (NPV) of a customer's purchases and anticipated costs of serving the customer.[4,5] Vendors can use such information to decide whether to remain in a given customer relationship and whether to change the nature and level of their customer management effort.

Although the sophistication of NPV models makes them excellent tools for valuing customers, the value of the models reflects the accuracy of the data inputs. A number of industrial marketing firms that have attempted to link their customer management efforts with customer responses have found NPV calculations of future revenues and cost streams to involve major assumptions that can render dubious customer valuations. Prescriptions for customer management based on such values can be entirely wrong. In such situations, more customer level information becomes a curse.

Field research suggests that rather than pursuing elusive customer profitability data, firms are better served by taking a more pragmatic view and splitting their customer base into two customer types: those that must be managed with a revenue focus; and those that can truly be managed for profit.

---

[3]Manohar U. Kalwani and Narakesari Narayandas, "Long-Term Manufacturer-Supplier Relationships: Do They Pay Off for Supplier Firms?" *Journal of Marketing* 59, no. 1 (1995): 1–16.
[4]Researchers who have developed sophisticated models for calculating the net present value of customers in a variety of market situations include Robert C. Blattberg and John Deighton, "Manage Marketing by the Customer Equity Test," *Harvard Business Review* 74, no. 4 (1995); 136–44, Robert C. Blattberg, Gary Getz, and Jacquelyn S. Thomas *Customer Equity: Building and Managing Relationships as Valuable Assets* (Boston, Mass.: Harvard Business School Press, 2001). Ronald T. Rust, Valarie A. Zeithaml, and Katherine N. Lemon, *Driving Customer Equity: How Customer Lifetime Value Is Reshaping Corporate Strategy* (New York: The Free Press, 2001).
[5]The strong assumption here is that the lagged effects of any action taken during the target period are negligible and that all anticipated customer response is recorded during the same period.

MANAGING CUSTOMERS FOR REVENUE

There are many situations in which revenues derived from a customer relationship are far more responsive to customer management effort than are costs, for example a rapid-growth business in which demand outstrips supply, and high-margin businesses such as specialty products and services. Vendors in such businesses are well advised to strive to maximize prices and volumes rather than focus on costs. Using a sales volume metric or Share of Customer Wallet (SCW) (in the presence of multiple suppliers) together with a price index can serve as a more than adequate measure of returns to vendor effort.

THE SCW INDEX

The commonly used SCW measure represents the portion of total purchases made by a customer that is accounted for by the focal vendor. Using SCW makes sense when the following are true:

- The customer routinely purchases the vendor's products or services and not much change is expected. The customer has an ongoing annual purchase volume that is known to all vendors. For example, Dell, Compaq, HP, and IBM have a good understanding of the annual Information Technology (IT) budgets of their large corporate customers. Grabbing as much as possible of each customer's total purchases is the goal of each of these competitors.

- There is little or no time lag between changes in the vendor's customer management effort and customer responses. For example, when customers place annual (or biannual) contracts, they typically rely on vendor performance in the previous period to guide the reallocation of their purchases among the different vendors. If the lag between vendor effort and customer response is high, it becomes difficult to pin down the efficacy of vendor effort on SCW and the measure loses its predictive power.

In a study of the link between customer satisfaction and SCW for an industrial packaging company, it was found that increasing customer satisfaction over time did not always correspond to an increase in sales. The link between increasing satisfaction and increasing sales held only among customers to whom the vendor was the primary supplier, that is, the vendor who had the major share of a customer's total purchases. Although they appreciated the vendor's efforts, other customers did not find increased satisfaction to be a compelling reason to shift business away from their primary supplier to this vendor. These customers unanimously explained that they would increase the proportion of sales to the vendor only if their primary supplier's performance slipped. Clearly, the incumbent supplier with a majority SCW accrued benefits that other suppliers could not usurp.

In addition to scale efficiencies gained in marketing, sales, manufacturing, and other functions, owning a majority share of a customer's purchases permits a vendor to build a relationship that leads the customer to display various loyalty behaviors. A classic example of a vendor benefiting from greater customer share is Dell Computer Corporation, a direct marketer of PCs. Dell's true power is its ability, not to customize products for individual customers, but to standardize its customized offerings. The more share of a customer's wallet Dell gets, the more it benefits from scale economies and lowers costs. Dell's costs are much lower for one customer who buys a hundred PCs than for a hundred customers for whom it has developed customized specifications who each buy one PC. Although both yield the same market share, Dell benefits from scale economies only when its customer share goes up. Let's consider how this happens.

When Dell receives a call from a corporate customer prospect that the telesales rep identifies as high potential, it sends a field account representative to meet with the prospect. Jointly with the customer, Dell develops customized system specification PC solutions that exactly meet the customer's needs. To customize unique product for each customer can be expensive. But whenever a customer needs a new PC, that customer need only to contact Dell and provide details of who they are. Based on its customer knowledge, Dell then knows exactly what that customer requires. Dell's benefit from standardizing all orders based in its existing customers' orders is that the cost of customizing a PC is close to zero.

But this is just part of the story. Consider what happens at the customer end. In being involved in creating a unique, customized solution to meet its own needs, the customer bears part of the customization cost. How likely is this customer to be willing to expend the same effort and incur additional costs with another PC vendor? Getting a consistent product specification and quality all the time is another enormous advantage of continuing to do business with Dell. Over time, as its installed base of Dell computers grows, a customer will become less willing to consider switching to another vendor. In essence, the customer now sees Dell as a deliverer of specialty solutions in a commodity market. Consequently, the customer might even be willing to pay a price premium for Dell products and display other loyalty behaviours.

PRICE PAID INDEX

Another powerful loyalty measure is a price paid index. Given that vendors typically sell a range of products and services, using raw price data (or an average of all prices) does not make sense. For example, if a customer bought just one unit of a high-end product at a very high price and a million units of a low-end product at a steep discount, simply averaging the two prices would yield an incorrect picture. A more correct picture is obtained by following a three-step process:

1. First, estimate the price paid by the customer for the high-end product relative to other customers using a scale anchored by a score of 100 for the average price paid for the high-end product across all customers.[6]
2. Repeat the process for the low-end product.
3. Take a weighted average of the two price scores, the weights being the percentage of the customer's total purchases from the vendor. For example, if a customer's purchases from the vendor totaled $200,000 and the high-end product accounted for $60,000, then the weights used would be .3 and .7 for the high- and low-end products, respectively.

The price and purchase volume information needed to construct this index is readily available to vendors in business and consumer markets.

---

[6]The lack of information can sometimes force the use of subjective scores where executives estimate the index rather than use hard data to calculate the index. While this can reduce the accuracy, it typically does not affect the effectiveness of the measure in subsequent analyses.

MANAGING CUSTOMERS FOR PROFIT

It makes sense to manage for profits only when customers' needs are well understood and not expected to change over time. Commodity products in mature markets are an example. There are nine steps to managing customers for profits:

1. Build a master customer database that contains information about who customers are, what they have bought, their total purchase volume, and so forth.
2. Next, based on past purchasing patterns, set a revenue target for the coming year (or quarter) for each customer.
3. Given the revenue target, set a profit goal.
4. Starting with information on the cost of goods sold, work backward to arrive at the target cost to serve for each customer.
5. Develop the portfolio of sales and marketing effort that can be used to contact customers; it is important that vendors have empirical evidence on the impact of each element on customer demand.
6. Understand cost per contact for each type of effort.
7. Develop a customer contact matrix, that is, the optimal mix of the various effort types that fit within the budget assigned to each customer. The plan should detail which marketing effort (for example, direct sales call, telesales, direct mail, Web-based contact) is to be used, when, and how frequently.
8. Adhere to the customer contact matrix plan.
9. Periodically review the customer database to verify customer-purchasing patterns and sales and marketing efforts and make changes in those customer relationships that are not meeting the profit target.

Although this approach does not preclude revenue increases arising from an increase in vendor share of customer wallet, its main limitation is that it begins with the assumption that the vendor is not able to increase market-level demand. The approach is thus applicable to mature and declining markets characterized by a high expectation of stable customer demand. The strength of the approach is that it forces discipline in a vendor's sales and marketing effort. Hunter Business Group, a business-to-business direct marketer, has successfully used variants of this approach to manage mature and declining businesses such as electrical typewriters, commercial building maintenance systems, and sales of automobile accessories such as tires, batteries, and chemicals to automobile service stations.[7]

Summary

In their desire to manage individual customers for profits, vendors rush to estimate customer profits using naïve, incorrect methodologies that can be very misleading. Decisions based on such models can undo vendors' efforts in the first three stages of the customer management framework. Instead of trying to manage all customers for

---

[7] Das Narayandas, "Hunter Business Group: Team TBA," Harvard Business School Case #500-030 (2000).

profits, vendors would find it more efficient to manage only a select set of customers for profits and use revenue-based metrics such as the SCW and price indices to gain a more realistic picture of their rewards in customer relationships.

Review Questions and Exercises

1. Why is it important to use metrics to gauge the status of customer–firm relationships?
2. Why is solely measuring customer satisfaction insufficient? What are the risks when customer satisfaction is the only metric?
3. When should the SCW index be used? When should the price paid index be used? What do these indices tell you about the health of the firm's relationship with the customer?

◆◆◆ **Hunter Business Group:** *TeamTBA*

Case 11-1   Hunter Business Group: *TeamTBA*

Das Narayandas

Sometimes you have a secondary product line that is moving in a direction different from that of the firm. . . . You think that everything is OK, that it is just an incremental business, but in fact, it becomes more like an anchor. . . .
—VIC HUNTER, CHAIRMAN AND CEO, HUNTER BUSINESS GROUP

Such was the dilemma that Star Oil faced during the summer of 1992. Its tire, battery, and accessory (TBA) business, the "ugly stepchild" of its gasoline station services division, was now unprofitable and consuming valuable field resources. Its downward trend in profitability had led to a growing sentiment within the firm toward abandoning Star's branded TBA business. Yet, a recent survey of the firm's service stations produced a surprise finding. Customers who had their cars serviced at the 2,200 U.S. gasoline service stations[1] selling Star-branded TBA products bought four times more gasoline than those who bought only gasoline there. This suggested that Star's branded TBA products played a strategic role in boosting Star's gasoline sales. The decision to exit the TBA business, therefore, no longer appeared easy. In the face of increasing competition, Star could not afford an erosion of customer loyalty that might damage its well-known brand. However, the unprofitable nature of the business was unacceptable to the firm's top management. Star executives sought a way to retain the branded TBA business and restore profitability. At this point Star turned to the Hunter Business Group (HBG) for assistance.

HUNTER BUSINESS GROUP

The Hunter Business Group (HBG) specialized in reorganizing the sales and marketing efforts of large and small firms, in industries ranging from computers and biomedical supplies to office supplies and auto parts. Vic Hunter (an alumnus of the Harvard Business School), the company's President and CEO, had founded HBG in 1981 after amassing a wealth of direct marketing and sales management experience. Hunter believed that strategic use of direct marketing technologies could revolutionize the face of business-to-business (b2b) marketing. Seeing direct marketing as more than just a technique, Hunter expressed his vision:

> Our goal is to facilitate the *transformation of change* within our clients' businesses. We believe that direct marketing is a *highly personal* form of marketing that respects and recognizes the unique needs of each customer. A properly designed and maintained database allows communications to be derived from specific information attached to a given customer account. When a seller's communications provide genuine value to a customer, direct marketing programs result in solid relationships, high retention rates and increased profitability.

HBG achieved these objectives by stepping beyond traditional approaches to sales and

---

The case was prepared by Research Associate Elizabeth Caputo (under the direction of Professor Das Narayandas). Copyright © 1999 by the President and Fellows of Harvard College. Harvard Business School Case 500-030.

[1] Gasoline service stations typically had one or more service bays in addition to multiple self-serve and full-service gasoline pumps. Based on the availability of labor, these establishments offered a range of services from simple maintenance jobs (replacement of tires/batteries/wiper blades/engine oil/transmission oil/windshield washer liquid) to more complex repairs (repairing brake pads/mufflers/struts, tuning engines, etc.).

marketing to find new ways to increase brand penetration and customer satisfaction, while cutting sales and marketing expense. Consequently, HBG had become widely recognized as a "Statue of Liberty," both for fatigued and impoverished divisions of large companies and for healthy firms looking to revolutionize their sales and marketing efforts. Over the years, HBG had built a highly diversified client base, including IBM, Du Pont, Hallmark Cards, 3M, Monsanto, and BellSouth.

When presented with the details of Star's dilemma, Hunter found it an ideal match for HBG's unique expertise. In fact, based on his experience, he was confident that HBG could turn around the TBA division and make it profitable within a year. Of course, this required fundamentally altering the way Star's gas station operators approached their business. It also meant that Star's sales reps would need to redefine the way they managed dealer relationships, using HBG's integrated direct marketing model to maximize their sales and marketing effectiveness.

DIRECT MARKETING AND HBG'S CUSTOMER CONTACT MATRIX

Direct marketing had long held a mixed reputation. In the consumer arena, for example, manufacturers and service providers saw it as the lowest-cost approach for promoting to attractive customer segments by using databases and linked, automated telephone and mailing systems. For many consumers this meant endless dinnertime phone calls offering low-rate credit cards, long-distance rate deals, and other kinds of "come-ons."

In the arena of business marketing, however, direct marketing techniques had not been fully explored until the 1980s. In this domain, telemarketing methods were often put to more careful use, supplementing rather than replacing expensive face-to-face sales calls. Hunter defined direct marketing as "an interactive marketing system that employs *integrated*, organized contacts to effect a measurable customer response." The effectiveness of integrating mail, telephone, and field contacts, he believed, would always be greater than that resulting from using each medium independently (Exhibit 1).

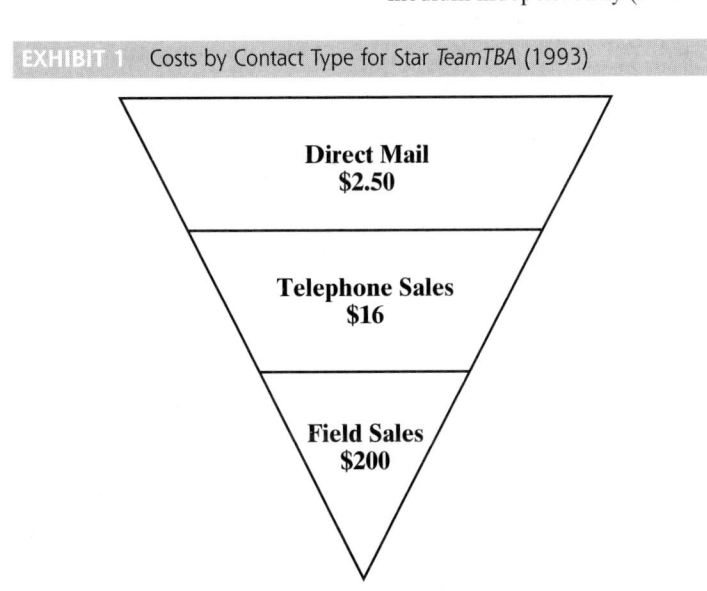

EXHIBIT 1 Costs by Contact Type for Star *TeamTBA* (1993)

- Direct Mail $2.50
- Telephone Sales $16
- Field Sales $200

- The dollar values above represent the costs per a single, completed contact with a prospective Star dealer.
- Telemarketing is best used as part of a total marketing and sales program.
- Cost per contact is not contiguous from medium to medium.
- Lower-cost contacts must leverage higher-cost contacts.

Source: Hunter Business Group, Inc.

Central to the HBG approach was the use of an economic model—a customer contact matrix—developed by Hunter. The foundation for the model (**Electronic Exhibit 1, Exhibit 4**) rested upon the research of the service management group at the Harvard Business School.[2] This group developed groundbreaking methods to measure customer loyalty and adjust customer contact frequency based on current and future revenues. Therefore, even in a dying industry like typewriters where sales had gone down 20% in one year, there would be stability and sustainability as long as selling expenses declined more rapidly than revenues.

THE EVOLUTION OF GASOLINE SERVICE STATIONS AND THE BRANDED TBA MARKET

The concept of the modern-day gasoline service station evolved during the 1950s with the advent of the U.S. interstate system. In order to differentiate themselves in a highly competitive gasoline market, service stations began providing "under the hood" checks during fill-ups and replaced worn-out tires, batteries, and other accessories with their own branded products.[3] Station operators discovered that offering these "expert/advisory" services gave them an opportunity to strengthen their bonds with customers. Many also discovered that their customers often were willing to pay a premium for branded TBA products. By the 1970s, it was common for major gasoline retailers, including Amoco, Shell, and Star (all of which had very strong brand images), to offer their own branded TBA products and services. These stations used their branded components to maintain a competitive edge in retail gasoline sales. In addition to providing a point of differentiation and margins of more than 20%, branded TBA products could often represent half or more of a service station's overall contribution while accounting for only a small portion its revenues.

Although gasoline retailers like Star dominated the TBA market during the 1960s and 1970s, the market's high margins soon attracted the attention of specialty competitors that included high-volume/low-price service models (Kmart, Wal-Mart), specialty service chains (NTB, Jiffy Lube), and independent dealers. These firms aggressively entered the TBA market in the 1980s and gained significant share at the expense of traditional players like Star, who encountered market share declines as high as 70% versus 1960s levels. This trend continued in the 1980s with the closing of nearly 72,000 service stations throughout the decade—an additional 35% decline. By 1990, 80% of repairs on the nation's 190 million automobiles were made, almost equally, by car dealerships, private garages, specialty repair shops, and gasoline service station dealers. The "do-it-yourself" market made up the remaining 20%.

THE STAR OIL ACCOUNT

The branded TBA business was not new to HBG. The firm had recently ended an eight-year relationship with Amoco, a global gasoline retailer like Star. Amoco had partnered with HBG to increase lagging TBA sales at its nearly 6,000 service stations (hereafter referred to as *dealers*). Despite the implementation of a highly successful, integrated, direct marketing program at Amoco, the HBG partnership was discontinued in 1991 when Amoco decided to outsource its entire branded TBA business to the National Automotive Parts Association Supply Company (NAPA).

When Star approached HBG soon thereafter, Vic Hunter was delighted. Star recognized the importance of the TBA business in supporting its ubiquitous, industry-dominant logo. To Hunter, the importance Star's management ascribed to preserving this brand image suggested its long-term commitment to the TBA business—something he had found lacking in the Amoco relationship.

Nonetheless, with revenues having fallen over 20% in the past 12 months, Star managers were finding it difficult to justify maintaining the TBA division despite its importance in supporting the brand. Hunter described the situation:

---

[2]James L. Heskett; Earl W. Sasser Jr.; and, Leonard A. Schlesinger, *The Service Profit Chain: How Leading Companies Link Profit And Growth To Loyalty, Satisfaction And Value* (New York: Free Press, 1997).

[3]Gasoline retailers like Star had traditionally sold branded TBA products through their gasoline service station dealers.

In 1991–92 Star was losing money. They were unsure how much but knew the amount was substantial. On a variable cost basis, the small part that they could track, the loss was about $8 million. Further, the TBA division had become unattractive not only from the financial standpoint, but also from that of human resources. TBA was not an exciting place to be. Yet, a significant amount of Star's brand equity rested in its TBA product lines. Strong customer relationships had been built around these products throughout the marketplace.

I was convinced that the integrated approach we had used at Amoco would also work well at Star. Consequently, we told them we would turn their business around within a year. We also promised that we would design a sales and marketing program to maintain their brand image and increase dealer satisfaction while simultaneously reducing sales and marketing expenses. Their reaction was "yes, but what about the dealer/employee relationships? We have seasoned people who were hired to work for Star forever and you're telling us that you can do things better and with a significantly lower budget?" Star's managers were clearly skeptical about our ability to deliver on our promises, but their only alternative was to give us a chance.

TEAMTBA

HBG began by establishing an entirely new company to address the Star business. It was named *TeamTBA*. The company operated out of HBG's Milwaukee headquarters under the leadership of Julie Kowalski, a member of HBG's management team. The initial agreement between the firms stated that HBG would license the Star brand, and independently manage a direct marketing operation that would include marketing, sales, manufacturing, and product design. Star would receive no compensation on sales below $20 million per year, but was entitled to 2% of *TeamTBA* revenues exceeding that. Additionally, Star would retain control over the product—HBG would need to obtain Star's approval before making changes to current TBA products. This included dropping existing products, changing vendors, and introducing new products and services. Star also wanted *TeamTBA* to live up to its word and reduce operating costs by 50% in the first year. Star retained the right to terminate the agreement if this condition was not met.

TeamTBA began operations by creating an extensive branded TBA dealer database. Prior to 1992, Star had maintained dealer profile databases by product line. However, like other firms in this industry, it maintained this information entirely on paper. Rebecca Nguyen, HBG's Information System Manager at the time, recalled:

> When we began work with Star, all service station (hereafter referred to as *dealer*) information was stored on paper and much of it was incomplete. We used that information to create a master that would then be updated as our salespeople called on the various dealers and collected current information. It took us more than six months to gather all the pertinent information. By September 1992, our dealer master database had grown to include all 2,200 dealers.

TeamTBA organized its sales and marketing effort around sales teams, each consisting of a field sales representative (FSR), an internal telesales representative (TSR), and a customer service representative (CSR). In contrast to Star's field sales force of 84 reps, *TeamTBA* began with just 18 sales people (16 HBD employees or new hires and two former Star field sales representatives). Hunter explained:

> It is not that we did not want to hire Star's reps. In fact, we gave them an option to join us. However, most stayed on at Star to focus on gasoline sales, or left because they lacked confidence in our approach. Some felt the transition would be too difficult to handle.

TeamTBA's FSRs were assigned sales territories and teamed with a headquarters-based TSR. This partnership formed the field customer interface (Exhibit 2). FSRs were to advise dealers on how to better manage and grow their service bay operations, thereby stimulating demand for TBA products. Also, internal TSRs would proactively initiate contacts with station owners, in close collaboration with FSRs, to solicit orders, conduct and coordinate predefined sales strategies, and maintain/update customer profiles in the dealer master database. Inbound CSRs, also located at

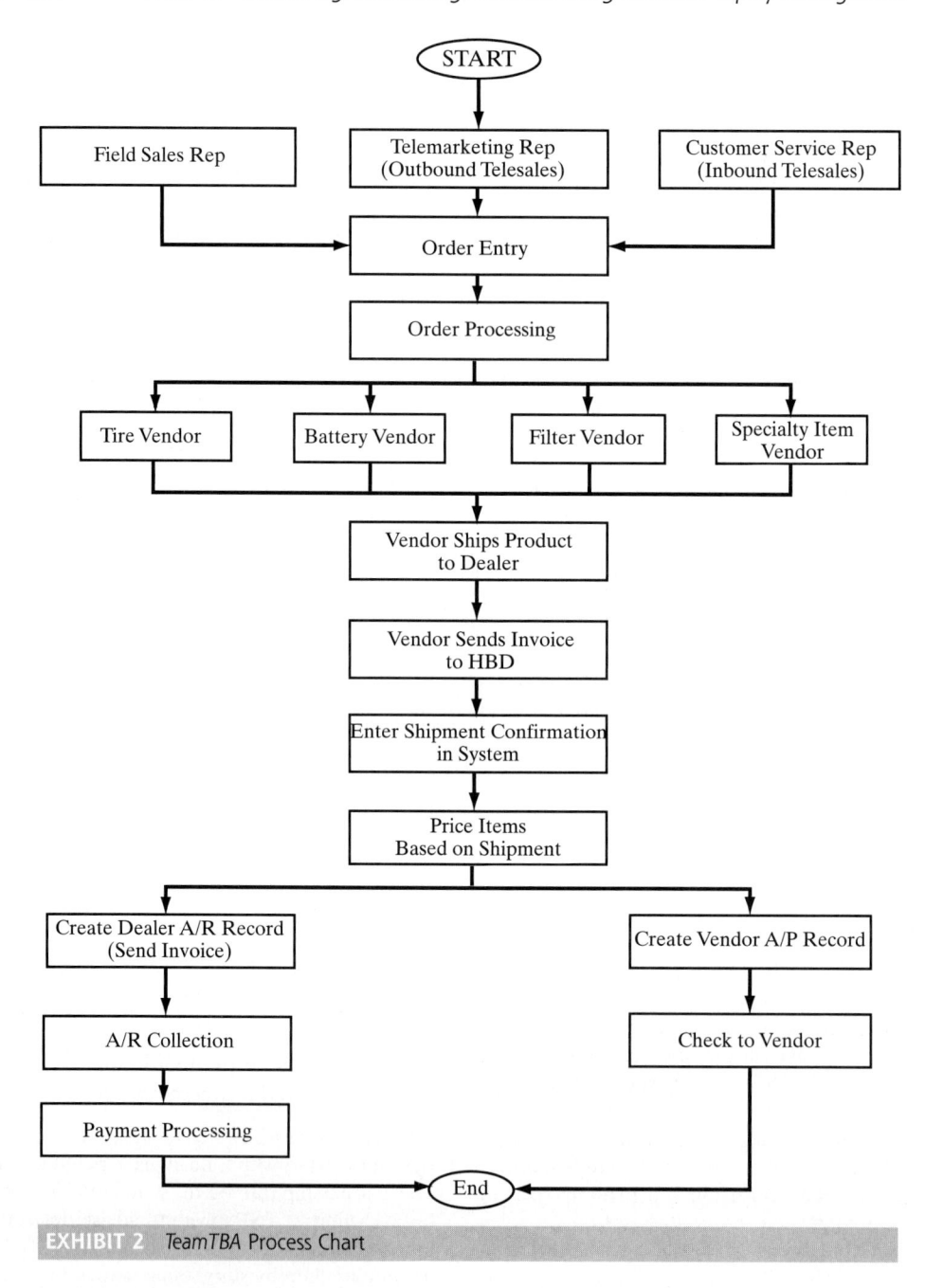

```
                           START
                             │
┌─────────────┐    ┌──────────────────┐    ┌──────────────────┐
│ Field Sales │    │ Telemarketing Rep│    │ Customer Service │
│    Rep      │    │(Outbound Telesales)│  │ Rep (Inbound     │
│             │    │                  │    │ Telesales)       │
└─────────────┘    └──────────────────┘    └──────────────────┘
        │                   │                       │
        └──────────────→ Order Entry ←──────────────┘
                             │
                      Order Processing
                             │
    ┌────────────┬───────────┼───────────┬──────────────┐
┌───────┐   ┌─────────┐  ┌────────┐  ┌──────────────┐
│ Tire  │   │ Battery │  │ Filter │  │Specialty Item│
│Vendor │   │ Vendor  │  │ Vendor │  │   Vendor     │
└───────┘   └─────────┘  └────────┘  └──────────────┘
    └────────────┴───────────┬───────────┴──────────────┘
                             │
                  Vendor Ships Product
                       to Dealer
                             │
                  Vendor Sends Invoice
                         to HBD
                             │
                 Enter Shipment Confirmation
                         in System
                             │
                       Price Items
                    Based on Shipment
                             │
        ┌────────────────────┴────────────────────┐
┌──────────────────────┐              ┌──────────────────────┐
│ Create Dealer A/R    │              │ Create Vendor A/P    │
│ Record (Send Invoice)│              │      Record          │
└──────────────────────┘              └──────────────────────┘
            │                                      │
     A/R Collection                         Check to Vendor
            │                                      │
     Payment Processing                            │
            │                                      │
            └────────────────→ End ←───────────────┘
```

EXHIBIT 2 *TeamTBA* Process Chart

headquarters, would augment the process by providing order status, order processing support, and immediate customer problem resolution. Weekly conference calls (between the FSR and the TSR) would be conducted to share information about recent dealer contacts and to develop future contact strategies. These calls would also be taped so that management could ensure that the sales teams were working effectively to develop value added, integrated contact plans. Further, contact and coordination with the existing Star gasoline sales force would be part of the overall contact plan and the responsibility of the FSRs.

Marketing and promotional resources were to be provided through a Marketing Coordinator located centrally. This coordinator was responsible for overseeing production and distribution of key marketing elements by working with Star (as required) and with outside vendors. An initial 1993 Promotion Calendar had already been created to guide these efforts.

Accounting resources had been established to handle order entry, vendor invoice processing, accounts receivable, financial analysis and reporting, pricing analysis, sales analysis, and auditing of intracompany transactions.

Information Systems was charged with maintaining and enhancing software and hardware resources, developing new systems to support the business process, training and communicating with all system users, managing a "help desk" function, and managing the EDI process with vendors.

Vendor negotiations and relationship management were the responsibilities of the general manager. Hunter explained:

> We took a radically different approach with vendors. To begin with, in each category we short-listed those vendors we thought capable of meeting our quality standards. Based on their experience, most of these vendors came to the negotiating table expecting to talk price and play "hardball." They were surprised when we refused to talk about price. Not that price was unimportant, we were more interested in hearing what these vendors had to offer in terms of added value that would help us differentiate *TeamTBA* products in the eyes of our dealers and the end consumers. We were looking for partners, not suppliers. We offered long-term, single-source contracts to these vendors in return for their commitment to customize existing products and to develop new ones for us. Interestingly, several vendors walked away from the table because they were unprepared to do business this way. Those that remained were committed to making *TeamTBA* a success.

By December 1992, *TeamTBA* had selected Kelly Springfield as its main tire vendor, Delco-Remy for batteries, and Champion for filters—each a well-known manufacturer in its industry. A vendor decision on chemicals was to be made before the end of December. All TBA products, regardless of vendor, would be labeled and marketed under the Star brand name.

In order to ensure a smooth transition, *TeamTBA* had assumed some of Star's telemarketing, order processing, and customer service responsibilities in August 1992. By the end of December of that year, *TeamTBA's* field sales representatives were in place, and the new sales plan was launched at the beginning of January 1993.

USING THE STAR CUSTOMER CONTACT MATRIX

Understanding and applying Hunter's customer contact matrix was the backbone of *TeamTBA's* customer (gasoline service station) management strategy. The process began by projecting revenues for 1993 (Exhibit 3). Hunter forecasted revenues at $20 million—a significant reduction from the 1991 and 1992 levels. *TeamTBA* made this downward projection based on their belief that the earlier Star TBA revenues had been overreported. Further, a large portion of the TBA volume had resulted from Star reps "pushing" TBA products. Finally, the negative impact of the Persian Gulf War was expected to hit the industry that year. Assuming reduced product costs (now budgeted at 80% of revenues) as a result of stronger relationship management and the consolidation of suppliers, *TeamTBA* projected a gross margin of $4 million for 1993. With this in mind, *TeamTBA* began to think about a reasonable estimate for direct marketing expense.

Star wanted *TeamTBA* to honor Hunter's verbal commitment that his team could implement their program successfully while reducing operating costs by 50% of the expected 1993 revenues. This meant that HBG's projected operating costs had to be reduced from 35.5% to 17.75% as a percentage of revenues, or to $3.55 million. "Operating costs," as noted in Exhibit 3, comprised two expenses: the direct marketing and sales expense (which included mail, phone, and field operations, salaries) and fixed operating expense (which included rent, salaries for internal office support, database management, and miscellaneous

	1991	As % of 1991 Revenues	1992	As % of 1992 Revenues	1993 (Team TBA Projection)	As % of 1993 Revenues	1994 (Team TBA Projection)	As % of 1994 Revenues
Revenue	$36.7		$39.4		$20.0		$16.0	
Product costs	32.3	88.0	33.6	85.3	16.0	80.0	12.8	80.0
Gross margin	4.4	12.0	5.8	14.7	4.0	20.0	3.2	20.0
Operating costs	11.3	30.8	14.0	35.5	3.55	17.75	2.84	17.75
Operating income	(6.9)	(18.8)	(8.2)	(20.8)	.45	2.25	.36	2.25

EXHIBIT 3 Star Financial Information, 1991–1992 (actual); 1993–1994 (projected); in $millions

Source: Hunter Business Group, Inc.

costs associated with *TeamTBA*'s Milwaukee headquarters). HBG's experience suggested that fixed expenses would run between 40%–45% of operating costs, or about $1.5 million. Consequently, the team established a baseline of $2 million for direct marketing and sales expense.

Exhibit 4 illustrates the cost and corresponding frequency of contacts by medium—mail ($2.50 per contact), phone ($16 per contact), and face-to-face meetings ($200 per contact)—and shows the number of active dealers by sales volume grade. *TeamTBA* knew from experience that as the amount of sales visits fell, the frequency of phone and mail contacts would need to go up. The question for *TeamTBA*, however, was whether or not this could be done more effectively given their $2 million budget. The next step was to determine the optimal combination of mail, phone, and field contacts within the budget, yet still meet the new sales target.

Dealers graded by purchase volume Dealers were sorted into buckets based on their TBA purchase volumes. The buckets were labeled "AA" (more than $30,000), "A" ($20,000–$30,000), "B" ($10,000–$20,000), "C" ($5,000–$10,000) and "D" (less than $5,000). Using past purchase data, *TeamTBA* established the average dollar sales for each grade, as shown in the table.

Number of dealers It was HBG's standard industry practice to sort customer accounts (dealers in this case) according to a 5/15/25/25/30 rule, designating the "top 20%" accounts as AA and A respectively. Thus, regardless of industry, the percentage of accounts allocated to each grade always remained constant.

Sales revenue HBG's customer contact matrix usually extended the "20/80" rule across industries—the AA and A accounts typically generated 80% of the overall sales revenues. However, this was not the case with TBA, where the AA and A dealers only accounted for about one-half of all sales revenue.

Average field calls per dealer account Field calls were the most expensive yet most effective component of the program, and therefore were the starting point for decisions on the allocation of marketing efforts. As Julie Kowalski, head of *TeamTBA*, described:

Profit for *TeamTBA* needed to be considered for each grade. For a dealer account in the D grade, bringing in around $1,650 of revenue and $330 of margin, a single field contact costing $200 would be ineffective and unprofitable, hence the zero demarcation in the model. In contrast, AA accounts might justify as many as 24 visits a year, or $4,800 in field expense.

Average mail contacts per dealer account The number of times a dealer would be contacted by mail was determined by HBG's experience. Virtually all direct mail solicitation was performed at least monthly; thus, even for C and D accounts, 12 contacts per year were reasonable. For higher-level accounts more frequent mailings (including targeted offerings and marketing calendars) were added (72, 48, 24 and 12).

EXHIBIT 4 Customer Contact Matrix

Customer Grade	Dollar Sales Range	Actual Avg Sales Revenue per Account	# of Accounts	Sales Revenue	Avg Mail Contacts per Account	Total Mail Contacts	Mail Cost Avg Cost per Contact $2.50	Avg Phone Calls per Account	Total Phone Calls	Phone Cost Avg Cost per Contact $16.00	Avg Field Calls per Account	Total Field Sales Calls	Field Sales Cost Avg Cost per Contact $200	Total Cost	Expense to Revenue Ratio
AA (5%)	>$30,000	$50,000	88	$4,400,000	72	6,336	$15,840	48	4,224	$67,584	24	2,112	$422,400	$505,824	11.50%
A (15%)	$20,000–$30,000	$25,000	264	$6,600,000	72	19,008	$47,520	24	6,336	$101,376	12	3,168	$633,600	$782,496	11.86%
B (25%)	$10,000–$20,000	$12,000	440	$5,280,000	48	21,120	$52,800	18	7,920	$126,720	4	1,760	$352,000	$531,520	10.07%
C (25%)	$5,000–$10,000	$6,500	440	$2,860,000	24	10,560	$26,400	12	5,280	$84,480	0	0	$0	$110,880	3.88%
D (30%)	<$5,000	$1,650	528	$871,200	12	6,336	$15,840	6	3,168	$50,688	0	0	$0	$66,528	7.64%
Total			1,760	$20,011,200		63,360	$158,400		26,928	$430,848		7,040	$1,408,000	$1,997,248	9.98%

Source: Hunter Business Group, Inc.

Average phone calls per dealer account Telephone contact frequency was also based on HBG's experience. *TeamTBA* believed that every dealer should be contacted at least every two months. As with mail contacts for higher volume dealers, more frequent phone contacts were planned.

TeamTBA planned to adjust the number of mail, phone, and field contacts to reflect changes in incoming revenue throughout the program.

"GOLD" ACCOUNTS

In order for the *TeamTBA* approach to be successful, sales teams had to provide incentives to dealers: not only so dealers would purchase larger volumes of Star products, but more importantly so they would purchase a *wider assortment* of these products. To do this, *TeamTBA* established the "Gold Account" program. A Gold Account was defined as a dealer who purchased $17,000 or more from *TeamTBA* during a given year. This $17,000 had to include at least 25 batteries ($1,250), 50 tires ($2,500), $250 in filters, and $250 in chemicals every 90 days. This translated to sales of $4,250 per quarter, or $17,000 annually. Kowalski explained:

> The heart of our methodology is to identify dealers who take a proactive approach to TBA products. Based on experience, we found that the easiest way to identify such accounts is to look at their purchase patterns. A dealer who routinely orders a certain amount of product in each category is presumably committed to selling those product categories. We are therefore interested not just in volume, but also the breadth of products purchased.

Based on this definition, an AA account that purchased $50,000 of "product" consisting only of tires would not receive Gold Account recognition. But, a B account purchasing an $18,000 combination of filters, batteries, tires, and chemicals would achieve Gold Account status due to the combination of products purchased. Consequently, Gold Accounts were not limited to AA accounts and included some in each of the AA, A, and B accounts.

Using Star information from the end of 1992, *TeamTBA* discovered that of 2,200 stations, only 14 qualified for Gold status. Vic Hunter remarked: "What looked like a very strong brand because

Month	Gold Accounts
January	–
February	14
March	46
April	55
May	87
June	116
July	105
August	122
September	136
October	145
November	154

EXHIBIT 6 Number of Gold Accounts—Year One (1993)

Source: Hunter Business Group, Inc.

80% of dealers purchased Star-branded products, proved to be poor brand foundation with weak market penetration. We were very disappointed."

TeamTBA encouraged its sales teams to increase the number of Gold Accounts by offering them $100 bonuses for each net addition to the number of Gold Accounts in their territory. Exhibit 6 shows the dramatic increase in the number of Gold accounts during 1993, the first year of the program. Hunter credited the surge to active management of customer needs. Unlike the past, when TBA representatives "pushed" products onto dealers, *TeamTBA* representatives now showed dealers how to sell TBA products more efficiently. Hunter explained:

> We helped dealers learn to market. Under the new model, our representative would notice, for instance, when a station had not purchased filters for a given time period. The *TeamTBA* rep would then demonstrate how offering a discounted oil change with every 50 gallons of gas purchased would increase the dealer's revenues.

TEAMTBA RESULTS

A few months after *TeamTBA* started operations it conducted a satisfaction survey of the 2,200 dealers (Exhibit 7). The survey results were encouraging and surprising. First, in all but one category dealer satisfaction had risen after *TeamTBA* had taken over the business. Second,

Change in Star Dealer Satisfaction Key Factor from Survey, 1993

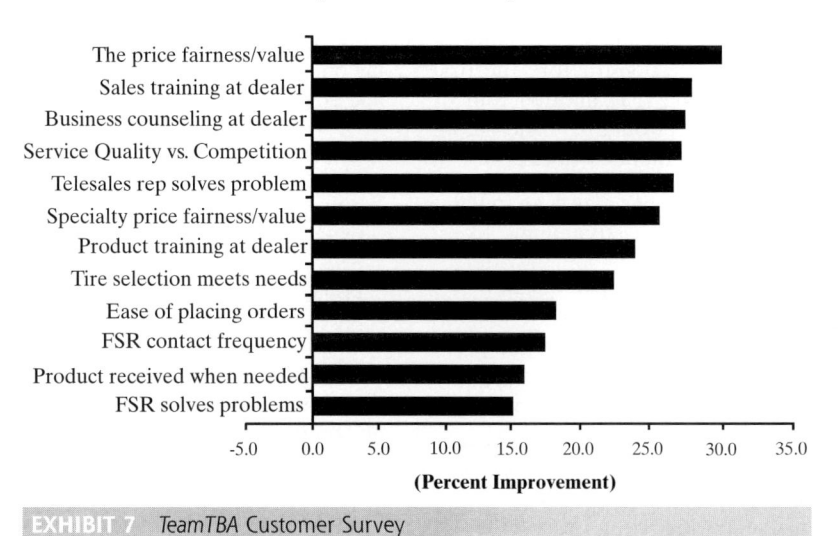

Factor	Percent Improvement
The price fairness/value	~30
Sales training at dealer	~28
Business counseling at dealer	~27
Service Quality vs. Competition	~27
Telesales rep solves problem	~26
Specialty price fairness/value	~25
Product training at dealer	~24
Tire selection meets needs	~22
Ease of placing orders	~18
FSR contact frequency	~17
Product received when needed	~15
FSR solves problems	~15

EXHIBIT 7 *TeamTBA* Customer Survey

Source: Hunter Business Group, Inc.

and perhaps more striking, was the seemingly counterintuitive increase in territory sales manager (TSM) contact frequency, despite *TeamTBA* decreasing its number of field representatives from 83 (Star) to 18 (*TeamTBA*), and decreasing its frequency of direct personal contact by 70%. Hunter clarified this point:

> Classic marketing suggests that if I [the Star rep] call dealers less frequently, I get less business . . . we went from 83 to 18 field reps—this should have spelled disaster. The survey showed that dealers' perceptions of the frequency of face-to-face contacts had actually risen. This is not as counterintuitive as it seems at first. People don't differentiate between contact media. They differentiate based on the frequency of "valued communications." If you generate valued communications by phone and through the mail that are seamlessly integrated with field activities, the overall perception is that face-to-face contact frequency has increased. Previously, a Star representative, for instance, would ordinarily visit a retailer or owner in San Antonio 50 times a year. Now, (with the *TeamTBA* model) field visits were reduced to 12 times a year, but when a dealer was asked the question "How many times does a TBA rep visit you?" they responded that the frequency had increased 17% (59 visits), much higher than it actually was (12 visits).

The survey results demonstrated the effectiveness of Hunter's integrated marketing approach. In fact, by contacting dealers through a variety of media, *TeamTBA* had actually increased the number of contacts by 600%. Hunter concluded:

> Star's main problem had been a lack of understanding about what dealers really needed—it was not face-to-face contact from field representatives. Before *TeamTBA*, Star reps had focused on the politics of the relationship between Star and its dealers, rather than focusing on tires, batteries, and accessories. Dealers saw their relationship as confrontational at best, involving prolonged meetings that accomplished little. Meetings typically had concluded with dealers buying Star's products based on a sense of obligation, or to gain access to co-op marketing funds.

Within the new business approach, the starting point was a dealer specific plan based on information recorded in the dealer master database. Next, a phone conversation between the *TeamTBA* telesales rep and the dealer would ensue to confirm the dealer's needs. More research would then be done before the first field visit. Following the visit, another four or five phone/mail contacts would be made before the next field trip. As Hunter described:

> When a *Team* member makes an initial phone contact, they say something like "I would like to talk to you about the battery program. What are some of the problems that you encounter that are not currently being addressed . . . ? And, by the way, Vic Hunter will be in your area next week. Would you like him to come in and show you our line?" If the dealer expressed an interest, the field rep would call on the dealer personally, discussing any unmet needs or other issues. Dealers then feel better about buying our products because their needs are addressed and value is being exchanged.

Other Survey Results

Several other dealer responses piqued HBG's interest. For instance, the survey confirmed the impression that a majority of the dealers carried branded TBA products. However, tires and batteries—which generated a significant portion of *TeamTBA* revenues—were being sold by only a small percentage of accounts. Secondly, it appeared that dealers' perceived value of the Star brand varied with the type of products they purchased. For example, across all dealers in the survey, 65% considered the Star brand to be of equal or greater importance than price. Yet, among those who also sold tires, this number rose to 80%. Finally, dealers reflected in their responses their reluctance "to throw out the TBA baby with the bath water." 80% of respondents reported that service bay repairs were highly important to their overall business, with an additional 16% describing such services as having average or above average importance.

EARLY SUCCESSES

Within six months of the *TeamTBA* launch, the program looked like a great success. The number of active Star accounts (those accounts having purchased within the previous 30 days) had increased 24%. Even more impressive was the significant increase in the number of Gold Accounts, which had exceeded 100 by June. Jim Jaskoske, chairman of Star's National Dealer Council, wrote a letter to council members reporting on a *TeamTBA* sales training meeting that he had attended in mid-1993:

> I can assure you that *TeamTBA*'s only objective is to help us earn a profit. Their only business is selling Star branded TBA products. We can look forward to competitive pricing, point-of-sale materials, award programs, quantity discounts, and the fastest possible delivery service.

Hunter was delighted that the results of the dealer satisfaction survey seemed to prove the merits of his firm's customer contact matrix. Even though face-to-face contact had decreased by 70% or more in many cases, dealers were more satisfied with the sales interactions they had under the *TeamTBA* program than they ever had been. Over 85% of respondents in the survey considered *TeamTBA* to offer equal or better service than that of Star, and nearly 30% found that service to be "much better" than previous service offerings. Nearly 40% of dealers reported that the Star brand added a 15% premium to the prices they were able to charge.

Through 1993, the good news continued for *TeamTBA*, as cumulative first year sales passed the target of $20 million. While this represented about half of the revenue generated a year earlier, the cost of sales had plummeted, thereby meeting the initial goal of attaining profitability for the *TeamTBA* program.

However, one concern was beginning to grow. By the beginning of 1994, it looked as though the number of active accounts and total sales volume had begun to level off. Further, Star had launched a program to convert franchised service stations at major intersections (usually *TeamTBA*'s best customers) into convenience stores with no service facilities. The number of service stations with service bays was also expected to fall from 2,200 to 1,700 in the next year or two.

PLANNING FOR THE JOURNEY AHEAD

As she reviewed the situation for the coming year, Julie Kowalski made an assumption that there would be 1,500 active accounts. Based on the data and projections she had before her, she also expected the average sales volume within each account grade to decline, and that *TeamTBA*'s sales revenues would drop to around $16 million in 1994. Along with Vic Hunter and the rest of the management team, she set out to develop a plan that would allow product costs and margins as a percentage of revenues to remain constant for the next year, leaving *TeamTBA* with an expected operating income of $360,000 for 1994. Based on this, Kowalski began evaluating her options, knowing that *TeamTBA*'s strategy could take any of several approaches.

As one approach, Kowalski could assume that *TeamTBA*'s fixed costs would remain constant at $1.5 million. This meant that they would not shut down any facilities, abandon any territories, or scale back operational expenses associated with running the TBA program. By freezing these fixed costs, *TeamTBA* would have only $1.34 million to spend on direct marketing and sales efforts. They would thus have to reduce sales and marketing expenditures by $660,000 from 1993 in order to meet their $360,000 profitability target.

This scenario raised several obstacles. First, there was the sales force question. At present, the cost of salaries for the *TeamTBA* sales force exceeded $1.6 million (Exhibit 5). It appeared impossible, then, to meet the new profitability target without drastically cutting back the sales and marketing force—whether in mail, telesales, or field sales. Indeed, Kowalski even wondered if there was any merit to eliminating the field sales force entirely and establishing *TeamTBA* as a premier telesales operation. Just looking at the original matrix, she recognized that such a move could eliminate $1.4 million in costs.

Kowalski knew that making such a move could create a serious morale problem within the team, so she weighed the expected cost recovery against the likely adverse reactions among the remaining *TeamTBA* sales force and the Star dealers who were their valued customers. She also knew that the fruits of such cost recovery would be partially consumed in the investments required to expand telemarketing capacity.

A second strategy would be to maintain the fixed component of *TeamTBA*'s operating expenses at a constant *percentage of revenue*, or 40%–45%. This would equal $1.28 million, given Kowalski's projection of $2.84 million for total 1994 operating costs. Such a move, however, would leave only $1.56 million for sales and marketing costs—a figure that included salary expense. Consequently, a certain number of jobs would still have to be cut.

A third alternative strategy would be a hybrid approach. This scenario involved reducing fixed costs as well as sales and marketing costs by 20%, consistent with the 20% decline in revenues from 1993. *TeamTBA* could do this in a variety of ways. They could make wholesale changes in the frequency of contacts by mail, phone, or field; they could try to increase the number of Gold Accounts and make an effort to boost sales volume among the highest performers, while decreasing or terminating contacts among C and D accounts; or they could experiment with a combination of the two: adjusting contact frequency and encouraging more dealers to "step up" to the Gold Account level.

EXHIBIT 5 *TeamTBA Direct Marketing Sales Force Salary Information (1993)*

Employee Category	Number of Employees	Fully Burdened Salary	Total Salary Cost to HBG	Total Contact Cost for HBG	% of Total Contact Cost Attributed to Employee Salary
Field sales	18	$70,000	$1,260,000	$1,408,000	89%
Telesales	6	$56,000	$336,000	$430,848	76%
Mail	1.5	$36,000	$54,000	$158,400	34%
Total	25		$1,650,000	$1,997,248	

There were several questions that needed to be addressed with this hybrid approach. Would reducing the number of contacts hasten the decline in revenues? Was it possible for *TeamTBA* to improve its effectiveness over 1993 levels by developing Gold accounts? Was the team capable of getting these dealers to buy more TBA products? After all, TBA products were not their primary source of revenues. Was this asking for too much from the dealers?

Amidst all this, Hunter, Kowalski, and the management team were debating whether this was the time to change their sales compensation structure from trying to maximize revenue to maximizing contribution margin. Hunter explained: "By educating the sales force on the costs of TBA products and the types of purchasing arrangements that would be most conducive to *maximizing contribution margin*, we could get them to make more autonomous decisions on how to manage individual dealer accounts. This would align their efforts with our goal of managing the sales-to-expense ratio." Would this move be counterproductive as well?

In the face of all the questions associated with each of the options, Hunter and Kowalski needed to come up with a plan to counter the forthcoming decline in revenues. ■

◆◆◆ CMR Enterprises

Case 11-2 CMR Enterprises

Mary Neuner Caravella and Das Narayandas

Sam Marcus ran his hand over the curved maple edge of the next day's shipment as he listened to his sales manager describe the latest telephone exchange with Blackstone Homes, one of their company's largest customers. The smooth wood of the custom desk contrasted sharply with his turbulent thoughts about the relationship with this customer, which promised such growth, but had grown increasingly difficult to manage. Marcus had been running CMR Enterprises (formerly Mike's Cabinets) since he and his partner had bought the 25-year-old architectural millwork company from its founder two years earlier. Revenues from Blackstone, a new customer, represented a significant part of 1998 sales growth for the small, Nebraska-based company, and he was counting on further growth to pay his debt and fund expansion efforts in 1999. But as the residential construction season warmed up with the spring sun, conversations with and about Blackstone had become increasingly heated. Marcus knew something had to change before the summer crunch.

BACKGROUND

The acquisition of Mike's Cabinets and creation of CMR Enterprises had grown out of a friendship born during Sam Marcus's second year at Harvard Business School (HBS). Asked to write a paper for his fall Entrepreneurial Management class on an admired entrepreneur, Marcus (HBS '94) had chosen William Walters, who had founded and successfully grown five businesses. Walters had turned 55 that fall and was in the process of selling his business interests to focus on more leisurely pursuits.

Impressed by Marcus and his desire to own a business, Walters had kept in touch as the HBS grad searched for a job that might present such an opportunity. Then one day in early February 1994, Walters had phoned Marcus: having just sold his last company he was looking for places to invest and had decided to invest in Marcus. If they could find the right $5 million business to acquire, Walters offered to partner with Marcus 50/50, with Walters providing the financing and Marcus the "sweat equity." "After I picked myself up off the floor and talked to my wife," Marcus recalled,

---

The case was prepared by E-Business Fellow Mary Neuner Caravella (under the direction of Professor Das Narayandas). Copyright © 2000 by the President and Fellows of Harvard College. Harvard Business School Case 501-012.

Walters and I discussed how we would find the right business to partner on. My previous employer was in restructuring mode and had offered me a position that provided opportunities to see deal flow in an industry where I had experience. I ended up taking that job with the understanding by all parties that I would continue to work with Walters and look for a company for us to acquire.

Sixteen months later, my employer offered me the opportunity to run a $25 million division, but with a catch; they wanted a five-year commitment and I had to stop the search with Walters. I resigned. My wife and I had still been living the student lifestyle to minimize burn; we had about six months before we maxed our credit cards. As it turned out, Walters agreed to fund our search and we investigated 22 companies before making an offer on Mike's Cabinets.

We were looking for a company with good cash flow in a "B" industry, someplace where I could "put together 'A' players and do well," but where I had some room to make mistakes without losing the company. We had a three-pronged strategy to our search: a focused search in industries and areas where I knew I could add value; a more general search of small-cap, publicly traded companies where we had access to financials; and, finally, the opportunistic "put out the word that we're looking and see what shows up search." Mike's Cabinets came from the last strategy. We made an offer in February 1997 and signed the deal on June 11.

MIKE'S CABINETS AND THE CUSTOM ARCHITECTURAL MILLWORK INDUSTRY

Mike's Cabinets was one of 1,500 mostly small companies that made up the custom architectural millwork industry, which produced custom installed woodwork, cabinetry, and furnishings for businesses and high-end homes. (See Exhibit 1 for examples of architectural millwork products.) Marcus explained:

> Most of the companies in the industry were started by guys who liked woodworking and had enough entrepreneurial drive to go it alone. You can enter the market with relatively little capital investment. But in many cases, the company grows only to the size where the owner can still "get sawdust on his hands." The owner starts making enough money in the business to be comfortable: any bigger and the owner isn't doing what he likes to do anymore. So there are a lot of little companies, each selling primarily to the local contractors in their regions.

Architectural millwork companies competed in both residential and commercial construction markets. To residential markets they provided custom cabinets and millwork for both new and remodeled homes. Most residential work was kitchen and bathroom cabinetry, a $4.8 billion market in the United States in 1996. Only about 15% of homebuilders contracted for custom cabinetry, typically for high-end homes that might include specialized items like entertainment centers in addition to kitchen and bathroom cabinetry. The more frequent choice was to use stock or semi-custom cabinets made and marketed nationally by companies such as Masco and Triangle Pacific and sold through dealers and home centers such as Home Depot.

The largest commercial market was for retail store fixtures, although architectural millwork companies also supplied executive suites and lobbies for office buildings and customized wood interior components for banks and doctors' offices, among other buildings. Commercial projects split relatively evenly between new construction and remodeling. Estimates of market size varied widely upwards of $5 billion in the United States in 1996.

Mike's Cabinets, based in Lincoln, Nebraska, when Marcus and Walters bought it in 1997, employed 115 people and was doing $6.8 million in annual sales, which put it in the top 5% in its industry. Started in 1975, it had been working in a subcontractor relationship supplying custom cabinetry to the general contractors who built homes. When the housing market entered a recession in the early 1980s, Mike's Cabinets had begun remodeling office buildings and other commercial spaces again in a subcontracting capacity. Although commercial work grew to two-thirds of its projects and 80% of its sales, much of the company's pride continued to derive from its residential work. Marcus remarked:

> Our residential products were something that every employee could relate to

EXHIBIT 1 Examples of Cabinetry and Millwork Manufactured by CMR Enterprises

Source: Company promotional materials.

and every employee had a story of a friend or family member who loved their cabinets from Mike's. At one of the first social events I attended in town I talked to a woman who told me about the wonderful person from Mike's who installed her cabinets and how he went back and strengthened a VCR shelf when he saw that her small children would end up climbing on it. This "Mike's Way" was something the employees, and I, were very proud of and it helped the company maintain premium pricing and good margins.

FROM MIKE'S CABINETS TO CMR ENTERPRISES

"When we bought the company in June 1997 and renamed it CMR Enterprises," recalled Marcus,

we were definitely a shock to the company and to the community. This is a small town. The previous owners grew up here, grew their business here, and had become very prominent in the business community. We were outsiders who didn't know the industry. We met with the entire company on the first day and our most important message was that we knew we had a lot to learn and that we weren't going to make major changes right away. No one was going to get fired tomorrow.

But we also made it clear from the start that we had aggressive goals for growth. At this first meeting we introduced our goal of $70 million in sales by 2007. For a company that had taken 22 years to get to $7 million this was really big really fast and I was looking out at a lot of skeptical faces.

Marcus spent much of his first few months with employees and customers. He got to know his employees personally at lunches, group events, or individual dinners to which he also invited spouses. He met with each of the company's top 50 customers to learn about their impressions of it and about the issues they faced. He also spent time in the shop learning the manufacturing processes, in the office learning how sales and project management worked, and with employees working to document all these processes. At the end of long days spent learning the business Marcus always came back to two issues:

Increasing profits and cash flow was always at the top of my list. The company had taken on a lot of debt, both in a note to the previous owners and the money that my partner had invested. The growth in the commercial business was tough on our cash flow since the project cycles were generally six months or more and we got paid mostly at the end. The growth of the residential business in that first year really helped a lot and their project cycles were more like four to six weeks. I knew I needed management help to get my arms around the financial issues, so a CFO was the first new person I hired, about four months after I took over.

I also thought a lot about how to lay a foundation for growing the kind of company I wanted to grow at the rate I wanted to grow it. Part of the challenge was how to make a scaleable and replicable business model in this industry. This business has an inherently geographic piece, based on economically delivering large, bulky products, and, we believe, developing personal relationships with the local decision makers. So I focused on building the foundation for a franchise-oriented business model, starting with documenting our processes. I envisioned franchises with $8–$15 million in sales, local sales operations and some amount of local production. To avoid setting premature expectations on what would actually be in any location, I used the term "footprint" instead of franchise. I would talk to employees about perfecting the footprint here in Nebraska, then branching out to other locations.

The second part of laying the foundation was making sure that the employees were actively involved in doing it. I wanted them to feel ownership for what we were building. This was personally important to me and I also believe it is the best way to attract and keep good people. So we spent time as a company developing a creed that described our core principles [see Exhibit 2].

As the first year drew to a close, Marcus began make more significant changes. First, he began to invest in information technology and develop information systems based on the process

> **Our Creed...**
>
> 1. **Vision:** *know the course*
> 2. **Integrity:** *habitual adherence to our standards*
> 3. **Custom:** *custom product & custom service*
> 4. **Teaching:** *a shared responsibility to educate*
> 5. **Quality:** *a mindset of all*
> 6. **Delivery:** *on time, every time*
> 7. **Productivity:** *low cost producer*
> 8. **Metrics:** *plan, measure and continuously improve*
> 9. **Technology:** *the right info to the right person the right way*
> 10. **Marketing:** *divide and conquer*
> 11. **Diversified Customer Base:** *achieve sustainable growth*
> 12. **Community:** *commitment to the communities we serve*

EXHIBIT 2 CMR Enterprises Creed (Company Records)

information that had been gathered. (There were only been three computers in the entire company when Marcus took over.) Second, he began to reconfigure the plant to improve productivity. Finally, he hired a VP of Sales and, after developing a list of target accounts for the next year (see Exhibit 3), added the company's first commercial salesperson.

Commercial Work

There were at least three roles involved in any commercial construction job that CMR Enterprises bid. The owner, who was the ultimate customer for the other two roles, paid for jobs. The architect or designer was responsible for designing and developing detailed drawings (or architectural plans) for the project, the general contractor for turning the plan into the finished project by a specified date. The latter roles might involve different companies or both be performed by the same company depending on the project. Often, for example, large retailers' in-house design firms developed store design plans for projects all over the world. For other design-build contracts, a single firm might both develop and execute the design.

General contractors solicited bids from subcontractors such as CMR for portions of a project as specified in the architectural plans. Large contractors often had many project managers and detailed processes for soliciting, comparing, and awarding subcontractor bids. CMR had traditionally subscribed to FW Dodge and MSA (Manufacturers Survey Association), plan services that listed active commercial projects and provided plans on paper or microfilm or electronically, from which it got about 50 projects per week, or about 75%–80% of the projects it looked at. These were generally "open market" projects, in which contractors bidding to project owners would accept unsolicited subcontractor bids.

CMR Enterprises had two goals for its new sales team: to improve the odds of winning open market bids by building relationships with contractors; and to find or create opportunities for negotiating bids among a limited number of acceptable bidders. Among the obstacles to these goals that had to be overcome, according to CMR's VP of Sales, was that

> The general contractors weren't used to having salespeople from this industry call on them; none of our competitors have a direct sales force. In fact, our customers often have "plan rooms" in the front office so that subcontractors can come in and get the information they need to bid from architectural drawings without ever talking to the general contractor.

Having identified a bid opportunity and secured the architectural drawings, CMR

EXHIBIT 3 Top 50 Contractor Prospects for Fiscal Year 1999 (ranked by sales team)

Target Rank	Market-Area Served	Metro Area (Commercial) Rank	Revenue	95-Present "Got Rate"	Revenues FY 1997	FY 1998
A1	Commercial-Metro	7	$116.5 MM	50%	$29,329	$239,878
A2	Commercial-Metro	3	232.2 MM	65%	47,561	370,369
A3	Commercial-Metro	11	87.0 MM	3%	18,273	90,776
A4	Commercial-Metro			42%	34,795	n/a
A5	Commercial-Metro	23	35.0 MM	23%	$304	n/a
A6	Commercial-Metro			42%	75,446	73,729
A7	Commercial-Metro			33%	28,261	76,553
A8	Commercial-Metro			38%	109,574	249,794
A9	Commercial-Metro	1	785.8 MM	15%	53,110	197,219
A10	Commercial-Metro			22%	55,575	n/a
A11	Commercial-Metro	2	450.0 MM	7%	109,648	9,927
A12	Commercial-Metro	4	183.0 MM	7%	31,158	3,414
A13	Commercial-Metro	6	130.5 MM	11%	5,511	102,704
A14	Commercial-Metro	5	172.0 MM	27%	287,504	154,507
A15	Commercial-Metro	20	42.0 MM	n/a	n/a	3,822
A16	Commercial-Metro	22	40.0 MM	44%	38,836	303,179
A17	Commercial-Metro	9	97.4 MM	50%	78,720	259,622
A18	Commercial-Metro			52%	204,726	360,169
A19	Commercial-Metro	24	32.0 MM	17%	n/a	84,489
A20	Commercial-Metro	12	53.2 MM	43%	41,630	26,601
A21	Commercial-Metro			43%	281,900	47,849
A22	Commercial-Metro			46%	n/a	n/a
A23	Commercial-Metro			40%	13,979	55,146
A24	Commercial-Metro	8	98.0 MM	25%	28,941	n/a
A25	Commercial-Metro			7%	30,384	66,434
B1	Commercial-Local			n/a	12,545	2,664
B2	Commercial-Local			21%	7,626	64,107
B3	Commercial-Local			72%	67,826	102,472
B4	Commercial-Local			51%	n/a	105,991
B5	Commercial-Local			21%	1,953	13,206
B6	Commercial-Local			86%	180,775	198,182
B7	Commercial-Local			85%	102,756	927
B8	Commercial-Local			71%	84,683	27,519
B9	Commercial-Local			n/a	41,760	7,309
B10	Commercial-Local			n/a	1,613	33,100
R1	Blackstone			n/a	32,295	303,237
R2	Residential-Local			n/a	27,188	75,298
R3	Residential-Local			n/a	n/a	438
R4	Residential-Local			n/a	13,199	37,156
R5	Residential-Local			n/a	2,898	32,713
R6	Residential-Local			n/a	43,668	22,813
R7	Residential-Local			n/a	60,684	36,210
R8	Residential-Local			n/a	296	42,176
R9	Residential-Local			n/a	850	19,792
R10	Residential-Local			n/a	114,842	117,245
R11	Residential-Local			n/a	6,663	17,816
R12	Residential-Local			n/a	7,453	8,943
R13	Residential-Local			n/a	34,085	60,869
R14	Residential-Local			n/a	9,262	n/a
R15	Residential-Local			n/a	3,753	51,695

Source: Company records

needed to develop a bid. The skills required to accurately estimate the time and materials needed to design, manufacture, and deliver the customized products it manufactured were considered fairly industry-specific. Because developing an estimate could take from half an hour to seven days, this task was closely monitored at CMR. Explained the head of the estimating team:

> I take a look at each plan to find sections of work we'd be interested in bidding. About 50% of the potential projects make it past our first cut, which is based on whether there is enough work to meet our minimum job size (currently $15K) and whether the delivery date is further out than our lead time (currently 12 weeks). At this point, I make an "estimate estimate," the time I think it will take to estimate the job, and add the job to the estimating schedule. If the schedule is full, then I'll start prioritizing estimates based on different markets. For example, we do better at winning jobs for doctors' offices than we do for apartment buildings.
>
> The estimator then does a "takeoff"— goes through the architectural plans and takes off the specifications, dimensions, materials, etc. for the sections of work we are bidding. From that the estimator determines the materials and labor it will take to deliver to the specification and also gets "buyout" pricing and lead time on anything that we won't actually manufacture, but instead will buy from an outside vendor.

Estimates were turned into one-page bid proposals. CMR bid a single price for each section designated by standardized industry descriptors such as "architectural woodwork" and "wood casework." Bid proposals were sent to the general contractors and incorporated into their project bids. The same bid proposal was sent to each of the general contractors for an open market job. The sales team was responsible for following up open bids; an inside salesperson spent most of the day on the phone with contractors following projects and trying to close orders. Between 15% and 20% of CMR's bid proposals resulted in orders. Price was always a factor and was rarely negotiated once a bid was submitted, although that was changing as CMR's salespeople created more negotiated bid situations.

Under Marcus, CMR had developed a formal hand-off procedure from sales to project management. When a contractor issued a purchase order, a file was generated with all the paper and electronic information about the job, an information checklist was used to ensure that required data were present and accurate, and a letter was sent to the contractor introducing the project manager who would be taking over the job. It was at this point that a project was considered a "got" and the salesperson credited with the order. Project managers were assigned as their schedules permitted, but each worked regularly with about half a dozen contractors. Explained a project manager, "When you have worked with a contractor for several jobs they trust that you'll get the job done without them calling to follow up all the time, which makes things easier for everyone." A project manager was typically responsible for 18–20 active projects each worth on average $30–$80,000.

Project managers met with the lead draftsman to develop the shop drawings and material selections needed to build the job. Completed drawings were sent via the general contractor to the architect for approval. About this time the project manager would visit the site to take field measurements to finalize the construction drawings. Explained a project manager:

> In addition to getting exact measurements that we'll use in construction, I'm also looking to see that there are no conflicts between what we're planning and the electrical, plumbing, and heating plans. If I see problems I'll alert the contractor. I'm also looking at things that will impact delivery, like how will our products get from the delivery truck to the space they will be installed in? How big are the elevators? Are there any tight corners? It's much better to build something in pieces that can be attached on site than for the contractor to find out when the delivery truck arrives that a desk won't fit into the elevator!

Other than this on-site visit, most communication with contractors was over the phone. CMR project managers spoke with contractors' project management teams at least once a week throughout a project, escalating to multiple times per day as material was delivered. A project manager described:

> While we are working on the shop drawings I'll talk by phone with the contractor or architect about design questions. Sometimes I'll suggest changes to details that allow us to reduce costs by using a more standardized cabinet or something that we've designed before. I'm also spending a lot of time on schedules. Millwork/cabinet companies have a reputation in the industry for being late, so contractors tend to build buffers into their dates. But if we deliver too early our products may be in the way of other contractors or ... get damaged while they're waiting to be installed. You have to build enough trust with the contractor to get realistic dates.

New management brought changes in the project manager role, as a project manager observed:

> It's more complicated now. In the past we didn't have a sales force and I would have done most everything myself. Things seem to take longer this way—you have to wait on people—but we're working on it because it's necessary for us to grow. The new ownership has set goals a lot higher. And we have a lot more information now; before we never really knew if we were doing well or doing poorly unless cabinets started coming back through the door.

Residential Work

CMR continued to sell to the residential market under the Mike's Cabinets name. Even as the new management team was adding sales resources to increase commercial sales, Mike's Cabinets' reputation and a booming construction market was increasing residential sales. Although some homeowners hired architects and interior designers, many relied on contractors for both design and construction. Because many design details were often left with the homeowner, most cabinet shops in the area, including Mike's Cabinets, maintained showrooms where homeowners could view options for cabinets. Mike's Cabinets' showroom was open from 7:30 a.m. to 4:30 p.m. and the 10 or so homeowners who visited per week could arrive at any time, though most made appointments. The residential sales manager described the buying process:

> For a new home, the contractor would give the homeowner an allowance, say, $6,000, for cabinets. The allowance is generally intended to cover a basic kitchen and bathroom layout, pre-finished and installed. The homeowner would then visit our showroom and maybe two or three other shops and decide on the specific cabinets, materials, and colors. We would work up drawings and a price for the job and send that price to the contractor to apply against the allowance. If the price was over the allowance the homeowner would have to pay the difference.
>
> I would try to pull out qualification information before I showed them anything. By the time the customer got to us, which was usually six weeks to two months before they closed on the house, they had already been dealing with other subcontractors, like the fixture people and the carpet people, and they knew that the allowance generally got them the low end. Just by talking with them and watching their reactions I could figure out how much extra cash they had for upgrades. Cabinetry is a big expense and it's one of the things that really stands out in a house. But buying custom cabinets is a new experience for most people and they don't necessarily know what to look for in construction quality, for example. By the end of that first hour-long meeting I generally knew whether or not I was going to get the order and that affected how I followed up and priced the job.

Mike's Cabinets developed from a customer's design choices a set of basic shop drawings and quote that would subsequently be sent to a contractor. This activity took about 90 minutes, including 30 minutes of estimating, which was a somewhat different task than for commercial projects. The estimating manager explained:

> There was rarely more than one contractor involved in a job; the homeowner picked a contractor before coming to us. And the plans

we were working from were less defined up front. We would do our estimate based on some basic plans that had a lot of notes added by our salesperson. There also tended to be more revisions, the more elaborate plans could go through three to four revisions before things were finalized.

The company estimated that between 45%–55% of homeowners who arrived at the showroom with an allowance ended up placing an order. As in commercial work, a project manager assumed responsibility for implementation, but the handoff from sales and project management was rarely as clean. There appeared to be a number of reasons for this. According to one project manager:

> The homeowner mostly drives this; they don't want to be handed off and they work with one person at most of our competitors. But also, a lot of the right questions about livability—the things that will make the homeowner happy with their decisions—can't be asked until you get on-site. Cabinetry is a particularly visual element in a home; everyone who comes in your house sees it, especially in upper-end homes with lots of custom shelving and entertainment systems in addition to the cabinets in the kitchen and bathrooms. But it can be difficult for a homeowner to look at standardized drawings and imagine what their customized house will look like when it actually is built. We end up doing individualized layouts for each family and about 30% of the time I'll end up re-doing a layout based on the conversation I have on-site with the homeowner. That extra touch is the reason we have such a good reputation in custom cabinetry.

Of the approximately 70 contractors within a 30-mile radius Mike's Cabinets had worked with about a dozen in the last year and with most of them at some point in its history. The company expended little effort marketing to residential contractors, letting its execution do its selling. With many choices now made by homeowners, this appeared to be working for Mike's Cabinets. Explained the company's residential sales manager: "Over the years we have built relationships with building contractors and we work to keep them as loyal customers. But there are a lot of small cabinet shops, so in today's market our goal is referrals from contractors, for them to say to the homeowner, 'Go to Mike's. They've got a good product. They're always on time.'"

DEVELOPING INFOCENTRAL

With both a new sales team and the project management team now interacting with customers, maintaining and communicating information about what was going on at customer accounts became extremely important. Remarked a project manager:

> Sales sets the stage, but selling doesn't stop once we get the order. My job is to maintain the relationship as the liaison between CMR and the contractor. We used to be called project coordinators and we actually did all the project tasks, like revising drawings. Now, as project managers, we are making sure that everything happens in engineering, drafting, purchasing, etc. so that the job gets done right. Keeping InfoCentral up-to-date and accurate is key. The information flow is too difficult to manage otherwise.

The InfoCentral the project manager referred to was a set of software tools CMR had begun to develop to document work flow and manage project and customer information. InfoCentral represented a significant commitment of time and resources. One of the first components to be developed supported the new commercial salespeople. CMR's VP of Sales described the effort that went into developing sales processes and the computer systems that supported them.

> To make our footprint (franchise) concept work we knew we had to distribute customer and opportunity information across the company, but both the salespeople and I initially resisted it. If I was going to have to use a system like this I was going to make it very useful for me and I felt the same way for my sales team. So we spent a lot of time customizing software to support the procedures we were putting in place and to get rid of administrative work. For example, the system now automatically generates sales calls that are due

based on the salesperson's assessment of how often the customer should be called.... The salesperson uses this to plan his week and then prints out a schedule and "road pack" with customer contacts, active projects and lots of other information that will help him during each call. Of course, I can then see where the salespeople are going each week. But the information that generates the recommended call list and the actual schedule is left up to the salespeople. Either they can believe in the system and adhere to it because they are making the decisions or I can tell them and they can resist me.

Marcus and I spent several weeks in early 1999 actually going on sales calls ourselves using the procedures and tools we had developed. We changed a lot after that based on what we learned on the ground! Now we have solid sales processes that we think will work as we expand to other footprints. The salespeople not only use it, they depend on it.

Marcus was also investing heavily in the job costing and project management components of InfoCentral, which were to be used for both commercial and residential projects. He explained:

I constantly pushed people to think of CMR as an information company that happened to make cabinets. To grow, we needed to improve how information moved around the company. Of more immediate concern to me was getting data to get our arms around what things cost and where we were making money. We were running pretty blind. For years the company had been using a rule of thumb about how much revenue they should generate per shop hour: around $65/hour. Our fully burdened shop rate for the 75 shop employees was $16/hour and we were adding lots of overhead. With the new salespeople and executive team our SG&A had grown to $2.9 million in 1998—investments for growth, but much more than we needed at our current sales level. I knew that ratio needed to go up, but I didn't know what it should be or even if it was still a useful metric.

Over time, the systems began to provide more granular data. For example, material costs for commercial jobs averaged 34% of revenue versus 26% for residential jobs. The systems also automated data gathering for a key customer measurement, what CMR called the "got rate" (i.e., the percentage of bids for which they got orders, contractor by contractor.) (See Exhibit 3.) Explained Marcus:

There are three steps that stand between us bidding a job and getting an order: the owner may get the bids from the contractors and decide to delay or cancel the project; the contractor we bid to may lose to another contractor; or we may lose to another cabinet shop. The got rate incorporated all three of these elements and we could pull got rates apart and look at them as we needed to. A lot of our relationship-building efforts were focused on increasing got rates.

VALUING RELATIONSHIPS

Process improvement-oriented investments in people and infrastructure notwithstanding, CMR still lost many bids. Marcus observed:

This is still fundamentally bid-spec work and low bids win. Some of my competitors don't bid at all when their shops are full, then they rush in with lowball bids once their shops are empty. I understand it—I have to keep my shop running, too—but it can be really depressing, not to mention expensive, to work your butt off selling to a customer and developing a bid proposal only to lose it to a competitor you haven't seen in six months.

CMR's VP of Sales offered this view of relationships in the commercial market:

Relationships are still important in a bid-spec environment; we can change our customers and our customers can change us. For example, our customers used to never give us delivery dates. Over time we learned how to ask the right questions and they learned how we used the information. Now we don't bid a project without a delivery date and as a result we can execute better, which helps both of us.

Added a project manager:

Ninety percent of the time our contact for commercial work is the general contractor. You could say there's a lot of wasted work going on there in bidding all those jobs that we end up losing. But if only one subcontractor bids on a project, then the general contractor is not really doing his job for his customer, the owner. So even unsuccessful bids help us build relationships with general contractors, since by bidding we are helping them do their job.

Marcus related one 1998 success story that appeared to show that CMR's new sales approach was paying off.

> A commercial contractor with almost $120 million in revenues hadn't solicited a bid from us in almost 10 years, ever since a project manager, who was now the president, had a bad experience with some of our product. We got lucky and our salesperson called on a new project manager who didn't know this history. We had also been calling on the owner of one of this contractor's big projects and the owner's endorsement really helped us get our first big bid opportunity, which opened the door to a meeting with the president at which we found out about his history. We got his backing, got the order, and grew that account from almost nothing in 1997 to almost $240 thousand in 1998. It was our sixth-largest account last year and things are really going well this year, too.

BLACKSTONE HOMES

Another relationship that had initially appeared even more promising was Blackstone Homes, a new residential customer founded by two young entrepreneurs in 1995. By early 1997 it had become one of the largest homebuilders in the area.

Blackstone started with open areas of land and developed entire subdivision communities, building the streets, installing utilities, in some cases building common use facilities such as playgrounds and tennis courts, and, finally, building the homes. The company had started in the first-time-homebuyer market, but by 1997 had three subdivisions in progress at different price points: small, often starter homes around $120,000; family homes from $150–$200,000; and luxury homes from $200,000 up. Blackstone was marketed to homebuyers as offering the best quality for the lowest prices. One of its strategies for making this approach profitable was to partner closely with subcontractors that could handle its entire demand and then permit the homeowners to make selections only from its partner subcontractors. This approach was unique in the market.

In the fall of 1997, a few months after Marcus took over Mike's Cabinets, Blackstone's president walked into the showroom to discuss a partnership. Marcus recalled:

> The shop he was working with was delivering late and he suspected they couldn't handle the workload. Cabinet installation was only a few weeks before closing so delays at this point were an especially critical problem for him. He came to us based on our reputation in the community and good experiences with a few projects we had recently done with him.
>
> The volume alone was compelling, but it also seemed like a great strategic fit. When we had bought the company the residential market seemed like a great opportunity for a company with a scaleable, replicable business model, and we had talked a lot with the employees about improving processes and growing the residential market. Unfortunately for us, others also saw the potential at about the same time and the market began consolidating literally under our feet. But here was one of the biggest customers in the area giving us an opportunity for immediate market share and his volume supported our goals to standardize our processes into flexible cells. We had heard that they were hard on their subs, but he saw the value we could provide and was willing to pay full price.

Blackstone was planning to build 40 homes in the next 12 months, 70 homes in the following 12 months, and then ramp a little more slowly. A partnership was established whereby Blackstone agreed to specify only CMR's cabinets in its homes and CMR to assign the project manager who had worked on the previous projects to work exclusively with Blackstone. The project manager began immediately to define and install cabinets in the model homes in the subdivisions that were Blackstone's primary sales tool. Blackstone developed cabinet allowances from those models, which it rolled into home prices and passed on to homeowners. Recounted Marcus:

> The first year was great. Blackstone did direct all its customers our way, and grew to be 25% of our residential business. The

ability to start with a standard plan for a model home and modify from there really fit well with the changes we were making in the manufacturing processes during that time. And with them growing so fast, it really appeared that their staff valued our expertise. I had heard from the sales manager that their staff was pretty overextended and that we would sometimes correct things that they otherwise would miss.

But I had some concerns, too. For example, I was out in the shop one day and noticed a whole set of cabinets sitting off to the side. I asked what was going on with them and the shop manager told me that Blackstone had changed a piece at the last minute and so the other pieces were waiting while that last piece was rushed through. I logged into our project management system to see if I could get details, but there wasn't any information about the change in there. So I went to talk to the project manager, who was on the phone, and I could hear yelling at the other end. Turns out it was someone from Blackstone screaming about that same delivery even though from everything we could tell the cabinets were late because of homeowner changes.

BLACKSTONE HOMES: YEAR 2

In the fall of 1998, after doing business with CMR for about a year, Blackstone's president called Marcus to discuss pricing.

He knew how much business he was sending our way and thought that we must be gaining operating efficiencies that would translate into lower prices. But we hadn't yet seen those efficiencies. For example, homeowners still came to our showroom, so we had to have our salesperson available. Also, neither of us seemed to be very good at limiting changes that homeowners wanted to make to the designs.

Marcus asked his residential team to meet with Blackstone to discuss ways they might work together to reduce costs and, ultimately, prices. The companies agreed to pursue cost reductions by limiting CMR's interaction with the homeowners. When Blackstone sold a home it would collect the cabinet selections from the homeowner based on the model home. The Blackstone project manager would then fax to the CMR project manager a cabinet specification sheet that included the name of the model home upon which the home design was based and the choices Blackstone had discussed with the homeowner. The CMR project manager would then have the appropriate design drawings the homeowner's cabinet choices and decisions, and the name of the company that would be supplying appliances (around which the kitchen cabinets would be built). Believing that this would reduce costs, CMR gave Blackstone a price reduction for the cabinets specified in the model homes.

But the agreement proved harder to enforce than either company had anticipated. Blackstone homeowners still worked directly with many other subcontractors; knowing that their cabinets were coming from Mike's they continued to visit CMR's showroom. Homeowners who could afford upgrades presented an opportunity for CMR to increase its profits; CMR billed Blackstone for upgrades and Blackstone, in turn, increased the price the homeowner paid at closing.

There were also, according to a residential project manager, project coordination problems:

Cabinetry often is the framework for other elements; the plumbers have to know where the sink will be to bring in the pipes to the faucet and drain. But we were working independently from the other subcontractors and each of us were making our own little modifications to the standard design based on discussions with the homeowners. So sometimes it wasn't until you got out to do field measurements that you realized that, for example, a cabinet you designed was going to end up right in front of a heating vent.

Ideally, the contractor is coordinating all of this. But regardless, if something is wrong you're going to be making a new cabinet and fighting about who pays for the mistake. And Blackstone yells a lot. After a while it became easier to spend the time going out to the site and making a detailed construction drawing up front in order to coordinate more easily with the other subcontractors and be clear about what were billable changes. Only then the other contractors started calling us instead of Blackstone to get drawings.

INCREASING CONCERNS

Marcus was also concerned that his focus on managing processes and information wasn't paying off on the residential side the way it was on the commercial side. With an experienced sales manager, two experienced project managers, and an operations manager with considerable experience in residential work, Marcus had taken a hands-off approach with residential sales. Marcus made one demand: that enough information was entered into InfoCentral to enable the CFO to roll up financials and operating measurements for the company. Acknowledged Marcus:

> I knew that the residential business was different enough from commercial that the same strategies and systems we had developed didn't quite fit. I wanted them to have ownership for managing their information and, to be fair, I was focused on the commercial side where we were bringing in people with less experience and creating things from scratch. But I worried that the company always seemed to be fighting fires with Blackstone business.
>
> For example, Blackstone had three or four homes they were rushing to finish for the Fall Parade of Homes.[1] They were rushing, we were rushing, we probably didn't get enough lead time, there were lots of changes, and we were doing lots of things without the paperwork complete. In the end, we delivered a few things late and changes that added up to three to four thousand dollars in extras didn't get back to Blackstone until after the house closings.

Concluding that internal miscommunication had played a part in this episode, Marcus insisted that the residential team use InfoCentral for all internal communications. This was met with some grumbling, as the residential team believed that the unique needs of the residential business were not captured in the software. But in other areas, InfoCentral was rapidly becoming the tool Marcus had hoped: "After over a year of running practically blind, I was finally able to get details we could use to analyze our customers and where our money was coming from." (See Exhibits 4 and 5.)

Marcus began to regularly receive reports showing differences between estimated and actual costs for each project (see Exhibit 6). As 1998 drew to a close he asked his CFO to pull together a detailed report on profitability by segment and, specifically, profitability on the Blackstone Homes jobs (see Exhibits 7a and 7b). Marcus noted:

> We only had four people—one sales person, two project managers, and one shop coordinator—as indirect costs for all the residential business That only cost us about $200,000, so residential was still dropping

---

[1] The Parade of Homes was one of the largest residential homebuilding marketing events in the area. Area builders held simultaneous open houses at recently completed homes in order to demonstrate their work to prospective homebuyers. A guide to all the open houses, as well as advertising and editorial reviews of the homes, was published in the local newspaper.

EXHIBIT 4 Revenue in First Years of New Ownership (to nearest thousand)

	Fiscal Year 1997 (ownership change mid-year)		Fiscal Year 1998	
	Amount	*Percent of Total*	*Amount*	*Percent of Total*
Commercial	$5,470,000	80%	$7,270,000	82%
"A" Commercial Accounts	$1,605,000	23%	$2,776,000	31%
"B" Commercial Accounts	$ 501,000	7%	$ 615,00	7%
Residential	$1,367,000	20%	$1,596,000	18%
Top 15 Residential Accounts	$ 387,000	6%	$ 826,000	9%
Total Revenue	$6,837,000	100%	$8,866,000	100%

Source: Company records.

Market Segment	Bid Qty	Got Qty	Got Rate (Qty)	Bid Value	Got Value	Got Rate (Val)	Avg Bid	Avg Got
Commercial	**1967**	**617**	**31.4%**	**$61,044,041**	**$9,507,814**	**15.6%**	**$31,034**	**$15,410**
Assisted Living	73	26	35.6%	5,897,404	1,116,072	18.9%	80,786	42,926
Apartments	23	7	30.4%	2,353,749	115,825	4.9%	102,337	16,546
Banks	53	17	32.1%	1,304,849	248,242	19.0%	24,620	14,602
Casinos	17	10	58.8%	424,118	284,754	67.1%	24,948	28,475
Churches	79	36	45.6%	1,294,647	502,782	36.1%	17,654	13,966
Conv. Stores	49	19	38.8%	365,553	140,745	38.5%	7,460	7,408
Courthouses	7	4	57.1%	187,951	79,581	42.3%	26,850	19,895
Government	104	38	36.5%	5,497,968	379,377	6.9%	52,865	9,984
Hotels	46	16	34.8%	2,916,381	536,180	18.4%	63,400	33,511
Libraries	17	6	35.3%	3,031,025	287,612	9.5%	178,296	47,935
Medical/ Dental	209	81	38.8%	7,516,096	1,117,040	14.9%	35,962	13,791
Manufacturing	31	14	45.2%	240,387	99,038	41.2%	7,754	7,074
Miscellaneous	141	42	29.8%	5,118,933	238,427	4.7%	36,304	5,677
Post Offices	535	67	12.5%	11,966,855	1,441,216	12.0%	22,368	21,511
Restaurants	31	11	35.5%	628,613	67,391	10.7%	20,278	6,126
Retail	136	61	44.9%	1,817,714	380,107	20.9%	13,366	6,231
Schools	120	44	36.7%	4,879,952	1,232,789	25.3%	40,666	28,018
Tenant Space (Office)	296	118	39.9%	5,501,846	1,240,636	22.5%	18,587	10,514
Residential	**604**	**416**	**68.8%**	**3,309,310**	**1,860,148**	**56.2%**	**5,479**	**4,472**
Totals	**2571**	**1033**	**40.2%**	**$64,353,351**	**$11,367,962**	**17.7%**	**$25,030**	**$11,005**

EXHIBIT 5 Bids, Orders, and Got Rates for FY 1999

Source: Company records.

great cash to the bottom line. But the contribution margins were definitely worse than we had expected—averaging 38% of sales for residential as opposed to 48% for commercial. We wanted to raise prices. We were a leader in the area; when the company raised prices in the past our competitors generally did, too. But now we had to consider Blackstone's reaction.

By mid-March we decided we had to go ahead and raise our residential prices, which we hadn't done since the ownership change. We raised them about 7% across the board and we also corrected prices for some individual items that we had discovered were mispriced. But Blackstone kept using the same amount for allowances. What started to happen was homeowners would come into the showroom expecting that their allowance would cover what they saw in a Blackstone model home and in the worst case, the model home configuration would price out 15%–20% high. It was easy for a Blackstone customer to go across the street and get a quote from another cabinet shop, and the word started getting out that our prices were too high.

Blackstone's president subsequently accused Marcus of having betrayed their agreement by raising prices. Collecting on change orders was another flash point in the relationship.

Job Started	Job ID	Job Description	Revenue	Budget Hours	Actual Hours	Favor (Unfavor) Variance	% Favor (Unfavor)
5/15/98	11844	Residence	$6,113	97	127	(30)	(31%)
6/4/98	10977-1	Family Room Cabinets	$2,561	40	56	(16)	(40%)
6/23/98	11872	Residence	$8,014	153	236	(83)	(54%)
6/26/98	11885	Residence	$7,620	121	161	(40)	(33%)
7/1/98	11872-1	Millwork	$1,674	35	50	(15)	(43%)
7/14/98	11954	Residence	$6,781	107	140	(33)	(31%)
7/20/98	12014	Residence	$6,762	107	145	(38)	(36%)
7/28/98	12032	Residence	$15,946	221	425	(204)	(92%)
7/28/98	11885-1	Wood Top and Vanity	$1,219	25	43	(18)	(72%)
7/28/98	12033	Residence	$7,694	122	207	(85)	(70%)
7/28/98	12034	Residence	$8,746	138	227	(89)	(64%)
7/28/98	12035	Residence	$8,628	137	206	(69)	(50%)
7/28/98	12036	Residence	$6,740	107	153	(46)	(43%)
8/3/98	12034-1	Prefinish Trim	$847	16	34	(18)	(113%)
8/13/98	12034-2	Doors	$1,240	23	43	(20)	(87%)
8/20/98	12034-3	Millwork	$864	17	41	(24)	(141%)
8/20/98	12033-1	Den Area	$5,355	85	170	(85)	(100%)
8/20/98	12215	Model Home Kitchen/Bath	$7,600	119	184	(65)	(55%)
8/20/98	12216	Model Home	$7,600	120	171	(51)	(43%)
8/20/98	12215-1	Model Home Additions	$1,314	24	34	(10)	(42%)
8/21/98	12223	Residence	$21,147	334	583	(249)	(75%)
8/21/98	12224	Kitchen and Bath	$7,841	124	163	(39)	(31%)
9/1/98	12223-1	Prefinish Trim	$1,176	20	37	(17)	(85%)
9/8/98	12308	Kitchen	$21,851	345	601	(256)	(74%)
9/9/98	12315	Kitchen	$10,433	165	417	(252)	(153%)
9/14/98	12315-1	Fireplace Front	$810	11	28	(17)	(155%)
9/14/98	12388	Kitchen and Bath	$8,934	142	313	(171)	(120%)
9/17/98	12388-1	Millwork	$970	17	40	(23)	(135%)
9/25/98	12422	Model Home	$9,815	155	251	(96)	(62%)
10/5/98	12388-2	Entertainment Center	$725	11	22	(11)	(100%)
10/12/98	12215-2	Model Home Trim	$1,333	23	48	(25)	(109%)
10/13/98	12556	Bookcase/Service Work	$1,575	30	39	(9)	(30%)
10/14/98	12558	Residence	$8,027	114	165	(51)	(45%)
10/22/98	12388-1	Fireplace & Bookcase	$2,359	31	83	(52)	(168%)
		TOTAL	$210,314	3336	5643	(2307)	(69%)

EXHIBIT 6 Completed Blackstone Homes Projects in InfoCentral as of December 15, 1998

Source: Company records.

Marcus wasn't sure how well the project manager was handling this. From the limited data in InfoCentral, he seemed to be conceding a lot of little change orders and the dollars that CMR didn't collect were adding up. The last angry phone call from Blackstone, apparently sparked by an invoice that included a change order Blackstone didn't want to pay, had escalated into

CHAPTER 11 *Managing Customer Profitability in Industrial Markets*   **457**

EXHIBIT 7A Profitability Study by Market (projects completed during January 1999)

	Commercial	Residential
Revenue	$542,528	$133,410
Actual shop hours	6,045 hrs	2,985 hrs
Actual revenue per shop hour	$89.75	$44.69
Budgeted shop hours[a]	6,275 hrs	2,465 hrs
Budgeted revenue per shop hour	$86.46	$54.12
Target revenue per shop hour	$65.00	$65.00

[a] The hours were planned for a project at the point it was considered a "got" (when the project was passed from sales to project management); CMR looked at pricing and estimating (sales processes) for sources of variance between target and budget and at operations (and project management) for sources of variance between budget and actual.

Source: Company records.

a tirade about high prices and late delivery (see Exhibit 8).

ALTERNATIVES

Marcus returned to his desk that April evening to try to plan a course of action for dealing with Blackstone. His residential team projected revenues from Blackstone at $400,000 for the year, making it CMR's largest account. Marcus reflected on all the discussions he had had recently about Blackstone. He had talked with CMR people who were involved with the account and sought advice from his business partner and several former HBS classmates. Opinions about what to do fell into three camps.

The first camp held that current problems with Blackstone were nothing that unusual and it was only a matter of time before they sorted themselves out if CMR would just hold on. It was pointed out that difficult times in the relationship seemed to correspond with Blackstone's own internal crises, over which CMR had no control. Being at the receiving end of a yelling match every once in a while was a small price to pay for the growth and steady cash flow provided by this account. Marcus, although not so

EXHIBIT 7B Profitability Study by Market & Project Manager (Projects Completed during January 1999)

	Commercial					Residential	
Revenue per Shop Hour	Comm 1 PM	Comm 2 PM	Comm 3 PM	Comm 4 PM	Comm 5 PM	Res 1 PM	Res 2 PM (Blackstone Homes)
Actual	$162.16	$64.35	$96.94	$75.32	$57.68	$48.13	$40.63
Difference	43.79	(17.95)	34.59	0.39	(5.55)	(9.10)	(11.14)
Budget	118.36	82.29	62.35	74.93	63.22	57.22	51.78
Difference	53.36	17.29	(2.65)	9.93	(1.78)	(7.78)	(13.22)
Target	65.00	65.00	65.00	65.00	65.00	65.00	65.00

Source: Company records.

EXHIBIT 8 Caldwell Home Project Timeline (from project file)

Date	Activities
January 25	Blackstone Homes project manager faxed notice of new project, provided location, homeowner name, date to measure cabinets (2/18/99), and date to install cabinets (3/22–3/23/99).
January 26	Homeowner visited showroom, met with sales manager to pick out materials and trim. Home based on Model #4. Sales manager filled out residential customer information form with materials and trim part numbers and sent estimation checklist to estimation department with request for quote by Fri, Jan 29 at 11am. Sales manager noted that customer was looking to add a laundry chute in a yet undetermined spot and also a fireplace front that did not appear in the model print. Sales manager provided homeowner with estimate of $875 for fireplace.
January 29	Quote faxed to Blackstone Homes project manager. Quote included kitchen, main bathroom and 1/2 bathroom, delivered and installed with completion date of 3/22/99. Total price quoted: $7571 (internal estimate of 106 shop hours).
January 30	Blackstone Homes project manager replied with fax to CMR project manager of cabinet spec sheet. Spec sheet confirmed that a fireplace and laundry chute would both be added. Provided colors and materials for fireplace, noted that location for laundry chute had not been determined.
February 1	Internal Job File initiated (project manager took over). Data in job file: delivery date 3/23/99, amount $7521, 141 shop hours.
February 9	Blackstone Homes project manager contacted sales manager. Homeowners had added a finished bathroom in the basement, needed quote for additional bathroom vanity and linen cabinet.
February 10	Sales manager faxed add-on quote for vanity ($819) and linen cabinet ($524). (No internal estimate of additional hours.) Sales manager also included $875 for fireplace front on this quote.
February 11	Blackstone Homes project manager re-faxed cabinet spec sheet: "Wasn't sure that I had sent specs" (no change from cabinet specs sent on Jan 30).
March 10	CMR drafting completed construction drawings for kitchen, main bath, half bath, bathroom in basement.
March 11	(Copy of handwritten note.) Additions to job: broom closet $375, pigeonholes under desk upper $90, no glass doors.
March 16	CMR drafting completed revised construction drawings for kitchen that included broom closet and pigeonholes under desk.
March 16	Job released to shop.
March 16	CMR buyer ordered bathroom countertops from supplier, requested delivery date: 3/30/99.
March 18	CMR buyer ordered kitchen countertop from supplier, requested delivery date: 3/24/99.
(no date)	Hand-drawn drawings of fireplace front construction detail.
March 18	CMR ordered marble fireplace surround from supplier, requested delivery date.
March 30	Cabinets and trim shipped to job site.
March 31	Final direct costs for total job: materials: $3263, shop labor: 228 hours
March 31	CMR invoiced Blackstone Homes for completed job:
	One set of kitchen and bath cabinets prefinished and installed $7571.00
	Lower level vanity prefinished and installed $819.00
	Linen cabinet prefinished and installed $524.00
	Fireplace front prefinished and installed $875.00
	Pigeonholes at desk upper and 15 broom closet in the kitchen pref. + $465.00
	Six oak shelves in master bedroom prefinished and installed $120.00
	Total $10,374.00

Source: Company records.

nonchalant about the impact of irate phone calls on the people in his company, was reluctant to intervene in the team's handling of Blackstone for that reason alone.

The second camp acknowledged that there were problems, but maintained that they were fixable. CMR's poor performance was deemed to be responsible for much of the deterioration in the relationship, and it was suggested that if the same focus were applied to the residential business that had been applied to the commercial business many of the problems would be resolved. It was pointed out that the business processes in residential, and the Blackstone account in particular, differed significantly from those in commercial, but newly developed processes and tools such as InfoCentral didn't reflect that difference.

Marcus took these points, but wondered to what degree the problems lay in inadequate systems and processes versus poor execution or reluctance by the Blackstone team to change. For example, whereas others in the company routinely used InfoCentral to share information about projects, including residential projects, there was little data about Blackstone in the system. Was that because the system was poorly designed for residential or for dealing with Blackstone or because the Blackstone team simply didn't want to use it? Marcus also was beginning to wonder if the Blackstone project manager, who had previously worked with smaller accounts, was up to the task of handling one large account of such importance. Or did he have the skills and was just not executing? Would he benefit from training, or did CMR perhaps need someone with a different skill set to handle Blackstone?

The last camp, deeming the relationship to be too far gone, believed that the best thing to do was to terminate, or at least significantly restructure, the agreement with Blackstone. Blackstone, it was suggested, was so different from any of CMR's other customers that it not only drained resources, but also got in the way of efforts to grow the business. Some went so far as to encourage Marcus to drop residential business altogether.

Marcus had a hard time with the latter option for a number of reasons. The first was that, for all its problems, Blackstone and the rest of the residential business still contributed a substantial amount of money, which Marcus needed to fund investments. Blackstone had the potential to provide steady, profitable income that could moderate the impact of wild swings in income often associated with commercial work. But as important to Marcus was the impact this move could have on company morale. He had made many commitments to growing the residential business. The people on his residential team were among the most experienced in the company and had worked hard to grow Blackstone from nothing to its largest account in less than two years. Marcus relied on their experience to help him run the business. Would terminating even just the Blackstone agreement affect how the company would view other commitments he had made?

Marcus had asked his residential team to meet with him the next morning to decide what to do. As he contemplated his options before heading home, he reflected on how this decision might affect his ability to implement the strategies he had laid out for CMR Enterprises:

> The footprint concept, all our plans for growth depend on everyone in the company being committed to the huge changes we need to make to get there. Is Blackstone an opportunity to raise the bar, or is it getting in the way? ■

CHAPTER 12

The Role of CRM Technologies in Customer Management

When developing and implementing a customer equity management approach, it is important to consider the technology necessary to collect, access, and use the appropriate information. The application of such technology is often called a customer relationship management (CRM) initiative—a software implementation by an outside vendor or by internal technical staff. However, focusing solely on the technology aspect of a customer management strategy undervalues the preparation and planning necessary to successfully implement what is typically a substantial investment of both human and financial capital. This chapter discusses CRM software technologies and how they integrate with key customer management strategies. We look at typical implementation issues to help ensure initial success and the eventual demonstration of return on investment (ROI) by measures defined in the planning process. Finally, we examine how current marketing trends are impacting CRM technology.

◆ BACKGROUND

CRM software is often confused with other enterprise-wide applications that coordinate corporate efforts on behalf of customers. Enterprise resource planning (ERP) and supply chain management (SCM) software are often critical to servicing the customer, but they are fundamentally not CRM products because they focus on the back office,[1] whereas CRM requires front office[2] components by definition. The fundamental objective of CRM software is to allow the customer to interact directly with the company via the Web, phone, e-mail, fax, and snail-mail,[3] while using

---

[1] Back office: Those elements of an operating system that are transparent to the customer and with which they cannot interact and are hidden. An operating system is the configuration of the activities concerned with transforming resources within an organization. (Oxford Reference Online)
[2] Front office: Those elements of an operating system that are transparent to the customer and with which they can interact. (Oxford Reference Online)
[3] Snail-mail: Mail sent via the postal system.

sophisticated software to provide a consistent level of service and gain more insight into customer preferences.

There are three other abbreviations sometimes used when discussing CRM software: SFA (sales force automation),[4] CCI (call center integration),[5] and ERM (enterprise relationship management).[6] SFA software focuses on activities specifically related to the sales process, such as contact management, proposal generation, and sales lead tracking. ERM is software that enables collaboration and coordination between sales, marketing, and customer support. It is sometimes referred to as comprehensive CRM.

◆ FITTING STRATEGY WITH FUNCTIONAL DESIGN

CRM technologies are enabled by a systems architecture with three distinct pieces of software functionality: operational, analytical, and collaborative.[7] The operational and analytical components create the backbone that allows the collaborative piece to function. By recognizing that the architecture is driven by the strategy needs, the operating system can be developed to support the critical success factors while maintaining a balance with the other architecture requirements.

Operational functionality includes integration of front and back office products and activities, such as ERP, SCM, customer service, sales automation, and marketing automation. The operational activities generate data that need to be analyzed to monitor business performance. Analytical functionality relies on the fact a CRM implementation keeps data in consolidated databases, making data collection and analysis much easier. Finally, CRM creates multiple customer touch point opportunities by enabling various communications channels. Not only can the customer communicate with the company, but the customer can also communicate with business partners (portals, cross selling), allowing him or her to collaborate with the company to service them better.

Given the three key components of the CRM architecture, we can consider the marketing strategies of customer intimacy, product innovation, and operational excellence. Each of these strategies could rely on different components of the architecture, depending on the customer management strategy. A strategy of customer intimacy could best be supported by an analytical component with data structures that are customer oriented. This allows the company to gain insight into customer behaviors and to create useful performance measures based on this information (e.g., customer segment profitability). A company with a strategy of product innovation would want data structures focused on products, allowing the company to create metrics around customer adoption and the product life cycle.

---

[4]SFA is considered to be the precursor of CRM.
[5]CCI or CTI (computer telephony integration) is the use of computers to manage phone calls, directing customers to the right departments.
[6]An integrated information system that serves the front office departments within an organization. (TechEncyclopedia).
[7]*The Customer Relationship Management Ecosystem*, META Group, Elizabeth Roche (March 1999), File No. 724, www.metagroup.com.

INTEGRATION—STAKEHOLDERS

CRM solutions are not just about software. If implemented correctly, they are reconfigurations of existing operating systems that leverage technology to create more value for both the customer and the company. They can represent significant changes to existing processes and can affect many parties in different departments. The key to success is to determine who the stakeholders are and what their perspective is on the proposed changes. Often, a successful CRM implementation is more about change management than it is about technology.

Armed with that information, leaders within the CRM initiative can develop tactics to defuse negative momentum created by the general aversion to change. As an example, salespeople will generally oppose a CRM solution with an SFA component. They will often view the software as an incremental burden, giving them less time to sell. Customer service representatives can perceive CRM software as increased management oversight with no incremental reward. Salespeople can be convinced of the initiative's value with the explanation that the automated letter and proposal templates inherent in SFA will save time and increase their efficiency—actually increasing their time interacting with customers point. Customer service representatives will also become more efficient by well-organized call routing. Rewards can also be tied to incremental results now observable through the CRM system. Additional stakeholders to consider include marketing, field service, IT, and executive management.

Given the wide range of stakeholders in the CRM implementation, it is important to build cross functional teams early in the process, even as business strategy is being developed. These teams will include an enterprise's business and technical personnel, vendor technical consultants, system integrators, and often management or strategy consultants.

INTEGRATION—CRITICAL TOUCH POINTS

When considering a CRM implementation, four integration perspectives should be considered: front office and back office, operational and analytical, internal and external, and multi-channel and cross channel coordination. To successfully achieve the business objectives inherent in the CRM strategies, it is important to understand the architecture trade-offs in each perspective.

FRONT OFFICE AND BACK OFFICE

A recent Gartner survey of IT executives found that high deployment costs and integration issues still top the list of CRM project roadblocks. The CRM implementation requires that front office systems be integrated with those in the back office. The back office systems are typically inventory control, order fulfillment, and accounting, sometimes ERP or SCM systems. Integration can involve sharing data or redesigning business processes to automate them across systems and functions. Each of the systems may have its own database and associated architecture, further complicating the integration. However, if the products being integrated are standardized, and not developed in house specifically for that system, middleware[8] may be an option for uniting the systems. A well-designed integration strategy will provide more responsive service and better customer information, in turn further increasing the CRM's success. It is important to have a very specific customer or partner service objective to make the most of the links between the back office and front office applications.

OPERATIONAL AND ANALYTICAL

Historically, customer information has been organized based on operational considerations, developed from the corporate focus on SFA and CCI solutions. Typically, these considerations support the day-to-day interactions with the customers by salespeople, customer service representatives, the Internet, interactive voice response (IVR),[9] and other automated channels. Often, each of these customer interaction channels uses different systems to support its activities. Subsequently, customer data often are dispersed throughout the company across many different databases in multiple locations. Even if the information in kept in a central data warehouse,[10] this information is not application or user friendly.

Although this kind of data organization may support the customer adequately, it does not support the requirements of CRM implementations with analytical components (customer intelligence, data mining, and automated marketing). Effective analytics requires the creation of functional data marts,[11] populated with comprehensive customer information including demographic data, past behavior, revenues generated, and costs incurred. Equally important is the development or acquisition of user-friendly tools able to extract useful information from the collection of data. Analytical components tend to drive up implementation costs, because they are incremental to a simple CRM implementation. However, they are required to provide performance metrics on the CRM solution and its impact on business.

INTERNAL AND EXTERNAL

A CRM implementation will have both internal and external "customers." Employees in various departments will use the software's functionality to better serve the customer and gain better insight into their preference and trends. The company's business partners (distributors, vendors, resellers) will use the information to see service trends, gain product feedback, and anticipate company needs. Customers will use the CRM software to order goods and services directly, provide feedback, and check on their accounts. Opening the CRM solution to a larger and larger user base increases the leverage created by sharing the information. However, openness must be balanced with the increased costs, poor data integrity, and security concerns created by such infrastructures.

---

[8]Middleware: Software that functions as a conversion or translation layer to enable one application to communicate with another.
[9]IVR: An automated telephone information system that speaks to the caller with a combination of fixed voice menus and real-time data from databases. Sometimes referred to as VRU (voice response unit).
[10]Data warehouse: A combination of different databases across an entire enterprise designed to support decision making in an organization.
[11]Data mart: A database, or collection of databases, designed to help managers make strategic decisions.

MULTI-CHANNEL AND CROSS CHANNEL COORDINATION

Often a company wants to communicate with a customer through as many different channels as possible. It is common place for companies to have enabled Web, phone (live and IVR), mobile, and traditional storefront channels for their customers. However, each of these channels has a different cost of service. Effective CRM implementations can help direct less-profitable customers to lower-cost channels. The solutions can also provide the information needed to create metrics that tell managers how they are doing with those customer relationships across channels and touch points.

Coordination between channels is very important to attract and maintain customers. Communication miscues are a common problem in multi-channel implementations. Some common examples are sending an e-mail touting the benefits of a new product that the e-mail's recipient already has purchased, and a new business phone solicitation to a current customer. Although neither of these customer inconveniences is overly significant, they do erode customer confidence. With careful planning and structuring they can be avoided.

♦ IMPLEMENTATION STUMBLING BLOCKS

In recent survey CEOs of global companies ranked customer loyalty and retention as their number one management challenge.[12] This has led many companies to pursue major CRM initiatives, spending millions of dollars in the process. A 2002 study by Nucleus Research Inc.[13] estimated the average cost of a Siebel systems customer relationship management deployment at $6.6 million. However, studies by Gartner and the META Group estimate that between 55 percent and 70 percent of CRM implementations fail, with sales force automation projects failing at the highest rate. What are the reasons something so critical to a company's success can be so poorly implemented?

Gartner identifies seven reasons why CRM implementations fail:[14]

1. **Data quality is ignored.** Personnel will not use the application if the data are suspect.
2. **Organizational politics are driving initiatives.** Politics are diluting the customer focus of the initiative. Lack of senior management sponsorship is often an issue.
3. **IT and business organizations can't work together.** Poor communication or organization biases contribute to this common problem.
4. **There is no plan.** Lack of resource commitment and proper strategy formulation can contribute here.
5. **CRM is implemented for the enterprise, not the customer.** Customer-focused stakeholders need to be part of the process.

---

[12]*The CEO Challenge, Top Marketplace and Management Issues'* (January 2001), Melissa, The Conference Board. Berman New York; Report R-1286-01-RR.
[13]Heather Harreld, "Siebel rejects negative report card," *Infoworld* (September 24, 2002), www.infoworld.com.
[14]*Management Update: CRM Success Is in Strategy and Implementation, Not Software*, March 12, 2003. Dale Hagemeyer and Scott D. Nelson, Gartner Group, *www.gartnergroup.com*, Stamford, CT.

CHAPTER 12 The Role of CRM Technologies in Customer Management

6. A flawed process is automated. CRM should be implemented to improve the customer relationship. Fixing flawed processes is part of this improvement process.
7. No attention is paid to skill sets. Management and organizational dynamics cannot be solved by adding software.

Notice that "software selection" is not listed as a reason. Each failure point is about a breakdown in strategy and implementation. Enterprises can significantly increase their chance of CRM success by focusing on strategy and the business process before focusing on the technology.

◆ HOW TO MEASURE SUCCESS

Because CRM solutions typically represent millions of dollars in financial and human resource commitments, most endeavors must pass through a capital budgeting decision process. In most organizations, these processes include return on investment (ROI) and business case analyses. CRM projects will have tangible benefits (reduced costs, revenue enhancements) that can be quantified and soft benefits (more intimate customer relationships) that are more difficult to measure. Although CRM initiatives are often initially justified by cost savings, they are unlikely to be authorized solely on this point. Revenue enhancements through efficiency and effectiveness gains span the multiple years necessary to rationalize the investment in CRM. Data can be gathered from the relevant departments to build a rationale based on such things as increased margins, decreased sales cycle, increased deal value, reduced training costs, and decreased head count. As the business case is assembled, it is critical to have agreement from functional and department champions to support the calculations. The calculations will also serve as the future measure of the project's success, so building the capability to calculate these metrics in the solution is also important. Each department should be committed to delivering its own estimated benefit per the business case.

◆ INDUSTRY OVERVIEW[15]

CRM software is designed to bring a wide array of information together to allow management to make decisions that maximize profits and increase customer satisfaction. Because this objective is so broad and cuts across almost all departments in a company, the industry has both generalists and specialty software. The industry contains four major segments: CRM suites, marketing, sales, and service.

- *Suites.* Suites are single products that attempt to aggregate all relevant CRM functionality. Suites are marketed to three segments: business-to-business (B2B), business-to-consumer (B2C), and small-to-midsize businesses (SMB).

- *Marketing.* Marketing functions across different industries can be varied. The CRM packages addressing this segment are subsequently numerous and varied in their functionality. This market is still emerging, and providers are continuing to enhance their offerings.

---

[15] Claudio Marcus, *Gartner's 2003 CRM Magic Quadrants,* (March 31, 2003) www.gartnergroup.com. Stamford, CT.

- *Sales.* Sales CRM products are highly specialized by industry. There is a wide variety of CRM offerings having the greatest functionality for niche markets. The type of industry should be a major consideration when evaluating sales application CRM solutions.

- *Service.* Service components for CRM solutions tend to focus on three elements: call center support, Web support, and field service automation.

INDUSTRY TRENDS

The CRM software industry is still relatively new and is undergoing significant refinement. Both the CRM vendors and the enterprise consumers are learning as the number of installations continues to grow and information is gathered on CRM software effectiveness.

The CRM software industry is embracing the overall software trend toward Web services.[16] This use of open standards is making integration easier, while at the same time allowing customers to no longer be held captive by vendors because of their proprietary standards. This should keep downward pressure on software license fees by lowering switching costs.

The CRM industry is one of the few areas that application service providers (ASPs)[17] have been successful in capturing market share from traditional license providers. Whereas most vendors sell traditional licenses,[18] ASPs offer what is more akin to a rental arrangement. This decreases the up-front costs and hence the failure risk of investing in CRM technology, which can be a sizable hurdle for most organizations. Vendors such as industry-leader SalesForce.com and others such as Salesnet and UpShot offer robust solutions that focus on configurability instead of customization through programming. Although this is a significant trade-off, especially for larger organizations with specific needs, smaller organizations will appreciate the shorter roll-out times while still extracting significant benefits.

Enterprise needs vary significantly across type, each with its own industry-specific data models, unique sales channels, and processes. Many vendors have carved niches in specific industries (utilities, pharmaceuticals, consumer products, telecommunication) based on a focused knowledge base of processes and customizations. This verticalization will continue as vendors develop their knowledge base from sales to new customers and acquisitions of niche players by the major industry players. This trend will help enterprises extract more value from CRM initiatives by decreasing integration costs and allowing for more industry customization.

Pressure from the CRM ASPs and tightened revenue reporting requirements for software license fees will force vendors to realign their sales model from traditional to

---

[16]Web services: Web-based applications that dynamically interact with other Web applications using open standards.
[17]ASP: An organization that hosts software applications on its own servers within its own facilities. Customers rent the use of the application and access it over the Internet or via a private line connection.
[18]Traditional licenses allow an individual or group to use a piece of software for a one-time fee. For enterprise software, a customer typically has to pay an ongoing maintenance fee to cover future upgrades.

subscription-based licensing.[19] This will provide customers the opportunity to spread out the licensing costs of a CRM implementation (typically, 50% of the total cost).

Industry surveys continue to point out integration and deployment as the top concerns of managers involved in CRM implementations. To address them, vendors will continue to focus on providing internal and third-party professional services.

Finally, the industry behemoth Microsoft has entered the CRM market with technology from its Great Plains unit. Although Microsoft is targeting the small-to-midsize businesses (SMB) market, the overall industry will benefit from the increased exposure and advertising Microsoft will bring out.

Summary

Implementing CRM software is not just a technology issue. CRM software is a tool to realize a business strategy of more closely understanding your customers—merely one aspect of implementing a customer management strategy. Senior management needs to proselytize the benefits of the initiative. Careful planning by stakeholders across all involved departments is imperative to ensure the success of the project. A CRM implementation is a significant investment and should be justified by a quantifiable business case that is supported by all parties. The execution of CRM software will often involve a restructuring of existing processes and data models to focus on the customer, instead of products or internal organizational needs. Trends in the CRM industry are making sophisticated technology cost effective for even smaller business, improving ROI.

Review Questions and Exercises

1. What are the biggest barriers to successful customer relationship management? How can you begin to overcome them?
2. Consider the four integration perspectives discussed in this chapter: front office and back office, operational and analytical, internal and external, and multi-channel and cross channel. What are the implications of these integration perspectives for customer equity management?
3. Which is more important for successful CRM implementations and why?
   - getting the right system and software
   - integrating the CRM system with existing structures and systems within the firm
   - managing the customer relationship from the customer's perspective

   What happens if the firm fails to get one of these aspects right?

---

[19]Subscription license: A suite of applications typically provided for a monthly fee.

◆◆◆ Moore Medical Corporation

Case 12-1   Moore Medical Corporation

Andrew Mcafee

INTRODUCTION

At the end of a hectic day in February 2001, Linda Autore, the CEO of Moore Medical, Inc., sat in her office reviewing a fax she'd just received (see Exhibit 1) from Clarify, a vendor of customer relationship management (CRM) software. Clarify had responded to her company's request for a quote on a CRM system to improve Moore's ability to sense and respond to customer desires. This had always been a crucial capability for Moore, a distributor of medical supplies that had built its business around taking excellent care of specific groups of practitioners such as podiatrists and emergency medical service personnel.

While Moore's strong tradition of accurately and quickly filling customer orders had not deteriorated, Autore had begun to question whether this was sufficient for the company to win new customers, or indeed even keep its existing ones. She wondered whether the kinds of capabilities that CRM software could provide—providing an integrated record of all customer contacts through all channels (phone, fax, Web, etc.), assembling an "optimal" schedule of appointments for salespeople, increasing the consistency of Moore's interactions with its customers—were the ones that might make a difference now and in the future. If so, the company needed to seriously consider investing in a CRM system.

Autore knew, however, that the decision to purchase CRM was not as simple as comparing costs and benefits, even assuming that benefits could be quantified. It was not clear that Moore's issues with customer acquisition and retention stemmed from deficiencies that could be corrected by CRM. If they did not, and there were other efforts that would be more productive, then the large investment in the Clarify system might not be a good one, especially since Moore had many other uses for any available funds.

Some of these funds could be used, for example, to purchase other software products, ones that were intended to correct shortcomings with another large system Moore had implemented previously. While this system, which automated and facilitated many internal functions such as finance and logistics, worked largely as intended, some problems had emerged. "Bolt-on" software was available to address these problems; should Moore purchase it instead of, or in addition to, the CRM system?

Or should the company simply stop spending money on enterprise-level software, at least for a while? Moore had spent heavily on information technology in recent years, and Autore wondered if it was time to slow the pace down. No new systems meant no new IT investments and expenses, and also meant no new large, lengthy implementation projects. All of this sounded good to Autore, but she wondered whether she had the luxury of turning her back, even for a while, on the promises and perils of "big" IT.

COMPANY HISTORY

Founding

In 1947 H. L. Moore founded the H. L. Moore Drug Exchange and began selling brand-name pharmaceuticals from the back office of Axelrod Pharmacy in New Britain, Connecticut. He also sold vitamins and cold medicines to pharmacies by mailing out postcards that listed products and prices. Moore took and filled orders through the mail.

New Products and Customers

Soon Moore expanded the original product line to provide drugstores across the country a wide

---

The case was prepared by Research Associate Gregory Bounds (under the direction of Assistant Professor Andrew McAfee). Copyright © 2001 by the President and Fellows of Harvard College. Harvard Business School Case 601-142.

CHAPTER 12 The Role of CRM Technologies in Customer Management

Clarify

Ex A ver 1.11.C
Moore Medical/att John Plummer
389 John Downey Drive
New Britain, CT 06050-2740

Order number: _____

		^Language	English
		*Database:	SQL/Server
		*Enhanced Server:	NT
		Flexible Deployment Server:	
		+Database Server:	
		+Traveler Server:	
		+Web Server:	

Discount**: 0.00%

Quantity	Product	List Price $	Extended List Price	Discount %	Total Discount $	Extended Total Net Amount $
1	Clear Support Applications	20,000	20,000			20,000.00
1	Account Manager Application	20,000	20,000			20,000.00
1	Full TextSearch and WebFTS Applications	20,000	20,000			20,000.00
1	Clear Call Center Applications	20,000	20,000			20,000.00
1	ClearCustomize Tools (DD,UI and ClearBasic Editors)	20,000	20,000			20,000.00
1	ClearEnterprise Flexible Deployment	0	0			0.00
100	Clarify Full Universal User (Concurrent)	4,000	400,000			400,000.00
	Total Extended List Price					500,000.00
	Totals		500,000	0.00%	0.00	500,000.00
	TOTAL NET PRODUCT AMOUNT					500,000.00

Quantity	Escrow	List Price $	Extended List Price	Discount %	Total Discount $	Extended Amount $
1	Technology Escrow Agreement General Account	2,500		N/A	N/A	2,500.00
	Total Net Escrow Amount					2,500.00

Quantity	Support* *NOTE: not all custom fit options are available from all Support Offices. Check with Regional Customer Care Mgmt. for availability and custom quotes.	Standard % of List Price	Extended List Price	Discount %	Total Discount $	Extended Total Net Amount $
12	CustomerCARE Annual Customer Service Programs (Per Month)	18.0%	7,500	N/A	N/A	90,000.00
	Total Net CustomerCARE Support (Per Month)					90,000.00
	Total Net Support Amount					90,000.00

Quantity	Training	List Price $	Extended List Price	Discount %	Total Discount $	Extended Total Net Amount $

Quantity	Consulting					
TBD	Consulting	See Notes				0.00
	Total Net Consulting Amount					0.00
	TOTAL CLARIFY SERVICES					592,500.00
	TOTAL CLARIFY PRODUCT & SERVICES QUOTATION					592,500.00

Orders must include Software License, Maintenance, and Consulting agreements.

Terms: Net 30 days from date of invoice.
This quotation is valid if accepted by March 15, 2000:

EXHIBIT 1 Clarify Proposal for CRM Software

Source: Company documents.

selection of products, ranging from cosmetics to crayons and cameras to clocks. In the 1950s and 1960s Moore expanded into fragrances, cosmetics, generic pharmaceuticals, and medical and surgical supplies.

In 1970 the company was renamed Moore Medical Corporation. In the decade that followed, Moore increased its base of pharmacy customers, did extensive mailings of catalogs and other product information, and added professional practitioners (doctors and other medical service providers) to its customer base.

In the 1980s, Moore experienced significant sales growth and acquired other companies. However, by the late 1980s, the number of independent pharmacies was shrinking significantly as drugstore chains expanded rapidly. In response to this, Moore concentrated on growing its practitioner business. In 1994 Moore became the first medical supplier to assemble a practitioner-friendly *Buyer's Guide* featuring 350 pages of detailed product information, including full-color pictures.

Exiting Pharmaceuticals

In 1997 Moore exited the wholesale pharmaceutical business, which accounted for 60% of its revenues at the time. Nearly 70% of this market belonged to five national distributors (Bergen Brunswig, McKesson, Cardinal, Amerisource, and Bindley Western). These larger players had invested heavily in technology (e.g., hand-held ordering devices for pharmacies) and warehousing infrastructure in order to drive down operating costs and increase customer service. Intense competition among these firms cut drug prices and margins, and Moore found that it could no longer profitably distribute pharmaceuticals to drugstores. Instead, the company turned its full attention to the practitioner business.

Practitioner Customers

Moore's practitioner customers included general physicians, podiatrists, rescue squads and emergency medical technicians, industrial sites, schools/universities, government facilities, and correctional facilities. Moore found that while practitioners typically placed smaller orders than drugstores had, they were willing to pay higher prices; gross margins were around 30% for practitioner orders vs. approximately 5% for those placed by pharmacies. Moore was one of the first national distributors to embrace this market, which was widely considered to be unattractive because order sizes were small and customers were unsophisticated and required a lot of "hand holding."

Moore began to pursue a strategy of serving the practitioner markets by offering a relatively broad product range (thereby providing "one-stop shopping") and fulfilling orders quickly, accurately, and reliably. To reach out to practitioners, the company relied heavily on catalogs, brochures, and other direct marketing materials, and decreased its emphasis on direct selling via a sales force, which had been important in the pharmaceutical industry. Moore's practitioner business tripled from approximately $40 million in 1990 to $125 million in 2000 (for company financial information, see Exhibit 2).

BUSINESS MODEL IN EARLY 2001
Product Line

Moore provided more than 8,500 products, ranging from disposables such as cotton balls and latex gloves to equipment such as stethoscopes, forceps, and stretchers. However, this number was only a fraction of the approximately half a million available products in the medical supplies marketplace. Moore sought to provide most of the products that its customers would want and so to be the single source for most of their orders.

Markets

The company divided its customers into six groups: Physicians (general and specialty groups); Podiatrists; Emergency Medical Services (EMS); Public Sector (schools, municipalities, correction facilities, federal and state facilities); Industrial (on-site occupational health facilities); and Resellers (dealers). During the year 2000, Physicians accounted for the most sales and Resellers the least at a ratio of 3 to 1.

Moore's penetration rates across these groups also varied widely; approximately 75% of U.S. podiatrists had ordered from the company, while fewer than 5% of physicians had. The company also came much closer to providing one-stop shopping in some segments than others. Its "share of wallet" (or percentage of an existing customer's total medical supply purchases that came from Moore) was 45% for podiatry, 37% for EMS, and much lower for some other segments.

Autore illustrated these issues of penetration and share of wallet using the podiatrists for context:

> Of the 12,000 active APMA domestic podiatrists, Moore regularly does business

	Years Ended		
	2000	1999	1998
ASSETS			
Current Assets:			
Cash	$ 5,233	$ 744	$ 3,250
Accounts receivable, less allowances of $200 and $372	12,326	11,488	9,385
Inventories	9,554	14,242	13,684
Prepaid expenses and other current assets	2,152	1,852	1,992
Deferred income taxes	3,692	2,330	2,500
Total Current Assets	32,957	30,656	31,081
Noncurrent Assets:			
Equipment and leasehold improvements, net	9,672	10,641	7,038
Other assets	2,500	669	362
Total Noncurrent Assets	12,172	11,310	7,400
	$45,129	$41,966	$38,481
LIABILITIES AND SHAREHOLDERS' EQUITY			
Current Liabilities:			
Accounts payable	$10,192	$ 7,483	$ 5,421
Accrued expenses	2,984	4,665	7,139
Total Current Liabilities	13,176	12,148	12,560
Deferred Income Taxes:	2,387	2,368	368
Long-Term Notes Payable	5,208	—	—
Shareholders' Equity:			
Preferred stock, no shares outstanding	—	—	—
Common stock—$.01 par value; 5,000 shares authorized; 3,246 shares issued	32	33	33
Capital in excess of par value	21,700	21,675	21,667
Retained earnings	3,913	8,449	6,597
	25,645	30,157	28,297
Less treasury shares, at cost, 305 and 308 shares	(1,287)	(2,707)	(2,744)
Total Shareholders' Equity	24,358	27,450	25,553
	$45,129	$41,966	$38,481

EXHIBIT 2A Consolidated Balance Sheets (amounts in $ thousands, except per-share data)

with around 8,000. Of the 8,000, we are the primary supplier to a portion. For many of the podiatry practices, though, which are very price sensitive, we operate as a secondary or even tertiary supplier, so there is opportunity for improved share of wallet among these practices. We'd like to seize this opportunity.

Moore did not fully understand why penetration rates and shares of wallet were so different across its customer segments, although

	Years Ended			
	2000	1999	1998	1997
Cash Flows from Operating Activities				
Net income (loss)	$(4,536)	$1,852	$2,809	$(2,921)
Adjustments to reconcile net income (loss) to net cash flow provided by operating activities:				
Depreciation and amortization	2,641	1,733	1,251	1,481
Deferred income taxes	(1,343)	2,170	1,008	(1,130)
Other	30	(262)	455	603
Changes in operating assets and liabilities:				
Accounts receivable	(838)	(2,103)	5,827	10,549
Inventories	4,688	(558)	(268)	30,412
Other current assets	(300)	140	968	1,157
Accounts payable	2,709	2,062	(3,632)	(18,018)
Other current liabilities	(1,681)	(2,474)	1,338	(221)
Net cash flows provided by operating activities	1,370	2,560	9,756	21,912
Cash Flows from Investing Activities				
Equipment and leasehold improvement acquired	(1,599)	(5,336)	(4,778)	(660)
Acquisition of business	(1,934)	—	—	
Net cash flows (used in) investing activities	(3,533)	(5,336)	(4,778)	
Cash Flows from Financing Activities				
Revolving credit financing decrease, net	—	—	(1,512)	(21,214)
Sale of treasury stock	1,444	56	121	
Long-term notes payable	5,208	—	—	
Net cash flows provided by (used in) financing activities	6,652	45		
(Decrease) increase in cash	4,489	(2,766)	3,466	38
Cash at the beginning of year	744	3,520	54	16
Cash at End of Year	$ 5,233	$744	$3,520	$54

EXHIBIT 2B Consolidated Statements of Cash Flows (amounts in thousands, except per-share data)

some of the reasons were clear. Within podiatry, for example, penetration was high partly because the company had invested heavily in direct marketing to these customers, and share of wallet was not higher partly because Moore did not offer capital goods such as X-rays and whirlpools, nor did it carry all categories of medical/surgical supplies.

Moore also did not completely understand why some of its customers left. Its churn rate, or percent of customers that stopped placing orders over the course of a year, was 30% (ranging as high as 35% in some of the segments); the industry average was approximately 25%. Autore believed that some of this churn was due to customers who cared only about price; they bought from Moore when Moore was cheapest (perhaps because of a special offer), but had no deep loyalty or connection to the company. However, Autore also felt that Moore's product family might be too narrow, and that this could be contributing to churn. If a customer wanted a single source for all of its medical purchases but found that Moore was unable to meet this need over time, it might switch to a competitor.

	Years Ended			
	2000	1999	1998	1997
Net sales	$123,555	$118,454	$120,846	$288,513
Cost of products sold	86,712	81,573	83,143	249,451
Gross profit	36,843	36,881	37,703	39,062
Selling, general, and administrative expenses	43,039	34,465	33,326	41,857
Operating income (loss)	(6,196)	2,416	4,377	(2,795)
Interest (income) expense, net	(228)	(8)	(82)	1,898
Income (loss) before income taxes	(5,968)	2,424	4,459	(4,693)
Income tax provision (benefit)	(1,432)	572	1,650	(1,772)
Net income (loss)	$ (4,536)	$ 1,852	$ 2,809	$ (2,921)
Basic net income (loss) per share	$(1.49)	$.63	$.96	$(1.00)
Diluted net income (loss) per share	$(1.49)	$.63	$.95	$(1.00)

EXHIBIT 2C Consolidated Statements of Operations (amounts in thousands, except per-share data)

Source: Company documents.

Competitors

Moore competed directly with distributors like Schein and PS&S, which were many times larger and served numerous other markets. For example, Schein provided dental equipment and supplies, as well as medical equipment. These larger competitors generally offered significantly more SKUs in their product mix. Likewise, they fielded larger numbers of sales representatives than did Moore. While Moore was a relatively small company in the medical supply distribution industry, it also competed with a cluster of even smaller companies that were anywhere from 5% to 30% of Moore's size and dedicated to a given health care specialty, such as EMS.

Interactions with Customers

Moore had a variety of representatives who worked on the customer interface. (See Exhibit 3 for the distribution of employees across various job functions.) The Customer Support Group was composed primarily of customer support representatives who provided the foundation of daily contact with customers by answering telephone calls to take orders. Moore averaged about 2,000 orders per day, with an average of 5 items and 2 shipping cartons per order. While the company had traditionally received most of its orders over the phone and by fax, it projected that the sources of orders for 2001 would be:

Inbound telephone (800#)	50%
Internet	10%
Outbound telemarketing/field sales	25%
Mail	5%
Bid & quote	3%
Fax	5%
Customer relations	2%
Total	100%

Besides customer service representatives, other customer support personnel included:

- *Market-specific representatives* who provided information to customers in different market segments;
- *New business representatives* who sought out new opportunities and customers in specific segments;
- *Key account representatives* who focused on large customers and buying groups;
- *Field sales representatives* who called on customers;
- *Bids and quotes contract specialists* who assisted customers with legal and technical details, such as bonds to ensure performance of the contract.

Supply Chain			Sales, Marketing, and e-Business		
Maint.	3		Marketing Operations	15	
Jacksonville	21	(3 pt)	Business Development	13	
Lemont	19	(2 pt)	Sales/Key Alliances	32	(1 pt)
New Britain	40		Customer Support	52	(7 pt)
Purch.	15				
Visalia	15				
	113			113	
HR			**Executive**		
HR	5			7	
Mailroom	3				
Receptionist	1				
	9			7	
Finance			**IS**		
Accounting/Financial Planning	22			23	
B/Q	8				
Regulatory	5				
	35			23	
			Total Headcount	**299**	
			299 =		
			Exempt	124	
			Nonexempt	175	
			(Part-time)	13	
			Full-time Equivalent Headcount	292.50	

EXHIBIT 3 Headcount Overview (as of 04-02-01)

Source: Company documents.

Moore sought to differentiate itself by its dedication to service, ease of ordering and knowledgeable, friendly operators, as well as its ability to provide one-stop shopping.

OPERATIONS

Distribution Centers and Shipment Policies

Moore had four distribution centers, located in Connecticut, Florida, Illinois, and California, to help ensure quick delivery across the country. They enabled the company to deliver over 87% of customers' orders within two days. [See Exhibit 4 for selected distribution center (DC) performance metrics.] Moore sought to keep exactly the same items in stock in each DC, and to ship complete orders from the distribution center closest to the customer. This was not always possible; depending on stock and availability, some orders would have to be split across distribution centers, so the customer would receive a "split shipment." Moore estimated that a typical split shipment cost an additional $2.82 to ship. Moore absorbed the incremental shipping costs associated with split shipments and never passed those costs on to the customer.

Moore drop-shipped some products to customers direct from the manufacturer in order to avoid stocking low volume items such as surgical instruments, as well as to minimize handling of sensitive instruments such as scales and bulky items such as office furniture. Moore paid freight charges on all orders over $100.

The "Perfect Order"

In late 2000 Moore instituted a performance measurement system based around "the

DC Location	% of Orders	Lines Processed per FTE	Error-free Lines Processed	Inventory Accuracy[a]	FTEs
New Britain, CT	40%	650	99.84%	100.00%	40
Lemont, IL	22%	664	99.88%	99.90%	20
Jacksonville, FL	24%	634	99.80%	99.55%	20
Visalia, CA	14%	631	99.79%	99.95%	14
	100%	645	99.83%	[b]	94

EXHIBIT 4 Distribution Center Performance Metrics for 2000

Source: Company documents.

[a]Physical inventory results (net $)—New Britain (2000), Jacksonville (2000), Visalia (1999), Lemont (1999). Perpetual inventory relative to book inventory.
[b]Cannot be averaged, as time frames are not the same and inventory levels are significantly different.

perfect order." A perfect order had all of its items in stock, was shipped on time and damage free from the closest DC, and arrived at the customer's location damage free and on time. Moore began tracking perfect orders in June 2000 and found that its overall "perfect percentage" was 68% (see Exhibit 5). The remaining 32% of the orders were split shipments (17% of total orders); back orders (10%); and late shipments (5%). Autore stated that, "Generally speaking, the biggest opportunity is with implementing proactive demand planning to make sure that the right product is available at the right location at the right time. Eighty-four percent of our opportunity (27% out of the 32% non-perfect orders) is related to resolving demand planning. The less significant opportunity (only 5%) is resolving shipping issues."

SUPPLIER RELATIONS

Moore dealt with more than 600 suppliers, communicating with them via EDI, phone, fax, e-mail, and postal mail. Lead time for orders averaged around 10 days, but could vary widely from just a few days to four weeks.

As it had done in seeking to improve customer relationships, Moore also worked to improve efficiencies with suppliers. For example, with many of its mid-sized suppliers Moore arranged to take responsibility for negotiating the costs of shipment to its distribution centers and to customers in the case of direct drop shipment because Moore had substantial negotiating power with carriers such as UPS. Moore had also recently launched a supplier rationalization effort to reduce the number of suppliers for each product it carried (this effort began when the company found that it had five different suppliers for latex rubber gloves). Moore planned to implement supplier rationalization throughout a number of product categories in 2001.

INFORMATION TECHNOLOGY
ERP (J. D. Edwards)

In late 1997, Moore began a project to select and implement a comprehensive enterprise resource planning (ERP) system. The system was intended to replace many of the systems in use within the company (some of which were not Y2K-compliant) with a single information platform.

Arthur Andersen Consulting assisted Moore with its selection and implementation of the ERP software from J. D. Edwards. (See Exhibit 6 for the list of software modules, or "suites," that Moore purchased.) In total, this effort cost nearly $7 million and included a significant cost overrun from the originally quoted system due to Arthur Andersen installation consultation fees and consulting service fees from a J. D. Edwards installation firm. The implementation began in earnest during early 1998 after several months of pre-project planning.

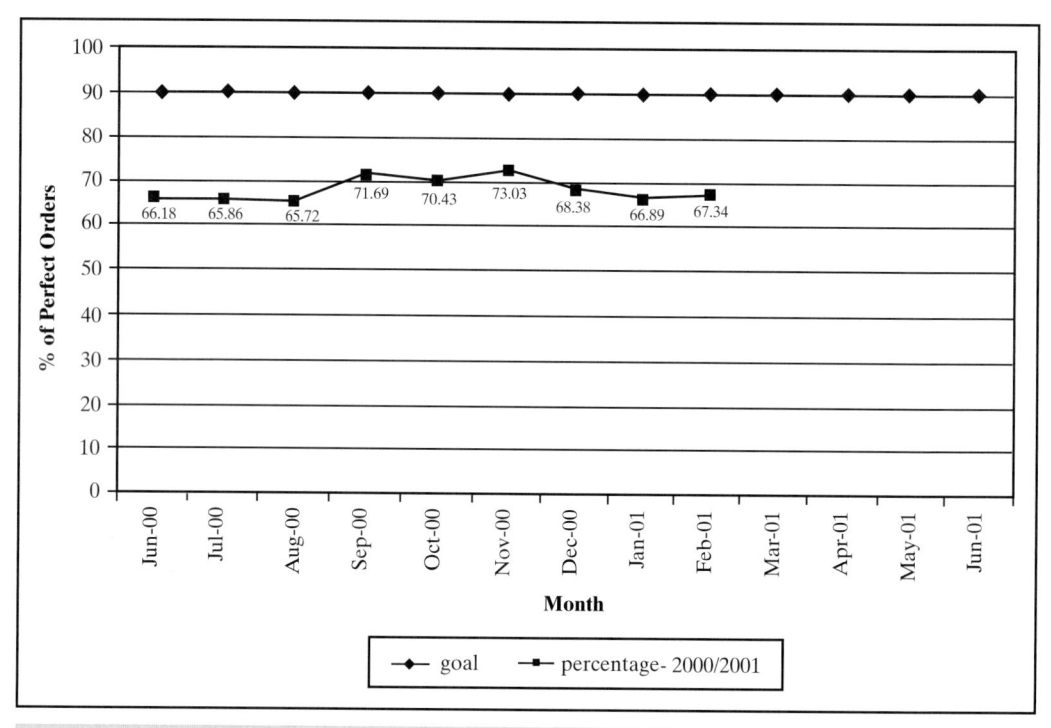

EXHIBIT 5 Moore's Performance on the Perfect Order Metric[a]

Source: Company documents.

[a]In late 2000, Moore instituted a performance measurement system based around "the perfect order." A perfect order had all of its items in stock and shipped on time and damage free from the closest DC, and arrived at the customer's location damage free and on time.

After the turmoil of implementation and adaptation to the new information system, Moore executives were generally pleased with the functionality provided by the J. D. Edwards system. However, they felt that Moore was not fully utilizing the information retained in the system, and that in some cases the new system's capabilities were actually inferior to what had been in place previously. These areas included:

Bids and quotes To create a bid and/or quote for a customer or group of customers was extremely cumbersome within the J. D. Edwards structure. There was not an efficient or easy mechanism within the new system to retrieve quotes attached to customers, expired quotes, etc. The legacy system that existed prior to J. D. Edwards was a customized program that allowed the Bid and Quote Department to manage their quotes efficiently.

Marketing The J. D. Edwards system did not provide a total campaign solution for managing marketing efforts, such as sending trade show materials, catalogs, or promotional flyers. Furthermore, the generic implementation of J. D. Edwards Advanced Pricing module was not conducive to Moore's preferred method of pricing. Moore adapted to the J. D. Edwards system, but began redefining the process. Within a market segment, for example, Moore began to do differentiated pricing by subsegment.

Order entry Moore customer service representatives found the order entry system in J. D. Edwards difficult to use in comparison to their old system. Representatives had to use many

Foundation Suite:
Technical Foundation (for Information Systems Staff)
Address Book (very robust system of customer master and additional data)
FASTR (financial reporting tool)
Conversion programs (necessary to convert legacy data to J. D. Edwards)
Documentation
Case Foundation Envelope
Security Officer (for Information Systems Staff)
Computer Operations (for Information Systems Staff)
Technical Aids (for Information Systems Staff)
Electronic mail
EDI-electronic data interchange
DREAM writer (ability to operate the same menu option with different criteria)
World Writer (reporting tool for databases)

Financial Suite:
General Ledger
Accounts Payable
Accounts Receivable
Fixed Assets
Time Accounting
Financial Reporting
Multi-currently processing
Financial modeling and budgeting
Cash Basis Account

Distribution Suite:
Sales Order Management (ability to take orders from customers)
Procurement
Transportation
Inventory

Advance Warehouse Management (for the distribution of product):
Requirements Planning
Basic Equipment Management
Enterprise Facility Planning
Quality Management
Advance Pricing
Advance Stock Valuation
Bulk Stock Management
Order Management – base
Work Order/Service Billing
Job Costing

EXHIBIT 6 Modules of J. D. Edwards Sold in "Suites" and Purchased by Moore

Source: Company documents.

function keys and drill down to customer or item information to access information during order entry. As a result, the order entry process was longer than it had been previously.

New account setup The lengthy new account setup process within J. D. Edwards also added time to customer calls. In addition, there was no system within J. D. Edwards that allowed new accounts to be reviewed against existing ones. This led to increased duplicate account records within the customer database.

Demand Planning System

The most serious problem Moore faced with its J. D. Edwards implementation was that the system proved to be passive and reactive to demand, rather than proactive in forecasting. Each item carried by Moore was initialized on the system with a minimum stocking level and an economic order quantity. When successive customer orders reduced the on-hand stock of an item to its minimum level, the system generated a recommended replenishment order to be sent to the supplier with the quantity equal to the economic order quantity.

Moore was investigating a new demand planning system, which would create purchasing requirements based on previous history *and* future planned activity, including promotions, as well as automate purchase order creation and execution. Once this new demand planning system was implemented, Moore expected to see a significant increase in customer service levels and a decrease in inventory expense. Planners would be able to set service levels by product to ensure that top moving products would always be in stock. Moore expected this new capability to lead to reduced costs, increased revenue, and better customer satisfaction. Since the proposed system would decrease the paperwork and manual tasks for buyers, they would hopefully become more productive.

Moore also considered purchasing three additional modules to go along with the demand planning system. One was a warehouse transfer system that looked for excess inventory within all four Moore DCs before looking to purchase more from a supplier. The second module facilitated deal management by allowing a buyer to analyze any special offers they received from a supplier. The module looked at what the usage had been and, together with the costs and savings involved, determined if it made financial sense to "stock up" on the item. The third module would provide the ability to do stock simulations to estimate, for example, the service levels that would result from different inventory levels. Moore estimated that each of the four modules under consideration would cost approximately $300,000 to purchase and implement.

Web Site

Moore's initial e-commerce capabilities came from a storefront established in early 1999 within the Yahoo! shopping environment at shopping.yahoo.com. Customer orders from the storefront were manually re-entered into the J. D. Edwards system. In May 2000, Moore launched its own e-commerce Web site, *www.mooremedical.com*. The company spent approximately $1.5 million developing the site, which fed orders directly into the J. D. Edwards system. From May through early October 2000, Moore kept both sites open, since many e-customers had bookmarked the Yahoo site.

Moore sought to encourage its customers to migrate to the Web. Autore and her colleagues were convinced that the Web would enhance service and availability to customers and reduce costs for the company. Moore discovered that 87% of the customers ordering through the Web site were those who converted from other methods of ordering (phone, fax, etc.), while 13% were new customers. Many of these new customers were individual consumers. In fact, Moore anticipated doing approximately $500,000 worth of consumer business in the coming year. To reduce the frustration of navigating the website for all of its customers, Moore also trained its sales representatives to seamlessly handle questions about the website over the phone without having to switch the customers to a technician for answers.

Moore promoted the use of its Web site through its catalogue, coupons for discounts on Web orders, mailed instructions on how to use the site, and the use of Net agents (who conducted text chats with online shoppers). Each promotion had noticeable effects on Web site usage. Since the introduction of its new Web site, the number of orders per month had grown from 1,423 to 2,218 (see Exhibit 7).

This transformation from traditional catalog marketer to a "bricks and clicks," or Internet-based business had been expensive for Moore. The costs associated with the

	Visitors per Month	Orders per Month	Income per month
Start of Yahoo site (8/98)	3,635	182	$ 36,866.00
End of Yahoo site (5/00)	23,486	1,392	$312,644.00
Start of new Web site (6/00)	8,458	1,423	$322,866.00
Last full month of new Web site (12/00)	41,517	2,218	$544,732.00

EXHIBIT 7 Web Site Traffic

Source: Company documents.

transformation, including website design and development, hiring of key personnel and consultants, and the acquisition of two specialty health care Web sites—Podiatry Online (*www.podiatryonline.com*) and Merginet (*www.merginet.com*), which was aimed at emergency responders—meant that the company was not profitable in 2000.[1] In a February 2001 press release accompanying its year-end financials, Moore stated that "Results are consistent with Management's expectations reported in the Company's 1999 Form 10K, and are tied to its investments in technology and ongoing two-year transformation to a multichannel, Internet-enabled direct marketer."

Moore was also considering adding two to three additional people with technology programming skills to keep its Web site current. Moore regarded this addition to be important since it took its own pictures of products and generated its own content for its catalogues and its Web site. The fully burdened cost for these new hires would be $75,000 to $100,000 per person.

CRM DECISION
Goals, Objectives, and Criteria

Through a series of interviews within the company, Moore developed a list of objectives and criteria to guide its investment decision. These interviews revealed a desire to use new technology to better service customers, generate new business, and give employees the tools to handle a growing number of customer communications more efficiently and effectively. Some of the specific objectives included items like "Increase cross-sell and up-sell options for rep," and "Reduce inventory shelf time." Additional technical objectives related to consolidation of data, creation of additional data fields, and elimination of the need for backup in existing information systems. (For the full report on requirements for the CRM system, see Exhibit 8.)

Moore had received responses from more than one CRM vendor, but the one from Clarify seemed most attractive in terms of both functionality and price. While it would be necessary to do more detailed comparisons of prospective vendors and their products, Clarify had emerged as the clear front runner to date in the selection process.

Conclusion

As Autore looked over the fax from Clarify, she was also reviewing the decisions she and Moore faced. Should the company invest in the CRM system, the demand planning bolt-ons to the ERP system, both, or neither? More fundamentally, what criteria should be used to make these decisions? How should she determine whether IT was the solution to a particular problem, such as customer acquisition and retention, or whether another approach was better? And how would she know if she were spending too much, too little, or just the right amount on information technology? ∎

---

[1] In 2000, Moore also took a one-time charge of $2.5 million, or $.79 per share, to settle with the U.S. government a pricing error dispute related to a 1991–1996 contract with the company's former Wholesale Drug Distribution division.

480 PART III *Measuring, Monitoring, and Evaluating Customer Equity Management*

EXHIBIT 8 Report on Customer Relationship Management System

In preparation for their decision about investing in CRM technology, Moore conducted a study to determine the company's goals, technical objectives, and needs. The following summary report on Moore's findings was supplied by internal analyst Erica LeBlanc.

OBJECTIVES

Moore Medical is looking to implement new technology to service its customers better, to generate new business, and to give its employees the tools to handle a growing number of customer communications more efficiently and effectively. The following key objectives were derived from interviews with various members of Moore Medical:

- Increase rep effectiveness and efficiency.
- Introduce single-point-of-contact philosophy by providing cradle-to-grave customer data/history information.
- Increase customer interaction consistency among all reps by increasing company control and manner of customer interaction.
- Minimize loss of customer interactions (via transfers or rep time off) by tracking interactions from start to finish regardless of channel.
- Increase cross-sell and up-sell options for reps.
- Increase effectiveness of campaigns and promotions.
- Increase and measure success rate of bids and quotes by introducing scheduled follow-ups.
- Increase accuracy and accessibility of information obtained from customers.
- Introduce business consistent customer interaction dispositioning regardless of interaction channel.
- Improve sales forecasting and supply chain management by providing sales pattern information for use with data mining and forecast modeling.
- Reduce inventory shelf time.
- Reduce learning curve for new reps.
- Increase cross utilization of reps between departments.
- Reduce time to implement script changes for outbound prospecting/customer service/etc.
- Capture and present data in a Windows GUI-based environment on the rep desktop.

TECHNICAL OBJECTIVES

- Consolidate customer relationship data in one database.
- Create additional customer data fields outside J. D. Edwards restricted DB2 AS400 keeping the J. D. Edwards system focused.
- Make stand-alone Goldmine and Act systems redundant, eliminating the need for support and backup.
- Provide standard service level reports on all interaction channels.

CRM SYSTEM SELECTION MATRIX

High-level evaluation categories, representing Moore Medical's key requirement areas for the solution, were utilized to check whether the various products evaluated provide functionality for the key requirement areas. The evaluation categories fall into three groups: Channels, Environment, and Customer Relationship Management and Channel Management solution.

1. **Channels** Multi-channel support is key for the CRM solution to enable Moore Medical to service its customers via the customers' channel of choice for both inbound and outbound interactions. Cost of channel operation will eventually become important in deciding the optimum interaction channels.
   - Phone channel includes inbound and/or outbound telephone interactions, IVR and VoIP.
   - Fax channel includes inbound and/or outbound hardcopy and/or softcopy faxes.
   - Email channel includes inbound and/or outbound emails, auto acknowledgements, and automatic responses.
   - Web channel includes self-service, personalization, and webinars as well as intranet.
   - Collaboration channel includes chat, form sharing, page push, and co-browsing.

2. **Environment** The environment-related issues have to do with interfacing any new applications with Moore Medical's existing systems to leverage their technology investments and to ensure a productive working environment for agents.
   - Nortel interface to leverage Moore Medical's investment in a Nortel switch.
   - J. D. Edwards or SQL Server 7.0 interface to ensure smooth integration with Moore Medical's ERP system.
   - Universal inbox where all inbound interactions, via multiple channels, are presented to the reps.
   - CTI capability to enable screen pops and automated dialing.

3. **CRM/CM** This includes high-level requirement categories for the Customer Relationship Management and Channel Management solution.
   - Multitasking capability to be able to process multiple communications concurrently.
   - Full-time tracking to enable cradle-to-grave monitoring of, and reporting on, interactions.
   - Account and contact management to capture and maintain pertinent business-to-business or business-to-consumer account information (addresses, phone numbers, contacts, profile information, interaction history) in a central repository.
   - Scripting to automate workflows.
   - Time management for scheduling/calendaring functionality for individual reps and groups.
   - Document Management to provide document templates and to capture inbound and outbound correspondence in interaction history.
   - Literature processing to automate literature requests for central fulfillment.
   - Call list management to create and process customer lists for outbound calling.
   - Multi-channel marketing so the channel of choice can be utilized for campaigns and promotions.
   - Cross-sell/up-sell capabilities to generate more business.
   - Knowledge base to create and maintain an online source of reference materials for the reps, e.g., procedure manuals and FAQs.
   - Sales Management to enable sales forecasting, capturing of reasons for winning and losing deals, and competitor information.

(Continued)

- Field sales module to provide a mobile, disconnected application for the field reps.
- Telecommuting capability to allow reps to access full functionality from an off-site location.
- Customer service functionality for complicated Customer Relations issues to track history against specific issues and provide customers self-help access to check issue status.
- Security to control view/edit capabilities on accounts (access to one's assigned accounts only) or specific fields (regulatory affairs issues).

EXHIBIT 8 *(cont.)*

Source: Company documents.

◆◆◆ **SaleSoft, Inc.**

Case 12-2 SaleSoft, Inc.

Das Narayandas

In September 1995, Gregory Miller, the President and CEO of SaleSoft was faced with the question of whether or not to introduce a Trojan Horse[1] product. Trojan Horse (TH) could potentially distract SaleSoft from its primary objective of becoming a leader in the high end of the sales automation (SA) software industry. In addition, there was a risk that it would cannibalize sales from the PROCEED product that SaleSoft was currently marketing. Finally, TH could potentially prevent SaleSoft from forming relationships with consultants whose support was critical to the success of PROCEED. Yet, TH might offer an easy way for SaleSoft to get into new customer accounts, gain quick sales, and generate much needed revenues.

Greg Miller had founded SaleSoft in June 1993 with the objective of marketing PROCEED, a comprehensive sales automation system (CSAS). In the past 18 months PROCEED had received very favorable responses from prospects. However, converting interest to actual sales was taking a long time. With limited funds and the need to show performance before seeking additional venture capital, Miller and Bill Tanner, executive vice president and CFO, had to decide whether to continue trying to sell PROCEED to select customers, or to make an all out effort to launch TH to a much larger customer base.

Further, the best place to launch TH would be the Sales Automation Conference in December that was expected to attract more than half the prospective customers for SA products. To have a demonstrable version of TH for the conference, SaleSoft would have to devote all its efforts in the next few months to TH.

THE SALES AUTOMATION INDUSTRY

Sales Automation (SA) could be broadly defined as any system that automated some or all processes used in the sales order cycle from lead

---

The case was prepared by Professor Das Narayandas with the assistance of Professor Benson P. Shapiro. Copyright © 1996 by the President and Fellows of Harvard College. Harvard Business School Case 596-112.

[1] The term "Trojan Horse" refers to an object or action used to gain easy entry into areas that might otherwise be difficult to access. The Trojan War is the subject of Homer's *Iliad* and is thought to reflect a real siege of Troy by the Greeks in 1200 BC. The fall of Troy is recounted in Virgil's *Aeneid:* according to Virgil, the Trojans, having held out against the Greeks for 10 years, were tricked into hauling inside their city walls a large wooden horse (the so-called Trojan Horse) left as a gift for the Trojans by the Greeks. The belly of the wooden horse was full of Greek soldiers who, once inside the walls, opened the city gates at night and thus let in their compatriots to sack Troy.

generation to post-sales service. This included marketing functions such as telemarketing, direct mail, and other modes of direct communication with the customer; sales functions such as account management, team selling, and sales force management; and customer service functions such as complaint tracking, service reports, and repurchase details. International Data Corporation, a respected market research organization, estimated the 1995 SA market at around $1 billion, and expected it to grow at over 40% annually over the next five years.

The rapid growth in SA was due to significant changes in three areas. The first was the dramatic drop in laptop computer prices with enhanced processing speed, increased storage capacity, color displays, and light weight. The second was the introduction and continuous enhancement of powerful and user-friendly software including operating systems such as Microsoft Windows, groupware such as Lotus' Notes that allowed for easy sharing of information, and networking software such as Novell's Netware for easy information transfer. The last was developments in communication technology that allowed remote laptop computers to link with central databases.

The potential U.S. market included over 9.2 million salespeople. The Gartner Group, a leading authority in SA, estimated current SA penetration at 2.4 million or 26% of the market. There were over 300 vendors that offered solutions addressing one or two SA areas. Most of them were small niche firms that had annual sales less than $5 million. Only a couple of vendors, such as Sales Technologies with sales over $50 million and Brock Control Systems with $25 million, were considered big players. These firms had been well established in the mainframe environment. However, the major shift from mainframes to PC-based client/server systems had recently forced these firms into the PC world where most SA action was now concentrated.

There were no integrated solutions currently available that addressed the complete automation of any customer. One industry expert stated:

> You cannot buy everything in an integrated fashion from one vendor. Although the industry is moving in that direction, it will be a long time before that's possible. So the customer will be forced to act as her own integrator and force different vendors to work together to provide a customized solution.
> —*Datamation*, May 1, 1995

One reason for this was a general belief that there was no standardized approach to the sales order cycle:

> People in sales are not willing to realize that the way they sell is similar to the way someone else sells, so we are not seeing the development of cross-industry SA applications.
> —*Datamation*, May 1, 1995

The time to sell and install a typical SA project took anywhere from 22 to 30 months. The extended time frame of implementation, high level of customization, and the rapid change in technology stretched the resources of small SA vendors and affected their ability to stay competitive and survive. In fact, seven out of 10 SA vendors were forced out of business by three years after startup. This high failure rate had led to a great deal of skepticism amongst potential customers.

Types of SA solutions

There were a variety of SA solutions available in the market ranging from simple Contact Management Systems (CMS) at the low end to Comprehensive Sales Automation Systems (CSAS) at the high end.

Over 80% of all SA efforts in the early 1990s were projects where the salespeople had been equipped with simple contact management software. Contact managers or Call Reporting systems allowed the user to maintain, access, and update details of the contact person (customer) in a database that resided in the salesperson's laptop computer. Typically, salespeople maintained customer names, telephone numbers, addresses, and personal details.

It was common to find salespeople within a firm using the same CMS in radically different ways. This restricted the usefulness of CMS. As one CEO put it:

> The bottom line of our SA initiative is that we provided our salespeople with an electronic card file costing $3,500 instead of a $100 paper organizer...

Most *Fortune* 1,000 firms had initiated their SA effort by equipping their salespeople with CMS. Several hundred SA vendors offered proprietary versionsof contact managers that did not allow for integration with other databases or software. The most popular CMS was ACT, sold by Symantec Corporation. Unlike most CMS vendors, Symantec was a large PC software company that offered a suite of productivity software for enterprise-level corporate computing and had over 1500 employees worldwide. ACT had an installed base of close to 1 million users and cost from $200 to $500 per user.

With an emphasis on providing individual products that performed one function in the sales and marketing process, CMSs lacked integration across all marketing, sales, and service functions. This severely limited the scope of CMS projects and reduced their bottom line impact. As one vice president (Management Information Systems) put it:

> Neither did the CMS help management leverage the market information to which our sales people are privy, nor did it help our sales reps and sales managers improve their management of the sales process/order cycle . . .

A New Wave in Sales Automation

As an answer to inherent limitations in CMS, and in response to growing customer needs, several firms had announced development of Comprehensive Sales Automation System (CSAS) solutions that took a process view to automating the sales order cycle. These solutions were expected to (1) provide sales, marketing, and service personnel with a suite of integrated tools to enable them to communicate better and to perform their jobs more efficiently and effectively; and (2) provide management with back-end decision support systems to enable them to manage marketing, sales, and service resources more proactively. Overall, the main objective was to increase productivity by improving efficiency and effectiveness, and reducing order cycle time. (See Exhibit 1 for more details.)

CSAS solutions were expected to provide greater value where there was greater variance and uncertainty in the sales order cycle. Tanner said:

We do not see the next generation of SA products being used in all situations. They are not useful in simple selling situations. Our ideal customer profile would face pressures to predict revenues correctly all the time, have a dispersed salesforce with a team selling approach—perhaps, multi-level or even cross functional, and have made significant investments in their sales force.

This narrowed the focus for CSAS solutions to industries that involved large ticket items with long, complex sales order cycles and/or that involved consultative team selling. The complexity of CSAS made it easier to implement in industries with computer literate salesforce. Exhibit 2 gives more details on the market potential for SA. Larger firms in most of these industries had installed CMSs like ACT with varying degrees of success in the first phase of their SA effort. Their salespeople were known to "swear by" and "swear at" CMS.

In June 1994, there were no integrated CSAS products available. Towards the end of 1994, several vendors announced their intent to develop and sell such systems. Some had even established beta[2] test sites by early 1995. By mid-95, more than a third of the vendors had dropped out. Exhibit 3 provides more detail on firms currently in the market with preliminary CSAS solutions.

A Typical CSAS Buying Cycle

The inefficiencies within and across most current sales, marketing, and service systems affected all levels from the CEO right down to the salesperson. Trying to undertake a selling effort that involved educating a potential customer at all levels on the benefits of a CSAS system was beyond the resources of most SA vendors (see Exhibit 4 for some of the important issues raised by the affected constituencies). It was easier for SA vendors to pursue prospects that had already decided to implement a CSAS solution.

---

[2]It was a common practice to install early software versions at a few, select customer sites for test. These were referred to as "beta" test sites.

EFFICIENCY BENEFITS

- Effective and timely distribution of sales leads and marketing literature to the field
- Increased customer contacts and face-to-face selling time
- Improved visibility to identify salesperson's weaknesses and developmental opportunities

More effective management by exception via sales process metrics for each rep, district, region, and for the entire company, including:

– Overall average sales cycle
– Average number of days in each segment of the sales process
– Yield by each segment of the sales process
– Win/loss rates

- Lower salesperson turnover and retraining costs
- Decreased paperwork and reporting (administrative) time
- Improved account planning and customer service
- Increased communication

EFFECTIVENESS BENEFITS

- Improved accuracy of forecasting
- Complete visibility into the buying cycle for each customer
- Immediate insight into all customer activity for entire sales team and management
- Improved timeliness and visibility of order cycle status and ability to effect closure
- Shorter non-productive time for new hires
- More effective sales management, training, and reinforcement of sales methodology
- Timeliness of correspondence, quotations, and proposals with fewer mistakes
- Easier territory maintenance
- Better and timely competitive information updates

ORDER CYCLE BENEFITS

- Reduced order cycle times because of greater efficiency and effectiveness

EXHIBIT 1 Benefits of CSAS

Source: Company product literature.

A typical customer buying cycle involved several steps. First, was the realization by senior management that CSAS might solve some of the existing sales, marketing, and service problems. Having reached this stage, it could take a customer another 21 to 30 months to implement CSAS.

It was rare for firms to automate all processes at the same time. Thus, the second step in the buying cycle was to evaluate the potential to automate existing processes and to specify the order of functions to be automated. Customers were usually not equipped to do this in-house. It was common for SA consultants to help them.

Industry	Total # of Firms with 50+ Sales Reps	Estimated Number of Employees	Estimated Number of Sales Reps
Software Industry			
Computers; periph. equip; software	46	68,642	6,864
Computer programming services	49	67,241	6,724
Prepackaged software	54	116,095	11,610
Aggregate total	149	251,978	25,198
Computers, office equipment			
Aggregate total	137	1,211,601	121,160
Commercial Banking			
National commercial banks	1,097	1,954,088	1,074,748
State commercial banks	1,299	781,603	429,882
Other banks	44	34,583	19,021
Aggregate total	2,440	2,770,274	1,523,651
Diversified Service Companies			
Computer programming, data processing, other Computer-related services.	113	427,393	21,370
Accounting, auditing, bookkeeping	19	218,998	10,950
Management consulting services	66	314,224	15,711
Aggregate total	198	960,615	48,031
Electronics, Electrical Equipment			
Aggregate total	479	2,043,614	143,053
Scientific, Photo, & Control Equip.			
Aggregate total	263	1,309,515	78,571
Diversified Financial Companies			
Aggregate total	547	891,611	276,399
Life Insurance Companies			
Aggregate total	370	1,049,653	293,903

EXHIBIT 2 Market Potential for CSAS

Note: SIC stands for Standard Industry Classification.

SA consultants typically specialized in implementing SA in one or a few vertical industry markets like health care, pharmaceuticals, etc. Their deep understanding of the industry, and their skills and experience made them the best option for this step, which took three to four months.

In the third step, the customer decided how the different functions to be automated were related, and determined how data was to be collected, stored, and analyzed. This again was usually done by SA consultants with the support of the customer's information systems department, and usually took two to three months to complete.

The customer decided the type of SA software and hardware to be purchased, at this point, the fourth step. Here again, the customer relied heavily on the consultant. Short listing[3] and selecting vendors typically took six to eight months. Even at this late stage in the buying cycle, it was not uncommon for CSAS vendors to face concerns about SA at all levels of the customer organization (see Exhibit 5 for a list of concerns and benefits sought).

---

[3]Detailed evaluation of all available products was a very expensive and time-consuming process. Therefore, based on preliminary analysis, business customers with the consultant's help would identify a few, select vendors that were likely to meet their specific needs. This reduced set of vendors was called a "short list." In the next stage, extensive comparative analysis across vendors in the short list was done prior to selecting a vendor for the project.

EXHIBIT 3 List of CSAS Competitors

Company/ Location	SaleSoft, Columbus, OH	Action Systems, Golden, CO.	SalesBook Systems, Pittford, NY	Sales Technologies, Atlanta	Saratoga Systems, Campbell, CA	Penultimate, Irvine, CA
Product	PROCEED	Heatseeker	SalesBook	SNAP for Windows	SPS (Windows version)	SalesForce
Client/user base 1993 Estimated/ 1994 projected revenues	5/500 $0/$0.3 million	7/1,700 ?/$8.5 million	5/3,000 ?/$5 million	27/1,500 $50/$50 million	80/3,200 $5/$10 million	15/1,600 $0/$3.5 million
Average price 200 users	$480,000	$250,000	$250,000	$400,000	$250,000	$260,000
Process- or data-driven application	Process	Process	Data; optional process module avail 6/94	Process	Data	Process
Primary system focus (account or opportunity mgmt.)	Opportunity and Account	Accounts	Accounts	Accounts	Accounts	Opportunity
Customization	Vendor-customized, client-customized (PowerBuilder source code is provided) or third parties (e.g., Affiliates) can customize.	Vendor-customized	Vendor-customized, or clients can add pieces using Visual Basic, PowerBuilder, etc.	Proprietary. Configurator tool for client customization, or vendor customized.	Proprietary. Saratoga Tools for client customization, or vendor-customized.	Proprietary tool for client customization, or vendor-customized.
Back-end system	Novell, Windows NT, OS/2, Unix	SQL Server, Windows NT, or any ODBC compliant database server	Back-end implementation available through mix of base product and customization	Unix, OS/2, Novell via NLMs	MVS, DOS, Windows under DOS, SCO Unix, OS/2, AIX	Windows NT (OS/2 and Novell available via NLMs)
Remote communications strategy	MAPI, VIM, (Microsoft Mail, CC Mail), Xcellenet	Remote LAN connectivity software (e.g., Microsoft's RAS, DCAs Remote LAN Node	Any network gateway product as a default, or any specialty product like Xcellenet or Intel	Xcellenet for OS/2 back end, proprietary for Unix back end, or standard e-mail packages	Proprietary or left to client's selection	Xcellenet; Microsoft's RAS for NT users; IBM's LAN Distance for OS/2 users

Source: Company records.

EXHIBIT 4 Typical Issues Raised by Decision Making Unit as Regards to Order Cycle and Possible Solutions

Who?	Issue	Possible Solution
Entire organization	• It is impossible to keep track and schedule everyone's time. If a meeting requires several people, we have to schedule it way into the future. If the meeting topic cannot wait, we end up making decisions without everyone's input.	• Group calendar • Time management
CEO	• Sales, marketing, and service have their customer information systems. None of them has a complete understanding of what is occurring in the account.	• Sales, marketing, and service activities are integrated into one database. This system shows every activity that has occurred with the account in the same format.
CEO	• My manufacturing cycle is greater than the customer backlog. Therefore, manufacturing tries to anticipate customer product demand and they always forecast wrong. We end up with to much of some products and not enough of the products we need to meet demand.	• Detailed product forecast with trend analysis and confidence indicators.
CEO	• I cannot tell if sales are doing their job.	• Sales management gives anyone the visibility to see everything that is going on in the sales cycle.
CEO	• Channel conflict is hurting my profits. When we do not effectively communicate among channels, we usually end up giving the customer two prices. In effect, we lose face with the account even if we win the business.	• Give your channel the same system. Allow salespeople in the channels to have visibility to each other's activities.
CEO/CFO	• Sales and marketing cannot identify their constraints with the demand and sales cycle. Therefore, resources are being allocated to perform the wrong activities.	• Order cycle management
VP sales	• We are not sure if the sales reps are using a sales process.	• Sales and marketing method/process steps
VP sales	• When a salesperson leaves us, it takes a year before we can effectively manage the territory again. This ends up costing us a lot money in training and lost revenue during the startup period.	• Develop a database that has a complete history of event by account and opportunity. This in combination with the marketing encyclopedia system will get new reps up to speed faster.
VP sales	• We do not have a means to understand our wins or losses. Therefore, we cannot learn from either.	• Record the wins and losses for each opportunity. Use the information gained to enhance the appropriate areas of the system.

VP sales	• The sales cycle is getting longer and longer and we are not sure why. This forces us to make decisions to close business that is not in our best interest.	• Measure each step in the sales cycle. Understand early on if the opportunity is taking too long or if the step is not being responsive.
VP sales/ sales managers	• We are not sure the reps are taking the right step to move the account through the pipeline.	• Process and activity review by opportunity.
VP sales/ sales managers	• Forecasting and call reports are the only way I can see what activities are taking place in the field. These items consume too much time away from selling.	• These items are a by-product of the salesperson using the system to do time management.
VP sales/ sales managers	• It takes us too long to acknowledge the receipt of an order from a customer. The customer thinks we are being unresponsive.	• Print a copy of the order acknowledgment for the customers to sign before you leave their offices.
VP sales/ sales managers	• Sales reps must come in to the office to get access to the information to do their jobs.	• Provide them with a store and forward remote client server platform. This platform allows the rep to do business anytime, anywhere.
VP marketing	• Telemarketing sends leads to the salesperson and never hears anything about them again.	• Give the telemarketers visibilityinto the sales cycle. This allows them to understand status without getting the rep involved
VP marketing	• Sales reps do not know which accounts are in their territories. They end up wasting resources on opportunities that belong to a different channel.	• Populate the local databases of all the accounts in each territory. This provides the ability to perform account, contact, and territory management in one system.
VP marketing	• Competitor information is out of date before it can be distributed.	• Marketing Encyclopedia System.
VP marketing	• We cannot measure the effectiveness of our marketing dollars or the messages they send. We know we are wasting resources, but where? and why?	• Keep track of each campaign, response rates, costs. Record this information by account. Allow the user to review before and after pipeline status.
Sales reps	• We spend too much time verifying and chasing down expense reports and commission checks.	• Provide status of these items on their local database.
Sales reps	• Every year the company raises my quota, which forces me to do more to keep my compensation the same. We need the ability to manage more opportunities at one time.	• Give the salesperson tools that allow them to manage more tasks. Address their administrative needs.

EXHIBIT 5 Typical Concerns Regarding CSAS Solutions

Who?	Typical Concerns	Benefits Sought
CEO, CFO	• Are the costs justified? • Who else is using it? Give us a reference list. • What's the guarantee that you will be around after a few years? • Can you prove that it will work in our selling environment?	• SG&A cost reductions • Process control and improvement • Sustainable competitive advantage • Reduced sales force turnover • Reduced sales cycle • Increase in opportunities addressed
VP MIS	• Is the system compatible with our existing systems? • Can you customize reports to our formats? • Who is going to maintain the system? • What is the guarantee that the system will work? • How do you know that our salespeople will use the system the right way? • Can you guarantee that sales will give us all the information required?	• Integrated with our other systems to allow for bi-directional information transfer • Transportable to the new hardware computing environments that we plan to buy in the future • Minimal increase in load on MIS department to support these systems
VP sales and sales managers	• Will my reps use it? • Will my salespeople use all the functions? • Will they spend all their time playing with it rather than using it properly? • Will my salespeople censor information that they need to report?	• Improved visibility of opportunities • Better forecasts • Better sales management • Improved work habits of salespeople • Improved coaching tools through exception reporting • Reduction in paperwork
Sales reps	• Will this lead to management trying to keep an eye on everything I do? • Is this extra work? • If I give away information about my customers then the firm will not need me anymore. • What is in it for me? • I do not need to be told how I should handle my customers. • I like working on my own and I do not like intrusion into my privacy. • As long as I deliver results, why should they care?	• More freedom through better and more efficient forecasting, call reporting, and account reviews • Better information flow on team accounts, new leads • Better and prompt customer service • Ability to identify areas/skills that need to be developed

Source: Company records.

After choosing the vendor, the fifth step was to pilot test the CSAS after customizing it to meet the customer's specific needs. It usually took three to five months to implement this step.

The sixth step was to modify the CSAS software in response to feedback from the pilot test, which took three to four months. Full scale roll out, the final step, typically took another four to six months.

Recent Trends in Partnering in the Sales Automation Industry

Recently, several CSAS vendors had announced partnerships with SA consultants. Partnering with consultants helped a CSAS vendor in two ways. First, it allowed the CSAS vendor to access the consultant's customers while potentially locking out other CSAS vendors. Second, it took care of training issues.[4] It was common for consultants to either have in-house training skills or long-standing partnerships with specialized training firms. The main drawback of partnering was that it could potentially alienate the CSAS vendor from other consultants and their customers. This was amplified by the fact that consultants expected the CSAS to be customized to proprietary specifications.

Currently, SaleSoft did not have any partnerships with any consultant. In preliminary discussions with Miller, several consultants had indicated that they needed to see a complete CSAS solution before they would even think about partnering.

THE PROCEED SMRP® (SALES AND MARKETING RESOURCE PLANNING) SYSTEM

SaleSoft's CSAS product, called PROCEED SMRP®, allowed customers to automate their entire marketing, sales, and customer service operations. PROCEED had eight modules:

Sales System	*Marketing System*	*Services System*
Field Sales	Campaign Management	Incident Tracking
Opportunity Management	Marketing Encyclopedia	Relationship Management
Sales Management	Literature Fulfillment	

Currently, only the three modules in PROCEED's Sales System were ready. Miller estimated that it would cost $1 million to develop and roll out the remaining five over the next eight months.

Sales system   The PROCEED Sales System consisted of three modules.

The *Field Sales* module recorded and displayed on an easy-to-use scheduling system all customer information, personal appointments, meetings, and "To Do" activities. It was designed to minimize keyboard and mouse entry to make it easier for salespeople to use. It also created a common database using information input from each salesperson that allowed the entire sales team to view the availability, allocation, and coordination of resources throughout the organization. The data collected in this module was the only input into the Opportunity Management and Sales Management modules reducing the "paperwork" burden on salespeople, an activity they generally despised.

The *Opportunity Management* module organized the flow of each prospective sale into pipeline segments. Each segment contained a user defined set of sales activities involving the salesperson and/or other sales team members. When all activities in a segment were completed, an opportunity was automatically moved to the next pipeline segment. Exhibit 6 gives one example of an opportunity pipeline. Used in conjunction with the Field Sales module, it allowed each sales person to constantly view her sales opportunities and the progress made toward closure.

---

[4]Training was a critical factor in CSAS vendor evaluation given product complexity and minimal prior user experience. In addition to using the CSAS system, users also had to be educated on using laptops, linking to central databases to transfer information, printing reports, and using application software such as word processors, spreadsheets, and electronic mail. Customers expected CSAS vendors either to have in-house training skills (which was usually not the case) or to partner with firms that specialized in training.

492 PART III *Measuring, Monitoring, and Evaluating Customer Equity Management*

EXHIBIT 6 Opportunity Pipeline Management in the PROCEED Sales System

Note: This pipeline is for Gregory Miller as of April 23 1996, for the current quarter. The pipeline has eight segments labeled I, F, P, S, PS, E, D, and C, respectively. Currently, Miller has opportunities worth $125,000 in the first segment (labeled I) against a target of $0. Similarly, he has opportunities worth $900,000 in segment PS against a forecast of $1.35 million.

For each opportunity, its current status in the pipeline, all associated current activities, and the probability of converting this opportunity into a sale can be input into PROCEED. For the example shown below, the opportunity is currently in pipeline segment E and has a 50% chance of being converted into a sale.

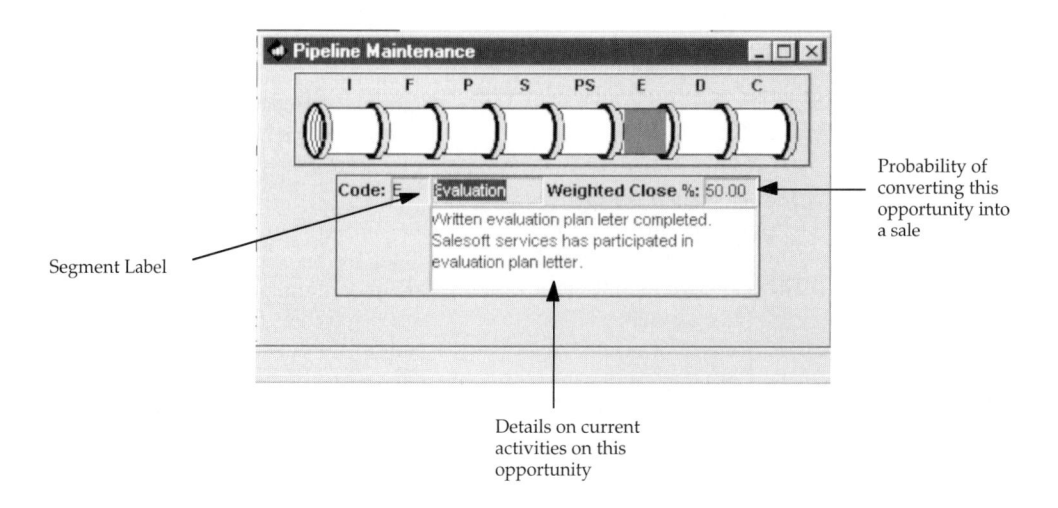

The number of pipeline segments, the name/label of each segment, and the probability of closing the sale can be specified based on user requirements.

The *Sales Management* module continuously updated and consolidated information by opportunity and provided up-to-date pipeline status on all opportunities. It also included a decision support and executive information system that allowed management to plan efficient resource deployment.

Marketing system The three modules in this system automated and integrated all the marketing processes within a firm.

The Campaign Management module automated telemarketing, direct mail, and advertising campaigns. It provided an effective and efficient means for rapidly transferring qualified leads to field sales. It also provided management with data for evaluating the cost/benefit of each campaign, including what-if campaign analysis.

The *Marketing Encyclopedia* module was a central repository for maintaining and updating all product information, pricing schedules, new product launch announcements, press releases, and other marketing material. This ensured consistency and timely availability of all marketing and sales support information.

The *Literature Fulfillment* module automated the identification, accumulation, and distribution of literature requests from all sources within the organization, customers, and prospects. It also tracked the usage and inventory of marketing resources.

Service system The customer service system was made up of two modules.

The *Incident Tracking* module captured all customer service issues and tracked them through to ultimate resolution. By maintaining information online, it provided management with continuous feedback from customers.

The *Relationship Management* module provided a repository for all customer contacts, activities, commitments, and correspondence that could be used to generate new sales opportunities from existing customers.

PROCEED System Design

PROCEED was developed to run on Microsoft Windows, an industry standard operating system. This was expected to shorten the learning time for the large installed base of Windows users. In addition, PROCEED was integrated with common e-mail, word processing, fax, spreadsheet, and presentation software. It used advanced software technologies that allowed the salesperson to use the complete functionality of the system unattached to the host system. The salesperson could, at any time, connect to the host to transfer data to and from a central corporate database.

Current PROCEED Sales

To date, SaleSoft had sold the three existing modules of PROCEED to five customers in the computer software industry and had an installed base of just under 300 users. SaleSoft had committed to these customers that it would release the remaining modules on a staged basis by June 1996.

SaleSoft was also pursuing sales opportunities with over 20 prospects in computer software and hardware, financial services, and banking. The number of users varied from 200 to 600 per prospect. Exhibit 7 gives more details on two of them. In each case, the customer wanted to see the total PROCEED product before making any purchase commitments. Barring any delays in product development, Miller felt at least a quarter of the current prospects would buy PROCEED over the next 12 to 15 months.

SALESOFT ORGANIZATION

SaleSoft Inc. was founded in July 1993, to develop and market CSAS systems (see Exhibit 8 for the organization structure).

Greg Miller, the President and CEO of SaleSoft, had spent over 12 years in the application software industry including positions in sales and marketing, product development, services, and general management. Before founding SaleSoft, Miller was president of Symix Computer Systems, Inc., a $30 million public company that developed and marketed manufacturing software. Prior to Symix, Miller was Vice President of Sales and Marketing and the third employee at a software company that

		Company A	*Company B*
1	Industry	Financial services	Computer hardware
2	Annual sales	$120 million	$350 million
3	Selling costs (% of revenues)	30%	35%
4	Variable component of sales expense (e.g., commissions)	10%	4%
5	Number of sales reps	120	250
6	Annual rep turnover (%)	20%	35%
7	Time for new reps to become productive	60 days	90 days
8	Number of PROCEED users	250	600
9	PROCEED License Fee	$600,000	$1,440,000
10	Implementation and training costs in the first year	$180,000	$430,000
11	Annual software support and maintenance (% of license fee)	20%	20%
12	Hardware costs	$1,500,000	$3,600,000
13	Project startup costs	$200,000	$450,000
14	Annual cost of internal resources	$150,000	$350,000
15	Current selling cycle	120 days	180 days
16	Estimated reduction in sales cycle using PROCEED	6 days	15 days
17	Estimated reduction in startup time for a new sales person using PROCEED	14 days	20 days
18	Estimated % reduction in rep turnover using PROCEED	10%	15%

EXHIBIT 7 Profile of Two Prospects for PROCEED

Source: Company records.
Note: Costs and benefits were estimated by the customer in each case.

developed and marketed one of the first integrated Manufacturing Resource Planning (MRP) systems. His experience in automating manufacturing environments convinced Miller that there was a tremendous opportunity for a solution that integrated a firm's sales, marketing, and service functions.

We were able to bring order to chaos in manufacturing and provide customers with huge savings by reducing wasted effort. I am sure that PROCEED will prove as effective as MRP packages that I have sold in the past.

Very few firms have any control over customer management processes. They are held hostage by their salespeople. By using CSAS, our customers will be able to drive out inefficiencies in their sales, marketing, and service cycles, and reduce their SG&A costs.

The benefits are so great that customers will be eager to adopt these systems at the earliest. If you thought MRP systems led to a revolution in manufacturing, wait till you see what CSAS will do to selling, marketing, and service.

William Tanner, the Executive Vice President and CFO, had over 14 years of work experience in finance and management of technology based businesses. Tanner's experience and contacts had been instrumental in SaleSoft's ability to get venture capital funding.

EXHIBIT 8 Organization Chart

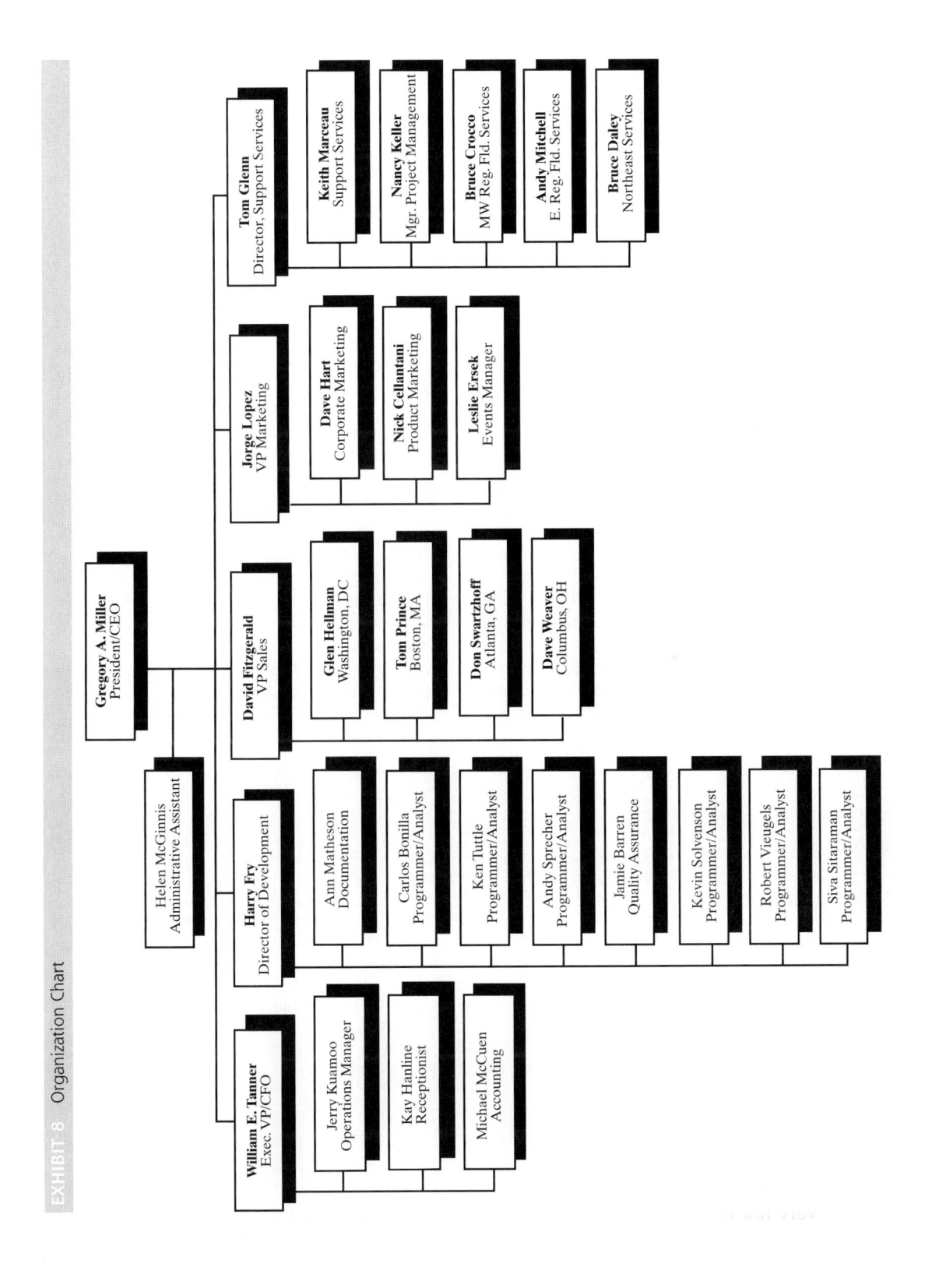

- **Gregory A. Miller** — President/CEO
  - Helen McGinnis — Administrative Assistant
  - **William E. Tanner** — Exec. VP/CFO
    - Jerry Kuamoo — Operations Manager
    - Kay Hanline — Receptionist
    - Michael McCuen — Accounting
  - **Harry Fry** — Director of Development
    - Ann Matheson — Documentation
    - Carlos Bonilla — Programmer/Analyst
    - Ken Tuttle — Programmer/Analyst
    - Andy Sprecher — Programmer/Analyst
    - Jamie Barren — Quality Assurance
    - Kevin Solvenson — Programmer/Analyst
    - Robert Vieugels — Programmer/Analyst
    - Siva Sitaraman — Programmer/Analyst
  - **David Fitzgerald** — VP Sales
    - Glen Hellman — Washington, DC
    - Tom Prince — Boston, MA
    - Don Swartzhoff — Atlanta, GA
    - Dave Weaver — Columbus, OH
  - **Jorge Lopez** — VP Marketing
    - Dave Hart — Corporate Marketing
    - Nick Cellantani — Product Marketing
    - Leslie Ersek — Events Manager
  - **Tom Glenn** — Director, Support Services
    - Keith Marceau — Support Services
    - Nancy Keller — Mgr. Project Management
    - Bruce Crocco — MW Reg. Fld. Services
    - Andy Mitchell — E. Reg. Fld. Services
    - Bruce Daley — Northeast Services

496 PART III Measuring, Monitoring, and Evaluating Customer Equity Management

TABLE A Summary of Revenues and Market Share for SaleSoft

Year	Revenue ('000 $)	Net Income ('000 $)	Total Market ($ million)	SaleSoft's Market Share
1993	0	(104)	600	0%
1994	305	(658)	780	0.1
1995[a]	2,000	(1,328)	1014	0.2
1996[a]	6,750	(413)	1318	0.5
1997[a]	15,000	1,395	1713	0.9
1998[a]	30,000	3,197	2227	1.3

[a]Projected.

The Financial Situation

By 1994, Miller and Tanner and a few other promoters had invested just over $800,000 in equity. This was supplemented in early 1995 with $2 million of venture capital. To support the firm's expenses through 1997, Miller and Tanner felt they would need to raise another $2 million in early 1996 (see Table A for a summary of projected revenues and market share for SaleSoft).

Exhibits 9 and 10 give more details of the financial projections for SaleSoft. As of September 1995, expenses were running at projected levels. Year-to-date revenues, however, were a little over half a million dollars.

THE TROJAN HORSE OPPORTUNITY

On several occasions, salespeople had told Miller that a large number of prospects, who were not ready for PROCEED, were desperately looking for a system to manage their sales forecasting process. These firms were involved in long, complex selling cycles that made it difficult to forecast revenues and affected overall operations including revenue planning, inventory management, capital

EXHIBIT 9 Statement of Operations

	1993	1994	1995[a]	1996[a]	1997[a]	1998[a]
Revenues:						
License fees	0	203	1,659	4,813	10,500	21,000
Services	0	102	350	1,937	4,500	9000
Total revenues	0	305	2,009	6,750	15,000	30,000
Expenses:						
Cost of license fees	0	0	143	546	1,155	2,310
Cost of services	0	0	377	1,146	2,700	5,400
Sales & marketing	3	192	1,527	3,524	5,700	10,500
Product development	90	384	516	1,007	2,100	4,200
Interest expense	2	4	0	0	0	0
General & admin. exp.	8	288	774	940	1,950	3,000
Total Expenses	103	868	3,337	7,163	13,605	25,410
Income before taxes	−103	−658	−1,328	−413	1,395	4,590
Provision for income taxes	0	0	0	0	0	−1,393
Net Income (Loss)	−103	−658	−1,328	−413	1,395	3,197

Source: Company records.
[a]Projected.

CHAPTER 12 The Role of CRM Technologies in Customer Management   **497**

	1993	1994	1995[a]	1996[a]	1997[a]	1998[a]
Current Assets:						
Cash	171	146	330	1,300	281	365
Accounts receivable	0	50	750	2,118	4,726	9,452
Other current	8	7	10	40	121	242
Total Current Assets	179	203	1,090	3,458	5,128	10,059
Equipment & improvements:		6	169	381	1,206	2,856
Less accumulated deprn	0	0	−43	−145	−386	−957
Net equip. & improvements	0	6	126	236	820	1,899
Capitalized software, net	0	0	0	0	0	0
Other assets	1	9	9	16	122	182
Total Assets	180	218	1,225	3,710	6,070	12,140
Current Liabilities:						
Acts payable & accr. expenses	5	25	254	481	1,379	2,645
Income taxes payable	0	0	0	0	0	557
Customer deposits	0	0	80	302	300	600
Deferred revenue	0	17	193	681	750	1,500
Total Current Liabilities	5	42	527	1,464	2,429	5,302
Debt	180	110	0	0	0	0
Stockholder equity:						
Common stock & paid-in capital	99	829	2,789	4,749	4,749	4,749
Retained earnings	−103	−763	−2,091	−2,503	−1,108	2,089
Total Stockholder Equity	−4	66	698	2,246	3,641	6,838
Total Liabilities & Equity	180	218	1,225	3,710	6,070	12,140

EXHIBIT 10 Balance Sheet

Source: Company records.
[a]Projected.

equipment budgeting, and human resource development. As a sales VP put it:

Our selling cycle is long and uncertain. Most of the time, until the order is in, I have no idea of what is going to happen and when it is going to happen. There are many cases when a sure-shot lead was left unanswered because the salesperson was chasing a low probability opportunity. There are other times when the salesperson did not push the customer along to the next stage in the buying cycle. This delayed the order and sent our forecast right out the window. Right now, it takes my team months to gather the data and by the time I get the information, it is too late to do anything.

I hate to go to management meetings with no clue of what is going to happen, when it's going to happen, and worst of all, why it did not happen. I want reports that will give me up-to-date status on every lead generated in the past 18 months. That will reduce my high blood pressure dramatically.

In my ideal world, my people can log onto their systems every morning and look at a plan for the day, week, month, quarter, and year. This would include the status of each opportunity, and what they need to do to close each sale. If we have this information available online, then we should be able to improve our selling effectiveness, reduce our selling time cycle by 2% to 3%, and impact our bottom line significantly.

I know I need more than a CMS. I also know that I do not need CSAS. I am not going to try to convince marketing and service about integrating their functions with sales. Give me a solution that will help *me* manage the sales pipeline better.

Miller knew that some of the functions currently available in the three modules of PROCEED's Sales System could serve as the basic building block to develop a product that provided answers for the sales VP's problems. Tanner called this the Trojan Horse. Miller added:

> Over the last couple months, we did try to push the current Sales System modules of PROCEED to various prospects. The response from these sales VPs was very discouraging. None of the prospects that saw the current product were even remotely serious about buying the product as it is today. They all said they needed a lot more functionalities than what we have right now. Frankly, I agree that PROCEED's sales system needs substantial work before it can be sold as a stand-alone Trojan Horse (TH) product.
>
> Unfortunately for us, when developing the sales system modules, we never thought they would be sold as stand-alone products. A lot of functions that the prospects want to see in TH are ones that we had planned to build into the other two systems of PROCEED. In order to add these functions and interfaces, we have to put in substantial effort in software design and development. Without this additional work, we do not have an adequate solution that will interest sales VPs.
>
> I wish we had known right in the beginning that we needed to develop TH. By now, for the same costs that we have already incurred in developing the three sales system modules of PROCEED, we would have developed TH as well. But, what's the point in crying over lost chances. We need to look ahead and make some decisions now. The most important question facing us is whether or not we should develop the TH product.
>
> If done right, using information provided by the salespeople for all their accounts, TH will allow a sales manager to review expected close dates of all opportunities and the probability of closing them on time. The sales manager can anticipate any shortfall in sales and set up early and timely intervention programs to manage the gaps in performance. Further, by archiving data over time,

a sales manager will be able to track and review previous wins and losses, associated sales activity, and competitive behavior to improve sales force performance.

Selling Cycle for TH Versus PROCEED

Selling TH was different from PROCEED in several ways. First, unlike PROCEED, TH was focused only on sales. This significantly reduced the number of people involved in the buying cycle. Second, it was easier to quantify the benefits of TH. This simplified the selling process for TH. Miller estimated that selling TH would take a third of the time to sell PROCEED. Finally, TH needed minimal customization. This included changing the number and names of segments in the opportunity pipeline and could be done at a fraction of the cost of customizing PROCEED.

Tanner believed that selling TH would be more like selling CMS. "We can go after this market by ourselves. We do not have to partner with SA consultants or other firms. Further, with low customization costs, we can afford to go after a much broader market than our current approach for PROCEED," he said.

THE DECISION

Miller and Tanner had to decide whether or not to go ahead with the launch of TH. Miller thought:

> PROCEED and TH will be targeted to different markets. Customers that are convinced about implementing CSAS are not going to be interested in looking at only TH.

Another issue that concerned Miller was the sales force:

> We do not have the resources to have separate sales forces for the two products. At the same time, I fear that if we ask our people to sell both, most of them will land up pushing TH rather than PROCEED. It gets worse if the customers of TH are unlikely to consider PROCEED in the long run.
>
> Pricing TH low to get entry into an account does not make sense. I do not think we will ever sell the whole system once we launch TH. If we decide to launch TH, we need to price it high. In addition, if the customers are really excited about TH, then they will be willing to pay almost any price for it.

PROCEED is priced at $2,400 per user and I think we should charge at least $1,000 per user for TH. At that price, we will extract a substantial part of the value of TH to a customer.

Tanner, on the other hand, felt that they should use TH to open customers doors. He preferred a low price approach for the TH:

> Setting a high price for TH will make it difficult to sell and will demand a lot more customer education effort on our part. It will put off potential customers who recently have spent a lot of money on hardware and software.
>
> TH should be priced at the same level as CMS. That is the reference customers will use to evaluate TH. A price of $400 is about right. At this price, our sales force will have to just go out and pick up orders. There is nothing more important to us today than orders in the book.
>
> I also believe that once we get into an account, it will just be a matter of time before we sell PROCEED. I realize we might not have PROCEED ready if we go ahead with TH. I do not think we will lose our first mover advantage if we were to pull out of the CSAS market for a couple of years.
>
> In fact, if we do well with TH, then we should have the resources to get back to PROCEED after a few years. That will be the right time to convert TH users to PROCEED.

Miller responded:

> I agree there is a crying need for TH. However, I do not share Tanner's feeling that customers will line up to buy TH. Further, I do not agree with his thought that we will not relinquish the CSAS market to others by temporarily pulling out of it.
>
> And then there is the issue of costs. I estimate that developing and fine-tuning TH will take the entire development team at least three months and cost about $200,000. This does not including marketing costs that could be very high.
>
> Educating customers about TH will demand a broad-based marketing strategy that could cost us half a million dollars over the next six to eight months. Once we create general awareness for TH, I estimate marketing costs per TH user will be a third that of PROCEED.

The Changing Competitive Environment

Recently, several things had changed at the low end of SA. Giants like Microsoft[5] and Lotus[6] had announced major strategic thrusts into this area. In addition, CMS vendors had announced their intent to upgrade existing CMS capabilities to allow users to hook onto networks, share information and manage sales opportunities. This would make the TH market extremely tough and competitive very quickly.

Staying on course and trying to sell PROCEED had its advantages. This market was less crowded with all CSAS vendors being small startups. And, this was not expected to change very soon. ■

---

[5]The maker of DOS and Windows operating system software and other application software such as Word, a word processor, and Excel, a spreadsheet software.
[6]The maker of Lotus 1-2-3 spreadsheet software and Notes groupware.

CHAPTER 13
How Customer Management Is Changing Marketing

Customer management involves a new mind-set and a new set of tools for interacting with the customer. More important, it is changing the nature of the marketing function itself. Marketing is in the process of transforming its focus on products and transactions to one on customers and relationships.

◆ HOW CUSTOMER EQUITY ANALYSIS CHANGES MARKETING

Traditional marketing was based on the "4 P's" (promotion, product, place, and price).[1] The customer equity perspective replaces this with the three drivers of customer equity (value equity, brand equity, and relationship equity). Superimposing the 4 P's on the three drivers of customer equity, we note that product, place, and price fit mostly into value equity, and promotion primarily serves to increase brand equity. There is nothing in the 4 P's about relationship equity! Marketing authors in recent years have realized this deficiency and have expanded the 4 P's to include a fifth P (people), but actually it is the people (customers) and the money that come from these customers that create all revenue, and creating revenue is what marketing is about.

Viewing profits as coming from customers rather than products should lead a company to organize its marketing function around customers rather than products. Databases for profitability analyses should be organized by customer rather than by product. For example, banks used to have separate databases for each of their products (checking account, savings account, home loans, etc.), but in recent years they have realized the importance of building databases that enable them to examine the relationship with a specific customer, across products. This implies one interrelated database rather than separate silos.[2]

---

[1] See, for example, Philip Kotler, *Managerial Marketing, Planning, Analysis, and Control* (Upper Saddle River, N.J.: Prentice Hall, 1967).
[2] See, for example, Frederick Newell, *Why CRM Doesn't Work: How to Win by Letting Customers Manage the Relationship* (New York: Bloomberg Press, 2003); and specific case studies profiled at *www.teradata.com*.

Likewise, brand managers should be replaced (or at least superseded) by customer managers. If customers are big, then the customer managers are key account managers, as are already common in business-to-business environments (B2B). If customers are small, then the customer managers are segment managers. Either way, the organization's resources should be allocated to customers or customer groups. The brand managers, if they still exist, should then obtain their resources from the customer managers. This alleviates the problem of brand managers behaving selfishly, and not in the best interest of the organization.

CUSTOMER MANAGEMENT AND MARKETING ACCOUNTABILITY

We have seen that customer management and measurement facilitate making marketing financially accountable. This has significant implications for the importance of the marketing function and even the emphasis of the firm itself. It has traditionally been the case that most marketing expenditures were unaccountable, as it was difficult to determine the extent to which specific marketing expenditures resulted in increases in revenve or profit. This has inevitably led to marketing being accorded less influence at the top levels of management. A company seeking to improve profits could account for initiatives that led to cost reductions, but could not confidently attribute revenue expansion to marketing initiatives. When revenues went up, companies could see that something had worked, but could not pinpoint the source of the good fortune.

The customer equity framework makes it possible to evaluate the return on investment (ROI) from marketing initiatives.[3] This not only makes marketing more efficient, by learning which initiatives are successful or unsuccessful, but it also gives marketing a more persuasive voice in the boardroom. The ability to show accountability gives marketing increased power at the top levels of the organization.[4]

Summary

The long-term shift from goods to services is happening in all sectors of every developed economy. Even goods firms are finding that the bulk of their profits come from service, rather than from the physical product itself. Successful service means knowing the customer, and knowing the customer means learning over time, and that, in turn,

---

[3]See for example, Jagdish N. Sheth and Rajendra S. Sisodia, "Marketing Productivity Issues and Analysis," *Journal of Business Research* 55 (May 2002): 349–63; Philip Kotler, "Driving Business Strategy," *Brand Strategy* 176 (October 2003): 13; and Peter Mitchell, "Demystifying Media Neutrality," *Journal of Database Marketing* 10 (July 2003): 303–12.

[4]For examples of research moving marketing in this direction, consider the following: Rajendra K. Srivastava, Tasadduq A. Shervani, and Liam Fahey, "Market-Based Assets and Shareholder Value: A Framework for Analysis," *Journal of Marketing* 62, no. 1 (1998): 2–18; Alan S. Dick and Kunal Basu, "Customer Loyalty: Toward an Integrated Conceptual Framework," *Journal of the Academy of Marketing Science* 22, no. 2 (1994): 99–113; and Ruth Bolton, "A Dynamic Model of the Duration of the Customer's Relationship with a Continuous Service Provider: The Role of Satisfaction," *Marketing Science* 17, no. 1 (1998): 45–65.

implies cultivating, measuring, and managing customer relationships. Marketing is changing by increasingly emphasizing these elements.[5]

So far, this shift is most evident in the service sector and in B2B. In both cases, businesses realize that their future success relies on the continuing relationships with profitable customers. The current areas of greatest change are the goods sector, especially consumer packaged goods and high technology—areas in which there has traditionally been much more of a product focus and a transaction mindset. Those areas are likely, over time, to become much more similar to the service sector and B2B in the way that they do marketing.

Managing customers is the emerging viewpoint for marketing, and is making marketing more efficient, more accountable, and more influential over time. This book has provided an introduction to some of the methods used to create this new marketing revolution.

Review Questions and Exercises

1. How has your view of marketing changed as a result of reading this book and taking this course? What are the most important trends influencing marketing? How will these changes influence the way managers practice marketing?
2. What are the implications of customer equity management for other functional areas in the corporation? How will customer equity management influence financial decision making? How might it influence accounting practices? How will it affect operations or information technology?
3. What critical skills will marketers need in the next ten years? What traditional marketing skills and approaches may diminish or disappear?

---

[5]For recent marketing management textbooks incorporating these elements see, for example, Roger J. Best, *Market-Based Management, 3rd ed.* (Upper Saddle River, N.J.: Prentice Hall, 2002); and Philip Kotler, *Marketing Management, 11th ed.* (Upper Saddle River, N.J.: Prentice Hall, 2002). For additional readings in this area, consider Christine Moorman and Roland T. Rust (1999), "The Role of Marketing," *Journal of Marketing*, 63 (JM/MSI special issue on fundamental issues in marketing, 1999): 180–97; Roland T. Rust, Tim Ambler, Gregory S. Carpenter, V. Kumar, and Rajendra K. Srivastava, "Measuring Marketing Productivity: Current Knowledge and Future Directions," *Journal of Marketing* (forthcoming); Roland T. Rust, Valarie A. Zeithaml, and Katherine N. Lemon, "Customer-Centered Brand Management" *Harvard Business Review*, (September 2004), 110–118. Stephen L. Vargo and Robert F. Lusch, "Evolving to a New Dominant Logic for Marketing," *Journal of Marketing* 68 (January 2004); 1–17.

Customer Profitability and Customer Relationship Management at RBC Financial Group (Abridged)

Case 13-1 Customer Profitability and Customer Relationship Management at RBC Financial Group (Abridged)

V. G. Narayanan

(1) Who are our most important customers? (2) How do we put them in charge of our Company?
—SCREEN SAVER[1] ON THE COMPUTER OF KEVIN PURKISS, SENIOR MANAGER, CUSTOMER VALUE ANALYTICS

INTRODUCTION

Richard McLaughlin looked again at the latest customer profitability reports. The new data mining capability that RBC Financial Group had pioneered was astonishing. The good news was that customer, customer segment, and product profitability numbers were more comprehensive and accurate than with the Bank's old profitability model. The bad news was that those precise numbers clearly showed major losses in the Bank's personal checking accounts. McLaughlin knew the Bank was also struggling with its seventh out of eight ranking among financial institutions in the Bank's internal value for money study. The Canadian public increasingly wanted value and personal service from its banks. Competition among Canada's leading financial institutions was fierce as the industry responded to deregulation and new niche-market entrants. McLaughlin's thoughts turned to how he would present this information to the Bank's segment and product managers, and questioned how the Bank should respond:

Now we have real customer profitability numbers and, through our customer relationship management (CRM) tools, we know an awful lot about customer preferences and needs. The question is, what do we do with this information? How can the Bank derive value from CRM and customer profitability? How can we turn unprofitable customers and products into profitable ones? Is there a way to enhance the Bank's value in the eyes of the banking public? How can we put the whole picture together and make decisions that work for both the Bank and our customers?

RBC FINANCIAL GROUP

RBC Financial Group entered the tumultuous twenty-first century as Canada's leading bank. With Canada's finance industry in flux from changes in banking regulations, many smaller banks changed their focus away from retail banking or were acquired by larger banks. In the early part of the new century, RBC emerged as one of Canada's few full-service, national, and international financial institutions.

RBC Financial Group, headquartered in Toronto, had five main lines of business: personal and commercial (retail) banking (RBC Royal Bank), insurance (RBC Insurance), wealth management (RBC Investments), corporate and investment banking (RBC Capital Markets), and transaction processing (RBC Global Services). Canada's largest bank when measured by assets and market capitalization, RBC owned

---

The case was prepared by Research Associate Lisa Brem (under the direction of Professor V. G. Narayanan). Copyright © 2002 by the President and Fellows of Harvard College. Harvard Business School Case 102-072.
[1] Downloaded from *www.fastcompany.com/homepage*.

$270 billion[2] in assets, had 23 million retail accounts,[3] 700 products, 58,000 employees, and served 10 million personal, commercial, corporate, and public sector customers in North America and around the world.

RBC Royal Bank (Royal Bank), which accounted for 50% of RBC's cash net income, had an extensive delivery network that included 1,300 branches, 4,800 automated banking machines (ABMs), 87,250 proprietary point-of-sale terminals, over 900 mobile sales staff, 1.4 million online banking customers, and 2 million telephone banking customers. The Bank also boasted an international network that included 300 offices in over 30 countries. The personal banking division encompassed consumer and small business banking and loans, while the commercial side served larger companies earning $5 million to $25 million. The multinational corporations were covered under the corporate and investment-banking business line and were not a part of Royal Bank. Royal Bank also included Card Services, which provided Visa credit cards and debit cards; RBC Centura, a U.S. retail bank acquired in June 2001; and RBC Prism, a U.S. mortgage originator.

HISTORY OF RBC FINANCIAL GROUP

In the post-war era beginning in 1946, the Royal Bank devised the philosophy of being "all things to all people." It began an expansion nationally and internationally that broadened its delivery network, while simultaneously developing new products and services. In the 1960s and 1970s, the Bank increased its commitment to technology and decentralization in response to changing market conditions. In 1968, 25 automatic banking machines (ABMs) were added to domestic operations.[4] During that time, the Royal Bank was already employing technology and a customer orientation philosophy to gain a competitive edge. As one history of the Bank cited:

> The 1971 Annual Report provided an interesting account of how automated back-room transactions improved both the cost and quality of operations ... this also helped to free up front-line people to deliver the services that required a personal touch. New possibilities for specialization were directed toward improving service to the customer.[5]

The 1980s were turbulent times for Canadian banks, as changes to the Bank Act of 1871[6] allowed foreign competitors limited access in the Canadian market (1980), and deregulation of the financial industry (1986 and 1987). Deregulation allowed crossover between the "four pillars"—banking, trust,[7] securities, and insurance—which had been kept separate since the original Bank Act.

Royal Bank responded by purchasing companies that allowed it to become a fully integrated financial service institution. By 1989 Royal had entered the securities market with a bang, capturing 50% of the mutual fund (offered through banks) market. In addition:

> The 1990 acquisition of 70% of Marcil Trust Company, specialists in real estate, strengthened [Royal Bank's] base in the trust industry.... Market-share received increased attention during the period because it was viewed both as a condition and a measure of success: size was important. The Royal did not intend to participate in domestic markets that it could not dominate....
>
> [I]n ... 1992, the Royal was the first to offer group retirement products. The thrust was to develop relationships with different

---

[2] All financial data reported in Canadian dollars.
[3] Canadian population was estimated at 30.75 million in 2000, with the largest concentration of people in Ontario, Quebec, and British Columbia. Average income after taxes for two people or more in the same household averaged $49,626 in 1998 (statistics provided by *www.statcan.ca*, accessed August 27, 2001).
[4] James L. Darroch, *Canadian Banks and Global Competitiveness* (McGill-Queen's University Press 1994), p. 136.

[5] Ibid.
[6] The Bank Act of 1871 created chartered banks that could engage only in banking. The Bank Act and charters were to be reviewed every 10 years. (Darroch, Appendix Two).
[7] Canadian Trusts were similar to U.S. Savings and Loans. They were typically smaller, regional companies that issued mortgages, set up and administered deposit accounts, wills, trust accounts, and engaged in estate planning. Some Trusts offered specialized investment services. Prior to deregulation, Trusts were the only financial entities allowed to issue mortgages.

target markets by offering products and delivery mechanisms that made customers feel comfortable as they discussed their personal financial affairs. Transactions at a teller's wicket [window] were no longer the model. Now bankers had to listen.[8]

CURRENT ENVIRONMENT

Throughout most of Canadian banking history, the six largest Canadian banks enjoyed a relatively undifferentiated and "friendly competition" industry structure. By the late 1990s, however, changes were on the horizon. The advent of Internet banking and the continued lowering of protections for domestic banks spelled an end to the banking oligopoly. While the Internet represented both opportunities and threats, the insurgence of foreign banks coupled with the minister of finance's halting of two important mergers was a warning call to Canada's banks that they would soon face competition from large out-of-country banks that could rival or exceed their own resources.[9]

While the big banks cast one wary eye offshore, the other was trained on the small Internet upstarts that threatened to eat away at their bread-and-butter personal and small business accounts. Being "all things to all people" suddenly became a lot harder.

Kevin Purkiss, Senior Manager, Customer Value Analytics, summed up Royal Bank's perception of the competitive landscape:

> We perceive TD Canada Trust as our nearest and most aggressive competitor at least as far as a full service bank is concerned. The rest of the large banks have slightly differentiated strategies in line with their expertise. The Bank of Nova Scotia, for example, has been redefining itself as a retail multi-national bank. CIBC (Canadian Imperial Bank of Commerce), the second-largest bank in Canada, is the largest bank credit card issuer and is also a close competitor in the Canadian mortgage market.
>
> Other types of competitors pose different threats. What we think of as non-traditional competitors entered the market with specialized products and low costs. ING Bank of Canada, for example, is a virtual bank that offers a very attractive rate on deposit accounts. In order to access the deposit account, the customer must transfer money from their existing checking account (in a rival brick and mortar bank) to ING's electronic repository. ING can offer high rates because it does not have the physical infrastructure that a bank like RBC Royal Bank has to maintain. ING has since expanded into a more complete product offering including mortgages and loans.
>
> Another emerging market is in "white labeling" or the use of bank services by non-bank companies. For example, one of Canada's largest supermarkets, Loblaw's, recently partnered with a division of CIBC to offer President's Choice Financial Services, which includes no-fee banking and a discount on groceries to Loblaw's customers. CIBC is providing the service, but it is marketed as a Loblaw service and physically located in the supermarket.
>
> The common denominator in all these new products and markets is the customer. How a financial entity focuses on customer needs is the differentiation point in our industry right now.

DEVELOPING A CRM PHILOSOPHY

The ultimate goal of CRM was to bring together in one place a view of all contacts, transactions, accounts and interactions with each customer. A financial institution's fully integrated CRM system could allow its personal bankers (PBs) to access a customer's transaction history. For example, the ideal CRM system could provide the following information to PBs[10] when triggered by a customer call or visit:

- address, age, and account balances,
- all contacts the customer had at any company location, phone center, or Internet site,
- what level of service the customer qualified for, based on current and future profitability,

---
[8]Darroch, pp. 146–147.
[9]Jordan Kendall, with Bruce D. Temkin, Emily Gaszynski, and Charles Finlay, The Forrester Report, *Canada's Big Banks Unravel*, May 2001, pp. 6–12.

[10]Royal Bank did not necessarily provide or want to provide this kind of information directly to the desktop due to client confidentiality and privacy.

- what products the customer held at the time of the call,
- what products the customer was targeted/approved for by sales and marketing,
- how the customer responded to targeted direct marketing campaigns.

Although the benefits promised to be great, CRM was expensive and difficult to deploy, particularly on a large scale. One U.S. industry journal survey in 2001 reported found that "although the vast majority of respondents—78%—consider CRM critical, just 35% have actually implemented it."[11] Costs could run into the millions for enterprise-wide systems. Various roadblocks stymied successful implementation, such as budget constraints, lack of coordination and cooperation within companies, lack of management commitment, unsupportive cultural climate, and inadequate technological infrastructure.[12]

Companies most successful with CRM created ongoing repeat purchase relationships with their customers and had the resources and infrastructure to capture detailed data about the customer's behavior when the customer purchased, used, and repurchased their products and services. Industries in which companies had made inroads to CRM included airlines, auto manufacturers, and financial services.

CRM at Royal Bank The seeds of the CRM program at Royal Bank were sown in 1997 as the result of several marketing projects within the Bank. The Strategic Marketing Research and Analytics (SMR&A) group had been conducting brand research, as well as segmentation and predictive modeling using information from Royal Bank's data mart.[13] This research was conducted with the objective of determining the image perceptions of major financial institutions and identifying the optimum positioning for RBC Royal Bank. In response to the competitive pressures nipping at its heels, Royal Bank wanted to actively use the information that it had been collecting on its customers to interact with them in a more informed way.

One study conducted in 1997 asked 2,000 customers of the large Canadian financial institutions (FIs) what aspects of banking they most highly valued and juxtaposed those findings with an assessment of FI strengths (see Exhibit 1). The results created the "burning platform" for CRM within the Bank. As Gaétane Lefebvre, Vice President of SMR&A, explained:

> What was most important to the customer was customer intimacy. It encompassed issues such as trust, reassurance, a feeling that the bank knows them, understands their needs, recognizes who they are and values their business. Conversely, banks offered more concrete things like large branch and ATM networks, convenient hours, and easy access to accounts.

Richard McLaughlin, Vice President of CRM and Information Management, added:

> Conventional wisdom up until this point was that the key differentiating factor for banks was a 24/7 call center and a branch on every corner. This study identified a whole new area of differentiation that Royal could explore.

Differentiation among the leading Canadian banks in the newly competitive environment was highly sought after. CRM was pitched up the ranks from marketing to the head office of Royal Bank as a business philosophy crucial for developing an expertise in customer intimacy. Royal Bank chose to deploy CRM in points of contact critical to the customer experience such as call centers, branches, and direct mail.

Reorganization Around CRM

Primary customer segments; Key, Growth, and Prime, were used to realign Royal Bank's business (see Exhibit 2). As Kevin Purkiss explained:

> The segment structure reflects life stages and the complexity of their financial needs. The groupings also reflect commonalities in service and product requirements. The interesting part to note is that the current

---

[11]Mario Apicella and Tom Yager, "Solid CRM Is Difficult, But Not Impossible," *InfoWorld*, April 16, 2001, proquest.com, accessed May 3, 2000, p. 55.
[12]Ibid.
[13]The data mart at Royal Bank used a hardware platform provided by NCR called TeraData, which housed the Bank's customer information files.

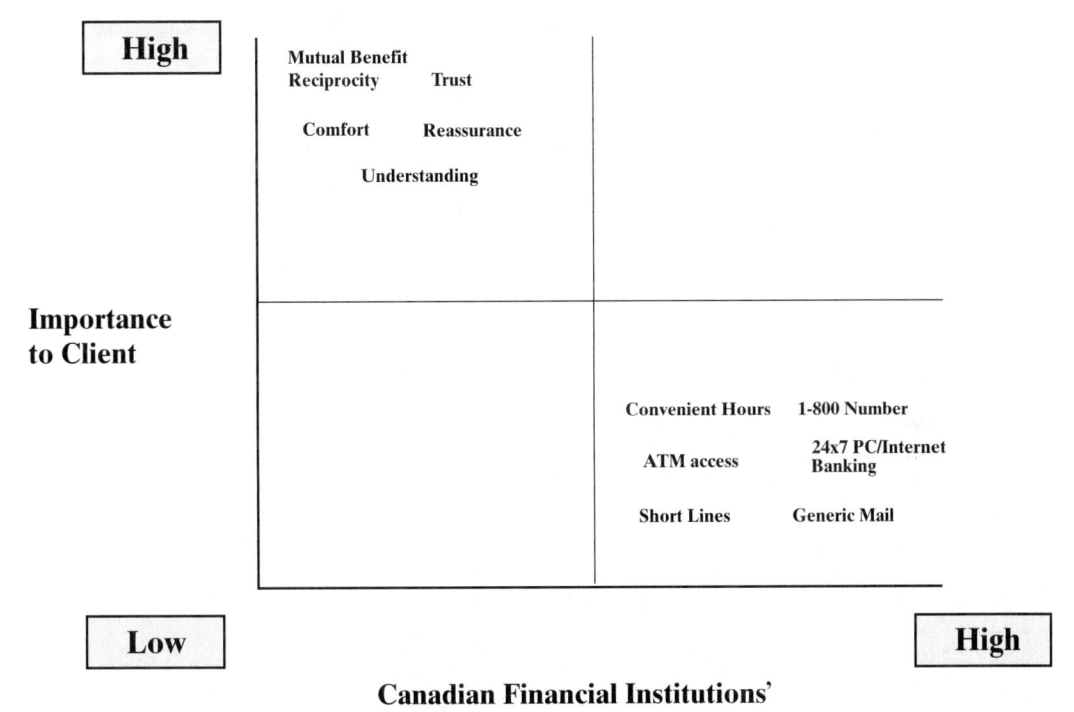

Exhibit 1 RCB Financial Group 1996 Marketing Study Results

Importance to Client (High / Low) vs. **Canadian Financial Institutions' Proficiency at Delivering** (Low / High)

High Importance / Low Proficiency quadrant:
- Mutual Benefit
- Reciprocity
- Trust
- Comfort
- Reassurance
- Understanding

Low Importance / High Proficiency quadrant:
- Convenient Hours
- 1-800 Number
- ATM access
- 24x7 PC/Internet Banking
- Short Lines
- Generic Mail

Source: Company records.

profitability between these groups is quite different. For example, the Key group comprises four sub-segments—Youth, Nexus, Small Business, and Farming & Lifestyle Agriculture. These sub-segments have low current value, but many within these sub-segments have the potential to provide higher levels of profit for the Bank.

The Growth stage represents clients in mid-life, and/or businesses that are still growing their assets and have high credit and financial advisory needs. Our strategy is to retain, grow, and consolidate these relationships.

The Prime grouping consists of more mature customers in the accumulation and

Exhibit 2 Royal Bank Personal Business Line Major Customer Segments and Subsegments

Key	*Growth*	*Prime*
Getting started stage—Youth	Life stage 2—Building Business	Life stage 3—Accumulating
Life stage 1—Nexus	Agriculture	Life stage 4—Preserving
Small Business		
Farming & Lifestyle Agriculture		

Source: Company records.

preservation phases with significant potential for full RBCFG offerings. The value proposition for the Prime segment is trusted service and referral to specialized resources.

Segment managers competed for resources along with product managers and functional area managers. This "friendly competition" was designed to foster close collaboration between functional areas, product and segment managers, and centers of expertise (such as marketing, CRM, and SMR&A). (See Exhibits 3a and b.)

The change, of course, was not entirely seamless. Richard McLaughlin recalled some of the resistance met by the new customer centered organization:

> We had some very traditional product and functional silos in this organization that had limited motivation for moving toward a more customer-centered framework. Part of the problem was our inability to fully communicate about how things would work. Our corporate processes were executed more from consensus and conversations than a clear road map, so when we started to insert new processes, we received some response that it would slow people's decision making down. Another problem was the power shift. We were taking some power out the product managers and putting it in the customer manager's realm. To make matters worse, customer managers tended to be marketing people, while product managers tended to be bankers. There was not a lot of understanding between the two groups about what each could bring to the table.

The consolidation of the regional sales and marketing groups meant that instead of calling regional offices for lead lists, branches received lists from the sales and marketing office in Toronto. Royal Bank also created a small, specialized group that produced ad hoc or follow-up leads as requested by the branch. The goal was to replace the often-haphazard sales lead process at the local level with centralized and standardized sales leads.

Account Manager for Investments (AMI) Jamie Reich explained how the process of building and using sales leads had changed since the Bank adopted CRM:

> Before CRM, every branch had a different way to generate sales leads and account managers were responsible for creating their own lists. One way to do this was to go to the regional credit department and ask for a list of people age 25 to 45 who held at least three products, for example. After a while the department would generate a list based on your query, and you'd make calls off that list. The leads were based on how good a query you put in, and you got new lists depending on when you had time to stop by the credit department. It wasn't very consistent or accessible across all branches.

> Now, the leads are generated centrally and everyone has direct access to them. The leads have gone from paper based to being available electronically. I also have seen the leads improve from rather generic to more customized. For example, I used to get a lot of leads for customers who might be interested in credit products. These weren't very helpful to me since I deal mainly in investments. Lately, the lead lists sent to me have been much more focused on investments and products that are of real interest to my customers.

Reich's job was to manage the accounts of customers that were chosen[14] for the Bank's relationship banking program. The program provided clients with a personal contact at the Bank who coordinated all aspects of the client's business with the Bank, from issuing mortgages, to lines of credit, to investment accounts. Reich managed roughly 200 clients at RBC Royal Bank's main Toronto branch. In a typical week, Reich would speak to 20 of his customers on the phone and meet another 10 in his office. CRM helped him and other account managers work more efficiently. As Reich explained:

> Account managers know their customers and know what their needs are, but these electronic lead lists help us to remember to call and offer products. They also save us

---

[14] Customers were chosen for the AMI program based on their current and potential profitability.

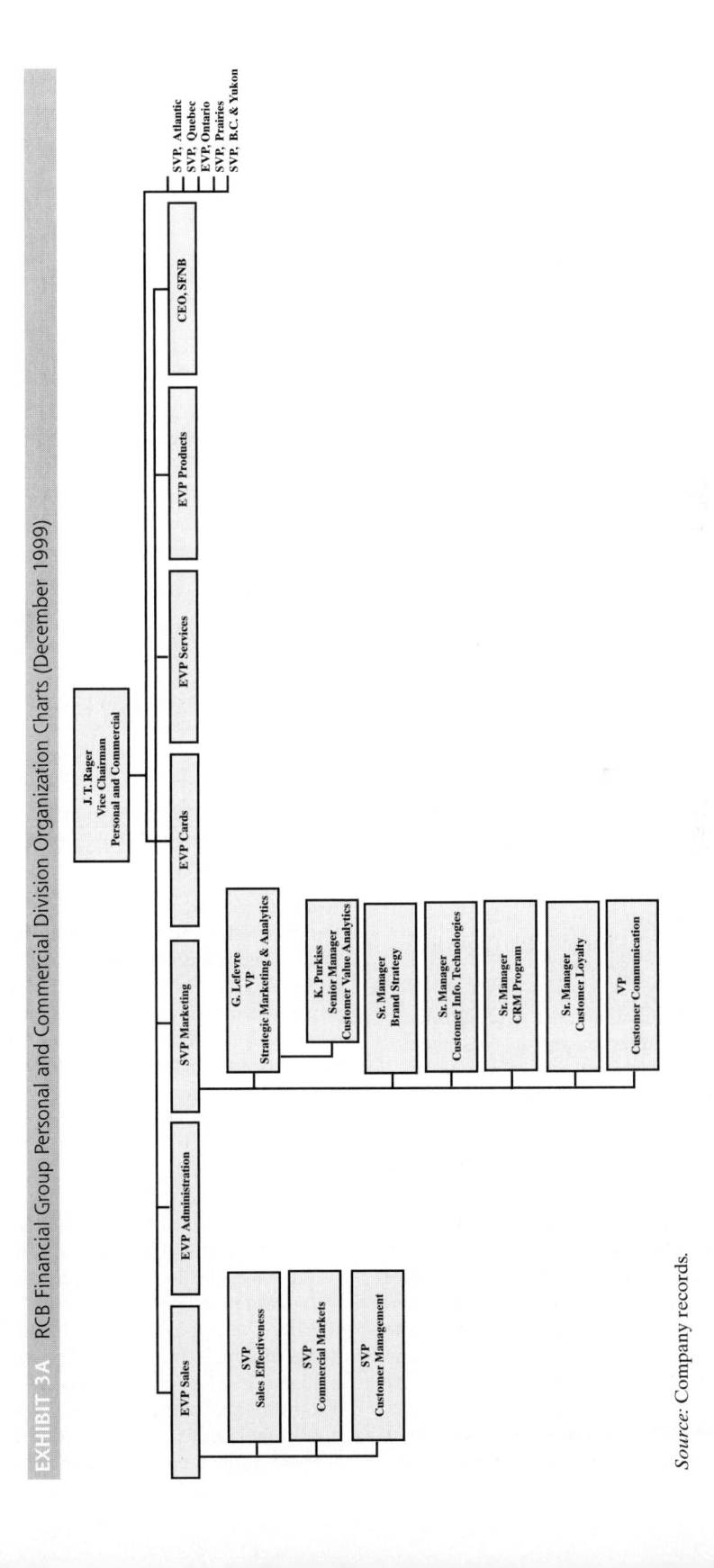

EXHIBIT 3A RCB Financial Group Personal and Commercial Division Organization Charts (December 1999)

```
                              J.T. Rager
                            Vice Chairman
                        Personal and Commercial
    ┌──────────┬──────────┬──────────┬─────────┬──────────┬──────────┬──────────┬──────────┐
    EVP        SVP        EVP        EVP       EVP        EVP        EVP        CEO,
    Sales      Marketing  Administration Cards  Services   Products            SFNB
                                                                                │
                                                                    ┌───────────┤
                                                                    SVP, Atlantic
                                                                    SVP, Quebec
                                                                    EVP, Ontario
                                                                    EVP, Prairies
                                                                    SVP, B.C. & Yukon
```

EVP Sales reports:
- SVP Sales Effectiveness
- SVP Commercial Markets
- SVP Customer Management

SVP Marketing reports:
- G. Lefevre, VP Strategic Marketing & Analytics
  - K. Purkiss, Senior Manager Customer Value Analytics
- Sr. Manager Brand Strategy
- Sr. Manager Customer Info. Technologies
- Sr. Manager CRM Program
- Sr. Manager Customer Loyalty
- VP Customer Communication

Source: Company records.

509

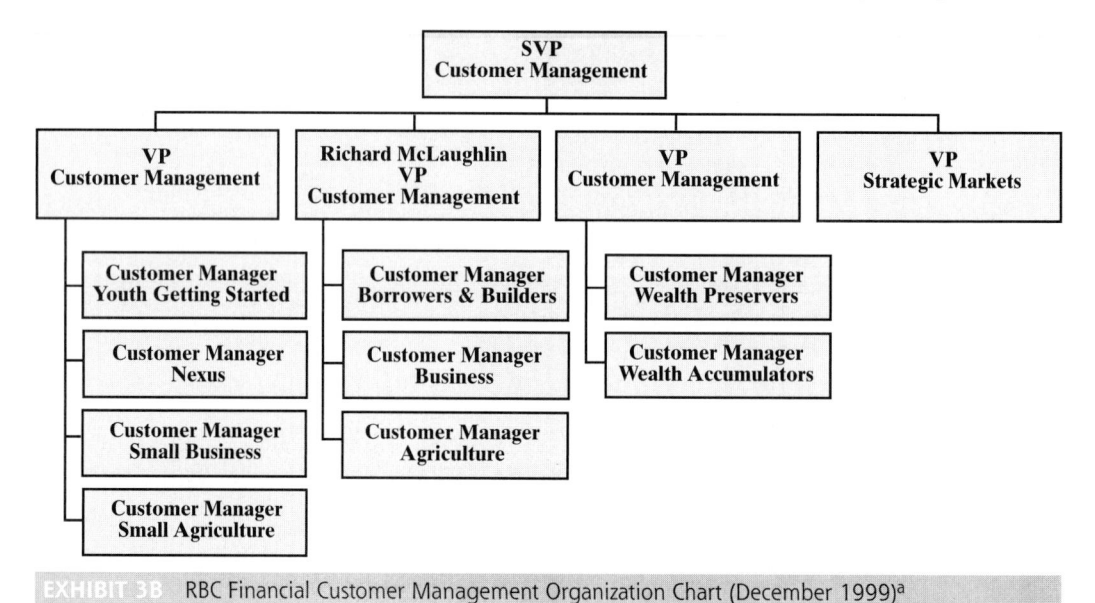

```
                        SVP
                 Customer Management
    ┌──────────────┬───────────────┬──────────────┐
    VP        Richard McLaughlin      VP              VP
Customer           VP              Customer       Strategic
Management      Customer           Management      Markets
                Management
```

- Customer Manager Youth Getting Started
- Customer Manager Nexus
- Customer Manager Small Business
- Customer Manager Small Agriculture

- Customer Manager Borrowers & Builders
- Customer Manager Business
- Customer Manager Agriculture

- Customer Manager Wealth Preservers
- Customer Manager Wealth Accumulators

EXHIBIT 3B RBC Financial Customer Management Organization Chart (December 1999)[a]

Source: Company records.

[a] In 1999, Richard McLaughlin serviced as a Vice President of Customer Management. In 2000, he returned to his prior position as Vice President of CRM & Information Management, reporting directly to the Senior Vice President of Marketing.

time and are generating better and better leads for new clients.

Richard McLaughlin explained how centralizing profitability measurement in the corporate office freed the frontline staff from having to collect customer information:

> We reach a decision in the central office, based on our information and analysis, about how valuable the customer is or will be. We then inform the salesperson who works directly with the customer. This process eliminates the need for a salesperson to capture and process customer information.

In addition to allowing the Bank to centralize sales lead generation, locating the sales and marketing groups in Toronto also made it easier for them to interface with SMR&A, CRM, and information management teams. One of the areas where these groups collaborated was in using current and future customer profitability to determine targeted direct marketing campaigns, levels of customer service, and other customer-oriented decision making.

CUSTOMER PROFITABILITY AND POTENTIAL MEASUREMENT AT ROYAL BANK

Royal Bank had been experimenting with customer profitability measurement since the early 1990s. The marketing group deployed a model on the personal banking side in 1992 that used aggregate information rather than actual data. The Bank analyzed its then customer base of approximately 8 million customers and distributed the customer profit over deciles. The Bank learned that roughly 20% of its customers accounted for 100% of its profit. As Kevin Purkiss explained:

> The model placed customers into three large "buckets": A, B, and C. The "A" customers made the most profit, the "B" customers made some, and the "C" customers broke even or lost money. This information was distributed to the field office. It helped align the sales force around customer profitability and planted the seeds for the new customer-centric organization. However, it wasn't refined enough for advanced channel

optimization or relationship pricing. In addition, we realized later that in some instances, customers were treated without consideration of the potential business they could contribute.

About the time Richard McLaughlin was hired to head the CRM implementation, the Bank realized it needed a "more robust profitability measurement." The search was on for a better model. By 1998, marketing had developed a prototype of the model it wanted to employ. The group went shopping for software packages that would fit the bill. While none seemed to be exactly right, the Bank found that NCR was developing a package called Value Analyzer that looked promising.[15] The Bank agreed to serve as a "beta site" for NCR, while tailoring Value Analyzer to its needs. The software promised to make profitability calculations much faster. The high volume and complexity of the Bank's accounts required high processing power. Since many groups depended on this information downstream, the raw data had to be processed within a few hours.

The SMR&A group was quite excited about the level of detail that this new model promised to deliver. As Purkiss explained: "The new model was to be a vast improvement over the 1992 measurement system. We would be going from using muskets to rifles, or from having a machete to a scalpel."

Once Value Analyzer came on line, the Bank found that profitability rankings changed by at least two deciles for 70% of customers. More accurate spread information, customer specific risk assessments, transaction based fee and costs elements contributed to these changes. However, the Bank realized that customer profitability calculations were not enough. As Lefebvre explained:

> We came to understand that customers can be both profitable and have the potential to be profitable, and that the bank needs

both kinds of customers. One big "Aha" came when we realized we had very deep relationships with wealth preservers, but very weak relationships with younger segments. We needed to shift our approach. We became willing to invest in some sub-segments such as Nexus, in order to nurture our relationship with potentially profitable customers. The customer potential calculation enabled us to determine on which customers we would be willing to take losses in the short term. SMR&A developed the notion of potential in 1997. This was part of the original reason for adopting CRM.

Our new strategy was to look at our customers' total holdings and figure out how to deepen their relationship with the bank if they had potential. For example, were we losing opportunities to sell products to those customers? Are potentially profitable and profitable customers being lured away?

Royal Bank found that truly useful customer profitability models had to begin with detailed, accurate account or customer level activity based costing information. Without this infusion of real data and accurate activity driver rates, customer profitability was scattershot. (See Exhibit 4.)

In addition to calculating current profitability for customers and customer segments, Royal Bank also began experimenting with ways to measure future profitability and lifetime value. The Bank looked at two ways to measure lifetime value: (1) assuming that the current profitability percentile of the customer would remain constant throughout his or her projected lifetime and calculating the present value of those profits, and (2) factoring in other variables such as: age, tenure with the Bank, number of products held, probability of acquisition (how likely to add products to portfolio), and attrition (of products). Lifetime value was calculated individually and could be aggregated up to segment level.

USING CUSTOMER PROFITABILITY FOR CUSTOMER DECISIONING

Once the Bank determined customer profitability and lifetime value, it included those measures when determining customer decisions. For Royal

---

[15] Other companies marketing CRM software at the time were ABC Technologies, PeopleSoft, PMG Systems, Oracle, Fiserv IPS/Sendero, HNC Financial Solutions, and Metavante (Meridien Research, "Putting ABC into Customer Profitability," *Customer Knowledge*, vol. 4, no. 1, Sepember 27, 2000, p. 10).

> **EXHIBIT 4** Components of Old Versus New Customer Profitability Model

As Table A illustrates, although the same process was used in the older profitability model, the new model required the ABC information to be much more precise.

Activity-based costs The Bank had been tracking ABC information for approximately 20 years. In the 1980s, it began to develop a system to calculate and update activity-based costs quarterly by transaction and product. The current system was implemented in 1991 and was enhanced during the late 1990s to differentiate costs by delivery channels such as branch, Internet, telephone, and ABM.

The cost system at Royal Bank started with the general ledger. Chitwant Kohli, Vice President of Costing and Profitability, explained the ABC system:

As a services company, we are most interested in tracking labor costs, which make up over 60% of non-interest expenses. We extract expense data quarterly from the general ledger for each individual cost center. These cost centers are then grouped with like units based on products services and activities performed by the unit. We refer to this as the processing path.

For example, domestic branches, which sell and service the same product lines using the same processes, become a unit group. Similarly, call centers, business-banking centers, and service delivery units that perform the same product-specific activities become unique groups. Through grouping units by product line and processing path, channel views are created. Head Office groups, regional offices, and IT costs are also identified in separate buckets.

Within the 30 to 40 unique unit type groups, we establish total staff time consumed by each activity based on unit time per activity multiplied by volumes processed. This enables the proper allocation of the unit's salary cost to products and activities and also

TABLE A Old versus New Customer Profitability Model

Input	*Old Model*	*New Model*
Interest revenue (funds transfer pricing)	Average revenue by product	Actual net interest revenue by account, using internal transfer pricing
Fees and commissions	Average fee per product	Actual fees by account
Direct expenses (event costing)	Average Activity-Based Costs	Transaction level cost, rolled up to individual account and customer
Indirect expenses (overhead)	Allocated across products	Allocated across products
Risk provision	Average risk per product	Expected risk score by account

Source: Company records and adapted from Meridien Research, Inc., "Putting ABC into Customer Profitability," *Customer Knowledge*, vol. 4, no. 1, September 27, 2000 and adapted from NCR Case Study, Royal Bank Finds Micro Markets with NCR Tool, www.ncr.com, accessed April 25, 2001, page 3.

forms the basis for apportioning premises and general operating costs. Once we have these drivers by product, activity and channel, we can aggregate costs across all units to arrive at both transaction and total product cost. These costs are then available for use in profitability models.

For example, we can report the full end-to-end product cost of residential mortgages including acquisition and renewal costs by channel, back office processing, call center support, system costs, Head Office and regional overheads. For every customer we can then arrive at costs associated with "ownership" of each separate product in the customer's portfolio, based on transaction usage and channel preference.

The amount of time spent on each activity is updated as needed. We have also recently instituted the idea of "champion branches"—a cross section of branches that provide activity times, volumes, and costs on an ongoing basis.

While labor costs are allocated based on studies of actual time spent on activities, indirect costs and the cost of excess capacity are allocated proportionately across all products based on the level of direct expense attracted.

Interest revenue and transfer pricing Royal Bank determined profits on an asset product, such as a mortgage, using actual interest income, less the transfer rate on the mortgage. Conversely, profits for a liability product, such as a savings account, were determined by subtracting the actual interest paid out by the Bank from the transfer rate on the money in the deposit account.

Risk calculation When a customer sought to purchase a loan product, the Bank determined whether to grant the loan, and at what price. The Bank used a number of factors, such as income, debt service ratio, cash flow, and third party–provided credit reports, to make this initial decision. Once the loan was granted, the Bank assigned a risk score (adjusted monthly) based on the nature and frequency of transactions in the customer's accounts. The score was converted to a cost driver that was then used to allocate the cost of expected credit losses to that customer. Once all the inputs were entered, the customer profitability software calculated the customer profitability. For example, one customer may have two accounts with the Bank, a home loan and a savings account. Although one account was losing money, the other was quite profitable. The customer as a whole was making a profit for the Bank. (See **Table B**.)

TABLE B Sample Customer Profitability Calculation for Customer John Doe (January 2001)

	Home Loan	Savings Account
Net interest revenue	$60	$2
Other revenue	$ 0	$0
Direct expense	$ 3	$5
Indirect expense	$ 1	$1
Risk provision	$ 5	$0
Total profitability per account	$51	($4)

Source: Company records.

Bank, decisioning encompassed customized marketing campaigns, alignment of pricing discretion, and alignment of level of service based on depth (how many products held) and potential (lifetime value) of a relationship.

As Gaétane Lefebvre explained:

> Customer decisioning refers to the customer strategies that are built in our decision engine. This engine contains a multitude of category trees. One of the most significant trees leverages four strategic predictive models: profitability, client (credit) risk, client vulnerability (how vulnerable the Bank is to losing the client), and lifetime value. Depending on how people rate, (high, medium, or low) for each model, they are placed into one of 14 categories, for which the Bank will have a primary objective: to retain, grow, manage client risk, or optimize costs. We can then use these categories (or grouping of categories) for marketing effectiveness, courtesy overdraft, allocation of rate discretion, and differentiated service. These categories are a proxy for the Bank's objectives, while the segments (such as Nexus and Wealth Accumulators) are a proxy for the client's needs. We strongly believe that it is the alignment of the Bank's and customers' objectives, which will allow us to differentiate ourselves in the marketplace. (See Exhibit 5.)

Although the marketing department started working with customer lifetime value and segmentation, the information given to the branches was limited to a profitability ranking that continued to use the three bucket (A, B, and C) system. Detailed information on segmentation was not disseminated to the branches.

Customized Marketing Campaigns

Customer profitability was one of the primary determinants the Bank used to segment its customers into groupings and sub-groupings in order to target these groups for marketing campaigns. SMR&A also conducted studies on customer segment goals, needs, likes and dislikes, the types of products from which they would most likely benefit, and developed models to determine their propensity to buy. Using this information, SMR&A targeted customers within segments or sub-segments for certain products, offers, and marketing channels (such as direct mail, telephone solicitation, or an in-person sales call).

As one report explained:

> At the Royal Bank, the 9 million personal retail clients are segmented into discrete segments based on attitudinal and behavioral factors, current and potential profitability, expected purchasing behavior, vulnerabilities, and channel preferences. Strategies are then developed, not only for each segment but also for hundreds of micro-segments within each segment—the ultimate objective of this quest being one-to-one marketing. Individual treatment strategies can be tested on small cells of clients to establish what works and what doesn't, and to test refinements on a continuing basis.[16]

Rather than passing raw data on to the customer contact points, SMR&A inserted the sales leads into the customer's file. Purkiss described a typical scenario for a customer coming into a branch seeking to open a line of credit:

> The customer enters the branch and gives the account manager her Royal Bank client card. Once it is swiped into the computer, the manager can access the client file, which includes information on her age, address, and what products she holds. It also notes that she has been targeted for a particular line of credit product. That information guides the manager through the interaction with the client. He no longer has to ask her for every detail about where she lives or what her financial situation is. He knows instantly that she is eligible for a credit line and can quickly and confidently answer her questions. This process is much more efficient and it eliminates a lot of stress for the

---

[16]NCR Case Study, "Royal Bank Finds Micro Markets with NCR Tool," www.NCR.com (accessed April 25, 2001), p. 5.

EXHIBIT 5 Royal Bank CRM Initiatives

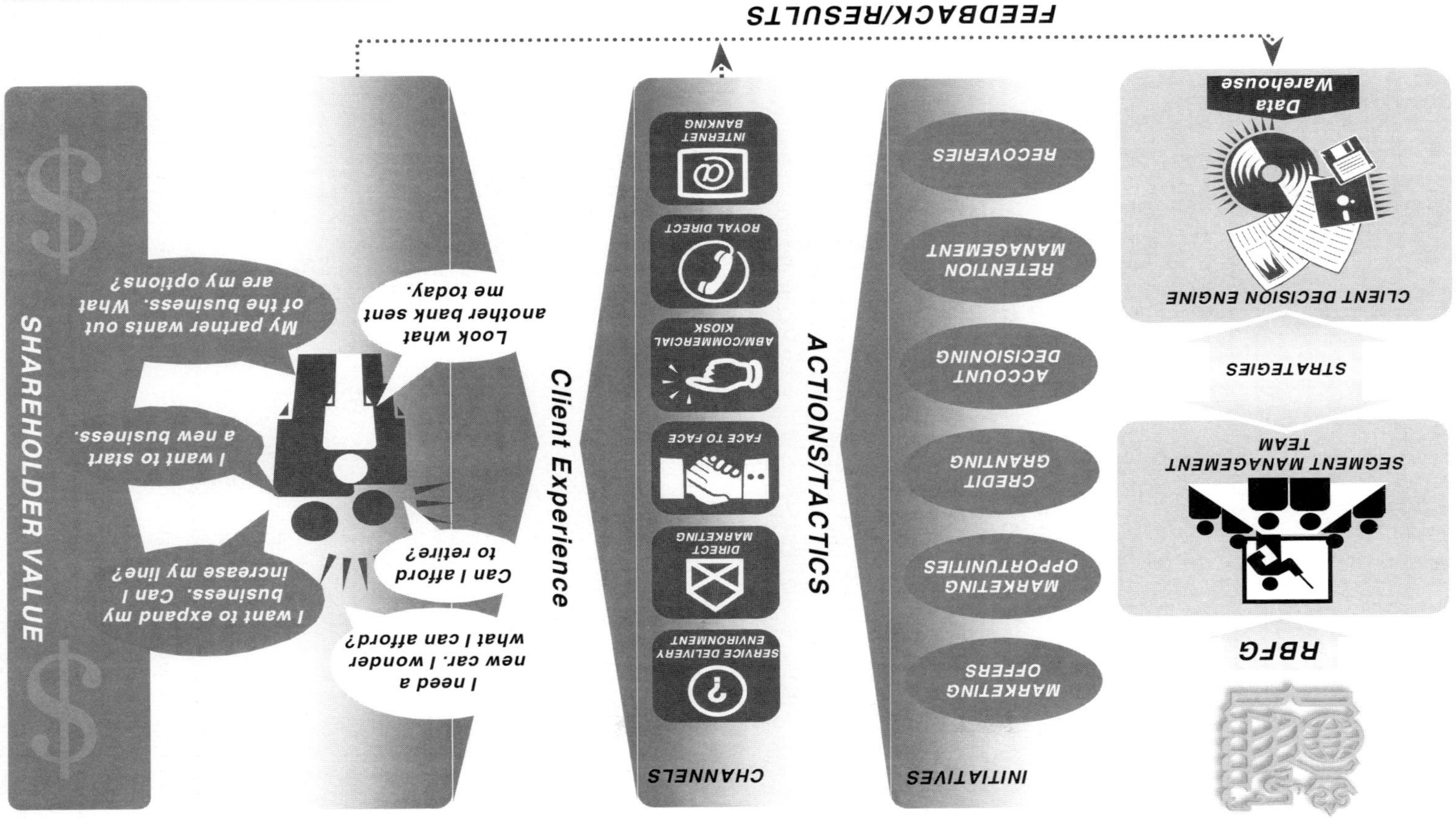

Source: Company records.

customer. It also empowers the branches to make better, more informed decisions because they have good information at their fingertips. We don't pass on the specific customer category or segment information to the branches. We want our branch personnel to focus on the customer, not the category.

Levels of Service

The Bank also determined a set of customer treatment strategies—such as the decision to offer pre-approved credit for credit lines—by the customer segment and category.

Lefebvre described one example of how the Bank planned to use present and future profitability to help determine levels of service:

> We are beginning to use the customer's category assignment to determine the length of wait time and the type of customer service representative that the customer talks to at our telephone-banking center. We always want to ensure that our very best clients, in terms of profitability and lifetime value, get the very best service. That's how we retain good customers.

Product Design and Pricing

Reich's decision The CRM system used customer profitability and future potential calculations to give pricing parameters to account managers like Jaime Reich. CRM and customer profitability was being used more and more by account managers to make difficult decisions on which customers to cultivate, how to treat existing customers, what products to offer, and what pricing levels were appropriate. Reich described his interactions with clients:

> Usually in the early part of the relationship, customers tend to negotiate pricing. In general, products are priced appropriately and we do not need to give special deals, since the sales leads on our computer already have discretionary pricing built in. Once clients realize that the Bank's rates are competitive, they start to trust me and negotiate less. For the vast majority of clients, the pricing on our products is sufficient to make them happy. It is quite rare for me to seek approval for a better price from my manager.

Those rare instances usually came about because of some new piece of information unknown to the CRM system. One example of such a decision was an instance when one of Reich's clients, a long-term and important customer of the Bank, introduced him to her niece, a 23-year-old MBA who recently graduated from business school and who was not in the AMI program.

The niece was hoping to get a position with a Toronto advertising firm, but was currently unemployed. She had accompanied her aunt to Reich's office in order to request a car loan. She wanted to get a loan with the Bank, the niece explained, because the Bank had a more flexible loan program than the dealership. Although Reich did not ordinarily work with Bank customers that were not in the AMI program, he looked up the niece's profile on the Bank's customer relationship management (CRM) system. The system, which calculated the rate discretion for a customer based on their potential and profit, allowed her a maximum of a 1% discount. The standard rate for the niece was prime plus 5%. The problem was that the niece wanted Reich to match what the dealership was offering—prime plus 2.5%.

Reich knew that making the niece a loan at prime plus 2.5 would be extremely difficult. He would have to go to his manager and argue the case that the Bank should make an exception for this customer, and even then it was doubtful he would get more than a 1% additional discount. Although Reich did not have access to the actual profit and potential information on this customer, he did know that she held a savings and a checking account with the Bank and had historically low balances in both (see Exhibit 6). To complicate matters further, the niece had told Reich that although she had a competitor's credit card, she currently did not hold one of the Bank's credit cards. Reich knew that there was a very high likelihood that the CRM system would eventually prompt a personal banking representative to attempt to sell her a credit card.

	Niece	*Aunt*
Age	23	68
Number of products held	2	8
Type of products held	Signature Plus checking account; Calculator Plus savings account	Signature Plus checking account, Royal Money Maker Plus savings account, mortgage on home, mortgage on second home, investment accounts, retirement account, line of credit, Visa
Tenure with Bank	6 years	50 years
Annual income	$23,000	$240,000
Net worth	$5,000	$2.8 million

EXHIBIT 6 Client Profiles[a]

Source: Casewriter.
[a] All information in this exhibit is disguised.

In order to provide this customer with the loan rate she wanted, Reich would have to persuade his manager that doing so was a good move for the Bank. The questions in Reich's mind as he mulled his decision were: was this really the best use of the Bank's funds? Would she take the credit card if he did not give her the rate she wanted on her car loan?

Packages versus fees: McLaughlin's decision
Another way the Bank used customer profitability data was to inform the debate over whether to charge for services using flat rate packages or to charge fees based on the amount and type of transactions the customer was generating with the Bank.

By 1998, with the new customer profitability model in place, the Bank became aware that many of its personal accounts were losing money. Looking more deeply into the data, the Bank found that the delivery channel producing the biggest drain on profits was the practice of customers using ABMs to pay their bills. This practice was widely in use in Canada by the late 1990s. While customers viewed this service as convenient, it was extremely costly for the Bank (see Exhibit 7). These higher costs led to negative customer profitability, particularly for customers who did not carry high balances, such as those in the Key/Nexus segment. Recovering those costs could be tricky, since marketing studies showed that customer valued predictability, fairness, and simplicity in their banking relationships, and that they felt "nickel and dimed" by the transaction fees charged by some banks. Many at the Bank felt that flat rate packages were one way to cover costs without subjecting customers to pages of fees on their bank statements (see Exhibit 8 for a sample of product pricing).

In addition to how to move CRM and customer profitability forward, the question for the Bank when trying to price products in the current CRM environment was: how to recover costs and make a profit while providing the type of service its customers would value and keeping customers that the Bank valued?

Richard McLaughlin knew that value for money was a particularly thorny issue for the Bank. The Bank asked customers to rank the leading Canadian banks in value for money, and RBC had ranked seventh out of eight. McLaughlin pondered how the Bank could boost the perception among its customers that they gained significant value for their money and guard against competitor encroachment, while simultaneously stemming the tide of red ink spilling from its personal accounts. ■

EXHIBIT 7 Royal Bank—Average Unit Costs by Channel[a]

	ABMs		Retail Branch	BBC[b]	Telephone Banking[c]		Internet/Web	Mortgage Reps
Activities	Full Function	Cash Counter			Agent	IVR[d]		
Open								
Products approved (credit check)								
RD (telephone banking) Enrollment	—	—	$104.03	$365.72	$158.36	$97.15	$194.35	$983.15
Business development (new business/growth)	—	—	—	—	14.89	—	—	—
Business development (retention)	—	—	67.44	90.36	4.26	—	—	—
Fulfillment	—	—	9.29	12.68	4.26	—	—	—
Renewal	—	—	19.14	17.16	—	—	—	—
Withdrawal	—	—	32.18	20.00	—	—	—	—
Deposit	0.40	$0.55	3.80	—	—	—	0.18	—
Transfer	0.97	—	2.87	—	—	—	—	—
Bill payment	2.26	2.38	21.36	3.84	8.39	0.30	0.18	—
Inquiry	0.90	—	2.69	—	8.15	0.30	0.18	—
Maintenance	0.31	0.54	9.19	7.18	8.52	0.30	0.19	—
Close	—	—	28.49	47.93	10.75	—	—	—

Source: Company records.

[a] All numbers in this exhibit have been disguised for confidentiality purposes.
[b] Business Banking Center marketed to and serviced small businesses from a centralized location.
[c] All costs are on a per call basis as opposed to a per transaction basis. In addition, back office operation (support costs outside of Royal Direct hierarchy) are included in the respective unit costs. All IVR costs except for loan applications are based on the average time per call.
[d] Interactive voice recognition.

Name of Service	Signature Plus Checking Account	Royal Money Maker Plus Savings Account
Free debits	2/monthly cycle and 1/payroll credit	2/monthly cycle and 1/payroll credit
Per check fee	$0.60	$1.35
In-branch withdrawals	$0.60	$1.35
PTB[a] withdrawals, payments, Transfers	$0.50	$1.35
Telephone banking debits	$0.50	$0.50
PC/Internet debits	$0.50	$0.50
IDP[b] purchases	$0.30	$0.30
ABM withdrawals at other FIs	$1.25 plus PTB Withdrawal Fee	
Flat fee options	15 full-service debits for $5/month	None
	15 self-service debits for $3/month	
	25 self-service debits for $5/month	
Overdraft protection option Account record		

EXHIBIT 8 1996 Personal Account Pricing and Service Levels

Source: Company records.

[a]Personal Touch Banking is the Bank's proprietary name for their automatic teller machines.
[b]Debit card payments at a retail outlet, such as a grocery store.

◆◆◆ **Citibank: Launching the Credit Card in Asia Pacific (A)**

Case 13-2 Citibank: Launching the Credit Card in Asia Pacific (A)

V. Kasturi Rangan

On a rainy afternoon in 1989, Rana Talwar, head of Citibank's Asia Pacific Consumer Bank, reflected upon the 11 years that had gone by since the Consumer Bank had established its consumer business in Asia. The branch banking business operations in 15 countries throughout Asia Pacific and the Middle East projected Citibank as a prestigious, consumer-oriented international bank and as the undisputed leader in most marketplaces. With earnings of $69.7 million in 1988, and a goal of $100 million in 1990, Talwar considered the launch of a new product (credit cards) as a way of growing future revenues. (See Exhibit 1 for 1988 performance.) Cards could prove to be an excellent way to overcome distribution limitations imposed on foreign banks in the Asia-Pacific region: first, by

The case was prepared by Professor V. Kasturi Rangan with the research assistance from Marie Bell and Melanie Alper. Copyright © 2002 by the President and Fellows of Harvard College. Harvard Business School Case 595-026.

	($ million)
Net revenue from fund (NRFF)	$209.0
Fees/commissions/insurance	31.3
Customer net revenue	$240.3
Net credit losses/fraud	4.8
Credit/collection	11.7
Total credit cycle	$ 16.5
Delivery expense	$138.3
Other revenues/(expense)	$(15.9)
Net earnings before tax	69.7
Tax	$ 23.5
Profit center earnings (PCE)	$ 46.2
Customer liabilities ($ billion)	4.9
Customer assets ($ billion)	2.3
Average total assets ($ billion)	3.0
Full-time equivalent employees	3,536
Number of accounts (000)	846
Number of branches	56

EXHIBIT 1 Citibank's Asia-Pacific Consumer Bank Performance (1988)

Source: Company documents.

Note: NRFF for the card business was about $10 million, with a PCE of (−$3) million. Concentrated in Hong Kong, this business was growing rapidly and by the middle of 1989 Citibank had nearly 100,000 customers.

acquiring card members, by targeting customers outside its branch business, and, then, by actively cross selling other Citibank products and services to these customers.

In the past, the credit card idea had met with skepticism from Citibank's New York headquarters as well as its country managers. Many in New York considered it a risky investment. Senior credit managers questioned the wisdom of issuing cards in markets with annual per capita income of $350 and also in markets with little credit experience and hardly any infrastructure. The Citibank management recognized that the economies of most Asia-Pacific countries were relatively underdeveloped compared with the United States and Europe; consumers' attitudes and credit card usage patterns differed country by country. In this context, several country managers were unsure whether the success of Citibank's U.S. card business could be projected onto Asia-Pacific. Further, they wondered whether Citibank could adopt a mass-market positioning to acquire enough credit card customers and still maintain its up-market positioning with the current upscale branch banking customers. A premium-priced card product would not sell in the marketplace in a large way, it was argued. Moreover, country managers were not comfortable with an unsecured credit product such as credit cards and did not want to take the large losses of a card business, in the initial years, that their projections seemed to indicate. Weak local infrastructure, limited distribution capabilities, and the experience with loss-making proprietary credit card businesses that some of the countries had, served to underline arguments against a credit card launch.

Pei Chia, who had been appointed in late 1987 to head Citibank's International Consumer businesses, had experience managing Citibank's huge U.S. card businesses and was favorably disposed toward international expansion. Confident of support from his boss if a viable proposition could be structured, Talwar pondered the pros and cons of a credit card product. If he decided to push for the product, he would need to articulate a viable business strategy.

Citibank's Asia-Pacific Operations

Unlike many of its competitors, Citibank operated on a view of the world as one marketplace and had consistently pursued a global strategy for growth. (See Exhibits 2 and 3 for a summary of Citibank's global operations.)

Citibank's mission in the Asia-Pacific region was to be the most profitable and preeminent provider of a wide array of financial services to an increasingly affluent upper- and middle-income market, and to reach the rapidly growing middle-income households in this region. The bank operated in 15 countries throughout Asia-Pacific and the Middle East: Hong Kong, Taiwan, Australia, the Philippines, Guam, Singapore, India, the Gulf (United Arab Emirates, Bahrain, Oman), Malaysia, Indonesia, Thailand, Pakistan, and Korea.

Rapid economic development (see Exhibit 4) had made these countries attractive business propositions for many international banks. However, most Asian governments had a number of regulations designed to protect local banks and limit the expansion of foreign banks. For instance, foreign banks in Indonesia could operate only two branches; in Malaysia and Singapore, they were limited to three; and in Thailand, each foreign bank was allowed only one branch.

Citibank's senior managers knew that they could not rely only on breakthroughs in the regulatory environment to gain increased access in the local market. Therefore, offering the most innovative and high-quality products, services, and technology was critical to acquiring and retaining customers. For example, Citibank pioneered telephone banking in much of Asia. It developed alternate distribution channels for products such as automobile loans. With the dealers acting as the bank's agents, customers did not ever have to visit the branch. (More details about Citibank's core products and services are provided in Exhibit 5.)

Against such a backdrop, it was felt that the introduction of a credit card in Asia would support Citibank's strategy of expanding its customer base from the upper-income segment to include the rapidly growing middle-income households. Supporters of the card product suggested:

> We do not need bricks-and-mortar branches to access the middle market in most of our countries. We can acquire card customers through innovative new channels. When we get card customers, we have the opportunity to cross-sell our entire product line: Auto Loans, Ready Credit, Deposits, and Mortgage Power. This could be a wonderful opportunity for us to add customers.

Country managers, on the other hand, sought to highlight realities of the local marketplace. Bob Thornton, Country Manager of Citibank Indonesia, argued:

> There is a history of poor consumer payment on installment debt in Indonesia, as has been our experience with the mortgage portfolio, and high level of fraud in the financial sector. I wonder if credit card customers will perform any differently. The legal infrastructure is inadequate so that we cannot collect legally, if necessary. Also, while there is a small market for a card product, I am not sure that we can get the right kind of staffing and infrastructure to run such a business successfully and profitably. Yet, with a population of 180 million, it is among the few potentially large markets in Asia Pacific.

According to Dave Smith, Country Manager for Singapore:

> We have a small 2 million population and an already saturated card market. Moreover, American Express has the market in its pocket. Entering this market this late will most likely result in us losing money. We can do without this distraction from our main banking business.

Jaitirth Rao, Country Manager for India, who had, in a matter of two years, made the consumer bank an innovator of products and a catalyst for service orientation in the Indian financial services sector, expressed his concern: "Launching a credit card in a large country like ours with little infrastructure has great potential to be a major headache down the road. It's a dog. Let us delay it."

EXHIBIT 2 Citibank Background

With about $228 billion in assets in 1989, Citicorp was the largest banking company in the United States and ranked eleventh in the world. Its operations were broadly diversified across the banking industry in order to serve a variety of individual, institutional, and commercial customers.

Global finance Citicorp's commercial banking operation served the needs of the world's business community. Recognized as the leader in the foreign exchange market, its wide range of services included commercial lending, real estate, and services to financial organizations, such as insurance companies, securities companies, institutional investors, and other banks.

Global consumer The Global Consumer business aimed to serve the fullest possible range of financial needs for individual consumers. Its $106 billion in assets constituted 50% of the bank's asset base. The majority of Citibank consumers were in the United States, where one out of six American households had a relationship with the bank. However, its international presence had been growing rapidly, and while other large banks had been scaling back their efforts overseas, Citibank had expanded its services into 9 million households in 15 countries outside the United States.

By 1989 Citibank, which had started as a commercial bank, offered a variety of products for consumers as well, especially in the United States. In the United States alone, Citibank had grown its card membership from a mere 6 million in 1980 to more than 27 million in 1987.

Citibank: Summary of Aggregate Performance

	1986 Net Income (loss) $ Millions	1986 Average Assets $ Billions	1987 Net Income (loss) $ Millions	1987 Average Assets $ Billions	1988 Net Income (loss) $ Millions	1988 Average Assets $ Billions
Global consumer	362	71	556	85	626	106
Global finance						
Developed economies	538	81	513	84	810	88
Developing economies	143	18	195	17	285	17
Corporate initiatives/information business	(34)	–	(89)	1	(105)	1
Cross-border refinancing portfolio	124	14	(3,288)	13	278	12
Other	(75)	–	931	(2)	(36)	(3)
Total	**1,058**	**184**	**(1,182)**	**198**	**1,858**	**221**

Offices and Branches (1988)

United States	
Citibank, N.A.	
Branches	293
Subsidiaries	71
Citibank (New York State)	
Branches	39
Subsidiaries	8
Citicorp savings	252
Other Citicorp subsidiaries	522
Total Domestic	**1,185**

Overseas (in 89 countries)	
Citibank branches and representative offices	291
Banking subsidiaries	653
Banking affiliates	115
Other financial affiliates and subsidiaries	1,121
Total overseas	**2,180**
Total	**3,365**

Source: Annual Reports.

	1986	1987	1988
Net revenue from fund	$5,638	$6,476	$6,899
Credit cycle expense	1,701	1,580	1,746
Delivery expense	3,392	3,952	4,295
Total expense	5,093	5,532	6,041
Other income (expense)	92	65	92
Income before taxes	637	1,009	950
Net Income	362	556	626
Average assets ($ billions)	$ 71	$ 85	$ 97
Return on assets (%)	.51	.65	.64
Return on equity (%)	12.7	16.3	16.1
Assets ($ billions)			
Revolving loans	NA	$ 17.2	$ 21.8
Shelter loans		39.7	41.6
Student loans		1.8	2.1
Other loans		21.8	25.5
Other assets		12.0	13.3
		$ 92.5	$104.3
Liabilities			
Transaction account deposits	NA	$ 11.6	$ 13.5
Savings deposits		60.0	65.0
Other		20.9	25.8
		$ 92.5	$104.3
No. of accounts (millions)	NA	42.0	45.0

EXHIBIT 3 Citibank: Global Consumer Bank ($ millions)

Source: Annual Reports.

Card Business Basics

Banks issued Visa or MasterCards, both of which were organized as international franchises. Any bank or financial institution could become a member of these franchises by fulfilling certain eligibility criteria. On becoming a member, they all had to follow a certain common set of practices. An example was Gold Cards; they had to be a gold color, and the issuing bank was obliged to provide travel accident insurance and a 24-hour help line for its cardholders. In general, Visa/MasterCard set common standards for card-logo design and operating rules that its member franchises all had to abide by. It was up to the individual banks, however, to decide on pricing, branding, positioning, and customer acquisition strategies. The franchisers, Visa or MasterCard, provided the banks an extensive information network both within the country and internationally to clear transactions.

Member banks and financial institutions paid Visa and MasterCard a fee in proportion to their volume of network usage, and a franchise royalty (a small percentage of sales volume) as well. Banks and financial institutions in addition to issuing cards could also participate in the Visa and MasterCard Merchant Acquisition franchise. The objective here was to enlist retail merchants to clear their credit card transactions through the "acquiring" bank. That is, regardless of which bank issued the card to the customer, the retail merchant would forward transactions to its "acquiring" bank for clearance. Visa and MasterCard provided a worldwide communication flow, via satellite hookups and computer networks, to enable a convenient consummation of the credit card transaction—often involving a merchant, a customer, an acquiring bank, and an issuing bank, all within a matter of seconds.

EXHIBIT 4 Country Profile

	Australia	Hong Kong	India	Indonesia	Malaysia	Philippines	Singapore	Taiwan	Thailand
Population (millions)	16.5	5.6	797.0	167.7	16.9	61.9	2.7	19.8	55.0
Urban population	85%	90%	23%	25%	38%	50%	100%	72%	20%
Economy									
1988 real GNP (US$ billion)	$196.8	$45.7	$222.5	$63.4	$34.1	$32.6	$23.8	$95.8	$51.1
Per capita (US$)	$11,929	$8,158	$279	$338	$2,018	$527	$8,817	$4,837	$930
1988 growth rate	4.0%	7.3%	9.7%	4.8%	8.1%	6.8%	11.0%	7.3%	10.8%
Five-year average growth rate	4.6%	8.4%	6.1%	4.2%	4.2%	0.5%	5.6%	9.3%	7.2%
Savings rate	6.7%	30.0%	19.6%	27.9%	23.8%	NA	NA	31.2%	10.3%
Inflation									
1988	7.6%	7.4%	9.8%	8.0%	2.0%	8.7%	1.5%	1.2%	3.8%
Five-year average	7.1%	5.5%	8.2%	7.6%	1.6%	16.6%	0.7%	0.5%	2.3%
Literacy rate	99%	88%	48%	72%	80%	88%	87%	90%	89%
Ethnic composition	95% Caucasian; 4% Asian; 1% other	98% Chinese; 2% other	80% Hindu; 10% Muslim; 10% Christian, Sikh, Parsi, and others	74% various Malay groups; 26% other (mainly Chinese)	60% Malay; 31% Chinese; 9% Indian	91% Christian Malay; 4% Muslim Malay; 2% Chinese; 3% other	76% Chinese; 15% Malay; 7% Indian; 2% other	84% Taiwanese; 14% Mainland Chinese; 2% other	75% Thai; 14% Chinese; 11% other
No. of passenger cars in use	7,244,000	250,000	1,351,200	1,170,100	1,578,900	352,900	251,400	650,000	770,400
No. of telephones in use	8,727,000	2,461,000	4,409,000	907,000	1,646,000	658,400	1,122,000	7,800,000	1,000,000
No. of televisions in use	7,900,000	1,400,000	6,000,000	7,112,000	2,350,000	2,200,000	570,000	6,386,000	5,600,000
(Some of these data are for 1985, others for 1987)									
Political/economic risk factor	A	B	C	C	B	D	B	A	B
A — Most stable D — Most risky	Highly Westernized economy with opportunities for development	1997 return to Mainland China causes political uncertainty	Unstable federal government, political corruption	Large national debt, political corruption, speculation on new political leadership	Low inflation and fast high-tech growth, but political infighting	Political corruption, threats of Communist insurgency	Transition to new leadership after 30-year reign of Lee Kuan Yew	Strong economic and political stability	Strong growth, but heavy reliance on tourism. Political corruption

Sources: United Nations *Statistical Yearbook for Asia and the Pacific,* 1991, and U.S. Central Intelligence Agency, *Handbook of the Nations,* 1991.

EXHIBIT 5 Citibank Asia-Pacific Consumer Bank: Core Products and Services

CORE PRODUCTS

In offering the *Citi-One* account, Citibank used its advances in technology to provide customers something none of its competitors could reproduce: a consolidated deposit and investment account based on the sum total of all of a customer's accounts with Citibank. By enrolling in Citi-One, customers benefited from

- a consolidated statement showing the status of all their Citibank accounts,
- banking by phone,
- an automatic checking overdraft facility,
- linked savings and checking accounts where funds were swept from checking into savings overnight in order to earn interest, and
- a designated customer service officer to manage their accounts.

In order to fully offer its resources to branch banking customers, Citibank imposed relatively high deposit requirements of its checking/savings customers—usually about $10,000.

Mortgage Power, targeted at housing loan customers, allowed those whose homes were worth more than the existing mortgage to obtain a revolving line of credit on top of their existing loan.

Citibank was also one of the largest providers of *auto loans* in Asia. The bank worked to establish and maintain relationships with car dealers as one way to gain access to new customers; auto loans were then sourced and marketed through car dealerships.

Unlike other credit line accounts, Citibank's *Ready Credit,* a revolving credit facility that worked like a checking account, enabled customers to apply for an overdraft line of credit without having to formally apply for a loan. This product was targeted at mid-level professionals and provided them a ready source of funds for unexpected expenditures or emergencies. It offered a number of benefits, including low mandatory repayment of the loan, no collateral or guarantors required, and ready cash withdrawals through ATMs (automated teller machines).

To attract the high net worth segment of the market, Citibank offered its exclusive, personalized *Citigold* service. Its creators likened the Citigold concept to traveling in the first class cabin of an airplane. With Citigold service, customers who met the minimum average deposit requirements (this varied from country to country but was usually around $100,000) did their banking in exclusive, lavishly furnished service areas where they did not have to wait in lines for teller service. Soft music, warm lighting, tastefully selected artwork, and service from immaculately groomed, more experienced representatives all served to differentiate this class of customer. Access to more sophisticated products, investment advisory services, complimentary magazine subscriptions, and updates on currency trends were just some of the additional benefits bestowed upon Citigold customers. The Asia-Pacific division innovated the Citigold idea, and a much larger proportion of its customers in Asia (compared with its U.S. operations) were Citigold customers.

CitiPhone banking enabled customers to complete routine banking transactions, such as fund transfers and account balance inquiries, via phone, from the privacy of their own homes or offices, or even from mobile phones. Moreover, with CitiPhone Banking, customers could access their accounts 24 hours a day, 7 days a week, and 365 days a year.

Citibank had also revolutionized the banking industry in Asia via *automated teller machines*. Customers could use ATM cards to access their funds from stylishly decorated, highly secured Citicard Banking Centers in the language of their choice, and all ATMs contained phones which automatically connected customers with a Citibank officer in case of a problem. With the International Citibank Citicard, customers could carry out transactions on their accounts virtually anywhere in the world.

(Continued)

Business Segments

In addition to its regular branches, Citibank operated separate offices to serve certain strategic customer segments. Each of these offered a portfolio of products designed to meet the unique needs of customers in those segments.

Citibank's *Non-Resident Indian Business (NRI)* was set up to capture the business of Indian customers who did not reside in India. Citibank offered special foreign currency time deposit accounts and rupee (local currency) savings accounts in India which enabled *NRI* customers to invest their overseas earnings in Indian rupees or in foreign currencies. The former earned a significantly higher interest rate. This helped Citibank develop relations with the Indian government by helping the Central Bank to procure foreign currencies. *NRI* had branches in major financial centers all over the world.

With 21 banking centers in 15 countries around the world, the *International Personal Banking (IPB)* business was designed to service the growing group of affluent Asian offshore clients with global financial needs. *IPB* provided such innovative products as the International University Plan, which would allow customers to create the funds necessary to send their children to prestigious universities in the United States, Canada, and Europe, while insuring the funding for college against death or disability. It helped them cushion political and economic instability, offering them foreign currency advisory services and access to global investment products, while providing unique local tax benefits. IPB's focus on personalized service (a personal finance manager specially trained in international transactions), confidentiality, and accessibility made Citibank the choice of more than 120,000 customers worldwide.

EXHIBIT 5 (cont.)

When a Citibank cardholder approached a Citibank merchant to purchase goods, the following round of transactions would result: say, the customer bought $100 worth of goods on her Citibank card. The merchant would present the $100 charge slip to the acquiring bank and receive $97.00 for the same transaction. Hence, in this transaction, the acquiring bank would generate a merchant discount revenue of $3.00 (or 3.0%) from which it would have to make franchise payment to Visa or MasterCard, pay the card issuer (Citibank) an interchange fee, and also cover all its expenses related to the acquiring business. Citibank, the card issuer, would bill the cardholder the $100 in full, in the monthly statement. The cardholder would then have the choice of making a part payment or full payment, depending upon the payment terms. (Exhibit 6 provides a graphical representation of a typical transaction cycle.)

The gross discount percentages shown in the above illustrations, though representative, differed from country to country, and even by merchant to merchant, depending on the competitive context.

Local banks held back merchant discounts in the 1.5% to 2.0% range—far lower than Citibank's 3.0%. As a result, merchant acquisition was getting to be very tough in developed markets. Citibank had enrolled about 3,000 merchants in Hong Kong. In order to compete effectively with the local banks, it guaranteed merchants a faster transaction settlement time. In most Asia-Pacific markets, American Express had the higher-caliber merchants. Even though, like Citibank, it charged a 3% discount rate, most quality hotels, restaurants, and retailers accepted its affiliation in order to attract and retain travel-related international clients.

As part of a strategy to counter American Express's growing international presence, Citibank decided to look for an international proprietary card payment system. In 1981, Citibank acquired Diners Club International (DCI), which managed an international franchise for the Diners Club card. DCI allowed only one franchisee to be signed up in each country. The franchisee would be the sole issuer of Diners Club cards and the sole acquirer of Diners Club merchant business in that

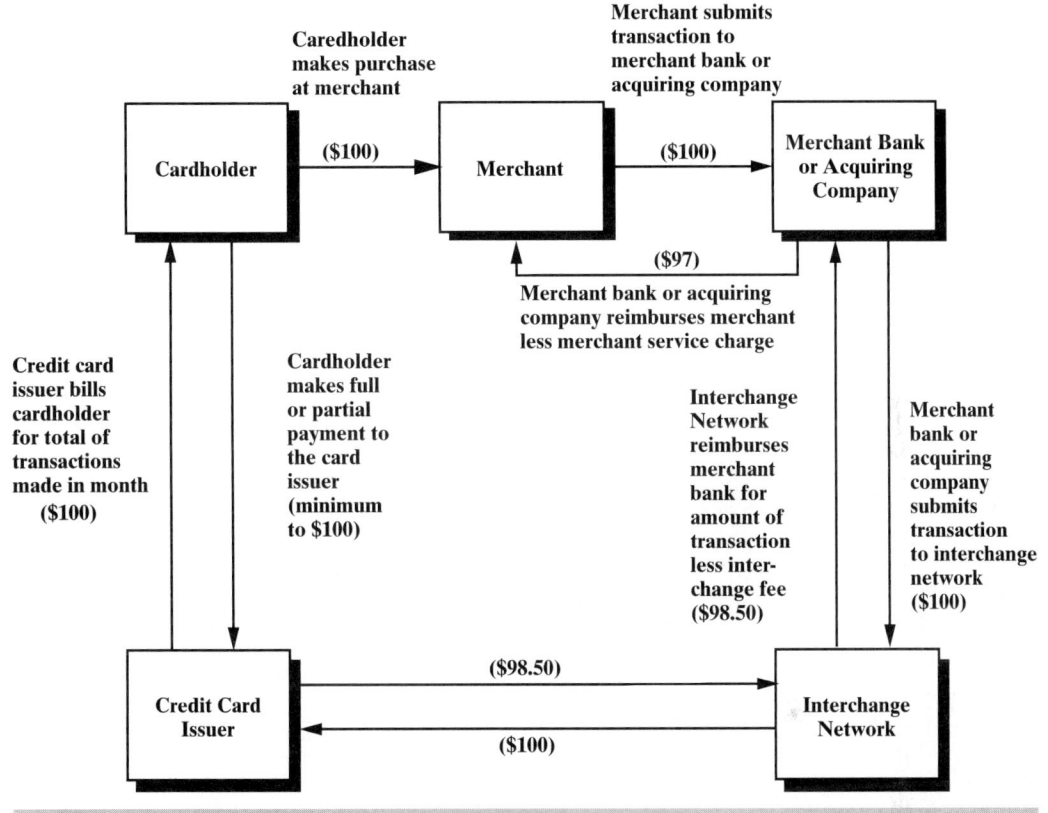

EXHIBIT 6 Typical Credit Card Purchase Transaction Cycle

Flow description:
- Cardholder makes purchase at merchant ($100)
- Merchant submits transaction to merchant bank or acquiring company ($100)
- Merchant bank or acquiring company reimburses merchant less merchant service charge ($97)
- Merchant bank or acquiring company submits transaction to interchange network ($100)
- Interchange Network reimburses merchant bank for amount of transaction less interchange fee ($98.50)
- Credit Card Issuer to Interchange Network ($98.50) / ($100)
- Cardholder makes full or partial payment to the card issuer (minimum to $100)
- Credit card issuer bills cardholder for total of transactions made in month ($100)

---

country. While Citibank owned the Diners Club franchise in some countries, private companies managed the franchise in most other countries.

Positioned as a travel and entertainment card for senior executives and successful businessmen, the Diners Club card is a charge card, i.e., all outstandings on the card have to be settled in full at the end of every billing month. With no interest revenue, unlike bank cards, the primary revenue sources are fees and merchant discounts.

LAUNCHING A CREDIT CARD IN ASIA-PACIFIC

While opinion was divided on whether a card launch made sense, Talwar wondered whether a staged, sequential plan could be the basis for any possible consensus and a regional thrust if he chose in favor of the credit card. This way, each subsequent country launch would benefit from the experience of all the countries preceding it. Management debated which country to lead off with, how to enter the market, and how to develop the rest of the region.

Profiles of the target countries in Citibank's Asia-Pacific markets are provided in Exhibit 7. Exhibit 8 provides a quick overview of the distribution of cards by income group for each country, and Exhibit 9a and b provides comparative information on card pricing.

Market Entry Costs

Citibank could enter the market either by acquiring an already existing card portfolio from another company, or do greenfield market development to build a customer base, or adopt a combination of the two.

EXHIBIT 7 Citibank Country Profile (1988)

	Australia	Hong Kong	India	Indonesia	Malaysia	Philippines	Singapore	Taiwan	Thailand
No. of branches	9	27	6	2	3	3	3	2	1
No. of bank customers ('000)	85	130	61	21	29	46	18	16	12
No. of bank accounts ('000)	150	250	165	25	58	85	67	30	16
No. of Citigold customers	–	7,600	1,000	550	487	2,300	1300	680	–
No. of IPB customers	–	9,900	–	–	–	–	12,800	–	–
No. of autoloan customers ('000)	36	200	15	13	–	4	10	11	4
No. of mortgage customers ('000)	27	22	–	2	9	–	3	2	5
No. of card customers	–	102	–	–	–	–	–	–	–
% of bank customers owning Citibank card	–	6	–	–	–	–	–	–	–
Net revenue from fund ($ millions)	59	67	6	12	11	19	16	11	8
Average annual customer income (US$)	$60,000	$36,000	$10,000	$24,000	$14,000	$10,000	$20,000	$25,000	$15,000
Average customer bank balance (US$)	$24,000	$20,000	$3,500	$9,000	$23,000	$4,000	$13,000	$9,000	$5,000

	Annual Income (head of household)					
	Above $25,000	$12,500 to $25,000	$6,000 to $12,500	$2,000 to $6,000	Below $2,000	Total $ (millions)
Australia						
% of population	12.5[a]	30	37.5	15	5	16.5
% of cards	30[b]	35	30	5	0	10.5
Hong Kong						
% of population	10	25	50	10	5	5.6
% of cards	15	25	50	10	0	2.0
India						
% of population	1	2	2	5	90	800
% of cards	10	10	10	70	0	.280
Indonesia						
% of population	3	2	2	3	90	168
% of cards	40	10	10	40	0	.120
Malaysia						
% of population	5	10	20	45	20	17
% of cards	10	45	45	0	0	.380
Philippines						
% of population	3	5	22	30	40	62
% of cards	50	45	5	0	0	.240
Singapore						
% of population	5	5	10	25	55	2.7
% of cards	30	70	0	0	0	.630
Taiwan						
% of population	12.5	30	35	10	5	20
% of cards	30	50	20	0	0	.100
Thailand						
% of population	5	10	10	20	55	55
% of cards	12.5	12.5	50	25	0	.210

EXHIBIT 8 Estimated Distribution of Population and Cards by Income

Note: The minimum age for cardholders was 18 years in Australia and 21 in the other countries. While the card issuers imposed their own income requirements, the government of Malaysia imposed a minimum income of $9,000/year, and Singapore imposed a minimum of $14,000/year.

[a] Of Australia's 16.5 million people, 12.5% were estimated to live in households where the head (of the household) had an income above $25,000.
[b] Of Australia's 10.5 million credit cards, 30% were owned by individuals with incomes above $25,000.

Acquiring an existing card portfolio would facilitate a quick entry into the market. Further, the bank could consider leveraging off an already developed operations infrastructure and trained human resources in the acquired company to further consolidate the market share. On the other hand, there were several arguments that questioned market entry through acquisition. Looking back at the Hong Kong entry, one manager reflected:

We never really started a credit card business in Hong Kong. We simply acquired the existing Bank of America business with all the baggage that usually accompanies such an acquisition. Further, the bulk of our branch banking business was aimed at a limited target market, whereas the credit card business was targeted at the mass market. There was a mismatch right there.

EXHIBIT 9A Competing Product Profiles: Pricing

	American Express		Diners Club	Local Banks	
	Green	Gold	Regular	Classic	Gold
1. Australia					
Joining Fee	$30	$45	$45	Nil	Nil
Annual Membership Fee	$45	$60	$60	Nil	Nil
Payment Terms	Balance due monthly	Balance due monthly	Balance due monthly	Balance due monthly (overdue int. 2% p.m.)	Balance due monthly (overdue int. 2% p.m.)
2. Hong Kong					
Joining Fee	$32	$50	$32	Nil	Nil
Annual Membership Fee	$50	$83	$54	$28	$61
Payment Terms	Monthly	Monthly	Monthly	Monthly (overdue int. 2%)	Monthly (overdue int. 2%)
3. India					
Joining Fee	NA	NA	$25	Nil	NA
Annual Membership Fee	NA	NA	$40	$10 to $19	NA
Payment Terms	NA	NA	Monthly	Monthly (overdue int. 2.5%)	NA
4. Indonesia					
Joining Fee	$60	$60	$40	$15 to $40	$30 to $60
Annual Membership Fee	$50	$60	$35	$20 to $30	$30 to $45
Payment Terms	Monthly	Monthly	Monthly	Monthly (overdue int. 2.5%)	Monthly (overdue int. 2.5%)
5. Malaysia					
Joining Fee	$31	$38	$40	0 to $30	0 to $50
Annual Membership Fee	$54	$75	$60	$20 to $50	$50 to $75
Payment Terms	Monthly	Monthly	Monthly	Monthly (overdue int. 2.5%)	Monthly (overdue int. 2.5%)
6. Philippines					
Joining Fee	$35	$50	$40	Nil	$5 to $20
Annual Membership Fee	$50	$60	$50	$20	$50
Payment Terms	Monthly	Monthly	Monthly	Monthly (overdue int. 3%)	Monthly (overdue int. 3%)
7. Singapore					
Joining Fee	$50	$50	$45	Nil	Nil
Annual Membership Fee	$60	$95	$60	0 to $50	0 to $65
Payment Terms	Monthly	Monthly	Monthly	Monthly (overdue int. 2%)	Monthly (overdue int. 2%)
8. Taiwan					
Joining Fee	$40	$60	$45	Nil	Nil
Annual Membership Fee	$72	$120	$80	$48	$96
Payment Terms	Monthly	Monthly	Monthly	Monthly (overdue int. 1.5%)	Monthly (overdue int. 1.5%)
9. Thailand					
Joining Fee	$40	$60	$40	Nil	Nil
Annual Membership Fee	$65	$120	$80	$20	$40
Payment Terms	Monthly	Monthly	Monthly	Monthly (overdue int. 1.5%)	Monthly (overdue int. 1.5%)

	American Express	*Diners Club*	*Banks*
Card replacement	24 hours or next business day at 1,500 locations worldwide	24 to 48 hours at Diners offices	1 to 2 weeks Written loss report required
Loss/misuse liability	$100 maximum	$100 maximum	Some provide no coverage until loss reported, others provide $100 maximum
Spending limits	None	None	Yes
Emergency check cashing	$1,000 (Green) $5,000 (Gold) at AMEX locations $250 at hotels $100 at airlines	$1,000 at Diners offices and Citibank branches $250 at hotels $100 at airlines	$250 at hotels $100 at airlines
Cash advance	None (except through Express Card ATM)	$1,000 at Diners office and Citibank branches	$1,000 to $10,000 or up to credit limit
Year-end summary	Gold Card only	No	No
Interest-free period	45 days	30 days	25 days
Minimum payment	Full	Full	10% of balance
Replacement card	Free	Free	$20 to $50

EXHIBIT 9B Competing Product Profiles: Services

If Citibank chose greenfield market development, it would need to invest in a direct marketing program, typically consisting of (1) direct mail, (2) take-ones, (3) direct sales force, and (4) bind-ins. Each had its advantages and drawbacks. Direct mail could target applications to the intended audience. However, it was much more expensive than some of the other methods available. "Take-Ones," applications distributed at in-store countertop displays, offered a much broader reach; yet being available to the general public regardless of qualification, more than half of the applicants usually would not qualify. Using direct sales representatives was very expensive, although a competitor had achieved enormous success at a very low per-customer acquisition cost in South Korea. Finally, newspaper and magazine inserts (known as bind-ins) were by far the least expensive to circulate but they had a very low response rate.

The Hong Kong launch following the acquisition had used a combination of widespread Take-One displays in more than 4,000 merchant locations and direct mailings as well as cross selling to existing branch customers. Bursts of thematic television and print advertising were also used to enforce brand positioning to achieve maximum effectiveness in customer acquisition efforts and to promote customers' spending on the card.

A regional market research agency estimated that in order to acquire about 25,000 customers in Singapore (see Table A), Citibank would typically need to invest in a multifaceted direct marketing program consisting of direct mail, take-ones, direct sales force (making about 10 calls a day), and bind-ins. The agency further estimated that of the prospects who had responded through direct mail or direct sales, nearly two-thirds would qualify for a card, and of those who responded to take-ones or bind-ins, nearly one-third would qualify for a card. Over 80% of those who qualified would usually become a card customer. An additional $1.6 million would also have to be invested in TV advertising to complement the direct marketing program. Such a budget would typically support 300 30-second spots during Christmas, New

TABLE A Customer Acquisition Cost

Channel	Unit Cost ($)	Prospects Reached	Response Rate
Direct mail	1.5	300,000	2%
Take-ones	0.25	2,000,000	1.5%
Direct sales	18,000/sales person	30,000	50%
Bind-ins	0.15	3,000,000	1%

Year's, Chinese New Year, and Eid ul Fitri (Islamic Festival of Breaking the Fast). Such image advertising not only helped to bring in prospects, but also converted qualified prospects into firm customers. While a $1.6 million to $2.5 million advertising budget was adequate to reach a broad customer base within a country, a similar expenditure would be needed in each country if Citibank chose to enter several markets.

In addition to the launch costs of the card program, the infrastructural support (that is, computer systems, software development, customer support, merchant liaison, and other such fixed overhead costs) were estimated at about $35 million per year for supporting about 250,000 customers. For every incremental 250,000 customers an additional $10 million per year to $15 million per year of overhead would result. The direct cost, including that of the card itself, mailing, correspondence, and so on, currently cost about $25 per card in 1989, but was expected to drop to $6 to $8 per card when volume reached about one million cards.

CARD BUSINESS OPERATION ECONOMICS

Revenues from cards could come on an ongoing basis from several sources: joining/annual fee, interest payment, merchant discounts, and other transaction-related fees. (Exhibit 9 provides some basic information on how the card transaction settlement cycle works.) Setting the proper joining/annual fee was of some concern. Pricing the card too low would conflict with Citibank's stated positioning and would have a major impact on break-even projections. However, pricing it too high might mean low customer acceptance. One proposal was to waive the joining fee to induce more customers to buy the product, and charge a higher annual fee to provide a steady recurring revenue. Conventional wisdom, however, dictated a joining fee to cover the cost of acquisition, and a low annual fee to retain customers. Results from the Hong Kong card operations could be used to estimate revenues based on the income levels of the customer base. As Table B shows, the Hong Kong business projected revenues of $16,279,144, or $162.65 per customer, in 1989.

OPTIONS AND CONTROVERSIES

Citibank's management was concerned that consumers' attitudes and credit card usage patterns differed by country. This formed the basis for debate on introducing one card with a single set of features versus developing customized offerings for each market. (Exhibit 10 provides a qualitative description of the various customer markets and their competitive environments.)

One of the most controversial ideas was that of premium pricing a card product. One of the proponents explained, "In Asia-Pacific, we started business as a commercial bank. Our relationships were with large business houses. As a result, we have had a steady flow of high-status clients. Reaching out to the mass market here would certainly kill our unique positioning in the consumer's mind." Opponents argued that a premium price might mean staying out of the market, since almost all local card issuers were giving away free or low-fee credit cards.

Opinion was divided on whether each country should issue a local-currency credit card or whether the U.S. dollar should be the standard currency for all cards. American Express, which had a dominant market position in terms of market share and image, issued only a U.S.-dollar card in the region, while local players in each

TABLE B Net Revenue Impact of Citibank Hong Kong Credit Card Business, 1989

Annual Income	Percent of Card Owners	Average No. of Cards Owned	No. of Card Owners	No. of Cards	Annual Interest Payment[a] per Customer	Other Annual Revenue[b] per Customer	Total Annual Revenue[c] per Customer
Less than $6,200	—	—	—	—	—	—	—
$6,200–$12,400	67.5%	1.49	67,507	100,633	$102.18	$34.70	$136.88
$12,400–$23,200	20.9%	1.96	20,938	41,118	$134.44	$62.87	$197.31
Greater than $23,000	11.6%	2.43	11,640	28,249	$166.97	$82.84	$249.81
Total	100.0%	1.70	100,985	170,000	$116.46	$46.19	$162.65

[a]The interest payment reported is net after subtracting the cost of working capital to the bank.
[b]This revenue consisted of merchant discounts and annual fee.
[c]Though a large proportion of customers usually paid the interest and other charges on time, about 3% to 7% usually defaulted on payments, of whom only about 50% were able to eventually pay.

EXHIBIT 10 Asia-Pacific Markets: Country Profiles

From the bustling financial metropolis of Singapore to the rice fields of Indonesia, the eight additional Asian markets Citibank considered for expanding its credit card business represented a broad spectrum of cultural, industrial, and economic diversity. Moreover, the level of credit card penetration and market development differed from one country to the next, as did consumers' attitudes toward card ownership and usage. Detailed descriptions of the market in each country follow.

Australia
With its highly developed service sector, high per capita GDP, and predominantly Caucasian population, Australia closely resembled the commercialized, industrialized nations of the West in many ways, including its financial services and banking infrastructure. Compared with other developed economies, Australia ranked second only to France in the number of outlets, such as branch offices and ATMs, offering banking services per capita.

In contrast to other Asia-Pacific markets, Australia's credit card market was already saturated by 1989. With about 10.5 million cards in force, the average Australian carried two cards. Of these, about half were Bankcards, cards issued by 10 local banks for local use only. Bankcards were an introduction to credit cards for many consumers, and most still reported owning at least one. Because they had been in use for so long, and because of their usage limitations outside the country, consumers perceived Bankcards as becoming less popular, if not almost obsolete.

Visa and MasterCard had also developed large franchises in Australia, with 17.6% and 16.8% of the market, respectively. Though both were known for their wide domestic and international retail acceptance and were highly regarded in overall reputation, consumers viewed the

(Continued)

EXHIBIT 10 (cont.)

Visa card as slightly more prestigious and higher in merchant acceptability. Twenty-three local banks and six foreign banks offered a total of 4.1 million Visas and MasterCards, though the majority were issued by Australia's four largest banks—Westpac, Commonwealth, ANZ, and National Australia Bank.

American Express and Diners Club also operated in Australia; with 600,000 and 180,000 cards in force, respectively, their franchises were much smaller than the other brands. Both cards had been known as symbols of status and had been very strong businesses at one time. However, by 1989 both were experiencing problems, due primarily to decreases in retailer acceptance and consumers' negative attitudes toward AMEX and Diners Club membership fees. Unlike the local banks, both AMEX and Diners Club charged consumers a joining fee as well as an annual membership fee.

In Australia, as in other parts of Asia, consumers recognized credit cards as an important shopping tool that freed them from carrying cash and allowed them to shop whenever and wherever they wanted. Credit card purchases varied, but most of them were related to travel, entertainment, or shopping. However, card usage had become so commonplace in Australia that prestige and image associated with the card or the issuing bank was no longer an important consideration when choosing a credit card. Australian consumers, more concerned with how credit cards could be used in conjunction with other banking services to better manage their finances, viewed credit cards as an extension of an existing relationship with their banks. Therefore, MasterCards and Visas that allowed for easy cash withdrawal through ATMs, provided for payment of monthly bills, linked all of a customer's bank accounts, provided lost wallet protection service, and had no annual fee were the most popular. The MasterCards and Visas offered by the four major national banks offered one or more of these features.

Debit cards were also available; however, penetration was less than 5% and these were primarily seen as a nonbank financial institution product linked to savings accounts.

Hong Kong

Citibank had been in the credit card business in Hong Kong since 1983, when it acquired the Diners Club card business from Hong Kong's Standard Chartered Bank. The business was expanded in 1987 through the acquisition of Bank of America's Visa card portfolio, that had grown to 75,000 customers over the previous 12 years.

With the country's impressive economic growth and rapid industrialization, the relatively affluent population of 5.6 million with an average annual income of $8,158, and a high concentration of people living in urban centers, the people of Hong Kong were no strangers to the use of credit cards. By the late 1980s, consumers were sophisticated in their knowledge and usage of credit cards—using them for a variety of occasions from daily trips to the grocery store to business travel to family vacations. They had a number of credit card options to choose from. Visas and MasterCards issued by the local Hong Kong Bank and Standard Chartered Bank were considered popular. By 1989, Hong Kong had nearly 2 million cards in force, with cardholders owning an average of 1.7 cards each.

Citibank viewed its Hong Kong card business as a way to grow its customer base by targeting customers outside its branch business; the bank would then deepen its relationships with these customers by actively cross selling other Citibank products and services. By 1989, Citibank's 140,000 Classic and Gold Visas held an 8.7% share of the credit card market. In addition, it owned 100,000 Diners Club card customers. This charge card competed directly with American Express, which had issued 175,000 cards in Hong Kong.

India

With 80% of the country's population living in rural areas, agriculture formed the foundation of India's economy. Growth in the country's key industries—textiles, food processing, and pharmaceuticals—and in the service sector contributed to India's strong economic development in the late 1980s.

Because the majority of the country's wealth was concentrated among a small group of urban households, credit card penetration in India was extremely low. Credit cards served as status symbols for India's upper-middle-class consumers and provided the convenience of not having to carry lots of cash. Consumers preferred to pay on time and not use the card as a means of revolving credit. Though merchant acceptance was generally not as high in India as in other Asian countries, consumers were able to use their cards for a variety of purchases, more than half of which were related to travel and entertainment.

To this select group of card owners, wide acceptance, brand/bank image, and ease of the application process were a card's most important features. With regard to these preferences, only Diners Club, with about 70,000 members, was strong and presented a distinct positioning. American Express did not issue a local credit card. The other major competitors were bank cards. Two of them with about 100,000 cards had already overtaken Diners Club. The local banks did not charge a joining fee and kept the annual fee at about $15. All foreign-exchange transactions in India were heavily regulated by the central bank. As a result credit cards issued in India could be used only for local transactions in local currency.

Indonesia

Despite its 9 billion barrels of proven oil reserves and its wealth of other minerals, Indonesia remained a relatively poor country, with about 80% of the population living in rural areas and earning less than $500 per year. A significant portion of Indonesia's small but rapidly growing wealthy class was the local Chinese business community—part of a larger network of some 27 million mainland Chinese whose growing international business interests had prompted them to settle in foreign places around the world. But many wealthy Indonesian business people shared a similar international outlook as their business travels took them frequently to Malaysia, Singapore, and Australia.

The government did not impose restrictions on card ownership, but because of low income levels many did not qualify for membership, and this severely limited the size of the customer base. Thus, Indonesians perceived card ownership as a measure of high social standing. Among the major competitors were Visa and MasterCard issued by local banks. American Express and Diners Club also operated there, offering products and services for the small pool of professionals and well-to-do citizens. Three local banks, American Express, and Diners Club shared the market equally. Whereas all charged a joining fee as well as an annual membership fee, the local banks priced their offerings significantly lower.

To those few who were able to use credit cards, a number of features were important in choosing which card to use, especially outstanding service, prestige, billing in rupiahs (local currency), and extra "perks" of membership, such as prizes for joining and purchase protection. Even among those eligible for membership, low credit limits kept consumers from using their cards intensely. Consumers were able to use their cards for a wide variety of purchases, including travel expenses, groceries, and hospital bills.

(Continued)

EXHIBIT 10 (cont.)

Malaysia

An important world producer of rubber and timber, Malaysia was largely a rural country, with 61% of the population living in rural areas. However, as a growing industrial nation, it was also the world's third-largest producer and largest exporter of semiconductors. As with neighboring Indonesia, Malaysia had a prosperous business population of nearly 1 million (half of whom were of Chinese origin) whose business interests took them to many countries in the Asia-Pacific region as well as to the United Kingdom.

Convenience and extra credit were important reasons for owning credit cards. Malaysians considered it acceptable to revolve credit, so that though some customers paid their monthly bills in full, many others relied on their cards to finance short-term expenses. Cards were used mostly to pay for personal and family retail purchases, with the exception of a small group of corporate customers who used the cards for business travel and entertainment.

Malaysians had plenty of card options to choose from in 1989. American Express, for instance, with a 15% share of the market, offered a charge card that was recognized internationally for its premium image and superior customer service and that had no preset spending limit. The rest of the market was divided between international banks, which used credit cards as a way of reaching new customers (foreign banks were limited to three branches in Malaysia), and local banks, which tapped into their base of branch customers to develop their card businesses. Established international banking groups, such as Hong Kong Bank and Standard Chartered Bank, offered their cards globally and were particularly attractive to customers with international interests. With its extensive branch and ATM network, Malayan Banking Berhad, with a 10% share, was viewed as an established local bank whose cards were a vehicle of convenience. Finally, offering high credit limits but lacking in customer service and prestige, Malayan Borneo Finance offered numerous card types with varied pricing levels in order to be all things to all people and gain the widest possible market share. In general, MasterCard and Visa were known for their flexibility and wide retail acceptance, and the reputations of the banks issuing these cards helped consumers decide which one to choose. Local banks usually did not charge a joining fee for the classic card, but they all charged an annual fee, and they all offered an exclusive Gold card. According to Malaysian law, only consumers with an annual income of $9,000 or more could own a credit card.

Philippines

After a deep recession from 1984 through 1986, the Philippines during the late 1980s was in the midst of a booming recovery. Jumps in consumer demand helped fuel the economy as more and more jobs became available through new sources of capital and government programs. Food and beverage consumption was rising tremendously, as were sales of "big-ticket" items.

Even in the context of this rapid economic growth, credit card penetration in the Philippines was extremely low.

The credit card market was relatively underdeveloped, with only two major banks issuing MasterCards and Visas. Consumers valued these cards for their wide acceptance and revolving credit facility. American Express, perceived as the card for the international consumer, and Diners Club, known as the prestigious card, were also available. Between the two, they had nearly 50% of the market.

To their owners, credit cards provided value by allowing them to make purchases and pay for services at any time without having to worry about carrying large amounts of cash. Groceries were the most common kinds of card purchases, followed by restaurant meals, clothing, and gasoline. Wide acceptance was therefore by far the most important factor considered in selecting a card, followed by its terms, such as interest rate, repayment terms, and credit limit. The reputation of a card and its issuing bank was also important to consumers, but far less critical than other factors. Credit cards issued in the Philippines could be used only for local transactions in local currency.

Singapore

Thirty years of political stability under the strong-handed rule of Prime Minister Lee Kuan Yew helped Singapore develop into one of the world's largest centers for international trade and services, as well as the site of one of the world's biggest oil refineries. A host of multinational corporations had clamored to set up operations in this "high-tech Mecca." With an average per capita income of $8,800, the standard of living in Singapore was closer to that of industrialized Westernized nations than to that of its neighbors.

By 1989, Singaporeans were quite familiar with credit cards. In fact, with cardholders owning an average of two credit cards each and with nearly 500,000 cards in force, many felt the market was already saturated. In consumers' minds, cards fell into three categories. First, American Express, with about a 15% share, the high-price charge card with no spending limit, was known for its prestige, worldwide acceptance, and outstanding global service. Second, large international banks such as Hong Kong Bank, Chase, and Standard Chartered Bank offered MasterCards and Visas with worldwide acceptance and an international image. Consumers perceived their service and prestige to be lower than that of American Express but greater than that of the local banks. Finally, a number of local banks such as UOB, DBS, OUB, and OCBC offered low-priced MasterCards and Visas with worldwide acceptance but no international image. These cards were considered to have minimum levels of service and prestige, but were seen as patriotic and conservative choices. Consumers attached a lot of importance to the reputation of the issuing bank when choosing a card. American Express was the only card to charge a joining fee. By also waiving annual membership fees, local banks UOB and DBS had each captured a 20% share of the market.

As members of a society that prided itself on introducing the latest technology and service to make things run most efficiently, Singaporean consumers viewed credit cards as vehicles of convenience. At the same time, because government regulations required all cardholders to be at least 21 years old and to earn at least $14,400 per year, credit cards were also considered a status symbol. Because the market was so well developed, cards were used to purchase high-priced and low-priced items alike, from clothing, appliances, and electronics to restaurants, entertainment, and travel.

Taiwan

As the world's twelfth-largest trading power, Taiwan was a major investor in the Philippines, Thailand, Malaysia, Indonesia, and Mainland China. Once a rural nation, Taiwan had rapidly developed its capital- and technology-intensive industries, making its population one of the wealthiest and best educated in the region.

Though heavy government protection and support helped foster this industrial growth, it was a barrier to growth in the credit card business. Prior to 1989, laws prohibited consumers from owning more than one credit card, from revolving credit, and from using their cards to obtain cash advances. Also, international cards could not be issued in Taiwan. Anyone wanting a charge card from Citibank, American Express, or Chase Manhattan had to obtain it in Hong Kong. (The Taiwanese branches of these companies supported the Hong Kong branches in promoting these cards.)

Reforms in banking regulations, passed in July 1989, lifted the restrictions on international cards, on multiple-card ownership, and on revolving credit. However, the government retained

(Continued)

EXHIBIT 10 *(cont.)*

much control over the entire industry through its National Credit Card Center (NCCC), which engaged in developing merchant acceptance, maintained an extensive database on all member cardholders, and settled overseas transactions. Though the government exempted American Express and Diners Club from NCCC control, any bank wanting to issue a MasterCard or Visa had to obtain authority from the NCCC.

Such heavy regulation had kept all but a few players out of the credit card business, making it an industry in relatively early stages of development. Based on their global networks and premium-quality service, American Express and Diners Club developed a prestigious reputation, which they used to attract their target customers: executives, world travelers, and upper-class Taiwanese. Conversely, China Trust and Cathay Trust provided a lower-cost MasterCard and Visa suited for a wider audience. Consumers perceived American Express as the card to use for travel, Diners Club as the highest symbol of prestige, Visa as the most popular, widely accepted card in the world, and MasterCard as the second card to have in the wallet. American Express had about 50% of the market share. Unlike American Express and Diners Club, the local banks did not charge a joining fee.

To the Taiwanese consumer, the charge card was a badge of status. Taiwan was a cash-oriented society in which it was considered unacceptable to owe other people money. Even when it became legal to revolve credit, the majority of Taiwanese refrained from doing so. With an average purchase valued at $80 to $110, most credit cards were used in department stores, supermarkets, nightclubs, restaurants, and, of course, for travel—50% of credit card purchases were made overseas.

Thailand

With its economy growing at an average of 11.6% from 1986 to 1989, Thailand was one of Asia's most rapidly developing nations; foreign investment was growing faster there than anywhere else in Southeast Asia. Most of the increases came from the country's small but strong industrialized sector and from tourism, Thailand's largest source of foreign exchange. This continued strong economic performance resulted in a growth in consumer affluence and spending.

Compared with the more industrialized nations such as Singapore and Hong Kong, the card market in Thailand had relatively few major players. Card products could be divided into two groupings. First, there was American Express and Diners Club, whose core business was charge cards and which issued about 50% of the cards in the market. Prestige was the key to their positioning, as they focused on acquiring an upscale customer base. Second, the local banks issued Visa or MasterCard credit cards. These were often aimed at the bank's customers and did not have the same upscale image among consumers.

Korea

Local regulations did not permit banks to issue cards with revolving credit. Further, due to strict foreign exchange control measures, only local currency cards could be issued. As a result, several local banks were issuing Visa/MasterCards as charge and debit cards. For many years, Citibank had been managing the Diners Club business in Korea. Management experience with the Korean card business was far from satisfactory with financial losses as well as labor problems.

Source: "The Worldwide Web of Chinese Business," *Harvard Business Review*, March–April 1993: 24–37.

market issued local-currency cards. A decision in this matter would have to take into account two aspects. First, local-card spend patterns versus overseas-card spend patterns in each market would help decide which currency type would appeal to customers. Second, asset growth of a local-currency card would hinge upon steady, matching growth of funding through local-currency deposits based on the limited branch network of Citibank.

There was considerable skepticism surrounding the idea of a centralized data processing setup, the Regional Card Center. Country managers feared that centralized processing would slow the speed of response, and system developers would be cut off from local markets. "I don't know how we can call ourselves a service company, if our systems are all centralized in Singapore," queried a country manager. "Also, it does not make cost sense to spend so much money on creating a huge centralized unit, and on leasing unreliable local and overseas communication lines when we can instead piggyback on our local systems, which can be upgraded with less expense." Moreover, if the centralized system broke down, the service platforms in all countries would suffer.

The advocates of a Regional Card Center, however (except Hong Kong, which had its own system capabilities), cited two important benefits:

1. Lower costs because of scale economies, especially with respect to software development. For example, if Citibank introduced a new reporting feature for its card customers, the programming could be done centrally, and simply downloaded to the countries. There would be no need to customize by country.
2. Capability to do quick card product launches in Asia-Pacific, because of the ease of transferring best practices.

Talwar attributed the root cause of his country managers' resistance to Citibank's Asia-Pacific organization structure. Responsibility for launching the card would rest with the country managers who were already handling the branch banking side of the business. In the United States and Europe, the card business was handled by a dedicated team outside the branch banking organization. Few country managers in Asia Pacific wished to take the initial huge losses of a credit card product their projections indicated was a distinct possibility. They argued that Citibank, instead of attempting to dilute its efforts in acquiring mass-market customers, should in fact focus on its upscale customers and reinforce its depth of relationship with Citi-One and Citigold types of products and services. Some of the country managers felt they were already stretched on resources, while aggressively developing the branch banking business. It would be difficult, they said, to fund the people needs in a demanding card business since the market had no trained talent available. Countries could, then, lose focus in branch banking and would not be able to do justice to the new card business either.

The credit card idea was not without its supporters. Rajive Johri, a business manager in Indonesia, expressed his exuberance:

> In a country of 180 million, it should not be difficult to find the right staff and a million customers. We have the expertise in the United States and other markets, and if we can source enthusiastic people, we can train them in the business too. We will not only be building new business in a virgin territory but be a catalyst for changing the cash societies in emerging and rapidly growing economies of Asia-Pacific.

If a decision to "go-ahead" was approved, then questions of positioning, pricing, and launch economics would have to be carefully addressed. Jeannine Farhi, who had moved to Asia from Citibank in the United States, cautioned:

> It is useful to remember that poor implementation can often kill great strategy. I am not really sure if the U.S. experience can be directly translated here. For example, I am not sure if the postal service here can handle the kind of direct mail program we often mount in the United States. Post offices here are not accustomed to handling such large masses of mail. Moreover, we have to be creative about how we put together the direct mailing lists to target customers. Ready-made lists, of course, are simply unavailable. The telecom infrastructure of many countries in

this region is inadequate. Some countries take several months, or even years, to provide new telephone connections at high costs, and their reliability is poor. I have not heard of any credit bureaus which could help us evaluate potential customers. All these difficult issues should be addressed in any launch plan.

At Singapore's Changi International Airport, as Rana Talwar boarded his flight to Australia, he contemplated the diversity of his markets as well as his management's views on the card product.

On the one hand, the expedient move would be to stick to our proven up-market branch banking strategy. This seems to have the support of a large majority of country managers. On the other hand, we cannot be unmindful of the growth opportunities that the card product offers us. It is not clear we have a strategy for the credit card positioning, pricing, or country selection.

We are never going to get a consensus; that's why it is important for me to make a decision soon, one way or the other.

Index

A

Aaker, David A., 24, 52, 147, 242
Abandoned drugs, 310
ABC, see Activity-based costing
ABMs, see Automatic banking machines
Account analysis, bottom-up account, 361
Ackerstein, Daniel, 244
Activity-based costing (ABC), 354, 512
Ader, Jason, 128, 133
Adoption process, 17, 163
Advanced Pricing module, J.D. Edwards, 476, 477
Advertisement, Bloomingdale's, 186
Advertising
 awareness, 47, 50, 54
 cable, 173
 campaign
  GoodFoods, 384
  investment in, 385
  Wendy's, 279
 catalog, 184
 direct-to-consumer, 242
 expenditures, 375
 image, 237
 journal, 296
 media, 241
 outdoor, 173
 print, 241, 261
 radio, 241
 revenues, Generation Y, 256
Affinity programs, 25
After-sales service, 72
Agarwal, Rajshree, 270
Airline
 industry, logit regression results, 55
 membership, 418
All-at-once approach, 316, 317
Ambler, Tim, 238, 502
American Customer Satisfaction Index, 196
Anderson, Eugene W., 47, 242, 383
Anderson, James C., 25, 52, 194, 313
Aoki, Naomi, 299
Apicella, Mario, 506
Application service providers (ASPs), 466
Architectural millwork companies, 443

Asia-Pacific markets, credit card, 533–538
 Australia, 533–534
 Hong Kong, 534
 India, 535
 Indonesia, 535
 Korea, 538
 Malaysia, 536
 Philippines, 536–537
 Singapore, 537
 Taiwan, 537–538
 Thailand, 538
ASPs, see Application service providers
ATMs, see Automated teller machines
Automated marketing, 463
Automated teller machines (ATMs), 525, 534
Automatic banking machines (ABMs), 504
Automatic Price Protection, Tweeter, Etc., 274
Availability, definition of, 278
Awareness advertising, 29

B

Baby Boomers, 368
Back office systems, 462
Balance sheet(s), 204
 consolidated, 357, 471
 Medicines Company, 304
 SaleSoft, 497
Baldwin, Carliss Y., 315
Bank
 acquiring, 523
 champion branches, 513
 virtual, 505
Banking
 branch, 519, 525
 relationship, 508
 telephone, 516
Barista coffee house environment, 273
BAS transaction, see Book and ship transaction
Bass, Elliot B., 319
Basu, Kunal, 501
Bayus, Barry L., 270
Berger, Paul D., 4, 42, 43, 45, 46, 141, 142, 381
Berry, Leonard L., 238, 277, 381

Best, Roger J., 502
Beverage market, growth of segments of U.S., 107
Bhattacharya, C. B., 238, 313
Bid(s)
 creation, 476
 preliminary, 294
 process, 230, 294
 proposals, 448
 -spec environment, relationships in, 451
 unsuccessful, 452
Biggest bang for the buck, 382
Big IT, 468
Binkley, Christina, 117, 134
Bitner, Mary Jo, 240, 273
Blattberg, Robert C., 2, 4, 22, 43, 45, 51, 141, 142, 276, 425
Blockbuster drugs, 302
Bogo (buy one, get one free) promotion, 109, 275
Bolt-on software, 468
Bolton, Ruth N., 4, 43, 46, 274, 313, 365, 381, 501
Bond, Jonathan, 7, 8
Book
 industry overview, 72
 publishers, world's leading, 76
 publishing industry, 73, 74
 retailers, 77
 wholesalers, 75
Book and ship (BAS) transaction, 352, 355
Bottom-up account analysis, 361
Boulding, William, 271
Bounds, Wendy, 248, 251
Bowman, Douglas, 4, 365, 366, 381
Brainstorming, 325
Branch banking, 519, 525
Brand
 awareness, 241
 chain, 411
 choice probabilities, 144
 competing, 142
 customer attitude toward, 243
 customer perception of, 237
 drivers, 95
 equity
  corporate ethics and, 91
  CRM to increase, 94
  drivers of, 97
  ethics driver of, 243
  role of, 24

541

Index

Brand *Continued*
  fashion, 12
  Hilton, 413
  image, corporate image and, 20
  lifestyle, 12
  loyalty, 158
  management, 13
  manager, 23
  partners, 242
  perceptions of, 38
  positioning, 242, 531
  report card priorities, 266
  strategy, 27, 382
  superpremium, 249
  switching, 43, 141, 142
    customer equity and, 48
    matrix, 46, 63, 99, 143, 146
  values, 243
Brand equity, building and
    managing, 237–266
  case (Alloy.com), 252–261
    Alloy.com, 256–261
    Generation Y market, 252–253
    online competition for
      Generation Y spending,
      254–256
  case (brand report card
    exercise), 262–266
    delivering on customers'
      desires, 262
    integrated marketing
      activities, 264
    management, 264–265
    monitoring, 265
    portfolio, 264
    positioning, 263
    relevance, 262–263
    support, 265
    value, 263
  case (Eastman Kodak
    Company), 248–251
    category pricing, 249–250
    consumer behavior, 250–251
    funtime strategy, 251
  definition and significance of
    brand equity, 237–238
  growth of brand equity, 240–245
    attitude toward brand,
      242–243
    building brand awareness,
      241–242
    corporate citizenship and
      ethics, 243–245
    importance of brand equity,
      238–240
Bricks and clicks business, 478
Briggs, Elton, 4, 381
Broadcast e-mail, 260
Brown box business, 190
Brown, Eryn, 253
Brown, Jeff, 87
Bugsy Siegel, 118

Business class hotel market,
    413, 422
Business groups, Xerox, 69
Buyer–seller relationships, 313
Buying decisions, teen, 257
Buyout pricing, 448

C

Cable advertising, 173
Calder, Bobby J., 237
Call center integration (CCI), 461
Call center, 210, 315, 506
Capacity forecasts, 230
Caravella, Mary Neuner, 442
Carpenter, Gregory S., 502
Carraway, Robert L., 47
Carrolo, Patricia Martone, 117
Cash flows, consolidated
    statements of, 472
Casino(s)
  facilities, Indian, 128
  Las Vegas, 139
  resort, 118
Catalog(s)
  advertising, 184
  average purchase, 374
  direct-mail, 32
  Eddie Bauer, 370
  e-mail, 261
  Japanese-language, 256
  mini-, 192
  -only product, 377
  print, 254
  production, 373
Category pricing, 249
Cattell, Raymond B., 53
CCI, see Call center integration
CEO, marketing-oriented, 23
CES, see Customer equity share
Chain brands, 411
Chamber of Commerce, 213
Chandy, Rajesh K., 241
Channel partners, 163
Charge card, 527, 537
Chief marketing officer, 1, 4
Childhood buddies, 238
Chintagunta, Pradeep, 56
CICs, see Customer-initiated
    contacts
CIG customers, see Commercial,
    industrial, and
    government customers
CIPAD, see Customer Value
    Improvement Process
    and Database
Citibank, 523
Clancy, Kevin J., 51, 114
Clark, Kim B., 315
Class to mass strategy, 111
Client
  database, Granny's Goodies, 222

  information, Granny's Goodies,
    214–217
  survey, 208
Cline, Craig E., 224
Clinical testing, 298, 301, 309
Cluttered packaging, 7
CLV, see Customer lifetime value
CM, see Contract Manufacturer
CMS, see Contact management
    systems
Cold calling, 210
Cold channel, 11
Collins, Glen, 7
Columbine High School shooting
    tragedy, 258
Columbo, Richard, 46
Commercial, industrial, and
    government (CIG)
    customers, 331
Communication(s)
  consumer-to-firm, 241
  customers and, 179
  direct-to-consumer, 241
  miscues, 464
  word-of-mouth, 241, 246
Community
  -building programs, 25, 26
  event sponsorship, 244
  virtual, 26
Company
  acquisition, 326
  debt, 445
Competition, 100
  Brita's, 113
  elevator market, 280, 293
  Fabtek, 226
  gift industry, 206
  Harrah's, 139
  online, 254
Competitive effects, modeling
    of, 142
Competitor(s)
  CSAS, 487
  Fabtek's, 235
  fighting back by, 385
  firm's performance and, 96
  Nortel Networks, 404
  performance, 31
  selling strategy of, 321
  WESCO, 332
Complaints, 366
Complex pricing, definition of, 276
Comprehensive sales automation
    system (CSAS), 482, 483
  benefits of, 485
  competitors, 487
  market potential for, 486
  products, 484, 491
  solutions, typical concerns
    regarding, 490
  vendors, 486
Computer server industry, 28

Index

Conference calls, 434
Consortium customer, 346
Construction market, booming, 449
Consumer
   attitudes, 104, 109
   decision making, brand name and, 250
   electronics retailer, 274
   -to-firm communications, 241
   -generated content, Alloy Web site, 258
   promotion, 115
Contact management systems (CMS), 483
Contract Manufacturer (CM), 350
Contracts, single-source, 435
Cooil, Bruce, 46
Cooper, Robin, 424
Copeland, Tom, 50
Corporate assets, evaluation of, 61
Corporate citizenship, 54, 243, 245
Corporate culture, congenial, 169
Corporate ethics, 91
Corporate gifts, 185, 200, 205
Corporate image, 20
Cost(s)
   activity-based, 354, 512
   customer acquisition, 532
   estimators, 234
   inventory-carrying, 355
   IT, 512
   marketing, 49, 415
   overtime, 235
   procurement, 335
   reductions, Blackstone Homes, 453
   to serve (CTS), 319, 320
   walking, 418
Countertop displays, Take-One, 541
Coupons, 187, 241
Cowboys, 293
Credit card(s)
   business operation economics, 532
   histories, 244
   launch, 521
   low-rate, 431
   markets, Asia-Pacific, 533–538
   pricing, 530
   product, premium-priced, 520
   purchases, 527, 534
   reasons for owning, 536
   use of in India, 535
Credit reports, third party–provided, 513
Crittenden, Victoria L., 241
Crittenden, William F., 241
CRM technologies, role of in customer management, 460–499
   background, 460–461

case (Moore Medical Corporation) 468–482
   business model, 470–474
   company history, 468–470
   CRM decision, 479–482
   information technology, 475–479
   operations, 474–475
   supplier relations, 475
case (SaleSoft, Inc.), 482–499
   decision, 498–499
   organization, 493–496
   PROCEED SMRP, 491–493
   sales automation industry, 482–491
   Trojan horse opportunity, 496–498
critical touch points, 462–464
   front office and back office, 462–463
   how to measure success, 465
   industry overview, 465–466
   industry trends, 466–467
   internal and external, 463
   multi-channel and cross channel coordination, 464
   operational and analytical, 463
   fitting strategy with functional design, 461
   implementation stumbling blocks, 464–465
   stakeholders, 462
CRM, see Customer relationship management
Cross-marketing, 138
CSAS, see Comprehensive sales automation system
CSR, see Customer service representative
CTS, see Cost to serve
Cultural logic, Snapple, 14
Customer(s)
   acquisition, 479
   cost, Citibank, 532
   efforts, 531
   awareness, building of, 238
   base, pyramid structure of, 195
   behavior, determinant of future, 33
   branch banking, 525
   brand-switching matrix, 63
   -centered thinking, 43
   -centric company, 196
   commercial, industrial, and government 331
   communications strategy, 241
   consolidation, 124, 194
   consortium, 346
   contact matrix, 435, 437
   database, 78, 201, 239, 365, 428
   decisioning, 231, 322, 511, 514
   demographics, 374

   external, 463
   feedback, 409
   fired, 325
   -firm relationship, 26
   -first culture, 398
   -friendly company, 84
   gaming, 132
   grateful, 322
   hostage, 323
   ignorant, 322
   industrial, 199
   -initiated contacts (CICs), 365, 366
   intelligence, 463
   internal, 463
   interview, 34, 35–41
   intimacy, 506
   investments, 198
   link between firm and, 268
   loyalty, 57
      casino, 129
      definition of, 404
   management
      strategies, 26, 29, 30
      systems, enterprise-level, 194
   mass-market, 539
   migration, 321, 323
   Moore Medical Corporation, 470
   needs, 337
   perceptions, 45
   potential, 32, 313
   preferences, 503
   profitability, 511, 512, 514
   purchasing decisions, 141, 401
   retention, 46, 199
   revenue stream, 424
   reward program, 239
   satisfaction issue resolution process, 405, 406
   satisfaction survey, 392, 399, 400
   segmentation, opportunity based, 133, 134
   service representative (CSR), 433
   -specific coupons, 29
   strategy, 2, 31
   target, 134
   testimonials, 408
   transactional, 355
   types, 322, 331, 425
   unconcerned, 323
   use of research to capture, 148
   value(s), 100, 318
      equation, 268
      management, 407
      research, implications for, 408
   Value Improvement Process and Database (CIPAD), 399
   voice of, 405
   worth, 133

Index

Customer equity, 22, 43, 387
  brand switching and, 48
  component of, 238–240
  definition of, 2, 144
  driver(s)
    diagram, 151
    importance of, 52
    efforts, Avis U.K., 143
    estimation of, 145
    management
      framework, 2
      process, steps in, 5
    measurement of, 388
    model of, 61
    restaurant chain, 146
    share (CES), 49, 98, 99
Customer equity analysis, 91–140, 382, 388, 290
  analysis of firm's performance, 93–96
  case (Brita Products Company), 103–117
    Brita Products Company, 104–113
    Clorox Company, 103–104
    Couric's decision, 116–117
    faucet-mounted filter entry, 113–116
  case (Harrah's Entertainment, Inc.), 117–140
    company background, 119–128
    competition, 139–140
    early strategy, 128–130
    gambling in United States, 117–119
    new approach, 130–139
  comparing firm's performance to that of competitors', 96–98
  data collection, 29
  firm and competitor performance, 31
  lessons from analysis, 100
  magnitude of opportunity, 98–99
  market analysis, 91–93
Customer equity approach and customer management plan, 22–90
  case (Coca-Cola), 83–90
    Big Brother, 87–88
    mean vending machines, 88–90
    testing of vending unit, 84–86
    vending machine technology, 86
  case (Xerox), 69–83
    book acquisition, 79
    book industry overview, 72
    Book-in-Time project, 79–83
    distribution value chain, 72–78
    economics of value chain, 78–79
    options, 83
    Xerox Corporation, 69–72
  customer equity approach, 23–26
    role of brand equity, 24–25
    role of relationship equity, 25–26
    role of value equity, 24
  customer equity exercise, 34–41
    directions for interview, 34–35
    participant to complete, 35
    possible introduction for customer interview, 35
    questions to ask customer, 35–41
  customer management plan, 29–31
    data collection, 29–31
    firm and competitor performance, 31
    measuring, monitoring, and evaluating, 31
    strategy development, 31
  customer management strategies, 26–29
    brand strategies, 27
    mixed strategies, 29
    relationship-brand strategies, 28–29
    relationship strategies, 27–28
    value-brand strategies, 28
    value-relationship strategies, 28
    value strategies, 26–27
  return on marketing, 42–64
    contribution of article, 43–45
    customer equity, 43
    discussion, 59–61
    estimation details, 61–64
    example application, 52–59
    example survey items, 64
    financial accountability, 42–43
    implementation issues, 50–52
    linking marketing actions to financial return, 45–50
    marketing strategy problem, 42
    overview of article, 45
Customer equity management strategy, 1–21
  benefits of, 4
  case (Snapple), 6–21
    glory years, 7–9
    origins of brand, 6–7
    Quaker takes command, 9–13
    Triarc acquires Snapple, 13–21
  importance of, 4
  overview, 2–3
Customer equity measurement, 141–193
  brand switching and customer lifetime value, 141–145
  case (aerosphere Airlines), 151–152
  case (Aqualisa Quartz), 152–166
    channels of distribution, 157–158
    development of quartz shower valve, 158–160
    initial sales results, 162–163
    Quartz, 160–162
    shift in marketing strategy,163–166
    U.S. shower market, 153–157
  case (Calyx & Corolla), 166–193
    Calyx & Corolla, 176–177
    customers and communication, 179–188
    fresh flower industry, 169–176
    management team, 167–169
    operations, 177 product line, 179
    relationship with Federal Express, 178–179
    relationship with growers, 177–178
    ultimate positioning, 188–193
  cross-sectional versus longitudinal data, 146–149
  modeling of switching matrix, 145–146
  return on investment, 146
Customer lifetime value (CLV),22, 42, 43, 141, 144
  American Airlines, 56
  estimating, 63
  model, 43, 45, 57, 60
Customer relationship management (CRM), 3, 94, 132, 320
  Harrah's, 132
  implementation failure, 464
  initiatives, 460, 515
  project roadblocks, 462
  reorganization around, 506
  software, 148 320, 460, 462, 468
  system selection matrix, 481
Customer selection, 194–236
  case (Fabtek), 224–236
    fabrication division, 224–225
    forecasts, 227
    manufacturing process, 227–230
    marketing, 230–231
    markets and customers, 225–226
    other considerations, 234–235
    prospective fabrication orders, 231–234
  case (Granny's Goodies, Inc.), 202–223

Index

challenges in sales planning process, 222–223
corporate gift market, 205–207
firm history, 202–205
marketing and lead generation, 210–221
sales process, 221–222
target markets, 207–210
criteria, 200
customer selection, 195–201
customer roles and management, 198–199
decision accountability, 199
decision evaluation basis and data quality, 199–201
effective customer management strategy, 194–195
Customized PCs, Dell, 197
Customized products, 39
Cut-flower industry, 189

D

Danaher, Peter J., 45, 141, 384
Darren, Chervitz, 257
Darroch, James L., 504, 505
Database
customer, 78, 201, 239, 365, 428
management, 368
marketing (DBM), 132, 133
Data mining, 463
DataStage, 148
Davis, Aaron, 107
Davis, Ricardo, 249
Day, George S., 147
DBM, see Database marketing
De Rosa, Fernando, 383
Deal clincher, 221
Debit card, virtual, 255
Decision calculus, 51
Decision making
processes, 270
unit (DMU), 322, 488–489
Degeratu, Alexandru M., 48
Deighton, John, 2, 6, 22, 43, 45, 51, 103, 141, 142, 240, 252, 410, 425
Demand
flow, supplier management of, 352
planning system, 478
Design registration, 351
Dick, Alan S., 501
Digital printing industry, 81
Digital sales channel, 221
Digital world, market in, 81
Direct mail, 32, 164, 296, 364
Direct marketing, 431, 531
campaign, 1
customer-centric approach to, 136
Direct-to-consumer advertising, 242

Direct-to-consumer communications, 241
Discounted share-of-wallet, 60
Distribution
channels, 75, 334
specialty, 332
value chain, 72
DIY market, see Do-it-yourself market
DMU, see Decision making unit
Document
solutions, 71
technology center (DTC), 82
Do-it-yourself (DIY) market, 155
Do-it-yourselfers, targeting of, 164
Dolan, Robert J., 248
Dowling, Grahame R., 25, 46
Drew James, 43
Driver(s)
brand equity, 97
coefficients, 55, 149
ethics, 243
relationship, 53, 95, 97
strategic expenditure to improve, 50
value equity, 91, 277
Drop shipping, 359
Drug(s)
abandoned, 310
anti–blood clotting, 303
blockbuster, 302
development industry, 298
fast-acting, 304
pipeline, 312
premium-priced, 309
DTC, see Document technology center
Duncan, Tom, 241
Dwyer, F. Robert, 46, 142, 270

E

Ease of use, definition of, 278
E-commerce, 221
store, 89
wave, 315
Web site, 478
Edell, Julie, 238
EDI, see Electronic Data Interchange
Ehrbar, Al, 50
Eisler, Peter, 107
Electrical equipment and supplies business, 328
Electronic Data Interchange (EDI), 339, 354, 435
Elevator(s)
industry, 280
machine room configurations, 283
price levels, 290

purchasing decision, 284
technology, 282
E-mail, 3, 364
broadcast, 260
catalog, 261
memo, company, 407
notifications of specials, 373
unsolicited, 241
voices, 378
Emergency care patients, 305
Energy savings, appeal of, 292
Enterprise relationship management (ERM), 461
Enterprise resource planning (ERP), 460, 475
ERM, see Enterprise relationship management
ERP, see Enterprise resource planning
Escarpit, R., 79
Estimate estimate, 448
Ethics
brand equity and, 247
corporate, 91
standards, 58
Everyday low pricing, 274
Expert/advisory services, 432
External customers, 463
Extreme sports clothing, 256
Extreme value, 145
E-Zine registrations, 261

F

FAEs, see Field application engineers
Fahney, Liam, 45, 98, 501
Falcone, Mark, 128, 133
Fashion brand, 12
Fashion trajectory, 17
Fashion water, 20
Fast-acting drugs, 304
Faucet filter, market simulation study, 114
Faxes, 364
FDA approval, 299, 301, 303
Fellman, Michelle Wirth, 50
Ferrell, O. C., 24
Field application engineers (FAEs), 353
Field sales representative (FSR), 352, 433, 473
Financial accountability, 42
Financial institutions (FIs), 506
Financial return
linking marketing actions to, 45
projected, 58
Financial summary, KONE, 286
Finlay, Charles, 505
First tier supplier/distributors, 343
FIs, see Financial institutions
FITD, see Foot-in-the-door

Index

Flings, 238
Focus groups, 7, 151
Foot-in-the-door (FITD), 314
  pricing strategies, 316
  product, 315, 316
Footprint, 445, 450, 459
Foreign exchange
    market, 522
    transactions, India, 535
Fornell, Claes, 365
Forward buying, 61
Fournier, Susan, 24, 238, 240
Francella, Kevin, 11
Franchisees, 419
Franchise-oriented business
    model, 445
Frank, Ildiko E., 51
Frank, Ronald E., 48
Franses, Philip Hans, 274
Frequent buyer cards, 147
Fresh flower industry, 169
Freund, Rudolf J., 51
Friedman, Jerome H., 51
Friendship networks, 18
FSR, see Field sales representative
Fulfillment company, 261

G

G&A, see General and
    Administrative expenses
Gale, Bradley T., 24, 43, 60, 268, 400
Gambling
  geographic expansion of
    legalized, 119
  relationship of United States
    with, 117
Games players, 420
Gaming
  customers, 132
  revenues, 128, 140
  value, 239
Garfield, Charles A., 244
Gasoline service stations,
    evolution of, 432
Gaszynski, Emily, 505
Geared traction elevators, 282
Gearless traction elevators, 282
General and Administrative
    expenses (G&A), 178
Generation Y
  advertising revenues, 256
  broadcast e-mail to, 260
  market, 252
  spending, online competition
    for, 254
Gerstner, Eitan, 274
Gessner, Guy, 51
Getz, Gary, 4, 43, 141, 142, 425
Ghemawat, Pankaj, 77
Gift industry competition, 206
Glazer, Rashi, 93

Global consumer bank,
Global value map, 397
Gold Account, TeamTBA, 438
Got rate, 451, 455
Gourville, John T., 274, 276, 297
Graphical User Interface (GUI),
    70, 71
Grateful customers, 322
Graves, Tom, 119
Great Attractor, 16
Greene, William H., 62
Grewal, Dhruv, 277
Gronstedt, Anders, 42
Guadagni, Peter M., 46, 145
GUI, see Graphical User
    Interface
Gummeson, Evert, 25, 52, 92
Gunthorpe, Deborah, 244
Gupta, Sunil, 57, 61, 98, 145
Gustafsson, Anders, 47

H

Hagan, Patti, 189, 190
Hagemeyer, Dale, 464
Hagerty, Michael R., 51
Håkansson, H., 43
Hansen, Barbara, 107
Harrah, William Fisk, 128
Harreld, Heather, 464
Hauser, John R., 141
Hausler, Eric, 128, 133
Hays, Constance L., 84
Henderson, Geraldine R., 237
Heparin, 305
Heskett, James L., 45, 432
High-risk patients, 307
High-tech Mecca, 537
Higie, Robin, 237
Hippel, Eric Von, 323, 325
Hocking, Ronald R., 51
Hoeffler, Steve, 244
Hoekstra, Janny C., 274
Hoerl, A. E., 384
Hogan, John, 4, 43, 47
Home pages, 359
Home water filtration
    industry, 103
Horticulture industry, 169
Hostage customers, 323
Hotel
  chains, segments served by
    major, 415
  corporate rates, 412
  industry, 411
  profitability, 418
  reimbursement, 421
Howard Stern, 8
Hu, Michael Y., 51
Hult, Thomas G., 24
Hunt, Shelby D., 96, 313
Hydraulic elevators, 282

I

Ignorant customers, 322
Image advertising, 237
I-media, 372
  customer, 373
  newness of, 376
  sales, 369
  success of, 380
Income statement(s), 202, 203
  comparative, 369
  consolidated, 349
  Hilton HHonors
    Worldwide, 416
Indian casino facilities, 128
Industrial customers, 199, 331
Industrial markets, managing
    customer profitability in,
    424–459
  case (CMR Enterprises),
    442–459
    alternatives, 457–459
    background, 442–443
    Blackstone Homes, 452–453
    developing InfoCentral,
      450–451
    increasing concerns, 454–457
    from Mike's Cabinets to
      CMR Enterprises,
      445–450
    Mike's Cabinets and custom
      architectural millwork
      industry, 443–445
    valuing relationships,
      451–452
  case (Hunter Business Group),
    430–442
    direct marketing and HBG's
      customer contact matrix,
      431–432
    early successes, 440
    evolution of gasoline service
      stations and branded
      TBA market, 432
    Gold Account, 438
    Hunter Business Group,
      430–431
    planning for journey ahead,
      440–442
    Star Oil account, 432–433
    TeamTBA, 433–435
    TeamTBA results, 438–440
    using Star customer contact
      matrix, 435–438
  managing customers for profit,
    428
  managing customers for rev-
    enue, 426–427
  price paid index, 427
  SCW index, 426–427
Industry networking
    meetings, 209

Information technology (IT), 317
   big, 468
   budgets, HP products, 317
   costs, 512
   ticket sales, 148
Initial public offering (IPO), 252
Instant Order Updates, Amazon.com, 196
In-store displays, 241
In-store sales, 1
Insurance service, 315
Interactive voice response (IVR), 463
Interest revenue, 512
Internal customers, 463
Internal memo, Nortel Networks, 395
Internet, 3, 364
   access, WiFi wireless, 279
   Arrow Schweber and, 359
   -based business, 478
   -based trading system, 347
   -enabled direct marketer, 479
   purchases, 244
   traffic, backbone, 398
Inventory, 276
   carrying costs, 355
   replenishment system, 354
   shelf time, 479, 480
   tracking of, 352
IPO, see Initial public offering
Irons, John S., 88, 90
IT, see Information technology
IVR, see Interactive voice response

J

Jackson, Barbara B., 46
Jain, Dipak, 56
Japanese-language catalog, 256
Job satisfaction, 169
Johnson, Michael D., 47
Joint strategy, 382
Jolliffe, I. T., 53
Journal advertising, 296
Jump balls, 351
Juran, Joseph M., 271

K

Kaiser, Henry F., 53
Kalra, Ajay, 271
Kalwani Manohar U., 46, 270, 425
Kamakura, Wagner A., 45, 383
Kaplan, Andrew, 12
Kaplan, Robert S., 319, 424
Kathleen, Kerwin, 252
Keiningham, Timothy L., 29, 45, 383, 384
Keller, Kevin L., 24, 52, 238, 244

Kendall, Jordan, 505
Kennard, R.W., 384
Khermouch, G., 251
King III, Charles, 83
Kirshenbaum, Richard, 7, 8
Knowledge-building programs, 25
Koller, Tim, 50
Konicki, Steve, 320
Kordupleski, Raymond, 43, 60, 384
Korman, Kathy, 202
Kotler, Philip, 43, 242, 500, 502
Krishnamurthi, Lakshman, 384
Kumar, Piyush, 25, 92
Kumar, V., 4, 43, 144, 147, 381, 383, 385, 389, 502

L

Labor market, Philadelphia, 227
Lal, Rajiv, 117
Lane, M., 79
Larreché, Jean-Claude, 43
Las Vegas casinos, 139
Lauterborn, Robert F., 241
Lead generation, marketing and, 210
Leading National Advertisers, 173
Leamon, Ann K., 367
Lee, Eunkyu, 51
Lehmann, Donald R., 57, 61, 98, 145, 238
Leithen, Francis, 3
Lemon, Katherine N., 2, 4, 23, 29, 41, 42, 43, 45, 47, 52, 94, 151, 238, 244, 246, 268, 274, 383, 391, 425, 502
Levey, Richard H., 138
Libai, Barak, 43, 47
Licensing, 433, 466
Liesse, Juline, 12
Lifestyle brand, 12
Lifetime value expressions, 49
LIMDEP, 62
Little, John D. C., 46, 51, 145, 386
Local-currency cards, Citibank, 539
Location, definition of, 277
Lodging industry, U.S., 412
Logit software, 62
Long-term relationship (LTR), 425
Loss leaders, 316
Loyalty program(s), 25, 47, 122, 411
   budget upside, 137
   frequency upside, 137
   Harrah's, 136
   improvement, 384
   investment in, 54
LTR, see Long-term relationship
Lusch, Robert F., 502

M

Madden, Normandy, 3
Maher, Brian, 119
Maignan, Isabelle, 24
Mail order, 188
   operation, 166
   reliability of, 192
Mailing lists, 213
Malkin, Lawrence, 191
Malls, upscale regional, 372
Management, value-based, 50
Mandel, Leon, 128
Manufacturers Survey Association, 446
Manufacturing process, second generation, 308
Manufacturing Resource Planning (MRP), 494
MAP, see Minimum advertised price
Marcus, Claudio, 465
Market(s)
   analysis, 91
   beverage, 107
   Book-in-Time, 80
   business class hotel, 413, 422
   construction, 449
   do-it-yourself, 155
   entry costs, Citibank, 527
   expansion, 204
   foreign exchange, 522
   Generation Y, 252
   globalization, 194
   launches, KONE, 288
   mature, 159
   photo film market, 248
   property developer, 156
   recruiting, 210
   research
      organization, 483
      survey, 367
   selection, importance of, 195
   share
      maintenance of, 291
      SaleSoft, 496
   simulation study, faucet filters, 114
   -specific representatives, 473
   strategies, KONE, 291
   target, 207
   test, 388
Marketer of the Year, 196
Marketing
   accountability, 501
   actions, evaluating potential, 383
   activities, design of, 141
   automated, 463
   campaigns, customized, 514
   challenges, 1
   classic, 439

Marketing Continued
  costs, 49, 415
  cross-, 138
  database, 132, 133
  direct, 136, 431
  emerging viewpoint for, 502
  events, residential home-
      building, 454
  expenditures, 52
    evaluation of, 59
    projected ROI from, 58
  experiments, 134
  financial return and, 45
  firms, industrial, 425
  highly personalized form of, 430
  initiatives, competing, 42
  investment, 147, 386, 390
  lead generation and, 210
  literature, ideas from, 145
  multi-channel, 363
  organization, Fabtek, 225
  -oriented CEO, 23
  Pavlovian, 140
  proactive, 133
  programs, loyalty, 411
  resources, KONE, 295
  strategy, 2
    customer-focused, 22, 33
    determination of, 20
    potential ROI of, 389
    shift in, 163
  study, RCB Financial Group, 507
  system, PROCEED, 493
  tactic, most used, 274
Marketing, how customer
      management is
      changing, 500–540
  case (Citibank), 519–540
    Asia-Pacific operations, 521
    card business basics, 523–527
    card business operation
      economics, 532
    launch of credit card in
      Asia-Pacific, 527–532
    options and controversies,
      532–540
  case (RBC Financial
      Group),503–519
    current environment, 505
    customer profitability and
      potential measurement
      at Royal Bank, 510–511
    developing CRM philosophy,
      505–510
    history, 504–505
    RBC Financial Group, 503–504
    using customer profitability
      for customer decisioning,
      511–519
  customer management
      and marketing
      accountability, 501
  how customer equity
      analysis changes
      marketing, 500–501
Markov matrix, 46, 47
Maselli, Jennifer, 320
Mass merchants, 111
Massy, William F., 46, 51, 142
Mature market, 159
Mazzon, Jose Afonso, 383
Mcafee, Andrew, 468
McFadden, Daniel S., 62
McWilliam, Gil, 25, 252
Media
  advertising, 241
  creative strategy, 242
Mehegan, Sean, 113
Membership cards, Harrah's, 239
Midstream business, 317
Mini-catalogs, 192
Minimum advertised price
    (MAP), 111
Mitchell, Peter, 501
Mittal, Vikas, 238, 383
Mobile-push-to-talk phone, 386
Model(s)
  brand-switching matrix, 46
  customer equity, 61
  customer lifetime value, 43, 45, 60
  customer profitability, 511, 512
  customer retention, 46
  estimates, reliability of, 56
  franchise-oriented business, 445
  multinomial logit, 48
  multinomial probit, 56
  new customer profitability, 517
  procurement, 344
  return on investment, 42, 59
  return on marketing, 44
  return on quality, 45
  switching matrix, 48, 145
  utility, 48
Mom-and-pop stores, 7
Money-back guarantee, 167
Monroe, Kent B., 274
Montgomery, David B., 46, 142
Moon, Youngme, 152
Moorman, Christine, 502
Morgan, Robert M., 96, 313
Moriarty, Rowland T., 195, 224,
    235, 319, 321, 322, 323
Moriarty, Sandra, 241
Morrison, Donald G., 46, 47, 142
MRP, see Manufacturing
    Resource Planning
Mucha, Thomas, 143
Mulhern, Francis J., 43
Multi-channel settings, managing
    customer relationships
    using multiple touch
    points in, 363–380
  case (Eddie Bauer, Inc.),
    367–380
    background, 367–369
    catalog, 369–372
    channel conflicts, 376–378
    customers, 374
    economics, 376
    I-media, 372–373
    marketing, 374–376
    marketing strategy, 378–380
    retail stores, 372
  customer's perspective, 365–366
  multi-channel marketing,
    363–364
Multinomial logit model, 48
Multinomial probit model, 56
Murrin, Jack, 50
Must-see properties, 119, 130,
    139, 140
Myers, Mark B., 71

N

Naik, Prasad, 51
NAMs, see National account
    managers
Narayanan, V. G., 319, 503
Narayandas, Das, 83, 194, 199, 200,
    201, 202, 280, 313, 326,
    347, 365, 366, 392, 424,
    425, 428, 442, 482
Narayandas, Narakesari, 270
Narus, James A., 25, 52, 194, 313
Narver John C., 43
Nasr, Nada I., 43, 45, 46, 141, 142
National account development, 340
National account managers
    (NAMs), 337, 338
National Credit Card Center
    (NCCC), 538
National implementation team
    (NIT), 338
NCCC, see National Credit
    Card Center
Nelson, Scott D., 464
Neslin, Scott A., 276
Net present value (NPV), 23, 425
Net Revenue from Fund (NRFF),
    541, 542
Network solutions, seamless
    access to, 398
Networking, 213
Neuborne, Ellen, 252
New age of procurement, 341
New Age, 15, 17
New Drug Application, 301, 308
Newell, Frederick, 25, 500
New-to-the-world products, 61
NIT, see National implementation
    team
Nobuhiko, Seraku, 271
Nolan, Paul, 205
Noreen, O'Leary, 252
Noriaki, Kano, 271

Index

Nowlis, Stephen M., 274
NPV, see Net present value
NRFF, see Net Revenue from Fund

O

OEMs, see Original equipment manufacturers
Ofir, Chezy, 274
Oh, Sejo, 270
Oliver, Richard L., 43, 93, 268, 272
On-air endorsement, 8
On-demand service, 83
One-shot deal, 197
Online shopping sites, 253
Open market projects, 446
Operating survey, FTD, 171
Opportunity portfolio management, 317
Order fulfillment, 254
Ordering devices, hand-held, 470
Organization chart
    Aqualisa, 153
    Arrow Electronics, Inc., 348
    Fabtek, 226
    KONE, 285
    RBC Financial Group, 509, 510
    SaleSoft, 495
    WESCO, 327
Original equipment manufacturers (OEMs), 347, 350
Outdoor advertising, 173
Outsourcing, 404
Overtime, cost of, 235

P

P&L statements, 167
Packaged goods manufacturers, 365
Parasuraman, A., 4, 24, 52, 381
Parvatiyar, Atul, 313
Pavlovian marketing, 140
Payment plans, 276
PBs, see Personal bankers
PCE, see Profit Center Earnings
Peer-reviewed scientific journals, 299
Perfect order, 474, 476
Perfect percentage, 475
Personal bankers (PBs), 505
Pessemier, Edgar A., 51
Peterson, Robert A., 51, 313
Pfeifer, Phillip E., 47
Pharmaceutical companies, leading, 300
Pharmaceutical product manager, 4
Phase-gate review process, 72
Photo film market, U.S., 248
Physical product, definition of, 271
PLDs, see Programmable logic devices
PMs, see Product managers

Polls, 107
Preferential treatment, 54
Preliminary bids, 294
Price to cost of goods sold ratio, 306
Price
    competitiveness, 230
    discounts, 275
    discrimination, rampant, 89
    justification, 356
    minimum advertised, 111
    paid index, 427
    promotions, 1
    sensitivity, 291, 358
    tiers, 249
    value equity and, 274
Price-and-availability business, 362
Pricing
    buyout, 448
    category, 249
    complex, 276
    credit card, 530
    everyday low, 274
    negotiated, 516
    situation-based, 274, 276
    strategies, FITD, 316
    value, 418
Principal components
    analysis, 53
    regression, 51, 61
Print advertising, 241, 261
Print catalogs, 254
Printing companies, 77
Privacy, 25, 366
Private label products, 250
Proactive marketing, 133
Procurement
    cost, 335
    models, 344
    new age of, 341
    process, 343
Product(s)
    availability, 394
    brand, perceptions of, 38
    catalog-only, 377
    -centered thinking, 43
    Citibank, 525
    competing, 270
    contracts for, 336
    CSAS, 484
    customized, 39
    deficiencies in, 163
    FITD, 315
    high-volume, 352
    innovation, 461
    managers (PMs), 23, 353
    new-to-the-world, 61
    physical, 271
    premium-priced credit card, 520
    private label, 250
    quality, 28, 37
    reliability, 403
    service, 272

    timing, 377
Trojan Horse, 498
value added, 358
Productivity software, Symantec, 484
Profit Center Earnings (PCE), 541
Profit margins, 276
Profitability
    analysis, databases for, 500
    customer, 514
    hotel, 418
    long-term, 381, 383
    study, Blackstone Homes, 457
Programmable logic devices (PLDs), 349
Promotion(s)
    bogo, 109
    consumer, 115
    price, 1
    run-of-press, 192
    sales, 241
    tie-ins, 184
Propeller heads, 133
Property
    developer market, 156
    investments, 139
    management industry, 222
Public relations, 188, 241
Publicity, 241
Publishing houses, trend among modern-day, 73
Purchase(s)
    agreement, 326
    credit card, 527, 534
    decision, 238, 401
    dollar volume, 339
    frequency, 146
    intent, 62
    Internet, 244
    manager, gatekeeper as, 358
    order creation, 478
    volume, 198, 436

Q

Quality
    product, 28, 37
    service, 47, 146
    sub-drivers of, 92, 96, 271, 279
Quantitative statistical analysis, implementation of, 31

R

R&D, see Research and development
Radio advertising, 241
Rangan, Kasturi V., 69, 198, 313, 319, 321, 322, 323, 519
Rangaswamy, Arvind, 384
RCV, see Relative Customer Value

Index

Recession-proof industry, 223
Recruiting market, 210
Regional ethos, 19
Reichheld, Fredrick, 141
Reinartz, Werner, 43, 46, 383
Relational cheating, 358
Relationship(s)
  banking program, 508
  bid-spec environment, 451
  -brand strategies, 28
  buyer–seller, 313
  drivers, 53, 95, 97
  equity, 23, 93
    definition of, 25
    4 P's about, 500
    role of, 25
  long-term, 425
  strategy, 27, 382
  valuing, 451
  vendor learning in, 198
Relationship equity management, 313–362
  approaches to managing customer relationship, 313–319
    all-at-once approach, 316–319
    foot-in-the-door approach, 313–316
  case (Arrow Electronics, Inc.), 347–362
    Arrow Electronics, 347–348
    Arrow/Schweber, 348–351
    Arrow's selling effort, 352–353
    A/S and Internet, 359
    A/S's relationship with suppliers, 351–352
    decisions, 359–362
    Express Parts. Inc., 359
    relationships with customers, 353–358
  case (WESCO Distribution, Inc.), 326–347
    electrical equipment and supplies business, 328
    going ahead, 345–347
    NA customer of next millennium, 341–345
    National Account program, 335–341
    preparing for NA review, 326–328
    trends in EES industry in 1980s and early 1990s, 333–335
    WESCO Distribution, Inc., 328–333
  managing different customer types concurrently, 319–325
    high price—high CTS, 321–322

high price—low CTS, 322–323
low price—low CTS, 323–324
low price—low CTS, 324–325
Relative Customer Value (RCV), 396
Repositioning, 251
Request for quote (RFQ), 335, 353
Research and development (R&D), 160
Residential homebuilding marketing events, 454
Retail management training program, 269
Retail market shares, home water treatment devices, 111
Retail outlet, 110, 157
Retail store fixtures, 443
Retention program, 123
Return on investment (ROI), 42, 381, 460, 465
  anticipated, 424
  calculation of, 50
  marketing actions based on, 386
  marketing initiatives and, 501
  model, 42, 59
  projection, 58, 60, 150
  total customer management effort, 425
Return on marketing model, 44
Return on quality models, 45
Revenue
  enhancements, 465
  interest, 512
  streams, 259, 424
  trajectory, vendor's, 314
RFQ, see Request for quote
Riggs, Cynthia, 6
Right to privacy, 366
Right-angle turn, Nortel Networks, 396, 407
Road show, 296
Road warrior business, 419
Roche, Elizabeth, 461
ROI, see Return on investment
ROP promotions, see Run-of-press promotions
Ross, Elliot B., 321, 322
Run-of-press (ROP) promotions, 192
Rust, Roland T., 2, 4, 23, 29, 41, 42, 43, 45, 46, 47, 51, 52, 60, 141, 151, 246, 268, 272, 383, 384, 391, 425, 502

S

Sacharow, Anya, 253
Sales and marketing representatives (SMRs), 352
Sales
  automation (SA) software industry, 482

compensation structure, 442
force automation (SFA), 461
forecast, 116, 332
I-media, 369
leads, 221
messages, 292
patterns, Granny's Goodies, 218–220
planning process, challenges in, 222
promotions, 241
system, PROCEED, 491
Same day cash, 136
Sampling
  bias, 51
  random, 52
SA software industry, see Sales automation software industry
Sasser, Earl W. Jr., 432
Satellite system, 269
Scheduling system, 491
Schmittlein, David C., 46
Schultz, Don E., 42, 241
Schurr, Paul H., 270
Scope creep, 324
SCW, see Share of Customer Wallet
Segment communication program, 135
Seiders, Kathleen, 277
Selling
  cycle, 497, 498
  effort, Arrow Electronics, Inc., 352
  story, WESCO, 333
  strategy, 321
Service
  automation, 315
  delivery
    definition of, 272
    process, 272
  driven economy, 4
  environment, definition of, 273
  product, definition of, 272
  profit chain, 45
  quality, 47, 146
  system, PROCEED, 493
SFA, see Sales force automation
Shankar, Venkatesh, 274
Shapiro, Benson p., 195, 224, 235, 319, 321, 322
Shapiro, Eben, 8
Share of Customer Wallet (SCW), 426
Share of wallet, 60, 470
Share-gaining attempts, 248
Shervani, Tasadduq A., 45, 98, 501
Sheth, Jagdish N., 313, 501
Shipment policies, 474
Shock radio, 8
Shoemaker, Stowe, 410

Index 551

Shop schedule, Fabtek, 229
Showcase accounts, 324
Showrooms, 157
Shulman, Robert S., 51, 114
SIC codes, see Standard industrial classification codes
Silk, Alvin J., 51
Simester, Duncan I., 45, 51, 141
Single-source contracts, 435
Sisodia, Rajendra S., 501
Situation-based pricing, 274, 276
Slater, Stanley F., 43
Small Business Administration loan, 205
Small-to-midsize business (SMB), 467
SMB, see Small-to-midsize business
Smith, Jennifer, 119
SMRs, see Sales and marketing representatives
Social reinforcement, 17
Soft drink industry, 13
Software
  bolt-on, 468
  CRM, 148, 320, 460, 462, 469
  freedom from defects, 409
  productivity, 484
  sales automation, 482
  selection, 465
SOHO (Small Office Home Office), 70
Soman, Dilip, 276
Spam, 241
Specialty distributors, 332
Spector, Robert, 367
Split shipment, 474
Srinivasan, V., 43
Srivastava, Rajendra K., 45, 98, 501, 502
Staelin, Richard, 271
Standard industrial classification (SIC) codes, 210
Start-up venture, 192–193
Steckel, Joel H., 93
Steenkamp, Jan-Benedict, 46
Stock performance, Medicines Company, 300
Storbacka, Kaj, 43
Store image, Web site and, 380
Strategic implementation, 381–423
  case (Aerospace Airlines), 391
  case (Hilton HHonors), 410–423
    hotel industry, 411–413
    loyalty marketing programs, 411
    marketing of Hilton brand, 413–421
    Starwood announcement, 421–423
  case (Nortel Networks), 392–410

    company background, 393–398
    customer satisfaction and loyalty survey, 399–405
    feedback on Optical Networks' traditional program, 408–409
    operationalizing CSAT, 405–407
    origins of customer measurement process, 398–399
    right-angle turn, 407–408
    what to do with information, 409–410
  for hands-on analysis, 385–386
  potential marketing actions, 383–385
  review, 381–383
  tracking results and monitoring of process, 386–389
    measurement of customer equity over time, 386–388
    test versus control, 388–389
Strategic investment categories, 47
Strategy
  brand, 382
  development, 382
  joint, 382
  relationship, 382
  triangle, 27
  value, 382
Stuart, Jennifer A., 57, 61, 145
Sub-drivers, quality, 92, 93, 96, 98
Sullivan, R. Lee, 250
Supermarket brand shares, 10
Superpremium brands, 249
Supersegment analysis, 375
Supplier relations, 362, 475
Supplier/distributors
  first tier, 343
  quality programs, 335
Supply chain management, 460
Survey
  customer, 34
  design, 399
  market research, 367
  methodology, 401
  questions, 402, 403
Swartz, Gordon S., 280, 319, 323
Switching matrix, 48, 58, 142, 143, 145
Synergy, payoff from, 376

T

Tacobucci, Dawn, 237
Takahashi, Fumio, 271
Take-One countertop displays, 541
Tannenbaum, Stanley, 241
Tapscott, Dan, 197
Target markets, 207

TBA business, see Tire, battery, and accessory business
Technology assistance, 267
Teen(s)
  buying decisions of, 257
  celebrities, 256
Telecommunications equipment provider, 396
Telemarketing, 3, 241, 296, 364
Telephone(s)
  banking center, 516
  mobile-push-to-talk, 386
  solicitation, 514
  Web-enabled, 320
Telesales representative (TSR), 433
Telesales, 364
Tellis, Gerard J., 241, 274
Temkin, Bruce D., 505
Territory sales manager (TSM), 439
Terry, Creed, 4, 381
Test market, 114, 388
Thaivanich, Pattana, 241
Thomas, Jacquelyn S., 4, 43, 141, 142, 385, 425
Thomke, Stefan, 323
Thrill of the hunt, 273
Tire, battery, and accessory (TBA) business, 430
Toh, Rex S., 51
Total cost of ownership, 354
Total Gold program, 130
Trade shops, 157
Trade shows, 310
Trademarks, 254
Trager, Cara, 6, 7
Transferability, 198
Travel managers, 420
Trojan horse approach, 314, 482, 496
Tsai, Chih-Ling, 51
TSM, see Territory sales manager
TSR, see Telesales representative
Tsuji, Shinichi, 271

U

Uncharted territory syndrome, 223
Uncles, Mark, 25, 46
Unconcerned customers, 323
Unstable angina, 304
Upstream business, 317
Urban, Glen L., 51
Utility model, 48

V

Value(s)
  -added products, 358
  -added services, 321, 336, 338
  brand, 28, 243
  chain, economics of, 78
  drivers, 95, 97, 394
  equation, 268

Value(s) *Continued*
  equity, 23, 93
    actionable drivers, 26
    building opportunity, 273
    definition of, 24
    drivers of, 91, 271, 277
    role of, 24
  extreme, 145
  gaming, 239
  -relationship strategies, 28
  strategy, 382
Value equity, building and managing, 267–312
  case (KONE), 280–297
    elevator industry, 280–284
    evolution of KONE MonoSpace, 286–288
    KONE, 284–286
    MonoSpace experience in Europe, 288–293
    preparing for German MonoSpace launch, 293–297
  case (Medicines Company), 297–312
    Angiomax, 303–308
    bringing Angiomax to market, 308–310
    company history, 302–303
    drug development industry, 298–302
    looking ahead, 312
    other drugs under development, 310–312
  convenience, 277–279
  customer's value equation, 268
  drivers of value equity, 271–277
    price, 274–277
    quality, 271–273
  importance of value equity, 270–271

Vargo, Stephen L., 502
Varki, Sajeev, 46, 272, 384
Vavra, Terry G., 43
Vehicle rental industry, 269
Vending machine technology, 86, 88
Vendor(s)
  CSAS, 486
  customer relationship management strategies, 424
  firing of customer by, 325
  investments, 319
  margins, 198
  revenue trajectory, 314
  scope creep and, 324
  turnkey solutions from, 321
  value-added services, 321
  value extracted by, 318
Venkatesan, Rajkumar, 144, 383, 385, 389
Verhoef, Peter, 4, 43, 274, 383
Vilcassim, Naufel, 56
Virtual bank, 505
Virtual community, 26
Virtual debit card, 255
Voice of the customer, 405

W

Waddock, Sandra A., 244
Walking cost, 418
Warehouse space, 177
Warm channel, 11
Waxler, Caroline, 255, 256
Web
  -based contact, 428
  -enabled phones, 320
  site
    consumer-generated content, 258
  e-commerce, 478
  Eddie Bauer, 367
  store image and, 380
  traffic, 260, 479
  use of as location strategy, 277
Wedel, Michel, 46
Wernerfelt, Birger, 141, 365
White labeling, 505
Wholesale pharmaceutical business, 470
WiFi networks, 270
WiFi wireless Internet access, 279
Wilson, William J., 51
Wilson, William R., 51
Winer, Russell S., 93
Winner's Information Network, 129
Wolf, Marianne, 51, 114
Wood, Robert Chapman, 400
Woodruff, Robert B., 24
Word-of-mouth communications, 241, 246
Wow factor, 162
Wu, George, 274
Wylie, David, 166

Y

Yager, Tom, 506

Z

Zahorik, Anthony J., 29, 43, 45, 60, 383, 384
Zaltman, Gerald, 237
Zeithaml, Valarie A., 2, 4, 23, 24, 29, 41, 42, 43, 45, 47, 52, 151, 240, 246, 268, 381, 383, 391, 425, 502
Zero-sum game, 313

SINGLE PC LICENSE AGREEMENT AND LIMITED WARRANTY

READ THIS LICENSE CAREFULLY BEFORE USING THIS PACKAGE. BY USING THIS PACKAGE, YOU ARE AGREEING TO THE TERMS AND CONDITIONS OF THIS LICENSE. IF YOU DO NOT AGREE, DO NOT USE THE PACKAGE. PROMPTLY RETURN THE UNUSED PACKAGE AND ALL ACCOMPANYING ITEMS TO THE PLACE YOU OBTAINED THEM FOR A FULL REFUND OF ANY SUMS YOU HAVE PAID FOR THE SOFTWARE. *THESE TERMS APPLY TO ALL LICENSED SOFTWARE ON THE DISK EXCEPT THAT THE TERMS FOR USE OF ANY SHAREWARE OR FREEWARE ON THE DISKETTES ARE AS SET FORTH IN THE ELECTRONIC LICENSE LOCATED ON THE DISK:*

1. **GRANT OF LICENSE AND OWNERSHIP:** The enclosed computer programs and data ("Software") are licensed, not sold, to you by Pearson Education, Inc. publishing as Prentice-Hall, Inc. ("We" or the "Company") and in consideration of the license fee, which is part of the price you paid and your agreement to these terms. We reserve any rights not granted to you. You own only the disk(s) but we and/or or licensors own the Software itself. This license allows you to use and display your copy of the Software on a single computer (i.e., with a single CPU) at a single location for academic use only, so long as you comply with the terms of this Agreement. You may make one copy for back up, or transfer your copy to another CPU, provided that the Software is usable on only one computer.

2. **RESTRICTIONS:** You may not transfer or distribute the Software or documentation to anyone else. Except for backup, you may not_copy the documentation or the Software. You may not network the Software or otherwise use it on more than one computer or computer terminal at the same time. You may not reverse engineer, disassemble, decompile, modify, adapt, translate, or create derivative works based on the Software or the Documentation. You may be held legally responsible for any copying or copyright infringement that is caused by your failure to abide by the terms of these restrictions.

3. **TERMINATION:** This license is effective until terminated. This license will terminate automatically without notice from the Company if you fail to comply with any provisions or limitations of this license. Upon termination, you shall destroy the Documentation and all copies of the Software. All provisions of this Agreement as to limitation and disclaimer of warranties, limitation of liability, remedies or damages, and our ownership rights shall survive termination.

4. **LIMITED WARRANTY AND DISCLAIMER OF WARRANTY:** Company warrants that for a period of 60 days from the date you purchase this SOFTWARE (or purchase or adp[t the accompanying textbook), the Software, when properly installed and used in accordance with the Documentation, will operate in substantial comformity with the description of the Software set forth in the Documentation, and that for a period of 30 days the disk(s) on which the Software is delivered shall be free from defects in materials and workmanship under normal use. The Company does not warrant that the Software is delivered shall be free from defects in materials and workmanship under normal use. The Company does not warrant that the Software will meet your requirements or that the operation of the Software will be uninterrupted or error-free. Your only remedy and the Company's only obligation under these limited warranties is, at the Company's option, return of the disk for a refund of any amounts paid for it by you or replacement of the disk. THIS LIMITED WARRANTY IS THE ONLY WARRANTY PROVIDED BY THE COMPANY AND ITS LICENSORS, AND THE COMPANY AND ITS LICENSORS DISCLAIM ALL OTHER WARRANTIES, EXPRESS OR IMPLIED, INCLUDING WITHOUT LIMITATION, THE IMPLIED WARRANTIES OF MERCHANTABILITY AND FITNESS FOR A PARTICULAR PURPOSE. THE COMPANY DOES NOT WARRANT, GUARANTEE OR MAKE ANY REPRESENTATION REGARDING THE ACCURACY, RELIABILITY, CURRENTNESS, USE, OR RESULTS OF USE, OF THE SOFTWARE.

5. **LIMITATION OF REMEDIES AND DAMAGES:** IN NO EVENT, SHALL THE COMPANY OR ITS EMPLOYEES, AGENTS, LICENSORS, OR CONTRACTORS BE LIABLE FOR ANY INCIDENTAL, INDIRECT, SPECIAL OR CONSEQUENTIAL DAMAGES ARISING OUT OF OR IN CONNECTION WITH THIS LICENSE OR THE SOFTWARE, INCLUDING FOR LOSS OF USE, LOSS OF DATA, LOSS OF INCOME OR PROFIT, OR OTHER LOSSES, SUSTAINED AS A RESULT OF INJURY TO ANY PERSON, OR LOSS OF OR DAMAGE TO PROPERTY, OR CLAIMS OF THIRD PARTIES, EVEN IF THE COMPANY OR AN AUTHORIZED REPRESENTATIVE OF THE COMPANY HAS BEEN ADVISED OF THE POSSIBILITY OF SUCH DAMAGES. IN NO EVENT SHALL THE LIABILITY OF THE COMPANY FOR DAMAGES WITH RESPECT TO THE SOFTWARE EXCEED THE AMOUNTS ACTUALLY PAID BY YOU, IF ANY, FOR THE SOFTWARE OR THE ACCOMPANYING TEXTBOOK. BECAUSE SOME JURISDICTIONS DO NOT ALLOW THE LIMITATION OF LIABILITY IN CERTAIN CIRCUMSTANCES, THE ABOVE LIMITATIONS MAY NOT ALWAYS APPLY TO YOU.

6. **GENERAL:** THIS AGREEMENT SHALL BE CONSTRUED IN ACCORDANCE WITH THE LAWS OF THE UNITED STATES OF AMERICA AND THE STATE OF NEW YORK, APPLICABLE TO CONTRACTS MADE IN NEW YORK, AND SHALL BENEFIT THE COMPANY, ITS AFFILIATES AND ASSIGNEES. HIS AGREEMENT IS THE COMPLETE AND EXCLUSIVE STATEMENT OF THE AGREEMENT BETWEEN YOU AND THE COMPANY AND SUPERSEDES ALL PROPOSALS OR PRIOR AGREEMENTS, ORAL, OR WRITTEN, AND ANY OTHER COMMUNICATIONS BETWEEN YOU AND THE SUBJECT MATTER OF THIS AGREEMENT. If you are a U.S. Government user, this Software is licensed with "restricted rights" as set forth in subparagraphs (a)-(d) of the Commercial Computer-Restricted Rights clause at FAR 52.227-19 or in subparagraphs (c)(1)(ii) of the Rights in Technical Data and Computer Software clause at DFARS 252.227-7013, and similar clauses, as applicable.

Should you have any questions concerning this agreement or if you wish to contact the Company for any reason, please contact in writing:

Director of New Media
Higher Education Division
Prentice Hall, Inc.
1 Lake Street
Upper Saddle River, NJ 07458